MICROECONOMICS

Fifteenth Canadian Edition

CAMPBELL R. MCCONNELL
University of Nebraska—Emeritus

STANLEY L. BRUE
Pacific Lutheran University

SEAN M. FLYNN
Scripps College

THOMAS P. BARBIERO
Ryerson University

Mc
Graw
Hill
Education

Microeconomics
Fifteenth Canadian Edition

Copyright © 2019, 2016, 2013, 2010, 2007, 2005, 2002, 1999, 1996, 1993, 1990, 1987, 1984, 1981, 1978 by McGraw-Hill Ryerson Limited. Copyright © 2015, 2012, 2009, 2008, 2005, 2002, 1999, 1996, 1993, 1990, 1987, 1984, 1981, 1978, 1975, 1972, 1969, 1966, 1963, 1960 by McGraw-Hill Education LLC. All rights reserved. No part of this publication may be reproduced or transmitted in any form or by any means, or stored in a database or retrieval system, without the prior written permission of McGraw-Hill Ryerson Limited, or in the case of photocopying or other reprographic copying, a licence from The Canadian Copyright Licensing Agency (Access Copyright). For an Access Copyright licence, visit www.accesscopyright.ca or call toll-free to 1-800-893-5777.

The Internet addresses listed in the text were accurate at the time of publication. The inclusion of a website does not indicate an endorsement by the authors or McGraw-Hill Ryerson, and McGraw-Hill Ryerson does not guarantee the accuracy of the information presented at these sites.

ISBN-13: 978-1-25-965488-6
ISBN-10: 1-25-965488-5

1 2 3 4 5 6 7 8 9 10   TCP   22 21 20 19

Printed and bound in Canada.

Care has been taken to trace ownership of copyright material contained in this text; however, the publisher will welcome any information that enables them to rectify any reference or credit for subsequent editions.

PRODUCT DIRECTOR: Rhondda McNabb
SENIOR PORTFOLIO MANAGER: Kevin O'Hearn
SENIOR MARKETING MANAGER: Loula March
CONTENT DEVELOPER: Melissa Hudson
SENIOR PORTFOLIO ASSOCIATE: Stephanie Giles
SUPERVISING EDITOR: Jeanette McCurdy
PHOTO/PERMISSIONS RESEARCH: Alison Lloyd Baker
COPY EDITOR: Rodney Rawlings
PLANT PRODUCTION COORDINATOR: Sarah Strynatka
MANUFACTURING PRODUCTION COORDINATOR: Jason Stubner
COVER AND INTERIOR DESIGN: Liz Harasymczuk
COVER IMAGE: Jean-Pierre Lescourret/Getty Images
PAGE LAYOUT: Aptara®, Inc.
PRINTER: Transcontinental Printing Group

Dedication

To my granddaughter, Serafina, and past instructors.

About the Authors

Campbell R. McConnell earned his Ph.D. from the University of Iowa after receiving degrees from Cornell College and the University of Illinois. He taught at the University of Nebraska–Lincoln from 1953 until his retirement in 1990. He is also coauthor of *Contemporary Labor Economics*, ninth edition; *Essentials of Economics*, second edition; *Macroeconomics: Brief Edition*; and *Microeconomics: Brief Edition* (all The McGraw-Hill Companies), and has edited readers for the principles and labour economics courses. He is a recipient of both the University of Nebraska Distinguished Teaching Award and the James A. Lake Academic Freedom Award and is past president of the Midwest Economics Association. Professor McConnell was awarded an honorary Doctor of Laws degree from Cornell College in 1973 and received its Distinguished Achievement Award in 1994. His primary areas of interest are labour economics and economic education. He has an extensive collection of jazz recordings and enjoys reading jazz history.

Stanley L. Brue carried out his undergraduate work at Augustana College (South Dakota) and received its Distinguished Achievement Award in 1991. He received his Ph.D. from the University of Nebraska–Lincoln. He is retired from a long career at Pacific Lutheran University, where he was honoured as a recipient of the Burlington Northern Faculty Achievement Award. Professor Brue has also received the national Leavey Award for excellence in economic education. He has served as national president and chair of the Board of Trustees of Omicron Delta Epsilon International Economics Honorary. He is coauthor of *Economic Scenes*, fifth edition (Prentice-Hall); *Contemporary Labor Economics*, ninth edition; *Essentials of Economics*, second edition; *Macroeconomics: Brief Edition*; *Microeconomics: Brief Edition* (all The McGraw-Hill Companies); and *The Evolution of Economic Thought*, seventh edition (South-Western). For relaxation, he enjoys international travel, attending sporting events, and skiing with family and friends.

Sean M. Flynn did his undergraduate work at the University of Southern California before completing his Ph.D. at U.C. Berkeley, where he served as the Head Graduate Student Instructor for the Department of Economics after receiving the Outstanding Graduate Student Instructor Award. He teaches at Scripps College (of the Claremont Colleges) and is the author of *Economics for Dummies* (Wiley) and coauthor of *Essentials of Economics*, second edition; *Macroeconomics: Brief Edition*; and *Microeconomics: Brief Edition* (all The McGraw-Hill Companies). His research interests include finance, behavioural economics, and health economics. An accomplished martial artist, he has represented the United States in international aikido tournaments and is the author of *Understanding Shodokan Aikido* (Shodokan Press). Other hobbies include running, travelling, and enjoying ethnic food.

Thomas P. Barbiero received his Ph.D. from the University of Toronto after completing undergraduate studies at the same university. He is a professor in the Department of Economics at Ryerson University in Toronto. His research interests include the economic history of Canada and modern Italy. He spends his summers in Fontanarosa, a small town in his native region of Campania in southern Italy. It is situated in the vineyards of the Taurasi wine-growing area. There he indulges in his favourite pastime: consuming good food and wine.

Brief Contents

Contents

xiv   CONTENTS

Preface

Welcome to the Fifteenth Canadian Edition of *Microeconomics*. Thousands of Canadian students have studied economics from the Canadian editions of *Macroeconomics* and *Microeconomics*. An estimated 15 million students worldwide have now used a version of the McConnell textbooks, making them the world's best-selling economic principles textbooks.

Fundamental Objectives

We have three main goals for *Microeconomics*:

- Help the beginning student master the principles essential for understanding economic problems, specific economic issues, and the policy alternatives
- Help the student understand and apply the economic perspective, and reason accurately and objectively about economic matters
- Promote a lasting student interest in economics and the economy

What's New and Improved?

One of the benefits of writing a successful text is the opportunity to revise—to delete the outdated and insert the new, to rewrite misleading or ambiguous statements, to introduce more relevant illustrations, to improve the organizational structure, and to enhance the learning aids.

We trust you will agree that we have used this opportunity wisely and fully. Some of the more significant changes include the following.

Separate Presentations of Monopolistic Competition and Oligopoly

In response to instructor feedback, we have split the material on monopolistic competition and oligopoly that in previous editions had made up a single chapter into two separate chapters. The separated chapters have been made modular, so skipping either or covering both will be equally viable options for instructors. This should be particularly helpful to instructors who want to spend more time on oligopoly.

New Chapter on Technology, R&D, and Efficiency

Technological change has picked up considerably since the information technology revolution began in the early 1980s. We have added a new chapter that considers technology and its impact on market structure, pricing, and efficiency.

New "Consider This" and "Last Word" Pieces

Our Consider This boxes are used to provide analogies, examples, or stories that help drive home central economic ideas in a student-oriented, real-world manner. For instance, a Consider This box titled "McHits and

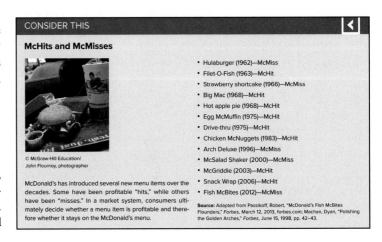

CONSIDER THIS

McHits and McMisses

© McGraw-Hill Education/
John Flournoy, photographer

McDonald's has introduced several new menu items over the decades. Some have been profitable "hits," while others have been "misses." In a market system, consumers ultimately decide whether a menu item is profitable and therefore whether it stays on the McDonald's menu.

- Hulaburger (1962)—McMiss
- Filet-O-Fish (1963)—McHit
- Strawberry shortcake (1966)—McMiss
- Big Mac (1968)—McHit
- Hot apple pie (1968)—McHit
- Egg McMuffin (1975)—McHit
- Drive-thru (1975)—McHit
- Chicken McNuggets (1983)—McHit
- Arch Deluxe (1996)—McMiss
- McSalad Shaker (2000)—McMiss
- McGriddle (2003)—McHit
- Snack Wrap (2006)—McHit
- Fish McBites (2012)—McMiss

Source: Adapted from Passikoff, Robert, "McDonald's Fish McBites Flounders," *Forbes*, March 12, 2013, forbes.com; Machan, Dyan, "Polishing the Golden Arches," *Forbes*, June 15, 1998, pp. 42–43.

Singapore's Efficient and Effective Health Care System

How does Singapore deliver some of the best health care in the world while spending less per person than Canada?

© Comstock Images/Picturequest

In every health-quality category monitored by the World Health Organization, the small island nation of Singapore is either number one in the world or near the top of the list. Among other achievements, Singapore has the world's lowest rate of infant mortality and the world's fourth-highest life expectancy.

One might expect that achieving these exceptional outcomes would be extremely expensive. But Singapore is also number one in another category: It spends less per person on health care than any other developed nation. In 2010 Canada spent about 10 percent of its GDP on health care. Singapore spent just 3.8 percent.

How does Singapore deliver world-class health care while spending less than any other developed nation? The answer is a unique combination of government mandates to encourage competition, high out-of-pocket costs for consumers, and laws requiring people to save for future health expenditures.

Competition is encouraged by forcing hospitals to post prices for each of their services. Armed with this information, patients can shop around for the best deal. The government also publishes the track record of each hospital on each service so that consumers can make informed decisions about quality as well as price. With consumers choosing on the basis of cost and quality, local hospitals compete to reduce costs and improve quality.

Singapore also insists upon high out-of-pocket costs in order to avoid the overconsumption and high prices that result when insurance policies pick up most of the price for medical procedures. Indeed, out-of-pocket spending repre-sents about 92 percent of all non-government health care spending in Singapore, as against just less than 10 percent in Canada.

Having to pay for most medical spending out of pocket, how-ever, means that Singapore's citizens are faced with having to pay for most of their health care themselves. How can this be done without bankrupting the average citizen? The answer is mandatory health savings accounts.

Singapore's citizens are required to save about 6 percent of their incomes into MediSave accounts. MediSave deposits are private property so that people have an incentive to spend the money in their accounts wisely. In addition, the citizens of Singapore also know that they won't be left helpless if the money in their MediSave accounts runs out. The government subsidizes the health care of those who have exhausted their MediSave accounts as well as the health care of the poor and others who have not been able to accumulate much money in their MediSave accounts.

Given the present universal health care system in Canada, which according to most Canadians functions quite well, it is unlikely that they would opt for a Singapore-style MediSave system.

Question

What are the three major cost-reducing features of the Singapore health care system? Which one do you think has the largest effect on holding down the price of medical care in Singapore? How difficult do you think it would be to implement the missing elements in Canada? Explain.

McMisses" illustrates consumer sovereignty through a listing of successful and unsuccessful products. How businesses exploit price discrimination is driven home in a Consider This box that explains why ballparks charge different admission prices for adults and children but only one set of prices at their concession stands. These brief vignettes, each accompanied by a photo, illustrate key points in a lively, colourful, and easy-to-remember way. We have added six new Consider This boxes in this edition.

Our Last Word boxes are lengthier applications or case studies placed near the end of each chapter. For example, the one for Chapter 1 (Limits, Alternatives, and Choices) examines pitfalls to sound economic reasoning, while the one for Chapter 4 (Market Failures: Public Goods and Externalities) examines cap-and-trade versus carbon taxes as policy responses to excessive carbon dioxide emissions. There are six new Last Words in this edition.

If you are unfamiliar with *Microeconomics*, we encourage you to thumb through the chapters to take a quick look at these highly visible features.

In previous editions, a substantial portion of our game theory coverage appeared in an appendix to a chapter that covered both monopolistic competition and oligopoly. With the material on monopolistic competition now located in a separate chapter, we have been able to eliminate the appendix and fully integrate the game theory material that had appeared there with the treatment of oligopoly that had appeared in the main body of text. The result is our new Chapter 13, Oligopoly and Strategic Behaviour.

This integrated presentation facilitates student comprehension of both game theory and oligopoly because strategic interactions are always presented in an accessible, intuitive context. Students already understand that Google's actions affect those of rivals such as Facebook, and vice versa. So integrating oligopoly with game theory illuminates both sets of material.

Tested Content for Peer Instruction

While technology has made learning with *Microeconomics* more efficient for the individual student, we wanted to offer new methods to enhance the effectiveness of the classroom experience as well. We are consequently proud that we are now going to offer Peer Instruction materials that are highly effective, comprehensive, and classroom-tested.

Peer Instruction was pioneered by Eric Mazur of Harvard University's Physics Department. It is a student-focused, interactive teaching method that has been shown to massively increase the depth of student understanding across a wide variety of disciplines. It works by having students, in groups, ponder and discuss questions about challenging scenarios before their instructor steps in to clear up any lingering misconceptions. Along the way, students first answer each question individually before voting as a team after a discussion. Those two answers—individual, then group—provided the evidence for the effectiveness of Peer Instruction.

As explained by Harvard psychologist Stephen Pinker, the group discussions lead to a deeper and more intuitive understanding of concepts and theories than can usually be achieved with lecture-based instruction. That is the case because beginners are often better than experts at explaining challenging ideas to other beginners. The problem with experts—that is, instructors like you and me—is that the process of becoming an expert rewires the brain so that the expert can no longer think like a beginner. Our own expertise makes it difficult to see where students are getting confused and it is consequently very useful to unleash the power of Peer Instruction to help beginners tackle new material.

The effectiveness of Peer Instruction depends, however, on the quality of the questions and scenarios that students are asked to ponder. Developing good questions and effective scenarios is highly time intensive and often a matter of experimentation; you just don't know how well a question or scenario will work until you try it. It is not a surprise, then, that today's busy instructors often shy away from Peer Instruction because of the high start-up costs and the time required to develop truly effective questions and scenarios.

Fortunately for you, we did all the work. Author Sean Flynn and Todd Fitch of the University of San Francisco have field-tested hundreds of questions and scenarios for effectiveness. The questions and scenarios have been adapted by Thomas Barbiero of Ryerson University and Jason Dean of Wilfred Laurier. So with this 15th Canadian edition of McConnell, we are ready to offer a fully supported set of Peer Instruction material tied directly to each of the learning objectives in *Microeconomics*. The questions and scenarios, as well as resources to help organize a Peer Instruction classroom can be found in Connect.

If you have ever been in a situation in which more experienced students helped to teach newer students, you have seen the power of Peer Instruction. Our new materials bring us back to that paradigm. So while we are first once again with Peer Instruction in economics, credit belongs to the pioneering work of dedicated teachers like Eric Mazur and Stephen Pinker for making this method available across disciplines.

Full Support for Flipped Classroom Teaching Strategies

We have also designed our new Peer Instruction materials to facilitate flipped-classroom teaching strategies, wherein students learn basic material at home, before lecture, before being challenged in class to reach higher levels of understanding. In K–12 math programs, for example, students study short videos on new content at home before coming to class to work problems. That sequence of learning activities assures that an instructor is present at the stage where students encounter the most difficulties, namely, when they attempt to apply the material. By contrast, the traditional (non-flipped) method for teaching elementary math presents new content in class before sending students home to work problems by themselves. That sequence leaves students without expert help when they are most vulnerable to misunderstandings and errors.

We have designed our new Peer Instruction materials to facilitate the flipped-classroom method by leveraging the adaptive learning materials that are already available in our Connect online learning platform. In particular, students can be assigned new material before lecture via SmartBook, which is an adaptive-learning technology that tutors students through the basic concepts and skills presented in each section of the book.

Those pre-class activities will allow students to master the lower levels of Bloom's Taxonomy of learning objectives—things like remembering and understanding—*before* they come to class. They will then be ready to attack the higher levels of Bloom's Taxonomy—things like applying, analyzing, and evaluating. That's where our new Peer Instruction material comes in. Students who have each already worked their way through the lower levels of Bloom's Taxonomy come together in class under the instruction of an expert—their teacher—to work in unison on the higher levels of understanding that are the ultimate goal of economics instruction.

Current Discussions and Examples

The Fifteenth Canadian Edition of *Microeconomics* refers to and discusses many current topics. Examples are surpluses and shortages of tickets at the Olympics; the myriad impacts of ethanol subsidies; creative destruction; applications of behavioural economics; applications of game theory; oil and gasoline prices; cap-and-trade systems and carbon taxes; occupational licensing; consumption versus income inequality; conditional and unconditional cash transfers; and many others.

Chapter-by-Chapter Changes

Each chapter of *Microeconomics*, Fifteenth Canadian Edition, contains updated data reflecting the current economy, revised Learning Objectives, and reorganized and expanded end-of-chapter content. Several chapters also contain one or more additional Quick Review boxes to help students review and solidify content as they are reading along. In addition to these changes, each chapter contains the following updates:

Chapter 1: Limits, Alternatives, and Choices features two refreshed Consider This pieces as well as revised new examples and working improvements to clarify the main concepts.

Chapter 2: The Market System and the Circular Flow contains updated examples and a brief new introduction to the concept of residual claimant.

Chapter 3: Demand, Supply, and Market Equilibrium includes a new Last Word on how student lending can raise university and college tuition, data updates, and example updates.

Chapter 4: Market Failures: Public Goods and Externalities features updated examples and a new Key Word on Pigovian taxes.

Chapter 5: Government's Role and Government Failure has a new Consider This on government agencies violating government laws, several new examples, and wording revisions for increased clarity.

Chapter 6: Elasticity contains several updated examples.

Chapter 7: Consumer Choice and Utility Maximization incorporates updated examples and a new Consider This vignette on consumers applying maximizing behaviour to the calorie data that are now printed on restaurant menus

Chapter 7B: Behavioural Economics contains a new Consider This piece on the myopia-busting business model employed by Solar City and a new Last Word describing the activities of the Behavioural Insights Team.

Chapter 8: The Firm and Costs of Production incorporates a few wording updates to facilitate rapid comprehension.

Chapter 9: Perfect Competition in the Short Run features several wording changes to improve student understanding of the end-of-chapter questions and problems.

Chapter 10: Perfect Competition in the Long Run contains several updated examples to keep the content relevant for today's students.

Chapter 11: Monopoly has a new Last Word about individualized online price discrimination and updated examples.

Chapter 12: Monopolistic Competition was previously part of a chapter that covered both monopolistic competition and oligopoly. We have split that chapter into two parts for the fifteenth edition so that instructors who wish to skip either set of material may easily do so.

Chapter 13: Oligopoly and Strategic Behaviour was previously part of a chapter that covered both monopolistic competition and oligopoly. The material on oligopoly constitutes the basis for this stand-alone chapter, which also extends the game theory material found in the previous edition. Our extended coverage of game theory and strategic behaviour includes extensive-form (game-tree) representations of sequential games and the concept of subgame-perfect Nash equilibrium. As in prior editions, all game theory material is kept concrete by presenting it in the context of strategic behaviour among oligopoly firms.

Chapter 14: Technology, R&D, and Efficiency is a new chapter that considers technology and its impact on market structure, pricing, and efficiency.

Chapter 15: Competition Policy and Regulations has a new Last Word that covers both anti-trust prosecutions against human managers who intentionally engage in anticompetitive practices and the newly evolving area of price-fixing by artificial intelligence algorithms that in effect "collude" to fix prices when they interact.

Chapter 16: The Demand for Factors of Production incorporates light data updates and an entirely new Last Word on capital–labour substitution. This discussion uses ABM machines as its main example, just as the Last Word in the previous edition did. But an update was required because recent research indicates that the main premise of the old Last Word no longer holds true: ABMs did not in fact replace human tellers in the aggregate, at least not after managers adjusted to the new technology. The new Last Word updates the story.

Chapter 17: Wage Determination features extensive data updates, improved wording for clarity, and a new Last Word on how unnecessary occupational licensing requirements are reducing employment opportunities.

Chapter 18: Rent, Interest, and Profit incorporates wording improvements, data updates, and a new Consider This on the subject of profits.

Chapter 18B: Income Inequality, Poverty, and Discrimination contains a new Consider This about welfare cliffs and some data updates and several new examples.

Chapter 19: International Trade is largely unchanged from the last edition.

Chapter 19B: Natural Resource and Energy Economics has extensive data updates and a new Consider This box on how the current limitations of electricity-storage technology stymie the wider adoption of renewable energy sources such as solar and wind power.

Integrated Text and Website

We continue to integrate the eBook with our extensive supplementary learning offerings.

WORKED PROBLEM 2.1   Least-Cost Production

Worked Problems are hyperlinked within the eBook and provide students with a step-by-step illustration of how to solve a problem. These pieces consist of side-by-side computational questions and the computational procedures used to derive the answers. In essence, they extend the textbook's explanations involving computations—for example, of real GDP, real GDP per capita, the unemployment rate, the inflation rate, per-unit production costs, and more. At relevant points in the text, the Worked Problem hyperlink directs the student to an online appendix for this additional support.

MATH 4.1   The Optimal Amount of a Public Good

For those students who want to explore the mathematical details of the theoretical concepts covered in the text, **Math** indicators direct the students to See the Math exercises in the online appendix.

To help students understand graphing concepts used in the text, Connect offers a Graphing Tool Introduction and assignable graphing exercises called Graphing Extras.

Bonus Chapters

Bonus chapters are available online. They are 7B, Behavioural Economics; 18B, Income Inequality, Poverty, and Discrimination; and 19B, Natural Resource and Energy Economics.

Distinguishing Features

- *Comprehensive Explanations at an Appropriate Level* *Microeconomics* is comprehensive, analytical, and challenging, yet fully accessible to a wide range of students. Its thoroughness and accessibility enable instructors to select topics for special classroom emphasis with confidence that students can independently read and comprehend other assigned material in the book. Where needed, an extra sentence of explanation is provided. Brevity at the expense of clarity is false economy.

- *Fundamentals of the Market System* Many economies throughout the world are making difficult transitions from planning systems to market systems. Our detailed description of the institutions and operation of the market system in Chapter 2 (The Market System and the Circular Flow) is even more relevant than before. We pay particular attention to property rights, entrepreneurship, freedom of enterprise and choice, competition, and the role of profits, because these concepts are often misunderstood by beginning students.

- *Extensive Treatment of International Economics* We give the principles and institutions of the global economy extensive treatment. The appendix to Chapter 3 (Demand, Supply, and Market Equilibrium) has an application on exchange rates. Chapter 19 (International Trade) examines key facts of international trade, specialization and comparative advantage.

  As noted previously, Chapter 19 (International Trade) is constructed so that instructors who want to cover international trade early in the course can assign it immediately after Chapter 3. Comprehending Chapter 19 requires only a good understanding of production possibilities analysis and of supply and demand analysis. International competition, trade flows, and financial flows are integrated throughout the micro and macro sections. Global Perspective boxes add to the international flavour of the book.

- *Early and Extensive Treatment of Government* The public sector is an integral component of modern capitalism. This book introduces the role of government early. Chapter 4 (Market Failures: Public Goods and Externalities) systematically discusses public goods and government policies toward externalities. Chapter 5 (Government's Role and Government Failure) details the factors that cause government failure.

- *Stress on the Theory of the Firm* We have given much attention to microeconomics in general and to the theory of the firm in particular, for two reasons. First, the concepts of microeconomics are difficult for most beginning students; abbreviated expositions usually compound these difficulties by raising more questions than they answer. Second, we wanted to couple analysis of the various market structures with a discussion of the impact of each market arrangement on price, output levels, resource allocation, and the rate of technological advance.

- *Emphasis on Technological Change* This edition has a new chapter on technological change and its impact on market structure pricing.

- *Integrated Text and Website* Selected interactive graphs are available on Connect.

Organizational Alternatives

Although instructors generally agree on the content of principles of economics courses, they sometimes differ on how to arrange the material. *Microeconomics* includes five parts, and that provides considerable organizational flexibility. For example, Chapter 19 on international trade can easily be covered immediately after Chapter 3 on supply and demand for instructors who want an early discussion of international trade.

Pedagogical Aids

Microeconomics is highly student-oriented. The Fifteenth Canadian Edition is accompanied by a variety of high-quality supplements that help students master the subject and help instructors implement customized courses.

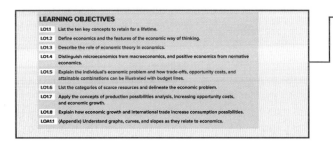

- **Learning Objectives** The Learning Objectives have been expanded in the fifteenth edition. We set out the Learning Objectives at the start of each chapter so the chapter's main concepts can be easily recognized. We have also tied the Learning Objectives to each of the numbered sections in each chapter and the Questions and Problems at the end of each chapter. In addition, the chapter summaries are organized by Learning Objective.

- **Terminology** A significant portion of any introductory course is terminology. Key terms are highlighted in bold type the first time they appear in the text. A glossary of definitions can be found at the end of the book. Users of the eBook can hover their cursor over each bolded term to see its definition.

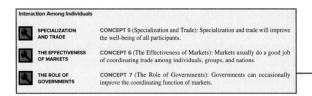

- **Ten Key Concepts** Ten Key Concepts have been identified to help students organize the main principles. The Ten Key Concepts are introduced in Chapter 1 and each one is reinforced throughout the textbook by an icon.

- **Graphics with Supporting Data** Where possible we have tried to provide data to support our graphs. In such cases a data table now appears in the same figure with the graph.

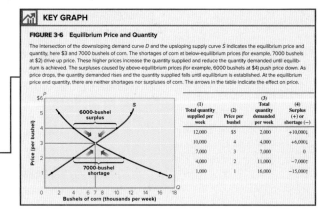

- **Key Graphs** We have labelled graphs having special relevance as Key Graphs. There is a quick quiz of four questions related to each Key Graph, with answers provided at the bottom of the graph.

- **Reviewing the Chapter** Important things should be said more than once. You will find a Chapter Summary at the conclusion of every chapter as well as two or three Quick Reviews within each chapter. The summary at the end of each chapter is presented by Learning Objective. These review statements will help the student to focus on the essential ideas of each chapter and also to study for exams.

Comprehensive Learning and Teaching Package

The Fifteenth Canadian Edition is also accompanied by a variety of high-quality supplements that help students master the subject and help instructors implement customized courses.

MARKET LEADING TECHNOLOGY

Learn Without Limits

McGraw-Hill Connect® is an award-winning digital teaching and learning platform that gives students the means to better connect with their coursework, with their instructors, and with the important concepts that they will need to know for success now and in the future. Using Connect, instructors can take advantage of McGraw-Hill's trusted content to seamlessly deliver assignments, quizzes and tests online. McGraw-Hill Connect is the only learning platform that continuously adapts to each student, delivering precisely what they need, when they need it, so class time is more engaging and effective. It makes teaching and learning personal, easy, and proven.

Connect Key Features

As the first and only adaptive reading experience, SmartBook is changing the way students read and learn. It creates a personalized reading experience by highlighting the most important concepts a student needs to learn at that moment. As a student engages with SmartBook, the reading experience continuously adapts by highlighting content according to what each student knows and doesn't know. This ensures that he or she is focused on the content needed to close specific knowledge gaps, while it simultaneously promotes long-term learning.

Connect Insight is a new, one-of-a-kind visual analytics dashboard—now available for both instructors and students—that provides at-a-glance, immediately actionable information regarding student performance. By presenting assignment, assessment, and topical performance results together with a time metric that is easily visible for aggregate or individual results, Connect Insight gives the user the ability to take a just-in-time approach to teaching and learning that was never before available. Connect Insight presents data that empowers students and helps instructors improve class performance in a way that is efficient and effective.

Simple Assignment Management

With Connect, creating assignments is easier than ever, so instructors can spend more time teaching and less time managing. Instructors can

- Assign SmartBook learning modules

- Edit existing questions and create their own questions

- Draw from a variety of text-specific questions, resources, and test bank material to assign online

- Streamline lesson planning, student progress reporting, and assignment grading to make classroom management more efficient than ever

Smart Grading

When it comes to studying, time is precious. Connect helps students learn more efficiently by providing feedback and practice material when they need it, where they need it.

- Automatically score assignments, giving students immediate feedback on their work and comparisons with correct answers.

- Access and review each response; manually change grades or leave comments for students to review.

- Track individual student performance—by question, by assignment, or in relation to the class overall—with detailed grade reports.

- Reinforce classroom concepts with practice tests and instant quizzes.

- Integrate grade reports easily with Learning Management Systems including Blackboard, D2L, and Moodle.

Instructor Library

The Connect Instructor Library is a repository for additional resources to improve student engagement in and out of class. It provides all the critical resources instructors need to build their course.

- Access Instructor resources.

- View assignments and resources created for past sections.

- Post your own resources for students to use.

Instructor Resources

- *Instructor's Manual*   The Instructor's Manual is available again in this edition as a Microsoft® Office Word document.

- *Solutions Manual*   includes the answers to all end-of-chapter questions and problems.

- *Microsoft® PowerPoint® Presentation Software*   This presentation system is found on the Instructor's Site of Connect. It offers visual presentations that may be edited and manipulated to fit a particular course format.

- *Computerized Test Banks*   The Computerized Test Bank contains about 6000 multiple-choice and true/false questions, and hundreds of short-answer questions with suggested answers.

Image Gallery

All figures that appear in this text can be downloaded from the image gallery on Connect and easily embedded into instructors' PowerPoint slides.

Superior Learning Solutions and Support

The McGraw-Hill Education team is ready to help instructors assess and integrate any of our products, technology, and services into your course for optimal teaching and learning performance. Whether it's helping your students improve their grades or putting your entire course online, the McGraw-Hill Education team is here to help you do it. Contact your Learning Solutions Consultant today to learn how to maximize all of McGraw-Hill Education's resources.

For more information, please visit us online:

http://www.mheducation.ca/highereducation/educators/digital-solutions

Acknowledgments

The Fifteenth Canadian Edition of *Microeconomics* has benefited from a number of perceptive reviewers, who were a rich source of suggestions for this revision. We extend our thanks to every one of them for their considerable help in improving *Microeconomics*.

We are greatly indebted to an all-star group of professionals at McGraw-Hill Education—in particular Kevin O'Hearn, Senior Portfolio Manager; Jeanette McCurdy, Supervising Editor; Melissa Hudson, Content Developer; Stephanie Giles, Senior Portfolio Associate; and Loula March, Marketing Manager—for their publishing and marketing expertise. We thank Rodney Rawlings for his thorough and sensitive editing, Alison Lloyd Baker for her selection of photos, Liz Harasymczuk for the cover and interior design, and Gianluigi Pelloni of the University of Bologna (Rimini Campus) and Jose Luis Alvarez Arce of the University of Navarra in Pamplona, Spain, for their helpful suggestions and insights.

Campbell R. McConnell
Stanley L. Brue
Sean M. Flynn
Thomas P. Barbiero

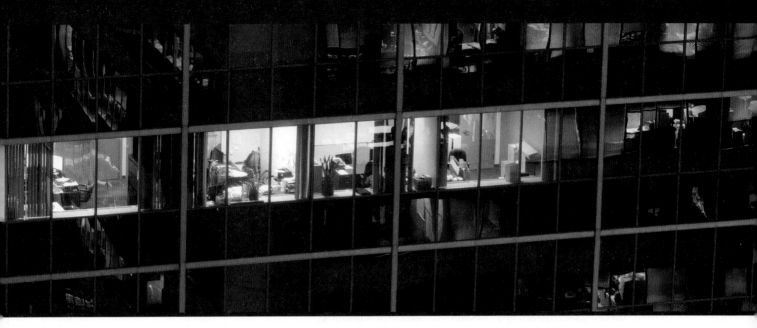

CHAPTER 1

Limits, Alternatives, and Choices

An appendix on understanding graphs follows this chapter. If you need a quick review of this mathematical tool, you might benefit from reading the appendix first.

LEARNING OBJECTIVES

LO1.1   List the ten key concepts to retain for a lifetime.

LO1.2   Define economics and the features of the economic way of thinking.

LO1.3   Describe the role of economic theory in economics.

LO1.4   Distinguish microeconomics from macroeconomics, and positive economics from normative economics.

LO1.5   Explain the individual's economic problem and how trade-offs, opportunity costs, and attainable combinations can be illustrated with budget lines.

LO1.6   List the categories of scarce resources and delineate the economic problem.

LO1.7   Apply the concepts of production possibilities analysis, increasing opportunity costs, and economic growth.

LO1.8   Explain how economic growth and international trade increase consumption possibilities.

LOA1.1   (Appendix) Understand graphs, curves, and slopes as they relate to economics.

People's wants are numerous and varied. Biologically, people need only air, water, food, clothing, and shelter. But in modern society people also desire goods and services that provide a more comfortable standard of living. We want bottled water, soft drinks, and fruit juices, not just water from the creek. We want salads, burgers, and pizzas, not just berries and nuts. We want jeans, suits, and coats, not just woven reeds. We want apartments, condominiums, and houses, not just mud huts. And, as the saying goes, "That's not the half of it." We also want flat-panel TVs, Internet service, education, cellphones, health care, and much more.

Fortunately, society possesses productive resources, such as labour and managerial talent, tools and machinery, and land and mineral deposits. These resources, employed in the economic system (or simply the economy), help us produce goods and services that satisfy many of our economic wants. But the blunt reality is that our economic wants far exceed the productive capacity of our scarce (limited) resources. We are forced to make choices. This unchanging truth underlies the definition of economics, which is the social science concerned with how individuals, institutions, and society make optimal (best) choices under conditions of scarcity.

Numerous problems and issues arise from the challenge of making optimal choices under conditions of scarcity. Although it is tempting to plunge into them, that sort of analysis must wait until we discuss some important preliminaries.

1.1   Ten Key Concepts to Retain for a Lifetime

LO1.1   List the ten key concepts to retain for a lifetime.

Suppose you unexpectedly meet your Introductory Economics professor on the street five or ten years after you complete this course. What will you be able to tell her you retained from the course? More than likely you will not be able to remember very much. To help you retain the main ideas that economics has to offer, we have come up with *ten key concepts* that we believe are essential to understanding the world around you and will help you in your chosen career. These concepts will be reinforced throughout the textbook so that you will, we hope, retain them long after the course is over. When a key concept is about to be discussed, you will be alerted with an icon and the concept description.

The ten concepts are simply listed here; you will find elaboration of each as we progress through the textbook. At the end of the course you should review them. They will help you to organize and better understand the materials you have studied. We have divided these key concepts into three categories: (a) concepts that pertain to the individual, (b) concepts that explain the interaction among individuals, and (c) concepts that deal with the economy as a whole and the standard of living.

Economics is concerned with the efficient use of scarce resources to obtain the maximum satisfaction of society's unlimited wants.

The Individual

 FACING TRADE-OFFS   **CONCEPT 1** (Facing Trade-offs): Scarcity in relation to wants means you face trade-offs; therefore, you have to make choices.

 OPPORTUNITY COSTS   **CONCEPT 2** (Opportunity Costs): The cost of the choice you make is what you give up for it, or the opportunity cost.

CHOOSING A LITTLE MORE OR LESS

CONCEPT 3 (Choosing a Little More or Less): Choices are usually made at the margin; we choose a little more or a little less of something.

 THE INFLUENCE OF INCENTIVES

CONCEPT 4 (The Influence of Incentives): The choices you make are influenced by incentives.

Interaction Among Individuals

 SPECIALIZATION AND TRADE

CONCEPT 5 (Specialization and Trade): Specialization and trade will improve the well-being of all participants.

 THE EFFECTIVENESS OF MARKETS

CONCEPT 6 (The Effectiveness of Markets): Markets usually do a good job of coordinating trade among individuals, groups, and nations.

 THE ROLE OF GOVERNMENTS

CONCEPT 7 (The Role of Governments): Governments can occasionally improve the coordinating function of markets.

The Economy as a Whole and the Standard of Living

 PRODUCTION AND THE STANDARD OF LIVING

CONCEPT 8 (Production and the Standard of Living): The standard of living of the average person in a particular country is dependent on its production of goods and services. A rise in the standard of living requires a rise in the output of goods and services.

 MONEY AND INFLATION

CONCEPT 9 (Money and Inflation): If the monetary authorities of a country annually print money in excess of the growth of output of goods and services, this practice will eventually lead to inflation.

INFLATION–UNEMPLOYMENT TRADE-OFF

CONCEPT 10 (Inflation–Unemployment Trade-off): In the short run, society faces a short-run trade-off between inflation and its level of unemployment.

As you read the text, be on the lookout for the icon that alerts you that one of these concepts is being discussed. We now turn to our first topic, the economic way of thinking.

1.2   The Economic Way of Thinking

LO1.2   Define economics and the features of the economic way of thinking.

Close your eyes for a minute and pretend you are in paradise, a place where you can have anything you want whenever you desire it. On a particular day, you might decide you want a new pair of jeans, a new notebook computer, a cellphone, tickets to see Justin Bieber, and a new red Ferrari sports car to cruise around in. Your friends might have a completely different list of wants, but in paradise all of their desires also will be satisfied. Indeed, everyone's desires are satisfied. The following day you can start all over and have any request fulfilled. And so it will continue, forever. Your body will never get old or sick, you will have all the friends and love you want, etc., etc.

Of course, paradise may be waiting for us in the afterlife, but in this world our wants greatly outstrip our ability to satisfy them. Whenever our wants are greater than the resources needed to meet those desires, we have an economic problem. It is this reality that gives economists their unique perspective. This **economic perspective** or *economic way of thinking* has several crucial and closely interrelated features.

Scarcity and Choice

The economic resources needed to make goods and services are in limited supply. This **scarcity** restricts options and requires choices. Because we can't have it all, we must decide what we will have and what we must forgo.

At the core of economics is the idea that "there is no free lunch." You may get treated to lunch, making it free to you, but there is a cost to someone—ultimately society. Scarce inputs of land, equipment, farm labour, the labour of cooks and waiters, and managerial talent are required. Because these resources might be used in other production activities, they and the other goods and services that might have been produced are sacrificed in making the lunch available. Economists call these sacrifices **opportunity costs**. To get more of one thing, you forgo the opportunity to get something else. That sacrifice is the opportunity cost of the choice. For example, you have $100 that you can spend on a pair of jeans or shoes. The opportunity cost of buying the shoes is the jeans you could have purchased, and vice versa.

 OPPORTUNITY COSTS

Purposeful Behaviour

Economics assumes that human behaviour reflects rational self-interest. Individuals look for and pursue opportunities to increase their **utility**—the pleasure, happiness, or satisfaction obtained from consuming a good or service. They allocate their time, energy, and money to maximize their satisfaction. Because they weigh costs and benefits, their decisions are purposeful or rational, not random or chaotic.

Consumers are purposeful in deciding what goods and services to buy. Business firms are purposeful in deciding what products to produce and how to produce them. Government entities are purposeful in deciding what public services to provide and how to finance them.

CONSIDER THIS

Free for All?

Free products are seemingly everywhere. Sellers from time to time offer free apps, free cellphones, and no-fee chequing accounts. Dentists give out free toothbrushes. At provincial visitor centres there are free brochures and maps.

Does the presence of so many free products contradict the economist's assertion that there is no free lunch? No! Scarce resources are used to produce each of these products, and because those resources have alternative uses, society gives up something else to get the "free" good. Because alternatives must be forsaken, there is no such thing as a free lunch.

So why are these goods offered for free? In a word: marketing. Firms sometimes offer free products to entice people to try them and perhaps subsequently purchase them. Getting to try out the free version of an app may eventually entice you to buy a payed version that has more features. In other cases, a product is free only in conjunction with a purchase. To get the soft drink, you must buy the large pizza. To get the free cellphone, you need to sign up for a year (or more) of cellphone service.

© Mar Photographics/Alamy Stock Photo

But while "free" products may come at no cost to the individuals receiving them, they are never free to society because their manufacture requires the use of resources that might have been put to alternative uses.

"Purposeful behaviour" does not assume that people and institutions are immune to faulty logic and therefore are perfect decision makers. They sometimes make mistakes. Nor does it mean that people's decisions are unaffected by emotion or the decisions of those around them. Indeed, economists acknowledge that people are sometimes impulsive or emulate what others do. "Purposeful behaviour" simply means that people make decisions with some desired outcome in mind.

Rational self-interest is not the same as selfishness. In the economy, increasing one's own wage, rent, interest, or profit normally requires identifying and satisfying *somebody else's* wants! Also, people make personal sacrifices for others. They contribute time and money to charities because they derive pleasure from doing so. Parents help pay for their children's education for the same reason. These self-interested but unselfish acts help maximize the giver's satisfaction as much as any purchase of goods or services. Self-interested behaviour is simply behaviour designed to increase personal satisfaction, however it may be derived.

Marginal Analysis: Comparing Benefits and Costs

The economic perspective focuses largely on **marginal analysis**—comparisons of *marginal benefits* and *marginal costs*. To economists, marginal means *extra*, *additional*, or *a change in*. Most choices or decisions involve changes in the status quo (the existing state of affairs). Should you attend school for another year or not? Should you study an extra hour for an exam? Should you add fries to your fast-food order? Similarly, should a business expand or reduce its output? Should government increase or decrease health care funding?

 CHOOSING A LITTLE MORE OR LESS

CONSIDER THIS

Fast-Food Lines

The economic perspective is useful in analyzing all sorts of behaviours. Consider an everyday example: the behaviour of customers at a fast-food restaurant. When customers enter the restaurant, they go to the shortest line, believing that line will minimize their time cost of obtaining food. They are acting purposefully; time is limited, and people prefer using it in some way other than standing in line.

If one line is temporarily shorter than other lines, some people will move to that one. They apparently view the time saving from the shorter line (marginal benefit) as exceeding the cost of moving from their present line (marginal cost). The line switching tends to equalize line lengths. No further movement of customers between lines occurs once all lines are about equal.

Fast-food customers face another cost–benefit decision when a clerk opens a new station at the counter. Should they move to the new station or stay put? Those who shift to the new line decide that the time saving from the move exceeds the extra cost of physically moving. In so deciding, customers must also consider just how quickly they can get to the new station compared with others who may be contemplating the same move. (Those who hesitate are lost!)

Customers at the fast-food establishment do not have perfect information when they select lines. Thus, not all decisions turn out as expected. For example, you might enter a short line only to find that the person in front of you is ordering hamburgers and fries

© Syracuse Newspapers/The Image Works RF

for forty people in the Greyhound bus parked out back (and also that the employee taking orders is a trainee!). Nevertheless, when you made your decision, you thought it was optimal.

Finally, customers must decide what food to order when they arrive at the counter. In making their choices, they again compare marginal costs and marginal benefits in attempting to obtain the greatest personal satisfaction for their expenditure.

Economists believe that what is true for the behaviour of customers at fast-food restaurants is true for economic behaviour in general. Faced with an array of choices, consumers, workers, and businesses rationally compare marginal costs and marginal benefits.

Each option will have marginal benefits and marginal costs. In making choices, the decision maker will compare those two amounts. For example, you and your fiancée are shopping for an engagement ring. Should you buy a ¼-carat, ½-carat, ¾-carat, or larger diamond? The marginal cost of the larger stone is the added expense beyond the smaller one. The marginal benefit is the greater lifetime pleasure (utility) from the larger one. If the marginal benefit of the larger diamond exceeds its marginal cost, you buy the larger one. But if the marginal cost is more than the marginal benefit, buy the smaller diamond instead, even if you can afford the larger.

In a world of scarcity, the marginal benefit associated with some specific option always includes the marginal cost of doing without something else. Spending money on the larger diamond may mean forgoing a honeymoon to an exotic location. Opportunity costs, the value of the next best thing forgone, are always present whenever a choice is made.

1.3   Theories, Principles, and Models

LO1.3   Describe the role of economic theory in economics.

Like the physical and life sciences, as well as other social sciences, economics relies on the **scientific method**. That procedure consists of several elements:

- Observing real-world behaviour and outcomes.

- Formulating a possible explanation of cause and effect (hypothesis) based on those observations.

- Testing this explanation by comparing the outcomes of specific events to the outcome predicted by the hypothesis.

- Accepting, rejecting, or modifying the hypothesis based on these comparisons.

- Continuing to test the hypothesis against the facts. As favourable results accumulate, the hypothesis evolves into a theory. A very well tested and widely accepted theory is referred to as an economic law or an **economic principle**—a statement about economic behaviour or the economy that enables prediction of the probable effects of certain actions. Combinations of such laws or principles are incorporated into models, which are simplified representations of how parts of the economy work, such as a market or segment of the economy.

Economists develop theories of the behaviour of individuals (consumers, workers) and institutions (businesses, governments) engaged in the production, exchange, and consumption of goods and services. Theories, principles, and models are *purposeful simplifications*. The full scope of economic reality itself is too complex and bewildering to be understood as a whole. In developing theories, principles, and models, economists remove the clutter and simplify.

Economic principles and models are highly useful in analyzing economic behaviour and understanding how the economy operates. They are the tools for ascertaining cause and effect (or action and outcome) within the economic system. Good theories do a good job of explaining and predicting. They are supported by facts concerning how individuals and institutions actually behave in producing, exchanging, and consuming goods and services.

Other things you should know about economic principles are as follows:

- *Generalizations* Economic principles are generalizations relating to economic behaviour or to the economy itself. Economic principles are expressed as the tendencies of typical or average consumers, workers, or business firms. For example, economists say that consumers buy more of a particular product when its price falls. Economists recognize that some consumers may increase their purchases by a large amount, others by a small amount, and a few not at all. This *price–quantity principle* holds both for the typical consumer and for consumers as a group.

- *Other-Things-Equal Assumption* In constructing their theories, economists use the *ceteris paribus* or **other-things-equal assumption**—the assumption that factors other than those being considered do not change. They assume that all variables except those under immediate consideration are held constant for a particular analysis. For example, consider the relationship between the price of Pepsi and the amount of it purchased. Assume that of all the factors that might influence the amount of Pepsi purchased (for example, the price of Pepsi, the price of Coca-Cola, and consumer incomes and preferences), only the price of Pepsi varies. This is helpful because the economist can then focus on the relationship between the price of Pepsi and purchases of Pepsi in isolation without being confused by changes in other variables.

MATH 1.1   Ceteris Paribus

- *Graphical Expression* Many economic models are expressed graphically. Be sure to read the appendix at the end of this chapter as a review of graphs.

1.4   Microeconomics and Macroeconomics

LO1.4   Distinguish microeconomics from macroeconomics, and positive economics from normative economics.

Economists develop economic principles and models at two levels.

Microeconomics

Microeconomics is the part of economics concerned with decision making by individual customers, workers, households, and business firms. At this level of analysis, we observe the details of their behaviour under a figurative microscope. We measure the price of a specific product, the number of workers employed by a single firm, the revenue or income of a particular firm or household, or the expenditures of a specific firm, government entity, or family. In microeconomics, we examine the grains of sand, the rocks, and the shells, but not the beach.

Macroeconomics

Macroeconomics examines the performance and behaviour of the economy as a whole. It focuses on economic growth, the business cycle, interest rates, inflation, and the behaviour of major economic aggregates such as the government, household, and business sectors. An **aggregate** is a collection of specific economic units treated as one unit. Therefore, we might lump together the millions of consumers in the Canadian economy and treat them as one huge unit called *consumers*.

In using aggregates, macroeconomics seeks to obtain an overview, or general outline, of the structure of the economy and the relationships of its major aggregates. Macroeconomics speaks of such economic measures as total output, total employment, total income, aggregate expenditures, and the general level of prices in analyzing various economic problems. Very little attention is given to the specific units that make up the various aggregates. Figuratively, macroeconomics looks at the beach, not the grains of sand, the rocks, and the shells.

The last decade has been an exciting time to study macroeconomics. The global financial crisis that spread to Canada in late 2008 resulted in a deep recession, which has been dubbed the Great Recession. You will have a much better understanding of what causes recessions, unemployment, inflation, and changes in the standard of living of the average Canadian once you have finished your course in introductory macroeconomics.

The micro–macro distinction does not mean that economics is so highly compartmentalized that every topic can be readily labelled as either macro or micro; many topics and subdivisions of economics are rooted in both. For example, while the problem of unemployment is usually treated as a macroeconomic topic (because unemployment relates to aggregate production), economists recognize that the decisions made by *individual* workers on how long to search for jobs and the ways in which *specific* labour markets encourage or impede hiring are also crucial in determining the unemployment rate.

Positive and Normative Economics

Both microeconomics and macroeconomics contain elements of positive economics and normative economics. **Positive economics** focuses on facts and cause-and-effect relationships. It includes description, theory development, and theory testing. Positive economics avoids value judgments. It tries to establish scientific statements about economic behaviour and deals with what the economy is actually like. Such analysis is essential to good policy analysis.

Economic policy, on the other hand, involves **normative economics**, which incorporates value judgments about what the economy *should* be like or what particular policy actions *should* be recommended to achieve a desirable goal. Normative economics looks at the desirability of certain aspects of the economy. It underlies expressions of support for particular economic policies.

Positive economics concerns *what is*, whereas normative economics embodies subjective feelings about *what ought to be*. For example, a positive statement would be "The unemployment rate in France is higher than that in Canada." A normative statement would be "France ought to undertake policies to make its labour market more flexible to reduce unemployment rates." When you see words such as "ought" or "should" in a sentence, you are likely encountering a normative statement.

Most of the disagreement among economists involves normative, value-based policy questions. Of course, there is often disagreement about which theories or models best represent the economy and its parts. But economists agree on a full range of economic principles. Most economic controversy thus reflects differing opinions or value judgments about what society should be like.

QUICK REVIEW 1.1

- Economics examines how individuals, institutions, and society make choices under conditions of scarcity.

- The economic way of thinking stresses (a) resource scarcity and the necessity of making choices, (b) the assumption of purposeful (or rational) behaviour, and (c) comparisons of marginal benefit and marginal cost.

- In choosing among alternatives, people incur opportunity costs—the value of the next-best option.

- Economists use the scientific method to establish economic theories, which are cause–effect generalizations about the economic behaviour of individuals and institutions.

- Microeconomics focuses on specific decision making within an economy; macroeconomics examines the economy as a whole.

- Positive economics deals with factual statements (what is); normative economics deals with value judgments (what ought to be).

1.5   The Individual's Economic Problem

> **LO1.5**   Explain the individual's economic problem and how trade-offs, opportunity costs, and attainable combinations can be illustrated with budget lines.

A close examination of the **economic problem**—the need to make choices because economic wants exceed economic means—will enhance your understanding of economic models and the difference between microeconomic and macroeconomic analysis. Let's first build a simple microeconomic model of the general economic problem faced by an individual.

Limited Income

We all have a finite amount of income, even the wealthiest among us. Even members of the Thomson and Weston families—Canada's richest—have to decide how to spend their money, and the majority of us have much more limited means. Our income comes to us in the form of wages, interest, rent, and profit, although we may also receive money from government programs or from family members. As Global Perspective 1.1 shows, the average income of Canadians in 2015 was US$47,250. In the poorest nations, it was less than $500.

1.1 GLOBAL PERSPECTIVE

Average Income, Selected Nations

Average income (total income/population), and therefore typical individual budget constraints, vary greatly among nations.

Country	Per capita income, 2015 (U.S. dollars, based on exchange rates)
Norway	$93,530
Switzerland	84,550
United States	55,980
Canada	47,250
France	40,710
Japan	38,840
South Korea	27,450
Brazil	9,990
Mexico	9,710
China	7,710
Pakistan	1,440
Mali	760
Rwanda	700
Congo	410

Source: World Bank. http://hdl.handle.net/123123123123/123. Licence: Creative Commons Attribution Licence (CC BY 3.0 IGO). The World Bank authorizes the use of this material subject to the terms and conditions on its website, http://www.worldbank.org/terms.

Unlimited Wants

For better or worse, most people have virtually unlimited wants. We desire various goods and services that provide utility. Our wants extend over a wide range of products, from *necessities* (food, shelter, and clothing) to *luxuries* (perfumes, yachts, and sports cars). Some wants, such as basic food, shelter, and clothing, have biological roots. Other wants—for example, specific kinds of food, shelter, and clothing—arise from the conventions and customs of society.

Over time, as new and improved products are introduced, economic wants tend to change and multiply, fuelled by new products. Only recently have people wanted Wi-Fi connections, tablets, or flying drones, because those products did not exist a few decades ago. Also, the satisfaction of certain wants may trigger others: the acquisition of a Ford Focus or a Honda Civic has been known to whet the appetite for a Lexus or a Mercedes.

Services, as well as goods, satisfy our wants. Car repair work, the removal of an inflamed appendix, legal and accounting advice, and haircuts all satisfy human wants. Actually, we buy many goods, such as automobiles and washing machines, for the services they render. The differences between goods and services are often smaller than they appear to be.

For most people, the desires for goods and services cannot be fully satisfied. Bill Gates may have all that he wants for himself, but it is clear from his massive charitable giving that he keenly wants better health care for the world's poor. Our desires for a particular good or service can be satisfied; over a short period of time we can surely get enough toothpaste or pasta. And one appendectomy is plenty. But our broader desire for more goods and services and higher-quality goods and services seems to be another story.

Because we have limited income (usually through our work) but seemingly insatiable wants, it is in our self-interest to pick and choose goods and services that maximize our satisfaction, given the limitations we face. It should be noted that while we are stressing limited income, there is rarely enough of all the other things people desire, such as health, time, physical/mental abilities, and much, much more.

The Budget Line

We can depict the economic problem facing individuals using a **budget line** (or, more technically, *budget constraint*), a schedule or curve that shows various combinations of two products a consumer can purchase with a specific money income. Although we assume two products, the analysis generalizes to the full range of products available to consumers.

To understand the idea of a budget line, suppose that you received an Amazon gift card as a birthday present. The $120 card is soon to expire. You go to Amazon.ca and confine your purchase decisions to two alternatives: movies and paperback books. Movies are $20 each and paperback books are $10 each. Your purchase options are shown in the table in Figure 1-1.

At one extreme, you might spend the entire $120 on 6 movies at $20 each and have nothing left to spend on books. Or, by giving up 2 movies and thereby gaining $40, you can have 4 movies at $20 each and 4 books at $10 each. And so on to the other extreme, at which you could buy 12 books at $10 each, spending your entire gift card on books with nothing left to spend on movies.

The graph in Figure 1-1 shows the budget line. Note that, unlike the table, the graph is not restricted to whole units of movies and books. Every point on the graph represents a possible combination of movies and books, including fractional quantities. The slope of the graphed budget line measures the ratio of the price of books (P_b) to the price of movies (P_m); more precisely, the slope is $P_b/P_m = \$(-10)/\$(+20) = -\frac{1}{2}$. So you must forgo 1 movie (measured on the vertical axis) to buy 2 books (measured on the horizontal axis). This yields a slope of $-\frac{1}{2}$ or -0.5.

The budget line illustrates several ideas.

ATTAINABLE AND UNATTAINABLE COMBINATIONS

All of the combinations of movies and books on or inside the budget line are *attainable* from the $120 of money income. You can afford to buy, for example, 3 movies at $20 each and 6 books at $10 each. You obviously can also

FIGURE 1-1   A Consumer's Budget Line

The budget line (or budget constraint) shows all the combinations of any two products that can be purchased, given the prices of the products and the consumer's money income.

THE BUDGET LINE: WHOLE-UNIT COMBINATIONS OF MOVIES AND PAPERBACK BOOKS ATTAINABLE WITH AN INCOME OF $120		
Units of movies (price = $20)	Units of books (price = $10)	Total expenditure
6	0	($120 = $120 + $0)
5	2	($120 = $100 + $20)
4	4	($120 = $80 + $40)
3	6	($120 = $60 + $60)
2	8	($120 = $40 + $80)
1	10	($120 = $20 + $100)
0	12	($120 = $0 + $120)

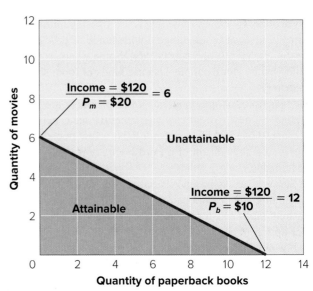

afford to buy 2 movies and 5 books, thereby using up only $90 of the $120 available on your gift card. But to achieve maximum utility you will want to spend the full $120. The budget line shows all combinations that cost exactly the full $120.

In contrast, all combinations beyond the budget line are *unattainable*. For example, the $120 limit does not allow you to purchase 5 movies at $20 each and 5 books at $10 each. That $150 expenditure would clearly exceed the $120 limit. In Figure 1-1 the attainable combinations are on and within the budget line; the unattainable combinations are beyond the budget line.

TRADE-OFFS AND OPPORTUNITY COSTS

The budget line in Figure 1-1 illustrates the idea of trade-offs arising from limited income. To obtain more movies, you have to give up some books. For example, to obtain the first movie you trade off 2 books. So the opportunity cost of the first movie is 2 books. To obtain the second movie, the opportunity cost is also 2 books. The straight-line budget constraint, with its constant slope, indicates constant opportunity cost. That is, the opportunity cost of 1 extra movie remains the same (= 2 books) as more movies are purchased. And the opportunity cost of 1 extra book does not change (= ½ movie) as more books are bought.

CHOICE

Limited income forces people to choose what to buy and what to forgo to fulfill wants. You will select the combination of movies and paperback books that you think is best. That is, you will evaluate your marginal benefits and marginal costs (here, product price) to make choices that maximize your satisfaction. Other people with the same $120 gift card would undoubtedly make different choices.

INCOME CHANGES

The location of the budget line varies with money income. An increase in money income shifts the budget line to the right; a decrease in money income shifts it to the left. To verify this, recalculate the table in Figure 1-1, assuming the card value (income) is (a) $240 and (b) $60, and then plot the new budget lines in the graph. No wonder people like to have more income: that shifts their budget line outward and enables them to buy more goods and services. But even with more income, people will still face spending trade-offs, choices, and opportunity costs.

CONSIDER THIS

Did Zuckerberg, Seacrest, and Swift Make Bad Choices?

Opportunity costs come into play in decisions well beyond simple buying decisions. Consider the different choices people make with respect to post-secondary education. The average salaries earned by college/university graduates are nearly twice as high as those earned by persons with just high school diplomas. For most capable students, "Go to college/university, stay in college/university, and earn a degree" is very sound advice.

Yet Facebook founder Mark Zuckerberg and media personality Ryan Seacrest both dropped out of university, while pop singer Taylor Swift never even bothered to start classes. What were they thinking? Unlike most students, Zuckerberg faced enormous opportunity costs for staying in post-secondaty education. He had a vision for his company, and dropping out helped to ensure Facebook's success. Similarly, Seacrest landed a professional DJ job at his local radio station when he was in high school before moving to Hollywood and eventually becoming America's top radio

© Helga Esteb/Shutterstock.com

and TV personality. Finishing his post-secondary education might have interrupted the string of successes that made his career possible. And Swift knew that staying on top in the world of pop takes unceasing work. So after her first album became a massive hit for her at age 16, it made sense for her to skip post-secondary education in order to relentlessly pursue continuing success.

So Zuckerberg, Seacrest, and Swift understood opportunity costs and made their choices accordingly. The size of opportunity costs matters greatly in making individual decisions.

QUICK REVIEW 1.2

- Because wants exceed incomes, individuals face an economizing problem; they must decide what to buy and what to forgo.

- A budget line (budget constraint) shows the various combinations of two goods that a consumer can purchase with a specific money income.

- Straight-line budget constraints imply constant opportunity costs for both goods.

WORKED PROBLEM 1.1   Budget Lines

1.6   Society's Economic Problem

LO1.6   List the categories of scarce resources and delineate the economic problem.

Society must also make choices under conditions of scarcity. It, too, faces the economic problem. Should it devote more of its limited resources to the criminal justice system (police, courts, and prisons) or to education (teachers, books, and schools)? If it decides to devote more resources to both, what other goods and services does it forgo? Health care? Energy development?

Scarce Resources

Society has limited or scarce **economic resources**, meaning all natural, human, and manufactured resources that go into the production of goods and services. This includes the entire set of factory and farm buildings and all the equipment, tools, and machinery used to produce manufactured goods and agricultural products; all transportation and communication facilities; all types of labour; and land and mineral resources.

Resource Categories

Economists classify economic resources into four general categories.

LAND

Land means much more to the economist than it does to most people. To the economist, **land** includes all natural resources ("gifts of nature") used in the production process. These include forests, mineral and oil deposits, water resources, wind power, sunlight, and arable land.

LABOUR

The resource **labour** consists of the physical actions and mental activities that people contribute to the production of goods and services. The work-related activities of a logger, retail clerk, machinist, teacher, professional hockey player, and nuclear physicist all fall under the general heading of labour.

CAPITAL

For economists, **capital** (or capital goods) includes all manufactured aids used in producing consumer goods and services. Included are all factory, storage, transportation, and distribution facilities, as well as tools and machinery. Economists refer to the purchase of capital goods as **investment** to describe spending that pays for the production and accumulation of capital goods.

Capital goods differ from consumer goods because consumer goods satisfy wants directly, while capital goods do so indirectly by aiding the production of consumer goods. For example, large commercial baking ovens (capital goods) help make loaves of bread (consumer goods). Note that the term *capital* as used by economists does not refer to money, but to tools, machinery, and other productive equipment. Because money produces nothing, economists do not include it as an economic resource. Money (or money capital or financial capital) is simply a means of purchasing capital goods.

ENTREPRENEURIAL ABILITY

Finally, there is the special human resource, distinct from labour, called **entrepreneurial ability**. It is supplied by **entrepreneurs**, who perform several crucial economic functions:

- The entrepreneur takes the initiative in combining the resources of land, labour, and capital to produce a good or a service. Both a spark plug and a catalyst, the entrepreneur is the driving force behind production and the agent who combines the other resources in what is hoped will be a successful business venture.

- The entrepreneur makes the strategic business decisions that set the course of an enterprise.

- The entrepreneur innovates. He or she commercializes new products, new production techniques, or even new forms of business organization.

- The entrepreneur bears risk. Innovation is risky, as nearly all new products and ideas can fail. Progress would cease without entrepreneurs who are willing to take on risk by devoting their time, effort, and ability—as well as their own money and the money of others—to commercializing new products and ideas that may raise society's standard of living.

Because land, labour, capital, and entrepreneurial ability are combined to produce goods and services, they are called the **factors of production**, or simply *inputs*.

1.7   Production Possibilities Model

LO1.7   Apply the concepts of production possibilities analysis, increasing opportunity costs, and economic growth.

Society uses its scarce resources to produce goods and services. The alternatives and choices it faces can best be understood through a macroeconomic model of production possibilities. To keep things simple, let's initially assume:

- *Full Employment* The economy is employing all its available resources.
- *Fixed Resources* The quantity and quality of the factors of production are fixed.
- *Fixed Technology* The state of technology (the methods used to produce output) is constant.
- *Two Goods* The economy is producing only two goods: pizzas and industrial robots. Pizzas symbolize **consumer goods**, products that satisfy our wants directly; industrial robots (for example, the kind used to weld automobile frames) symbolize **capital goods**, products that satisfy our wants indirectly by making possible more efficient production of consumer goods.

Production Possibilities Table

A production possibilities table lists the different combinations of two products that can be potentially produced with a specific set of resources, assuming full employment. Table 1-1 contains such a simple economy that is producing pizzas and industrial robots; the data are, of course, hypothetical. At alternative A, this economy would be devoting all its available resources to the production of industrial robots (capital goods); at alternative E, all resources would go to pizza production (consumer goods). Those alternatives are unrealistic extremes; an economy typically produces both capital goods and consumer goods, as in B, C, and D. As we move from alternative A to E, we increase the production of pizzas at the expense of the production of industrial robots.

Because consumer goods satisfy our wants directly, any movement toward E looks tempting. In producing more pizzas, society increases the satisfaction of its current wants. But there is a cost: More pizzas means fewer industrial robots. This shift of resources to consumer goods catches up with society over time because the stock of capital expands more slowly, thereby reducing potential future production. By moving toward alternative E, society chooses "more now" at the expense of "much later."

By moving toward A, society chooses to forgo current consumption, thereby freeing up resources that can be used to increase the production of capital goods. By building up its stock of capital this way, society will have

TABLE 1-1	Production Possibilities of Pizzas and Robots with Full Employment and Productive Efficiency				
	PRODUCTION ALTERNATIVES				
Type of product	**A**	**B**	**C**	**D**	**E**
Pizzas (in hundred thousands)	0	1	2	3	4
Robots (in thousands)	10	9	7	4	0

greater future production and, therefore, greater future consumption. By moving toward A, society is choosing "more later" at the cost of "less now."

It is generally true that, at any point in time, a fully employed economy must sacrifice some of one good to obtain more of another good. Scarce resources prohibit such an economy from having more of both goods. Society must choose among alternatives. There is no such thing as a free pizza or a free industrial robot. Having more of one thing means having less of something else. For example, if Canadians want more spending on health care, they may have to be satisfied with less spending on education.

Production Possibilities Curve

The data presented in a production possibilities table are shown graphically as a **production possibilities curve**. Such a curve displays the different combinations of goods and services that society can potentially produce in a fully employed economy, assuming a fixed availability of supplies of resources and fixed technology. We arbitrarily represent the economy's output of capital goods (here, industrial robots) on the vertical axis and the output of consumer goods (here, pizzas) on the horizontal axis, as shown in Figure 1-2 (Key Graph).

 # KEY GRAPH

FIGURE 1-2   The Production Possibilities Curve

Each point on the production possibilities curve represents some maximum combination of two products that can be produced if full employment and full production are achieved. When operating on the curve, more robots means fewer pizzas, and vice versa. Limited resources and a fixed technology make any combination of robots and pizzas lying outside the curve (such as at *W*) unattainable. Points inside the curve are attainable, but they indicate that full employment and productive efficiency are not being realized.

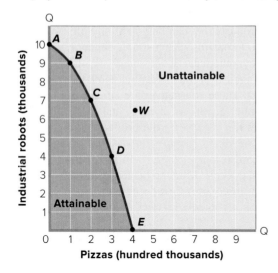

	PRODUCTION ALTERNATIVES				
Type of product	**A**	**B**	**C**	**D**	**E**
Pizzas (in hundred thousands)	0	1	2	3	4
Robots (in thousands)	10	9	7	4	0

QUICK QUIZ

1. **Production possibilities curve *ABCDE* is bowed out from the origin because**

    a. The marginal benefit of pizzas declines as more pizzas are consumed.

    b. The curve gets steeper as we move from E to A.

    c. It reflects the law of increasing opportunity costs.

    d. Resources are scarce.

2. **The marginal opportunity cost of the second unit of pizzas is**

    a. 2 units of robots

    b. 3 units of robots

    c. 7 units of robots

    d. 9 units of robots

3. **The total opportunity cost of 7 units of robots is**

    a. 1 unit of pizzas

    b. 2 units of pizzas

    c. 3 units of pizzas

    d. 4 units of pizzas

4. **All points on this production possibilities curve necessarily represent**

    a. Society's optimal choice

    b. Less than full use of resources

    c. Unattainable levels of output

    d. Full employment

Answers   1. c; 2. a; 3. b; 4. d

Each point on the production possibilities curve represents some maximum output of the two products. The curve is a *constraint* because it shows the limit of attainable outputs. Points on the curve are attainable as long as the economy uses all of its available resources. Points lying inside the curve are also attainable, but they reflect less total output and therefore are not as desirable as points on the curve. Points inside the curve imply that the economy could have more of both industrial robots and pizzas if it achieved full employment. Economic fluctuations are inherent in any economy, and when economic downturns occur, unemployment rises, characterized by points inside the production possibilities curve. One of the main goals of macroeconomics is to understand why an economy can settle inside the production possibilities curve and what policy measures should be undertaken to get the economy back to the **full employment** of all its resources, particularly labour. Points lying beyond the production possibilities curve, like *W*, would represent a greater output than the output at any point on the curve. Such points are, however, unattainable with the current availability of resources and technology.

Law of Increasing Opportunity Costs

Figure 1-2 clearly shows that more pizzas means fewer industrial robots. The number of units of industrial robots that must be given up to obtain another unit of pizzas is, of course, the opportunity cost of that unit of pizzas.

In moving from alternative *A* to alternative *B* in Table 1-1, the cost of 1 additional unit of pizzas is 1 less unit of industrial robots. But when additional units are considered—*B* to *C*, *C* to *D*, and *D* to *E*—an important economic principle is revealed: For society, the opportunity cost of each additional unit of pizzas is greater than the opportunity cost of the preceding one. When we move from *A* to *B*, just 1 unit of industrial robots is sacrificed for 1 more unit of pizzas; but in going from *B* to *C* we sacrifice 2 additional units of industrial robots for 1 more unit of pizzas; then 3 more of industrial robots for 1 more of pizzas; and finally 4 for 1. Conversely, confirm that as we move from *E* to *A*, the cost of an additional unit of industrial robots (on average) is ¼, ⅓, ½, and 1 unit of pizzas, respectively, for the four successive moves.

Our example illustrates the **law of increasing opportunity costs**. As the production of a particular good increases, the opportunity cost of producing an additional unit rises.

SHAPE OF THE CURVE

The law of increasing opportunity costs is reflected in the shape of the production possibilities curve: The curve is bowed out from the origin of the graph. Figure 1-2 shows that when the economy moves from *A* to *E*, it must give up successively larger amounts of industrial robots (1, 2, 3, and 4) to acquire equal increments of pizzas (1, 1, 1, and 1). This is shown in the slope of the production possibilities curve, which becomes steeper as we move from *A* to *E*.

ECONOMIC RATIONALE

The economic explanation for the law of increasing opportunity costs is that *economic resources are not completely adaptable to alternative uses*. Many resources are better at producing one type of good than at producing others. Consider land. Some land is highly suited to growing the ingredients necessary for pizza production. But, as pizza production expands, society has to start using land that is less bountiful for farming. Other land is rich in mineral deposits and therefore well suited to producing the materials needed to make industrial robots. That land will be the first land devoted to the production of industrial robots. But as society steps up the production of robots, it must use land that is less and less suited to making their components.

If we start at *A* and move to *B* in Figure 1-2, we can shift resources whose productivity is relatively high in pizza production and low in industrial robots. But as we move from *B* to *C*, *C* to *D*, and so on, resources highly productive in making pizzas become increasingly scarce. To get more pizzas, resources will be needed whose productivity in making industrial robots is relatively great. It will take increasingly more of such resources, hence greater sacrifices of industrial robots, to achieve each 1-unit increase in pizzas. This lack of perfect flexibility, or interchangeability, on the part of resources is the cause of increasing opportunity costs for society.

WORKED PROBLEM 1.2   Production Possibilities

Optimal Allocation

Of all the attainable combinations of pizzas and industrial robots on the curve in Figure 1-2, which is optimal (best)? That is, what specific quantities of resources should be allocated to pizzas and what specific quantities to industrial robots in order to maximize satisfaction?

Recall that economic decisions centre on comparisons of marginal benefit (MB) and marginal cost (MC). Any economic activity should be expanded as long as marginal benefit exceeds marginal cost and should be reduced if marginal cost exceeds marginal benefit. The optimal amount of the activity occurs where MB = MC. Society needs to make a similar assessment about its production decision.

Consider pizzas. We already know from the law of increasing opportunity costs that the marginal cost of additional units of pizzas will rise as more units are produced. At the same time, we need to recognize that the extra or marginal benefits that come from producing and consuming pizza decline with each successive unit of pizza. Consequently, each successive unit of pizza brings with it both increasing marginal costs and decreasing marginal benefits.

The optimal quantity of pizza production is indicated in Figure 1-3 by point *e* at the intersection of the MB and MC curves: 200,000 units. Why is this amount the optimal quantity? If only 100,000 units of pizzas were produced,

FIGURE 1-3   Optimal Allocation: MB = MC

Optimal allocation requires the expansion of a good's output until its marginal benefit (MB) and marginal cost (MC) are equal. No resources beyond that point should get allocated to the product. Here, allocative efficiency occurs when 200,000 pizzas are produced.

the marginal benefit of an extra unit of them (point *a*) would exceed its marginal cost (point *b*). In money terms, MB is $15, while MC is only $5. When society gains something worth $15 at a marginal cost of only $5, it is better off. In Figure 1-3, net gains can continue to be realized until pizza production has been increased to 200,000.

In contrast, the production of 300,000 units of pizzas is excessive. There the MC of an added unit is $15 (point *c*) and its MB is only $5 (point *d*). This means that 1 unit of pizzas is worth only $5 to society but costs society $15 to obtain. This is a losing proposition for society!

So resources are being efficiently allocated to any product when the marginal benefit and marginal cost of its output are equal (MB = MC). Suppose that by applying the above analysis to industrial robots, we find their optimal (MB = MC) quantity is 7000. This would mean alternative *C* (200,000 units of pizzas and 7000 units of industrial robots) on the production possibilities curve in Figure 1-2 would be optimal for this economy.

QUICK REVIEW 1.3

- Economists categorize economic resources as land, labour, capital, and entrepreneurial ability.

- The production possibilities curve illustrates (a) scarcity of resources, implied by the area of unattainable combinations of output lying outside the production possibilities curve; (b) choice among outputs, reflected in the variety of attainable combinations of goods lying along

the curve; (c) opportunity cost, illustrated by the downward slope of the curve; and (d) the law of increasing opportunity costs, reflected in the bowed-outward shape of the curve.

- A comparison of marginal benefits and marginal costs is needed to determine the best or optimal output mix on a production possibilities curve.

1.8 Unemployment, Growth, and the Future

LO1.8 **Explain how economic growth and international trade increase consumption possibilities.**

In the depths of the Great Depression of the 1930s, almost 20 percent of workers were unemployed and one-quarter of Canadian production capacity was idle. Subsequent downturns have been much less severe. During the relatively deep 2008–2009 recession, for instance, production fell by a comparably smaller 2.8 percent and the unemployment rate peaked at 8.7 percent. Almost all nations have experienced widespread unemployment and unused production capacity from business downturns at one time or another. Since 2010, for example, many nations—including Argentina, Italy, Russia, Japan, and France—have had economic downturns and unemployment.

How do these realities relate to the production possibilities model? Our analysis and conclusions change if we relax the assumption that all available resources are fully employed. The five alternatives in Table 1-1 represent maximum outputs; they illustrate the combinations of pizzas and industrial robots that can be produced when the economy is operating at full employment. With unemployment, this economy would produce less than each alternative shown in the table.

Graphically, we represent situations of unemployment by points inside the original production possibilities curve (reproduced here in Figure 1-4). Point *U* is one such point. Here the economy is falling short of the various maximum combinations of pizzas and industrial robots represented by the points on the production possibilities curve. The arrows in Figure 1-4 indicate three possible paths back to full employment. A move toward full employment would yield a greater output of one or both products.

A Growing Economy

When we drop the assumptions that the quantity and quality of resources and technology are fixed, the production possibilities curve shifts position and the potential maximum output of the economy changes.

INCREASES IN FACTOR SUPPLIES

Although factor supplies are fixed at any specific moment, they change over time via more education and training. Historically, the economy's stock of capital has increased at a significant, though unsteady, rate. And although

FIGURE 1-4   Unemployment, Productive Inefficiency, and the Production Possibilities Curve

Any point inside the production possibilities curve, such as *U*, represents unemployment or a failure to achieve productive efficiency. The arrows indicate that, by realizing full employment and productive efficiency, the economy could operate on the curve. This means it could produce more of one or both products than it is producing at point *U*.

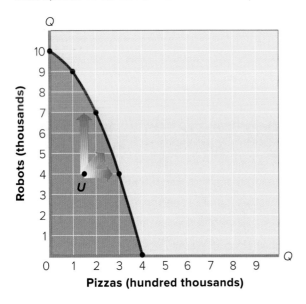

some of our energy and mineral resources are being depleted, new sources are also being discovered. The development of irrigation systems, for example, adds to the supply of arable land.

The net result of these increased supplies of the factors of production is the ability to produce more of both consumer goods and capital goods. Thus, twenty years from now the production possibilities may supersede those shown in Table 1-1. The new production possibilities might look like those in the table in Figure 1-5. The greater abundance of resources will result in a greater potential output of one or both products at each alternative. The economy will have achieved economic growth in the form of expanded potential output. Thus, when an increase in the quantity or quality of resources occurs, the production possibilities curve shifts outward and to the right, as illustrated by the move from the inner curve to curve *A′B′C′D′E′* in Figure 1-5. This sort of shift represents growth of economic capacity that, when used, means **economic growth**: a larger total output.

ADVANCES IN TECHNOLOGY

An advancing technology brings both new and better goods and improved ways of producing them. For now, let's think of technological advance as being only improvements in the methods of production—for example, the introduction of computerized systems to manage inventories and schedule production. These advances alter our previous discussion of the economic problem by allowing society to produce more goods with available resources. As with increases in resource supplies, technological advances make possible the production of more industrial robots *and* more pizzas.

A real-world example of improved technology is the recent surge of new innovations relating to computers, communications, and biotechnology. Technological advances have dropped the prices of computers and greatly increased their speed. Improved software has greatly increased the everyday usefulness of computers. Cellphones and the Internet have increased communications capacity, enhancing production and improving the efficiency of markets. Advances in biotechnology have resulted in important agricultural and medical discoveries. These and other new and improved technologies have contributed to both global and Canadian economic growth (outward shifts of the nation's production possibilities curve).

Conclusion: Economic growth is the result of (1) increases in supplies of factors of production, (2) improvements in factor quality, and (3) technological advances. The consequence of growth is that a full-employment economy can enjoy a greater output of both consumption goods and capital goods. While static, no-growth economies must sacrifice some of one good to obtain more of another, dynamic, growing economies can have larger quantities of both goods.

FIGURE 1-5   Economic Growth and the Production Possibilities Curve

The increase in supplies of resources, the improvements in resource quality, and the technological advances that occur in a dynamic economy move the production possibilities curve outward and to the right, allowing the economy to have larger quantities of both types of goods.

	PRODUCTION ALTERNATIVES				
Type of product	**A′**	**B′**	**C′**	**D′**	**E′**
Pizzas (in hundred thousands)	0	2	4	6	8
Robots (in thousands)	14	12	9	5	0

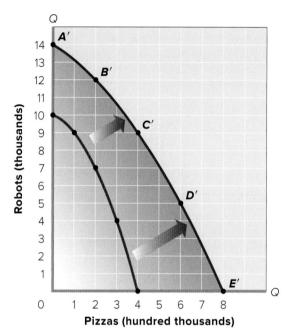

Present Choices and Future Possibilities

An economy's current chosen position on its production possibilities curve helps determine the future location of that curve. Let's designate the two axes of the production possibilities curve as *goods for the future* and *goods for the present*, as in Figure 1-6 (Key Graph). Goods for the future are such things as capital goods, research and education, and preventive medicine. They increase the quantity and quality of property resources, enlarge the stock of technological information, and improve the quality of human resources. As we have already seen, goods for the future, such as capital goods, are the ingredients of economic growth. Goods for the present are consumer goods, such as food, clothing, and entertainment.

CONSIDER THIS

Women, the Workforce, and Production Possibilities

We have seen that more and better-quality factors of production and improved technology shift a nation's production possibilities curve outward. An example of more resources is the large increase in the number of employed women in Canada within the past five decades: 62 percent of adult Canadian women work full-time or part-time in paid jobs today, as against only 40 percent in 1965.

Over recent decades, women have greatly increased their productivity in the workplace, mostly by becoming better educated and professionally trained. As a result, they can earn higher wages. Because those higher wages have increased the opportunity cost—the forgone wage earnings—of staying at home, women have substituted employment in the labour market for the now more "expensive" traditional home activities. This substitution has been particularly pronounced among married women. Along with other factors, such as changing attitudes and expanded job access, the rising earnings of women have produced a substantial increase in the number of women workers in Canada. This increase in the quantity of available resources has helped push the Canadian production possibilities curve outward.

© Shutterstock/Monkey Business Images

KEY GRAPH

FIGURE 1-6   Present Choices and Future Locations of a Production Possibilities Curve

(a) Presentville's current choice to produce more present goods and fewer future goods, as represented by point *P*, will result in a modest outward shift of the production possibilities curve in the future. (b) Futureville's current choice of producing fewer present goods and more future goods, as depicted by point *F*, will lead to a greater outward shift of the production possibilities curve in the future.

Now suppose there are two hypothetical economies, Presentville and Futureville, which are initially identical in every respect except one: Presentville's current chosen position on its production possibilities curve strongly favours present goods over future goods. Point *P* in Figure 1-6a indicates that choice. It is located quite far down the curve to the right, indicating a high priority for goods for the present, at the expense of fewer goods for the future. Futureville, in contrast, makes a current choice that stresses larger amounts of future goods and smaller amounts of present goods, as shown by point *F* in Figure 1-6b.

Now, other things equal, we can expect Futureville's future production possibilities curve to be farther to the right than Presentville's future production possibilities curve. By currently choosing an output more favourable to technological advances and to increases in the quantity and quality of resources, Futureville will achieve greater economic growth than Presentville. In terms of capital goods, Futureville is choosing to make larger current additions to its "national factory" by devoting more of its current output to capital than Presentville. The payoff from this choice for Futureville is greater future production capacity and economic growth. The opportunity cost is fewer consumer goods in the present for Futureville to enjoy.

Is Futureville's choice "better" than Presentville's? That we cannot say. The different outcomes simply reflect different preferences and priorities in the two countries. But each country will have to live with the economic consequences of its choice.

A Qualification: International Trade

Production possibilities analysis implies that an individual nation is limited to the combinations of output indicated by its production possibilities curve. But we must modify this principle when international specialization and trade exist.

You will see in later chapters that an economy can circumvent, through international specialization and trade, the output limits imposed by its domestic production possibilities curve. Under international specialization and trade, each nation first specializes in the production of those items for which it has the lowest opportunity costs (due to an abundance of the necessary resources). Countries then engage in international trade, with each country exchanging the items that it can produce at the lowest opportunity costs for the items that other countries can produce at the lowest opportunity costs.

International specialization and trade allow a nation to get more of a desired good at less sacrifice of some other good. Rather than sacrifice three units of domestically produced robots to get a third unit of domestically produced pizza, as in Table 1-1, a nation that engages in international specialization and trade might be able to do much better. If it specializes in robots while another country specializes in pizza, then it may be able to obtain the third unit of pizza by trading only two units of domestically produced robots for one unit of foreign-produced pizza. Specialization and trade have the same effect as having more and better resources or discovering improved production techniques; both increase the quantities of capital and consumer goods available to society. Expansion of domestic production possibilities and international trade are two separate routes for obtaining greater output.

QUICK REVIEW 1.4

- Unemployment causes an economy to operate at a point inside its production possibilities curve.

- Increases in resource supplies, improvements in resource quality, and technological advances cause economic growth, which is depicted as an outward shift of the production possibilities curve.

- An economy's present choice of capital and consumer goods helps determine the future location of its production possibilities curve.

- International specialization and trade enable a nation to obtain more goods than its production possibilities curve would indicate.

The **LAST WORD**

Pitfalls to Sound Economic Reasoning

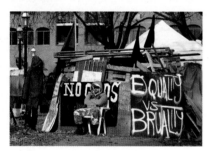

© Deborah Baic/The Globe and Mail

Because they affect us so personally, we often have difficulty thinking accurately and objectively about economic issues.

Here are some common pitfalls to avoid in successfully applying the economic perspective.

Biases Most people bring a bundle of biases and preconceptions to the field of economics. For example, some might think that corporate profits are excessive or that lending money is always superior to borrowing money. Others might believe that government is necessarily less efficient than businesses, or that more government regulation is always better than less. Biases cloud thinking and interfere with objective analysis. All of us must be willing to shed biases and preconceptions that are not supported by facts.

Loaded Terminology The economic terminology used in newspapers and broadcast media is sometimes emotionally biased, or loaded. The writer or spokesperson may have a cause to promote or an axe to grind and may slant comments accordingly. High profits may be labelled "obscene," low wages may be called "exploitive," or self-interested behaviour may be identified as "greed." Government workers may be referred to as "mindless bureaucrats" and those favouring stronger government regulations may be

called "socialists." To analyze economic issues objectively, you must be prepared to reject or discount such terminology.

Fallacy of Composition Another pitfall in economic thinking is the assumption that what is true for one individual or part of a whole is necessarily true for a group of individuals or the whole. This is a logical fallacy called the *fallacy of composition*. A statement valid for an individual or part is not necessarily valid for the larger group or whole. A noneconomic analogy might be that you can see the action better if you leap to your feet to see an outstanding play at a football game. But if everyone leaps to their feet at the same time, nobody—including you—will have a better view than when all remained seated.

Here are two economic examples: An individual shareholder can sell shares of, say, BlackBerry Limited stock without affecting the price of the stock. This is because the sale is a negligible fraction of the total shares of BlackBerry being bought and sold. If, however, all BlackBerry shareholders decide to sell their shares on the same day, the market will be flooded with shares and the price will fall precipitously. Similarly, a single cattle ranch can increase its revenue by expanding the size of its livestock herd. The extra cattle will not affect the price of cattle when they are brought to market. But if all ranchers as a group expand their herds, the total output of cattle will increase so much that the price of cattle will decline when the cattle are sold. If the price reduction is relatively large, ranchers as a group might find that their income has fallen despite their having sold a greater number of cattle because the fall in price overwhelms the increase in quantity.

Post Hoc Fallacy You must think very carefully before concluding that because event A precedes event B, A is the cause of B. This kind of faulty reasoning is known as the *post hoc, ergo propter hoc* or "after this, therefore because of this" fallacy. To give another noneconomic example: The Calgary Flames hire a new coach and the team's record improves. Is the new coach the cause? Maybe. But it might be that the presence of more experienced and talented players or an easier schedule is the true cause. Another example is that the rooster crows before dawn, but does not cause the sunrise.

Correlation and Causation Do not confuse correlation, or connection, with causation. Correlation between two events or two sets of data indicates only that they are associated in some systematic and dependable way. For example, we may find that when variable X increases, Y also increases. But this correlation does not necessarily mean that there is causation—that is, that increases in X cause increases in Y. The relationship might be purely coincidental or dependent on some other factor, Z, not included in the analysis.

Here is an example: Economists have found a positive correlation between education and income. In general, people with more education earn higher incomes than those with less education. Common sense suggests that education is the cause and higher incomes are the effect; more education implies a more knowledgeable and productive worker, and such workers receive larger salaries.

But causation could also partly run the other way. People with higher incomes could buy more education, just as they buy more furniture and steaks. Or is part of the relationship explainable in still other ways? Are education and income correlated because the characteristics required for succeeding in education—ability and motivation—are the same ones required to be a productive and highly paid worker? If so, then people with those traits will probably both obtain more education and earn higher incomes. But greater education will not be the sole cause of the higher income.

Question

Studies indicate that married men on average earn more income than unmarried men of the same age and education level. Why must we be cautious in concluding that marriage is the cause and higher income is the effect?

Chapter Summary

LO1.1   List the ten key concepts to retain for a lifetime.

- The ten key concepts can be divided into three categories: (a) concepts that pertain to the individual (Facing Trade-offs, Opportunity Costs, Choosing a Little More or Less, and The Influence of Incentives); (b) concepts that explain the interaction among individuals (Specialization and Trade, The Effectiveness of Markets, and The Role of Governments); and (c) concepts that deal with the economy as a whole and the standard of living (Production and the Standard of Living, Money and Inflation, and Inflation–Unemployment Trade-off).

LO1.2   Define economics and the features of the economic way of thinking.

- Economics is the social science that examines how individuals, institutions, and society make choices under conditions of scarcity. Central to economics is the idea of opportunity cost: the value of the good, service, or time forgone to obtain something else.

- The economic perspective includes three elements: scarcity and choice, purposeful behaviour, and marginal analysis. It sees individuals and institutions as making rational decisions based on comparisons of marginal benefits and marginal costs.

LO1.3   Describe the role of economic theory in economics.

- Economists employ the scientific method, in which they form and test hypotheses of cause-and-effect relationships to generate theories, principles, and laws. Economists often combine principles and laws into representations called models.

LO1.4   Distinguish microeconomics from macroeconomics, and positive economics from normative economics.

- Microeconomics examines specific economic units or institutions. Macroeconomics looks at the economy as a whole or its major aggregates.

- Positive economics deals with facts; normative economics reflects value judgments.

LO1.5   Explain the individual's economic problem and how trade-offs, opportunity costs, and attainable combinations can be illustrated with budget lines.

- Individuals face an economic problem. Because their wants exceed their incomes, they must decide what to purchase and what to forgo. Society also faces the economic problem. Societal wants exceed the available resources necessary to fulfill them. Society, therefore, must decide what to produce and what to forgo.

- Graphically, a budget line (or budget constraint) illustrates the economic problem for individuals. The line shows the various combinations of two products that a consumer can purchase with a specific money income, given the prices of the two products.

LO1.6   List the categories of scarce resources and delineate the economic problem.

- Economic resources are inputs into the production process and can be classified as land, labour, capital, and entrepreneurial ability. Economic resources are also known as factors of production or inputs.

- Economists illustrate society's economic problem through production possibilities analysis. Production possibilities tables and curves show the different combinations of goods and services that can be produced in a fully employed economy assuming that resource quantity, resource quality, and technology are fixed.

LO1.7   Apply the concepts of production possibilities analysis, increasing opportunity costs, and economic growth.

- An economy that is fully employed and thus operating on its production possibilities curve must sacrifice the output of some types of goods and services to increase the production of others. The gain in one type of good or service is always accompanied by an opportunity cost in the form of the loss in some other type of good or service.

- Because resources are not equally productive in all possible uses, shifting resources from one use to another creates increasing opportunity costs. The production of additional units of one product requires the sacrifice of increasing amounts of the other product.

- The optimal (best) point on the production possibilities curve represents the most desirable mix of goods and is determined by expanding the production of each good until its marginal benefit (MB) equals its marginal cost (MC).

LO1.8   Explain how economic growth and international trade increase consumption possibilities.

- Over time, technological advances and increases in the quantity and quality of resources enable the economy to produce more of all goods and services—that is, to experience economic growth.

- Society's choice as to the mix of consumer goods and capital goods in current output is a major determinant of the future location of the production possibilities curve and thus of the extent of economic growth.

- International trade enables a nation to obtain more goods from its limited resources than its production possibilities curve would indicate.

Terms and Concepts

economics	budget line
economic perspective	economic resources
scarcity	land
opportunity cost	labour
utility	capital
marginal analysis	investment
scientific method	entrepreneurial ability
economic principle	entrepreneurs
other-things-equal assumption	factors of production
microeconomics	consumer goods
macroeconomics	capital goods
aggregate	production possibilities curve
positive economics	law of increasing opportunity costs
normative economics	economic growth
economic problem	

Discussion Questions

1. What is an opportunity cost? How does the idea relate to the definition of economics? Which of the following decisions would entail the greater opportunity cost: allocating a square block in the heart of Toronto for a surface parking lot or allocating a square block at the edge of a typical suburb for such a lot? Explain.   [**LO1.2**]

2. Cite three examples of recent decisions that you made in which you (at least implicitly) weighed marginal cost and marginal benefit.   [**LO1.2**]

3. What is meant by the term *utility* and how does the idea relate to purposeful behaviour?   [**LO1.2**]

4. What are the key elements of the scientific method and how does this method relate to economic principles and laws?   [**LO1.3**]

5. State (a) a positive economic statement of your choice, and then (b) a normative economic statement relating to your first statement.   [**LO1.4**]

6. How does the slope of a budget line illustrate opportunity costs and trade-offs? How does a budget line illustrate scarcity and the effect of limited incomes? [LO1.5]

7. What are economic resources? What categories do economists use to classify them? Why are resources also called factors of production? Why are they called inputs? [LO1.6]

8. Why is money not considered a capital resource in economics? Why is entrepreneurial ability considered a category of economic resource, distinct from labour? What are the major functions of the entrepreneur? [LO1.6]

9. Specify and explain the typical shapes of marginal benefit and marginal cost curves. How are these curves used to determine the optimal allocation of resources to a particular product? If current output is such that marginal cost exceeds marginal benefit, should more or fewer resources be allocated to this product? Explain. [LO1.7]

10. Suppose that, on the basis of a nation's production possibilities curve, an economy must sacrifice 10,000 pizzas domestically to get the one additional industrial robot it desires, but that it can get the robot from another country in exchange for 9000 pizzas. Relate this information to the following statement: "Through international specialization and trade, a nation can reduce its opportunity cost of obtaining goods and thus move outside its production possibilities curve." [LO1.8]

Review Questions

1. Match each term with the correct definition. [LO1.2]

   economics

   opportunity cost

   marginal analysis

   utility

   a. The next-best thing that must be forgone in order to produce one more unit of a given product.

   b. The pleasure, happiness, or satisfaction obtained from consuming a good or service.

   c. The social science concerned with how individuals, institutions, and society make optimal (best) choices under conditions of scarcity.

   d. Making choices based on comparing marginal benefits with marginal costs.

2. Indicate whether each of the following statements applies to microeconomics or macroeconomics: [LO1.3]

   a. The unemployment rate in Canada was 5.9 percent in January 2018.

   b. A software firm discharged fifteen workers last month and transferred the work to India.

   c. An unexpected freeze in central Florida reduced the citrus crop and caused the price of oranges to rise.

   d. Canadian output, adjusted for inflation, increased by 3.0 percent in 2017.

   e. Last week Scotiabank lowered its interest rate on business loans by one-half of one percentage point.

   f. The consumer price index rose by 1.7 percent from January 2017 to January 2018.

3. Suppose that you initially have $100 to spend on books or movie tickets. The books start off costing $25 each and the movie tickets start off costing $10 each. For each of the following situations, would the attainable set of combinations that you can afford increase or decrease? [LO1.5]

   a. Your budget increases from $100 to $150 while the prices stay the same.

   b. Your budget remains $100, the price of books remains $25, but the price of movie tickets rises to $20.

   c. Your budget remains $100, the price of movie tickets remains $10, but the price of a book falls to $15.

4. Suppose that you are given a $100 budget at work that can be spent only on two items: staplers and pens. If staplers cost $10 each and pens cost $2.50 each, then the opportunity cost of purchasing one stapler is [LO1.5]

   a. 10 pens

   b. 5 pens

   c. No pens

   d. 4 pens

5. For each of the following situations involving marginal cost (MC) and marginal benefit (MB), indicate whether it would be best to produce more, fewer, or the current number of units. [LO1.5]

   a. 3000 units at which MC = $10 and MB = $13

   b. 11 units at which MC = $4 and MB = $3

   c. 43,277 units at which MC = $99 and MB = $99

   d. 82 units at which MC < MB

   e. 5 units at which MB < MC

6. Explain how (if at all) each of the following events affects the location of a country's production possibilities curve: [LO1.7]

   a. The quality of education increases.

   b. The number of unemployed workers increases.

   c. A new technique improves the efficiency of extracting copper from ore.

   d. A devastating earthquake destroys numerous production facilities.

7. What are the two major ways in which an economy can grow and push out its production possibilities curve? [LO1.8]

   a. Better weather and nicer cars

   b. Higher taxes and lower spending

   c. Increases in resource supplies and advances in technology

   d. Decreases in scarcity and advances in auditing

Problems

1. Potatoes cost Janice $1 per kilogram, and she has $5 that she could possibly spend on potatoes or other items. If she feels that the first kilogram of potatoes is worth $1.50, the second kilogram is worth $1.14, the third kilogram is worth $1.05, and all subsequent kilograms are worth $0.30, how many kilograms of potatoes will she purchase? What if she only had $2 to spend?   [**LO1.2**]

2. Pham can work as many or as few hours as she wants at the university bookstore for $9 per hour. But due to her hectic schedule, she has just 15 hours per week that she can spend working either at the bookstore or at other potential jobs. One potential job, at a café, will pay her $12 per hour for up to 6 hours per week. She has another job offer at a garage that will pay her $10 an hour for up to 5 hours per week. And she has a potential job at a daycare centre that will pay her $8.50 per hour for as many hours as she can work. If her goal is to maximize the amount of money she can make each week, how many hours will she work at the bookstore?   [**LO1.2**]

3. Suppose you won $15 on a lottery ticket at the local 7-Eleven and decided to spend all the winnings on candy bars and bags of peanuts. Candy bars cost $0.75 each while bags of peanuts cost $1.50 each.   [**LO1.6**]

    a. Construct a table showing the alternative combinations of the two products that are available.

    b. Plot the data in your table as a budget line in a graph. What is the slope of the budget line? What is the opportunity cost of one more candy bar? Of one more bag of peanuts? Do these opportunity costs rise, fall, or remain constant as each additional unit of the product is purchased?

    c. Does the budget line tell you which of the available combinations of candy bars and bags of peanuts to buy?

    d. Suppose that you had won $30 on your ticket, not $15. Show the $30 budget line in your diagram. Has the number of available combinations increased or decreased?

4. Suppose that you are on a desert island and possess exactly 20 coconuts. Your neighbour, Friday, is a fisher, and he is willing to trade 2 fish for every 1 coconut you are willing to give him. Another neighbour, Kwame, also a fisher, is willing to trade 3 fish for every 1 coconut.   [**LO1.6**]

    a. On a single figure, draw budget lines for trading with Friday and for trading with Kwame. (Put coconuts on the vertical axis.)

    b. What is the slope of the budget line from trading with Friday?

    c. What is the slope of the budget line from trading with Kwame?

    d. Which budget line features a larger set of attainable combinations of coconuts and fish?

    e. If you are going to trade coconuts for fish, would you rather trade with Friday or with Kwame?

5. Below is a production possibilities table for consumer goods (automobiles) and capital goods (forklifts).   [**LO1.7**]

    a. Show these data graphically. Upon what specific assumptions is this production possibilities curve based?

    b. If the economy is at point C, what is the cost of one more automobile? Of one more forklift? Which characteristic of the production possibilities curve reflects the law of increasing opportunity costs, its shape or its length?

    c. If the economy characterized by this production possibilities table and curve were producing 3 automobiles and 20 forklifts, what could you conclude about its use of its available resources?

    d. Is production at a point outside the production possibilities curve currently possible? Could a future advance in technology allow production beyond the current production possibilities curve? Could international trade allow a country to consume beyond its current production possibilities curve?

PRODUCTION ALTERNATIVES

Type of production	A	B	C	D	E
Automobiles	0	2	4	6	8
Forklifts	30	27	21	12	0

6. Look at Figure 1-3. Suppose that the cost of cheese falls, so that the marginal cost of producing pizza decreases. Will the MC curve shift up or down? Will the optimal amount of pizza increase or decrease?   [**LO1.7**]

7. Referring to the table in Problem 5, suppose that improvement occurs in the technology of producing forklifts but not in the technology of producing automobiles. Draw the new production possibilities curve. Now assume that a technological advance occurs in producing automobiles but not in producing forklifts. Draw the new production possibilities curve. Now draw a production possibilities curve that reflects technological improvement in the production of both goods.   [**LO1.8**]

8. Because investment and capital goods are paid for with savings, higher savings rates reflect a decision to consume fewer goods for the present in order to be able to invest in more goods for the future. On average, households in China save 40 percent of their annual income each year, whereas households in Canada save less than 5 percent. Production possibilities are growing at roughly 9 percent annually in China and 3.5 percent in Canada. Use graphical analysis of *present goods* versus *future goods* to explain the differences in growth rates.   [**LO1.8**]

A1.1 Graphs and Their Meanings

LOA1.1 Understand graphs, curves, and slopes as they relate to economics.

If you glance quickly through this text, you will find many graphs. Some seem simple, while others are more complicated. All are included to help you visualize and understand economic relationships. Physicists and chemists sometimes illustrate their theories by building arrangements of multicoloured wooden balls, representing protons, neutrons, and electrons, which are held in proper relation to one another by wires or sticks. Economists use graphs to illustrate their models. By understanding these illustrations you can more readily make sense of economic relationships.

Construction of a Graph

A *graph* is a visual representation of the relationship between two economic quantities or variables. Figure A1-1 is a hypothetical illustration showing the relationship between income and consumption for the economy as a whole. Without even studying economics, we would logically expect that people would buy more goods and services when their incomes go up. Thus, it is not surprising to find in Figure A1-1 that total consumption in the economy increases as total income increases.

The information in Figure A1-1 is expressed both graphically and in table form. Here is how it is done: We want to show graphically how consumption changes as income changes. We therefore represent income on the **horizontal axis** of the graph and consumption on the **vertical axis**.

Now we arrange the vertical and horizontal scales of the graph to reflect the ranges of values of consumption and income, and mark the scales in convenient increments. As you can see in Figure A1-1, the values marked on the scales cover all the values in the table. The values on both axes are indicated in $100 increments.

Because the graph has two dimensions, each point within it represents an income value and its associated consumption value. To find a point that represents one of the five income–consumption combinations in the table, we draw straight lines from the appropriate values on the vertical and horizontal axes. For example, to plot point *c* ($200 income, $150 consumption), draw straight lines up from the horizontal (income) axis at $200 and across from the vertical (consumption) axis at $150. These straight lines intersect at point *c*, which represents this particular income–consumption combination. You should verify that the other income–consumption combinations shown in the table are properly located on the graph. Finally, by assuming that the same general relationship between income and consumption prevails for all other

FIGURE A1-1   The Relationship Between Income and Consumption

Two sets of data that are positively or directly related, such as consumption and income, graph as an upsloping line.

Income per week	Consumption per week	Point
$ 0	$ 50	a
100	100	b
200	150	c
300	200	d
400	250	e

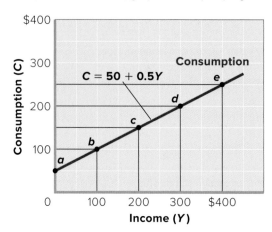

incomes, we draw a line or smooth curve to connect these points. That line or curve represents the income–consumption relationship.

If the curve is a straight line, as in Figure A1-1, we say that the relationship is *linear*. (It is permissible, and even customary, to refer to straight lines in graphs as "curves.")

Direct and Inverse Relationships

The line in Figure A1-1 slopes upward to the right, depicting a direct relationship between income and consumption. By a **direct relationship** (or positive relationship) we mean that two variables—in this case, consumption and income—change in the *same* direction. An increase in consumption is associated with an increase in income; a decrease in consumption accompanies a decrease in income. When two sets of data are positively or directly related, they always graph as an *upsloping* line, as in Figure A1-1.

In contrast, two sets of data may be inversely related. Consider Figure A1-2, which shows the relationship between the price of basketball tickets and game attendance at Informed University (IU). Here we have an **inverse relationship** (or negative relationship) because the two variables change in *opposite* directions. When ticket prices decrease, attendance increases. When ticket prices increase, attendance decreases. The six data points in the table are plotted in the graph. Observe that an inverse relationship always graphs as a *downsloping* line.

Dependent and Independent Variables

Although it is not always easy, economists seek to determine which variable is the *cause* and which the *effect*. Or, more formally, they seek the independent variable and the dependent variable. The **independent variable** is the cause or source; it is the variable that changes first. The **dependent variable** is the effect or outcome; it is the variable that changes because of the change in the independent variable. As in our income–consumption example, income generally is the independent variable and consumption the dependent variable. Income causes consumption to be what it is rather than the other way around. Similarly, ticket prices (set in advance of the season and printed on the ticket) determine attendance at Informed University basketball games; attendance at games does not determine the printed ticket prices for those games. Ticket price is the independent variable, and the quantity of tickets purchased is the dependent variable.

You may recall from your high school courses that mathematicians put the independent variable (cause) on the horizontal axis and the dependent variable (effect) on the vertical axis. Economists are less tidy; their graphing of independent and dependent variables is more arbitrary. Their conventional graphing of the income–consumption relationship is consistent with mathematical convention but economists put price and cost data on the vertical axis. Hence, economists' graphing of IU's ticket price–attendance data differs from the normal mathematical procedure. This does not present a problem, but we want you to be aware of this fact to avoid any confusion.

Other Things Equal

Our simple two-variable graphs purposely ignore many other factors that might affect the amount of consumption occurring at each income level or the number of people who

FIGURE A1-2 The Relationship Between Ticket Prices and Attendance

Two sets of data that are negatively, or inversely, related, such as ticket price and the attendance at basketball games, graph as a downsloping line.

Ticket price	Attendance, thousands	Point
$50	0	*a*
40	4	*b*
30	8	*c*
20	12	*d*
10	16	*e*
0	20	*f*

attend IU basketball games at each possible ticket price. When economists plot the relationship between any two variables, they employ the *ceteris paribus* (other things equal) assumption. Thus, in Figure A1-1, all factors other than income that might affect the amount of consumption are held constant. Similarly, in Figure A1-2, all factors other than ticket price that might influence attendance at IU basketball games are assumed constant. In reality, other things are not equal; they often change and when they do, the relationship represented in our two tables and graphs will change. Specifically, the lines we have plotted will *shift* to new locations.

Consider a stock market "crash." The dramatic drop in the value of stocks might cause people to feel less wealthy and therefore less willing to consume at each level of income. The result might be a downward shift of the consumption line. To see this, you should plot a new consumption line in Figure A1-1, assuming that consumption is, say, $20 less at each income level. Note that the relationship remains direct; the line merely shifts downward to reflect less consumption spending at each income level.

Similarly, factors other than ticket prices might affect IU game attendance. If IU loses most of its games, attendance at IU games might fall at each ticket price. To see this, redraw the graph in Figure A1-2, assuming that 2000 fewer fans attend IU games at each ticket price.

Slope of a Line

Lines can be described in terms of their slopes and their intercepts. The **slope of a straight line** is the ratio of the vertical change (the rise or drop) to the horizontal change (the run) between any two points of the line—or rise over run.

POSITIVE SLOPE

Between point *c* and point *d* in Figure A1-1 the rise or vertical change (the change in consumption) is +$50 and the run or horizontal change (the change in income) is +$100. Therefore

$$\text{Slope} = \frac{\text{vertical change}}{\text{horizontal change}} = \frac{+50}{+100} = \frac{1}{2} = 0.5$$

Note that our slope of ½ or 0.5 is positive because consumption and income change in the same direction; that is, consumption and income are directly or positively related.

The slope of 0.5 tells us that there will be $0.50 increase in consumption for every $1 increase in income. Similarly, there will be a $0.50 decrease in consumption for every $1 decrease in income.

NEGATIVE SLOPE

Between any two of the identified points in Figure A1-2— say, point *c* and point *d*—the vertical change is −10

(the drop) and the horizontal change is +4 (the run). Therefore

$$\text{Slope} = \frac{\text{vertical change}}{\text{horizontal change}} = \frac{-10}{+4} = -2\frac{1}{2} = -2.5$$

This slope is negative because ticket price and attendance have an inverse or negative relationship.

Note that on the horizontal axis attendance is stated in thousands of people. So the slope of −10/+4 or −2.5 means that lowering the price by $10 will increase attendance by 4000 people. That ratio also implies that a $2.50 price reduction will increase attendance by 1000 people.

SLOPES AND MEASUREMENT UNITS

The slope of a line will be affected by the choice of units for either variable. If, in our ticket–price illustration, we had chosen to measure attendance in individual people, our horizontal change would have been 4000 and the slope would have been

$$\text{Slope} = \frac{-10}{+4000} = \frac{-1}{+400} = -0.0025$$

The slope depends on the units by which variables are measured.

SLOPES AND MARGINAL ANALYSIS

Recall that economics largely deals with changes from the status quo. The concept of slope is important in economics because it reflects marginal changes—those involving one more (or one less) unit. For example, in Figure A1-1 the 0.5 slope shows that $0.50 of extra or marginal consumption is associated with each $1 change in income. In this example, people collectively will consume $0.50 of any $1 increase in their incomes and reduce their consumption by $0.50 for each $1 decline in income.

INFINITE AND ZERO SLOPES

Many variables are unrelated, or independent of one another. For example, the quantity of digital cameras purchased is not related to the price of bananas. In Figure A1-3a we represent the price of bananas on the vertical axis and the quantity of digital cameras demanded on the horizontal axis. The graph of their relationship is the line parallel to the vertical axis. The line's vertical slope indicates that the same quantity of cameras is purchased no matter what the price of bananas. The slope of the vertical line is *infinite*.

Similarly, aggregate consumption is completely unrelated to the nation's divorce rate. In Figure A1-3b we put consumption on the vertical axis and the divorce rate on the horizontal axis. The line parallel to the horizontal axis represents this lack of relatedness. This line has a slope of *zero*.

FIGURE A1-3   Infinite and Zero Slopes

(a) A line parallel to the vertical axis has an infinite slope. Here, purchases of digital cameras remain the same no matter what happens to the price of bananas. (b) A line parallel to the horizontal axis has a slope of zero. In this case, consumption remains the same no matter what happens to the divorce rate. In both parts (a) and (b), the two variables are totally unrelated to each other.

Vertical Intercept

A line can be positioned on a graph (without plotting points) if we know its slope and its vertical intercept. We have already discussed the slope. The **vertical intercept** of a line is the point where the line meets the vertical axis. In Figure A1-1 the intercept is $50. This intercept means that if current income were zero, consumers would still spend $50. They might do this through borrowing or by selling some of their assets. Similarly, the $50 vertical intercept in Figure A1-2 shows that at a $50 ticket price, IU's basketball team would be playing in an empty arena.

Equation of a Linear Relationship

If we know the vertical intercept and slope, we can describe a line succinctly in equation form. In its general form, the equation of a straight line is

$$y = a + bx$$

where y = dependent variable

a = vertical intercept

b = slope of line

x = independent variable

For our income–consumption example, if C represents consumption (the dependent variable) and Y represents income (the independent variable), we can write $C = a + bY$. By substituting the known values of the intercept and the slope, we get

$$C = 50 + 0.5\,Y$$

This equation also allows us to determine the amount of consumption C at any specific level of income. You should

use it to confirm that at the $250 income level, consumption is $175.

When economists reverse mathematical convention by putting the independent variable on the vertical axis and the dependent variable on the horizontal axis, then y stands for the independent variable, rather than the dependent variable, in the general form. We noted previously that this case is relevant for our IU ticket price–attendance data. If P represents the ticket price (independent variable) and Q represents attendance (dependent variable), their relationship is given by

$$P = 50 - 2.5\,Q$$

where the vertical intercept is 50 and the negative slope is −2½ or −2.5. Knowing the value of P lets us solve for Q, our dependent variable. You should use this equation to predict IU ticket sales when the ticket price is $15.

Slope of a Non-linear Curve

We now move from the simple world of linear relationships (straight lines) to the more complex world of non-linear relationships (curvy line). The slope of a straight line is the same at all its points. The slope of a line representing a non-linear relationship changes from one point to another. Such lines are always referred to as *curves*.

Consider the downsloping curve in Figure A1-4. Its slope is negative throughout, but the curve flattens as we move down along it. Thus, its slope constantly changes; the curve has a different slope at every point.

To measure the slope at a specific point, we draw a straight line tangent to the curve at that point. A straight line is

KEY GRAPH

FIGURE A1-4   Determining the Slopes of Curves

The slope of a non-linear curve changes from point to point on the curve. The slope at any point (say *B*) can be determined by drawing a straight line that is tangent to that point (line *bb'*) and calculating the slope of that line.

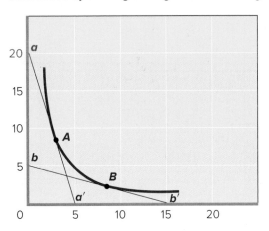

tangent at a point if it touches, but does not intersect, the curve at that point. Thus line *aa'* is tangent to the curve in Figure A1-4 at point *A*. The slope of the curve at that point is equal to the slope of the tangent line. Specifically, the total vertical change (drop) in the tangent line *aa'* is −20 and the total horizontal change (run) is +5. Because the slope of the

tangent line *aa'* is −20/+5, or −4, the slope of the curve at point *A* is also −4.

Line *bb'* in Figure A1-4 is tangent to the curve at point *B*. Following the same procedure, we find the slope at *B* to be −5/+15, or −⅓. Thus, in this flatter part of the curve, the slope is less negative.

APPENDIX Summary

LOA1.1 Understand graphs, curves, and slopes as they relate to economics.

- Graphs are a convenient and revealing means of representing economic relationships.

- Two variables are positively or directly related when their values change in the same direction. The line (curve) representing two directly related variables slopes upward.

- Two variables are negatively or inversely related when their values change in opposite directions. The line (curve) representing two inversely related variables slopes downward.

- The value of the dependent variable (the effect) is determined by the value of the independent variable (the cause).

- When the other factors that might affect a two-variable relationship are allowed to change, the graph of the relationship will likely shift to a new location.

- The slope of a straight line is the ratio of the vertical change to the horizontal change between any two points. The slope of an upsloping line is positive; the slope of a downsloping line is negative.

- The slope of a line or curve depends on the units used in measuring the variables. It is especially relevant for economics because it measures marginal changes.

- The slope of a horizontal line is zero; the slope of a vertical line is infinite.

- The vertical intercept and slope of a line determine its location; they are used in expressing the line—and the relationship between the two variables—as an equation.

- The slope of a curve at any point is determined by calculating the slope of a straight line tangent to the curve at that point.

APPENDIX Terms and Concepts

horizontal axis
vertical axis
direct relationship
inverse relationship

independent variable
dependent variable
slope of a straight line
vertical intercept

APPENDIX Discussion Questions

LOA1.1 Understand graphs, curves, and slopes as they relate to economics.

1. Briefly explain the use of graphs as a means of representing economic relationships.   [**LOA1.1**]

2. Describe the graphical relationship between ticket prices and the number of people choosing to visit amusement parks. Is that relationship consistent with the fact that, historically, park attendance and ticket prices have both risen? Explain.   [**LOA1.1**]

3. Look back at Figure A1-2, which shows the inverse relationship between ticket prices and game attendance at Informed University (IU).   [**LOA1.1**]

   a. Interpret the meaning of both the slope and the intercept.

   b. If the slope of the line were steeper, what would that say about how ticket sales respond to increases in ticket prices?

   c. If the slope of the line stayed the same but the intercept increased, what could you say about how ticket sales respond to increases in ticket prices?

APPENDIX Review Questions

1. Indicate whether each of the following relationships is usually a direct relationship or an inverse relationship. [**LOA1.1**]

   a. A sports team's winning percentage and attendance at its home games

   b. Higher temperatures and sweater sales

   c. A person's income and how often he or she shops at discount stores

   d. Higher gasoline prices and kilometres driven in automobiles

2. Erin grows pecans. The number of bushels (B) that she can produce depends on the number of centimetres of rainfall (R) that her orchards get. The relationship is given algebraically as follows: $B = 3000 + 800R$. Match each part of this equation with the correct term.   [**LOA1.1**]

B	slope
3000	dependent variable
800	vertical intercept
R	independent variable

APPENDIX Problems

1. Graph and explain the relationships you would expect to find between the following: [**LOA1.1**]

   a. The number of centimetres of rainfall per month and the sale of umbrellas

   b. The amount of tuition and the level of enrolment at a college or university

   c. The popularity of a music artist and the price of her concert tickets

2. Indicate how each of the following might affect the data shown in Figure A1-2 of this appendix: [**LOA1.1**]

   a. IU's athletic director schedules higher-quality opponents.

   b. A National Basketball Association (NBA) team locates in the city where IU also plays.

   c. IU signs a contract to have all of its home games televised.

3. The following table contains data on the relationship between saving and income. Rearrange these data into a meaningful order and graph them on the accompanying grid. What is the slope of the line? What is the vertical intercept? Write the equation that represents this line. What would you predict saving to be at the $12,500 level of income?   [**LOA1.1**]

Income (per year)	Saving (per year)
$15,000	$1,000
0	−500
10,000	500
5,000	0
20,000	1,500

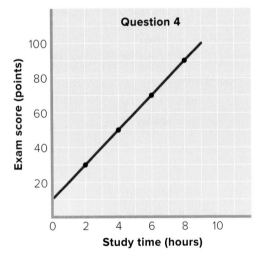

4. Construct a table from the data shown in the accompanying graph. Which is the dependent variable and which the independent variable? Summarize the data in equation form.   [**LOA1.1**]

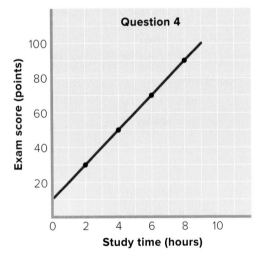

5. Suppose that when the interest rate on loans is 16 percent, businesses find it unprofitable to invest in machinery and equipment. However, when the interest rate is 14 percent, $5 billion worth of investment is profitable. At 12 percent interest, a total of $10 billion of investment is profitable. Similarly, total investment increases by $5 billion for each successive 2-percentage-point decline in the interest rate.   [**LOA1.1**]

Describe the relevant relationship between the interest rate and investment in a table, graphically, and as an equation. Put the interest rate on the vertical axis and investment on the horizontal axis. In your equation, use the form $i = a - bl$, where i is the interest rate, a is the vertical intercept, $-b$ is the slope of the line (which is negative), and l is the level of investment.

6. Suppose that $C = a + bY$, where C = consumption, a = consumption at zero income, b = slope, and Y = income.   [**LOA1.1**]

  a. Are C and Y positively related or negatively related?

  b. If graphed, would the curve for this equation slope upward or downward?

  c. Are the variables C and Y inversely or directly related?

  d. What is the value of C if $a = 10$, $b = 0.50$, and $Y = 200$?

  e. What is the value of Y if $C = 100$, $a = 10$, and $b = 0.25$?

7. The accompanying graph shows curve XX' and tangents at points A, B, and C. Calculate the slope of the curve at these three points.   [**LOA1.1**]

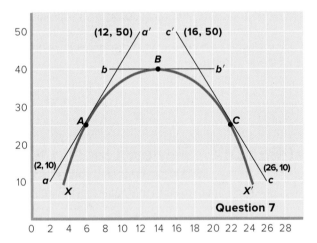

8. In the accompanying graph, is the slope of curve AA' positive or negative? Does the slope increase or decrease as we move along the curve from A to A'? Answer the same two questions for curve BB'.   [**LOA1.1**]

CHAPTER 2

The Market System and the Circular Flow

Suppose you are at a mall in Edmonton and are assigned to compile a list of all the individual goods and services there, including the different brands and variations of each type of product. That task would be daunting and the list would be long! And even though a single shopping mall in Edmonton contains a remarkable quantity and variety of goods, it is only a tiny part of the Canadian economy.

Who decided that the particular goods and services available at the mall and in the broader Canadian economy should be produced? How did the producers determine which technology and types of factors to use in producing these particular goods? Who will obtain these products? What accounts for the new and improved products among these goods? This chapter will answer these and related questions.

2.1 Economic Systems

LO2.1 Differentiate between laissez-faire capitalism, the command system, and the market system.

Every society needs to develop an **economic system**—a particular set of institutional arrangements and a coordinating mechanism—to respond to the economic problem. The economic system determines what goods are produced, how they are produced, who gets them, how to accommodate change, and how to promote technological progress.

Economic systems differ as to (1) who owns the factors of production and (2) the method used to motivate, coordinate, and direct economic activity.

Economic systems can be classified by the degree to which they rely on decentralized decision making based on markets and prices or centralized government control based on orders and mandates. At one extreme lies *laissez-faire capitalism*, in which government intervention is at a very minimum, and markets and prices are allowed to direct nearly all economic activity. At the other extreme lie *command systems* in which governments have total control over all economic activity. The vast majority of national economies lie somewhere in the middle, using some mixture of centralized government regulation and decentralized markets and prices. These economies are said to have *market systems* or *mixed economies.*

Laissez-Faire Capitalism

In **laissez-faire capitalism**—or pure capitalism—the government's role is limited to protecting private property from theft and aggression, and establishing a legal environment in which contracts can be enforced and people can interact in markets to buy and sell goods, services, and resources.

The term *laissez-faire* is French for "let it be"—that is, keep the government from interfering with the economy. Proponents of laissez-faire believe that such interference reduces human welfare. They maintain that any government that intervenes widely in the economy will end up being corrupted by special interests who will use the government's economic influence to benefit themselves rather than society at large.

To prevent that from happening, the proponents of laissez-faire argue that government should restrict itself to preventing individuals and firms from coercing each other. By doing so, it will ensure that only mutually beneficial economic transactions are negotiated and completed. That should lead to the highest possible level of human satisfaction because, after all, who knows better what people want than the people themselves?

It is important to note, however, that no society has ever employed a laissez-faire system. In fact, no government has *ever* limited its economic actions to the short list of functions that would be allowed under laissez-faire. Instead, every government known to history has undertaken a wider range of economic activities, many of which are widely popular, including industrial safety regulations, various taxes and subsidies, occupational licensing requirements, and income redistribution.

Thus, you should think of laissez-faire capitalism as a hypothetical system that is viewed by proponents as the ideal to which all economic systems should strive—but which is opposed by those who welcome greater government intervention in the economy.

The Command System

The polar opposite of laissez-faire capitalism is the **command system**, in which government owns most property resources and in which economic decisions are made according to a central economic plan created and enforced by the government. The command system is also known as *socialism* or *communism.*

Under the command system, a central planning board appointed by the government makes all major decisions concerning the use of resources, the composition and distribution of output, and the organization of production. The government owns most of the business firms, which produce according to government directives. The central planning board determines production goals for each enterprise and specifies the amount of resources to be allocated to each enterprise so that it can reach its production goals. The division of output between capital and consumer goods is centrally decided, and capital goods are allocated among industries on the basis of the central planning board's long-term priorities.

A pure command economy would rely exclusively on a central plan to allocate the government-owned property resources. But, in reality, even the preeminent command economy—the Soviet Union—tolerated some private ownership and incorporated some markets before its collapse in 1992. Recent reforms in Russia and most of the eastern European nations have, to one degree or another, transformed their command economies to capitalistic, market-oriented systems. China's reforms have not gone as far, but they have greatly reduced the reliance on central planning. Although government ownership of resources and capital in China is still extensive, the nation has increasingly relied on free markets to organize and coordinate its economy. North Korea and Cuba are the last prominent remaining examples of largely centrally planned economies. Other countries using mainly the command system include Turkmenistan, Laos, Belarus, Myanmar, and Iran. Later in this chapter we will explore the main reasons for the general demise of command systems.

The Market System

The vast majority of the world's economies use the **market system**, which is also known as *capitalism* or a *mixed economy*.

The market system is characterized by a mixture of centralized government economic initiatives, and decentralized actions taken by individuals and firms. The precise mixture varies from country to country, but in each case the system features the private ownership of resources, and the use of markets and prices to coordinate and direct economic activity.

In the market system, individuals and businesses seek to achieve their economic goals through their own decisions regarding work, consumption, and production. The system allows for the private ownership of capital, communicates through prices, and coordinates economic activity through markets—places where buyers and sellers come together to buy and sell goods, services, and resources.

Participants act in their own self-interest, and goods and services are produced and resources are supplied by whoever is willing and able to do so. The result is competition among independently acting buyers and sellers of each product and resource, and an economic system in which decision making is widely dispersed.

The market system also offers high potential monetary rewards that create powerful incentives for existing firms to innovate and for entrepreneurs to pioneer new products and processes despite the financial risks involved and despite most innovations failing to catch on with consumers.

In the capitalism practised in Canada and most other countries, the government plays a substantial role in the economy. It not only provides the rules for economic activity but also promotes economic stability and growth, provides certain goods and services that would otherwise be underproduced or not produced at all, and modifies the distribution of income. The government, however, is not the dominant economic force in deciding what to produce, how to produce it, and who will get it. That force is the market.

2.2 Characteristics of the Market System

LO2.2 List the main characteristics of the market system.

An examination of some of the key features of the market system in detail will be instructive.

Private Property

In a market system, private individuals and firms, not the government, own most of the property resources (land and capital). It is this extensive private ownership of capital that gives capitalism its name. This right of **private property**, coupled with the freedom to negotiate binding legal contracts, enables individuals and businesses to obtain, use, and dispose of property resources as they see fit. The right of property owners to designate who will receive their property when they die sustains the institution of private property.

The most important consequence of property rights is that they encourage people to cooperate by helping to ensure that only *mutually agreeable* economic transactions take place. To consider why this is true, imagine a world without legally enforceable property rights. In such a world, the strong could simply take whatever they wanted from the weak without giving them any compensation. But in a world of legally enforceable property rights, any person wanting something from you has to get you to agree to give it to them. And you can say no. The result is that if they really want what you have, they must offer you something that you value more highly in return. That is, they must offer you a mutually agreeable economic transaction—one that benefits you as well as them.

Property rights also encourage investment, innovation, exchange, maintenance of property, and economic growth. Nobody would stock a store, build a factory, or clear land for farming if someone else, or the government itself, could take that property for his or her own benefit.

Property rights also extend to intellectual property through patents, copyrights, and trademarks. Such long-term protection encourages people to write books, music, and computer programs, and to invent new products and production processes without fear that others will steal them and the rewards they may bring.

Moreover, property rights facilitate exchange. The title to an automobile or the deed to a cattle ranch assures the buyer that the seller is the legitimate owner. Also, property rights encourage owners to maintain or improve their property so as to preserve or increase its value. Finally, property rights enable people to use their time and resources to produce more goods and services, rather than using them to protect and retain the property they have already produced or acquired.

Freedom of Enterprise and Choice

Closely related to private ownership of property is freedom of enterprise and choice. The market system requires that various economic units make certain choices, which are expressed and implemented in the economy's markets:

- **Freedom of enterprise** ensures that entrepreneurs and private businesses are free to obtain and use economic resources to produce their choice of goods and services and to sell them in their chosen markets.

- **Freedom of choice** enables owners to employ or dispose of their property and money as they see fit. It also allows workers to enter any line of work for which they are qualified. Finally, it ensures that consumers are free to buy the goods and services that best satisfy their wants and that their budgets allow.

These choices are free only within broad legal limitations, of course. Illegal choices—such as selling human organs or buying illicit drugs—are punished through fines and imprisonment. Global Perspective 2.1 reveals that the degree of economic freedom varies greatly from economy to economy.

2.1 GLOBAL PERSPECTIVE

Index of Economic Freedom, Selected Nations

The Index of Economic Freedom measures economic freedom using ten broad categories, such as trade policy, property rights, and government intervention, with each category containing more than 50 specific criteria. It then ranks 180 nations according to the degree of economic freedom. A few selected rankings for 2017 are listed here.

FREE
- 1 Hong Kong
- 2 Singapore
- 5 Australia

MOSTLY FREE
- 7 Canada
- 17 United States
- 34 Botswana

MODERATELY FREE
- 36 Israel
- 69 Spain
- 79 Italy

MOSTLY UNFREE
- 94 Cambodia
- 127 Greece
- 156 Argentina

REPRESSED
- 158 Mozanbique
- 172 Algeria
- 180 North Korea

Self-Interest

In the market system, **self-interest** is the motivating force of the various economic units as they express their free choices. Self-interest simply means that each economic unit tries to achieve its own particular goal, which usually requires delivering something of value to others. Entrepreneurs try to maximize profit and minimize loss. Property owners try to get the highest price for selling or renting their resources. Workers try to maximize their utility (satisfaction) by finding jobs that offer the best combination of wages, hours, fringe benefits, and working conditions. Consumers try to obtain the products they want at the lowest possible price and apportion their expenditures to maximize their utility. The motive of self-interest gives direction and consistency to what might otherwise be a chaotic economy.

Competition

The market system depends on **competition** among economic units. The basis of this competition is freedom of choice exercised in pursuit of a monetary return. Very broadly defined, competition requires the following:

- Independently acting sellers and buyers operating in a particular product or factor market
- Freedom of sellers and buyers to enter or leave markets, on the basis of their economic self-interest

Competition among buyers and sellers diffuses economic power within the businesses and households that make up the economy. When there are independently acting sellers and buyers in a market, no single buyer or seller is able to dictate the price of the product or factor because others can undercut that price.

Competition also implies that producers can enter or leave an industry; there are no insurmountable barriers to an industry's expanding or contracting. This freedom of an industry to expand or contract provides the economy with the flexibility needed to remain efficient over time. Freedom of entry and exit enables the economy to adjust to changes in consumer tastes, technology, and factor availability.

The diffusion of economic power inherent in competition limits the potential abuse of that power. A producer that charges more than the competitive market price will lose sales to other producers. An employer who pays less than the competitive market wage rate will lose workers to other employers. A firm that fails to exploit new technology will lose profits to firms that do. And a firm that produces shoddy products will be punished as customers switch to higher-quality items made by rival firms. Competition is the basic regulatory force in the market system.

Markets and Prices

We may wonder why an economy based on self-interest does not collapse into chaos. If consumers should want breakfast cereal while businesses choose to produce running shoes and resource suppliers to make computer software, it might seem that production would be deadlocked by the apparent inconsistencies of free choices.

In reality, however, markets and prices, which are key components of the market system, give it the ability to coordinate millions of daily economic decisions. A **market** is an institution or mechanism that brings buyers (demanders) and sellers (suppliers) into contact. A market system conveys the decisions made by buyers and sellers of products and factors. The decisions made on each side of the market determine a set of product and factor prices that guide resource owners, entrepreneurs, and consumers as they make and revise their choices and pursue their self-interest.

Just as competition is the regulatory mechanism of the market system, the market system itself is the organizing and coordinating mechanism. It is an elaborate communication network through which innumerable individual free choices on the part of consumers and producers are recorded, summarized, and balanced. Those who respond to market signals and heed market dictates are rewarded with greater profit and income; those who do not are penalized. Thus society decides what the economy should produce, how production can be organized efficiently, and how the fruits of production are to be distributed among the various units that make up the economy.

QUICK REVIEW 2.1

- The market system rests on the private ownership of property, freedom of enterprise, and freedom of choice.

- Property rights encourage people to cooperate and make mutually agreeable economic transactions.

- The market system permits consumers, resource suppliers, and businesses to pursue and further their self-interest.

- Competition diffuses economic power and limits the actions of any single seller or buyer.

- The coordinating mechanism of capitalism is a system of markets and prices.

Technology and Capital Goods

In the market system, competition, freedom of choice, self-interest, and personal reward provide the opportunity and motivation for technological advance. The monetary rewards for new products or production techniques accrue directly to the innovator. The market system, therefore, encourages extensive use and rapid development of complex capital goods: tools, machinery, large-scale factories, and facilities for storage, communication, transportation, and marketing.

Advanced technology and capital goods are important because the most direct methods of production are often the least efficient. The only way to avoid that inefficiency is to rely on capital goods. It would be ridiculous for a modern farmer to go at production with bare hands. There are huge benefits to be derived from creating and using such capital equipment as plows, tractors, storage bins, and so on. More efficient production means much more abundant output.

Specialization

The extent to which market economies rely on **specialization** is astonishing. Specialization is the use of resources of an individual, region, or nation to produce one or a few goods or services rather than the entire range of goods and services. Those goods and services are then exchanged for a full range of desired products. The majority of consumers produce virtually none of the goods and services they consume, and they consume little or nothing of the items they produce. The person working nine to five installing windows in commercial aircraft may rarely fly. Many farmers sell their milk to the local dairy and then buy butter at the local grocery store. Society learned long ago that self-sufficiency breeds inefficiency. The jack-of-all-trades may be a very colourful individual but is certainly not an efficient producer.

DIVISION OF LABOUR

Human specialization—called the **division of labour**—contributes to a society's output in several ways:

- *Specialization Makes Use of Differences in Ability* Specialization enables individuals to take advantage of existing differences in their abilities and skills. If LeBron is strong, athletic, and good at shooting a basketball while Beyoncé is beautiful, agile, and can sing, their distribution of talents can be most efficiently used if LeBron plays professional basketball while Beyoncé records songs and gives concerts.

- *Specialization Fosters Learning-by-Doing* Even if the abilities of two people are identical, specialization may still be advantageous. By devoting time to a single task, a person is more likely to develop the skills required and to improve techniques than they are if they work at a number of different tasks. You learn to be a good lawyer by studying and practising law.

- *Specialization Saves Time* By devoting time to a single task, a person avoids the loss of time incurred in shifting from one job to another. Also, time is saved when people don't fumble around with tasks they are not trained to do.

For all these reasons, specialization increases the total output society derives from limited resources.

GEOGRAPHIC SPECIALIZATION

Specialization also works on a regional and international basis. Apples might conceivably be grown in Saskatchewan, but because of the unsuitability of the land, rainfall, and temperature, the costs would be very high. And wheat might conceivably be grown in British Columbia, but such production would be costly for similar geographical reasons. So Saskatchewan farmers produce products—wheat in particular—for which their resources are best suited, and British Columbians (especially in the Okanagan Valley) do the same, producing apples and other fruits. By specializing, both regional economies produce more than is needed locally. Then, very sensibly, Saskatchewan and British Columbia exchange some of their surpluses—wheat for apples, apples for wheat.

Similarly, on an international scale, Canada specializes in producing such items as commercial aircraft (Bombardier) and communication equipment and software (BlackBerry Limited), which it sells abroad in exchange for mobile phones from China, bananas from Honduras, and woven baskets from Thailand. Both human specialization and geographic specialization are needed to achieve efficiency in the use of limited resources.

Use of Money

A rather obvious characteristic of any economic system is the extensive use of money. Money performs several functions, but first and foremost it is a **medium of exchange**. It makes trade easier.

Specialization requires exchange. Exchange can, and sometimes does, occur through **barter**—swapping goods for goods (say wheat for apples). But barter poses serious problems because it requires a *coincidence of wants* between the buyer and the seller. In our example, we assumed that Saskatchewan had excess wheat to trade and wanted apples, and that British Columbia had excess apples to trade and wanted wheat. So an exchange occurred. But if such a coincidence of wants is missing, trade will not occur.

Suppose that Saskatchewan has no interest in British Columbia's apples but wants potatoes from Prince Edward Island. And suppose that Prince Edward Island wants British Columbia's apples but not Saskatchewan's wheat. And, to complicate matters, suppose that British Columbia wants some of Saskatchewan's wheat but none of Prince Edward Island's potatoes. We summarize the situation in Figure 2-1.

FIGURE 2-1   Money Facilitates Trade When Wants Do Not Coincide

The use of money as a medium of exchange permits trade to be accomplished despite a non-coincidence of wants. (1) Saskatchewan trades the wheat that British Columbia wants for money; (2) Saskatchewan trades the money it receives from British Columbia for the potatoes it wants from Prince Edward Island; (3) Prince Edward Island trades the money it receives from Saskatchewan for the apples it wants from British Columbia.

In none of the cases shown in the figure is there a coincidence of wants. Trade by barter would obviously be difficult. Instead, people in each province use **money**, which is simply a convenient social invention to facilitate exchanges of goods and services. Historically, people have used cattle, cigarettes, shells, stones, pieces of metal, and many other commodities as money with varying degrees of success. To serve as money, an item needs to pass only one test. It must be generally acceptable to sellers in exchange for their goods and services. Money is socially defined: Whatever society accepts as a medium of exchange *is* money.

Today, most economies use pieces of paper as money. The use of paper dollars (currency) as a medium of exchange is what enables Saskatchewan, British Columbia, and Prince Edward Island to overcome their trade stalemate, as demonstrated in Figure 2-1.

On a global basis, specialization and exchange are complicated by the fact that different nations have different currencies. But swapping dollars, yen, euros, pounds, and pesos for one another in markets in which currencies are bought and sold makes it possible for people living in different countries to exchange goods and services without resorting to barter.

Active but Limited Government

An active but limited government is the final characteristic of market systems in modern advanced industrial economies. Although a market system promotes a high degree of efficiency in the use of its resources, it has certain inherent shortcomings called *market failures*. We will discover in subsequent chapters that governments can often increase the overall efficiency of the economic system in several ways. However, governments have their own set of shortcomings that can themselves cause substantial misallocations of resources. Consequently, we will also investigate several types of so-called government failures.

QUICK REVIEW 2.2

- The market systems of modern industrial economies are characterized by extensive use of technologically advanced capital goods. Such goods help these economies achieve greater efficiency in production.

- Specialization is extensive in market systems; it enhances efficiency and output by enabling individuals, regions, and nations to produce the goods and services for which their resources are best suited.

- The use of money in market systems facilitates the exchange of goods and services that specialization requires.

2.3   Five Fundamental Questions

LO2.3   Explain how the market system answers the five fundamental questions of what to produce, how to produce, who obtains the output, how to adjust to change, and how to promote progress.

The key features of the market system help explain how market economies respond to five fundamental questions:

1. What goods and services will be produced?
2. How will the goods and services be produced?
3. Who will get the goods and services?
4. How will the system accommodate change?
5. How will the system promote progress?

These five questions highlight the economic choices underlying the production possibilities curve discussed in Chapter 1. They reflect the reality of scarce resources in a world of unlimited wants. All economies, whether market or command, must address these five questions.

What Will Be Produced?

How will a market system decide on the specific types and quantities of goods and services to be produced? The simple answer is this: The goods and services that can be produced at a continuing profit will be produced, while those whose production generates a continuing loss will be discontinued. Profits and losses are the difference between the total revenue (TR) a firm receives from the sale of its products and the total cost (TC) of producing those products. (For economists, the total cost includes not only wage and salary payments to labour, and interest and rental payments for capital and land, but also payments to the entrepreneur for organizing and combining the other resources to produce a product.)

Continuing economic profit (TR > TC) in an industry results in expanded production and the movement of resources toward that industry. Existing firms grow and new firms enter. The industry expands. Continuing losses (TC > TR) in an industry lead to reduced production and the departure of resources from that industry. Some existing firms shrink in size; others go out of business. The industry contracts.

In the market system, consumers are sovereign (in command). **Consumer sovereignty** is crucial in determining the types and quantities of goods produced. Consumers spend their income on the goods they are most willing and able to buy. Through these **dollar votes** they register their wants in the market. If the dollar votes for a certain product are large enough to create a profit, businesses will produce that product and offer it for sale. In contrast, if the dollar votes do not create sufficient revenues to cover costs, businesses will not produce the product. Through their dollar votes consumers collectively direct resources to industries that are meeting their wants and away from industries that are not.

The dollar votes of consumers determine not only which industries will continue to exist but also which products will survive or fail. Only profitable industries, firms, and products survive, so firms are not really free to produce whatever products they want. Consumers' buying decisions make the production of some products profitable and the production of other products unprofitable, thus restricting the choice of businesses in deciding what to produce. Businesses must match their production choices with consumer choices or else face losses and eventual bankruptcy.

The same holds true for resource (factor) suppliers. The employment of resources derives from the sale of the goods and services that the resources help produce. Autoworkers are employed because automobiles are sold. There are few remaining professors of early Latin because few people want to learn the Latin language any more. Resource suppliers that want to earn income are not truly free to allocate their resources to the production of goods

---

CONSIDER THIS

McHits and McMisses

© McGraw-Hill Education/
John Flournoy, photographer

McDonald's has introduced several new menu items over the decades. Some have been profitable "hits," while others have been "misses." In a market system, consumers ultimately decide whether a menu item is profitable and therefore whether it stays on the McDonald's menu.

- Hulaburger (1962)—McMiss
- Filet-O-Fish (1963)—McHit
- Strawberry shortcake (1966)—McMiss
- Big Mac (1968)—McHit
- Hot apple pie (1968)—McHit
- Egg McMuffin (1975)—McHit
- Drive-thru (1975)—McHit
- Chicken McNuggets (1983)—McHit
- Arch Deluxe (1996)—McMiss
- McSalad Shaker (2000)—McMiss
- McGriddle (2003)—McHit
- Snack Wrap (2006)—McHit
- Fish McBites (2012)—McMiss

Source: Adapted from Passikoff, Robert, "McDonald's Fish McBites Flounders," *Forbes*, March 12, 2013, forbes.com; Machan, Dyan, "Polishing the Golden Arches," *Forbes*, June 15, 1998, pp. 42–43.

or services that consumers do not value highly. Consumers register their preferences in the market; producers and resource suppliers, prompted by their own self-interest, try to satisfy those preferences.

How Will the Goods and Services Be Produced?

What combinations of resources and technologies will be used to produce goods and services? How will the production be organized? The answer is that it will be done in ways that minimize the cost per unit of output, because inefficiency drives up costs and lowers profits. As a result, any firm wishing to maximize its profits will make great efforts to minimize production costs. These efforts will include using the right mix of labour and capital, given the prices and productivity of those resources. They also mean locating production facilities optimally to minimize production and transportation expenses.

Those efforts will be intensified if the firm faces competition, as consumers strongly prefer low prices and will shift their purchases over to the firms that can produce a quality product at the lowest possible price. Any firm foolish enough to use higher-cost production methods will go bankrupt as it is undersold by its more efficient competitors who can still make a profit when selling at a lower price, because competition eliminates high-cost producers.

WORKED PROBLEM 2.1   Least-Cost Production

Least-cost production means that firms must employ the most economically efficient technique of production in producing their output. The most efficient production technique depends on the following:

- The available technology—that is, the available body of knowledge and techniques that can be used to combine economic resources to produce the desired results

- The prices of the needed resources

A technique that requires just a few inputs of resources to produce a specific output may be highly inefficient economically if those resources are valued very highly in the market. Economic efficiency requires obtaining a particular output of product with the least input of scarce resources, when both output and resource inputs are measured in dollars and cents. The combination of resources that will produce, say, $15 worth of bathroom soap at the lowest possible cost is the most efficient.

Suppose there are three possible techniques for producing the desired $15 worth of bars of soap. Suppose also that the quantity of each resource required by each production technique and the prices of the required resources are as shown in Table 2-1. By multiplying the required quantities of each resource by its price in each of the three techniques, we can determine the total cost of producing $15 worth of soap by means of each technique.

Technique 2 is economically the most efficient, because it is the least costly. It enables society to obtain $15 worth of output by using a smaller amount of resources—$13 worth—than the $15 worth required by the two other

TABLE 2-1		Three Techniques for Producing $15 Worth of Bar Soap					
		UNITS OF RESOURCE					
		Technique 1		**Technique 2**		**Technique 3**	
Resource	**Price per unit of resource**	**Units**	**Cost**	**Units**	**Cost**	**Units**	**Cost**
Labour	$2	4	$ 8	2	$ 4	1	$ 2
Land	1	1	1	3	3	4	4
Capital	3	1	3	1	3	2	6
Entrepreneurial ability	3	1	3	1	3	1	3
Total cost of $15 worth of bar soap			$15		$13		$15

techniques. Competition will dictate that producers use technique 2. Thus, the question of how goods will be produced is answered. They will be produced in a least-cost way.

A change in either technology or resource prices, however, may cause a firm to shift from the technology it is using. If the price of labour falls to $0.50, technique 1 becomes more desirable than technique 2. Firms will find they can lower their costs by shifting to a technology that uses more of the resource whose price has fallen. *Exercise:* Would a new technique involving 1 unit of labour, 4 of land, 1 of capital, and 1 of entrepreneurial ability be preferable to the techniques listed in Table 2-1, assuming the resource prices shown there?

Who Will Get the Output?

The market system enters the picture in two ways when determining the distribution of total output. Generally, any product will be distributed to consumers on the basis of their ability and willingness to pay its existing market price. If the price of some product—say a small sailboat—is $3000, then buyers who are willing and able to pay that price will get it; those unwilling or unable to pay the price will not.

The ability to pay the prices for sailboats and other products depends on the amount of income that consumers have, along with the prices of, and preferences for, various goods. If consumers have sufficient income and want to spend their money on a particular good, they can have it. And the amount of income they have depends on (1) the quantities of the property and human resources they supply and (2) the prices those resources command in the factor market. Factor prices (wages, interest, rent, profit) are crucial in determining the size of each person's income and therefore each person's ability to buy part of the economy's output. If a lawyer earning $130 an hour and a janitor earning $13 an hour both work the same number of hours each year, then each year the lawyer will be able to purchase ten times more of society's output than the janitor.

How Will the System Accommodate Change?

Market systems are dynamic: Consumer preferences, technology, and supplies of resources can all change at the same time. This means that the particular allocation of resources that is now the most efficient for a specific pattern of consumer tastes, range of technological alternatives, and amount of available resources will become obsolete and inefficient as consumer preferences change, new techniques of production are discovered, and resource supplies change over time. Can the market economy adjust to such changes?

Suppose consumer tastes change. For instance, assume that consumers decide they want more fruit juice and less milk than the economy currently provides. Those changes in consumer tastes will be communicated to producers through an increase in spending on fruit juice and a decline in spending on milk. Other things equal, prices and profits in the fruit juice industry will rise and those in the milk industry will fall. Self-interest will induce existing competitors to expand output and entice new competitors to enter the prosperous fruit juice industry and will, in time, force firms to scale down—or even exit—the depressed milk industry.

The higher prices and greater economic profit in the fruit juice industry will not only induce that industry to expand but will give it the revenue needed to obtain the resources necessary to its growth. Higher prices and profits will permit fruit juice producers to draw more resources from less urgent alternative employment. The reverse occurs in the milk industry, where fewer workers and other resources are employed. These adjustments in the economy are automatic responses to the changes in consumer tastes. This is consumer sovereignty at work.

The market system is a gigantic communications network. Through changes in prices and profits it communicates changes in consumer demand and elicits appropriate responses from businesses and resource suppliers. By affecting price and profits, changes in consumer demand direct the expansion of some industries and the contraction of others. Those adjustments are conveyed to the factor market. As expanding industries employ more factors of production and contracting industries employ fewer, the resulting changes in factor prices (wages and salaries, for example) and the flow of income steer resources from the contracting industries to the expanding industries.

This directing or guiding function of prices and profits is a core element of the market system. Without such a system, a government planning board or some other administrative agency would have to direct businesses and resources into the appropriate industries. A similar analysis shows that the system can and does adjust to other fundamental changes—for example, to changes in technology and in the prices of various resources.

How Will the System Promote Progress?

Society desires economic growth (greater output) and higher standards of living (greater output *per person*). How does the market system promote technological improvements and capital accumulation, both of which contribute to a higher standard of living for society?

TECHNOLOGICAL ADVANCE

The market system provides a strong incentive for technological advance and enables better products and processes to supplant inferior ones. An entrepreneur or firm that introduces a popular new product will gain revenue and economic profit at the expense of rivals.

Technological advance also includes new and improved methods that reduce production or distribution costs. By passing on part of its cost reduction to the consumer through a lower product price, the firm can increase sales and obtain economic profit at the expense of rival firms.

Moreover, the market system promotes the rapid spread of technological advance throughout an industry. Rival firms must follow the lead of the most innovative firm or else suffer immediate losses and eventual failure. In some cases, the result is **creative destruction**: the creation of new products and production methods completely destroys the market positions of firms that are wedded to existing products and older ways of doing business. For example, compact discs largely demolished vinyl records before MP3 players and then online streaming subsequently supplanted compact discs.

CAPITAL ACCUMULATION

Most technological advances require additional capital goods. The market system provides the resources necessary to produce additional capital goods through increased dollar votes for those goods.

But who will count the dollar votes for capital goods? Entrepreneurs and business owners. As receivers of profit income, they often use part of that income to purchase capital goods. Doing so yields even greater profit income in the future if the technological innovation that required the additional capital good is successful. Also, by paying interest or selling ownership shares, the entrepreneur and firm can attract some of the income of households to cast dollar votes for the production of more capital goods.

QUICK REVIEW 2.3

- The output mix of the market system is determined by profits, which in turn depend heavily on consumer preferences. Economic profits cause industries to expand; losses cause industries to contract.

- Competition forces industries to use the least costly production methods.

- Competitive markets reallocate resources in response to changes in consumer tastes, technological advances, and changes in availability of resources.

- In a market economy, consumer income and product prices determine how output will be distributed.

- Competitive markets create incentives for technological advance and capital accumulation, both of which contribute to increases in standards of living.

2.4 The Invisible Hand

LO2.4   Explain the operation of the "invisible hand" and why market economies usually do a better job than command economies at transforming economic resources into desirable output.

In his 1776 book *The Wealth of Nations*, Adam Smith first noted that the operation of a market system creates a curious unity between private interests and social interests. Firms and resource suppliers, seeking to further their own self-interest and operating within the framework of a highly competitive market system, will simultaneously, as though guided by an **invisible hand**, promote the public or social interest. For example, we have seen that in a competitive environment, businesses seek to build new and improved products to increase profits. Those enhanced products increase society's well-being. Businesses also use the least costly combination of resources to produce a specific output because it is in their self-interest to do so. To act otherwise would be to forgo profit or even to risk business failure. But, at the same time, to use scarce resources in the least costly way is clearly in the social interest as well. It frees up resources to produce something else that society desires.

Self-interest, awakened and guided by the competitive market system, is what induces responses appropriate to the changes in society's wants. Businesses seeking to make higher profits and to avoid losses, and resource suppliers pursuing greater monetary rewards, negotiate changes in the allocation of resources and end up with the output that society wants. Competition guides self-interest such that self-interest automatically and quite unintentionally furthers the best interest of society. The invisible hand ensures that when firms maximize their profits and resource suppliers maximize their incomes, these groups also help maximize society's output and income.

Of the various virtues of the market system, three merit emphasis:

- *Efficiency* The market system promotes the efficient use of resources, by guiding them into the production of the goods and services most wanted by society. It forces the use of the most efficient techniques in organizing resources for production, and it encourages the development and adoption of new and more efficient production techniques.

- *Incentives* The market system encourages skill acquisition, hard work, and innovation. Greater work skills and effort mean greater production and higher incomes, which usually translate into a higher standard of living. Similarly, the assumption of risk by entrepreneurs can result in substantial profit incomes. Successful innovations generate economic rewards.

- *Freedom* The major noneconomic argument for the market system is its emphasis on personal freedom. In contrast to central planning, the market system coordinates economic activity without coercion. The market system permits—indeed, it thrives on—freedom of enterprise and choice. Entrepreneurs and workers are free to further their own self-interest, subject to the rewards and penalties imposed by the market system itself.

Of course, no economic system, including the market system, is flawless. In Chapter 4 we will explain two well-known shortcomings of the market system and examine the government policies that try to remedy them.

The Demise of the Command System

Our discussion of how a market system answers the five fundamental questions yields insight into why the command systems of the Soviet Union, Eastern Europe, and China (prior to its market reforms) failed. Those systems encountered two insurmountable problems: the coordination problem and the incentive problem.

THE COORDINATION PROBLEM

The first problem was coordination. The central planners had to coordinate millions of individual decisions by consumers, resource suppliers, and businesses. Consider what it takes to set up a factory to produce tractors. The central planners had to establish a realistic annual production target: for example, 1000 tractors. They then had to make available all the necessary inputs—labour, machinery, electric power, steel, tires, glass, paint, and transportation—for the production and delivery of those 1000 tractors.

Because the outputs of many industries serve as inputs to other industries, the failure of any single industry to achieve its output target caused a chain reaction of repercussions. For example, if iron mines, for want of machinery or labour or transportation, did not supply the steel industry with the required inputs of iron ore, the steel mills were unable to fulfill the input needs of the many industries that depended on steel. Steel-using industries that produced capital goods (such as factory equipment and modes of transportation) were unable to meet their planned production goals. Eventually the repercussions spread to all firms that used steel as an input and from there to other input buyers or final consumers.

The coordination problem got worse as the economies expanded. Products and production processes grew more complex, and the number of industries requiring planning increased. Planning techniques that worked for the simpler economy proved highly inadequate and inefficient for the larger economy. Bottlenecks and production stoppages became the norm, not the exception. In trying to cope, planners further suppressed product variety, focusing on one or two products in each product category.

A lack of a reliable success indicator added to the coordination problem in the Soviet Union and China (prior to its market reforms). We have seen that market economies rely on profit as a success indicator. Profit depends on consumer demand, production efficiency, and product quality. In contrast, the major success indicator for the command economies usually was a quantitative production target that the central planners assigned. Production costs, product quality, and product mix were secondary considerations. Managers and workers often sacrificed product quality because they were being awarded bonuses for meeting quantitative, not qualitative, targets. If meeting production goals meant sloppy assembly work, so be it.

It was difficult at best for planners to assign quantitative production targets without unintentionally producing distortions in output. If the plan specified a production target for producing nails in terms of *weight* (tonnes of nails), the enterprise made only large nails. But if it specified the target as a *quantity* (thousands of nails), the firm made small nails and lots of them! That is precisely what happens in centrally planned economies.

THE INCENTIVE PROBLEM

The command economies also faced an incentive problem. Central planners determined the output mix. When they misjudged how many automobiles, shoes, shirts, and chickens were wanted at the government-determined prices, persistent shortages and surpluses of those products often arose. But as long as the managers who oversaw the production of those goods were rewarded for meeting their assigned production goals, they had no incentive to adjust production in response to the shortages and surpluses. And there were no fluctuations in prices and profitability to signal that more or less of certain products was desired. Thus, many products were unavailable or in short supply, while other products were overproduced and sat for months or years in warehouses.

The command systems of the former Soviet Union and of China before its market reforms also lacked entrepreneurship. Central planning did not trigger the profit motive, nor did it reward innovation and enterprise. The route for getting ahead was through participation in the political hierarchy of the Communist Party. Moving up the hierarchy meant better housing, better access to health care, and the right to shop in special stores. Meeting production targets and navigating the minefields of party politics were measures of success in "business." But a definition of business success based solely on political savvy is not conducive to technological advance, and is often disruptive to existing products, production methods, and organizational structures.

CONSIDER THIS

The Two Koreas

North Korea is one of the few command economies still standing. After the World War II, Korea was divided into North Korea and South Korea. North Korea, under the influence of the Soviet Union, established a command economy that emphasized government ownership and central government planning. South Korea established a market economy based upon private ownership and the profit motive. Today, the differences in the economic outcomes of the two systems are striking.

	North Korea	South Korea
GDP	$40 billion*	$1.8 trillion*
GDP per capita	$1,800*	$34,200*
Exports	$3.8 billion	$911 billion
Imports	$4.4 billion	$815 billion
Agriculture as % of GDP	23%	2.3%

*Based on purchasing power equivalencies to the U.S. dollar.

Source: *CIA World Fact Book*, 2014, www.cia.gov.

© Stocktrek Images/Getty Images RF

2.5　The Circular Flow Model

LO2.5　Describe the mechanics of the circular flow model.

The dynamic market economy creates continuous, repetitive flows of goods and services, resources, and money. The **circular flow diagram**, shown in Figure 2-2 (Key Graph), illustrates those flows for a simplified economy in which there is no government. Observe that in the diagram we group this economy's decision makers into *businesses* and *households*. Additionally, we divide this economy's markets into the *factor market* and the *product market*.

Households

The yellow-coloured rectangle on the right side of the circular flow diagram in Figure 2-2 represents **households**, which are defined as one or more persons occupying a housing unit. There are currently about nine million households in the Canadian economy. Households buy the goods and services that businesses make available in the product market. Households obtain the income needed to buy those products by selling resources in the factor market.

　　All the resources in our no-government economy are ultimately owned or provided by households. For instance, the members of one household or another directly provide all of the labour and entrepreneurial ability in the economy. Households also own all of the land and all of the capital in the economy either directly, as

KEY GRAPH

FIGURE 2-2　The Circular Flow Diagram

Factors of production flow from households to businesses through the factor market, and products flow from businesses to households through the product market. Opposite these real flows are monetary flows. Households receive income from businesses (their costs) through the factor market, and businesses receive revenue from households (their expenditures) through the product market.

QUICK QUIZ

1. **The factor market is where**
   a. Households sell products and businesses buy products.
   b. Businesses sell factors of production and households sell products.
   c. Households sell factors of production and businesses buy factors of production (or the services of factors).
   d. Businesses sell factors of production and households buy factors of production (or the services of factors).

2. **Which of the following would be determined in the product market?**
   a. A manager's salary
   b. The price of equipment used in a bottling plant
   c. The price of 80 hectares of farm land
   d. The price of a new pair of athletic shoes

3. **In Figure 2-2,**
   a. Money flows counterclockwise.
   b. Resources flow counterclockwise.
   c. Goods and services flow clockwise.
   d. Households are on the selling side of the product market.

4. **In Figure 2-2,**
   a. Households spend income in the product market.
   b. Firms sell resources to households.
   c. Households receive income through the product market.
   d. Households produce goods.

Answers   1. c; 2. d; 3. b; 4. a

personal property, or indirectly, as a consequence of owning all of the businesses in the economy (and thereby controlling all of the land and capital owned by businesses). Thus, all income in the economy—all wages, rents, interest, and profits—flows to households, because they provide the economy's labour, land, capital, and entrepreneurial ability.

Businesses

The yellow-coloured rectangle on the left side of the circular flow diagram represents **businesses**, which are economic entities (firms) that purchase factors of production and provide goods and services to the economy. These commercial establishments attempt to earn profits for their owners by offering goods and services for sale. Businesses fall into three main categories.

- A **sole proprietorship** is an unincorporated business owned and operated by a single person. The proprietor (the owner) provides all of the labour and produces all of the output. Examples are an arborist who runs her own tree-cutting business and an independent accountant who helps his clients with their taxes.

- A **partnership** is a natural outgrowth of the sole proprietorship. In a partnership, two or more individuals (the partners) agree to own and operate a business together. They pool their financial resources and business skills to operate the business, and they share any profits or losses that the business may generate. Many law firms and dental practices are organized as partnerships, as are a wide variety of firms in many other industries.

- A **corporation** is an independent legal entity that can—on its own behalf—acquire resources, own assets, produce and sell products, incur debts, extend credit, sue and be sued, and otherwise engage in any legal business activities.

The fact that a corporation is an independent legal entity means that its owners bear no personal financial responsibility for the fulfillment of the corporation's debts and obligations. For instance, if a corporation has failed to repay a loan to a bank, the bank can sue the corporation but not its owners. Professional managers run most corporations. They are hired and supervised by a board of directors that is elected annually by the corporation's owners. BlackBerry Limited, Bombardier, Ford, and Air Canada are examples of large corporations, but corporations come in all sizes and operate in every type of industry.

There are currently about 1.1 million businesses in Canada, ranging from enormous corporations like the Royal Bank of Canada, with 2016 revenues of over $38 billion and 78,000 employees, to one-person sole proprietorships with sales of less than $100 per day.

Businesses sell goods and services in the product market in order to obtain revenue, and they incur costs in the resource market when they purchase the labour, land, capital, and entrepreneurial ability that they need to produce their respective goods and services.

Product Market

The purple rectangle at the bottom of Figure 2-2 represents the **product market**, where the goods and services produced by businesses are bought and sold. Households use the income they receive from the sale of resources to buy goods and services. The money that they spend on goods and services flows to businesses as revenue.

Factor Market

Finally, the purple rectangle at the top of the circular flow diagram in Figure 2-2 represents the **factor market**, or resource market, in which households sell resources to businesses. The households sell resources to generate income, and the businesses buy resources to produce goods and services. Productive resources flow from households to businesses while money flows from businesses to households in the form of wages, rents, interest, and profits.

To summarize, the circular flow model depicts a complex web of economic activity in which businesses and households are both buyers and sellers. Businesses buy resources and sell products. Households buy products and sell resources. The counterclockwise flow of economic resources and finished products in Figure 2-2 is paid for by the clockwise flow of money income and consumption expenditures.

QUICK REVIEW 2.4

- Competition directs individuals and firms to unwittingly promote the social interest, as if guided by a benevolent invisible hand.

- The command systems of the Soviet Union and pre-reform China failed as a result of the coordination problem and the incentive problem.

- The circular flow model illustrates how resources flow from households to businesses and how payments for those resources flow from businesses to households.

2.6   How the Market System Deals with Risk

LO2.6   Explain how the market system deals with risk.

Producing goods and services is risky. Input shortages can suddenly arise. Consumer preferences can quickly change. Natural disasters can destroy factories and cripple supply chains. For an economic system to maximize its potential, it must develop methods for assessing and managing risk. The market system does so by confronting business owners with the financial consequences of their decisions. If they manage risks well, they may prosper. If they manage risks poorly, they may lose everything.

The Profit System

As explained in Chapter 1, entrepreneurial ability is the economic resource that organizes and directs the other three resources of land, labour, and capital toward productive uses. The owners of a firm may attempt to supply the entrepreneurial ability themselves. Or they can hire professional managers to supply the necessary leadership and decision making. Either way, it falls to those acting as the firm's entrepreneurs to deal with risk.

They are guided toward sensible decisions by the so-called *profit system*. This system is actually a *profit-and-loss* system because the entrepreneurs who must deal with risk and uncertainty gain profits if they choose wisely, but suffer losses if they choose poorly. That provides them with a large financial incentive to avoid unnecessary risks and make prudent decisions.

By contrast, risk management tends to be done very poorly in command economies, because the central planners who must allocate resources and deal with risk do not themselves face the possibility of losing money if they make bad decisions. As government employees, they tend to receive the same salaries whether things go well or poorly.

Shielding Employees and Suppliers from Business Risk

Under the market system, only a firm's owners are subject to business risk and the possibility of losing money. By contrast, the firm's employees and suppliers are shielded from business risk because they are legally entitled to receive their contracted wages and payments on time and in full regardless of whether the firm is earning a profit or generating a loss.

To see how this works, consider a pizza parlour that is being started in a small town. Its investors put up $50,000 to get it going. They rent a storefront, lease ovens, purchase computers, and set some money aside as a reserve. The firm then has to attract employees. To do so, it will offer wage contracts that promise to pay employees every two weeks, whether or not the firm is making a profit or generating a loss. This shields the firm's employees from the risks of owning and operating the business; they will get paid even if the pizza parlour is losing money.

In the same way, the contracts that the firm signs with its suppliers and with anyone who loans the firm money (for instance, the local bank) will also specify that they will be paid on time and in full no matter how the firm is doing in terms of profitability.

Because everyone else is legally entitled to get paid before the firm's owners, the firm's owners are referred to as **residual claimants** in business law. The owners are obligated to receive (claim) whatever profit or loss remains (is residual) after all other parties have been paid.

DEALING WITH LOSSES

So what happens if the firm starts losing money? In that case, the owners will take the financial hit. To be specific, suppose the pizza parlour loses $1500 during the month of October because it runs up $11,500 in costs

---

CONSIDER THIS

Insurance

Insurance promotes economic growth and investment by transferring risk from those who have a low tolerance for risk to those who have a high tolerance for risk. Consider fire insurance. Homeowners pay a monthly premium in exchange for which their insurance company guarantees to reimburse them if their house burns down. That guarantee transfers the risk of fire damage from the homeowners (who do not want to bear the risk) to the insurance company's owners (who are happy to bear the risk as a business proposition).

The insurance company will save the premiums that it receives from homeowners to help cover the rebuilding costs of any homes that do end up burning down. It is quite possible that there will be so many fires that the insurance company will spend more money repairing fire damage than it received in premiums. If that happens, the insurance company will suffer a loss that will fall on the company's owners. Their personal wealth will decline in order to make up for the

unexpectedly high number of fires. Thus, the insurance company's owners ultimately bear the fire risk; it is to them that the insurance contract transfers risk.

But if the number of fires is unexpectedly small, the insurance company will turn a nice profit and its

© Robert J. Bennett/AGE Fotostock RF

owners will benefit from having been willing to bear the risk that the homeowners did not wish to bear. More importantly, the economy's overall level of investment rises because the availability of insurance means those who dislike risk are much more willing to invest their savings in the construction and purchase of capital goods like houses, cars, and factories.

but generates only $10,000 in revenue. In that situation, the investors' wealth will shrink by $1500 as the firm is forced to dip into its reserve to cover the loss. If the firm continues to lose money in subsequent months and exhausts the reserve, the owners will then have to decide whether they want to close the shop or put in additional money in hopes that things will turn around.

All through those months of losses, the suppliers and employees are safeguarded. Because they are paid on time and in full, they are shielded from the firm's business risks and whether it is generating a profit or a loss. As a result, however, they are not legally entitled to share in the profits if the firm does end up being profitable. That privilege is reserved under the market system for the firm's owners as their reward for bearing business risk. In exchange for making sure that everyone else is shielded if things go badly, the owners are legally entitled to take all of the profits if things go well.

Benefits of Restricting Business Risk to Owners

There are two major benefits that arise from the market system's restriction of business risk to owners and investors.

ATTRACTING INPUTS

Many people deeply dislike risk and would not be willing to participate in a business venture if they were exposed to the possibility of losing money. That is the case with many workers, who just want to do their jobs and get paid twice a month without having to worry about whether their employer is doing well. The same is true for most suppliers, who just want to get paid on time and in full for the inputs they supply to the firm.

For both groups, the concentration of business risk on owners and investors is very welcome, because they can supply their resources to a firm without having to worry about the firm's profitability. That sense of security makes it much easier for firms to attract labour and other inputs, which in turn helps the economy innovate and grow.

FOCUSING ATTENTION

The profit system helps to achieve prudent risk management by focusing both the responsibility and the rewards for successfully managing risk onto a firm's owners. They can provide the risk-managing input of entrepreneurial ability themselves or hire it by paying a skilled manager. But either way, some individual's full-time job includes the specialized task of managing risk and making prudent decisions about the allocation of resources. By contrast, in a command system, the responsibility for managing risk tends to be spread out over several layers of government and many different committees so that nobody is personally responsible for bad outcomes.

QUICK REVIEW 2.5

- The market system incentivizes the prudent management of business risk by concentrating any profit or loss upon a firm's owners and investors.

- The market system shields employees, suppliers, and lenders from business risks but in exchange for that protection, they are excluded from any profit that may be earned.

- By focusing risk on owners and investors, the market system (a) creates an incentive for owners and investors to hire managerial and entrepreneurial specialists to prudently manage business risks and (b) encourages the participation of workers, suppliers, and lenders who dislike risk.

The LAST WORD

Shuffling the Deck

© Mpfaff/Dreamstime.com/GetStock.com

Economist Donald Boudreaux marvels at the way the market system systematically and purposefully arranges the world's tens of billions of individual resources.

In *The Future and Its Enemies*, Virginia Postrel notes the astonishing fact that if you thoroughly shuffle an ordinary deck of 52 playing cards, chances are practically 100 percent that the resulting arrangement of cards has never before existed. Never. Every time you shuffle a deck, you produce an arrangement of cards that exists for the first time in history.

The arithmetic works out that way. For a very small number of items, the number of possible arrangements is small. Three items, for example, can be arranged only six different ways. But the number of possible arrangements grows very quickly. The number of different ways to arrange five items is 120 . . . for ten items it's 3,628,800 . . . for fifteen items it's 1,307,674,368,000.

The number of different ways to arrange 52 items is 8.066×10^{67}. This is a big number. No human can comprehend its enormousness. By way of comparison, the number of possible ways to arrange a mere 20 items is 2,432,902,008,176,640,000—a number larger than the total number of seconds that have elapsed since the beginning of time ten billion years ago—and this number is Lilliputian compared to 8.066×10^{67}.

What's the significance of these facts about numbers? Consider the number of different resources available in the world—my labour, your labour, your land, oil, tungsten, cedar, coffee beans, chickens, rivers, the Empire State Building, [Microsoft] Windows, the wharves at Houston, the classrooms at Oxford, the airport at Miami, and on and on and on. No one can possibly count all of the different, productive resources available for our use. But we can be sure that this number is at least in the tens of billions.

When you reflect on how incomprehensibly large is the number of ways to arrange a deck containing a mere 52 cards, the mind boggles at the number of different ways to arrange all the world's resources.

If our world were random—if resources combined together haphazardly, as if a giant took them all into his hands and tossed them down like so many [cards]—it's a virtual certainty that the resulting combination of resources would be useless. Unless this chance arrangement were quickly rearranged according to some productive logic, nothing worthwhile would be produced. We would all starve to death. Because only a tiny fraction of possible arrangements serves human ends, any arrangement will be useless if it is chosen randomly or with inadequate knowledge of how each and every resource might be productively combined with each other.

And yet, we witness all around us an arrangement of resources that's productive and serves human goals. Today's arrangement of resources might not be perfect, but it is vastly superior to most of the trillions upon trillions of other possible arrangements.

How have we managed to get one of the minuscule number of arrangements that works? The answer is private property—a social institution that encourages mutual accommodation.

Private property eliminates the possibility that resource arrangements will be random, for each resource owner chooses a course of action only if it promises rewards to the owner that exceed the rewards promised by all other available courses.

[The result] is a breathtakingly complex and productive arrangement of countless resources. This arrangement emerged over time (and is still emerging) as the result of billions upon billions of individual, daily, small decisions made by people seeking to better employ their resources and labour in ways that other people find helpful.

Source: Abridged from Donald J. Boudreaux, "Mutual Accommodation," *Ideas on Liberty*, May 2000, pp. 4–5. Reprinted with permission.

Question

What explains why millions of economic resources tend to get arranged logically and productively rather than haphazardly and unproductively?

Chapter Summary

LO2.1   Differentiate between laissez-faire capitalism, the command system, and the market system.

- Laissez-faire capitalism is a hypothetical economic system in which government's role would be restricted to protecting private property and enforcing contracts. All real-world economic systems have featured a more extensive role for government. Governments in command systems own nearly all property and resources and make nearly all decisions about what to produce, how to produce it, and who gets the output. Most countries today, including Canada, have market systems in which the government does play a large role, but in which most property and resources are privately owned and markets are the major force in determining what to produce, how to produce it, and who gets it.

LO2.2   List the main characteristics of the market system.

- The market system is characterized by the private ownership of resources, including capital, and the freedom of individuals to engage in economic activities of their choice to advance their material well-being. Self-interest is the driving force of such an economy, and competition functions as a regulatory or control mechanism.

- In the market system, markets, prices, and profits organize and make effective the many millions of individual economic decisions that occur daily.

- Specialization, the use of advanced technology, and the extensive use of capital goods are common features of market systems. Functioning as a medium of exchange, money eliminates the problems of bartering and permits easy trade and greater specialization, both domestically and internationally.

LO2.3   Explain how the market system answers the five fundamental questions of what to produce, how to produce, who obtains the output, how to adjust to change, and how to promote progress.

- Every economy faces five fundamental questions: (1) What goods and services will be produced? (2) How will the goods and services be produced? (3) Who will get the goods and services? (4) How will the system accommodate change? (5) How will the system promote progress?

- The market system produces products whose production and sale yield total revenue sufficient to cover total cost. It does not produce products for which total revenue continually falls short of total cost. Competition forces firms to use the lowest-cost production techniques.

- Economic profit (total revenue minus total cost) indicates that an industry is prosperous and promotes its expansion. Losses

signify that an industry is not prosperous and hasten its contraction.

- Consumer sovereignty means that both businesses and resource suppliers are subject to the wants of consumers. Through their dollar votes, consumers decide on the composition of output.

- The prices that a household receives for the resources it supplies to the economy determine that household's income. This income determines the household's claim on the economy's output. Those who have income to spend get the products produced in the market system.

- By communicating changes in consumer tastes to entrepreneurs and resource suppliers, the market system prompts appropriate adjustments in the allocation of the economy's resources. The market system also encourages technological advance and capital accumulation, both of which raise a nation's standard of living.

LO2.4   Explain the operation of the "invisible hand" and why market economies usually do a better job than command economies at transforming economic resources into desirable output.

- Competition, the primary mechanism of control in the market economy, promotes a unity of self-interest and social interests. As if directed by an invisible hand, competition harnesses the self-interest motives of businesses and resource suppliers to further the social interest.

- The command systems of the former Soviet Union and pre-reform China met their demise because of coordination difficulties caused by central planning and the lack of profit incentives that encourage product improvement, produce new products, and give rise to entrepreneurship.

LO2.5   Describe the mechanics of the circular flow model.

- The circular flow model illustrates the flow of resources and products from households to businesses and from businesses to households, along with the corresponding monetary flows. Businesses are on the buying side of the resource market and the selling side of the product market. Households are on the selling side of the resource market and the buying side of the product market.

LO2.6   Explain how the market system deals with risk.

- By focusing business risks onto owners, the market system encourages the participation of workers and suppliers who dislike risk, while at the same time creating a strong incentive for owners to manage business risks prudently.

Terms and Concepts

economic system
laissez-faire capitalism
command system

market system
private property
freedom of enterprise

freedom of choice
self-interest
competition
market
specialization
division of labour
medium of exchange
barter
money
consumer sovereignty
dollar votes

creative destruction
invisible hand
circular flow diagram
household
businesses
sole proprietorship
partnership
corporation
product market
factor market
residual claimant

Discussion Questions

1. Contrast how a market system and a command economy try to cope with economic scarcity.   [**LO2.1**]

2. How does self-interest help achieve society's economic goals? Why is there such a wide variety of desired goods and services in a market system? In what way are entrepreneurs and businesses at the helm of the economy but commanded by consumers?   [**LO2.2**]

3. Why is private property, and the protection of property rights, essential to the success of the market system? How do property rights encourage cooperation?   [**LO2.2**]

4. What are the advantages of using capital goods in the production process? What is meant by the term *division of labour*? What are the advantages of specialization in the use of human and material resources? Explain why exchange is the necessary consequence of specialization.   [**LO2.2**]

5. What problem does barter entail? Indicate the economic significance of money as a medium of exchange. What is meant by the statement "We want money only to part with it"?   [**LO2.2**]

6. Evaluate and explain each of the following hypothetical statements: [**LO2.2**]

    a. The market system is a profit-and-loss system.

    b. Competition is the disciplinarian of the market economy.

7. Some large hardware stores such as Canadian Tire boast of carrying as many as 20,000 different products in each store. What motivated the producers of those individual products to make them and offer them for sale? How did the producers decide on the best combinations of factors to use? Who made those factors available, and why? Who decides whether these particular hardware products should continue to be produced and offered for sale?   [**LO2.3**]

8. What is meant by the term *creative destruction*? How does the emergence of MP3 (or iPod) technology relate to this idea?   [**LO2.3**]

9. In a sentence, define the phrase *invisible hand*.   [**LO2.3**]

10. In market economies, firms rarely worry about the availability of inputs to produce their products, whereas in command economies input availability is a constant concern. Why is there a difference?   [**LO2.4**]

11. Distinguish between the factor market and the product market in the circular flow model. In what way are businesses and households both sellers and buyers in this model? What are the flows in the circular flow model?   [**LO2.5**]

12. How does shielding employees and suppliers from business risk help to improve economic outcomes? Who is responsible for managing business risks in the market system?   [**LO2.6**]

Review Questions

1. Decide whether each of the following describes a command system, a market system, or a laissez-faire system.   [**LO2.1**]

    a. A woman cannot open a flower shop unless the central government decides to allow it.

    b. Shops stock and sell the goods their customers want but the government levies a sales tax on each transaction in order to fund elementary schools, public libraries, and welfare programs for the poor.

    c. The only taxes levied by the government are to pay for national defence, law enforcement, and a legal system designed to enforce contracts between private citizens.

2. Match each term with the correct definition.   [**LO2.2**]

    private property   self-interest

    freedom of enterprise   competition

    mutually agreeable   market

    freedom of choice

    a. An institution that brings buyers and sellers together.

    b. The right of private persons and firms to obtain, control, employ, dispose of, and bequeath land, capital, and other property.

c. The presence in a market of independent buyers and sellers who compete with one another and who are free to enter and exit the market as they each see fit.

d. The freedom of firms to obtain economic resources, decide what products to produce with those resources, and sell those products in markets of their choice.

e. What each individual or firm believes is best for itself and seeks to obtain.

f. Economic transactions willingly undertaken by both the buyer and the seller because each feels that the transaction will make him or her better off.

g. The freedom of resource owners to dispose of their resources as they think best, of workers to enter any line of work for which they are qualified, and of consumers to spend their incomes in whatever way they feel is most appropriate.

3. True or False? Money must be issued by a government for people to accept it.   [**LO2.2**]

4. Assume that a business firm finds that its profit is greatest when it produces $40 worth of product A. Suppose also that each of the three techniques shown in the table below will produce the desired output.   [**LO2.3**]

a. With the factor prices shown, which technique will the firm choose? Why? Will production using that technique entail profit or loss? What will be the amount of that profit or loss? Will the industry expand or contract? When will that expansion or contraction end?

b. Assume now that a new technique, called technique 4, is developed. It combines 2 units of labour, 2 of land, 6 of capital, and 3 of entrepreneurial ability. In view of the resource prices in the table, will the firm adopt technique 4? Explain your answer.

c. Suppose that an increase in the labour supply causes the price of labour to fall to $1.50 per unit, all other resource prices remaining unchanged. Which technique will the producer now choose? Explain.

d. "The market system causes the economy to conserve most in the use of resources that are particularly scarce in supply. Resources that are scarcest relative to the demand for them have the highest prices. As a result, producers use these resources as sparingly as is possible." Evaluate this statement. Does your answer to part (c) above bear out this contention? Explain.

5. Identify each of the following quotes as being an example of either the coordination problem, the invisible hand, creative destruction, or the incentive problem.   [**LO2.4**]

a. "If you compare a list of today's most powerful and profitable companies with a similar list from 30 years ago, you will see lots of new entries."

b. "Managers in the old Soviet Union often sacrificed product quality and variety because they were being awarded bonuses for quantitative, not qualitative, targets."

c. "Each day, central planners in the old Soviet Union were tasked with setting 27 million prices—correctly."

d. "It is not from the benevolence of the butcher, the brewer, or the baker that we expect our dinner, but from their regard to their own interest."

6. True or False? Households sell finished products to businesses. [**LO2.6**]

7. Franklin, John, Henry, and Harry have decided to pool their financial resources and business skills in order to open up and run a coffee shop. They will share any profits or losses that the business generates and will be personally responsible for making good on any debt that their business undertakes. Their business should be classified as a   [**LO2.6**]

a. Corporation

b. Sole proprietorship

c. Partnership

d. None of the above

8. Ted and Fred are the owners of a gas station. They invested $150,000 each and pay an employee named Lawrence $35,000 per year. This year revenues are $900,000, while costs are $940,000. Who is legally responsible for bearing the $40,000 loss?   [**LO2.6**]

a. Lawrence

b. Ted

c. Fred

d. Ted and Fred

e. Lawrence, Ted, and Fred

RESOURCE UNITS REQUIRED

Resource	Price per unit of resource	Technique 1	Technique 2	Technique 3
Labour	$3	5	2	3
Land	4	2	4	2
Capital	2	2	4	5
Entrepreneurial ability	2	4	2	4

Problems

1. Suppose Natasha currently makes $50,000 per year working as a manager at a cable TV company. She develops two possible entrepreneurial business opportunities. In one, she will quit her job to start a hand-made soap company. In the other, she will try to develop an Internet-based competitor to the cable company. For the soap-making opportunity, she anticipates annual revenue of $465,000 and costs for the necessary land, labour, and capital of $395,000 per year. For the Internet opportunity, she anticipates costs for land, labour, and capital of $3,250,000 per year as compared to revenues of $3,275,000 per year.   [**LO2.3**]

   a. Should she quit her current job to become an entrepreneur?

   b. If she does quit her current job, which opportunity should she pursue?

2. With current technology, suppose a firm is producing 400 loaves of banana bread daily. Also assume that the least-cost combination of resources in producing those loaves is 5 units of labour, 7 units of land, 2 units of capital, and 1 unit of entrepreneurial ability, selling at per-unit prices of $40, $60, $60, and $20, respectively.   [**LO2.3**]

   a. If the firm can sell these 400 loaves at $2 per unit, what is its total revenue? Its total cost? Its profit or loss? Will it continue to produce banana bread?

   b. If this firm's situation is typical for the other makers of banana bread, will resources flow toward or away from this bread?

3. Let us put dollar amounts on the flows in the circular flow diagram of Figure 2-2.   [**LO2.5**]

   a. Suppose that businesses buy a total of $100 billion of the four resources (labour, land, capital, and entrepreneurial ability) from households. If households receive $60 billion in wages, $10 billion in rent, and $20 billion in interest, how much are households paid for providing entrepreneurial ability?

   b. If households spend $55 billion on goods and $45 billion on services, how much in revenues do businesses receive in the product market?

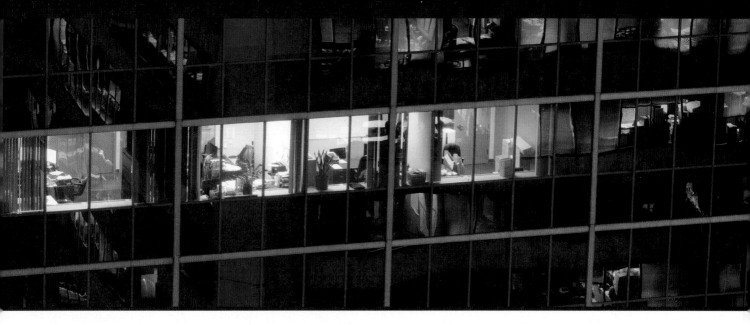

CHAPTER 3

Demand, Supply, and Market Equilibrium

LEARNING OBJECTIVES

LO3.1   Characterize and give examples of markets.

LO3.2   Describe *demand* and explain how it can change.

LO3.3   Describe *supply* and explain how it can change.

LO3.4   Relate how supply and demand interact to determine market equilibrium.

LO3.5   Explain how changes in supply and demand affect equilibrium prices and quantities.

LO3.6   Identify what government-set prices are and how they can cause surpluses and shortages.

LOA3.1   (Appendix) Illustrate how supply and demand analysis can provide insights into
actual-economy situations.

The model of supply and demand is the economics profession's greatest contribution to human understanding, because it explains the operation of the markets on which we depend for nearly everything that we eat, drink, or consume. The model is so powerful and so widely used that, to many people, it *is* economics.

This chapter explains how the model works and how it can explain both the *quantities* that are bought and sold in markets and the *prices* at which they trade.

3.1 Markets

LO3.1 Characterize and give examples of markets.

Markets bring together buyers (demanders) and sellers (suppliers). The corner gas station, an e-commerce website, the local bakery shop, a farmer's roadside stand—all are familiar markets. The Toronto Stock Exchange and the Winnipeg Commodity Exchange are markets where buyers and sellers of stocks, bonds, and farm commodities from all over the world communicate with one another to buy and sell. Auctioneers bring together potential buyers and sellers of art, livestock, used farm equipment, and sometimes real estate. In labour markets, new college or university graduates sell and employers buy specific labour services.

Some markets are local, while others are national or international. Some are highly personal, involving face-to-face contact between demander and supplier; others are faceless, with buyer and seller never seeing or knowing each other.

To keep things simple, in this chapter we will focus on markets in which large numbers of independently acting buyers and sellers come together to buy and sell standardized products. Markets with these characteristics are the economy's most highly competitive, and include the wheat market, the stock market, and the market for foreign currencies. All such markets involve demand, supply, price, and quantity. As you will soon see, the price is discovered through the interacting decisions of buyers and sellers.

3.2 Demand

LO3.2 Describe *demand* and explain how it can change.

Demand is a schedule or a curve that shows the various amounts of a product that consumers are willing and able to purchase at each of a series of possible prices during a specified period of time.[1] Demand shows the quantities of a product that will be purchased at various possible prices, *other things equal*. Demand can easily be shown in table form. Figure 3-1 shows a hypothetical demand schedule for a single consumer purchasing bushels of corn.

The table in Figure 3-1 reveals the relationship between the various prices of corn and the quantity of corn a particular consumer would be willing *and able* to purchase at each of these prices. We say willing *and able* because willingness alone is not effective in the market. You may be willing to buy a plasma television set, but if that willingness is not backed by the necessary dollars, it will not be effective, and therefore will not be reflected in the market. If the price of corn were $5 per bushel, our consumer would be willing and able to buy 10 bushels per week; if it were $4, the consumer would be willing and able to buy 20 bushels per week; and so forth.

The table in Figure 3-1 does not tell us which of the five possible prices will actually exist in the corn market. That depends on the interaction between demand and supply. Demand is simply a statement of a buyer's plans, or intentions, with respect to the purchase of a product.

As price falls the quantity demanded rises, and as price rises the quantity demanded falls.

---

[1] This definition is obviously worded to apply to product markets. To adjust it to apply to factor markets, substitute the word *factor* for *product* and the word *businesses* for *consumers*.

FIGURE 3-1   An Individual Buyer's Demand for Corn

Because price and quantity demanded are inversely related, an individual's demand schedule graphs as a downsloping curve such as *D*. Specifically, the law of demand says that, other things equal, consumers will buy more of a product as its price declines. Here and in later figures, *P* stands for price and *Q* stands for quantity (either demanded or supplied).

Price per bushel	Quantity demanded (bushels per week)
$5	10
4	20
3	35
2	55
1	80

To be meaningful, the quantities demanded at each price must relate to a specific period—a day, a week, a month, etc. Saying, "A consumer will buy 10 bushels of corn at $5 per bushel" is meaningless. Saying, "A consumer will buy 10 bushels of corn per week at $5 per bushel" is meaningful. Unless a specific time period is stated, we do not know whether the demand for a product is large or small.

Law of Demand

A fundamental characteristic of demand is this: Other things equal, as price falls the quantity demanded rises, and as price rises the quantity demanded falls. There is a negative or *inverse* relationship between price and quantity demanded. This inverse relationship is called the **law of demand**.

The *other-things-equal* assumption is crucial here (see Chapter 1). Many factors other than the price of the product being considered affect the amount purchased. The quantity of Nike shoes purchased will depend not only on the price of Nike shoes but also on the prices of substitutes such as Reebok, Adidas, and New Balance. The law of demand in this case says that fewer Nikes will be purchased if the price of Nikes rises and if the prices of Reebok, Adidas, and New Balance shoes all remain constant. In other words, if the *relative price* of Nikes rises, fewer Nikes will be bought.

Why is there an inverse relationship between price and quantity demanded? Let's look at three explanations, beginning with the simplest:

- The law of demand is consistent with common sense. People ordinarily *do* buy more of a product at a low price than at a high price. Price is an obstacle that deters consumers from buying. The higher that obstacle, the less of a product they will buy; the lower the price obstacle, the more they will buy. The fact that businesses hold "sales" to clear out unsold items is evidence of their belief in the law of demand.

- In any specific time period, each buyer of a product will derive less satisfaction (or benefit, or utility) from each successive unit of the product consumed. The second Big Mac will yield less additional satisfaction to the consumer than the first, and the third still less than the second. That is, consumption is subject to **diminishing marginal utility**. And because successive units of a particular product yield less and less marginal utility, consumers will buy additional units only if the price of those units is progressively reduced.

- We can also explain the law of demand in terms of *income* and *substitution* effects. The **income effect** indicates that a lower price increases the purchasing power of a buyer's money income, enabling the buyer to purchase more of the product than she or he could buy before. A higher price has the opposite effect. The **substitution effect** suggests that at a lower price buyers have the incentive to substitute what is now a less expensive product for other products that are now *relatively* more expensive. The product whose price has fallen is now a better deal relative to the other products.

For example, a decline in the price of chicken will increase the purchasing power of consumer incomes, enabling them to buy more chicken (the income effect). At a lower price, chicken is relatively more attractive and consumers tend to substitute it for pork, beef, and fish (the substitution effect). The income and substitution effects combine to make consumers able and willing to buy more of a product at a low price than at a high price.

The Demand Curve

The inverse relationship between price and quantity demanded for any product can be represented on a simple graph, in which, by convention, we measure *quantity demanded* on the horizontal axis and *price* on the vertical axis. In Figure 3-1 we plotted the five price–quantity data points listed in the table and connected the points with a smooth curve, labelled *D*. Such a curve is called a **demand curve**. Its downward slope reflects the law of demand—people buy more of a product, service, or factor as its price falls. The relationship between price and quantity demanded is inverse (or negative). We also refer to the demand curve as the *marginal benefit curve*, a concept introduced in Chapter 1. The demand curve tells us the extra benefit the consumer derives from one more unit of a good or service.

MATH 3.1   The Demand Curve

The table and the graph in Figure 3-1 contain exactly the same data and reflect the same relationship between price and quantity demanded. But the graph shows that relationship more simply and clearly than a table or a description in words.

Market Demand

So far, we have concentrated on just one consumer. By adding the quantities demanded by all consumers at each of the various possible prices, we can get from *individual* demand to *market* demand. If there are just three buyers in the market, as represented in Figure 3-2, it is relatively easy to determine the total quantity demanded at each price. Figure 3-2 shows the graphical summing procedure: At each price we sum horizontally the individual quantities demanded to obtain the total quantity demanded at that price; we then plot the price and the total quantity demanded as one point of the market demand curve. At the price of $3, for example, the three individual curves yield a total quantity demanded of 100 bushels (= 35 + 39 + 26).

Competition, of course, ordinarily entails many more than three buyers of a product. To avoid hundreds or thousands or millions of additions, we suppose that all the buyers in a market are willing and able to buy the same amounts at each of the possible prices. Then we just multiply those amounts by the number of buyers to obtain the market demand. This is how we arrived at the demand schedule and demand curve D_1, in Figure 3-3, for a market with 200 corn buyers. The table in Figure 3-3 shows the calculations for 200 corn buyers.

Determinants of Demand

In constructing a demand curve such as D_1 in Figure 3-3, we assume that price is the most important influence on the amount of any product purchased, even though other factors can and do affect purchases. These factors, called **determinants of demand**, are assumed to be constant when a demand curve like D_1 is drawn. They are the *other things equal* in the relationship between price and quantity demanded. When any of these determinants changes, the demand curve will shift to the right or left.

The basic determinants of demand are (1) consumers' tastes (preferences), (2) the number of consumers in the market, (3) consumers' incomes, (4) the prices of related goods, and (5) consumers' expectations.

Changes in Demand

A change in one or more of the determinants of demand will change the demand data (the demand schedule) in the table accompanying Figure 3-3, and therefore the location of the demand curve there. A change in the demand schedule—or, graphically, a shift in the demand curve—is called a *change in demand*.

FIGURE 3-2   Market Demand for Corn, Three Buyers

The market demand curve D is the horizontal summation of the individual demand curves (D_1, D_2, and D_3) of all the consumers in the market. At the price of $3, for example, the three individual curves yield a total quantity demanded of 100 bushels.

Price per bushel	QUANTITY DEMANDED							Total quantity demanded per week
	Joe		Jen		Jay			
$5	10	+	12	+	8	=		30
4	20	+	23	+	17	=		60
3	35	+	39	+	26	=		100
2	55	+	60	+	39	=		154
1	80	+	87	+	54	=		221

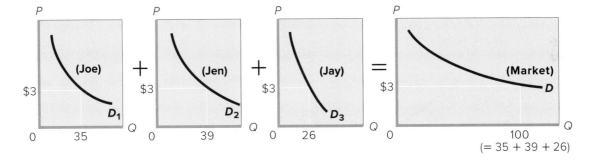

If consumers desire to buy more corn at each possible price than is reflected in column 2 of the table in Figure 3-3, that *increase in demand* is shown as a shift of the demand curve to the right—from, say, D_1 to D_2. Conversely, a *decrease in demand* occurs when consumers buy less corn at each possible price than is indicated in column 2 of the table in Figure 3-3. The leftward shift of the demand curve from D_1 to D_3 in Figure 3-3 shows that situation.

Now let's see how changes in each determinant affect demand.

TASTES

A favourable change in consumer tastes (preferences) for a product—a change that makes the product more desirable—means that more of it will be demanded at each price. Demand will increase; the demand curve will shift rightward. An unfavourable change in consumer preferences will decrease demand, shifting the demand curve to the left.

New products may affect consumer tastes; for example, the introduction of digital cameras has greatly decreased demand for film cameras. Consumers' concern over the health hazards of cholesterol and obesity have increased the demand for broccoli, low-calorie sweeteners, and fresh fruit, while decreasing the demand for beef, veal, eggs, and whole milk. Over the past twenty years, the demand for coffee drinks and table wine has greatly increased, driven by changes in tastes. So, too, has the demand for touch-screen mobile phones and fuel-efficient hybrid vehicles.

NUMBER OF BUYERS

An increase in the number of buyers in a market increases demand; a decrease in the number of buyers decreases demand. For example, the rising number of older persons in Canada in recent years has increased the demand for motor homes, medical care, and retirement communities.

Immigration to Canada from many parts of the world has greatly increased the demand for a whole range of ethnic goods and services, particularly in southern Ontario and British Columbia. Improvements in communications have given financial markets international range and have thus increased the demand for stocks and bonds.

FIGURE 3-3 Changes in the Demand for Corn

A change in one or more of the determinants of demand causes a change in demand. An increase in demand is shown as a shift of the demand curve to the right, as from D_1 to D_2. A decrease in demand is shown as a shift of the demand curve to the left, as from D_1 to D_3. These changes in demand are to be distinguished from a change in quantity demanded, which is caused by a change in the price of the product, as shown by a movement from, say, point *a* to point *b* on fixed demand curve D_1.

MARKET DEMAND FOR CORN, 200 BUYERS, D_1	
(1) Price per bushel	(2) Total quantity demanded per week
$5	2,000
4	4,000
3	7,000
2	11,000
1	16,000

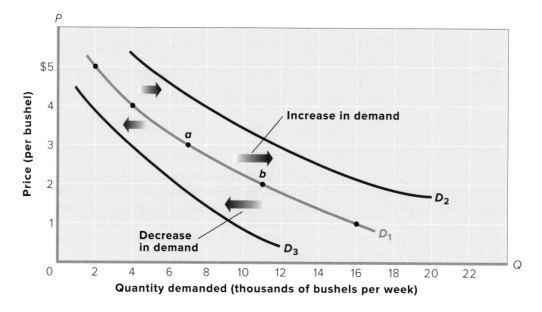

International trade agreements have reduced foreign trade barriers to Canadian farm commodities, increasing the number of buyers and the demand for those products.

In contrast, the emigration (out-migration) from many small rural communities has reduced the population and thus the demand for housing, home appliances, and auto repair in those towns.

INCOME

How changes in income affect demand is more complex. For most products, a rise in income causes an increase in demand. Consumers typically buy more steaks, furniture, and electronic equipment as their incomes increase. Conversely, the demand for such products declines as income falls. A product for which demand varies directly with money income is called a **normal good**.

Although most products are normal goods, there are some exceptions. As incomes increase beyond some point, the demand for used clothing, retread tires, and third-hand automobiles may decrease, because the higher incomes enable consumers to buy new versions of those products. Similarly, rising incomes may cause the demand for charcoal grills to decline as wealthier consumers switch to gas grills. Goods for which demand varies *inversely* with money income are called **inferior goods**.

PRICES OF RELATED GOODS

A change in the price of a related good may either increase or decrease the demand for a product, depending on whether the related good is a substitute or a complement. A **substitute good** is one that can be used in place of another good. A **complementary good** is one that is used together with another good.

- *Substitutes* Häagen-Dazs ice cream and Baskin-Robbins ice cream are substitute goods (or, simply, *substitutes*). When two products are substitutes, an increase in the price of one will increase the demand for the other. Conversely, a decrease in the price of one will decrease the demand for the other. For example, when the price of Häagen-Dazs ice cream rises, consumers will demand less of it and increase their demand for Baskin-Robbins ice cream. When the price of Colgate toothpaste declines, the demand for Crest declines. So it is with other product pairs such as Nike and Reebok shoes, Molson and Labatt beer, or Chevrolet and Ford pickup trucks. They are *substitutes in consumption.*

- *Complements* Because complementary goods (or simply *complements*) are used together, they are typically demanded jointly. Examples are computers and software, cellphones and cellular service, and snowboards and lift tickets. If the price of a complement (for example, lettuce) goes up, the demand for the related good (salad dressing) will decline. Conversely, if the price of a complement (for example, tuition) falls, the demand for a related good (textbooks) will increase.

- *Unrelated Goods* The vast majority of goods that are not related to one another are called *independent goods*. Examples are butter and golf balls, potatoes and automobiles, and bananas and wristwatches. A change in the price of one does not affect the demand for the other.

CONSUMER EXPECTATIONS

Changes in consumer expectations may shift demand. A newly formed expectation of higher future prices may cause consumers to buy now in order to beat the anticipated price rises, thus increasing current demand. That is often what happens in so-called hot real estate markets, such as Vancouver and Toronto. Buyers rush in because they think the price of new homes will continue to escalate rapidly. Some buyers fear being priced out of the market and therefore not obtaining the home they desire. Other buyers—speculators—believe they will be able to sell the houses later at a higher price. Whichever their motivation, these buyers increase the demand for houses.

Similarly, a change in expectations concerning future income may prompt consumers to change their current spending. For example, first-round NHL draft choices may splurge on new luxury cars in anticipation of lucrative professional hockey contracts. Or workers who become fearful of losing their jobs may reduce their demand for, say, vacation travel.

In summary, an *increase* in demand—the decision by consumers to buy larger quantities of a product at each possible price—may be caused by

- A favourable change in consumer tastes
- An increase in the number of buyers
- An increase in incomes if the product is a normal good
- A decrease in incomes if the product is an inferior good
- An increase in the price of a substitute good
- A decrease in the price of a complementary good
- A new consumer expectation that prices and incomes will be higher in the future

Reverse these generalizations to explain a *decrease* in demand. Table 3-1 provides additional illustrations of the determinants of demand.

Changes in Quantity Demanded

A *change in demand* must not be confused with a *change in quantity demanded*. A **change in demand** is a shift of the entire demand curve to the right (an increase in demand) or to the left (a decrease in demand). It occurs because the consumer's state of mind about purchasing the product has been altered in response to a change in one or more of the determinants of demand. Recall that *demand* is a schedule or a curve; therefore, a *change in demand* means a change in the schedule and a shift of the curve.

TABLE 3-1	Determinants of Demand Curve Shifts
Determinant	**Examples**
Change in buyer tastes	Physical fitness rises in popularity, increasing the demand for jogging shoes and bicycles; cellphone popularity rises, reducing the demand for landline phones.
Change in number of buyers	A decline in the birth rate reduces the demand for children's toys.
Change in income	A rise in incomes increases the demand for such normal goods as restaurant meals, sports tickets, and tablet computers, while reducing the demand for such inferior goods as cabbage, turnips, and inexpensive wine.
Change in the prices of related goods	A reduction in airfares reduces the demand for bus transportation (substitute goods); a decline in the price of Blu-ray DVD players increases the demand for Blu-ray DVD movies (complementary goods).
Change in consumer expectation	Inclement weather in South America creates an expectation of higher future coffee bean prices, increasing today's demand for coffee beans.

In contrast, a **change in quantity demanded** is a movement from one point to another point—from one price–quantity combination to another—on a fixed demand curve. The cause of such a change is an increase or decrease in the price of the product under consideration. In Figure 3-3, for example, a decline in the price of corn from $5 to $4 will increase the quantity of corn demanded from 2000 to 4000 bushels.

In Figure 3-3, the shift of the demand curve D_1 to either D_2 or D_3 is a change in demand. But the movement from point a to point b on curve D_1 represents a change in quantity demanded: Demand has not changed; demand is represented by the entire curve, which remains fixed in place.

QUICK REVIEW 3.1

- Demand is a schedule or a curve showing the amount of a product that buyers are willing and able to purchase at each possible price in a series of prices, in a particular time period.

- The law of demand states that, other things equal, the quantity of a good purchased varies inversely with its price.

- The demand curve shifts because of changes in (a) consumer tastes, (b) the number of buyers in the market, (c) consumer income, (d) the prices of substitute or complementary goods, and (e) consumer expectations.

- A change in demand is a shift of the demand curve; a change in quantity demanded is a movement from one point to another on a fixed demand curve.

3.3 Supply

LO3.3 Describe *supply* and explain how it can change.

Supply is a schedule or curve that shows the amounts of a product that producers are willing and able to make available for sale at each of a series of possible prices during a specific period.[2] Figure 3-4 is a hypothetical supply schedule for a single producer of corn. It shows the quantities of corn that will be supplied at various prices, other things equal.

Law of Supply

The table in Figure 3-4 shows a direct relationship between price and quantity supplied. As price rises, the quantity supplied rises; as price falls, the quantity supplied falls. This relationship is called the **law of supply**. A supply schedule tells us that, other things equal, firms will produce and offer for sale more of their product at a high price

[2]This definition is worded to apply to product markets. To adjust it to apply to factor markets, substitute the word *factor* for *product* and the word *owner* for *producer*.

FIGURE 3-4   An Individual Producer's Supply of Corn

Because price and quantity supplied are positively related, a firm's supply schedule is an upsloping curve such as *S*. Specifically, the law of supply says that, other things equal, firms will supply more of a product as its price rises.

Price per bushel	Quantity demanded (bushels per week)
$5	60
4	50
3	35
2	20
1	5

than at a low price. The higher the price, the greater the incentive and the greater the quantity supplied. This, again, is basically common sense.

Price is an obstacle from the standpoint of the consumer, who is on the paying end. The higher the price, the less the consumer will buy. But the supplier is on the receiving end of the product's price. To the supplier, price represents *revenue*, which serves as an incentive to produce and sell a product. The higher the price, the greater the incentive and the greater the quantity supplied.

Consider a farmer in Ontario who is deciding how much corn to plant. As corn prices rise, as shown in the table in Figure 3-4, the farmer finds it profitable to plant more. And the higher corn prices enable the Ontario farmer to cover the increased costs associated with more intensive cultivation and the use of more seed, fertilizer, and pesticide. The overall result is more corn.

Now consider a manufacturer. Beyond some quantity of production, manufacturers usually encounter increasing *marginal cost*—the added cost of producing one more unit of output. Certain productive resources—in particular, the firm's plant and machinery—cannot be expanded quickly, so the firm uses more of other resources, such as labour, to produce more output. But as labour becomes more abundant relative to the fixed plant and equipment, the additional workers have relatively less space and access to equipment. For example, the added workers may have to wait to gain access to machines. As a result, each added worker produces less added output, and the marginal cost of successive units of output rises accordingly. The firm will not produce the more costly units unless it receives a higher price for them. Again, price and quantity supplied are directly related.

The Supply Curve

As with demand, it is convenient to represent individual supply graphically. In Figure 3-4, curve *S* is the **supply curve** that corresponds to the price–quantity data in the accompanying table. The upward slope of the curve reflects the law of supply—a producer will offer more of a good, service, or factor for sale as its price rises. The relationship between price and quantity supplied is positive or direct.

MATH 3.2   The Supply Curve

Market Supply

Market supply is derived from individual supply in exactly the same way that market demand is derived from individual demand. We sum the quantities supplied by each producer at each price. That is, we obtain the market supply

FIGURE 3-5   Changes in the Supply of Corn

A change in one or more of the determinants of supply causes a shift in supply. An increase in supply is shown as a rightward shift of the supply curve, as from S_1 to S_2. A decrease in supply is depicted as a leftward shift of the curve, as from S_1 to S_3. In contrast, a change in the quantity supplied is caused by a change in the product's price and is shown by a movement from one point to another, as from point *a* to point *b*, on a fixed supply curve.

MARKET SUPPLY OF CORN, 200 PRODUCERS, S_1	
(1) Price per bushel	(2) Total quantity supplied per week
$5	12,000
4	10,000
3	7,000
2	4,000
1	1,000

curve by horizontally adding the supply curves of the individual producers. The price–quantity supplied data in the table in Figure 3-5 are for an assumed 200 identical producers in the market, each willing to supply corn according to the supply schedule shown in Figure 3-4. Curve S_1 in Figure 3-5 is a graph of the market supply data. Note that the axes in Figure 3-5 are the same as those used in our graph of market demand (Figure 3-2). The only difference is that we change the label on the horizontal axis from *quantity demanded* to *quantity supplied*.

Determinants of Supply

In constructing a supply curve, we assume that price is the most significant influence on the quantity supplied of any product. But other factors (the "other things equal") can and do affect supply. The supply curve is drawn on the assumption that these other things are fixed and do not change. If one of them does change, a *change in supply* will occur, meaning that the entire supply curve will shift.

The basic **determinants of supply** are (1) factor prices, (2) technology, (3) taxes and subsidies, (4) prices of other goods, (5) price expectations, and (6) the number of sellers in the market. A change in any one or more of these determinants of supply will move the supply curve for a product either to the right or to the left. A shift to the *right*, as from S_1 to S_2 in Figure 3-5, signifies an *increase* in supply: Producers supply larger quantities of the product at each possible price. A shift to the *left*, as from S_1 to S_3, indicates a *decrease* in supply. Producers offer less output at each price.

Changes in Supply

Let's consider how changes in each of the determinants affect supply. The key idea is that costs are a major factor underlying supply curves; anything that affects costs (other than changes in output itself) usually shifts the supply curve.

FACTOR PRICES

The prices of the factors used as inputs in the production process determine the costs of production. Higher *factor* prices raise production costs and, assuming a particular *product* price, squeeze profits. That reduction in profits reduces the incentive for firms to supply output at each product price. For example, an increase in the prices of iron ore and coke will increase the cost of producing steel for Dofasco and reduce its supply.

In contrast, lower *factor* prices reduce production costs and increase profits. So, when input prices fall, firms supply greater output at each product price. For example, a decrease in the price of iron ore will decrease the price of steel.

TECHNOLOGY

Improvements in technology (techniques of production) enable firms to produce units of output with fewer inputs. Because inputs are costly, using fewer of them lowers production costs and increases supply. For example, technological advances in producing flat-panel computer monitors have greatly reduced their cost. The manufacturers now offer more such monitors than previously at various prices; the supply of flat-panel monitors has increased.

TAXES AND SUBSIDIES

Businesses treat most taxes as costs. An increase in sales or property taxes will increase production costs and reduce supply. In contrast, subsidies are taxes in reverse. If the government subsidizes the production of a good, that lowers the producers' costs and increases supply.

PRICES OF OTHER GOODS

Firms that produce a particular product, say soccer balls, can sometimes use their plants and equipment to produce alternative goods, say basketballs and volleyballs. The higher prices of these other goods may entice soccer ball producers to switch production to those other goods to increase profits. This substitution in production results in a decline in the supply of soccer balls. Alternatively, when the prices of basketballs and volleyballs decline relative to the price of soccer balls, producers of those goods may decide to produce more soccer balls instead, increasing their supply.

PRODUCER EXPECTATIONS

Changes in expectations about the future price of a product may affect the producer's current willingness to supply that product. Saskatchewan farmers anticipating a higher wheat price in the future might withhold some of their current wheat harvest from the market, thereby causing a decrease in the current supply of wheat. In contrast, in many types of manufacturing industries, expectations that price will increase may induce firms to add another shift of workers or to expand their production facilities, causing current supply to increase.

NUMBER OF SELLERS

Other things equal, the larger the number of suppliers, the greater the market supply. As more firms enter an industry, the supply curve shifts to the right. Conversely, the smaller the number of firms in the industry, the less the market supply. This means that as firms leave an industry, the supply curve shifts to the left. Canada and the United States, for example, have imposed restrictions on haddock fishing to replenish dwindling stocks. As part of that policy, the federal government has bought the boats of some of the haddock fishers as a way of putting them out of business and decreasing the catch. The result has been a decline in the market supply of haddock.

Table 3-2 is a checklist of the determinants of supply, along with further illustrations.

Changes in Quantity Supplied

The distinction between a *change in supply* and a *change in quantity supplied* mirrors the distinction between a change in demand and a change in quantity demanded. Because supply is a schedule or curve, a **change in supply** means a change in the entire schedule and a shift of the entire curve. An increase in supply shifts the curve to the

TABLE 3-2	Determinants of Supply Curve Shifts

Determinant	Examples
Change in factor prices	A decrease in the price of microchips increases the supply of computers; an increase in the price of crude oil reduces the supply of gasoline.
Change in technology	The development of more effective wireless technology increases the supply of cellphones.
Change in taxes and subsidies	An increase in the excise tax on cigarettes reduces the supply of cigarettes; a decline in subsidies to universities reduces the supply of higher education.
Change in prices of other goods	An increase in the price of cucumbers decreases the supply of watermelons.
Change in producer expectations	An expectation of a substantial rise in future log prices decreases the supply of logs today.
Change in number of suppliers	An increase in the number of tattoo parlours increases the supply of tattoos; the formation of women's professional basketball leagues increases the supply of women's professional basketball games.

right; a decrease in supply shifts it to the left. The cause of a change in supply is a change in one or more of the determinants of supply.

In contrast, a **change in quantity supplied** is a movement from one point to another on a fixed supply curve. The cause of such a movement is a change in the price of the specific product being considered. Consider supply curve S_1 in Figure 3-5. A decline in the price of corn from \$4 to \$3 decreases the quantity of corn supplied per week from 10,000 to 7000 bushels. This movement from point b to point a along S_1 is a change in quantity supplied, not a change in supply. Supply is the full schedule of prices and quantities shown, and this schedule does not change when the price of corn changes.

QUICK REVIEW 3.2

- A supply schedule or curve shows that, other things equal, the quantity of a good supplied varies directly with its price.

- The supply curve shifts because of changes in (a) factor prices, (b) technology, (c) taxes and subsidies, (d) prices of other goods, (e) producer expectations, and (f) the number of sellers.

- A change in supply is a shift of the supply curve; a change in quantity supplied is a movement from one point to another on a fixed supply curve.

3.4 Market Equilibrium

LO3.4   Relate how supply and demand interact to determine market equilibrium.

With our understanding of demand and supply, we can now show how the decisions of buyers of corn interact with the decisions of the sellers to determine the price and quantity of corn. In the table in Figure 3-6 (Key Graph), columns 1 and 2 repeat the market supply of corn (from Figure 3-5), and columns 2 and 3 repeat the market demand for corn (from the table in Figure 3-3). We assume this is a competitive market, so that neither buyers nor sellers can set the price.

Equilibrium Price and Quantity

We are looking for the equilibrium price and equilibrium quantity. The **equilibrium price** (or market-clearing price) is the price at which the intentions of buyers and sellers match. It is the price at which quantity demanded equals quantity supplied. The table in Figure 3-6 reveals that at \$3, *and only at that price*, the number of bushels of corn that sellers

KEY GRAPH

FIGURE 3-6   Equilibrium Price and Quantity

The intersection of the downsloping demand curve *D* and the upsloping supply curve *S* indicates the equilibrium price and quantity, here $3 and 7000 bushels of corn. The shortages of corn at below-equilibrium prices (for example, 7000 bushels at $2) drive up price. These higher prices increase the quantity supplied and reduce the quantity demanded until equilibrium is achieved. The surpluses caused by above-equilibrium prices (for example, 6000 bushels at $4) push price down. As price drops, the quantity demanded rises and the quantity supplied falls until equilibrium is established. At the equilibrium price and quantity, there are neither shortages nor surpluses of corn. The arrows in the table indicate the effect on price.

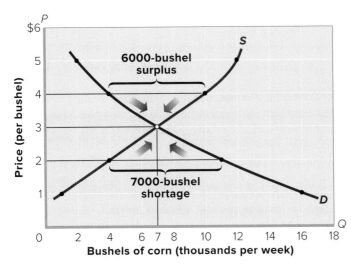

(1) Total quantity supplied per week	(2) Price per bushel	(3) Total quantity demanded per week	(4) Surplus (+) or shortage (−)
12,000	$5	2,000	+10,000↓
10,000	4	4,000	+6,000↓
7,000	3	7,000	0
4,000	2	11,000	−7,000↑
1,000	1	16,000	−15,000↑

QUICK QUIZ

1. **Demand curve *D* in Figure 3-6 is downsloping because**
   a. Producers offer less product for sale as the price of the product falls.
   b. Lower prices of a product create income and substitution effects, which lead consumers to purchase more of it.
   c. The larger the number of buyers in a market, the lower the product price.
   d. Price and quantity demanded are directly (positively) related.

2. **Supply curve *S***
   a. Reflects an inverse (negative) relationship between price and quantity supplied.
   b. Reflects a direct (positive) relationship between price and quantity supplied.

   c. Depicts the collective behaviour of buyers in this market.
   d. Shows that producers will offer more of a product for sale at a low product price than at a high product price.

3. **At the $3 price**
   a. Quantity supplied exceeds quantity demanded.
   b. Quantity demanded exceeds quantity supplied.
   c. The product is abundant and a surplus exists.
   d. There is no pressure on price to rise or fall.

4. **At price $5 in this market**
   a. There will be a shortage of 10,000 units.
   b. There will be a surplus of 10,000 units.
   c. Quantity demanded will be 12,000 units.
   d. Quantity demanded will equal quantity supplied.

Answers   1 b; 2 b; 3 d; 4 b.

wish to sell (7000) is identical to the number consumers want to buy (also 7000). At $3 and 7000 bushels of corn, there is neither a shortage nor a surplus of corn. So 7000 bushels of corn is the **equilibrium quantity**: the quantity at which the intentions of buyers and sellers match so that the quantity demanded and the quantity supplied are equal.

Graphically, the equilibrium price is indicated by the intersection of the supply curve and the demand curve in Figure 3-6. (The horizontal axis now measures both quantity demanded and quantity supplied.) With neither a shortage nor a surplus at $3, the market is *in equilibrium*, meaning "in balance" or "at rest."

MATH 3.3   Equilibrium Price and Quantity

Competition among buyers and among sellers drives the price to the equilibrium price, where it will remain unless it is subsequently disturbed by changes in demand or supply (shifts of the curves). To better understand the uniqueness of the equilibrium price, let's consider other prices. At any above-equilibrium price, quantity supplied exceeds quantity demanded. For example, at the $4 price, sellers will offer 10,000 bushels of corn, but buyers will purchase only 4000. The $4 price encourages sellers to offer lots of corn but discourages many consumers from buying it. The result is a **surplus** (or *excess supply*) of 6000 bushels. If corn sellers produced them all, they would find themselves with 6000 unsold bushels of corn.

Surpluses drive prices down. Even if the $4 price existed temporarily, it could not persist. The large surplus would prompt competing sellers to lower the price to encourage buyers to take the surplus off their hands. As the price fell, the incentive to produce corn would decline and the incentive for consumers to buy corn would increase. As shown in Figure 3-6, the market would move to its equilibrium at $3.

Any price below the $3 equilibrium price would create a shortage; quantity demanded would exceed quantity supplied. Consider a $2 price, for example. We see both from column 2 of the table and from the demand curve in Figure 3-6 that quantity demanded exceeds quantity supplied at that price. The result is a **shortage** (or *excess demand*) of 7000 bushels of corn. The $2 price discourages sellers from devoting resources to corn and encourages consumers to desire more bushels than are available. The $2 price cannot persist as the equilibrium price. Many consumers who want to buy corn at this price will not obtain it. They will express a willingness to pay more than $2 to get corn. Competition among these buyers will drive up the price, eventually to the $3 equilibrium level. Unless disrupted by supply or demand changes, the $3 price of corn will continue to prevail.

Rationing Function of Prices

The ability of the competitive forces of supply and demand to establish a price at which selling and buying decisions are consistent is called the *rationing function of prices*. In our case, the equilibrium price of $3 clears the market, leaving no burdensome surplus for sellers and no inconvenient shortage for potential buyers. It is the combination of freely made individual decisions that sets this market-clearing price. In effect, the market outcome says that all buyers who are willing and able to pay $3 for a bushel of corn will obtain it; all buyers who cannot or will not pay $3 will go without corn. Similarly, all producers who are willing and able to offer corn for sale at $3 a bushel will sell it; all producers who cannot or will not sell for $3 per bushel will not sell their product.

Efficient Allocation

A competitive market such as we have described not only rations goods to consumers but also allocates society's resources efficiently to the particular product. Competition among corn producers forces them to use the best technology and right mix of productive resources. If they didn't, their costs would be too high relative to the market price, and they would be unprofitable. The result is **productive efficiency**: the production of any particular good in the least costly way. When society produces corn at the lowest achievable per-unit cost, it is expending the smallest amount of resources to produce that product and therefore is making available the largest amount of resources to produce other desired goods. Suppose society has only $100 worth of resources available. If it can produce a bushel of corn using $3 of those resources, it will have available $97 of resources remaining to produce other goods. This is clearly better than producing the corn for $5 and having only $95 of resources available for the alternative uses.

Competitive markets also produce **allocative efficiency**: the *particular mix* of goods and services most highly valued by society (minimum-cost production assumed). For example, society wants land suitable for growing corn to be used for that purpose, not to grow dandelions. It wants diamonds to be used for jewellery, not to be crushed up and used as an additive to give concrete more sparkle. It wants streaming on-line music, not cassette players and tapes. Moreover, society does not want to devote all its resources to corn, diamonds, and portable digital music players. It wants to assign some resources to wheat, gasoline, and cellphones. Competitive markets make those proper assignments.

MATH 3.4   Allocative Efficiency

CONSIDER THIS …

Uber and Dynamic Pricing

The ride-sharing service known as Uber rose to prominence in 2013 by offering consumers an alternative to government-regulated taxi companies. Uber works via the Internet, matching people who need a ride with people who are willing to use their own vehicles to provide rides. Both parties can find each other easily and instantly via a mobile phone app and Uber makes its money by taking a percentage of the fare.

Uber is innovative in many ways, including empowering anybody to become a paid driver, breaking up local taxi monopolies, and making it effortless to arrange a quick pickup. But Uber's most interesting feature is dynamic pricing, under which Uber sets equilibrium prices in real time, constantly adjusting fares so as to equalize quantity demanded and quality supplied. The result is extremely short waiting times for both

SURGE PRICING   ✕

Demand is off the charts! Rates have increased to get more Ubers on the road.

1.75X
TIMES THE NORMAL RATE

Uber Manila Tips, http:// ubermanilatips.com/wp-content/ uploads/2015/02/surge-price-icon.jpg

riders and drivers as Uber will, for instance, set a substantially higher "surge price" in a given location if demand suddenly increases due to, say, a bunch of people leaving a concert all at once and wanting rides. The higher fare encourages more Uber drivers to converge on the area, minimizing wait times for both drivers and passengers.

The short wait times created by Uber's use of dynamic pricing stand in sharp contrast to taxi fares, which are fixed by law and therefore unable to adjust to ongoing changes in supply and demand. On days when demand is high relative to supply, taxi shortages arise. On days when demand is low relative to supply, drivers sit idle for long stretches of time. All of that inefficiency and inconvenience is eliminated by Uber's use of market equilibrium prices to equalize the demand and supply of rides.

The equilibrium price and quantity in competitive markets usually produce an assignment of resources that is "right" from an economic perspective. Demand essentially reflects the marginal benefit (MB) of the good (the extra benefit received from consuming one more unit of a good or service) and supply reflects the marginal cost (MC) of the good (the extra cost associated with producing one more unit of a good or service). The market ensures that firms produce all units of goods for which MB exceeds MC, and no units for which MC exceeds MB. At the intersection of the demand and supply curves, MB equals MC and allocative efficiency results. As economists say, there is neither an "underallocation of resources" nor an "overallocation of resources" to the product.

3.5   Changes in Supply, Demand, and Equilibrium

LO3.5   Explain how changes in supply and demand affect equilibrium prices and quantities.

We know that demand might change because of fluctuations in consumer tastes or incomes, changes in consumer expectations, or variations in the prices of related goods. Supply might change in response to changes in resource prices, technology, or taxes. What effects will such changes in supply and demand have on equilibrium price and quantity?

Changes in Demand

Suppose that the supply for some good (for example, potatoes) is constant and demand increases, as shown in Figure 3-7a. As a result, the new intersection of the supply and demand curves is at higher values on both the price and quantity axes. An increase in demand raises both equilibrium price and equilibrium quantity. Conversely, a decrease in demand, such as that shown in Figure 3-7b, reduces both equilibrium price and equilibrium quantity. (The value of graphical analysis is now apparent: We need not fumble with columns of figures to determine the outcomes; we need only compare the new and the old points of intersection on the graph.)

FIGURE 3-7   Changes in Demand and Supply, and the Effects on Price and Quantity

The increase in demand from D_1 to D_2 in panel (a) increases both equilibrium price and quantity. The decrease in demand from D_1 to D_2 in panel (b) decreases both equilibrium price and quantity. The increase in supply from S_1 to S_2 in panel (c) decreases equilibrium price and increases equilibrium quantity. The decline in supply from S_1 to S_2 in panel (d) increases equilibrium price and decreases equilibrium quantity. The boxes in the top right corners summarize the respective changes and outcomes. The upward arrows in those boxes signify increases in demand (D), supply (S), equilibrium price (P), and equilibrium quantity (Q); the downward arrows signify decreases in these items.

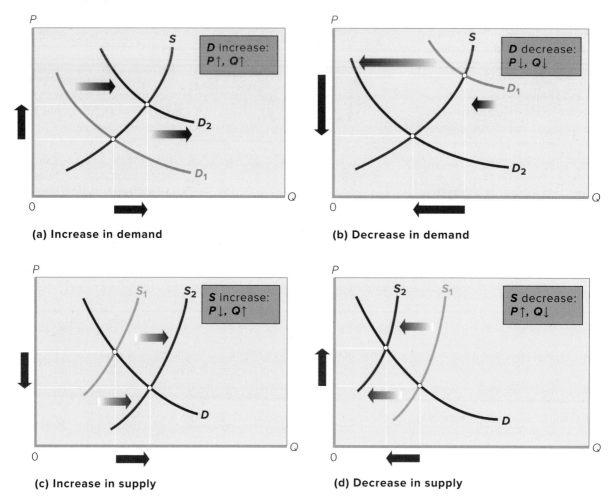

(a) Increase in demand

(b) Decrease in demand

(c) Increase in supply

(d) Decrease in supply

Changes in Supply

What happens if demand for some good (for example, automobiles) is constant but supply increases, as in Figure 3-7c? The new intersection of supply and demand is located at a lower equilibrium price but at a higher equilibrium quantity. An increase in supply reduces equilibrium price but increases equilibrium quantity. In contrast, if supply decreases, as in Figure 3-7d, equilibrium price rises while equilibrium quantity declines.

Complex Cases

When both supply and demand change, the effect is a combination of the individual effects. As you study the following cases, keep in mind that each effect on the demand and supply curves has to be considered independently.

1. ***Supply Increase, Demand Decrease*** What effect will a supply increase and a demand decrease for some good (for example, apples) have on equilibrium price? Both changes decrease price, so the net result is a price drop greater than that resulting from either change alone.

What about equilibrium quantity? Here the effects of the changes in supply and demand are opposed: The increase in supply increases equilibrium quantity, but the decrease in demand reduces it. The direction of the change in equilibrium quantity depends on the relative sizes of the changes in supply and demand. If the increase in supply is larger than the decrease in demand, the equilibrium quantity will increase. But if the decrease in demand is greater than the increase in supply, the equilibrium quantity will decrease.

2. *Supply Decrease, Demand Increase* A decrease in supply and an increase in demand for some good (for example, gasoline) both increase price. Their combined effect is an increase in equilibrium price greater than that caused by either change separately. But their effect on the equilibrium quantity is again indeterminate, depending on the relative sizes of the changes in supply and demand. If the decrease in supply is larger than the increase in demand, the equilibrium quantity will decrease. In contrast, if the increase in demand is greater than the decrease in supply, the equilibrium quantity will increase.

3. *Supply Increase, Demand Increase* What if supply and demand both increase for some good (for example, cellphones)? A supply increase drops equilibrium price, while a demand increase boosts it. If the increase in supply is greater than the increase in demand, the equilibrium price will fall. If the opposite holds, the equilibrium price will rise.

The effect on equilibrium quantity is certain: The increases in supply and demand both raise the equilibrium quantity. Therefore, the equilibrium quantity will increase by an amount greater than that caused by either change alone.

MATH 3.5 Changes in Supply, Demand, and Equilibrium

4. *Supply Decrease, Demand Decrease* What about decreases in both supply and demand? If the decrease in supply is greater than the decrease in demand, equilibrium price will rise. If the reverse is true, equilibrium price will fall. Because the decreases in supply and demand each reduce equilibrium quantity, we can be sure that equilibrium quantity will fall.

Table 3-3 summarizes these four cases. To understand them fully you should draw supply and demand diagrams for each case to confirm the effects listed in Table 3-3.

CONSIDER THIS

Salsa and Coffee Beans

If you forget the other-things-equal assumption, you can encounter situations that seem to be in conflict with the laws of demand and supply. For example, suppose salsa manufacturers sell 1 million bottles of salsa at $4 a bottle in one year, 2 million bottles at $5 in the next year, and 3 million at $6 in the year thereafter. Price and quantity purchased vary directly, and these data seem to be at odds with the law of demand.

But there is no conflict here; the data do not refute the law of demand. The catch is that the law of demand's other-things-equal assumption has been violated over the three years in the example. Specifically, because of changing tastes and rising incomes, the demand for salsa has increased sharply, as in Figure 3-7a. The result is higher prices and larger quantities purchased.

Another example is the fact that the price of coffee beans has occasionally shot upward at the same time that the quantity of coffee beans harvested has declined. These events seemingly contradict the direct relationship between price and quantity denoted by supply. The other-things-equal assumption underlying the upsloping supply curve was violated. Poor coffee harvests decreased supply, as in Figure 3-7d, increasing the equilibrium price of coffee and reducing the equilibrium quantity.

The laws of demand and supply are not refuted by observations of price and quantity made over periods of time in which either demand or supply changes.

© Nancy R. Cohen/Getty Images RF

TABLE 3-3	Effects of Changes in Both Supply and Demand			
	Change in supply	**Change in demand**	**Effect on equilibrium price**	**Effect on equilibrium quantity**
1	Increase	Decrease	Decrease	Indeterminate
2	Decrease	Increase	Increase	Indeterminate
3	Increase	Increase	Indeterminate	Increase
4	Decrease	Decrease	Indeterminate	Decrease

Special cases arise when a decrease in demand and a decrease in supply, or an increase in demand and an increase in supply, exactly cancel each other out. In both cases, the net effect on equilibrium price will be zero; price will not change.

The optional appendix accompanying this chapter provides additional examples of situations in which both supply and demand change at the same time.

3.6 Application: Government-Set Prices

LO3.6 Identify what government-set prices are and how they can cause surpluses and shortages.

Prices in most markets are free to rise or fall to their equilibrium levels, no matter how high or low that might be. However, government sometimes concludes that supply and demand will produce prices that are unfairly high for buyers or unfairly low for sellers. So government may place legal limits on how high or low a price or prices may go. Is that a good idea?

Price Ceilings

A **price ceiling** is the maximum legal price a seller may charge for a product or service. A price at or below the ceiling is legal; a price above it is not. The rationale for establishing price ceilings (or ceiling prices) on specific products is that they purportedly enable consumers to obtain some essential good or service that they could not afford at the equilibrium price. Examples are rent controls and usury laws, which specify maximum prices in the forms of rent and the interest that can be charged to borrowers.

GRAPHICAL ANALYSIS

We can easily demonstrate the effects of price ceilings graphically using the example of gasoline. Let's suppose that rapidly rising world income boosts the purchase of automobiles and shifts the demand for gasoline to the right so that the equilibrium or market price reaches $1.25 per litre, shown as P_0 in Figure 3-8. The rapidly rising price of gasoline greatly burdens low-income and moderate-income households, who pressure the federal government to "do something." To keep gasoline prices down, the government imposes a ceiling price, P_c, of $0.75 per litre. To be effective, a price ceiling must be below the equilibrium price. A ceiling price of $1.50, for example, would have no effect on the price of gasoline in the current situation.

To be effective, a price ceiling on gasoline must be below the equilibrium price.

FIGURE 3-8   A Price Ceiling Results in a Shortage

A price ceiling is a maximum legal price, such as P_c. When the ceiling price is below the equilibrium price, a persistent product shortage results. Here, that shortage is shown by the horizontal distance between Q_d and Q_s.

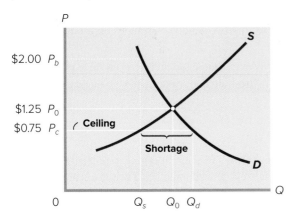

What are the effects of this $0.75 ceiling price? The rationing ability of the free market is rendered ineffective. Because the ceiling price, P_c, is below the market-clearing price, P_0, there is a shortage of gasoline. The quantity of gasoline demanded at P_c is Q_d and the quantity supplied is only Q_s; an excess demand or shortage of amount $Q_d - Q_s$ occurs.

The price ceiling, P_c, prevents the usual market adjustment in which competition among buyers bids up price, inducing more production and rationing some buyers out of the market. That process would normally continue until the shortage disappeared at the equilibrium price and quantity, P_0 and Q_0.

RATIONING PROBLEM

How will the government apportion the available supply, Q_s, among buyers who want the greater amount, Q_d? Should gasoline be distributed on a first-come, first-served basis—that is, to those willing and able to get in line the soonest or stay in line the longest? Or should gas stations distribute it on the basis of favouritism? Since an unregulated shortage does not lead to an equitable distribution of gasoline, the federal government must establish some formal system for rationing it to consumers. One option is to issue ration coupons, which allow coupon-holders to purchase a fixed amount of gasoline per month. The rationing system might require the printing of coupons for Q_s litres of gasoline and then the equal distribution of the coupons among consumers so that the wealthy family of four and the poor family of four both receive the same number of coupons.

BLACK MARKETS

But ration coupons would not prevent a second problem from arising. The demand curve in Figure 3-8 reveals that many buyers are willing to pay more than the ceiling price P_c. And, of course, it is more profitable for gasoline stations to sell at prices above the ceiling. Thus, despite a sizable enforcement bureaucracy that would have to accompany the price controls, *black markets* in which gasoline is illegally bought and sold at prices above the legal limits will flourish. Counterfeiting of ration coupons will also be a problem. And since the price of gasoline is now "set by government," government might face political pressure to set the price even lower.

CREDIT CARD INTEREST CEILINGS

Over the years there have been many calls in Canada for interest-rate ceilings on credit card accounts. The usual rationale is that the chartered banks and retail stores issuing such cards are presumably taking unfair advantage of users—and, in particular, lower-income users—by charging interest rates that average about 20 percent per year.

What might be the response if the Canadian government imposed a below-equilibrium interest rate on credit cards? The lower interest income associated with a legal interest ceiling would require the issuers of cards to reduce their costs or enhance their revenues:

- Card issuers might tighten credit standards to reduce losses due to nonpayment and collection costs. Then, low-income and young Canadians who have not yet established their creditworthiness would find it more difficult to obtain credit cards.

- The annual fee charged to cardholders might be increased, as might the fee charged to merchants for processing credit card sales. Similarly, card users might be charged a fee for every transaction.

- Card users now have a post-purchase grace period during which the credit provided is interest-free. That period might be shortened or eliminated.

- Certain enhancements that accompany some credit cards (for example, extended warranties on products bought with a card) might be eliminated.

- Oil companies such as Petro-Canada, that issue their own cards to consumers who buy from their gasoline stations, might increase their prices to help offset the decline of interest income; customers who pay cash would in effect be subsidizing customers who use credit cards.

Rent Controls

Some cities in Canada have at one time or another enacted rent controls: maximum rents established by law (or, more recently, maximum rent increases for existing tenants). Such laws are well intended. Their goals are to protect low-income families from escalating rents caused by perceived housing shortages and to make housing more affordable to the poor.

What have been the actual economic effects? On the demand side, the below-equilibrium rents attract a larger number of renters. Some are locals seeking to move into their own places after sharing housing with friends or family. Others are outsiders attracted into the area by the artificially lower rents. But a large problem occurs on the supply side. Price controls make it less attractive for landlords to offer housing on the rental market. In the short run, owners may sell their rental units or convert them to condominiums. In the long run, low rents make it unprofitable for owners to repair or renovate their rental units. (Rent controls are one cause of the many abandoned apartment buildings found in larger cities.) Also, insurance companies, pension funds, and other potential new investors in housing will find it more profitable to invest in office buildings, shopping malls, or motels, where rents are not controlled.

In brief, rent controls distort market signals and thus resources are misallocated: Too few resources are allocated to rental housing and too many to alternative uses. Ironically, although rent controls are often legislated to lessen the effects of perceived housing shortages, controls in fact are a primary cause of such shortages. For that reason, most American cities either have abandoned or are in the process of dismantling rent controls.

Price Floors

A **price floor** is a minimum price fixed by the government. A price at or above the price floor is legal; a price below it is not. Price floors above equilibrium prices are usually invoked when society believes that the free functioning of the market system has not provided a sufficient income for certain groups of resource suppliers or producers. Supported prices for some agricultural products and current minimum wages are two examples of price (or wage) floors. Let's analyze the results of imposing a price floor on wheat.

Suppose that many farmers have extremely low incomes when the price of wheat is at its equilibrium value of $3 per bushel. The federal government decides to help by establishing a legal price floor or price support of $4 per bushel.

What will be the effects? At any price above the equilibrium price, quantity supplied will exceed quantity demanded—that is, there will be an excess supply or surplus of the product. Prairie farmers will be willing to produce and offer for sale more than private buyers are willing to purchase at the price floor. As we saw with a price ceiling, an imposed legal price disrupts the rationing ability of the free market.

Supported prices for some agricultural products are an example of price floors.

FIGURE 3-9   A Price Floor Results in a Surplus

A price floor is a minimum legal price, such as P_f. When the price floor is above the equilibrium price, a persistent product surplus results. Here that surplus is shown by the horizontal distance between Q_s and Q_d.

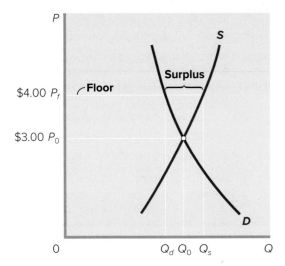

GRAPHICAL ANALYSIS

Figure 3-9 illustrates the effect of a price floor on wheat. Suppose that S and D are the supply and demand curves for wheat. Equilibrium price and quantity are P_0 and Q_0, respectively. If the federal government imposes a price floor of P_f, farmers will produce Q_s, but private buyers will purchase only Q_d. The surplus is the excess of Q_s over Q_d. The government can cope with the surplus resulting from a price floor in only two ways:

1. It can restrict supply (for example, by asking farmers in Alberta, Saskatchewan, and Manitoba to agree to take a certain amount of land out of production) or increase demand (for example, by researching new uses for the product involved). These actions may reduce the difference between the equilibrium price and the price floor and thereby reduce the size of the resulting surplus.

2. It can purchase the surplus output at the $4 price (thereby subsidizing Prairie farmers) and store or otherwise dispose of it.

ADDITIONAL CONSEQUENCES

Price floors such as P_f in Figure 3-9 not only disrupt the rationing ability of prices but also distort resource allocation. Without the price floor, the $3 equilibrium price of wheat would cause financial losses and force high-cost wheat producers to plant other crops or abandon farming altogether. But the $4 price floor allows them to continue to grow wheat and remain farmers. So society devotes too many of its scarce resources to wheat production and too few to producing other, more valuable goods and services. It fails to achieve allocative efficiency.

That's not all. Consumers of wheat-based products pay higher prices because of the price floor. Taxpayers pay higher taxes to finance the government's purchase of the surplus. Also, the price floor causes potential environmental damage by encouraging wheat farmers to bring marginal land into production. The higher price also prompts imports of wheat. But, since such imports would increase the quantity of wheat supplied and thus undermine the price floor, the government needs to erect tariffs (taxes on imports) to keep the foreign wheat out. Such tariffs usually prompt other countries to retaliate with their own tariffs against Canadian agricultural or manufacturing exports.

It is easy to see why economists sound the alarm when politicians advocate imposing price ceilings or price floors such as price controls, interest-rate caps, or agricultural price supports. In all these cases, good intentions lead to bad economic outcomes. Government-controlled prices cause shortages or surpluses, distort resource allocation, and produce negative side effects.

QUICK REVIEW 3.3

- In competitive markets, prices adjust to the equilibrium level at which quantity demanded equals quantity supplied.

- The equilibrium price and quantity are those indicated by the intersection of the supply and demand curves for any product or resource.

- An increase in demand increases equilibrium price and quantity; a decrease in demand decreases equilibrium price and quantity.

- An increase in supply reduces equilibrium price but increases equilibrium quantity; a decrease in supply increases equilibrium price but reduces equilibrium quantity.

- Over time, equilibrium price and quantity may change in directions that seem at odds with the laws of demand and supply because the other-things-equal assumption is violated.

- Government-controlled prices in the form of ceilings and floors stifle the rationing functions of prices, distort resource allocations, and cause negative side effects.

The LAST WORD

Student Loans and Tuition Costs

© baona/Getty Images RF

By increasing demand, student loans increase the price of higher education.

It is estimated that the average total debt load in Canada for graduating post-secondary school student is about $27,000. In Nova Scotia, that figure rises to more that $40,000, if one includes both provincial and federal student debt. Student debt has gone up significantly in the last decade, as have tuition fees. While tuition fees are set by each institution, and are a provincial matter, in the last decade tuition fees have risen as much as 40 percent in some provinces and have tripled in the last 20 years.

It may seem obvious that student loans have helped students keep up with rising costs for post-secondary education. Under this commonly held hypothesis, university and college costs have risen over time due to outside factors like having to pay higher salaries to faculty and administrators, having to install the equipment necessary for digital classrooms and Internet connectivity, and having to hire larger staffs as colleges and universities added a wider variety of student services, including career centres and tutoring programs. From this point of view, outside factors increased costs and one of the only ways for students to keep up was by taking out loans.

Recent research in the United States, where the cost of post-secondary education has skyrocketed in the past decade, actually suggests that as student loans become easier to get, colleges and universities find it easier to raise tuition. These results may also hold for Canada, even if our system of post-secondary education

is different. According to one U.S. study,* each $1 increase in the average amount of student loans received per full-time student increases tuition costs by an average of 70 cents. In addition, researchers were able to demonstrate the order of causation, because the U.S. federal government increased the borrowing limits on student loans in the mid-2000s. When the limits were raised, students borrowed more. And when they did, tuition increased. So it was clear: More loans lead to higher tuition (rather than higher tuition causing students to take out more loans).

The model of demand and supply can explain why taking out more loans raises tuition. Take a look at the accompanying figure. At any given time, the quantity supplied of higher education is essentially fixed, because it is not easy for colleges and universities to expand enrolments without constructing new classrooms. But the demand curve for higher education is not fixed. It shifts rightward whenever any factor increases either the willingness or the ability of students to pay for higher education.

That is important because student loans increase the ability to pay. Student loans consequently shift the demand curve for higher education to the right from D_1 to D_2. That rightward shift in

*David O. Lucca, Taylor Nauld, and Karen Shen, "Credit Supply and the Rise in College Tuition: Evidence from the Expansion in Federal Student Aid Programs," Staff Report No. 733, Federal Reserve Bank of New York, July 2015.

demand coupled with the fixed supply results in the equilibrium price of higher education rising from P_1 to P_2. More loans mean higher tuition costs.

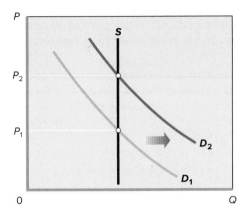

This suggests that student loans are the wrong approach for the government to be taking in its attempt to increase access to higher education. With each $1 increase in the average amount of student loans received per full-time student causing a 70-cent

increase in tuition, the student lending program is largely self-defeating, as it ends up dramatically raising the price of the very thing it is striving to make more affordable.

One alternative would be for the government to redirect its efforts toward subsidizing supply rather than demand. If the government set up programs to increase the supply of higher education, the equilibrium price of higher education would naturally fall as the supply curve for higher education S shifted rightward. This was the approach taken after World War II, when the heavily subsidized state university systems in the U.S. expanded rapidly.

Question

Real (inflation-adjusted) tuition costs were nearly constant during the 1960s despite a huge increase in the number of college and university students as the very large Baby Boom generation came of age. What does this suggest about the supply of higher education during that period? When the much smaller Baby Bust generation followed in the 1970s, real tuition costs fell. What does that suggest about demand relative to supply during the 1970s?

Chapter Summary

LO3.1   Characterize and give examples of markets.

- Markets bring buyers and sellers together. Some markets are local, others international. Some have physical locations while others are online. For simplicity, this chapter focuses on highly competitive markets in which large numbers of buyers and sellers come together to buy and sell standardized products. All such markets involve demand, supply, price, and quantity, with price being discovered through the interacting decisions of buyers and sellers.

LO3.2   Describe *demand* and explain how it can change.

- Demand is a schedule or curve representing the willingness of buyers in a specific period to purchase a particular product at each of various prices. The law of demand implies that consumers will buy more of a product at a low price than at a high price. Therefore, other things equal, the relationship between price and quantity demanded is negative or inverse and is graphed as a downsloping curve.

- Market demand curves are found by adding horizontally the demand curves of the many individual consumers in the market.

- Changes in one or more of the determinants of demand (consumer tastes, the number of buyers in the market, the money incomes of consumers, the prices of related goods, and consumer expectations) shift the market demand curve. A shift to the right is an increase in demand; a shift to the left is a decrease in demand. A change in demand is different from a change in the quantity demanded, the latter being a movement

from one point to another point on a fixed demand curve because of a change in the product's price.

LO3.3   Describe *supply* and explain how it can change.

- Supply is a schedule or curve showing the amounts of a product that producers are willing to offer in the market at each possible price during a specific period. The law of supply states that, other things equal, producers will offer more of a product at a high price than at a low price. Thus, the relationship between price and quantity supplied is positive or direct, and supply is graphed as an upsloping curve.

- The market supply curve is the horizontal summation of the supply curves of the individual producers of the product.

- Changes in one or more of the determinants of supply (factor prices, technology, taxes and subsidies, price expectations, or the number of sellers in the market) shift the supply curve of a product. A shift to the right is an increase in supply; a shift to the left is a decrease in supply. In contrast, a change in the price of the product being considered causes a change in the quantity supplied, which is shown as a movement from one point to another point on a fixed supply curve.

LO3.4   Relate how supply and demand interact to determine market equilibrium.

- The equilibrium price and quantity are established at the intersection of the supply and demand curves. The interaction of market demand and market supply adjusts the price to the point at which the quantity demanded and quantity supplied are equal. This is the equilibrium price. The corresponding quantity is the equilibrium quantity.

- The ability of market forces to synchronize selling and buying decisions to eliminate potential surpluses and shortages is known as the *rationing function of prices*.

LO3.5   Explain how changes in supply and demand affect equilibrium prices and quantities.

- A change in either demand or supply changes the equilibrium price and quantity. Increases in demand raise both equilibrium price and equilibrium quantity; decreases in demand lower both equilibrium price and equilibrium quantity. Increases in supply lower equilibrium price and raise equilibrium quantity; decreases in supply raise equilibrium price and lower equilibrium quantity.

- Simultaneous changes in demand and supply affect equilibrium price and quantity in various ways, depending on their direction and relative magnitude (see Table 3-3).

LO3.6   Identify what government-set prices are and how they can cause surpluses and shortages.

- A price ceiling is a maximum price set by government and is designed to help consumers. Effective price ceilings produce persistent product shortages, and if an equitable distribution of the product is sought, government must ration the product to consumers

- A price floor is a minimum price set by government and is designed to aid producers. Effective price floors lead to persistent product surpluses; the government must either purchase the product or eliminate the surplus by imposing restrictions on production or increasing private demand.

- Government-set prices stifle the rationing function of prices and distort the allocation of resources.

Terms and Concepts

demand	law of supply
law of demand	supply curve
diminishing marginal utility	determinants of supply
income effect	change in supply
substitution effect	change in quantity supplied
demand curve	equilibrium price
determinants of demand	equilibrium quantity
normal good	surplus
inferior goods	shortage
substitute goods	productive efficiency
complementary goods	allocative efficiency
change in demand	price ceiling
change in quantity demanded	price floor
supply	

Discussion Questions

1. Explain the law of demand. Why does a demand curve slope downward? How is a market demand curve derived from individual demand curves?   [LO3.2]

2. What are the determinants of demand? What happens to the demand curve when any of these determinants changes? Distinguish between a change in demand and a change in the quantity demanded, noting the cause(s) of each.   [LO3.2]

3. Explain the law of supply. Why does the supply curve slope upward? How is the market supply curve derived from the supply curves of individual producers?   [LO3.2]

4. What are the determinants of supply? What happens to the supply curve when any of these determinants changes? Distinguish between a change in supply and a change in the quantity supplied, noting the cause(s) of each.   [LO3.3]

5. In 2001, an outbreak of foot-and-mouth disease in Europe led to the burning of millions of cattle carcasses. What impact do you think this had on the supply of cattle hides, hide prices, the supply of leather goods, and the price of leather goods?   [LO3.5]

6. For each stock in the stock market, the number of shares sold daily equals the number of shares purchased. That is, the quantity of each firm's shares demanded equals the quantity supplied. So, if this equality always occurs, why do the prices of stock shares ever change?   [LO3.5]

7. What do economists mean when they say "Price floors and ceilings stifle the rationing function of prices and distort resource allocation"?   [LO3.6]

Review Questions

1. What effect will each of the following have on the demand for small automobiles such as the Mini-Cooper and Fiat 500? [**LO3.2**]

   a. Small automobiles become more fashionable.

   b. The price of large automobiles rises (with the price of small autos remaining the same).

   c. Income declines and small autos are an inferior good.

   d. Consumers anticipate that the price of small autos will greatly come down in the near future.

   e. The price of gasoline substantially drops.

2. True or False? A change in quantity demanded is a shift of the entire demand curve to the right or to the left. [**LO3.2**]

3. What effect will each of the following have on the supply of auto tires? [**LO3.3**]

   a. A technological advance in the methods of producing tires

   b. A decline in the number of firms in the tire industry

   c. An increase in the prices of rubber used in the production of tires

   d. The expectation that the equilibrium price of auto tires will be lower in the future than currently

   e. A decline in the price of the large tires used for semi trucks and earth-hauling rigs (with no change in the price of auto tires)

   f. The levying of a per-unit tax on each auto tire sold

   g. The granting of a 50-cent-per-unit subsidy for each auto tire produced

4. "In the corn market, demand often exceeds supply and supply sometimes exceeds demand." "The price of corn rises and falls in response to changes in supply and demand." In which of these two statements are the terms "supply" and "demand" used correctly? Explain. [**LO3.3**]

5. Suppose that in the market for computer memory chips, the equilibrium price is $50 per chip. If the current price is $55 per chip, there will be _____ of memory chips. [**LO3.4**]

   a. A shortage

   b. A surplus

   c. An equilibrium quantity

   d. None of the above

6. Critically evaluate the following statement: "In comparing the two equilibrium positions in Figure 3-7b, I note that a smaller amount is actually demanded at a lower price. This refutes the law of demand." [**LO3.5**]

7. Label each of the following scenarios with the set of symbols that best indicates the price change and quantity change that occur in the scenario. In some scenarios, it may not be possible from the information given to determine the direction of a particular price change or a particular quantity change. We will symbolize those cases as, respectively, P? and Q?. The four possible combinations of price and quantity changes are [**LO3.5**]

   P↑ Q?   P? Q↑

   P↑ Q?   P? Q↓

   a. On a hot day, both the demand for lemonade and the supply of lemonade increase.

   b. On a cold day, both the demand for ice cream and the supply of ice cream decrease.

   c. When Hawaii's Mt. Kilauea erupts violently, the demand on the part of tourists for sightseeing flights increases but the supply of pilots willing to provide these dangerous flights decreases.

   d. In a hot area of Arizona where they generate a lot of their electricity with wind turbines, the demand for electricity falls on windy days as people switch off their air conditioners and enjoy the breeze. But at the same time, the amount of electricity supplied increases as the wind turbines spin faster.

8. Suppose the total demand for wheat and the total supply of wheat per month in the Winnipeg grain market are as shown in the table here. Suppose also that the government establishes a price ceiling of $3.70 for wheat. What might prompt the government to establish this ceiling? Explain carefully the main effects. Demonstrate your answer graphically. Next, suppose the government establishes a price floor of $4.60 for wheat. What will be the main effects of this price floor? Demonstrate your answer graphically. [**LO3.6**]

Thousands of bushels demanded	Price per bushel	Thousands of bushels supplied
85	$3.40	72
80	3.70	73
75	4.00	75
70	4.30	77
65	4.60	79
60	4.90	81

9. A price ceiling will result in a shortage only if the ceiling price is _____ the equilibrium price. [**LO3.6**]

   a. Less than

   b. Equal to

   c. Greater than

   d. Louder than

Problems

1. Suppose there are three buyers of candy in a market: Tex, Dex, and Rex. The market demand and the individual demands of Tex, Dex, and Rex for candy are given in the table below.   **[LO3.2]**

    a. Fill in the missing values in the table.

    b. Which buyer demands the least at a price of $5? The most at a price of $7?

    c. Which buyer's quantity demanded increases the most when the price is lowered from $7 to $6?

    d. In which direction would the market demand curve shift if Tex withdrew from the market? What if Dex doubled his purchases at each possible price?

    e. Suppose that, at a price of $6, the total quantity demanded increases from 19 to 38. Is this a change in the quantity demanded or a change in demand?

	INDIVIDUAL QUANTITIES DEMANDED								
PRICE PER CANDY	Tex		Dex		Rex			TOTAL QUANTITY DEMANDED
$8	3	+	1	+	0	=		—
7	8	+	2	+	_	=		12
6	—	+	3	+	4	=		19
5	17	+	_	+	6	=		27
4	23	+	5	+	8	=		—

2. The figure that follows shows the supply curve for tennis balls, S_1. Use the figure and the table to give your answers to the following questions.   **[LO3.3]**

    a. Use the figure to fill in the quantity supplied on supply curve S_1 for each price in the table below.

Price	S_1 Quantity supplied	S_2 Quantity supplied	Change in quantity supplied
$3	_____	4	_____
2	_____	2	_____
1	_____	0	_____

    b. If production costs were to increase, the quantities supplied at each price would be as shown by the third column of the table (S_2 Quantity supplied). Use that data to draw supply curve S_2 on the same graph as supply curve S_1.

    c. In the fourth column of the table, enter the amount by which the quantity supplied at each price changes due to the increase in product costs. (Use positive numbers for increases and negative numbers for decreases.)

    d. Did the increase in production costs cause a decrease in supply or a decrease in quantity supplied?

3. Refer to the expanded table below from Review Question 8.   **[LO3.4]**

    a. What is the equilibrium price? At what price is there neither a shortage nor a surplus? Fill in the surplus–shortage column and use it to confirm your answers.

    b. Graph the demand for wheat and the supply of wheat. Be sure to label the axes of your graph correctly. Label equilibrium price P and equilibrium quantity Q.

    c. How big is the surplus or shortage at $3.40? At $4.90? How big a surplus or shortage results if the price is 60 cents higher than the equilibrium price? If it is 30 cents lower than the equilibrium price?

Thousands of bushels demanded	Price per bushel	Thousands of bushels supplied	Surplus (+) or shortage (−)
85	$3.40	72	_____
80	3.70	73	_____
75	4.00	75	_____
70	4.30	77	_____
65	4.60	79	_____
60	4.90	81	_____

4. How will each of the following changes in demand and/or supply affect equilibrium price and equilibrium quantity in a competitive market? That is, do price and quantity rise, fall, or remain unchanged, or are the answers indeterminate because they depend on the magnitudes of the shifts? Use supply and demand to verify your answers.   **[LO3.5]**

    a. Supply decreases and demand is constant.

    b. Demand decreases and supply is constant.

    c. Supply increases and demand is constant.

    d. Demand increases and supply increases.

    e. Demand increases and supply is constant.

    f. Supply increases and demand decreases.

    g. Demand increases and supply decreases.

    h. Demand decreases and supply decreases.

5. **Advanced Analysis** Assume that demand for a commodity is represented by the equation $P = 10 - 0.2Q_d$ and supply by the equation $P = 2 + 0.2Q_s$, where Q_d and Q_s are quantity demanded and quantity supplied, respectively, and P is price. Using the equilibrium condition $Q_s = Q_d$, solve the equations to determine equilibrium price. Now determine equilibrium quantity. Graph the two equations to substantiate your answers.   [**LO3.5**]

6. Suppose that the demand and supply schedules for rental apartments in the city of Gotham are as given in the table below.   [**LO3.6**]

Monthly rent	Apartments demanded	Apartments supplied
$2,500	10,000	15,000
2,000	12,500	12,500
1,500	15,000	10,000
1,000	17,500	7,500
500	20,000	5,000

a. What are the market equilibrium rental price per month and the market equilibrium number of apartments demanded and supplied?

b. If the municipal government can enforce a rent-control law that sets the maximum monthly rent at $1500, will there be a surplus or a shortage? Of how many units? How many units will actually be rented each month?

c. Suppose that a new government wants to keep out the poor. It declares that the minimum allowable rent is $2500 per month. If the government can enforce that price floor, will there be a surplus or a shortage? Of how many units? How many units will actually be rented each month?

d. Suppose that the government wishes to decrease the market equilibrium monthly rent by increasing the supply of housing. Assuming demand remains unchanged, by how many units of housing would the government have to increase the supply of housing in order to get the market equilibrium rental price to fall to $1500 per month? To $1000 per month? To $500 per month?

A3.1 Additional Examples of Supply and Demand

Our discussion has clearly demonstrated that supply and demand analysis is a powerful tool for understanding equilibrium prices and quantities. The information provided in the main body of this chapter is fully sufficient for moving forward in the book, but you may find that additional examples of supply and demand are helpful. This optional appendix provides several concrete illustrations of changes in supply and demand. It also applies supply and demand analysis to non-priced goods (goods owned in common and not bought and sold in markets).

Your instructor may assign all, some, or none of this appendix, depending on time availability and personal preference.

Changes in Supply and Demand

As Figure 3-7 demonstrates, changes in supply and demand cause changes in price, quantity, or both. The following applications illustrate this fact in several real-world markets. The simplest situations are those in which either supply changes while demand remains constant or demand changes while supply remains constant. Let's consider two such simple cases first, before looking at more complex applications.

LETTUCE

Every now and then, the media report that extreme weather has severely reduced the size of some crop. Suppose, for example, that a severe freeze destroys a sizable portion of the lettuce crop. This unfortunate situation implies a significant decline in supply, which we represent in Figure A3-1 as a leftward shift of the supply curve from S_1 to S_2. At each price, consumers desire as much lettuce as before, so the freeze does not affect the demand for lettuce. That is, demand curve D_1 does not shift.

What are the consequences of the reduced supply of lettuce for equilibrium price and quantity? As shown in Figure A3-1, the leftward shift of the supply curve disrupts the previous equilibrium in the market for lettuce and drives the equilibrium price up from P_1 to P_2.

Consumers respond to that price hike by reducing the quantity of lettuce demanded from Q_1 to Q_2. Equilibrium in the market is restored at P_2 and Q_2. Consumers who are willing and able to pay price P_2 obtain lettuce; consumers unwilling or unable to pay that price do not. Some consumers continue to buy as much lettuce as before, even at the higher price. Others buy some lettuce but not as much as before, and still others forgo lettuce altogether. The latter two groups use the money they would have spent on lettuce to obtain other

FIGURE A3-1 The Market for Lettuce

The decrease in the supply of lettuce, shown here by the shift from S_1 to S_2, increases the equilibrium price of lettuce from P_1 to P_2 and reduces the equilibrium quantity from Q_1 to Q_2.

products, say carrots. (Because of our other-things-equal assumption, the prices of other products have not changed.)

EXCHANGE RATES

Exchange rates are the prices at which one currency can be traded (exchanged) for another. Exchange rates are normally determined in foreign exchange markets. One exchange market is the euro–Canadian dollar market, in which the currency used in most of Europe, the euro, is exchanged for Canadian dollars. In Canada, this market is set up so that euros are priced in dollars—that is, the "product" being traded is the euro and the "price" to buy that product is quoted in dollars. Thus, the market equilibrium price one day might be $1.25 to buy one euro, while on another day it might be $1.50 to buy one euro.

Foreign exchange markets are used by individuals and companies that need to make purchases or payments in a different currency. Canadian companies exporting goods to Germany, for instance, wish to be paid in Canadian dollars. Thus, their German customers will need to convert euros into dollars. The euros that they bring to the euro–dollar market will become part of the overall market supply of euros. Conversely, a Canadian mutual fund may wish to purchase some real estate in France, but will need to pay in euros since the current French owners will accept only euros as payment. Thus, the Canadian mutual fund has a demand to purchase euros that will form part of the overall market demand for euros. The mutual fund will bring dollars to the euro–dollar foreign exchange market in order to purchase the euros it desires.

Sometimes the demand for euros increases. This might be because a European product surges in popularity in foreign countries. For example, if a new German-made automobile is a big hit in Canada, car dealers here will demand more euros with which to pay for more units of that new model. This will shift the demand curve for euros to the right, as from D_1 to D_2

in Figure A3-2. Given the fixed euro supply curve S_1, the increase in demand raises the equilibrium exchange rate (the equilibrium number of dollars needed to purchase one euro) from $1.25 to $1.50. The equilibrium quantity of euros purchased increases from Q_1 to Q_2. Because a higher dollar amount is now needed to purchase one euro, economists say that the dollar has *depreciated*—gone down in value—relative to the euro. Alternatively, the euro has *appreciated*—gone up in value—relative to the Canadian dollar because one euro now buys $1.50 rather than $1.25.

PINK SALMON

Now let's see what happens when both supply and demand change at the same time. Several decades ago, people who caught salmon earned as much as $2 for each kilogram of pink salmon—the type used mainly for canning—brought to the buyer. In Figure A3-3 that price is represented as P_1, at the intersection of supply curve S_1 and demand curve D_1. The corresponding quantity of pink salmon is shown as Q_1 kilograms. As time passed, supply and demand changed in the market for pink salmon.

On the supply side, improved technology in the form of larger, more efficient fishing boats greatly increased the catch and lowered the cost of obtaining it. Also, high profits at price P_1 encouraged many new fishers to enter the industry. As a result of these changes, the supply of pink salmon greatly increased and the supply curve shifted to the right, as from S_1 to S_2 in Figure A3-3.

Over the same years, the demand for pink salmon declined, as represented by the leftward shift from D_1 to D_2 in Figure A3-3. That decrease resulted from increases in consumer income and reductions of the price of substitute products. As buyers' incomes rose, consumers shifted demand away from canned fish and toward higher-quality fresh or frozen fish, including more-valued Atlantic, chinook, sockeye, and coho salmon. Moreover,

FIGURE A3-2   The Market for Euros

The increase in the demand for euros, shown here by the shift from D_1 to D_2, increases the equilibrium price of a euro from $1.25 to $1.50 and increases the equilibrium quantity of euros from Q_1 to Q_2. The Canadian dollar has depreciated.

FIGURE A3-3   The Market for Pink Salmon

In the last two decades, the supply of pink salmon has increased and the demand for pink salmon has decreased. As a result, the price of pink salmon has declined, as from P_1 to P_2. Because supply has increased more than demand has decreased, the equilibrium quantity of pink salmon has increased, as from Q_1 to Q_2.

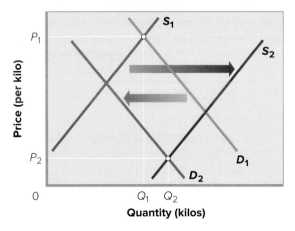

the emergence of fish farming, in which salmon are raised in ocean net pens, lowered the prices of these substitute species. That, too, reduced the demand for pink salmon.

The altered supply and demand reduced the price of pink salmon to as low as \$0.20 per kilogram, as represented by the drop in price from P_1 to P_2 in Figure A3-3. Both the supply increase and the demand decrease helped reduce the equilibrium price. However, in this particular case the equilibrium quantity of pink salmon increased, as represented by the move from Q_1 to Q_2. Both shifts of the curves reduced the equilibrium price, but equilibrium quantity increased because the increase in supply exceeded the decrease in demand.

GASOLINE

The price of gasoline has increased rapidly in Canada over the past several years. For example, the average price of a litre of

gasoline rose from around \$0.60 in 2004 to about \$1.40 in 2011. What caused the price of gasoline to more than double? How would we diagram this increase?

We begin in Figure A3-4 with the price of a litre of gasoline at P_1, representing the \$0.60 price. Simultaneous supply and demand factors disturbed this equilibrium. On the supply side, supply uncertainties relating to Middle East politics and warfare, and expanded demand for oil by fast-growing countries such as China, pushed up the price of a barrel of oil from \$37 in 2004 to over \$100 in 2011. Oil is the main input for producing gasoline, so any sustained rise in its price boosts the per-unit cost of producing gasoline. Such cost rises decrease the supply of gasoline, as represented by the leftward shift of the supply curve from S_1 to S_2 in Figure A3-4. At times, refinery breakdowns in North America also contributed to this reduced supply.

FIGURE A3-4   The Market for Gasoline

An increase in the demand for gasoline, as shown by the shift from D_1 to D_2, coupled with a decrease in supply, as shown by the shift from S_1 to S_2, boosts equilibrium price (here, from P_1 to P_2). In this case, equilibrium quantity increases from Q_1 to Q_2 because the increase in demand outweighs the decrease in supply.

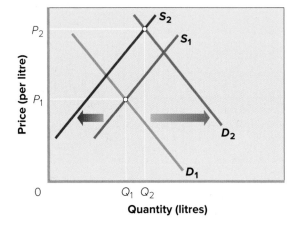

FIGURE A3-5   The Market for Sushi

Equal increase in the demand for sushi, as from D_1 to D_2, and in the supply of sushi, as from S_1 to S_2, expand the equilibrium quantity of sushi (here from Q_1 to Q_2), while leaving the price of sushi unchanged at P_1.

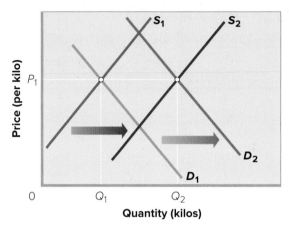

While the supply of gasoline declined between 2004 and 2011, the demand for gasoline increased, as depicted by the rightward shift of the demand curve from D_1 to D_2. Incomes in general were rising over these years because the Canadian economy was rapidly expanding. Rising incomes raise demand for all normal goods, including gasoline. An increased number of more fuel-efficient SUVs and light trucks on the road also contributed to growing gas demand.

The combined decrease in gasoline supply and increase in gasoline demand boosted the price of gasoline from $0.60 to $1.40, as represented by the rise from P_1 to P_2 in Figure A3-4. Because the demand increase outweighed the supply decrease, the equilibrium quantity expanded here, from Q_1 to Q_2.

In other periods the price of gasoline has *declined* as the demand for gasoline has increased. Test your understanding of the analysis by explaining how such a price decrease could occur.

SUSHI

Consumption of sushi has soared in Canada in recent years. Nevertheless, the price of sushi has remained relatively constant.

Supply and demand analysis helps explain this circumstance of increased quantity and constant price. A change in tastes has increased the Canadian demand for sushi. Many first-time consumers of sushi find it highly tasty. And, as implied by the growing number of sushi bars in Canada, the supply of sushi has also expanded.

We represent these supply and demand changes in Figure A3-5 as the rightward shift of the demand curve from D_1 to D_2 and the rightward shift of the supply curve from S_1 to S_2. Observe that the equilibrium quantity of sushi increases from Q_1 to Q_2 and the equilibrium price remains constant at P_1. The increase in supply, which taken alone would reduce the price, has perfectly offset the increase in demand, which taken alone would raise the price. The price of sushi does not

change but the equilibrium quantity greatly increases, because both the increase in demand and the increase in supply act to expand purchases and sales.

Simultaneous increases in demand and supply can cause the price to rise, fall, or remain constant, depending on the relative magnitudes of the supply and demand increases. In this case, the price remained constant.

A3.2 Upsloping Versus Vertical Supply Curves

As you already know, the typical good or service possesses an upsloping supply curve, because a higher market price will cause producers to increase the quantity supplied. There are, however, some goods and services whose quantities supplied are fixed and totally unresponsive to changes in price. Examples include the amount of land in a given area, the number of seats in a stadium, and the limited part of the electromagnetic spectrum that is reserved for cellular telephone transmissions. These sorts of goods and services have vertical supply curves because the same fixed amount is available no matter what price is offered to suppliers.

Reactions to Demand Shifts

Markets react very differently to a shift in demand depending upon whether they have upsloping or vertical supply curves.

UPSLOPING SUPPLY CURVES

When a market has an upsloping supply curve, any shift in demand will cause both the equilibrium price and the equilibrium quantity to adjust. Consider Figure A3-2. When the demand for euros increases, the movement from the initial

FIGURE A3-6   The Market for Land in Toronto

Because the quantity of land in Toronto is fixed at Q_0, the supply curve is vertical above Q_0 in order to indicate that the same quantity of land will be supplied no matter what the price is. As demand increases from D_1 to D_2, the equilibrium price rises from P_1 to P_2. Because the quantity of land is fixed at Q_0, the movement from equilibrium a to equilibrium b involves only a change in the equilibrium price; the equilibrium quantity remains at Q_0 because land is in fixed supply.

equilibrium to the final equilibrium involves the equilibrium price rising from $1.25 to $1.50 while the equilibrium quantity increases from Q_1 to Q_2. Price and quantity both change.

VERTICAL SUPPLY CURVES

When a market has a vertical supply curve, any shift in demand will cause only the equilibrium price to change; the equilibrium quantity remains the same because the quantity supplied is fixed and cannot adjust.

Consider Figure A3-6, in which the supply of land in Toronto is fixed at quantity Q_0. If demand increases from D_1 to D_2, the movement from the initial equilibrium at point a to the final equilibrium at point b is accomplished solely by a rise in the equilibrium price from P_1 to P_2. Because the quantity of land is fixed, the increase in demand cannot cause any change in the equilibrium quantity supplied. The entire adjustment from the initial equilibrium to the final equilibrium has to come in the form of a higher equilibrium price.

This fact explains why real estate prices are so high in Toronto and other major cities. Any increase in demand cannot be met by a combination of increases in price and increases in quantity. With the quantity of land in fixed supply, any increase in demand results solely in higher equilibrium land prices.

Preset Prices

In the body of this chapter we saw that an effective government-imposed price ceiling (legal maximum price) causes quantity demanded to exceed quantity supplied—a shortage. An effective government-imposed price floor (legal minimum price) causes quantity supplied to exceed quantity demanded—a surplus. Put simply, shortages result when prices are set below

equilibrium prices, and surpluses result when prices are set above equilibrium prices. We now want to establish that shortages and surpluses can occur in markets other than those in which government imposes price floors and ceilings. Such market imbalances happen when the seller or sellers set prices in advance of sales and the prices selected turn out to be below or above equilibrium prices. Consider the following two examples.

OLYMPIC FIGURE SKATING FINALS

Tickets for the women's figure skating championship at the Olympics are among the world's hottest tickets. The popularity of this event and the high incomes of buyers translate into tremendous ticket demand. Olympic officials set the price for the tickets in advance. Invariably, the price, although high, is considerably below the equilibrium price that would equate quantity demanded and quantity supplied. A severe shortage of tickets therefore occurs in this *primary market*—the market involving the official ticket office. The shortage, in turn, creates a *secondary market* in which buyers bid for tickets held by initial purchasers rather than the original seller.

Scalping tickets—selling them above the original ticket price—may be legal or illegal, depending on local laws. Figure A3-7 shows how the shortage in the primary ticket market looks in terms of supply and demand analysis. Demand curve D represents the strong demand for tickets, and supply curve S represents the supply of tickets. The supply curve is vertical because a fixed number of tickets are printed to match the capacity of the arena. At the printed ticket price of P_1, the quantity of tickets demanded, Q_2, exceeds the quantity supplied, Q_1. The result is a shortage of ab—the horizontal distance between Q_2 and Q_1 in the primary market.

FIGURE A3-7   The Market for Tickets to Olympic Women's Figure Skating Finals

The demand curve D and the supply curve S produce an equilibrium price above the P_1 price printed on the ticket. At price P_1 the quantity of tickets demanded, Q_2, greatly exceeds the quantity of tickets available (Q_1). The resulting shortage of ab (= $Q_2 - Q_1$) gives rise to a legal or illegal secondary market.

If the printed ticket price had been the higher equilibrium price, P_2, no shortage of tickets would have occurred. But at the lower price P_1, a shortage and secondary ticket market will emerge among those buyers willing to pay more than the original price and those sellers willing to sell their purchased tickets for more than the printed price. Wherever there are shortages and secondary markets, we can safely assume that the original price was set below the equilibrium price.

OLYMPIC CURLING PRELIMINARIES

Contrast the shortage of tickets for the women's figure skating finals at the Olympics to the surplus of tickets for one of the preliminary curling matches. Curling is a popular spectator sport in Canada and a few other nations, but it does not draw many fans in most countries, so the demand for tickets to most of the preliminary curling events is not very strong. We demonstrate this weak demand as D in Figure A3-8. As in our previous example, the supply of tickets is fixed by the size of the arena and is shown as vertical line S.

We represent the printed ticket price as P_1 in Figure A3-8. In this case the printed price is much higher than the equilibrium price of P_2. At the printed ticket price, quantity supplied is Q_1 and quantity demanded is Q_2. So a surplus of tickets of ba (= $Q_1 - Q_2$) occurs. No ticket scalping occurs and there are numerous empty seats. Only if Olympic officials had priced the tickets at the lower price, P_2, would the event have sold out. (Actually, Olympic officials try to adjust to demand realities for curling contests by holding them in smaller arenas and by charging less for tickets. Nevertheless, the stands are rarely full for the preliminary contests, which compete against final events in other winter Olympic sports.)

FIGURE A3-8   The Market for Tickets to the Olympic Curling Preliminaries

The demand curve D and the supply curve S produce an equilibrium price below the P_1 price printed on the ticket. At price P_1 the quantity of tickets demanded is less than the quantity of tickets available. The resulting surplus of ba (= $Q_1 - Q_2$) means the event is not sold out.

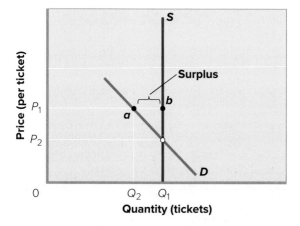

APPENDIX Summary

LOA3.1 Illustrate how supply and demand analysis can provide insights into actual-economy situations.

- A decrease in the supply of a product increases its equilibrium price and reduces its equilibrium quantity. In contrast, an increase in the demand for a product boosts both its equilibrium price and its equilibrium quantity.

- Simultaneous changes in supply and demand affect equilibrium price and quantity in various ways, depending on the relative magnitudes of the changes in supply and demand. Equal increases in supply and demand, for example, leave equilibrium price unchanged.

- Products (such as land) whose quantities supplied do not vary with price have vertical supply curves. For these products, any shift in demand will lead to a change in the equilibrium price but no change in the equilibrium quantity.

- Sellers set prices of some items, such as tickets, in advance of the event. These items are sold in the primary market that involves the original seller and buyers. If preset prices turn out to be below the equilibrium prices, shortages occur and scalping in legal or illegal secondary markets arises. The prices in the secondary market then rise above the preset prices. In contrast, surpluses occur when the preset prices happen to exceed the equilibrium prices.

APPENDIX Discussion Questions

1. Why are shortages or surpluses more likely with preset prices, such as for tickets, than with flexible prices, such as for gasoline? [**LOA3.1**]

2. Most scalping laws make it illegal to sell—but not to buy—tickets at prices above those printed on the tickets. Assuming that is the case, use supply and demand analysis to explain why the equilibrium ticket price in an illegal secondary market tends to be higher than in a legal secondary market. [**LOA3.1**]

3. How high (or how low) are gasoline prices now? Go to Gas-Buddy.com and follow the links to find the current retail price of gasoline in your area. How does the current price of regular gasoline compare with the price a year ago? What must have happened to either supply, demand, or both to explain the observed price change? [**LOA3.1**]

4. Suppose the supply of apples sharply increases because of perfect weather conditions throughout the growing season. Assuming no change in demand, explain the effect on the equilibrium price and quantity of apples. Explain why quantity demanded increases even though demand does not change. [**LOA3.1**]

5. Assume the demand for lumber suddenly rises because of a rapid growth of demand for new housing. Assume no change in supply. Why does the equilibrium price of lumber rise? What would happen if the price did not rise under the demand and supply circumstances described? [**LOA3.1**]

6. Assume that both the supply of bottled water and the demand for bottled water rise during the summer but that supply increases more rapidly than demand. What can you conclude about the directions of the impacts on equilibrium price and equilibrium quantity? [**LOA3.1**]

7. When asked for investment advice, humourist Will Rogers joked that people should "Buy land. They ain't making any more of the stuff." Explain his advice in terms of the supply and demand model. [**LOA3.1**]

APPENDIX Review Questions

1. Will the equilibrium price of orange juice increase or decrease in each of the following situations? [**LOA3.1**]

   a. A medical study reporting that orange juice reduces cancer is released at the same time that a freak storm destroys half of the orange crop in Florida.

   b. The prices of all beverages except orange juice fall by half while unexpectedly perfect weather in Florida results in an orange crop that is 20 percent larger than normal.

2. Consider the market for coffee beans. Suppose that the prices of all other caffeinated beverages go up 30 percent while at the same time a new fertilizer boosts production at coffee plantations dramatically. Which of the following best describes what is likely to happen to the equilibrium price and quantity of coffee beans? [**LOA3.1**]

   a. Both the equilibrium price and the quantity will rise.

   b. The equilibrium price will rise but the equilibrium quantity will fall.

   c. The equilibrium price may rise or fall but the equilibrium quantity will rise for certain.

   d. Neither the price change nor the quantity change can be determined for certain.

   e. None of the above.

3. A price ceiling will result in a shortage only if the ceiling price is _____ the equilibrium price. [**LOA3.1**]

   a. Less than   c. Greater than

   b. Equal to   d. Faster than

4. Suppose that you are the economic advisor to a municipal government that has to deal with a politically embarrassing surplus caused by a price floor that the government recently imposed. Your first suggestion is to get rid of the price floor, but the politicians don't want to do that. Instead, they present you with the following list of options that they hope will get rid of the surplus while keeping the price floor. Identify each one as either *could work* or *can't work*. [**LOA3.1**]

   a. Restricting supply

   b. Decreasing demand

   c. Purchasing the surplus at the floor price

5. Suppose both the demand for olives and the supply of olives decline by equal amounts over some time period. Use graphical analysis to show the effect on equilibrium price and quantity. [**LOA3.1**]

6. Governments can use subsidies to increase demand. For instance, a government can pay farmers to use organic fertilizers rather than traditional fertilizers. That subsidy increases the demand for organic fertilizer. Consider two industries, one in which supply is nearly vertical and the other in which supply is nearly horizontal. Assume that firms in both industries would prefer a higher market equilibrium price because a higher market equilibrium price would mean higher profits. Assuming that both industries have similarly sloped demand curves, which industry would probably spend more resources lobbying the government to increase the demand for its output? [**LOA3.1**]

   a. The industry with a nearly flat supply curve

   b. The industry with a nearly vertical supply curve

APPENDIX Problems

1. Demand and supply often shift in the retail market for gasoline. Here are two demand curves and two supply curves for litres of gasoline in the month of May in a small town in New Brunswick. Some of the data are missing. [**LOA3.1**]

	QUANTITIES DEMANDED		QUANTITIES SUPPLIED	
Price	D_1	D_2	S_1	S_2
$4.00	5000	7500	9000	9500
____	6000	8000	8000	9000
2.00	____	8500	____	8500
____	____	9000	5000	____

   a. Use the following facts to fill in the missing data in the table. If demand is D_1 and supply is S_1, the equilibrium quantity is 7000 litres per month. When demand is D_2 and supply is S_1, the equilibrium price is $3 per litre. When demand is D_2 and supply is S_1, there is an excess demand of 4000 litres per month at a price of $1 per litre. If demand is D_1 and supply is S_2, the equilibrium quantity is 8000 litres per month.

   b. Compare two equilibriums. In the first, demand is D_1 and supply is S_1. In the second, demand is D_1 and supply is S_2. By how much does the equilibrium quantity change? By how much does the equilibrium price change?

   c. If supply falls from S_2 to S_1 while demand declines from D_2 to D_1, does the equilibrium price rise, fall, or stay the same? What if only supply falls? What if only demand falls?

   d. Suppose that supply is fixed at S_1 and that demand starts at D_1. By how many litres per month would demand have to increase at each price level such that the equilibrium price per litre would be $3? $4?

2. The table below shows two demand schedules for a given style of men's shoes—that is, how many pairs per month will be demanded at various prices at a men's clothing store in Winnipeg called Stromnord. [**LOA3.1**]

Price	D_1 Quantity demanded	D_2 Quantity demanded
$75	53	13
70	60	15
65	68	18
60	77	22
55	87	27

Suppose that Stromnord has exactly 65 pairs of this style of shoe in inventory at the start of the month of July and will not receive any more pairs of this style until at least August 1.

   a. If demand is D_1, what is the lowest price that Stromnord can charge so that it will not run out of this model of shoe in the month of July? What if demand is D_2?

   b. If the price of shoes is set at $75 for both July and August and demand will be D_2 in July and D_1 in August, how many pairs of shoes should Stromnord order for August if it wants to end the month of August with exactly zero pairs of shoes in its inventory? What if the price is set at $55 for both months and demand is D_1 in July and D_2 in August?

3. Answer the following questions using the table that follows. [**LOA3.1**]

   a. If this table reflects the supply of and demand for tickets to a particular World Cup soccer game, what is the stadium capacity?

b. If the preset ticket price is $45, would we expect to see a secondary market for tickets? Explain why or why not. Would the price of a ticket in the secondary market be higher than, the same as, or lower than the price in the primary (original) market?

c. Suppose for some other World Cup game that the quantities of tickets demanded are 20,000 lower at each ticket price than shown in the table. If the ticket price remains $45, would the event be a sellout? Explain why or why not.

Quantity demanded, thousands	Price	Quantity supplied, thousands
80	$25	60
75	35	60
70	45	60
65	55	60
60	65	60
55	75	60
50	85	60

A3.1 The Mathematics of Market Equilibrium

A market equilibrium is the price and the quantity, denoted as the pair (Q^*, P^*), of a commodity bought or sold at price P^*. The following mathematical note provides an introduction to how a market equilibrium (Q^*, P^*) is derived.

The market equilibrium is found by using the market demand (buyers' behaviour), the market supply (sellers' behaviour), and the negotiating process (to find the agreed-upon price and quantity, namely P^* and Q^*, on which to transact). The market equilibrium is identified by the condition reached at the end of the negotiating process, that at the price they negotiated, P^*, the quantity of the commodity that buyers are willing to buy, denoted Q_d, and the quantity sellers are willing to sell, denoted Q_s, match exactly.

The Demand Curve

The equation describing the downsloping demand when the demand curve is a straight line, in which Q_d represents the quantity demanded by buyers and P the price, is

$$P = a - bQ_d$$

The demand equation and curve below tell us that if the price is higher than a, the buyers will not buy; thus, for a transaction to occur the price must be lower. The demand equation and curve also tell us that at a price lower than a the quantity demanded by the buyers increases. Buyers' behaviour, as described by the demand equation, is that at lower prices buyers buy more quantity.

The Supply Curve

The equation describing the upsloping market supply function when the supply curve is a straight line, in which Q_s represents the quantity supplied by sellers and P the price, is

$$P = c + dQ_s$$

If the price is lower than c, the sellers will sell nothing, as the figure below shows. If the price is c or higher, then the supply equation states that sellers facing higher prices sell more quantity. Sellers' behaviour, as described by the supply curve and equation, is that at higher prices sellers make more quantity available.

The Market Equilibrium

The negotiating process (in which price or quantity or both adjust) provides the mechanism by which, eventually, buyers and sellers agree upon a price, P^*, and a quantity, Q^*, at which they can buy and sell and thus complete the transaction. At the end of the negotiating process, the quantity demanded by the buyers, Q_d, is equal to the quantity supplied by the sellers, Q_s (at the agreed-upon price), and thus the market is in equilibrium. The mathematical representation of such a negotiating process is described as follows.

At the agreed price, P^*, the equilibrium condition of the negotiating process—the equality in the quantity demanded and supplied—is

$$Q_d = Q_s$$

Having denoted Q^* as the equilibrium quantity, then it must be that $Q^* = Q_d = Q_s$. To solve for the equilibrium quantity Q^* and the equilibrium price P^*, the demand and supply functions are used. With Q^* the equilibrium quantity, for the buyers is

$$P^* = a - bQ^*$$

and for the sellers is

$$P^* = c + dQ^*$$

Now, since P^* is the same agreed-upon price by both buyer and seller, then

$$a - bQ^* = c + dQ^*$$

giving the equilibrium quantity, Q^*, as

$$Q^* = \frac{(a - c)}{(b + d)}$$

To find P, substitute $\dfrac{(a - c)}{(b + d)}$ in the supply (or demand) function.

$$P^* = c + d\,\frac{(a - c)}{(b + d)}, \text{ thus}$$

$$P^* = \frac{(ad - bc)}{(b + d)}$$

The equilibrium is $(Q^*, P^*) = \left[\dfrac{(a - c)}{(b + d)}, \dfrac{(ad - bc)}{(b + d)}\right]$

The market equilibrium may also be represented diagrammatically, as shown below.

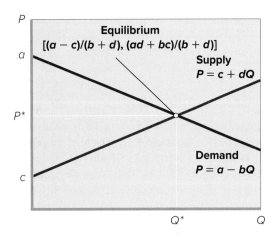

Example

Assume the demand for a pair of jeans is represented by the equation

$$P = 100 - 0.2Q_d$$

Assume the supply of a pair of jeans is represented by the equation

$$P = 20 + 0.2Q_s$$

Assume quantities are expressed in pairs of jeans per day, and the price in dollars.

To find the equilibrium price, P^*, and equilibrium quantity, Q^*, substitute Q^* for Q_d and Q_s and P^* for P in the demand and supply equations. To solve for Q^*:

$$100 - 0.2Q^* = 20 + 0.2Q^*$$
$$0.4Q^* = 80$$
$$Q^* = 200$$

To solve for P^*:

$$P^* = 100 - 0.2(200)$$
$$= 60$$

The equilibrium quantity of pairs of jeans is 200 per day, and the equilibrium price is $60 per pair of jeans.

CHAPTER 4

Market Failures: Public Goods and Externalities

LEARNING OBJECTIVES

LO4.1 Differentiate between demand-side market failures and supply-side market failures.

LO4.2 Explain the origin of both consumer surplus and producer surplus, and explain how properly functioning markets maximize their sum, economic surplus, while optimally allocating resources.

LO4.3 Describe free riding and public goods, and illustrate why private firms cannot normally produce public goods.

LO4.4 Explain how positive and negative externalities cause underallocations and overallocations of resources.

LO4.5 Show why we normally won't want to pay what it would cost to eliminate every last bit of a negative externality such as air pollution.

LOA4.1 (Appendix) Describe how information failures may justify government intervention in some markets.

Competitive markets usually do a remarkably effective job of allocating society's scarce resources to their most highly valued uses. Thus, we begin this chapter by demonstrating how properly functioning markets efficiently allocate resources. We then explore what happens when markets don't function properly. In some circumstances, economically desirable goods are not produced at all. In other situations, they are either overproduced or underproduced. This chapter focuses on these situations, which economists refer to as **market failures**.

In such situations, an economic role for government may arise. We will examine that role as it relates to public goods and so-called externalities—situations where market failures lead to sub-optimal outcomes that the government may be able to improve upon by using its powers to tax, spend, and regulate. The government may, for instance, pay for the production of goods that the private sector fails to produce. It may also act to reduce the production of goods and services that the private sector overproduces. Implementing such policies can, however, be both costly and complicated. We will conclude the chapter by noting the government inefficiencies that might hinder government's efforts to improve economic outcomes.

4.1 Market Failures in Competitive Markets[1]

LO4.1   Differentiate between demand-side market failures and supply-side market failures.

In Chapter 3 we said that "competitive markets usually produce an assignment of resources that is 'right' from an economic perspective." We now want to focus on the word "usually" and discuss exceptions. We must do this because unfortunately the presence of robust competition involving many buyers and many sellers may not, by itself, be enough to guarantee that a market will allocate resources correctly. Market failures sometimes happen in competitive markets. The focus of this chapter is to explain how and why such market failures can arise.

Fortunately, the broad picture is simple. Market failures in competitive markets fall into just two categories:

- A **demand-side market failure** happens when demand curves do not reflect consumers' full willingness to pay for a good or service.

- A **supply-side market failure** occurs when supply curves do not reflect the full cost of producing a good or service.

Demand-Side Market Failures

Demand-side market failures arise because it is impossible in certain cases to charge consumers what they are willing to pay for a product. Consider outdoor fireworks displays. People enjoy fireworks and would therefore be *willing* to pay to see them if the only way to see them was to have to pay for the right to do so. But because such displays are outdoors and in public, people don't actually *have* to pay to see them, because there is no way to exclude those who haven't paid from also enjoying the show. Private firms will therefore be unwilling to produce outdoor fireworks displays, as it will be nearly impossible for them to raise enough revenue to cover production costs.

Supply-Side Market Failures

Supply-side market failures arise in situations in which a firm does not have to pay the full cost of producing its output. Consider a coal-burning power plant. The firm running the plant will have to pay for all of the land, labour, capital, and entrepreneurship that it uses to generate electricity by burning coal. But if the firm is not charged for the smoke that it releases into the atmosphere, it will fail to pay another set of costs—the costs that its pollution imposes on other people. These include future harm from global warming, toxins that affect wildlife, and possible damage to agricultural crops downwind.

A market failure arises because it is not possible for the market to correctly weigh costs and benefits in a situation in which some of the costs are completely unaccounted for. The coal-burning power plant produces more electricity and generates more pollution than it would if it had to pay for each tonne of smoke that it released into the atmosphere. The extra units that are produced are units of output for which the costs are *greater than* the benefits. Obviously, these units should not be produced.

4.2 Efficiently Functioning Markets

LO4.2   Explain the origin of both consumer surplus and producer surplus, and explain how properly functioning markets maximize their sum, economic surplus, while optimally allocating resources.

The best way to understand market failure is to understand how properly functioning competitive markets achieve economic efficiency. We touched on this subject in Chapter 3, but we now want to expand and deepen that analysis, both for its own sake and to set up our discussion of public goods and externalities. Two conditions must hold if a competitive market is to produce efficient outcomes: (1) the demand curve in the market must reflect consumers' full willingness to pay and (2) the supply curve in the market must reflect all the costs

---

[1] Other market failures arise when there are not enough buyers or sellers to ensure competition. In those situations, the lack of competition allows either buyers or sellers to restrict purchases or sales below optimal levels for their own benefit. As an example, a monopoly—a firm that is the only producer in its industry—can restrict the amount of output that it supplies to drive up the market price and increase its own profit.

of production. If these conditions hold, then the market will produce only units for which benefits are at least equal to costs. It will also maximize the amount of benefits surpluses that are shared between consumers and producers.

Consumer Surplus

The benefit surplus received by a consumer or consumers in a market is called **consumer surplus**. It is defined as the difference between the maximum price a consumer is (or consumers are) willing to pay for a product and the actual price they do pay.

The maximum price that a person is willing to pay for a unit of a product depends on the opportunity cost of his consumption alternatives. Suppose that Ted is offered the chance to purchase an apple. He would of course like to have it for free, but the maximum amount he would be willing to pay depends on the alternative uses to which he can put his money. If his maximum willingness to pay for that particular apple is $1.25, then we know that he is willing to forgo up to—but not more than—$1.25 of other goods and services. Paying even one cent more would entail having to give up too much of other goods and services.

It also means that if Ted is charged any market price less than $1.25, he will receive a consumer surplus equal to the difference between the $1.25 maximum price that he would have been willing to pay and the lower market price. For instance, if the market price is $0.50 per apple, Ted will receive a consumer surplus of $0.75 per apple (= $1.25 − $0.50). In nearly all markets, consumers individually and collectively gain greater total utility or satisfaction in dollar terms from their purchases than the amount of their expenditures (= product price × quantity). This utility surplus arises because each consumer who buys the product only has to pay the market equilibrium price even though many of them would have been willing to pay more than the equilibrium price to obtain the product.

The concept of maximum willingness to pay also gives us another way to understand demand curves. Consider Table 4-1, where the first two columns show the maximum amounts that six consumers would each be willing to pay for a bag of oranges. Bob, for instance, would be willing to pay a maximum of $13 for a bag of oranges. Betty, by contrast, would only be willing to pay a maximum of $8 for a bag of oranges.

Notice that the maximum prices these individuals are willing to pay represent points on a demand curve because the lower the market price, the more bags of oranges will be demanded. At a price of $12.50, for instance, Bob will be the only person listed in the table who will purchase a bag. But at a price of $11.50, both Bob and Beata will want to purchase a bag. And at a price of $10.50, Bob, Beata, and Bill will each purchase a bag. The lower the price, the greater the total quantity demanded as the market price falls below the maximum prices of more and more consumers.

Lower prices also imply larger consumer surpluses. When the price is $12.50, Bob only gets $0.50 in consumer surplus because his maximum willingness to pay of $13 is only $0.50 higher than the market price of $12.50. But if the market price were to fall to $8, then his consumer surplus would be $5 (= $13 − $8). The third and fourth columns of Table 4-1 show how much consumer surplus each of our six consumers will receive if the market price of a bag of oranges is $8. Only Betty receives no consumer surplus because her maximum willingness to pay exactly matches the $8 equilibrium price.

TABLE 4-1	**Consumer Surplus**		
(1) **Person**	**(2)** **Maximum price** **willing to pay**	**(3)** **Actual price** **(equilibrium price)**	**(4)** **Consumer surplus**
Bob	$13	$8	$5 (= $13 − $8)
Beata	12	8	4 (= $12 − $8)
Bill	11	8	3 (= $11 − $8)
Bella	10	8	2 (= $10 − $8)
Brent	9	8	1 (= $9 − $8)
Betty	8	8	0 (= $8 − $8)

FIGURE 4-1 Consumer Surplus

Consumer surplus—shown as the green triangle—is the difference between the maximum price consumers are willing to pay for a product and the lower equilibrium price, here assumed to be $8. For quantity Q_1, consumers are willing to pay the sum of the amounts represented by the green triangle and the blue rectangle. Because they need to pay only the amount shown as the blue rectangle, the green triangle shows consumer surplus.

It is easy to show on a graph both the individual consumer surplus received by each particular buyer in a market and the collective consumer surplus received by all buyers. Consider Figure 4-1, which shows the market equilibrium price $P_1 = \$8$ as well as the downsloping demand curve D for bags of oranges. Demand curve D includes not only the six consumers named in Table 4-1 but also every other consumer of oranges in the market. The individual consumer surplus of each particular person who is willing to buy at the $8 market price is simply the vertical distance from the horizontal line that marks the $8 market price up to that particular buyer's maximum willingness to pay. The collective consumer surplus obtained by all of our named and unnamed buyers is found by adding together each of their individual consumer surpluses.

To obtain the Q_1 bags of oranges represented, consumers collectively are willing to pay the total amount shown by the sum of the green triangle and blue rectangle under the demand curve and to the left of Q_1. But consumers need to pay only the amount represented by the blue rectangle ($= P_1 \times Q_1$). So the green triangle is the consumer surplus in this market. It is the sum of the vertical distances between the demand curve and the $8 equilibrium price at each quantity up to Q_1. Alternatively, it is the sum of the gaps between maximum willingness to pay and actual price, such as those we calculated in Table 4-1. Thus, consumer surplus can also be defined as the area that lies below the demand curve and above the price line that extends horizontally from P_1.

Consumer surplus and price are inversely (negatively) related. Given the demand curve, higher prices reduce consumer surplus; lower prices increase it. To test this generalization, draw in an equilibrium price above $8 in Figure 4-1 and observe the reduced size of the triangle representing consumer surplus. When price goes up, the gap narrows between the maximum willingness to pay and the actual price. Next, draw in an equilibrium price below $8 and see that consumer surplus increases. When the price declines, the gap widens between maximum willingness to pay and actual price.

Producer Surplus

Like consumers, producers also receive a benefit surplus in markets. This **producer surplus** is the difference between the actual price a producer receives (or producers receive) and the minimum acceptable price that a consumer would have to pay the producer to make a particular unit of his or her product.

A producer's minimum acceptable price for a particular unit will equal the producer's marginal cost of producing that particular unit. That marginal cost will be the sum of the rent, wages, interest, and profit that the producer will need to pay in order to obtain the land, labour, capital, and entrepreneurship required to produce that particular unit. In this section, we are assuming that the marginal cost of producing a unit will include *all* of the costs of production. Unlike in the case of the coal-burning power plant mentioned above, the producer must pay for all of the costs, including the cost of pollution. In later sections, we will explore the market failures that arise in situations where firms do not have to pay all of their costs.

In addition to equalling marginal cost, a producer's minimum acceptable price can also be interpreted as the opportunity cost of bidding resources away from the production of other products. To see why this is true, suppose that for Leah, an apple grower, the resources necessary to produce one apple could be used to produce other things. To direct the resources toward producing an apple, it is necessary to pay Leah what it will cost her to bid the necessary resources away from other entrepreneurs who would like to use them to produce other products. Leah would naturally like to get paid as much as possible to produce the apple for you. But her minimum acceptable price is the lowest price you could pay her such that she can just break even after bidding away from other uses the land, labour, capital, and entrepreneurship necessary to produce the apple.

WORKED PROBLEM 4.1 Consumer and Producer Surplus

The size of the producer surplus earned on any particular unit will be the difference between the market price that the producer actually receives and the producer's minimum acceptable price. Consider Table 4-2, which shows the minimum acceptable prices of six different orange growers. With a market price of $8, Carlos—for instance—has a producer surplus of $5, which is equal to the market price of $8 minus his minimum acceptable price of $3. Chad, by contrast, receives no producer surplus because his minimum acceptable price of $8 just equals the market equilibrium price of $8.

Carlos's minimum acceptable price is lower than Chad's minimum acceptable price because Carlos is a more efficient producer than Chad, by which we mean that Carlos produces oranges using a less-costly combination of resources than Chad uses. The differences in efficiency between Carlos and Chad are likely due to differences in the type and quality of resources available to them. Carlos, for instance, may own land perfectly suited to growing oranges, while Chad has land in the desert that requires costly irrigation if it is to be used to grow oranges. Thus, Chad has a higher marginal cost of producing oranges.

The minimum acceptable prices that producers are willing to accept form points on a supply curve because the higher the price, the more bags of oranges will be supplied. At a price of $3.50, for instance, only Carlos would be willing to supply a bag of oranges. But at a price of $5.50, Carlos, Courtney, and Carla would all be willing to supply a bag of oranges. The higher the market price, the more oranges will be supplied as the market price surpasses the marginal costs and minimum acceptable prices of more and more producers. Thus, supply curves shown in this competitive market are both marginal-cost curves and minimum-acceptable-price curves.

The supply curve in Figure 4-2 includes not only the six producers named in Table 4-2 but also every other producer of oranges in the market. At the market price of $8 per bag, Q_1 bags are produced because only those producers whose minimum acceptable prices are less than $8 per bag will choose to produce oranges with their resources. Those lower acceptable prices for each of the units up to Q_1 are shown by the portion of the supply curve lying to the left of and below the assumed $8 market price.

TABLE 4-2	**Producer Surplus**		
(1) **Person**	(2) **Minimum acceptable price**	(3) **Actual price (equilibrium price)**	(4) **Producer surplus**
Carlos	$3	$8	$5 (= $8 − $3)
Courtney	4	8	4 (= $8 − $4)
Carla	5	8	3 (= $8 − $5)
Cindy	6	8	2 (= $8 − $6)
Carmela	7	8	2 (= $8 − $7)
Chad	8	8	0 (= $8 − $8)

FIGURE 4-2   Producer Surplus

Producer surplus—shown as the blue triangle—reflects the difference between the equilibrium price producers receive for a product (here, $8) and the lower minimum payments they are willing to accept. For quantity Q_1, producers receive the sum of the amounts represented by the blue triangle plus the green triangle. Because they need to receive only the amount shown by the green triangle to produce Q_1, the blue triangle represents producer surplus.

The individual producer surplus of each of these sellers is thus the vertical distance from each seller's respective minimum acceptable price on the supply curve up to the $8 market price. Their collective producer surplus is shown by the blue triangle in Figure 4-2. In that figure, producers collect revenues of $P_1 \times Q_1$, which is the sum of the blue and green triangles. As shown by the supply curve, however, revenues of only those illustrated by the green triangle would be required to entice producers to offer Q_1 bags of oranges for sale. The sellers therefore receive a producer surplus shown by the blue triangle. That surplus is the sum of the vertical distances between the supply curve and the $8 equilibrium price at each of the quantities to the left of Q_1.

There is a direct (positive) relationship between equilibrium price and the amount of producer surplus. Given the supply curve, lower prices reduce producer surplus; higher prices increase it. If you pencil in a lower equilibrium price than $8, you will see that the producer surplus triangle gets smaller. The gaps between the minimum acceptable payments and the actual prices narrow when the price falls. If you pencil in an equilibrium price above $8, the size of the producer surplus triangle increases. The gaps between minimum acceptable payments and actual prices widen when the price increases.

Efficiency Revisited

In Figure 4-3 we bring together the demand and supply curves of Figures 4-1 and 4-2 to show the equilibrium price and quantity and the previously described regions of consumer and producer surplus. All markets that have downsloping demand curves and upsloping supply curves yield consumer and producer surplus.

Because we are assuming in Figure 4-3 that the demand curve reflects buyers' full willingness to pay and the supply curve reflects all the costs facing sellers, the equilibrium quantity in Figure 4-3 reflects economic efficiency, which consists of productive efficiency and allocative efficiency.

- *Productive Efficiency* is achieved because competition forces orange growers to use the best technologies and combinations of resources available. Doing so minimizes the per-unit cost of the output produced.

- *Allocative Efficiency* is achieved because the correct quantity of oranges—Q_1—is produced relative to other goods and services.

There are two ways to understand why Q_1 is the correct quantity of oranges. Both involve realizing that any resources directed toward the production of oranges are resources that could have been used to produce other products. Thus, the only way to justify taking any amount of any resource (land, labour, capital, entrepreneurship, etc.)

FIGURE 4-3   Efficiency: Maximum Combined Consumer and Producer Goods

At quantity Q_1 the combined amount of consumer surplus, shown as the blue triangle, and producer surplus, shown as the green triangle, is maximized. Efficiency occurs because, at Q_1, maximum willingness to pay, indicated by the points on the demand curve, equals minimum acceptable price, shown by the points on the supply curve.

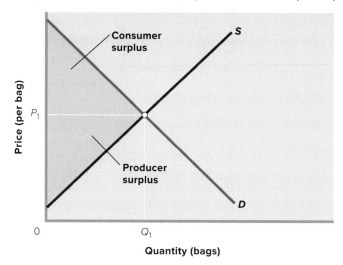

away from the production of other products is if it brings more utility or satisfaction when devoted to the production of oranges than it would if it were used to produce other products.

The first way to see why Q_1 is the allocatively efficient quantity of oranges is to note that demand and supply curves can be interpreted as measuring marginal benefit (MB) and marginal cost (MC). Recall from the discussion relating to Figure 1-3 that optimal allocation is achieved at the output level where MB = MC. We have already seen that supply curves are marginal cost curves. As it turns out, demand curves are marginal benefit curves. This is true because the maximum price that a consumer would be willing to pay for any particular unit is equal to the benefit of consuming that unit. Thus, each point on a demand curve represents both some consumer's maximum willingness to pay and the marginal benefit gained from consuming the particular unit in question.

Thus, combining the fact that supply curves are MC curves with the fact that demand curves are MB curves, we see that points on the demand curve in Figure 4-3 measure the marginal benefit of oranges at each level of output, while points on the supply curve measure the marginal cost of oranges at each level of output. As a result, MB = MC where the demand and supply curves intersect—which means that the equilibrium quantity Q_1 must be allocatively efficient.

To gain a deeper understanding of why Q_1 is allocatively efficient, notice that for every unit up to Q_1 marginal benefit exceeds marginal cost (MB > MC). And because marginal cost includes the opportunity cost of not making other things with the resources needed to make these units, we know that people are better off when the resources necessary to make these units are allocated to producing oranges rather than to producing anything else.

The second way to see why Q_1 is the correct quantity of oranges is based on our analysis of consumer and producer surplus and the fact that we can interpret demand and supply curves in terms of maximum willingness to pay and minimum acceptable price. In Figure 4-3, the maximum willingness to pay on the demand curve for each bag of oranges up to Q_1 exceeds the corresponding minimum acceptable price on the supply curve. Thus, each of these bags adds a positive amount (= maximum willingness to pay *minus* minimum acceptable price) to the *total* of consumer and producer surplus.

The fact that maximum willingness to pay exceeds minimum acceptable price for every unit up to Q_1 means that people gain more utility from producing and consuming those units than they would if they produced and consumed anything else that could be made with the resources that went into making those units. This is true because both the maximum willingness to pay and the minimum acceptable price take opportunity costs into account. As long as the maximum willingness to pay exceeds the minimum acceptable price, people are willing to pay more to consume a unit of the good in question (here, bags of oranges) than they would pay to consume anything else that could be made with the same resources. Only at the equilibrium quantity Q_1—where the maximum willingness to pay exactly equals the minimum acceptable price—does society exhaust all opportunities to produce units for which benefits exceed costs (including opportunity costs). Producing Q_1 units therefore achieves allocative efficiency because the market is producing and distributing only those units that make people happier with bags of oranges than they would be with anything else that could be produced with the same resources.

Geometrically, producing Q_1 units maximizes the combined area of consumer and producer surplus in Figure 4-3. In this context, the combined area is referred to as *total surplus*. Thus, when Q_1 units are produced, total surplus is equal to the large triangle formed by the green consumer surplus triangle and the blue producer surplus triangle.

When demand curves reflect buyers' full willingness to pay and when supply curves reflect all the costs facing sellers, competitive markets produce equilibrium quantities that maximize the sum of consumer and producer surplus. Allocative efficiency occurs at the market equilibrium quantity, where three conditions exist simultaneously:

1. MB = MC (Figure 1-3).

2. Maximum willingness to pay = minimum acceptable price.

3. Total surplus (= sum of consumer and producer surplus) is at a maximum.

Economists are enamoured of markets because properly functioning markets automatically achieve allocative efficiency. Other methods of allocating resources—such as government central planning—do exist. But since they cannot do any better than properly functioning markets—and may in many cases do much worse—economists usually prefer that resources be allocated through markets whenever properly functioning markets are available.

Efficiency Losses (or Deadweight Losses)

Figures 4-4a and 4-4b demonstrate that **efficiency losses (or deadweight losses)**—reductions of combined consumer and producer surplus—result from both underproduction and overproduction. First, consider Figure 4-4a, which analyzes the case of underproduction by considering what happens if output falls from the efficient level Q_1 to the smaller amount Q_2. When that happens, the sum of consumer and producer surplus, previously *abc*, falls to *adec*. So the combined consumer and producer surplus declines by the amount of the blue triangle to the left of Q_1. That triangle represents an efficiency loss to buyers and sellers. And because buyers and sellers are members of society, it represents an efficiency loss to society.

For output levels from Q_2 to Q_1, the maximum willingness to pay by consumers (as reflected by points on the demand curve) exceeds the minimum acceptable price of sellers (as reflected by points on the supply curve). By failing to produce units of this product for which a consumer is willing to pay more than a producer is willing to accept, society suffers a loss of net benefits. As a concrete example, consider a particular unit for which a consumer is willing to pay $10 and a producer is willing to accept $6. The $4 difference between those values is a net benefit that will not be realized if this unit is not produced. In addition, the resources that should have gone to producing this unit will go instead to producing other products that will not generate as much utility as if those resources had

FIGURE 4-4   Efficiency Losses (or Deadweight Losses)

Quantity levels less than or greater than the efficient quantity Q_1 create efficiency losses. Triangle *dbe* shows the efficiency loss associated with underproduction at output Q_2. Triangle *bfg* in panel (b) illustrates the efficiency loss associated with overproduction at output level Q_3.

(a)   Quantity (bags)

(b)   Quantity (bags)

been used here to produce this unit of this product. The triangle *dbe* in Figure 4-4a shows the total loss of net benefits that results from failing to produce the units from Q_2 to Q_1.

In contrast, consider the case of overproduction shown in Figure 4-4b, in which the number of oranges produced is Q_3 rather than the efficient level Q_1. In Figure 4-4b the combined consumer and producer surplus therefore declines by *bfg*—the blue triangle to the right of Q_1. This triangle subtracts from the total consumer and producer surplus of *abc* that would occur if the quantity had been Q_1. That is, for all units from zero to Q_1, benefits exceed costs, so that those units generate the economic surplus shown by triangle *abc*. But the units from Q_1 to Q_3 are such that costs exceed benefits. Thus, they generate an economic loss shown by triangle *bfg*. The total economic surplus for all units from zero to Q_3 is therefore the economic surplus given by *abc* for the units from 0 to Q_1 *minus* the economic loss given by *bfg* for the units from Q_1 to Q_3.

Producing any unit beyond Q_1 generates an economic loss because the willingness to pay for such units on the part of consumers is less than the minimum acceptable price to produce such units on the part of producers. As a concrete example, note that producing an item for which the maximum willingness to pay is, say, \$7 and the minimum acceptable price is, say, \$10 subtracts \$3 from society's net benefits. Such production is uneconomical and creates an efficiency loss (or deadweight loss) for society. Because the net benefit of each bag of oranges from Q_1 to Q_3 is negative, we know that the benefits from these units are smaller than the opportunity costs of the other products that could have been produced with the resources that were used to produce these bags of oranges. The resources used to produce the bags from Q_1 to Q_3 could have generated net benefits instead of net losses if they had been directed toward producing other products. The brown triangle *bfg* to the right of Q_1 in Figure 4-4b shows the total efficiency loss from overproduction at Q_3.

The magic of markets is that when demand reflects consumers' full willingness to pay and when supply reflects all costs, the market equilibrium quantity will automatically equal the allocatively efficient output level. Under these conditions, the market equilibrium quantity will ensure that there are neither efficiency losses from underproduction nor efficiency losses from overproduction. As we are about to see, however, such losses do happen when either demand does not reflect consumers' full willingness to pay or supply does not reflect all costs.

QUICK REVIEW 4.1

- Market failures in competitive markets have two possible causes: demand curves that do not reflect consumers' full willingness to pay and supply curves that do not reflect producers' full cost of production.

- Consumer surplus is the difference between the maximum price a consumer is willing to pay for a product and the lower price actually paid.

- Producer surplus is the difference between the minimum price a producer is willing to accept for a product and the higher price actually received.

- At the equilibrium price and quantity in competitive markets, marginal benefit equals marginal cost, maximum willingness to pay equals minimum acceptable price, and the total of consumer surplus and producer surplus is maximized. These individual conditions each define allocative efficiency.

- Quantities less than or greater than the allocatively efficient level of output create efficiency losses, also called deadweight losses.

4.3 Public Goods

LO4.3   Describe free riding and public goods, and illustrate why private firms cannot normally produce public goods.

Demand-side market failures arise in competitive markets when demand curves fail to reflect consumers' full willingness to pay for a good or service. In such situations, markets fail to produce all of the units for which there are net benefits because demand curves underreport how much consumers are willing and able to pay. This problem reaches its most extreme form in the case of a public good: Markets may fail to produce *any* of the public good because its demand curve may reflect *none* of its consumers' willingness to pay.

To understand public goods, we first need to understand the characteristics that define private goods.

Private Good Characteristics

We have seen that a full range of **private goods** are produced through the competitive market system. These are the goods offered for sale in stores, in shops, and on the Internet. Examples include automobiles, clothing, personal computers, household appliances, and sporting goods. Private goods have two characteristics: rivalry and excludability.

- **Rivalry** (in consumption) means that when one person buys and consumes a product, it is not available for another person to buy and consume. When Adams purchases and drinks a bottle of mineral water, it is not available for Benson to purchase and consume.

- **Excludability** means that sellers can keep people who do not pay for a product from obtaining its benefits. Only people who are willing and able to pay the market price for bottles of water can obtain these drinks and the benefits they confer.

Consumers fully express their personal demands for private goods in the market. If Adams likes bottled mineral water, that fact will be known by her desire to purchase the product. Other things equal, the higher the price of bottled water, the fewer bottles she will buy. So Adams's demand for bottled water will reflect an inverse relationship between the price of bottled water and the quantity of it demanded. This is simply *individual* demand, as described in Chapter 3.

The *market* demand for a private good is the horizontal summation of the individual demand schedules (review Figure 3-2). Suppose there are just two consumers in the market for bottled water and the price is $1 per bottle. If Adams will purchase 3 bottles and Benson will buy 2, the market demand will reflect that consumers demand 5 bottles at the $1 price. Similar summations of quantities demanded at other prices will generate the market demand schedule and curve.

Suppose the equilibrium price of bottled water is $1. Adams and Benson will buy a total of 5 bottles, and the sellers will obtain total revenue of $5 (= $1 × 5). If the sellers' cost per bottle is $0.80, their total cost will be $4 (= $0.80 × 5). So sellers charging $1 per bottle will obtain $5 of total revenue, incur $4 of total cost, and earn $1 of profit for the 5 bottles sold.

Because firms can profitably tap market demand for private goods, they will produce and offer them for sale. Consumers demand private goods, and profit-seeking suppliers produce goods that satisfy the demand. Consumers willing to pay the market price obtain the goods; nonpayers go without.

A competitive market not only makes private goods available to consumers but also allocates society's resources efficiently to the particular product. There is neither underproduction nor overproduction of the product.

Public Good Characteristics

Goods that have the opposite characteristics of private goods are called **public goods**. Public goods are distinguished by nonrivalry and nonexcludability.

- **Nonrivalry** (in consumption) means that one person's consumption of a good does not preclude consumption of the good by others. Everyone can simultaneously obtain the benefit from a public good such as national defence, street lighting, a global positioning system, or environmental protection.

- **Nonexcludability** means there is no effective way of excluding individuals from the benefit of the good once it comes into existence. Once in place, you cannot exclude someone from benefiting from national defense, street lighting, a global positioning system, or environmental protection.

These two characteristics create a **free-rider problem**. Once a producer has provided a public good, everyone—including nonpayers—can obtain the benefit. Because most people do not voluntarily pay for something that they can obtain for free, most people become free riders. They like the public good and would be willing to pay for it if producers could somehow force them to pay—but nonexcludability means that there is no way for producers to withhold the good from the free riders without also denying it to the few who do pay. As a result, free riding means that the free riders' willingness to pay is not expressed in the market. From the viewpoint of producers, free riding reduces demand. The more free riding, the less demand. And if all consumers free ride, demand will collapse all the way to zero.

The low or even zero demand caused by free riding makes it virtually impossible for private firms to profitably provide public goods. With little or no demand, firms have no potential to tap market demand for revenues and profits. As a result, they will not produce public goods. Society will therefore suffer efficiency losses because

CONSIDER THIS

Street Entertainers

Street entertainers are often found in tourist areas of major cities. These entertainers illuminate the concepts of free riders and public goods. Most street entertainers have a hard time earning a living from their activities (unless event organizers pay them) because they have no way of excluding nonpayers from the benefits of their entertainment. They essentially are providing public, not private, goods and must rely on voluntary payments. The result is a significant free-rider problem. Only a few in the audience put money in the container or instrument case, and many who do so contribute only token amounts. The rest are free riders who obtain the benefits of the street entertainment and retain their money for purchases that *they* initiate.

© Colin Young-Wolff/PhotoEdit

Street entertainers are acutely aware of the free-rider problem, and some have found creative ways to lessen it. For example, some entertainers involve the audience directly in the act. This usually creates a greater sense of audience willingness (or obligation) to contribute money at the end of the performance. "Pay for performance" is another creative approach to lessening the free-rider problem. A good example is the street entertainer painted up to look like a statue. When people drop coins into the container, the "statue" makes a slight movement. The greater the contribution, the greater the movement. But these entertainers still face a free-rider problem: Nonpayers also get to enjoy the acts.

goods for which marginal benefits exceed marginal costs are not produced. Thus, if society wants a public good to be produced, it will have to direct government to provide it. Because the public good will still feature nonexcludability, the government won't have any better luck preventing free riding or charging people for it. But because the government can finance the provision of the public good through the taxation of other things, the government does not have to worry about profitability. It can therefore provide the public good even when private firms can't.

Examples of public goods include national defence, outdoor fireworks displays, the light beams thrown out by lighthouses, public art displays, public music concerts, MP3 music files posted to file-sharing websites, and ideas and inventions not protected by patents or copyrights. Each of these goods or services shows both nonrivalry and nonexcludability.

In a few special cases, private firms can provide public goods, because the production costs of these public goods can be covered by the profits generated by closely related private goods. For instance, private companies can make a profit providing broadcast TV—which is a nonrival, nonexcludable public good—because they control who gets to air TV commercials, which are rival and excludable private goods. The money that broadcasters make from selling airtime for ads allows them to turn a profit despite having to give their main product, broadcast TV, away for free.

Unfortunately, only a few public goods can be subsidized in this way by closely related private goods. For the large majority of public goods, private provision is unprofitable. As a result, there are only two remaining ways for a public good to be supplied: private philanthropy or government provision. For many less expensive or less important public goods, like fireworks displays or public art, society may feel comfortable relying on private philanthropy. But when it comes to public goods like national defence, people normally look to the government.

One person's consumption of a public good does not preclude consumption of the same good by others.

© David Toase/Getty Images

This leads to an important question: Once a government decides to produce a particular public good, how can it determine the optimal amount that it should produce? How can it avoid either underallocating or overallocating society's scarce resources to the production of the public good?

MATH 4.1   Optimal Amount of a Public Good

Optimal Quantity of a Public Good

If consumers need not reveal their true demand for a public good in the marketplace, how can society determine the optimal amount of that good? The answer is that the government has to try to estimate the demand for a public good through surveys or public votes. It can then compare the marginal benefit (MB) of an added unit of the good against the government's marginal cost (MC) of providing it. Adhering to the MB = MC rule, government can provide the right—meaning efficient—amount of the public good.

Demand for Public Goods

The demand for a public good is somewhat unusual. Suppose Adams and Benson are the only two people in the society, and their marginal willingness to pay for a public good—this time, national defence—is as shown in columns 1, 2, and 3 in Table 4-3.

Notice that the schedules in Table 4-3 are demand schedules. Rather than depicting demand in the usual way—the quantity of a product someone is willing to buy at each possible price—these schedules show the price someone is willing to pay for an extra unit of each possible quantity. That is, Adams is willing to pay $4 for the first unit of the public good, $3 for the second, $2 for the third, and so on.

Suppose the government produces one unit of this public good. Because of the nonexcludability characteristic of a public good, Adams's consumption of the good does not preclude Benson from also consuming it, and vice versa. So both consume the good, and neither volunteers to pay for it. But from Table 4-3, column 4, we can find the amount these two people would be willing to pay, together. Columns 1 and 2 show that Adams would be willing to pay $4 for the first unit of the public good; columns 1 and 3 show that Benson would be willing to pay $5 for it. So the two people are jointly willing to pay $9 (= $4 + $5) for this unit.

For the second unit of the public good, the collective price they are willing to pay is $7 (= $3 from Adams plus $4 from Benson), for the third unit they will pay $5 (= $2 plus $3), and so on. By finding the collective willingness to pay for each additional unit (column 4), we can construct a collective demand schedule (a willingness-to-pay schedule) for the public good. Here, we are not adding the quantities demanded at each possible price as when we determine the market demand for a private good. Instead, we are adding the prices that people are willing to pay for the last unit of the public good at each possible quantity demanded.

Figure 4-5 shows the same adding procedure graphically, using the data from Table 4-3. Note that we sum Adams's and Benson's willingness-to-pay curves *vertically* to derive the collective willingness-to-pay curve (demand curve). The summing procedure is upward from the lower graph to the middle graph to the top (total) graph. For example, the height of the collective demand curve D_c at two units of output in the top graph is $7, the

TABLE 4-3	Demand for a Public Good, Two Individuals				
(1) Quantity of public good	(2) Adams's willingness to pay (price)		(3) Benson's willingness to pay (price)		(4) Collective willingness to pay (price)
1	$4	+	$5	=	$9
2	3	+	4	=	7
3	2	+	3	=	5
4	1	+	2	=	3
5	0	+	1	=	1

FIGURE 4-5   The Optimal Amount of a Public Good

Two people—Adams and Benson—are the only members of a hypothetical economy. (a) D_1 shows Adams's willingness to pay for various quantities of a particular public good. (b) D_2 shows Benson's willingness to pay for these same quantities of this public good. (c) The collective demand for this public good is shown by D_c and is found by summing vertically Adam's and Benson's individual willingness-to-pay curves. The supply (S) of the public good is upsloping, reflecting rising marginal costs. The optimal amount of the public good is 3 units, determined by the intersection of D_c and S. At that output, marginal benefit (reflected in the collective demand curve D_c) equals marginal cost (reflected in the supply curve S).

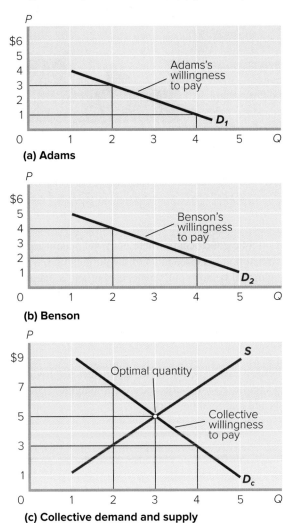

(a) Adams

(b) Benson

(c) Collective demand and supply

sum of the amounts that Adams and Benson are each willing to pay for the second unit (= $3 + $4). Likewise, the height of the collective demand curve at four units of the public good is $3 (= $1 + $2).

What does it mean in Figure 4-5a that, for example, Adams is willing to pay $3 for the second unit of the public good? It means that Adams expects to receive $3 of extra benefit or utility from that unit. And we know from the law of diminishing marginal utility that successive units of any good yield less and less added benefit. This is also true for public goods, explaining the downward slope of the willingness-to-pay curves of both Adams and Benson, and of the collective demand curve. These curves, in essence, are marginal benefit curves.

WORKED PROBLEM 4.2   Optimal Amount of a Public Good

Comparing MB and MC

We can now determine the optimal quantity of the public good. The collective demand curve D_c in Figure 4-5c measures society's marginal benefit of each unit of this particular good. The supply curve S in that figure measures

Responding to Digital Free Riding

Four teenage friends start a rock band. They practise hard, master their instruments, write their own songs, and do gig after gig for nearly nothing at local bars to gain experience and perfect their music. After nearly five years of effort, they get signed to a major record label. But the year is 2005 and record sales are collapsing due to digital piracy. The rise of Internet file sharing has turned music into a public good and sales of recorded music are shrinking as hundreds of millions of music lovers have become digital free riders.

At first, the band struggles with the new reality. If they can't make a living selling music, they might have to quit music and get regular jobs. But then they realize that while recorded music is now free for anyone who wants it to be free, live music isn't. And neither are T-shirts or memorabilia.

So the band promotes itself online and allows free downloads to help propel its popularity. Then it charges steep prices at live concerts and makes sure that its T-shirts and memorabilia also generate substantial revenues. By doing so, the band adjusts to the new reality in which music has become a public good but live concerts and T-shirts have not. They charge for the items that are still private goods.

© Robert Kohlhuber/Getty Images RF

society's marginal cost of each unit. The optimal quantity of this public good occurs where marginal benefit equals marginal cost, or where the two curves intersect. In Figure 4-5c that point is three units of the public good, where the collective willingness to pay for the last (third) unit—the marginal benefit—just matches that unit's marginal cost ($5 = $5). As we saw in Chapter 1, equating marginal benefit and marginal cost efficiently allocates society's scarce resources.

Cost–Benefit Analysis

The above example suggests a practical means, called **cost–benefit analysis**, for deciding whether to provide a particular public good and how much of it to provide. Like our example, cost–benefit analysis (or marginal benefit–marginal cost analysis) involves a comparison of marginal costs and marginal benefits.

CONCEPT

Suppose the federal government is contemplating a highway construction plan. Because the economy's resources are limited, any decision to use more resources in the public sector will mean fewer resources for the private sector. There will be both a cost and a benefit. The cost is the loss of satisfaction resulting from the accompanying decline in the production of private goods; the benefit is the extra satisfaction resulting from the output of more public goods. Should the needed resources be shifted from the private to the public sector? The answer is yes if the benefit from the extra public goods exceeds the cost that results from having fewer private goods. The answer is no if the cost of the forgone private goods is greater than the benefit associated with the extra public goods.

Cost–benefit analysis, however, can indicate more than whether a public program is worth doing. It can also help the government decide on the *extent* to which a project should be pursued. Real economic questions cannot usually be answered simply yes or no; rather, they involve such questions as "How much?" or "How little?"

ILLUSTRATION

Roads and highways can be run privately, as excludability is possible by using toll gates. However, the federal highway system is almost entirely nonexclusive, because anyone with a car can get on and off most federal highways without restriction anytime they want. Federal highways therefore satisfy one characteristic of a public good, nonexcludability. The other characteristic, nonrivalry, is also satisfied by the fact that unless a highway is already extremely crowded, one person's driving on the highway does not preclude another's. Thus, the federal highway

TABLE 4-4	Cost–Benefit Analysis for a National Highway Construction Project (billions of dollars)				
(1) Plan	(2) Total cost of project	(3) Marginal cost	(4) Total benefit	(5) Marginal benefit	(6) Net benefit (4) – (2)
No new construction	$ 0	$ 4	$ 0	$ 5	$0
A: Widen existing highways	4	6	5	8	1
B: Two–lane highways	10	**8**	13	10	3
C: Four–lane highways	**18**	10	**23**	**10**	**5**
D: Six–lane highways	28		26		–2

system is effectively a public good. This leads us to ask: Should the federal government expand the national highway system? If so, what would be the proper size or scope for the overall project?

Table 4-4 lists a series of increasingly costly highway projects: widening existing two-lane highways, building new two-lane highways, building new four-lane highways, and building new six-lane highways. The extent to which government should undertake highway construction depends on the costs and benefits. The costs are largely the costs of constructing and maintaining the highways; the benefit is an improved flow of people and goods throughout the country.[2]

The table shows that total benefit (column 4) exceeds total cost (column 2) for plans A, B, and C, indicating that some highway construction is economically justifiable. We see this directly in column 6, where total costs (column 2) are subtracted from total annual benefits (column 4). Net benefits are positive for plans A, B, and C. Plan D is not justifiable because net benefits are negative.

But the question of optimal size or scope for this project remains. Comparing the marginal cost (the change in total cost) and the marginal benefit (the change in total benefit) relating to each plan determines the answer. The guideline is well known to you from previous discussions: Increase an activity, project, or output as long as the marginal benefit (column 5) exceeds the marginal cost (column 3). Stop the activity at, or as close as possible to, the point at which the marginal benefit equals the marginal cost. Do not undertake a project for which marginal cost exceeds marginal benefit.

In this case, plan C (building new four-lane highways) is the best plan. For plans A and B, the marginal benefits exceed the marginal costs. Plan D's marginal cost ($10 billion) exceeds the marginal benefit ($3 billion) and therefore cannot be justified; it overallocates resources to the project. Plan C is closest to the optimum because its marginal benefit ($10 billion) still exceeds marginal cost ($8 billion) but approaches the MB = MC (or MC = MB) ideal.

This **marginal cost = marginal benefit rule** actually tells us which plan provides society with the maximum net benefit. You can confirm directly in column 6 that the maximum net benefit (= $5 billion) is associated with plan C.

Cost–benefit analysis shatters the myth that "economy in government" and "reduced government spending" are synonymous. "Economy" is concerned with using scarce resources efficiently. If the costs of a proposed government program exceed its benefits, the proposed public program should not be undertaken; but if the benefits exceed the costs, it would be uneconomical or wasteful not to spend on that government program. Economy in government does not mean minimization of public spending; it means allocating resources between the private and public sectors and among public goods to achieve maximum net benefit.

QUASI-PUBLIC GOODS

The government provides many goods that fit the economist's definition of a public good. However, it also provides other goods and services that could be produced and delivered in such a way that exclusion would be possible. Such

---

[2] Because the costs of public goods typically are immediate while the benefits often accrue over longer time periods, economists convert both costs and benefits to present values for comparison. Using present value properly accounts for the time value of money.

goods, called **quasi-public goods**, include education, streets and highways, police and fire protection, libraries and museums, preventive medicine, and sewage disposal. They could all be priced and provided by private firms through the market system. But, as we noted earlier, because they all have substantial positive externalities, they would be underproduced by the market system. Therefore, government often provides them to avoid the underallocation of resources that would otherwise occur.

THE REALLOCATION PROCESS

How are resources reallocated from the production of private goods to the production of public and quasi-public goods? If the resources of the economy are fully employed, government must free up resources from the production of private goods and make them available for producing public and quasi-public goods. It does so by reducing private demand for them. And it does that by levying taxes on households and businesses, taking some of their income out of the circular flow. With lower incomes and hence less purchasing power, households and businesses must curtail their consumption and investment spending. As a result, the private demand for goods and services declines, as does the private demand for resources. So by diverting purchasing power from private spenders to government, taxes remove resources from private use.

Government then spends the tax proceeds to provide public and quasi-public goods and services. Taxation releases resources from the production of private consumer goods (food, clothing, television sets) and private investment goods (Wi-Fi networks, boxcars, warehouses). Government shifts those resources to the production of public and quasi-public goods (post offices, submarines, parks), changing the composition of the economy's total output.

QUICK REVIEW 4.2

- Public goods are characterized by nonrivalry and nonexcludability.

- The demand (marginal benefit) curve for a public good is found by vertically adding the prices all the members of society are willing to pay for the last unit of output at various output levels.

- The socially optimal amount of a public good is the amount at which the marginal cost and marginal benefit of the good are equal.

- Cost–benefit analysis is the method of evaluating alternative projects by comparing the marginal cost and marginal benefit and applying the MC = MB rule.

- The government uses taxes to allocate resources from the production of private goods to the production of public and quasi-public goods.

4.4 Externalities

LO4.4   Explain how positive and negative externalities cause underallocations and overallocations of resources.

In addition to providing public goods, governments can also improve the allocation of resources in the economy by correcting for market failures caused by externalities. An **externality** occurs when some of the costs or the benefits of a good or service are passed on to or spill over to someone other than the immediate buyer or seller. Such spillovers are called externalities because they are benefits or costs that accrue to some third party that is external to the market transaction.

There are both positive and negative externalities. An example of a spillover cost or a *negative externality* is the cost of breathing polluted air; an example of a spillover benefit or a *positive externality* is the benefit of having everyone else inoculated against some communicable disease. When there are negative externalities, there is an overproduction of the product and an overallocation of resources to this product. Conversely, positive externalities result in underproduction of the product and an underallocation of resources. We can demonstrate both graphically.

Negative Externalities

Negative externalities cause supply-side market failures. These failures happen because producers do not take into account the costs that their negative externalities impose on others. This failure to account for all production costs causes firms' supply curves to shift to the right of (or below) where they would be if firms properly accounted for all costs. Consider the costs of breathing polluted air that are imposed on third parties living downwind of smoke-spewing factories. Because polluting firms do not take account of such costs, they oversupply the products they make, producing units for which total costs (including those that fall on third parties) exceed total benefits. The same is true when airlines fail to account for the costs that noisy jet engines impose on people living near airports and when biodiesel factories that convert dead animal parts into fuel release foul-smelling gases that disgust those living nearby.

An example of a negative externality is the cost of breathing polluted air.

© Glow Images

Figure 4-6a illustrates how negative externalities affect the allocation of resources. When producers shift some of their costs onto the community as externality costs, producers' marginal costs are lower than they would be if they had to pay for these costs. So their supply curves do not include or capture all the costs associated with the production of their goods. A polluting producer's supply curve, such as S in Figure 4-6a, therefore understates the total cost of production. The firm's supply curve lies to the right of the full-cost supply curve S_t, which would include the spillover cost. Through polluting and thus transferring cost to others in society, the firm enjoys lower production costs and has the supply curve S.

The outcome is shown in Figure 4-6a, where equilibrium output Q_e is larger than the optimal output Q_o. This means that resources are overallocated to the production of this commodity; too many units of it are produced. In fact, there is a net loss to society for every unit from Q_o to Q_e because, for those units, the supply curve that accounts for all costs, S_t, lies above the demand curve. Therefore, MC exceeds MB for those units. The resources that went into producing those units should have been used elsewhere in the economy to produce other things.

In terms of our previous analysis, the negative externality results in an efficiency loss represented by triangle *abc*.

FIGURE 4-6   Negative Externalities and Positive Externalities

(a) With negative externalities borne by society, the producers' supply curve S is to the right of (below) the full-cost curve S_t. Consequently, the equilibrium output Q_e is greater than the optimal output Q_o and the efficiency loss is *abc*. (b) When positive externalities accrue to society, the market demand curve D is to the left of (below) the full-benefit demand curve D_t. As a result, the equilibrium output Q_e is less than the optimal output Q_o and the efficiency loss is *xyz*.

(a) Negative externalities

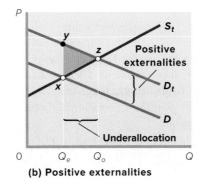

(b) Positive externalities

Positive Externalities

Positive externalities cause demand-side market failures. These failures happen because market demand curves in such cases fail to include the willingness to pay of the third parties who receive the external benefits caused by the positive externality. This failure to account for all benefits shifts market demand curves to the left of (or below) where they would be if they included all benefits and the willingness to pay of both the third parties and the primary beneficiaries. Because demand curves fail to take into account all benefits when there are positive externalities, markets in such cases fail to produce all units for which benefits (including those that are received by third parties) exceed costs. As a result, products featuring positive externalities are underproduced.

Vaccinations are a good example of how positive externalities reduce demand and shift demand curves down and to the left. When John gets vaccinated against a disease, he benefits not only himself (because he can no longer contract the disease) but also everyone else around him (because they know that in the future he will never be able to infect them). These other people would presumably be willing to pay some positive amount of money for the benefits they receive when John is vaccinated. But because his vaccination is a public good, there is no way to make them pay.

To see why his vaccination is a public good, note that the vaccination benefits that John provides to others feature nonrivalry and nonexcludability. There is nonrivalry because the protection his vaccination provides to one person does not lessen the protection that it provides to other people. There is nonexcludability because once he is vaccinated, there is no way to exclude anyone in particular from benefiting from his vaccination. Thus, the market demand for vaccinations will only include John's personal willingness to pay for the benefits that he personally receives from the vaccination. The market demand will fail to include the benefits that others receive. As a result, demand will be too low and vaccinations will be underproduced.

Figure 4-6b shows the impact of positive externalities on resource allocation. When external benefits occur, the market demand curve D lies to the left of the full-benefits demand curve, D_t. That is, D does not include the external benefits of the product, whereas D_t does. The outcome is that the equilibrium output, Q_e, is less than the optimal output, Q_o. The market fails to produce enough vaccinations and resources are underallocated to this product. The underproduction implies that society is missing out on a significant amount of potential net benefits. For every unit from Q_e to Q_o, the demand curve that accounts for all benefits, D_t, lies above the supply curve that accounts for all costs—including the opportunity cost of producing other items with the resources that would be needed to produce these units. Therefore, MB exceeds MC for each of these units and we know that society should redeploy some of its resources away from the production of other things in order to produce these units that generate net benefits.

In terms of our previous analysis, the positive externality results in an efficiency loss represented by triangle xyz.

Government Intervention

Government intervention may be called upon to achieve economic efficiency when externalities affect large numbers of people or when community interests are at stake. Government can use direct controls and taxes to counter negative externalities; it may provide subsidies or public goods to deal with positive externalities.

DIRECT CONTROLS

The direct way to reduce negative externalities from a certain activity is to pass legislation limiting that activity. Such direct controls force the offending firms to incur the actual costs of the offending activity. To date, this approach has dominated public policy in Canada. Historically, direct controls in the form of uniform emissions standards—limits on allowable pollution—have been a significant factor in Canadian air pollution policy. Clean-air legislation forces factories, cars, and businesses to install "maximum achievable control technology" to reduce emissions. Clean-water legislation limits the amount of heavy metals, detergents, and other pollutants firms can discharge into rivers and bays. Toxic-waste laws mandate special procedures and dump sites for disposing of contaminated soil and solvents. Violating these laws means fines and, in some cases, imprisonment.

Direct controls raise the marginal cost of production because the firms must operate and maintain pollution-control equipment. The supply curve S in Figure 4-7b, which does not reflect the external costs, shifts leftward (upward) to the full-cost supply curve, S_t. Product price increases, equilibrium output falls from Q_e to Q_o, and the

CONSIDER THIS

The Fable of the Bees

Economist Ronald Coase received the Nobel Prize for his **Coase theorem**, which pointed out that, under the right conditions, private individuals can often negotiate their own mutually agreeable solutions to externality problems through *individual bargaining* without the need for government interventions like pollution taxes.

© Digital Vision/Getty Images

This is a very important insight, because it means that we shouldn't automatically call for government intervention every time we see a potential externality problem. Consider the positive externalities that bees provide by pollinating farmers' crops. Should we assume that beekeeping will be underprovided unless the government intervenes with, for instance, subsidies to encourage more hives and hence more pollination?

As it turns out, no. Research has shown that farmers and beekeepers long ago used individual bargaining to

develop customs and payment systems that avoid free riding by farmers and that encourage beekeepers to keep the optimal number of hives. Free riding is avoided by the custom that all farmers in an area simultaneously hire beekeepers to provide bees to pollinate their crops. And farmers always pay the beekeepers for their pollination services, because if they didn't, no beekeeper would ever work with them in the future—a situation that would lead to massively reduced crop yields due to a lack of pollination.

The Fable of the Bees is a good reminder that it is a fallacy to assume that the government must always get involved to remedy externalities. In many cases, the private sector can solve both positive and negative externality problems on its own.

initial overallocation of resources shown in Figure 4-7a is corrected. Observe that the efficiency loss shown by triangle *abc* in Figure 4-7a disappears after the overallocation is corrected in Figure 4-7b.

PIGOVIAN TAXES

A second policy approach to negative externalities is for government to levy taxes or charges specifically on the related good. These targeted tax assessments are often referred to as **Pigovian taxes** in honour of Arthur Pigou, the

FIGURE 4-7   Correcting for Negative Externalities

(a) Negative externalities result in an overallocation of resources. (b) Government can correct this overallocation in two ways: (1) using direct controls, which would shift the supply curve from S to S_t and reduce output from Q_e to Q_o, or (2) imposing a specific tax, T, that would also shift the supply curve from S to S_t, eliminating the overallocation of resources and thus the efficiency loss.

(a) Negative externalities

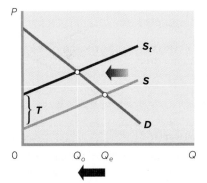

(b) Correcting the overallocation of resources via direct controls or via a tax

first economist to study externalities. *Example:* The government has put a manufacturing tax on CFCs, which deplete the stratospheric ozone layer protecting Earth from excessive solar ultraviolet radiation. Facing such a tax, manufacturers must decide whether to pay the tax or expend additional funds to purchase or develop substitute products. In either case, the tax raises the marginal cost of producing CFCs, shifting the private supply curve for this product leftward.

In Figure 4-7b, a tax equal to T per unit increases the firm's marginal cost, shifting the supply curve from S to S_t. The equilibrium price rises and the equilibrium output declines from Q_e to the economically efficient level Q_o. The tax eliminates the initial overallocation of resources and therefore the efficiency loss.

SUBSIDIES AND GOVERNMENT PROVISION

Where positive externalities are large and diffuse, as in our earlier example of vaccinations, government has three options for correcting the underallocation of resources:

1. **Subsidies to Buyers** Figure 4-8a shows the supply–demand situation for positive externalities. Government could correct the underallocation of resources—for example, to inoculations—by subsidizing consumers of the product; it could give each new mother a discount coupon to be used to obtain a series of vaccinations for her child. The coupon would reduce the price to the mother by, say, 50 percent. As shown in Figure 4-8b, this program would shift the demand curve for inoculations from too-low D to the appropriate D_t. The number of vaccinations would rise from Q_e to the optimal Q_o, eliminating the underallocation of resources and efficiency loss shown in Figure 4-8a.

2. **Subsidies to Producers** A subsidy to producers is a specific tax in reverse. Taxes impose an extra cost on producers, while subsidies reduce producers' costs. As shown in Figure 4-8c, a subsidy of U per inoculation to physicians and medical clinics would reduce their marginal costs and shift their supply curve rightward from S_t to S'_t. The output of inoculations would increase from Q_e to the optimal level Q_o, correcting the underallocation of resources and efficiency loss shown in (a).

3. **Government Provision** Finally, where positive externalities are large, the government may decide to provide the product for free to everyone. The Canadian government largely eradicated the crippling disease polio by administering free vaccines to all children. India ended smallpox by paying people in rural areas to come to public clinics to have their children vaccinated.

Table 4-5 lists several methods for correcting externalities, including those we have discussed thus far.

FIGURE 4-8   Correcting for Positive Externalities

(a) Positive externalities result in an underallocation of resources. (b) This underallocation can be corrected by a subsidy to consumers, which shifts market demand from D to D_t and increases output from Q_e to Q_o. (c) Alternatively, the underallocation can be eliminated by providing producers with a subsidy of U, which shifts their supply curve from S_t to S'_t, increasing output from Q_e to Q_o and eliminating the underallocation and thus the efficiency loss shown in (a).

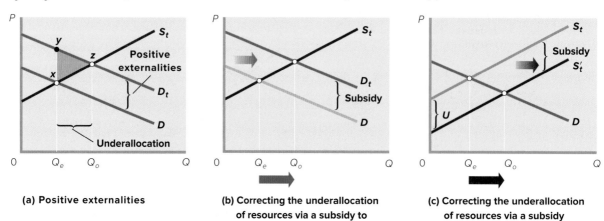

(a) Positive externalities

(b) Correcting the underallocation of resources via a subsidy to consumers

(c) Correcting the underallocation of resources via a subsidy to producers

TABLE 4-5	Methods for Dealing with Externalities	
Problem	**Resource allocation outcome**	**Ways to correct**
Negative externalities (spillover costs)	Overproduction of output and therefore overallocation of resources	1. Private bargaining 2. Liability rules and lawsuits 3. Tax on producers 4. Direct controls 5. Market for externality rights
Positive externalities (spillover benefits)	Underproduction of output and therefore underallocation of resources	1. Private bargaining 2. Subsidy to consumers 3. Subsidy to producers 4. Government provision

4.5 Society's Optimal Amount of Externality Reduction

LO4.5 Show why we normally won't want to pay what it would cost to eliminate every last bit of a negative externality such as air pollution.

Negative externalities such as pollution reduce the utility of those affected. These spillovers are not economic goods but economic "bads." If something is bad, shouldn't society eliminate it? Why should society allow firms or municipalities to discharge *any* impure waste into public waterways or to emit *any* pollution into the air?

 CHOOSING A LITTLE MORE OR LESS

Economists answer these questions by pointing out that reducing pollution and negative externalities is not free. There are costs as well as benefits to reducing pollution. As a result, the correct question to ask when it comes to cleaning up negative externalities is not "Do we pollute a lot or pollute zero?"—an all-or-nothing question that ignores marginal costs and marginal benefits. Instead, the correct question is "What is the optimal amount to clean up—the amount that equalizes the marginal cost of cleaning up with the marginal benefit of a cleaner environment?"

If we ask that question, we see that reducing a negative externality has a price. Society must decide how much of a reduction it wants to buy. High costs may mean that totally eliminating pollution entirely might not be desirable, even if it is technologically feasible. Because of the law of diminishing returns, cleaning up the last 10 percent of pollutants from an industrial smokestack is normally far more costly than cleaning up the prior 10 percent.

The marginal cost (MC) to the firm and hence to society—the opportunity cost of the extra resources used—rises as pollution is reduced further. At some point MC may rise so high that it exceeds society's marginal benefit (MB) of further pollution abatement (reduction). Additional actions to reduce pollution will therefore lower society's well-being; total cost will rise more than total benefit, as the more pollution reduction society accomplishes, the lower the utility (and benefit) of the next unit of pollution reduction.

MC, MB, and Equilibrium Quantity

Figure 4-9 shows both the rising marginal-cost curve, MC, for pollution reduction and the downsloping marginal-benefit curve, MB, for pollution reduction. MB slopes downward because of the law of diminishing marginal utility: The more pollution reduction society accomplishes, the lower the utility (and benefit) of the next unit of pollution reduction.

The **optimal reduction of an externality** occurs when society's marginal cost and marginal benefit of reducing that externality are equal (MC = MB). In Figure 4-9 this optimal amount of pollution abatement is Q_1 units. When MB exceeds MC, additional abatement moves society toward economic efficiency; the added benefit of cleaner air

FIGURE 4-9   Society's Optimal Amount of Pollution Abatement

The optimal amount of externality reduction—in this case, pollution abatement—occurs at Q_1, where society's marginal cost (MC) and marginal benefit (MB) of reducing the spillover are equal.

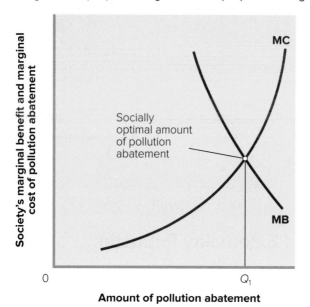

Amount of pollution abatement

or water exceeds the benefit of any alternative use of the required resources. When MC exceeds MB, additional abatement reduces economic efficiency; there would be greater benefits from using resources in some other way than to further reduce pollution.

In reality, it is difficult to measure the marginal costs and benefits of pollution control. Nevertheless, Figure 4-9 demonstrates that some pollution may be economically efficient. This is so not because pollution is desirable but because, beyond some level of control, further abatement may reduce society's net well-being. As an example, it would cost the government billions of dollars to clean up every last piece of litter in Canada. Thus, it would be better to tolerate some trash blowing around if the money saved by picking up less trash would yield larger net benefits when spent on other things.

Shifts in Locations of the Curves

The locations of the marginal-cost and marginal-benefit curves in Figure 4-9 are not forever fixed. They can, and probably do, shift over time. For example, suppose that the technology of pollution-control equipment improved noticeably. We would expect the cost of pollution abatement to fall, society's MC curve to shift rightward and the optimal level of abatement to rise. Or suppose that society were to decide that it wanted cleaner air and water because of new information about the adverse health effects of pollution. The MB curve in Figure 4-9 would shift rightward, and the optimal level of pollution control would increase beyond Q_1. Test your understanding of these statements by drawing the new MC and MB curves in Figure 4-9.

Government's Role in the Economy

Market failures can be used to justify government interventions in the economy. The inability of private-sector firms to break even when attempting to provide public goods and the overproduction and underproduction problems caused by positive and negative externalities mean that government can have an important role to play if society's resources are to be efficiently allocated to the goods and services that people most highly desire.

Correcting for market failures is not, however, an easy task. To begin with, government officials must correctly identify the existence and the cause of any given market failure. That, by itself, may be difficult, time-consuming, and costly. But even if a market failure is correctly identified and diagnosed, government may still fail to take appropriate corrective action due to the context of politics. To serve the public, politicians need to get elected. To stay elected, officials (prime ministers, members of parliament, mayors, council members, or school board members) need to satisfy their particular constituencies. At best, the political realities complicate government's role in the economy; at worst, they produce undesirable economic outcomes.

In the political context, overregulation can occur in some cases, underregulation in others. Some public goods and quasi-public goods can be produced not because their benefits exceed their costs but because their benefits accrue to firms located in regions served by powerful elected officials. Inefficiency can easily creep into government activities because of the lack of a profit incentive to hold down costs. Policies to correct negative externalities can be politically blocked by the very parties that are producing the spillovers. In short, the economic role of government, although critical to a well-functioning economy, is not always perfectly carried out.

Economists use the term *government failure* to describe economically inefficient outcomes caused by shortcomings in the public sector.

QUICK REVIEW 4.3

- Policies for coping with the overallocation of resources caused by negative externalities are (1) private bargaining, (2) liability rules and lawsuits, (3) direct controls, (4) specific taxes, and (5) markets for externality rights.

- Policies for correcting the underallocation of resources associated with positive externalities are (1) private bargaining, (2) subsidies to producers, (3) subsidies to consumers, and (4) government provision.

- The optimal amount of negative-externality reduction occurs where society's marginal cost and marginal benefit of reducing the externality are equal.

- Political pressures often lead governments to respond inefficiently when attempting to correct for market failures.

The LAST WORD

Carbon Dioxide Emissions, Cap and Trade, and Carbon Taxes

Cap-and-trade systems and carbon taxes are two approaches to reducing carbon dioxide (CO_2) emissions.

Externality problems are property rights problems. Consider a trash dump. Because the owner of the landfill has full rights to his land, people wishing to dump their trash into the landfill have to pay him. This payment implies that there is no externality: He happily accepts their trash in exchange for a dumping fee. By contrast, because nobody owns the atmosphere, all air pollution is an externality since there is no way for those doing the polluting to work out a payment to compensate those affected by the pollution, or for those threatened with pollution to simply refuse to be polluted upon.

Conventional property rights therefore cannot fix the externalities associated with air pollution. But that does not mean property rights can't help fight pollution. The trick to making them work is to assign property rights not to the atmosphere itself, but to *polluting* the atmosphere. This is done in cap-and-trade systems, under which the government sets an annual limit, or cap, on the number of tonnes of a pollutant that firms can emit into the atmosphere.

Consider carbon dioxide, or CO_2—a colourless, odourless gas that many scientists consider to be a contributing cause of climate change, specifically global warming. To reduce CO_2 emissions, the Canadian government might set a cap of 5 billion tonnes of CO_2 emissions per year (which would be about 10 percent below 2009 emissions levels). The government then prints out emissions permits that add up to the limit set in the cap and distributes them to polluting firms. Once they are distributed, the only way a firm can legally emit a tonne of CO_2 is if it owns a permit to do so.

Under this policy, the government can obviously adjust the total amount of air pollution by adjusting the cap. This by itself improves efficiency, because the cap imposes scarcity. Each firm has only a limited number of permits, so it has a strong incentive to maximize the net benefits it produces from every tonne of pollution it emits. But cap and trade leads to even greater improvements in efficiency, because firms are free to "trade"—sell them to each other.

For instance, suppose Smokestack Toys owns permits for 100 tonnes of CO_2 emissions and could use them to produce toy cars that would generate profits of $100,000. There is a power plant, however, that could make up to $1 million of profits by using those 100 tonnes of emissions permits to generate electricity. Because firms can trade their permits, Smokestack Toys will sell its permits to the power plant for more than the $100,000 in profits that it could make if it kept them and produced toy cars. And the power plant will gladly pay more than $100,000 for those permits, because it can turn around and use them to make up to $1 million of profits by using them to generate electricity.

Society will benefit hugely from this transaction: While 100 tonnes of CO_2 will be emitted no matter which firm uses the permits, society will receive much greater net benefits when they are used by the power plant, as indicated by the fact that the power plant can produce much larger profits than the toy company when using the same amount of this scarce resource.

Several words of caution are in order, however. Cap-and-trade systems have proven very difficult to implement in cases where it is difficult for regulators to effectively check whether firms are obeying the system. This has been a major problem with the European Union's system for CO_2 emissions. Because nearly every type of industrial activity releases CO_2 into the atmosphere, enforcement involves monitoring many thousands of factories of all sizes. That is very difficult and cheating has resulted. In addition, politically connected industries got politicians to give them exemptions or free permits.

By contrast, a cap-and-trade system on sulfur dioxide emissions from coal-burning public utilities has worked very well in Canada since the 1980s. But in that case, there were only a few polluting utilities and they were already being monitored for emissions. So there was very little ability to cheat. In addition, all of the firms were treated equally, with no firms allowed exemptions or free permits.

Due to the mixed results, many economists have concluded that cap and trade would not be the best way to curb CO_2 emissions. They believe that there are simply too many sources of pollution to make monitoring either possible or cost-effective. And it seems likely that politically connected industries will be granted exemptions. So, instead, many economists favour a carbon tax, which would involve taxing each tonne of coal, each litre of gasoline, and each barrel of oil on the basis of how much carbon it contains (and thus how much CO_2 will eventually be released into the atmosphere when it is used). By raising the cost of polluting, the tax would reduce consumption and lessen the externalities associated with CO_2 emissions. It would also be nearly impossible to evade so that we would not have to worry about cheating.

Question

Distinguish between a carbon tax and a cap-and-trade strategy for reducing carbon dioxide and other so-called "greenhouse gases" (believed by many scientists to be causing global warming). Which of the two strategies do you think would have the most political support in an election in your home province? Explain your thinking.

Chapter Summary

LO4.1 Differentiate between demand-side market failures and supply-side market failures.

- A market failure happens in a particular market when the market produces an equilibrium level of output that either overallocates or underallocates resources to the product being traded in the market.

- In competitive markets that feature many buyers and many sellers, market failures can be divided into two types. Demand-side market failures occur when demand curves do not reflect consumers' full willingness to pay. Supply-side market failures occur when supply curves do not reflect all production costs, including those that may be borne by third parties.

LO4.2 Explain the origin of both consumer surplus and producer surplus, and explain how properly functioning markets maximize their sum, economic surplus, while optimally allocating resources.

- Consumer surplus is the difference between the maximum price that a consumer is willing to pay for a product and the lower price actually paid. Producer surplus is the difference between the minimum price that a producer is willing to accept for a product and the higher price actually received. Collectively, consumer surplus is represented by the triangle under the demand curve and above the actual price, whereas producer surplus is shown by the triangle above the supply curve and below the actual price.

- Graphically, the combined amount of producer and consumer surplus is represented by the triangle to the left of the intersection of the supply and demand curves that is below the demand curve and above the supply curve. At the equilibrium price and quantity in competitive markets, marginal benefit equals marginal cost, maximum willingness to pay equals minimum acceptable price, and the combined amount of consumer surplus and producer surplus is maximized.

- Output levels less than or greater than the equilibrium output create efficiency losses—reductions in the combined amount of consumer surplus and producer surplus.

Underproduction creates efficiency losses because output is not being produced for which maximum willingness to pay exceeds minimum acceptable price. Overproduction creates efficiency losses because output is being produced for which minimum acceptable price exceeds maximum willingness to pay.

LO4.3 Describe free riding and public goods, and illustrate why private firms cannot normally produce public goods.

- Public goods are distinguished from private goods. Private goods are characterized by rivalry (in consumption) and excludability. One person's purchase and consumption of a private good precludes others from also buying and consuming it. Producers can exclude nonpayers (free riders) from receiving the benefits. In contrast, public goods are characterized by nonrivalry (in consumption) and nonexcludability. Public goods are not profitable to private firms because nonpayers (free riders) can obtain and consume those goods. Only government is willing to provide desirable public goods, financing them through taxation.

- The collective demand schedule for a particular public good is found by summing the prices each individual is willing to pay for an additional unit. Graphically, that demand curve is therefore found by summing vertically the individual demand curves for that good. The resulting total demand curve indicates the collective willingness to pay for (or marginal benefit of) the last unit of any given amount of the public good.

- The optimal quantity of a public good occurs where the society's willingness to pay for the last unit—the marginal benefit of the good—equals the marginal cost of the good.

LO4.4 Explain how positive and negative externalities cause underallocations and overallocations of resources.

- Externalities or spillovers are costs or benefits that accrue to someone other than the immediate buyer or seller. Such costs or benefits are not captured in market demand or supply curves and therefore cause the output of certain goods to vary from society's optimal output. Negative externalities (or spillover costs or external costs) result in an overallocation of resources to a particular product. Positive externalities (or spillover benefits or external benefits) are accompanied by an underallocation of resources to a particular product.

- Direct controls and Pigovian taxes can improve resource allocation in situations where negative externalities affect many people and community resources. Both direct controls (such as smokestack emission standards) and Pigovian taxes (such as taxes on firms producing toxic chemicals) increase production costs and hence product price. As product price rises, the externality and overallocation of resources are reduced, because less of the output is produced.

- Government can correct the underallocation of resources that results from positive externalities in a particular market either by subsidizing consumers (which increases market demand) or subsidizing producers (which increases market supply). Such subsidies increase the equilibrium output, reducing or eliminating the positive externality and consequent underallocation of resources.

- The Coase theorem suggests that under the right circumstances private bargaining can solve externality problems. Thus, government intervention is not always needed to deal with externality problems.

LO4.5 Show why we normally won't want to pay what it would cost to eliminate every last bit of a negative externality such as air pollution.

- The socially optimal amount of externality abatement occurs where society's marginal cost and marginal benefit of reducing the externality are equal. This optimal amount of pollution abatement is likely to be less than a 100 percent reduction. Changes in technology or changes in society's attitudes toward pollution can affect the optimal amount of pollution abatement.

- Market failures present government with opportunities to improve the allocation of society's resources and thereby enhance society's total well-being. But even when government correctly identifies the existence and cause of a market failure, political pressures may make it difficult or impossible for government officials to implement a proper solution.

Terms and Concepts

market failures	nonrivalry
demand-side market failure	nonexcludability
supply-side market failure	free-rider problem
consumer surplus	cost–benefit analysis
producer surplus	marginal cost = marginal benefit rule
efficiency losses (or deadweight losses)	quasi-public goods
private goods	externality
rivalry	Coase theorem
excludability	Pigovian tax
public goods	optimal reduction of an externality

Discussion Questions

1. Explain the two causes of market failures. Given their definitions, could a market be affected by both types of market failures simultaneously? [**LO4.1**]

2. Use the ideas of consumer surplus and producer surplus to explain why economists say competitive markets are efficient. Why are below- or above-equilibrium levels of output inefficient, according to these two sets of ideas? [**LO4.2**]

3. What are the two characteristics of public goods? Explain the significance of each for public provision as opposed to private provision. What is the free-rider problem as it relates to public goods? Is Canadian border patrol a public good or a private good? Why? How about satellite TV? Explain. [**LO4.3**]

4. What divergences arise between equilibrium output and efficient output when (a) negative externalities and (b) positive externalities are present? How might government correct these divergences? Cite an example (other than the text examples) of an external cost and an external benefit. [**LO4.4**]

5. Why are spillover costs and spillover benefits also called negative and positive externalities? Show graphically how a tax can correct for a negative externality and how a subsidy to producers can correct for a positive externality. How does a subsidy to consumers differ from a subsidy to producers in correcting for a positive externality? [**LO4.4**]

6. An apple grower's orchard provides nectar to a neighbour's bees, while the beekeeper's bees help the apple grower by pollinating his apple blossoms. Use Figure 4-6b to explain why this situation of dual positive externalities might lead to an underallocation of resources to both apple growing and beekeeping. How might this underallocation get resolved via the means suggested by the Coase theorem? [**LO4.4**]

7. The Lojack car recovery system allows the police to track stolen cars. As a result, they not only recover 90 percent of Lojack-equipped stolen cars but also arrest many auto thieves and shut down many chop shops that dismantle stolen vehicles to get at their used parts. Thus, Lojack provides both private benefits and positive externalities. Should the government consider subsidizing Lojack purchases? [**LO4.4**]

8. Explain why zoning laws, which allow certain land uses only in specific locations, might be justified in dealing with a problem of negative externalities. Explain why, in areas where buildings sit close together, tax breaks to property owners for installing extra fire prevention equipment might be justified in view of positive externalities. Explain why excise taxes on beer might be justified in dealing with a problem of external costs. [**LO4.5**]

Review Questions

1. Draw a supply-and-demand graph and identify the areas of consumer surplus and producer surplus. Given the demand curve, what impact will an increase in supply have on the amount of consumer surplus shown in your diagram? Explain why. [**LO4.2**]

2. Assume that candle wax is traded in a perfectly competitive market in which the demand curve captures buyers' full willingness to pay while the supply curve reflects all production costs. For each of the following situations, indicate whether the total output should be increased, decreased, or kept the same in order to achieve allocative and productive efficiency. [**LO4.2**]

    a. Maximum willingness to pay exceeds minimum acceptable price.

    b. MC > MB.

    c. Total surplus is at a maximum.

    d. The current quantity produced exceeds the market equilibrium quantity.

3. Efficiency losses _____. [**LO4.2**]

    a. Are not possible if suppliers are willing to produce and sell a product

    b. Can only result from underproduction

    c. Can only result from overproduction

    d. None of the above

4. Draw a production possibilities curve with public goods on the vertical axis and private goods on the horizontal axis. Assuming the economy is initially operating on the curve, indicate how the production of public goods might be increased. How might the output of public goods be increased if the economy is initially operating at a point inside the curve? [**LO4.3**]

5. Use the distinction between the characteristics of private and public goods to determine whether the following should be produced through the market system or provided by government: (a) French fries, (b) airport screening, (c) court systems, (d) mail delivery, and (e) medical care. State why you answered as you did in each case. [**LO4.3**]

6. Match each of the following characteristics or scenarios with either the term *negative externality* or the term *positive externality*. [**LO4.4**]

    a. Overallocation of resources

    b. Tammy installs a very nice front garden, raising the property values of all the other houses on her block.

    c. Market demand curves are too far to the left (too low).

    d. Underallocation of resources exists.

    e. Water pollution from a factory forces neighbours to buy water purifiers.

7. Use marginal cost/marginal benefit analysis to determine if the following statement is true or false: "The optimal amount of pollution abatement for some substances, such as dirty water from storm drains, is very low; the optimal amount of abatement for other substances, such as cyanide poison, is close to 100 percent." [**LO4.5**]

Problems

1. Refer to Table 4-1. If the six people listed in the table are the only consumers in the market and the equilibrium price is $11 (not the $8 shown), how much consumer surplus will the market generate? [**LO4.2**]

2. Refer to Table 4-2. If the six people listed in the table are the only producers in the market and the equilibrium price is $6 (not the $8 shown), how much producer surplus will the market generate? [**LO4.2**]

3. Look at Tables 4-1 and 4-2 together. What is the total surplus if Bob buys a unit from Carlos? If Beata buys a unit from Courtney? If Bob buys a unit from Chad? If you match up pairs of buyers and sellers so as to maximize the total surplus of all transactions, what is the largest total surplus that can be achieved? [**LO4.2**]

4. **Advanced Analysis** Assume the following values for Figures 4-4a and 4-4b: $Q_1 = 20$ bags, $Q_2 = 15$ bags, $Q_3 = 27$ bags. The market equilibrium price is $45 per bag. The price at point a is $85 per bag. The price at point c is $5 per bag. The price at point f is $59 per bag. The price at point g is $31 per bag. Apply the formula for the area of a triangle (area $= \frac{1}{2} \times$ base $\times$ height) to answer the following questions. [**LO4.2**]

   a. What is the dollar value of the total surplus (producer surplus plus consumer surplus) when the allocatively efficient output level is being produced? How large is the dollar value of the consumer surplus at that output level?

   b. What is the dollar value of the deadweight loss when output level Q_2 is being produced? What is the total surplus when output level Q_2 is being produced?

   c. What is the dollar value of the deadweight loss when output level Q_3 is produced? What is the dollar value of the total surplus when output level Q_3 is produced?

5. On the basis of the following three individual demand schedules for a particular good, and assuming these three people are the only ones in the society, determine (a) the market demand schedule on the assumption that the good is a private good and (b) the collective demand schedule on the assumption that the good is a public good. [**LO4.3**]

P	$Q_d (D_1)$	$Q_d (D_2)$	$Q_d (D_3)$
$8	0	1	0
7	0	2	0
6	0	3	1
5	1	4	2
4	2	5	3
3	3	6	4
2	4	7	5
1	5	8	6

6. Use your demand schedule for a public good, determined in Problem 5, and the following supply schedule to ascertain the optimal quantity of this public good. [**LO4.3**]

P	Q_S
$19	10
16	8
13	6
10	4
7	2
4	1

7. Look at Tables 4-1 and 4-2, which show, respectively, the willingness to pay and willingness to accept of buyers and seller of bags of oranges. For the following questions, assume that the equilibrium price and quantity will depend on the indicated changes in supply and demand. Assume that the only market participants are those listed by name in the two tables. [**LO4.4**]

   a. What is the equilibrium price and quantity for the data displayed in the two tables?

   b. What if, instead of bags of oranges, the data in the two tables dealt with a public good like fireworks displays. If all the buyers free ride, what will be the quantity supplied by private sellers?

   c. Assume that we are back to talking about bags of oranges (a private good), but that the government has decided that tossed orange peels impose a negative externality on the public that must be rectified by imposing a $2-per-bag tax on sellers. What is the new equilibrium price and quantity? If the new equilibrium quantity is the optimal quantity, by how many bags were oranges being overproduced before?

A4.1 Information Failures

LOA4.1 Describe how information failures may justify government intervention in some markets.

This chapter discussed the two most common types of market failure: public goods and externalities. But there is also another, subtler, type of market failure. This one results when either buyers or sellers have incomplete or inaccurate information and their cost of obtaining better information is prohibitive. Technically stated, this market failure is the result of **asymmetric information**—information unequally available to buyers and sellers about price, quality, or some other aspect of the good or service.

Sufficient market information is normally available to ensure that goods and services are produced and purchased efficiently. But in some cases, inadequate information makes it difficult to distinguish trustworthy from untrustworthy sellers or buyers. In these markets, society's scarce resources may not be used efficiently, implying that the government should intervene by increasing the information available to the market participants. Under rare circumstances the government may itself supply a good for which information problems have prohibited efficient production.

 THE ROLE OF GOVERNMENTS

Inadequate Buyer Information About Sellers

Inadequate information among buyers about sellers and their products can cause market failure in the form of underallocation of resources. Two examples will help you understand this point.

EXAMPLE: GASOLINE MARKET

Assume an absurd situation: Suppose there is no system of weights and measures established by law, no government inspection of gasoline pumps, and no law against false advertising. Each gas station can use whatever measure it chooses; it can define a litre of gas as it pleases. A station can advertise that its gas is 87 octane when, in fact, it is only 75. It can rig its pumps to indicate that it is providing more gas than the amount being delivered.

Obviously, the consumer's cost of obtaining reliable information under such chaotic conditions is exceptionally high, if not prohibitive. Customers or their representatives would have to buy samples of gas from various gas stations, have them tested for octane level, and test the accuracy of calibrations at the pump. And these activities would have to be repeated regularly, since a station owner could alter the product quality and the accuracy of the pump at will.

Because of the high cost of obtaining information about the seller, many consumers would opt out of this chaotic market. One tankful of a 50 percent mixture of gasoline and water would be enough to discourage most motorists from further driving. More realistically, the conditions in this market would encourage consumers to vote for political candidates who promise to provide a government solution. The oil companies and honest gasoline stations would most likely welcome government intervention. They would realize that accurate information, by enabling this market to work, would expand their total sales and profits.

The government has in fact intervened in the market for gasoline and other markets with similar potential information difficulties. It has established a system of weights and measures, employed inspectors to check the accuracy of gasoline pumps, and passed laws against fraudulent claims and misleading advertising. Clearly, these government activities have produced net benefits for society.

EXAMPLE: LICENSING OF SURGEONS

Suppose anyone could hang out a shingle and claim to be a surgeon, much as anyone can become a house painter. The market would eventually sort out the true surgeons from those who were learning by doing or were fly-by-night operators. As people died from unsuccessful surgery, lawsuits for malpractice eventually would identify and eliminate most of the medical impostors. People needing surgery for themselves or their loved ones could obtain information from newspaper reports or from people who had undergone similar operations. But this process of obtaining information for those needing surgery would take considerable time and would impose unacceptably high human and economic costs. There is a fundamental difference between getting an amateurish paint job on one's house and being on the receiving end of heart surgery by a bogus physician! The marginal cost of obtaining information about surgeons would be excessively high. The risk of proceeding without good information would result in much less surgery than is desirable—an underallocation of resources to surgery.

The government has remedied this market failure through a system of qualifying tests and licensing. The licensing provides consumers with inexpensive information about a service they buy infrequently. The government has taken a similar role in several other areas of the economy. For example, it approves new medicines, regulates the securities industry, and requires warnings on containers of potentially hazardous substances. It also requires warning labels on cigarette packages and disseminates information about communicable diseases. And it issues warnings about unsafe toys and inspects restaurants for health-related violations.

Inadequate Seller Information About Buyers

Just as inadequate information about sellers can keep markets from achieving economic efficiency, so can inadequate information about buyers. The buyers may be consumers who buy products, or firms that buy resources.

MORAL HAZARD PROBLEM

Private markets may underallocate resources to a particular good or service for which there is a severe **moral hazard problem**. The moral hazard problem is the tendency of one party to a contract to alter her or his behaviour after the contract is signed in ways that could be costly to the other party.

Suppose a firm offers an insurance policy that pays a set amount of money per month to couples that divorce. The attractiveness of such insurance is that it would pool the economic risk of divorce among thousands of people and, in particular, would protect spouses and children from the economic hardship that divorce often brings. Unfortunately, the moral hazard problem reduces the likelihood that insurance companies can profitably provide this type of insurance. After taking out such insurance, married couples would have less incentive to get along and to iron out marital difficulties. Some couples might be motivated to obtain a divorce, collect the insurance, and then continue to live together. Such insurance could even promote more divorces, the very outcome it is intended to protect against. The moral hazard problem would force the insurer to charge such high premiums for this insurance that few policies would be bought. If the insurer could identify in advance those people most prone to altering their behaviour, the firm could exclude them from buying it. But the firm's marginal cost of getting such information is too high compared with the marginal benefit. Thus, this market would fail. Although divorce insurance is not available in the marketplace, society recognizes the benefits of insuring against the hardships of divorce. It has corrected for this underallocation of hardship insurance through child-support laws that dictate payments to the spouse who retains the children, when the economic circumstances warrant such payments. Alimony laws also play a role.

The moral hazard problem is also illustrated in the following statements:

- Drivers may be less cautious because they have car insurance.
- Medical malpractice insurance may increase the amount of malpractice.
- Guaranteed contracts for professional athletes may reduce the quality of their performance.
- Employment compensation insurance may lead some workers to shirk.
- Government insurance on bank deposits may encourage banks to make risky loans.

ADVERSE SELECTION PROBLEM

Another problem resulting from inadequate information about buyers is the **adverse selection problem**. This problem arises when information known by the first party to a contract is not known by the second and, as a result, the second party incurs major costs. Unlike the moral hazard problem, which arises after a person signs a contract, the adverse selection problem arises at the time a person signs a contract.

In insurance, the adverse selection problem is that people who are most likely to need insurance payouts are those who buy insurance. For example, those in poorest health are more likely to buy the most generous health insurance policies. Or, at the extreme, a person planning to hire an arsonist to torch his failing business has an incentive to buy fire insurance.

The adverse selection problem thus tends to eliminate the pooling of low and high risks, which is the basis of profitable insurance. Insurance rates then must be so high that few people would want to (or be able to) buy such insurance.

Where private firms underprovide insurance because of information problems, the government often establishes some type of social insurance. It can require everyone in a particular group to take the insurance and thereby can overcome the adverse selection problem. For example, in Canada every citizen is covered by publicly funded health care insurance. The national health care program requires universal participation: People who are most likely to need the health care benefits are automatically participants in the program. So, too, are those not likely to need the benefits. Consequently, no adverse selection problem emerges.

Advocates of our publicly funded health care system point out that we need such a system because private markets would make it impossible for many Canadians who are seriously ill, or are at high risk of serious diseases, to get adequate health insurance. Private insurers would be unwilling to take on clients at high risk for developing serious diseases because of the very high costs this would entail for the insurer. Thus, advocates of our present health care system claim that private markets would underallocate resources to health care. Such underallocation of resources in private markets is a powerful argument for a fully publicly funded health care system.

Qualification

Households and businesses have found ingenious ways to overcome information difficulties without government intervention. For example, many firms offer product warranties to overcome the lack of information about themselves and their products. Franchising also helps overcome this problem. When you visit a McDonald's or a Holiday Inn, you know precisely what you are going to get, unlike when you stop at Slim's Hamburger Shop or the Ghost Buster Motel.

Also, some private firms and organizations specialize in providing information to buyers and sellers. Credit reports provide information about credit histories and past bankruptcies to lending institutions and insurance companies. Brokers, bonding agencies, and intermediaries also provide information to clients.

Economists agree, however, that the private sector cannot remedy all information problems. In some situations, government intervention is desirable to promote an efficient allocation of society's scarce resources.

APPENDIX Summary

A4.1 **Describe how information failures may justify government intervention in some markets.**

- Asymmetric information occurs when buyers and sellers do not have the same information about a product. It is a source of potential market failure, causing society's scarce resources to be allocated inefficiently.

- Asymmetric information can cause a market to fail if the party that has less information decides to withdraw from the market because it fears that that its lack of knowledge may be exploited the party that has more information.

- If the party that has less information reduces its participation in a market, the reduction in the size of the market may cause

an underallocation of resources to the product produced for the market.

- The moral hazard problem is the tendency of one party to a contract to alter its behaviour in ways that are costly to the other party; for example, a person who buys insurance may willingly incur added risk.

- The adverse selection problem arises when one party to a contract has less information than the other party and incurs a cost because of that asymmetrical information. For example, an insurance company offering no-medical-exam-required life insurance policies may attract customers who have life-threatening diseases.

APPENDIX Terms and Concepts

asymmetric information
moral hazard problem

adverse selection problem

APPENDIX Discussion Questions

1. Because medical records are private, an individual applying for private health insurance in Canada will know more about his own health conditions than will the insurance companies to which he is applying for medical services not covered by our national health care system. Is this likely to increase or decrease the insurance premium that he will be offered? Why? **[LOA4.1]**

2. Why is it in the interest of new homebuyers as well as builders of new homes to have government building codes and building inspectors? **[LOA4.1]**

3. Put an M beside the items in the following list that describe a moral hazard problem and an A beside those that describe an adverse selection problem: **[LOA4.1]**

   a. A person with a terminal illness buys several life insurance policies through the mail.

   b. A person drives carelessly because he or she has automobile insurance.

   c. A person who intends to torch his warehouse takes out a large fire insurance policy.

   d. A professional athlete who has a guaranteed contract fails to stay in shape during the off-season.

   e. A woman who anticipates having a large family takes a job with a firm that offers exceptional child care benefits.

APPENDIX   Review Questions

1. People drive faster when they have auto insurance. This is an example of   [**LOA4.1**]

   a. Adverse selection

   b. Asymmetric information

   c. Moral hazard

2. Government inspectors who check on the quality of services provided by retailers as well as government requirements for licensing in various professions are both attempts to resolve   [**LOA4.1**]

   a. The moral hazard problem

   b. The asymmetric information problem

3. True or False? A market may collapse and have relatively few transactions between buyers and sellers if buyers have more information than sellers.   [**LOA4.1**]

APPENDIX   Problems

1. Consider a used-car market with asymmetric information. Owners of used cars know what their vehicles are worth but have no way of credibly demonstrating those values to potential buyers. Thus, potential buyers must always worry that the used car they are being offered may be a "lemon" (a car with significant defects).   [**LOA4.1**]

   a. Suppose that there are equal numbers of good and bad used cars in the market and that good used cars are worth $13,000 while bad used cars are worth $5000. What is the average value of a used car?

   b. By how much does the average value exceed the value of a bad used car? By how much does the value of a good used car exceed the average value?

   c. Would a potential seller of a good used car be willing to accept the average value as payment for her vehicle?

   d. If a buyer negotiates with a seller to purchase the seller's used car for a price equal to the average value, is the car more likely to be good or bad?

   e. Will the used car market come to feature mostly—if not exclusively—lemons? How much will used cars end up costing if all the good cars are withdrawn?

CHAPTER 5

Government's Role and Government Failure

LEARNING OBJECTIVES

LO5.1 Describe how government's power to coerce can be economically beneficial and list some of the difficulties associated with managing and directing the government.

LO5.2 Discuss *government failure* and explain why it happens.

LOA5.1 (Appendix) Explain the difficulties of conveying economic preferences through majority voting.

Governments perform a variety of tasks in market economies. As discussed in various places in the book, these include promoting production and trade by defining property rights, enforcing contracts, and settling disputes; enforcing laws designed to maintain competition; redistributing income via taxes and transfers; reallocating resources by producing public goods and intervening to correct negative and positive externalities; and promoting economic growth and full employment.

In this chapter, we deepen our understanding of government's role in the market economy by examining some of the difficulties that democratic governments face when making specific laws related to the economy.

We will find that governments sometimes pursue policies for which costs outweigh benefits. These inefficient outcomes happen often enough that we need to be just as vigilant in looking for instances of *government failure* as we are in looking for instances of *market failure*.

5.1 Government's Economic Role

LO5.1 Describe how government's power to coerce can be economically beneficial and list some of the difficulties associated with managing and directing the government.

As discussed in Chapter 2, the Canadian economy is a *market system* that uses mostly markets and prices to coordinate and direct economic activity. But the government also has a prominent role in how the economy functions. Among other things, the government sets the laws governing economic activity, provides goods and services that would otherwise be underproduced by private firms, and modifies the distribution of income. The government also promotes both economic stability and economic growth.

Government's Right to Coerce

One key difference between the economic activities of government and those of private firms and individuals is that government possesses the legal right to force people to do things. Whereas private-sector economic activities consist primarily of voluntary transactions, government has the legal right to enforce involuntary transactions. Among other things, the government can put you in jail if you do not pay your taxes, fine you if you violate pollution laws, jail you if you commit fraud, and remove your business licence if you violate health and safety regulations.

FORCE AND ECONOMIC EFFICIENCY

From an economic perspective, the government's ability to force people to do things can be quite beneficial because it can be used to increase economic efficiency.

Correcting for Market Failures

Consider public goods and externalities. As discussed in Chapter 4, these market failures cause resource misallocations. When it comes to both public goods and products offering positive externalities, private producers fail to produce enough output because it is impossible to charge many of the beneficiaries for the benefits that they receive from the producers' products. In such cases, the government can improve economic efficiency by using involuntarily collected tax money to subsidize production.

By contrast, products that generate negative externalities are overproduced by the private sector because many of their costs are borne by third parties rather than by their producers. The government can reduce that overproduction and improve economic efficiency by using involuntary policies such as direct controls, pollution taxes, and cap-and-trade schemes to force producers to bear higher costs.

Reducing Private-Sector Economic Risks

Government's ability to force people to do things is also crucial in reducing private-sector economic risks. To begin with, the government helps to ensure that only mutually agreeable transactions take place by making blackmail, extortion, and other forms of private coercion illegal. The government also uses its legal powers to outlaw various forms of theft, deception, and discrimination as well as restraints on trade, price-fixing, and refusal to honour a contract.

CONSIDER THIS

Market Failure and the Need for Government

Suppose a municipality—such as Saskatoon—requires a new road. In the absence of a government request that a private firm build it, it is unlikely that a private firm will build the required road on its own initiative. To put it another way, private markets will not make available public goods. The citizens of Saskatoon have to elect a government to either direct a private firm to build the road or hire the people and buy the capital equipment needed to construct the road on its own.

Why would a private firm not undertake to build a road on its own? The obstacle is common property rights. The land on which the road is to be built must be owned by the firm before it would consider building the road. Lands used by all citizens are most often held publicly. The firm would thus need to get the consent of all the citizens affected. Such unanimity would be difficult to achieve. Indeed, it is the difficulty of making collective decisions that makes government action essential in the creation of an infrastructure—such as roads and airports—necessary to facilitate the functioning of

© BartCo/Getty Images

markets. Not only must a decision be made to build the road, but also the decision must be made on who should bear the cost. The free-rider problem arises here. Every individual hopes someone else will pay for the needed road. In this way, he or she can have the benefits without contributing to the cost. The free-rider problem can potentially arise in all situations where collective action must be taken. Unless we have a central authority—government—with the monopoly power to impose costs on all members of a society, many socially useful projects will not be undertaken.

In a pathbreaking book, *The Logic of Collective Action*,* Mancur Olson pointed out more than 50 years ago that, contrary to popular belief, groups of individuals with common interests do not necessarily attempt to further those common interests. In many instances, group members attempt to further their own personal interests. A few years later, the political scientist Garrett Hardin popularized the term "the tragedy of the commons"** to describe the problems that arise when there are common property rights. For example, where there are common property rights to a natural resource, it is typically over-exploited. The cod stocks on Canada's east coast have suffered just that fate.

*Olson, M. *The Logic of Collective Action*, Harvard University Press, 1965.
**Hardin, G. "The Tragedy of the Commons," *Science*, Vol. 162, No. 3859, 1968.

These limitations encourage economic activity by giving greater security to both individuals and firms. Because they know that the government will use its massive resources to arrest and punish those who break the law, they know that other individuals and firms are less likely to try to take advantage of them. That reduction in risk encourages higher levels of investment, the formation of more new businesses, and the introduction of more new goods and services. In economic terminology, both allocative and productive efficiency increase.

The Problem of Directing and Managing Government

As just discussed, the government can substantially improve allocative and productive efficiency if it directs its awesome coercive powers toward rectifying market failures and providing a low-risk economic environment for the private sector. However, it has only been in recent centuries that democratic political institutions have been able to tame government and direct it toward those goals. Until that happened, most governments were tyrannical, with their powers almost always directed toward enriching the small minority that controlled each government.

Because modern democratic governments serve much broader constituencies, they are much more likely to pursue economic policies with widespread social benefits. Their ability to deliver economically optimal outcomes is hindered, however, by the wide variety of government failures that this chapter will discuss in detail.

But before discussing them, it should be pointed out that governing a nation is not easy. In particular, governments face the daunting challenge of organizing hundreds of thousands of employees to carry out thousands of tasks—everything from cleaning sewers to researching cures for cancer to delivering the mail. An understanding of those challenges and complexities will give you a better sense of how well most governments manage to do despite all of the problems associated with government failure.

NO INVISIBLE HAND

Government economic policies are not self-correcting. Unlike the private sector—where competitive forces and Adam Smith's *invisible hand* help to automatically direct resources to their best uses—poorly designed government policies can misallocate resources indefinitely unless active steps are taken by legislators or administrators.

MASSIVE SIZE AND SCOPE

Identifying and correcting inefficient government policies is hampered by government's massive size and scope. Consider the Canadian federal government. In 2016, it had about 259,000 employees spread over 225 agencies that were collectively charged with enforcing hundreds of thousands of pages of laws and regulations while attempting to wisely spend about $295 billion.

CONSIDER THIS

Does Big Government Equal Bad Government?

You will sometimes hear politicians (and maybe your grumpy uncle) complaining about Big Government. Their implication is that large government initiatives are inherently inefficient or incompetent.

Since economics is focused on efficiency, you might wonder where economists stand on the subject.

The answer is that economists focus not on bigness or smallness per se, but on marginal benefits (MB) and marginal costs (MC). Spending should be increased up to the point where MB = MC. For some programs that will be a small dollar amount. For other programs that will be a large dollar amount.

Thus, economists don't see much point in having an abstract debate over Big versus Little Government. What matters is allocative and productive efficiency and directing government's limited resources toward the programs that generate the largest net benefits for society.

© Photawa I Dreamstime.com

From that vantage point, we should not condemn large government programs just for being large. We must first compare MB with MC. Only if MB < MC should large programs be reduced or eliminated.

THE NEED FOR BUREAUCRACY

By law, those 263,000 federal employees are ultimately supervised and directed by just 338 elected officials. Since 338 elected officials could never hope to directly supervise 263,000 people, governments rely on many layers of supervisors, and supervisors of supervisors, to manage the government's affairs. They collectively form a massive, hierarchical, many-layered bureaucracy.

THE NEED FOR PAPERWORK AND INFLEXIBILITY

To make sure that laws are uniformly enforced and do not vary at the whim of individual bureaucrats, the bureaucracy is regulated by detailed rules and regulations governing nearly every possible action that any individual bureaucrat might be called upon to make. These rules and regulations ensure that laws and regulations are uniformly applied. But they do so at the cost of massive amounts of paperwork and an inability to expeditiously process nonroutine situations and requests.

THE INFORMATION AGGREGATION PROBLEM

Because of their massive size and scope, bureaucracies have difficulty effectively aggregating and conveying information from their bottom to their top layers. As a result, top officials will tend to make many inefficient choices because they do not have enough information to sensibly compare the marginal benefit and marginal cost of individual programs, and because they are unable to comprehensively assess opportunity costs and where to best spend funds across the wide variety of programs run by the government.

LACK OF ACCOUNTABILITY

Governments also struggle with accountability. Democratic elections do take place for the elected officials at the top, but because the government undertakes so many activities simultaneously, it is difficult for the electorate to know the details of even a small fraction of what the government is up to at any particular time. As a result, hundreds of individual programs may be poorly run without affecting the re-election chances of the incumbent politicians who are supposed to be supervising everything.

Within the bureaucracy itself, individual accountability is also hard to enforce because most bureaucrats have civil service protections that effectively guarantee them a job for life. Those protections reduce corruption by shielding bureaucrats from political pressures. But they also severely constrain the ability of elected officials to hold individual bureaucrats personally responsible for bad decisions.

QUICK REVIEW 5.1

- Government's ability to enforce nonvoluntary transactions can improve economic outcomes by compensating for resource misallocations and by providing a low-risk economic environment for individuals and firms.

- Government economic actions are not automatically self-correcting (as with the invisible hand in competitive markets).

- Democratic governments face several challenges in directing and supervising government's actions, including inflexibility, information aggregation, comparing of marginal costs with marginal benefits, assessment of opportunity costs, and accountability.

5.2 Government Failure

LO5.2   Discuss *government failure* and explain why it happens.

The term **government failure** refers to economically inefficient outcomes caused by shortcomings in the public sector. One cause of government failure is the voting issue that we discuss at length in this chapter's appendix. But government failures caused by voting problems are somewhat unique in that they are driven by a lack of information about voter preferences. By contrast, most instances of government failure happen *despite* government officials knowing what voters prefer.

In these situations, government failures occur because the incentive structures facing government officials lead them either to put their own interests ahead of voter interests or to put the interests of a minority of voters ahead of those of a majority of voters. Let's examine what public interest theory has to say about these situations.

Representative Democracy and the Principal–Agent Problem

Our system of representative democracy has the advantage of allowing us to elect full-time representatives who can specialize in understanding the pros and cons of different potential laws and who have more time to digest their details than the average citizen.

But the system also suffers from conflicts known as **principal–agent problems**, which arise when tasks are delegated by one group of people (principals) to another group of people (agents). The interests of the agents may not be the same as the interests of the principals, so that the agents may end up taking actions opposed by the principals whom they are supposed to be representing.

In the business world, principal–agent problems often arise when the managers of a company (the agents) take actions that are not in the best interests of the company's shareholders (the principals). Examples include the managers spending huge amounts of company money on executive jets and lavish offices or holding meetings at expensive resorts. These luxuries are obviously very enjoyable to managers. But they are not in the best interests of shareholders, because the money spent on them might be either reinvested in the firm to increase future profits or paid out to shareholders immediately as dividends. To the extent that managers are free to follow their own interests, they may indeed take these and other actions; hence the conflicts.

In a representative democracy, principal–agent problems often arise because politicians have goals such as re-election that may be inconsistent with pursuing the best interests of their constituents. Indeed, casual reflection suggests that *sound economics* and *good politics* often differ. Sound economics calls for the public sector to pursue various programs as long as marginal benefits exceed marginal costs. Good politics, however, suggests that politicians support programs and policies that will maximize their chances of getting re-elected and staying in office. The result may be that the government will promote the goals of groups of voters that have special interests to the detriment of the larger public.

SPECIAL-INTEREST EFFECT

Efficient public decision making is often impaired by the **special-interest effect**. This is any outcome of the political process where a small number of people obtain a government program or policy that gives them large gains at the expense of a much greater number of persons who individually suffer small losses.

The small group of potential beneficiaries is well informed and highly vocal on the issue in question, and they press politicians for approval by making campaign contributions and by hiring well-connected professional advocates known as *lobbyists* to aggressively make their case. By contrast, the large number of people facing very small individual losses are generally uninformed on the issue. So politicians feel they will lose the campaign contributions and votes of the small special-interest group that backs the issue if they legislate against it but will not lose the support of the large group of uninformed voters, who are likely to evaluate the politicians on other issues of greater importance to them.

The special-interest effect is also evident in so-called *pork-barrel politics*, a means of securing a government project that yields benefits mainly to a single political district and its political representative. In this case, the special-interest group comprises local constituents, while the larger group consists of relatively uninformed taxpayers scattered across a much larger geographic area. Politicians clearly have a strong incentive to secure government projects ("pork") for their local constituents.

Finally, a politician's inclination to support the smaller group of special beneficiaries is enhanced because special-interest groups are often quite willing to help finance the campaigns of "right-minded" politicians and politicians. The result is that politicians may support special-interest programs and projects that cannot be justified on economic grounds.

RENT-SEEKING BEHAVIOUR

The appeal to government for special benefits at taxpayers' or someone else's expense is called **rent seeking**. The term *rent* in rent seeking is used loosely to refer to any payment in excess of the minimum needed to keep a resource employed in its current use. Those engaged in rent seeking are attempting to use government influence to get themselves into a situation in which they will get paid more for providing a good or service than the minimum amount you would actually have to pay them. (These excess, or surplus, payments are akin to *land rent*, which is also a surplus payment.)

Rent seeking goes beyond the usual profit seeking through which firms try to increase their profits by adjusting their output levels, improving their products, and incorporating cost-saving technologies. Rent seeking looks to obtain extra profit or income by influencing government policies. Corporations, trade associations, labour unions, and professional organizations employ vast resources to secure favourable government policies that result in rent— higher profit or income than would otherwise occur. The government is able to dispense such rent directly or indirectly through laws, rules, hiring, and purchases. Elected officials are willing to provide it because they want to be responsive to key constituents, who in turn help them remain in office.

Here are some examples of rent-providing legislation or policies: tariffs on foreign products that limit competition and raise prices to consumers, tax breaks that benefit specific corporations, government construction projects that create union jobs but cost more than the benefits they yield, occupational licensing that goes beyond what is needed to protect consumers, and large subsidies to farmers by taxpayers. None of these is justified by economic efficiency.

Clear Benefits, Hidden Costs

Some critics say that vote-seeking politicians will ignore economic rationality by failing to weigh costs and benefits objectively when deciding which programs to support. Because political officeholders must seek voter support every few years, they favour programs that have immediate and clear-cut benefits and vague or deferred costs.

Such biases may lead politicians to reject economically justifiable programs and to accept programs that are economically irrational. For example, a proposal to construct or expand mass-transit systems in large metropolitan areas may be economically rational on the basis of benefit–cost analysis; but if (1) the program is to be financed by immediate increases in highly visible income or sales taxes and (2) benefits will occur only years from now when the project is completed, the vote-seeking politician may oppose the program.

Another example of possible political bias is the distribution of health care expenditures by both the federal and provincial governments in Canada. Certain government health care expenditures on a relatively small number of Canadians may garner a lot of positive and visible front-page coverage and media attention, but may not be the most efficient expenditures of resources from society's standpoint.

Unfunded Liabilities

The political tendency to favour spending priorities that have immediate payouts but deferred costs also leads to many government programs having unfunded liabilities. A government creates an **unfunded liability** when it commits to making a series of future expenditures without simultaneously committing to collect enough tax revenues to pay for those expenditures.

Chronic Budget Deficits

A government runs an annual **budget deficit** whenever its tax revenues are less than its spending during a particular year. To make up for the shortfall, the government must borrow money, usually by issuing bonds. Whatever it borrows in a given year gets added to its overall pile of debt, which is the accumulation of all past budget deficits and budget surpluses.

Many governments run budget deficits year after year. These chronic deficits can be attributed to a pair of conflicting incentives that confront politicians. On the one hand, many government programs are highly popular with voters, so that there is almost always political pressure to either maintain or increase spending. On the other hand, hardly anyone likes paying taxes, so there is almost always political pressure to reduce taxes. Faced with those two conflicting pressures, politicians tend to opt for spending levels that exceed tax revenues. That may be problematic because chronic deficits can pose several economic challenges, including:

- *Economic Inefficiency* Deficits may allow the government to control and direct an inefficiently large fraction of the economy's resources. To the extent that deficit spending facilitates an underallocation of resources to the private sector and an overallocation of resources to the government sector, there will be a tendency to underproduce private goods and overproduce public goods. If that occurs, the economy will experience a decrease in both allocative and productive efficiency.

- *Debt Crises* A government's accumulated debt level may rise so high that investors lose faith in the government's ability or willingness to repay its debts. If that happens, the government will find itself in the middle of a **debt crisis**, unable to borrow any more money. Cut off from borrowing, the government will be forced to undertake some combination of drastic spending cuts or massive tax increases. Either of those actions will tend to plunge the economy into a recessionary period in which unemployment rises and output falls.

Misdirection of Stabilization Policy

Economies go through alternating periods of expansion and recession. These are multiyear periods during which output expands, employment increases, and living standards rise alternating with shorter periods during which output contracts, employment decreases, and living standards fall.

Governments often attempt to smooth out these so-called *business cycles* by using two types of macroeconomic stabilization policies:

- **Fiscal policy** attempts to use changes in tax rates and spending levels to offset the business cycle. For example, if the economy is going into a recessionary period with falling output and rising unemployment, the government may attempt to stimulate the economy by lowering tax rates or increasing government spending. Either action should increase spending on goods and services and consequently induce business to produce more output and hire more workers.

- **Monetary policy** attempts to use changes in interest rates to regulate the economy. In particular, the government can use its control over the money supply to lower interest rates during a recession. The lower interest rates stimulate spending by making it cheaper for individuals and businesses to borrow money to pay for capital goods such as houses, cars, and machinery. As spending on those items increases, firms are induced to produce more output and hire more workers.

POLITICIZATION OF FISCAL AND MONETARY POLICY

Fiscal and monetary policy are both subject to politicization. In the case of fiscal policy, if the economy goes into recession and there are calls to stimulate the economy through lower taxes or increased spending, politicians often spend more time attempting to target any tax cuts or spending increases toward special interests than they do making sure that their fiscal policy actions will actually stimulate the overall economy. The recession also provides political cover for increasing the size of the deficit.

Monetary policy can be similarly politicized, the biggest problem being that incumbent politicians will want to cut interest rates to boost the economy right before they are up for re-election. That is problematic because monetary stimulus is only helpful if the economy is in recession. If the economy is doing well, monetary stimulus can actually make things worse because it can raise the rate of inflation and drive up prices all over the economy.

To prevent that, most countries have put politically independent central banks in charge of monetary policy. In Canada, the Bank of Canada serves this function. Other top central banks include the Federal Reserve (U.S.), the Bank of Japan, the Bank of England, and the European Central Bank. Each is run by professional economists insulated from political pressures so that they may use their independent expertise and judgment to decide if and when monetary stimulus should be used.

QUICK REVIEW 5.2

- Principal–agent problems are conflicts that occur when the agents who are supposed to be acting in the best interests of their principals instead take actions that help themselves but hurt their principals.

- Because larger groups are more difficult to organize and motivate than smaller groups, special interests can often obtain what they want politically even when what they want is opposed by a majority of voters.

- Rent seeking involves influencing government policies so that one can get paid more for providing a good or service than it costs to produce.

- Political pressures cause politicians to favour policies such as unfunded liabilities and budget deficits that have immediate benefits and delayed costs.

Limited and Bundled Choice

Public choice theorists point out that the political process forces citizens and their elected representatives to be less selective in choosing public goods and services than they are in choosing private goods and services.

In the marketplace, the citizen as a consumer can exactly satisfy personal preferences by buying certain goods and not buying others. However, in the public sector the citizen as a voter is confronted with, say, only two or three candidates for an office, each representing a different bundle of programs (public goods and services). None of these bundles of public goods is likely to fit exactly the preferences of any particular voter, yet the voter must choose one of them. The candidate who comes closest to voter Smith's preference may endorse universal health care, increases in Canada Pension Plan benefits, subsidies to wheat farmers, and tariffs on imported goods. Smith is likely to vote for that candidate even though Smith might strongly oppose subsidies.

Parliament is confronted with a similar limited-choice, bundled-goods problem. Appropriations legislation combines hundreds, even thousands, of spending items into a single bill. Many of these spending items may be completely unrelated to the main purpose of the legislation, yet members of parliament must vote the entire package—yea or nay. Unlike consumers in the marketplace, they cannot be selective.

Bureaucracy and Inefficiency

Some economists contend that public agencies are generally less efficient than private businesses. The reason is that the market system creates incentives and pressures for internal efficiency that are absent from the public sector. The market system imposes a very obvious test of performance on private firms: the test of profit and loss. An efficient firm is profitable and therefore successful; it survives, prospers, and grows. An inefficient firm is unprofitable and unsuccessful; it declines and in time goes bankrupt and ceases to exist. But no similar, clear-cut test exists with which to assess the efficiency or inefficiency of public agencies.

Furthermore, economists assert that government employees, together with the special-interest groups they serve, often gain sufficient political clout to block attempts to pare down or eliminate their agencies. Politicians who attempt to reduce the size of huge federal bureaucracies such as those relating to agriculture, education, and health and welfare incur sizable political risk because bureaucrats and special-interest groups will team up to defeat them.

Finally, critics point out that there is a tendency for government bureaucrats to justify their continued employment by looking for and eventually finding new "problems" to solve. It is not surprising that social problems, as defined by government, tend to persist or even expand.

INEFFICIENT REGULATION AND INTERVENTION

Governments regulate many aspects of the market economy. Examples include health and safety regulations, environmental laws, banking supervision, restrictions on monopoly power, and the imposition of wage and price controls. These interventions are designed to improve economic outcomes, but several forms of regulation and intervention have been known to generate outcomes that are less beneficial than intended.

Regulatory Capture

A government agency that is supposed to supervise a particular industry is said to have suffered from **regulatory capture** if its regulations and enforcement activities come to be heavily influenced by the industry that it is supposed to be regulating. Regulatory capture is often facilitated by the fact that nearly everyone who knows anything about the details of a regulated industry works in the industry. So when it comes time for the regulatory agency to find qualified people to help write intelligent regulations, it ends up hiring a lot of people from regulated firms. Those individuals bring their old opinions and sympathies with them when they become bureaucrats. As a result, many regulations end up favouring the interests of the regulated firms.

Deregulation as an Alternative

Economists are divided about the intensity and inefficiency of regulatory capture as well as what to do about it. One potential solution is for the government to engage in **deregulation** and intentionally remove most or even all of the regulations governing an industry. Deregulation solves the problem of regulatory capture because there is no regulatory agency left to capture. But it only works well in terms of economic efficiency if the deregulated industry becomes competitive and is automatically guided toward allocative and productive efficiency by competitive forces and the invisible hand. If the deregulated industry instead tends toward monopoly or ends up generating substantial negative externalities, continued regulation might be the better option.

Proponents of deregulation often cite the deregulation of interstate trucking, railroads, and airlines in the 1970s and 1980s as examples of competition successfully replacing regulation. They do so because after regulation was removed, robust competition led to lower prices, increased output, and higher levels of productivity and efficiency. But for government agencies tasked with environmental protection, human safety, and financial regulation, there is less confidence as to whether competitive pressures might be able to replace regulation. For those industries, regulation may always be necessary. If so, some amount of regulatory capture may always be likely due to the fact that regulated firms will always want to capture their regulators.

Government's Poor Investment Track Record

Governments are often asked to use taxpayer money to directly invest in private businesses that have been unable to secure funding from private sources such as banks. Unfortunately, researchers have found that low and negative rates of return are the norm for government investments. In addition, government funding often allows inefficient firms to persist in operation long after competitive forces would have put them out of operation and freed up their resources for higher-valued projects elsewhere in the economy.

Critics also note that many government investments look like prime examples of rent seeking and the special-interest effect, especially when the firms receiving government investments are found to have made substantial financial contributions to influential politicians. In too many cases, the government's investment decisions appear to be based on political connections rather than on whether specific investments can produce substantial net benefits for society.

Loan Guarantees

The government also tends to earn low or negative returns when it subsidizes private-sector investments with **loan guarantees**.

Socializing Losses, Privatizing Gains

Government loan guarantees can be socially beneficial if they help to increase the production of beneficial products that are being underproduced by the private sector—as would be the case for products that generated positive externalities. But the loan guarantees also provide an inducement toward reckless investing, because they remove from private investors any consideration of losses. Indeed, loan guarantees are often criticized for "socializing losses and privatizing gains": If things go wrong, any losses fall on the taxpayer; if things go well, any profits go to private investors.

In addition, the process by which loan guarantees are awarded is often criticized for being highly politicized and likely to award loan guarantees not to the firms whose projects are the most likely to increase economic efficiency but to those with the best political connections. On the other hand, there may be legitimate cases where a new technology that would generate net benefits cannot be developed without government loan guarantees, so proponents of loan-guarantee programs argue that the programs should remain in place, but with tight controls against rent seeking and the special-interest effect.

Corruption

Political corruption is the unlawful misdirection of governmental resources or actions that occurs when government officials abuse their entrusted powers for personal gain. For instance, a police supervisor engages in political corruption if she accepts a bribe in exchange for illegally freeing a thief who had been lawfully arrested by another officer. Similarly, a government bureaucrat engages in political corruption if he refuses to issue a building permit to a homebuilder who is in full compliance with the law unless the homebuilder makes a "voluntary contribution" to the bureaucrat's favourite charity.

While relatively uncommon in Canada, political corruption is a daily reality in many parts of the world, as can be seen in Global Perspective 5.1, which gives the percentages of survey respondents in fifteen

5.1 GLOBAL PERSPECTIVE

Percentage of Households Paying a Bribe in the Past Year

The Global Corruption Barometer is compiled from a series of international surveys that ask individuals about their personal experiences with government corruption. The 2013 survey of over 114,000 people in 107 countries included a question that asked participants whether they or anyone in their respective households had paid a bribe in any form during the previous twelve months. Here are the results for ten selected countries.

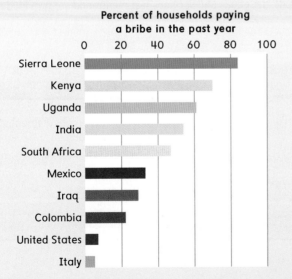

countries who reported that they or someone else in their household had paid a bribe during the previous twelve months.

Political corruption comes in two basic forms. In the first, a government official must be bribed to do what he should be doing for free as part of his job—as with the bureaucrat in our earlier example who demands a bribe to issue a permit to a homebuilder who is in full compliance with the law. In the second, a government official demands a bribe to do something that she is not legally entitled to do—as with the police supervisor in our earlier example who illegally freed a thief.

If a candidate accepts campaign contributions from a special-interest group and then shows subsequent support for that group's legislative goals, has a subtle form of political corruption taken place? While there are strong opinions on both sides of the issue, it is often hard to tell in any particular case whether a special interest's campaign contribution amounts to a bribe. On the one hand, the special interest may indeed be trying to influence the politician's vote. On the other hand, the special interest may simply be trying to support and get elected a person who already sees things their way and who would vote the way they wanted no matter what anyone did.

That said, the impression of impropriety lingers and so laws have been passed in Canada limiting the amount of money that individuals can donate to specific candidates and making it illegal for certain groups such as companies to donate money directly to individual politicians (as distinct from directing funds toward supporting specific issues or advocacy groups—which is both legal and unrestricted). Proponents of these laws hope that the limitations strike a good balance—allowing contributions to be large enough that individuals and groups can meaningfully support candidates they agree with but keeping contributions small enough that no one individual or group can singlehandedly donate enough money to sway a politician's vote.

Imperfect Institutions

Such criticisms of public-sector inefficiency shatter the concept of a benevolent government that responds with precision and efficiency to the wants of its citizens. The market system of the private sector is far from perfectly efficient, and government's economic function is mainly to correct that system's shortcomings; but the public sector, too, is subject to deficiencies in fulfilling its economic function.

Because the market system and public agencies are both imperfect, it is sometimes difficult to determine whether a particular activity can be performed with greater success in the private sector or the public sector. It is easy to reach agreement on opposite extremes: national defence must lie with the public sector, while automobile production can best be accomplished by the private sector. But what about health insurance? Parks and recreation areas? Fire protection? Garbage collection? Housing? Education? It is hard to say absolutely that it should be assigned to either the public or the private sector. After all, the goods and services just mentioned are provided in part by *both* private enterprises and public agencies.

QUICK REVIEW 5.3

- Unlike the private sector—where the profit motive helps to ensure efficiency and variety—government lacks a strong incentive to be efficient and typically offers only limited and bundled choices.

- Regulatory capture occurs when a regulated industry can control its government regulator and get it to implement policies that favour the industry.

- Political corruption occurs when government officials abuse their powers for personal gain.

The **LAST WORD**

Singapore's Efficient and Effective Health Care System

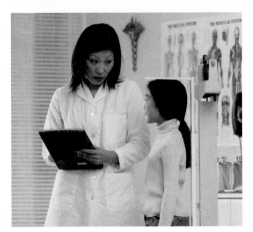

© Comstock Images/Picturequest

How does Singapore deliver some of the best health care in the world while spending less per person than Canada?

In every health-quality category monitored by the World Health Organization, the small island nation of Singapore is either number one in the world or near the top of the list. Among other achievements, Singapore has the world's lowest rate of infant mortality and the world's fourth-highest life expectancy.

One might expect that achieving these exceptional outcomes would be extremely expensive. But Singapore is also number one in another category: It spends less per person on health care than any other developed nation. In 2010 Canada spent about 10 percent of its GDP on health care. Singapore spent just 3.8 percent.

How does Singapore deliver world-class health care while spending less than any other developed nation? The answer is a unique combination of government mandates to encourage competition, high out-of-pocket costs for consumers, and laws requiring people to save for future health expenditures.

Competition is encouraged by forcing hospitals to post prices for each of their services. Armed with this information, patients can shop around for the best deal. The government also publishes the track record of each hospital on each service so that consumers can make informed decisions about quality as well as price. With consumers choosing on the basis of cost and quality, local hospitals compete to reduce costs and improve quality.

Singapore also insists upon high out-of-pocket costs in order to avoid the overconsumption and high prices that result when insurance policies pick up most of the price for medical procedures. Indeed, out-of-pocket spending repre-

sents about 92 percent of all non-government health care spending in Singapore, as against just less than 10 percent in Canada.

Having to pay for most medical spending out of pocket, however, means that Singapore's citizens are faced with having to pay for most of their health care themselves. How can this be done without bankrupting the average citizen? The answer is mandatory health savings accounts.

Singapore's citizens are required to save about 6 percent of their incomes into MediSave accounts. MediSave deposits are private property so that people have an incentive to spend the money in their accounts wisely. In addition, the citizens of Singapore also know that they won't be left helpless if the money in their MediSave accounts runs out. The government subsidizes the health care of those who have exhausted their MediSave accounts as well as the health care of the poor and others who have not been able to accumulate much money in their MediSave accounts.

Given the present universal health care system in Canada, which according to most Canadians functions quite well, it is unlikely that they would opt for a Singapore-style MediSave system.

Question

What are the three major cost-reducing features of the Singapore health care system? Which one do you think has the largest effect on holding down the price of medical care in Singapore? How difficult do you think it would be to implement the missing elements in Canada? Explain.

Chapter Summary

LO5.1   Describe how government's power to coerce can be economically beneficial and list some of the difficulties associated with managing and directing the government.

- Government's legal right to use coercion and force can help to improve economic efficiency by correcting for market failures and by enforcing laws and regulations that reduce the risk that individuals and firms will be taken advantage of.

LO5.2   Discuss *government failure* and explain why it happens.

- Special interests can succeed in perpetuating policies that are opposed by the majority of voters because the costs of organizing and motivating groups to take political action increase with group size. This collective action problem implies that special interests can perpetuate unpopular policies as long as the costs of organizing an opposition exceed the costs that the general public is currently suffering as a result of those policies.

- There are powerful incentives for politicians to accommodate rent seeking and support special-interest legislation.

- Because voters like receiving the benefits of government programs but do not like having to pay the taxes necessary to finance them, politicians tend to favour programs that offer easily identified immediate benefits but vague or deferred costs.

- When the economy goes into recession, politicians often use the need for fiscal policy stimulus as political cover to direct lower taxes or increased spending towards politically powerful special-interest groups. To prevent politicians from using lower interest rates and monetary stimulus as a way of increasing their re-election chances, most governments have put politically independent central banks in charge of monetary policy.

- Economic theorists cite several reasons why government might be inefficient in providing public goods and services: (a) citizens as voters as well as governmental representatives face limited and bundled choices of public goods and services, whereas consumers in the private sector can be highly selective in their choices; (b) government bureaucracies have less incentive to operate efficiently than do private businesses; (c) regulated industries may sometimes capture their government regulatory agencies and mould government policies that are in their own best interests.

- Government's track record as an investor in private-sector firms is very poor, with most government investments into private sector businesses generating low or negative returns for taxpayers.

- Government attempts to increase private investment by offering loan guarantees often cause resources to be misdirected to high-risk projects that have an extremely low likelihood of success. These arrangements "socialize losses and privatize gains," because if the businesses go bankrupt, the government bears the losses, but if they do well, private individuals receive the profits.

- Political corruption may cause governmental resources or actions to be misdirected.

- Neither governments nor markets are perfect economic institutions. Each sector has its own set of shortcomings and citizens should be aware of where each is likely to fail and where each is likely to succeed.

Terms and Concepts

government failure
principal–agent problems
special-interest effect
rent seeking
unfunded liability
budget deficit
debt crisis

fiscal policy
monetary policy
regulatory capture
deregulation
loan guarantees
political corruption

Discussion Questions

1. Why might citizens interested in maximizing economic efficiency be happy to invest their government with the right to coerce them in at least some situations?   [**LO5.1**]

2. Jean Baptiste Colbert was the minister of finance under King Louis XIV of France. He famously observed that "The art of taxation consists in so plucking the goose as to obtain the largest possible amount of feathers with the smallest possible amount of hissing." How does his comment relate to special interests and the collective action problem?   [**LO5.2**]

3. What is rent seeking, and how does it differ from the kinds of profit maximization and profit seeking that we discussed in previous chapters? Provide an actual or a hypothetical example of rent seeking by a firm in an industry, a union, and a professional association (for example, physicians or lawyers).

Why do elected officials often accommodate rent-seeking behaviour, particularly by firms, unions, and professional groups located in their home ridings?   [**LO5.2**]

4. How does the problem of limited and bundled choice in the public sector relate to economic efficiency? Why are public bureaucracies possibly less efficient than business firms?   [**LO5.2**]

5. Explain the reasoning behind the following statement: "Politicians would make more rational economic decisions if they weren't running for re-election every few years."   [**LO5.2**]

6. Critique the following statement: "Thank goodness we have so many government regulatory agencies. They keep Big Business in check."   [**LO5.2**]

Review Questions

1. Select all of the following that correctly complete the following sentence: To an economist, a coercive government can be useful in order to   [**LO5.1**]

   a. Reallocate resources in order to improve efficiency

   b. Fight negative externalities

   c. Ensure low gasoline prices

   d. Provide a low-risk economic environment for individuals and firms

2. To an economist, a government program is too big if an analysis of that program finds that MB _____ MC.   [**LO5.1**]

   a. Is greater than

   b. Is less than

   c. Is equal to

   d. Is less than twice as large as

   e. Is more than twice as large as

3. Tammy Hall is the mayor of a large Canadian city. She has just established the Office of Window Safety. Because windows sometimes break and spray glass shards, every window in the city will now have to pass an annual safety inspection. Property owners must pay the $5-per-window cost—and, by the way, Tammy has made her nephew the new head of the Office of Window Safety. This new policy is an example of   [**LO5.2**]

   a. Political corruption

   b. Earmarks

   c. Rent seeking

   d. Adverse selection

4. _____ occur when politicians commit to making a series of future expenditures without simultaneously committing to collect enough tax revenues to pay for those expenditures.   [**LO5.2**]

   a. Budget deficits

   b. Debt crises

   c. Loan guarantees

   d. Unfunded liabilities

Problems

1. Suppose that there are 1 million federal workers at the lowest level of the federal bureaucracy and that above them are multiple layers of supervisors and supervisors of supervisors. Assume that each higher level is one-tenth the size of the one below it because the government is using a 10:1 ratio of supervisees to supervisors. That is, for every 10 workers at the bottom, there is 1 supervisor; for every 10 of those supervisors, there is 1 supervisor of supervisors; for every one of those supervisors of supervisors, there is a supervisor of supervisors of supervisors and so on, all the way up the bureaucratic pyramid to the prime minister.   [**LO5.1**]

   a. How many supervisors will there be in each supervisory layer of the federal bureaucracy? Start with the layer of supervisors directly above the 1 million workers at the bottom.

   b. How many supervisors are there in total at all levels of the federal bureaucratic pyramid, including the prime minister?

2. Consider a corrupt provincial government in which each housing inspector examines two newly built structures each week. All the builders in the province are unethical and want to increase their profits by using substandard construction materials, but they can't do that unless they can bribe a housing inspector into approving a substandard building.   [**LO5.2**]

   a. If bribes cost $1000 each, how much will a housing inspector make each year in bribes? (Assume that each inspector works 52 weeks a year and gets bribed for every house he inspects.)

   b. There is a provincial construction supervisor who gets to hire all of the housing inspectors. He himself is corrupt and expects his housing inspectors to share their bribes with him. Suppose that 20 inspectors work for him and that each passes along half the bribes collected from builders. How much will the construction supervisor collect each year?

c. Corrupt officials may have an incentive to reduce the provision of government services to help line their own pockets. Suppose that the provincial construction supervisor decides to cut the total number of housing inspectors from 20 to 10 in order to decrease the supply of new housing permits. This decrease in the supply of permits raises the equilibrium bribe from $1000 to $2500. How much per year will the construction supervisor now receive if he is still getting half of all the bribes collected by the 10 inspectors? How much more is the construction supervisor getting now than when he had 20 inspectors working in part (b)? Will he personally be happy with the reduction in government services?

d. What if reducing the number of inspectors from 20 to 10 only increased the equilibrium bribe from $1000 to $1500? In this case, how much per year would the construction supervisor collect from his 10 inspectors? How much less is the construction supervisor getting than when he had 20 inspectors working in part (b)? In this case, will the construction supervisor be happy with the reduction in government services? Will he want to go back to using 20 inspectors?

Public Choice Theory and Voting Paradoxes

LOA5.1 Explain the difficulties of conveying economic preferences through majority voting.

A5.1 Public Choice Theory

Market failures, such as public goods and externalities, impede economic efficiency and justify government intervention in the economy. But the government's response to market failures is not without its own problems and pitfalls. In fact, government can sometimes fail as badly or even worse than markets in terms of delivering economic efficiency and directing resources to the uses where they will bring the largest net benefits.

That is why it is important to study **public choice theory**—the economic analysis of government decision making, politics, and elections. Just as the study of *market failure* helps us to understand how regulating markets may help to improve the allocation of resources, the study of *government failure* can help us to understand how changes in the way government functions might help it to operate more efficiently.

As we will discuss shortly, many instances of government failure can be traced to incentive structures that lead political representatives to pursue policies that go against the preferences of the people that they are representing. But an even more fundamental problem exists: The majority voting systems that we rely upon may make it difficult or even impossible to discern voter preferences correctly. In such cases, it is not surprising that government fails to deliver what the voters actually want.

Revealing Preferences Through Majority Voting

Society must decide in some way what public goods and services it wants and in what amounts. It must also determine the extent to which it wants government to intervene in private markets to correct externalities. Decisions needed to be made about how much regulation of business is necessary, the amount of income redistribution that is desirable, what policies the government might enact to mitigate asymmetric information problems, and more. Furthermore, society must determine the set of taxes it thinks best for financing government. How should the total tax burden be apportioned (divided) among the public?

Decisions such as these are made collectively in Canada through a democratic process that relies heavily on majority voting. Candidates for office offer alternative policy packages,

and citizens elect the people they think will make the best decisions on their collective behalf. Voters retire officials who do not adequately represent their collective wishes. Citizens also periodically have opportunities at the provincial and municipal levels to vote directly on public expenditures or new legislation.

Although the democratic process does a reasonably good job of revealing society's preferences, it is imperfect. Public choice theory demonstrates that majority voting can produce inefficiencies and inconsistencies.

Inefficient Voting Outcomes

Society's well-being is enhanced when government provides a public good whose total benefit exceeds its total cost. Unfortunately, majority voting does not always deliver that outcome.

INEFFICIENT "NO" VOTE

Assume that the government can provide a public good, say national defence, at a total expense of $900. Assume there are only three individuals—Adams, Benson, and Conrad—in the society and that they will share the $900 tax expense equally, each being taxed $300 if the proposed public good is provided. And assume, as Figure A5-1a illustrates, that Adams would receive $700 worth of benefits from having this public good, Benson $250, and Conrad $200.

What will be the result if a majority vote determines whether this public good is provided? Although people do not always vote strictly according to their own economic interest, it is likely that Benson and Conrad will vote no because they will incur tax costs of $300 each while gaining benefits of only $250 and $200, respectively. Adams will vote yes. So the majority vote will defeat the proposal even though the total benefit of $1150 (= $700 for Adams + $250 for Benson + $200 for Conrad) exceeds the total cost of $900.

INEFFICIENT "YES" VOTE

Now consider a situation in which the majority favours a public good even though its total cost exceeds its total benefit. Figure A5-1b shows the details. Again, Adams, Benson, and Conrad will equally share the $900 cost of the public good; they will each be taxed $300. But since Adams's benefit now is only $100 from the public good, she will vote against it.

FIGURE A5-1   Inefficient Voting Outcomes

Majority voting can produce inefficient decisions. (a) Majority voting leads to rejection of a public good that has greater total benefit than total cost. (b) Majority voting results in acceptance of a public good that has a higher total cost than total benefit.

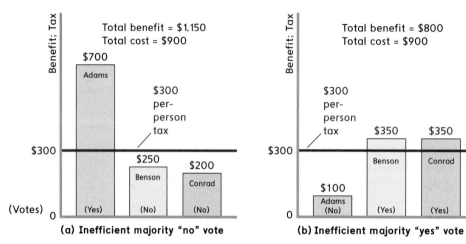

(a) Inefficient majority "no" vote

(b) Inefficient majority "yes" vote

Meanwhile, Benson and Conrad will benefit by $350 each. They will vote for the public good because that benefit ($350) exceeds their tax payments ($300). The majority vote will provide a public good costing $900 that produces total benefits of only $800 (= $100 for Adams + $350 for Benson + $350 for Conrad). Society's resources will be inefficiently allocated to this public good, and there will be too much of it.

IMPLICATIONS

The point is that an inefficient outcome may occur as either an overproduction or an underproduction of a specific public good and, therefore, as an overallocation or underallocation of resources for that particular use. In Chapter 4 we saw that government can improve economic efficiency by providing public goods that the market system will not make available. Now we have extended that analysis to reveal that government might fail to provide some public goods whose production is economically justifiable while providing other goods that are not economically warranted.

In our examples, each person has only a single vote, no matter how much he or she might gain or lose from a public good. In the first example (inefficient "no" vote), Adams would be willing to purchase a vote from either Benson or Conrad if buying votes were legal. That way Adams could be assured of obtaining the national defence she so highly values. But since buying votes is illegal, many people with strong preferences for certain public goods may have to go without them.

When individual consumers have a strong preference for a specific *private good*, they usually can find that good in the marketplace even though it may be unpopular with the majority of consumers. A consumer can buy beef tongue, liver, and squid in some supermarkets, although it is doubtful that any of these products would be available if majority voting stocked

the shelves. But a person cannot easily buy a *public good* such as national defence once the majority has decided against it.

Conversely, a consumer in the marketplace can decide against buying a particular product, even a popular one. But although you may not want national defence, you must pay for it through your taxes when it is favoured by the majority.

Conclusions: Because majority voting fails to incorporate the *strength* of the preferences of the individual voter, it may produce economically inefficient outcomes.

Interest Groups and Logrolling

Some, but not all, of the inefficiencies of majority voting get resolved through the political process. Two examples follow.

INTEREST GROUPS

Those who have a strong preference for a public good may band together into an interest group and use advertisements, mailings, and direct persuasion to convince others of the merits of that public good. Adams might try to persuade Benson and Conrad that it is in their best interests to vote for national defence—that national defence is much more valuable to them than their $250 and $200 valuations. Such appeals are common in democratic politics. Sometimes they are successful, sometimes not.

POLITICAL LOGROLLING

Perhaps surprisingly, logrolling—the trading of votes to secure favourable outcomes—can also turn an inefficient outcome into an efficient one. In our first example (Figure A5-1), perhaps Benson has a strong preference for a different public good—for example, a new road—which Adams and Conrad do not think is worth the tax expense. That would provide an opportunity for Adams and Benson to trade votes to ensure provision of both national defence and the new road. That is,

Adams and Benson would each vote yes on both measures. Adams would get the national defence and Benson would get the road. Without the logrolling, both public goods would have been rejected. Logrolling will add to society's well-being if, as was true for national defence, the road creates a greater overall benefit than cost.

Logrolling need not increase economic efficiency. Even if national defence and the road each cost more than the total benefit they produced, both might still be provided because of the vote trading.

Paradox of Voting

Another difficulty with majority voting is the **paradox of voting**, a situation in which society may not be able to rank its preferences consistently through paired-choice majority voting.

PREFERENCES

Consider Table A5-1, in which we again assume a community of three voters: Adams, Benson, and Conrad. Suppose the community has three alternative public goods from which to choose: national defence, a road, and a weather warning system. We expect that each member of the community prefers the three alternatives in a certain order. For example, one person might prefer national defence to a road, and a road to a weather warning system. We can attempt to determine the preferences of the community through paired-choice majority voting. Specifically, a vote can be held between any two of the public goods, and the winner of that vote can then be matched against the third public good in another vote.

The three goods and the assumed individual preferences of the three voters are listed in the top part of Table A5-1. The data indicate that Adams prefers national defence to the road and the road to the weather warning system. This implies also that Adams prefers national defence to the weather warning system. Benson values the road more than the weather warning system and the weather warning system more than national

defence. Conrad's order of preference is weather warning system, national defence, and road.

VOTING OUTCOMES

The lower part of Table A5-1 shows the outcomes of three hypothetical decisions of the majority vote. In the first, national defence wins against the road because a majority of voters (Adams and Conrad) prefer national defence to the road. In the second election to see whether this community wants a road or a weather warning system, a majority of voters (Adams and Benson) prefer the road.

We have determined that the majority of people in this community prefer national defence to a road and prefer a road to a weather warning system. It seems logical to conclude that the community prefers national defence to a weather warning system, but, in fact, the community does not!

To demonstrate this conclusion, we hold a direct election between national defence and the weather warning system. Row (3) shows that a majority of voters (Benson and Conrad) prefer the weather warning system to national defence. As listed in Table A5-1, then, the three paired-choice majority votes imply that this community is irrational: it seems to prefer national defence to a road and a road to a weather warning system, but would rather have a weather warning system than national defence.

The problem is not irrational community preferences, but rather a flawed procedure for determining those preferences. We see that the outcome from paired-choice majority voting may depend on the order in which the votes are taken. Different sequences of majority votes can lead to different outcomes, many of which may fail to reflect the electorate's underlying preferences. As a consequence, government may find it difficult to provide the "correct" public goods by acting in accordance with majority voting. One important note: This critique is not meant to suggest that some better procedure exists. Majority voting is much more likely to reflect community preferences than decisions made by, say, a dictator or a group of self-appointed leaders.

TABLE A5-1	Paradox of Voting		
	PREFERENCES		
Public good	**Adams**	**Benson**	**Conrad**
National defence	1st choice	3rd choice	2nd choice
Road	2nd choice	1st choice	3rd choice
Weather warning system	3rd choice	2nd choice	1st choice
Election	**Voting outcomes: Winner**		
1. National defence vs. road	National defence (preferred by Adams and Conrad)		
2. Road vs. weather warning system	Road (preferred by Adams and Benson)		
3. National defence vs. weather warning system	Weather warning system (preferred by Benson and Conrad)		

Median-Voter Model

One other aspect of majority voting reveals further insight into real-world phenomena. The median-voter model suggests that, under majority rule and consistent voting preferences, the median voter will, in a sense, determine the outcomes of elections. The median voter is the person holding the middle position on an issue; half the other voters have stronger preferences for a public good, amount of taxation, or degree of government regulation, while half have weaker or negative preferences. The extreme voters on each side of an issue prefer the median choice to the other extreme position, so the median voter's choice predominates.

EXAMPLE

Suppose a society composed of Adams, Benson, and Conrad has reached agreement that as a society it needs a weather warning system. Independently each is to submit a total dollar amount he or she thinks should be spent on the weather warning system, assuming each will be taxed one-third of that amount. An election will determine the size of the system. Because each person can be expected to vote for his or her own proposal, no majority will occur if all the proposals are placed on the ballot at the same time. Thus, the group decides on a paired-choice vote: They will first vote between two of the proposals and then match the winner of that vote against the remaining proposal.

The three proposals are as follows: Adams wants a $400 system; Benson wants an $800 system; Conrad wants a $300 system. Which proposal will win? The median-voter model suggests it will be the $400 proposal submitted by the median voter, Adams. Half the other voters favour a more costly system; half

favour a less costly system. To understand why the $400 system will be the outcome, let's conduct the two elections.

First, suppose that the $400 proposal is matched against the $800 proposal. Adams naturally votes for her $400 proposal, and Benson votes for his own $800 proposal. Conrad, who proposed the $300 expenditure for the weather warning system, votes for the $400 proposal because it is closer to his own. So Adams's $400 proposal is selected by a 2-to-1 majority vote.

Next, we match the $400 proposal against the $300 proposal. Again the $400 proposal wins. It gets a vote from Adams and one from Benson, who proposed the $800 expenditure and for that reason prefers a $400 expenditure to a $300 one. Adams, the median voter in this case, is in a sense the person who has decided the level of expenditure on a weather warning system for this society.

REAL-WORLD APPLICABILITY

Although our illustration is simple, it explains a great deal. We do note a tendency for public choices to match the median view most closely. Political candidates, for example, take one set of positions to win the nomination of their political parties; in so doing, they tend to appeal to the median voter within their party to get the nomination. They then shift their views more closely to the political centre when they square off against opponents from the opposite political party. In effect, they redirect their appeal toward the median voter within the total population. They also try to label their opponents as too liberal, or too conservative, and out of touch with mainstream Canada. They then conduct polls and adjust their positions on issues accordingly.

CONSIDER THIS

Voter Failure

Inefficient voting outcomes and the paradox of voting imply that governments may sometimes fail to deliver the best combination of public goods because it may be very difficult for politicians to discern what voters actually want. In other cases, though, economists worry that governments may end up failing to deliver allocative and productive efficiency, not because politicians can't tell what people want—but because they *can*.

The problem is that voters sometimes support policies that reduce rather than enhance allocative and productive efficiency. Examples include several types of wage and price controls, punitive tariffs on foreign products, and various industrial and agricultural subsidies.

These policies almost always reduce economic efficiency, but they are also extremely popular with voters in many countries. Faced with that reality, a politician may well end up

supporting such policies even if he personally understands that they will create more economic harm than benefit.

That behaviour makes some observers wish

© Tzogia Kappatou | Dreamstime.com

for braver politicians who might be willing to oppose these instances of "voter failure." But others argue that it is too much to hope for braver politicians. Instead, efforts should be directed toward educating the public and convincing them to support government policies that are economically efficient.

IMPLICATIONS

The median-voter model has two important implications:

1. At any point in time, many people will be dissatisfied by the extent of government involvement in the economy. The size of government will largely be determined by the median preference, leaving many people desiring a much larger, or a much smaller, public sector. In the marketplace you can buy no zucchinis, two zucchinis, or 200 zucchinis, depending on how much you enjoy them. In the public sector you will tend to get the public health funding that the median voter prefers.

2. Some people may "vote with their feet" by moving into political jurisdictions where the median voter's preferences are closer to their own. They may move from one province to another where the level of government services, and therefore taxes, is lower. Or they may move into an area known for its excellent but expensive school system. Some may move to other provinces; a few may even move to other countries.

For these reasons, and because our personal preferences for publicly provided goods and services are not static, the median preference shifts over time. Moreover, information about people's preferences is imperfect, leaving much room for politicians to misjudge the true median position. When they misjudge, they may have a difficult time getting elected or re-elected.

APPENDIX Summary

LOA5.1 Explain the difficulties of conveying economic preferences through economic preferences through majority voting.

- Public choice theory suggests that governments may sometimes suffer from government failures because majority voting fails to correctly indicate voter preferences.

- Majority voting creates the possibility of (a) underallocations or overallocations of resources to particular public goods and (b) inconsistent voting outcomes that make it impossible for a democratic political system to definitively determine the will of the people.

- The median-voter model predicts that, under majority rule, the person holding the middle position on an issue will determine the outcome of an election involving that issue.

APPENDIX Terms and Concepts

public choice theory
logrolling

paradox of voting
median-voter model

APPENDIX Discussion Questions

1. Explain how affirmative and negative majority votes can sometimes lead to inefficient allocations of resources to public goods. Is this problem likely to be greater under a benefits-received or an ability-to-pay tax system? Use the information in both panels of Figure A5-1 to show how society might be better off if Adams were allowed to buy votes. [**LOA5.1**]

2. Discuss the following: Majority voting ensures that government will produce only those public goods for which benefits exceed costs. [**LOA5.1**]

3. Critique this statement: "The problem with our democratic institutions is that they don't correctly reflect the will of the people! If the people—rather than self-interested politicians or lobbyists—had control, we wouldn't have to worry about government taking actions that don't maximize allocative and productive efficiency." [**LOA5.1**]

APPENDIX Review Questions

1. Explain the paradox of voting through reference to the accompanying table, which shows the ranking of three public goods by voters Jay, Dave, and Conan: [**LOA5.1**]

	RANKINGS		
Public good	**Jay**	**Dave**	**Conan**
Courthouse	2nd choice	1st choice	3rd choice
School	3rd choice	2nd choice	1st choice
Park	1st choice	3rd choice	2nd choice

2. We can apply voting paradoxes to the highway construction example of Chapter 4. Suppose there are only five people in a society and each favours one of the five highway construction options listed in Table 4.4. ("No new construction" is one of the five options.) Explain which of these highway options will be selected using a majority paired-choice vote. Will this option be the optimal size of the project from an economic perspective? [**LOA5.1**]

3. True or False? The median-voter model explains why politicians so often stake out fringe positions that appeal only to a small segment of the electorate. [**LOA5.1**]

APPENDIX Problems

1. Look back at Figures A5-1a and 1b, which show the costs and benefits to voters Adams, Benson, and Conrad of two different public goods that the government will produce if a majority of Adams, Benson, and Conrad support them. Suppose that Adams, Benson, and Conrad have decided to have a single vote at which the funding for both public goods will be decided simultaneously. [**LOA5.1**]

   a. Given the $300 cost per person of each public good, what are Adams's net benefits for each public good individually and for the two combined? Will he want to vote yes or no on the proposal to fund both projects simultaneously?

   b. What are Conrad's net benefits for each public good individually and for the two combined? Will he want to vote yes or no on the proposal to fund both projects simultaneously?

   c. What are Benson's net benefits for each public good individually and for the two combined? Will he want to vote yes or no on the proposal to fund both projects simultaneously—or will he be indifferent?

   d. Who is the median voter here? Who will the two other voters be attempting to persuade?

2. Political advertising is often directed at winning over so-called swing voters, whose votes might go either way. Suppose that two political parties—the Freedom Party and the Liberty Party—

disagree on whether to build a new road. Polling shows that of 1000 total voters, 450 are firmly for the new road and 450 are firmly against the new road. Thus, each party will try to win over a majority of the 100 remaining swing voters. [**LOA5.1**]

   a. Suppose that each party spends $5000 on untargeted TV, radio, and newspaper ads that are equally likely to reach any and all voters. How much per voter will be spent by both parties combined?

   b. Suppose that, instead, each party could direct all of its spending toward just the swing voters by using targeted ads that exploit social media. If all of the two parties' combined spending were targeted at just swing voters, how much would be spent per swing voter?

   c. Suppose that only the Freedom Party knows how to target voters using social media. How much per swing voter will it be spending? If at the same time the Liberty Party is still using only untargeted TV, radio, and newspaper ads, what portion of its total spending is likely to be reaching the 100 swing voters? How much per swing voter does that portion amount to?

   d. Looking at your answers to part (c), how much more per swing voter will the Freedom Party be spending than the Liberty Party? If spending per swing voter influences elections, which party is more likely to win?

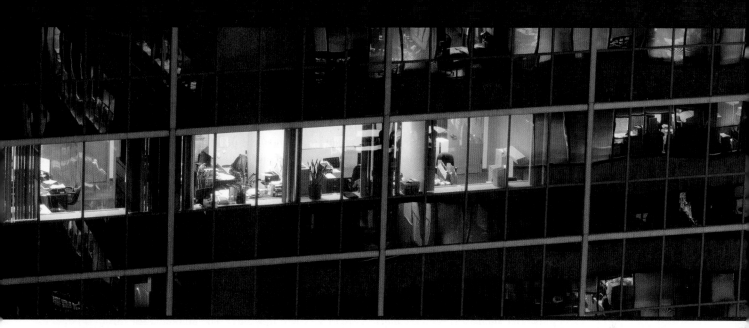

CHAPTER 6

Elasticity

LEARNING OBJECTIVES

LO6.1 Discuss price elasticity of demand and how it is calculated.

LO6.2 Explain the usefulness of the total-revenue test for price elasticity of demand.

LO6.3 List the factors that affect price elasticity of demand and describe some applications of price elasticity of demand.

LO6.4 Describe price elasticity of supply and how it can be applied.

LO6.5 Apply cross elasticity of demand and income elasticity of demand.

LO6.6 Apply the concept of elasticity to real-world situations.

In this chapter we extend Chapter 3's discussion of demand and supply by explaining *elasticity*, an extremely important concept that will help us answer several important questions: Why do buyers of some products (for example, ocean cruises) respond to price increases by substantially reducing their purchases, while buyers of other products (for example, gasoline) respond by only slightly cutting back? Why do higher market prices for some products (for example, chicken) cause producers to greatly increase their output, while price rises for other products (for example, gold) cause only limited increases in output? Why does the demand for some products (for example, books) rise a great deal when household income increases, while the demand for other products (for example, green beans) rises just a little?

Elasticity extends our understanding of markets by letting us know the degree to which changes in prices and incomes affect supply and demand. Sometimes the responses are substantial; at other times, the responses are minimal or even non-existent. But by knowing what to expect, businesses and the government can do a much better job of deciding what to produce, how much to charge, and, surprisingly, what items to tax.

6.1   Price Elasticity of Demand

LO6.1   Discuss price elasticity of demand and how it is calculated.

The law of demand tells us that, other things equal, consumers will buy more of a product when its price declines and less when its price increases. But *how much* more or less will they buy? The amount varies from product to product and over different price ranges for the same product. It also may vary over time. And such variations matter. For example, a firm contemplating a price hike will want to know how consumers will respond. If they remain highly loyal and continue to buy, the firm's revenue will rise. But if consumers defect en masse to other sellers or other products, the firm's revenue will tumble.

The responsiveness (or sensitivity) of consumers to a price change is measured by a product's **price elasticity of demand**. For some products—for example, restaurant meals—consumers are highly responsive to price changes. Modest price changes cause very large changes in the quantity purchased. Economists say that the demand for such products is *relatively elastic* or simply *elastic*.

For other products—for example, toothpaste—consumers are less responsive to price changes. Substantial price changes cause only small changes in the amount purchased. The demand for such products is *relatively inelastic* or simply *inelastic*.

The Price Elasticity Coefficient and Formula

We measure the degree to which demand is elastic or inelastic with the coefficient E_d, defined as

$$E_d = \frac{\text{percentage change in quantity demanded of product X}}{\text{percentage change in price of product X}}$$

MATH 6.1   Elasticity

Let's look at a specific example from Table 6-1, rows 1 to 3, to see how the price elasticity of demand is calculated (don't worry about columns 4 and 5 for now; they will be discussed later). This table shows the number of movie tickets demanded (in thousands) per week at each specified price. Let's calculate E_d for, say, the \$5 to \$4 price range. But before we do so, let's look at how we calculate a percentage.

CALCULATING A PERCENTAGE CHANGE

To calculate the percentage change in quantity demanded between two points, we divide the change in quantity demanded (ΔQ_d) by the original quantity demanded (Q_0) that we are considering. (Note that the Greek letter delta [Δ] signifies "change in.")

$$\% \Delta Q_d = \frac{\text{change in quantity demanded of product X}}{\text{original quantity of product X}} \times 100\%$$

TABLE 6-1	Price Elasticity of Demand for Movie Tickets as Measured by the Elasticity Coefficient and the Total-Revenue Test			
(1) Total quantity demanded per week (thousands)	(2) Price per ticket	(3) Elasticity coefficient, E_d	(4) Total revenue (1) × (2)	(5) Total-revenue test
1	$8		$ 8,000	
		5.00		Elastic
2	7		14,000	
		2.60		Elastic
3	6		18,000	
		1.57		Elastic
4	5		20,000	
		1.00		Unit elastic
5	4		20,000	
		0.64		Inelastic
6	3		18,000	
		0.38		Inelastic
7	2		14,000	
		0.20		Inelastic
8	1		8,000	

For example, if the quantity demanded increases from 4 to 5 units, the percentage change in quantity demanded is calculated as follows:

$$\% \Delta Q_d = \frac{\Delta Q_d}{Q_0} = \frac{1}{4} \times 100\% = 25\%$$

To calculate the percentage change in price between two points, we divide the change in price (ΔP) by the original price (P_0):

$$\% \Delta P = \frac{\text{change in price of product X}}{\text{original price of product X}} \times 100\%$$

For example, if the price dropped from $5 to $4, the percentage change in price is calculated as follows:

$$\% \Delta P = \frac{\Delta P}{P_0} = \frac{1}{5} \times 100\% = 20\%$$

USING AVERAGES

Unfortunately, an annoying problem arises in computing the price elasticity coefficient. A price change, say from $4 to $5, is a 25 percent (= $1/$4) increase; the quantity change from 5 to 4 units is a 20 percent (= 1/5) decrease in quantity, resulting in a price elasticity of 0.8 (= 20/25). But an opposite price change, from $5 to $4, is a 20 percent (= $1/$5) decrease; the quantity change from 4 to 5 units is a 25 percent increase, resulting in a price elasticity of 1.25 (= 25/20). Which percentage change in price should we use in the denominator to compute the price elasticity coefficient? And when quantity changes, for example, from 10 to 20, it is a 100 percent (=10/10) increase. But when quantity falls from 20 to 10 along the identical demand curve, it is a 50 percent (10/20) decrease. Should we use 100 percent or 50 percent in the numerator of the elasticity formula? Elasticity should be the same whether price rises or falls!

The simplest solution to the problem is to use the **midpoint formula** for calculating elasticity. This formula simply averages the two prices and the two quantities as the reference points for computing the percentages. That is,

$$E_d = \frac{\text{change in quantity}}{\text{sum of quantities}/2} \div \frac{\text{change in price}}{\text{sum of prices}/2}$$

In symbols, the formula becomes

$$E_d = \frac{\Delta Q}{(Q_0 + Q_1)/2} \div \frac{\Delta P}{(P_0 + P_1)/2}$$

WORKED PROBLEM 6.1   Elasticity of Demand

For the same $5 to $4 price range, the price reference is $4.50 (= ($5 + $4)/2), and for the same 10 to 20 quantity range, the quantity reference is 15 units (= (10 + 20)/2). The percentage change in price is now $1/$4.50, or about 22 percent, and the percentage change in quantity is 10/15, or also about 67 percent. So E_d is about 3. This solution eliminates the "up versus down" problem. All the price elasticity coefficients that follow are calculated using this midpoint formula.

USING PERCENTAGES

Why use percentages rather than absolute amounts in measuring consumer responsiveness? There are two reasons.

First, if we use absolute changes, the choice of units will arbitrarily affect our impression of buyer responsiveness. To illustrate, if the price of a bag of popcorn at the local hockey game is reduced from $3 to $2, and consumers increase their purchases from 60 to 100 bags, it appears that consumers are quite sensitive to price changes and, therefore, that demand is elastic. After all, a price change of 1 unit has caused a change of 40 units in the amount demanded. But by changing the monetary unit from dollars to pennies (why not?), we find that a price change of 100 units (pennies) causes a quantity change of 40 units. This result may falsely lead us to believe that demand is inelastic. We avoid this problem by using percentage changes. This particular price decline is the same whether we measure in dollars or pennies.

Second, by using percentages, we can correctly compare consumer responsiveness to changes in the prices of different products. It makes little sense to compare the effects on quantity demanded of a $1 increase in the price of a $10,000 used car with a $1 increase in the price of a $1 soft drink. Here the price of the used car increased by 0.01 percent, while the price of the soft drink increased by 100 percent. We can more sensibly compare the consumer responsiveness to price increases by using some common percentage increase in price for both.

ELIMINATING THE MINUS SIGN

We know from the downsloping demand curve shown in Chapter 3 that price and quantity demanded are inversely related. Thus, the price elasticity coefficient of demand E_d will always be a negative number. Economists usually ignore the minus sign and simply present the absolute value of the elasticity coefficient to avoid an ambiguity that might otherwise arise. It can be confusing to say that an E_d of -4 is greater than an E_d of -2. This possible confusion is avoided when we say that an E_d of 4 reveals greater elasticity than an E_d of 2. Incidentally, the ambiguity does not arise with supply because price and quantity supplied are positively related. All elasticity of supply coefficients, therefore, are positive numbers.

Interpretation of E_d

We interpret the coefficient of price elasticity of demand (E_d) as follows.

ELASTIC DEMAND

Demand is elastic (**elastic demand** exists) if a specific percentage change in price results in a larger percentage change in quantity demanded. In such cases, E_d will be greater than 1. For example, suppose that a 2 percent decline in the price of cut flowers results in a 4 percent increase in quantity demanded. Then demand for cut flowers is elastic and

$$E_d = 0.04/0.02 = 2$$

INELASTIC DEMAND

If a specific percentage change in price produces a smaller percentage change in quantity demanded, demand is inelastic (**inelastic demand** exists). In such cases, E_d will be less than 1. For example, suppose that a 2 percent decline in the price of coffee leads to only a 1 percent increase in quantity demanded. Then demand is inelastic and

$$E_d = 0.01/0.02 = 01 = 0.5$$

FIGURE 6-1   Perfectly Inelastic and Perfectly Elastic Demand

Demand curve D_1 in panel (a) represents perfectly inelastic demand ($E_d = 0$). A price increase does not change the quantity demanded. Demand curve D_2 in panel (b) represents perfectly elastic demand. A price increase causes quantity demanded to decline from an infinite amount to zero ($E_d = \infty$).

(a) Perfectly inelastic demand

(b) Perfectly elastic demand

UNIT ELASTICITY

The case separating elastic and inelastic demands occurs when a percentage change in price and the resulting percentage change in quantity demanded are the same. For example, suppose that a 2 percent drop in the price of chocolate causes a 2 percent increase in quantity demanded. This special case is termed **unit elasticity**, because E_d is exactly 1, or unity. In this example,

$$E_d = 0.02/0.02 = 1$$

EXTREME CASES

When we say demand is *inelastic,* we do not mean that consumers are completely unresponsive to a price change. In that extreme situation, when a price change results in no change whatsoever in the quantity demanded, economists say that demand is **perfectly inelastic**. The price elasticity coefficient is zero, because there is no response to a change in price. Think of a diabetic's demand for insulin or an addict's demand for heroin. A line parallel to the vertical axis, such as D_1 in Figure 6-1a, shows perfectly inelastic demand graphically.

Conversely, when we say that demand is *elastic,* we do not mean that consumers are fully responsive to a price change. In that extreme situation, when a small price reduction causes buyers to increase their purchases from zero to all they can obtain, the elasticity coefficient is infinite ($= \infty$), and economists say it is a **perfectly elastic demand**. A line parallel to the horizontal axis, such as D_2 in Figure 6-1b, shows perfectly elastic demand. You will see in Chapter 8 that such a demand applies to a firm—for example, a mining firm—that is selling in a perfectly competitive market.

6.2   The Total-Revenue Test

LO6.2   Explain the usefulness of the total-revenue test for price elasticity of demand.

The importance of elasticity for firms is due to the effect of price changes on **total revenue (TR)** and thus on profits (= total revenue − total costs).

FIGURE 6-2   The Total-Revenue Test for Price Elasticity

(a) Price declines from $2 to $1, and total revenue increases from $20 to $40. So demand is elastic. The gain in revenue (green area) exceeds the loss of revenue (blue area). (b) Price declines from $4 to $1, and total revenue falls from $40 to $20. So demand is inelastic. The gain in revenue (green area) is less than the loss of revenue (blue area). (c) Price declines from $3 to $1, and total revenue does not change. Demand is unit elastic. The gain in revenue (green area) equals the loss of revenue (blue area).

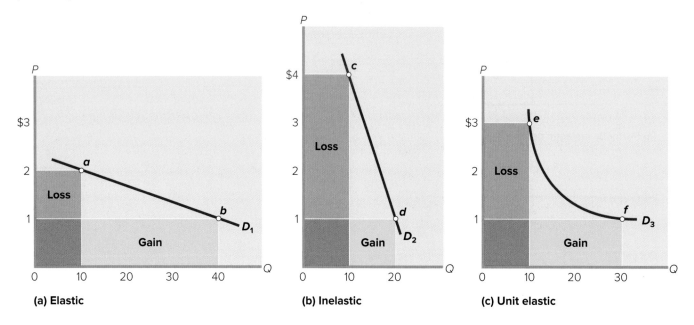

(a) Elastic   (b) Inelastic   (c) Unit elastic

Total revenue (TR) is the total amount the seller receives from the sale of a product (or service) in a particular time period; it is calculated by multiplying the product price (P) by the quantity demanded and sold (Q). In equation form,

$$TR = P \times Q$$

MATH 6.2   The Total-Revenue Test

Graphically, total revenue is represented by the $P \times Q$ rectangle lying below a point on a demand curve. At point *a* in Figure 6-2a, for example, price is $2 and quantity demanded is 10 units. So total revenue is $20 (= $2 × 10), shown by the rectangle composed of the blue and purple areas under the demand curve. We know from basic geometry that the area of a rectangle is found by multiplying one side by the other. Here, one side is price ($2) and the other is quantity demanded (10 units).

Total revenue and the price elasticity of demand are related. In fact, the easiest way to determine whether demand is elastic or inelastic is to employ the **total-revenue test**. Note what happens to total revenue when price changes. If total revenue changes in the opposite direction from price, demand is elastic. If total revenue changes in the same direction as price, demand is inelastic. If total revenue does not change when price changes, demand is unit elastic.

Elastic Demand

If demand is elastic, a decrease in price will increase total revenue. Even though a lesser price is received per unit, enough additional units are sold to more than make up for the lower price. For example, look at demand curve D_1 in Figure 6-2a. We have already established that at point *a*, total revenue is $20 (= $2 × 10), shown as the purple plus blue areas. If the price declines from $2 to $1 (point *b*), the quantity demanded becomes 40 units and total revenue is $40 (= $1 × 40). As a result of the price decline, total revenue has increased from $20 to $40. Total revenue has increased in this case because the $1 decline in price applies to 10 units, with a consequent revenue

CONSIDER THIS

A Bit of a Stretch

The following analogy might help you remember the distinction between *elastic* and *inelastic*. Imagine two objects—one an Ace elastic bandage used to wrap injured joints and the other a relatively firm bungee cord (rubber strap) used for securing items for transport. The Ace bandage stretches a great deal when pulled with a particular force; the bungee cord stretches some, but not a lot.

Similar differences occur for the quantity demanded of various products when their prices change. For some products, a price change causes a substantial "stretch" of quantity demanded. When this stretch in percentage terms exceeds the percentage change in price, demand is elastic. For other products,

© Nancy R. Cohen/Getty Images

quantity demanded stretches very little in response to the price change. When this stretch in percentage terms is less than the percentage change in price, demand is inelastic.

In summary:

- Elastic demand displays considerable "quantity stretch" (as with the Ace bandage).

- Inelastic demand displays relatively little "quantity stretch" (as with the bungee cord).

And by extension:

- Perfectly elastic demand has infinite quantity stretch.
- Perfectly inelastic demand has zero quantity stretch.

loss of $10 (the blue area). But 30 more units are sold at $1 each, resulting in a revenue gain of $30 (the green area). Visually, it is apparent that the gain of the green area exceeds the loss of the blue area. As indicated, the overall result is a net increase in total revenue of $20 (= $30 − $10).

The analysis is reversible. If demand is elastic, a price increase will reduce total revenue. The revenue gained on the higher-priced units will be more than offset by the revenue lost from the lower quantity sold. So, other things equal, when price and total revenue move in opposite directions, demand is elastic. *Elastic demand* occurs when E_d is greater than 1, meaning the percentage change in quantity demanded is greater than the percentage change in price.

Inelastic Demand

If demand is inelastic, a price decrease will reduce total revenue. The increase in sales will not fully offset the decline in revenue per unit, and total revenue will decline. To see this, look at demand curve D_2 in Figure 6-2b. At point *c* on the curve, price is $4 and quantity demanded is 10. So total revenue is $40, shown by the combined purple and blue rectangles. If the price drops to $1 (point *d*), total revenue declines to $20, which obviously is less than $40. Total revenue has declined because the loss of revenue (the blue area) from the lower unit price is larger than the gain in revenue (the green area) from the accompanying increase in sales. Price has fallen, and total revenue has also declined.

The analysis is again reversible. If demand is inelastic, a price increase will increase total revenue. So, other things equal, when price and total revenue move in the same direction, demand is inelastic. *Inelastic demand* occurs when E_d is less than 1, meaning the percentage change in quantity demanded is less than the percentage change in price.

WORKED PROBLEM 6.2   The Total-Revenue Test

Unit Elasticity

In the special case of unit elasticity, an increase or a decrease in price leaves total revenue unchanged. The loss in revenue from a lower unit price is exactly offset by the gain in revenue from the accompanying increase in sales. Conversely, the gain in revenue from a higher unit price is exactly offset by the revenue loss associated with the accompanying decline in the amount demanded.

In Figure 6-2c (demand curve D_3) we find that at the price of $3, 10 units will be sold, yielding total revenue of $30. At the lower $1 price, a total of 30 units will be sold, again resulting in $30 of total revenue. The $2 price reduction causes the loss of revenue shown by the blue area, but this is exactly offset by the revenue gain shown by the green area. Total revenue does not change. In fact, that would be true for all price changes along this particular curve.

Other things equal, when price changes and total revenue remains constant, demand is unit elastic (or unitary). *Unit elasticity* occurs when E_d is 1, meaning the percentage change in quantity demanded equals the percentage change in price.

Price Elasticity Along a Linear Demand Curve

Now a major confession! Although the demand curves depicted in Figure 6-2 nicely illustrate the total-revenue test for elasticity, two of the graphs involve specific movements along linear (straight-line) demand curves. That presents no problem for explaining the total-revenue test. However, you need to know that elasticity typically varies over different price ranges of the same demand curve. (The exception is the curve in Figure 6-2c, where elasticity is 1 along the entire curve.)

Table 6-1 and Figure 6-3 demonstrate that elasticity typically varies over the different price ranges of the same demand curve. Plotting the hypothetical data for movie tickets shown in columns 1 and 2 of Table 6-1 yields demand curve D in Figure 6-3. Observe that the demand curve is linear. But we see from column 3 of the table that the price elasticity coefficient for this demand curve declines as we move from higher to lower prices. For all downsloping, straight-line, and most other demand curves, demand is more price elastic toward the upper left (here, the $5 to $8 price range of D) than toward the lower right (here, the $4 to $1 price range of D).

 KEY GRAPH

FIGURE 6-3   The Relation Between Price Elasticity of Demand for Movie Tickets and Total Revenue

(a) Demand curve D is based on Table 6-1 and marked to show that the hypothetical weekly demand for movie tickets is elastic at higher price ranges and inelastic at lower price ranges. (b) The total-revenue curve TR is derived from demand curve D. When price falls and TR increases, demand is elastic; when price falls and TR is unchanged, demand is unit elastic; when price falls and TR declines, demand is inelastic.

(a) Demand curve

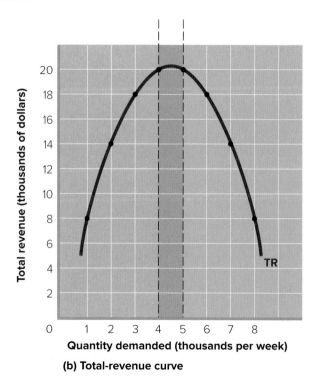

(b) Total-revenue curve

This is the consequence of arithmetic properties of the elasticity measure. Specifically, in the upper left segment of the demand curve, the percentage change in quantity is large because the original reference quantity is small. Similarly, the percentage change in price is small in that segment because the original reference price is large. The relatively large percentage change in quantity divided by the relatively small change in price yields a large E_d—an elastic demand.

The reverse holds true for the lower right segment of the demand curve. Here the percentage change in quantity is small because the original reference quantity is large; similarly, the percentage change in price is large because the original reference price is small. The relatively small percentage change in quantity divided by the relatively large percentage change in price results in a small E_d—an inelastic demand.

The demand curve in Figure 6-3a also illustrates that the slope of a demand curve—its flatness or steepness—is not a sound basis for judging elasticity. The catch is that the slope of the curve is computed from *absolute* changes in price and quantity, while elasticity involves *relative* or *percentage* changes in price and quantity. The demand curve in Figure 6-3a is linear, which by definition means that the slope is constant throughout, but we have demonstrated that such a curve is elastic in its high-price ($8 to $5) range and inelastic in its low-price ($4 to $1) range.

Price Elasticity and the Total-Revenue Curve

In Figure 6-3b we plot the total revenue per week to the theatre owner that corresponds to each price–quantity combination indicated along demand curve D in Figure 6-3a. The price–quantity-demanded combination represented by point a on the demand curve yields total revenue of $8000 (= $8 × 1000 tickets). In Figure 6.3b, we plot this $8000 amount vertically at 1 unit (1000 tickets) demanded. Similarly, the price–quantity-demanded combination represented by point b in the upper panel yields total revenue of $14,000 (= $7 × 2000 tickets). This amount is graphed vertically at 2 units (2000 tickets) demanded in the lower panel. The ultimate result of such graphing is total-revenue curve TR, which first slopes upward, then reaches a maximum, and finally turns downward.

Comparing curves D and TR sharply focuses the relationship between elasticity and total revenue. Lowering the ticket price in the elastic range of demand—for example, from $8 to $5—increases total revenue. Conversely, increasing the ticket price in that range reduces total revenue. In both cases, price and total revenue change in opposite directions, confirming that demand is elastic.

The $5 to $4 price range of demand curve D reflects unit elasticity. When price either decreases from $5 to $4 or increases from $4 to $5, total revenue remains $20,000. In both cases, price has changed and total revenue has remained constant, confirming that demand is unit elastic when we consider these particular price changes.

In the inelastic range of demand curve D, lowering the price—for example, from $4 to $1—decreases total revenue, as shown in Figure 6-3b. Raising the price boosts total revenue. In both cases, price and total revenue move in the same direction, confirming that demand is inelastic.

Table 6-2 summarizes the characteristics of price elasticity of demand. You should review it carefully.

TABLE 6-2	**Price Elasticity of Demand: A Summary**			
Absolute value of elasticity coefficient	Demand	Description	**IMPACT ON TOTAL REVENUE OF A:**	
			Price increase	Price decrease
Greater than 1 ($E_d > 1$)	Elastic or relatively elastic	Quantity demanded changes by a larger percentage than does price	Total revenue decreases	Total revenue increases
Equal to 1 ($E_d = 1$)	Unit or unitary elastic	Quantity demanded changes by the same percentage as does price	Total revenue is unchanged	Total revenue is unchanged
Less than 1 ($E_d < 1$)	Inelastic or relatively inelastic	Quantity demanded changes by a smaller percentage than does price	Total revenue increases	Total revenue decreases

6.3 Determinants of Price Elasticity of Demand

LO6.3 List the factors that affect price elasticity of demand and describe some applications of price elasticity of demand.

We cannot say just what will determine the price elasticity of demand in each individual situation. However, the following generalizations are often helpful.

Substitutability

Generally, the larger the number of substitute goods available, the greater the price elasticity of demand. Various brands of candy bars are usually substitutable for one another, making the demand for one brand of candy bar, say Snickers, highly elastic. At the other extreme, the demand for corrective lenses (glasses or contacts) is highly inelastic because there are simply no close substitutes.

The elasticity of demand for a product depends on how narrowly the product is defined. Demand for Reebok sneakers is more elastic than is the overall demand for shoes. Many other brands could substitute for Reebok sneakers, but there are few, if any, good substitutes for shoes.

Proportion of Income

Other things equal, the greater the proportion of income spent on a good, the greater the price elasticity of demand for it. A 10 percent increase in the price of relatively low-priced pencils or chewing gum amounts to a very small proportion of a consumer's income, and quantity demanded will probably decline only slightly. Thus, price elasticity for such items tends to be low. But a 10 percent increase in the price of relatively high-priced automobiles or houses means additional expenditures of perhaps $3000 or $20,000, respectively. These price increases are significant fractions of the annual incomes and budgets of most families, and quantities demanded will likely diminish significantly. The price elasticities for such items tend to be high.

Luxuries Versus Necessities

In general, the more a good is considered a luxury rather than a necessity, the greater the price elasticity of demand. Electricity is generally considered a necessity; a price increase will not significantly reduce the amount of lighting and power used in a household. (Note the very low price elasticity coefficient of electricity in Table 6-3.) In an extreme example, a person does not decline an operation for acute appendicitis because the surgeon has found a way to increase the cost.

On the other hand, vacation travel and jewellery are luxuries, which, by definition, can easily be forgone. If the prices of vacation travel or jewellery rise, a consumer need not buy them and will suffer no greater hardship without them.

What about the demand for a common product like salt? It is highly inelastic on three counts: Few good substitutes are available, salt is a negligible item in the family budget, and it is a "necessity" rather than a luxury.

Time

Generally, product demand is more elastic the longer the period under consideration. Consumers often need time to adjust to changes in prices. When the price of a product rises, it takes time to find and experiment with other products to see whether they are acceptable. Consumers may not immediately reduce their purchases very much when the price of beef rises by 10 percent, but in time they may switch to chicken, pork, or fish.

In general, the more a good is considered a luxury rather than a necessity, the greater the price elasticity of demand.

© Pixtal/age fotostock

TABLE 6-3	Selected Price Elasticities of Demand		
Product or service	**Coefficient of price elasticity of demand, E_d**	**Product or service**	**Coefficient of price elasticity of demand, E_d**
Newspapers	0.10	Household appliances	0.63
Electricity (household)	0.13	Movies	0.87
Bread	0.15	Beer	0.90
Major League Baseball tickets	0.23	Shoes	0.91
Telephone service	0.26	Motor vehicles	1.14
Sugar	0.30	Beef	1.27
Eggs	0.32	China, glassware, tableware	1.54
Legal services	0.37	Residential land	1.60
Automobile repair	0.40	Restaurant meals	2.27
Clothing	0.49	Lamb and mutton	2.65
Gasoline	0.60	Fresh peas	2.83
Milk	0.63		

Source: Compiled from numerous studies and sources reporting price elasticity of demand.

Another consideration is product durability. Studies show that short-run demand for gasoline is more inelastic ($E_d = 0.2$) than long-run demand ($E_d = 0.7$). In the short run, people are stuck with their present cars and trucks, but with rising gasoline prices they will eventually replace them with smaller, more fuel-efficient vehicles, or switch to mass transit where it is available.

Table 6-3 shows estimated price-elasticity coefficients for a number of products. Each reflects some combination of the elasticity determinants just discussed.

Applications of Price Elasticity of Demand

The concept of price elasticity of demand has great practical significance, as the following examples suggest.

LARGE CROP YIELDS

The demand for most farm products is highly inelastic; E_d is perhaps 0.20 or 0.25. As a result, increases in the supply of farm products arising from a good growing season or from increased productivity tend to depress both the prices of farm products and the total revenues (incomes) of farmers. For farmers as a group, the inelastic demand for their product means that a large crop may be undesirable. For policymakers it means that achieving the goal of higher total farm income requires that farm output be restricted.

SALES TAXES

Both federal and provincial governments pay attention to elasticity of demand when selecting goods and services on which to levy sales taxes. If a $1 tax is levied on a product and 10,000 units are sold, tax revenue will be $10,000 (= $1 × 10,000 units sold). If the government raises the tax to $1.50 but the higher price reduces sales to 5000 because of elastic demand, tax revenue will decline to $7500 (= $1.50 × 5000 units sold). Because a higher tax on a product with elastic demand will bring in less tax revenue, legislatures seek out products that have inelastic demand—such as liquor, gasoline, and cigarettes—when levying sales tax.

DECRIMINALIZATION OF ILLEGAL DRUGS

In recent years proposals to legalize drugs have been widely debated. Proponents contend that drugs should be treated like alcohol: made legal for adults and regulated for purity and potency. Efforts to reduce consumption of illegal drugs by cracking down on users, it is argued, have been unsuccessful and the associated costs—including enlarged police forces, the construction of more prisons, an overburdened court system, and untold human costs—have increased markedly. Some contend that legalization would reduce drug trafficking significantly by taking the profit out of it. Cocaine and heroin, for example, are cheap to produce and could be sold at low prices in legal markets. Because the demand of addicts is highly inelastic, the amounts consumed at the lower prices would increase only modestly. Addicts' total expenditures for cocaine and heroin would decline and so would the street crime that finances those expenditures.

Opponents of legalization say that the overall demand for cocaine and heroin is far more elastic than proponents think. In addition to the inelastic demand of addicts, there is the relatively elastic demand of another market segment consisting of occasional users, who use hard drugs when the prices are low but who abstain or substitute, say, alcohol when the prices are high. Thus, the lower prices associated with the legalization of hard drugs would increase consumption by occasional users. Also, removal of the legal prohibitions against using drugs might make drug use more socially acceptable, increasing the demand for cocaine and heroin.

Many economists predict that the legalization of cocaine and heroin would reduce street prices by up to 60 percent, depending on whether and how much it was taxed. According to an important study, price declines of that size would increase the number of occasional users of heroin by 54 percent and the number of occasional users of cocaine by 33 percent. The total quantity of heroin demanded would rise by an estimated 100 percent and the quantity of cocaine demanded would rise by 50 percent.[1] Moreover, many existing and first-time dabblers might in time become addicts. The overall result, say the opponents of legalization, would be higher social costs, possibly including an increase in street crime.

QUICK REVIEW 6.1

- The price elasticity of demand coefficient E_d is the ratio of the percentage change in quantity demanded to the percentage change in price. The averages of the two prices and two quantities are used as the base references in calculating the percentage changes.

- When E_d is greater than 1, demand is elastic; when E_d is less than 1, demand is inelastic; when E_d is equal to 1, demand is unit elastic.

- When price changes, total revenue will change in the opposite direction if demand is price elastic, in the same direction if demand is price inelastic, and not at all if demand is unit elastic.

- Demand is typically elastic in the high-price (low-quantity) range of the demand curve and inelastic in the low-price (high-quantity) range of the demand curve.

- Price elasticity of demand is greater (a) the larger the number of substitutes available, (b) the higher the price of a product relative to one's income, (c) the greater the extent to which the product is a luxury, and (d) the longer the time period involved.

6.4 Price Elasticity of Supply

LO6.4   Describe price elasticity of supply and how it can be applied.

The concept of price elasticity also applies to supply. If producers are relatively responsive to price changes, supply is elastic. If they are relatively insensitive to price changes, supply is inelastic.

We measure the degree of **price elasticity of supply** with the coefficient E_s, defined almost like E_d except that we substitute "percentage change in quantity supplied" for "percentage change in quantity demanded":

$$E_s = \frac{\text{percentage change in quantity supplied of product X}}{\text{percentage change in price of product X}}$$

---

[1] Henry Saffer and Frank Chaloupka, "The Demand for Illegal Drugs," *Economic Inquiry,* July 1999, pp. 401–411.

For reasons explained earlier in the chapter, the averages, or midpoints, of the before and after quantities supplied and the before and after prices are used as reference points for the percentage changes. Suppose an increase in the price of a good from $4 to $6 increases the quantity supplied from 10 units to 14 units. The percentage change in price would be 2/5, or 40 percent, and the percentage change in quantity would be 4/12, or 33 percent. Consequently

$$E_s = 0.33/0.40 = 0.83$$

In this case, supply is inelastic because the price elasticity coefficient is less than 1. If E_s is greater than 1, supply is elastic. If it is equal to 1, supply is unit elastic. Also, E_s is never negative, since price and quantity supplied are directly related. Thus there are no minus signs to drop, as was necessary with elasticity of demand.

The degree of **price elasticity of supply** depends on how easily—and therefore quickly—producers can shift resources between alternative uses. The more easily and quickly producers can shift resources, the greater the price elasticity of supply. A firm's response to, say, an increase in the price of Christmas trees depends on its ability to shift resources from the production of other products (whose prices we assume remain constant) to the production of trees. And shifting resources takes time: the longer the time available, the greater the resource "shiftability." So we can expect a greater response, and therefore greater elasticity of supply, the longer a firm has to adjust to a price change.

In analyzing the impact of time on elasticity, we distinguish among the immediate market period, the short run, and the long run.

Price Elasticity of Supply: The Immediate Market Period

The **immediate market period** is the length of time over which producers are unable to respond to a change in price with a change in quantity supplied. Suppose the owner of a small farm in southwestern Ontario brings to market one truckload of tomatoes, which is the entire season's output. The supply curve for the tomatoes is perfectly inelastic (vertical): The farmer will sell the truckload whether the price is high or low. Why? Because the farmer can offer only one truckload of tomatoes even if the price of tomatoes is much higher than anticipated. The farmer would like to offer more tomatoes, but tomatoes cannot be produced overnight. Another full growing season is needed to respond to a higher-than-expected price by producing more than one truckload. Similarly, because the product is perishable, the farmer cannot withhold it from the market. If the price is lower than anticipated, the farmer will still sell the entire truckload.

The farmer's costs of production, incidentally, will not enter into this decision to sell. Though the price of tomatoes may fall far short of production costs, the farmer will nevertheless sell everything he brought to market to avoid a total loss through spoilage. In the immediate market period, both the supply of tomatoes and the quantity of tomatoes supplied are fixed. The farmer offers only one truckload no matter how high or low the price.

Figure 6-4a shows the farmer's vertical supply curve during the immediate market period. Supply is perfectly inelastic because the farmer does not have time to respond to a change in demand, say from D_1 to D_2. The resulting price increase from P_0 to P_m simply determines which buyers get the fixed quantity supplied; it elicits no increase in output.

However, not all supply curves are perfectly inelastic immediately after a price change. If the product is not perishable and the price rises, producers may choose to increase quantity supplied by drawing down their inventories of unsold, stored goods, causing the market supply curve to attain some positive slope. For our tomato farmer, the immediate market period may be a full growing season; for producers of goods that can be inexpensively stored, there may be no immediate market period at all.

Price Elasticity of Supply: The Short Run

The **short run** in microeconomics is a period of time too short to change plant capacity but long enough to use the fixed plant capacity more or less intensively. In the short run, our farmer's plant (land and farm machinery) is fixed, but time is available to cultivate tomatoes more intensively by applying more labour and more fertilizer and pesticides to the crop. The result is a greater output in response to an increase in demand; this greater output is reflected in a more elastic supply of tomatoes, as shown by S_s in Figure 6-4b. Note that the increase in demand from D_1 to D_2 is met by an increase in quantity (from Q_0 to Q_s), so there is a smaller price adjustment

FIGURE 6-4 Time and Elasticity of Supply

The greater the amount of time producers have to adjust to a change in demand, here from D_1 to D_2, the greater will be their output response. (a) In the immediate market period, producers have insufficient time to change output, and so supply is perfectly inelastic. (b) In the short run, plant capacity is fixed, but changing the intensity of its use can alter output; supply is therefore more elastic. (c) In the long run, all desired adjustments, including changes in plant capacity, can be made, and supply becomes still more elastic.

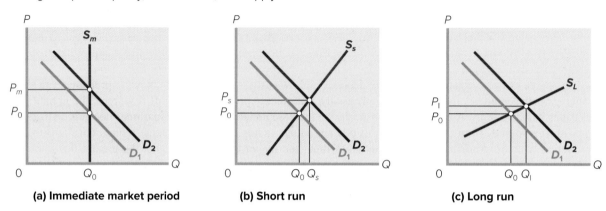

| (a) Immediate market period | (b) Short run | (c) Long run |

(from P_0 to P_s) than in the market period. The equilibrium price is, therefore, lower in the short run than in the market period.

Price Elasticity of Supply: The Long Run

The **long run** is a period long enough for firms to adjust their plant sizes and for new firms to enter (or existing firms to leave) the industry. In the tomato industry, for example, our farmer has time to acquire additional land and buy more machinery and equipment. Furthermore, other farmers may, over time, be attracted to tomato farming by the increased demand and higher price. Such adjustments create a larger supply response, as represented by the more elastic supply curve S_L in Figure 6-4c. The outcome is a smaller price rise (P_0 to P_1) and a larger output increase (Q_0 to Q_1) in response to the increase in demand from D_1 to D_2.

There is no total-revenue test for elasticity of supply. Supply shows a positive or direct relationship between price and amount supplied; the supply curve is upsloping. Regardless of the degree of elasticity or inelasticity, price and total revenue always move together.

Applications of Price Elasticity of Supply

The idea of price elasticity of supply has widespread applicability, as suggested by the following examples.

ANTIQUES AND REPRODUCTIONS

In several places across Canada, people take antiques to a central location for appraisal by experts. Some people are pleased to learn that their old piece of furniture or funky folk art is worth a large amount, say, $30,000 or more.

The high price of an antique results from strong demand and limited, highly inelastic supply. Because a genuine antique can no longer be produced, the quantity supplied either does not rise or rises only slightly as its price goes up. The higher price might prompt the discovery of a few more of the remaining originals and thus add to the quantity available for sale, but this quantity response is usually quite small. So the supply of antiques and other collectibles tends to be inelastic. For one-of-a-kind antiques, the supply is perfectly inelastic.

Factors such as increased population, higher income, and greater enthusiasm for collecting antiques have increased the demand for antiques over time. Because the supply of antiques is limited and inelastic, those increases in demand have greatly boosted the prices of antiques.

Contrast the inelastic supply of original antiques with the elastic supply of modern made-to-look-old reproductions. Such faux antiques are quite popular and widely available. When the demand for reproductions increases, the firms making them simply boost production. Because the supply of reproductions is highly elastic, increased demand raises their price only slightly.

VOLATILE GOLD PRICES

The price of gold is quite volatile, sometimes shooting upward one period and plummeting downward the next. The main sources of these fluctuations are shifts in demand interacting with highly inelastic supply. Gold production is a costly and time-consuming process of exploration, mining, and refining. Moreover, the physical availability of gold is highly limited. For both reasons, increases in gold prices do not bring forth substantial increases in quantity supplied. Conversely, gold mining is costly to shut down and existing gold bars are expensive to store. Price decreases therefore do not produce large drops in the quantity of gold supplied. In short, the supply of gold is inelastic.

The demand for gold is partly derived from the demand for its uses in jewellery, dental fillings, and coins. But people also demand gold as a speculative financial investment, increasing their demand when they fear general inflation or domestic or international turmoil that might undermine the value of currency and more traditional investments, and reducing their demand when events settle down. Because of the inelastic supply of gold, even relatively small changes in demand produce relatively large changes in price.

6.5   Cross Elasticity and Income Elasticity of Demand

LO6.5   Apply cross elasticity of demand and income elasticity of demand.

Price elasticities measure the responsiveness of the quantity of a product demanded or supplied when its price changes. The consumption of a good is also affected by a change in the price of a related product or by a change in income.

Cross Elasticity of Demand

The **cross elasticity of demand** measures how responsive consumer purchases of one product (say X) are to a change in the price of some other product (say Y). We calculate the coefficient of cross elasticity of demand E_{xy} just as we do the coefficient of simple price elasticity, except that we relate the percentage change in the consumption of X to the percentage change in the price of Y:

$$E_{xy} = \frac{\text{percentage change in quantity demanded of product X}}{\text{percentage change in price of product Y}}$$

The concept of cross elasticity (or cross price elasticity) allows us to quantify and more fully understand substitute and complementary goods, introduced in Chapter 3. Unlike price elasticity, we allow the coefficient of cross elasticity of demand to be either positive or negative.

SUBSTITUTE GOODS

If cross elasticity of demand is positive, meaning that sales of X move in the same direction as a change in the price of Y, then X and Y are substitute goods. An example is Evian water (X) and Dasani water (Y). An increase in the price of Evian causes consumers to buy more Dasani, resulting in a positive cross elasticity. The larger the positive cross elasticity coefficient, the greater the substitutability between the two products.

COMPLEMENTARY GOODS

When cross elasticity is negative, we know that X and Y "go together." An increase in the price of one decreases the demand for the other, so the two are complementary goods. For example, a decrease in the price of digital cameras will increase the amount of photo paper purchased. The larger the negative cross elasticity coefficient, the greater the complementarity between the two goods.

INDEPENDENT GOODS

A zero or near-zero cross elasticity indicates that the two products being considered are unrelated or independent goods. An example is walnuts and photo paper; we would not expect a change in the price of walnuts to have any effect on purchases of photo paper and vice versa.

APPLICATIONS

The degree of product substitutability, measured by the cross elasticity coefficient, is important to businesses and government. Suppose Coca-Cola is considering whether to lower the price of its Sprite brand. It will want to know not only the price elasticity of demand for Sprite (Will the price cut increase or decrease total revenue?), but also whether the increased sale of Sprite will come at the expense of its Coke brand. How sensitive are the sales of one of its products (Coke) to a change in the price of another of its products (Sprite)? By how much will the increased sales of Sprite reduce the sales of Coke? A low cross elasticity would indicate that Coke and Sprite are weak substitutes for each other and that a lower price for Sprite would have little effect on Coke sales.

Government also implicitly uses the concept of cross elasticity of demand in assessing whether a proposed merger between two large firms will substantially reduce competition and violate the anticombines laws. For example, the cross elasticity between Coke and Pepsi is high, making them strong substitutes for each other. In addition, Coke and Pepsi together sell about 70 percent of all carbonated cola drinks consumed in Canada. Taken together, the high cross elasticities and the large market shares suggest that the government would likely block a merger between Coke and Pepsi because it would substantially lessen competition. In contrast, the cross elasticity between photo paper and gasoline is low or zero. A merger between Coke and Petro-Canada would have a minimal effect on competition, so government would be more likely to allow it.

Income Elasticity of Demand

Income elasticity of demand measures the degree to which consumers respond to a change in their incomes by buying more or less of a particular good. The coefficient of income elasticity of demand, E_i, is determined using the formula

$$E_i = \frac{\text{percentage change in quantity demanded}}{\text{percentage change in income}}$$

NORMAL GOODS

For most goods, the income elasticity coefficient E_i is positive, meaning that more of them are demanded as incomes rise. Such goods are called normal goods (and were first described in Chapter 3). But the value of E_i varies greatly among normal goods. For example, income elasticity of demand for automobiles is about +3.00, while income elasticity for most farm products is only about +0.20.

INFERIOR GOODS

A negative income elasticity coefficient designates an inferior good. Retread tires, cabbage, long-distance bus tickets, and used clothing are likely candidates. Consumers decrease their purchases of inferior goods as incomes rise.

INSIGHTS

Coefficients of income elasticity of demand provide insight into the Canadian economy. For example, when recessions (business downturns) occur and incomes fall, income elasticity of demand helps predict which products will decline in demand more rapidly than others.

Products with relatively high income-elasticity coefficients, such as automobiles ($E_i = +3$), housing ($E_i = +1.5$), and restaurant meals ($E_i = +1.4$), are generally hit hardest by recessions. Those with low income-elasticity coefficients are much less affected. For example, food products prepared at home ($E_i = +0.20$) respond relatively little to income fluctuations. When incomes drop, purchases of food (and toothpaste and toilet paper) drop little compared to purchases of movie tickets, luxury vacations, and plasma-screen TVs. Products we view as essential tend to have

TABLE 6-4	Cross Elasticity and Income Elasticity of Demand	
Value of coefficient	**Description**	**Type of good(s)**
Cross elasticity:		
Positive ($E_{wz} > 0$)	Quantity demanded of W changes in same direction as change in price of Z.	Substitutes
Negative ($E_{xy} < 0$)	Quantity demanded of X changes in opposite direction from change in price of Y.	Complements
Income elasticity:		
Positive ($E_i > 0$)	Quantity demanded of the product changes in same direction as change in income.	Normal
Negative ($E_i < 0$)	Quantity demanded of the product changes in opposite direction from change in income.	Inferior

lower income-elasticity coefficients than products we view as luxuries. When our incomes fall, we cannot easily eliminate or postpone the purchase of essential products.

Table 6-4 provides a convenient synopsis of the cross elasticity and income elasticity concepts.

QUICK REVIEW 6.2

- Price elasticity of supply measures the sensitivity of suppliers to changes in the price of a product. The price elasticity of supply coefficient E_s is the ratio of the percentage change in quantity supplied to the percentage change in price. The elasticity of supply varies directly with the amount of time producers have to respond to the price change.

- The cross elasticity of demand coefficient E_{xy} is computed as the percentage change in the quantity demanded of

product X divided by the percentage change in the price of product Y. If the cross elasticity coefficient is positive, the two products are substitutes; if it is negative, they are complements.

- The income elasticity coefficient E_i is computed as the percentage change in quantity demanded divided by the percentage change in income. A positive coefficient indicates a normal or superior good. The coefficient is negative for an inferior good.

6.6   Elasticity and Tax Incidence

LO6.6   Explain the principles relating to tax shifting, tax incidence, and the efficiency losses caused by taxes.

Demand and supply analysis and the elasticity concept are applied repeatedly in the remainder of this book. Let's strengthen our understanding of these analytical tools and their importance by examining elasticity and **tax incidence**, the degree to which a tax falls on a particular person or group. In recent years many provinces (Ontario, New Brunswick, Nova Scotia, Prince Edward Island, and Newfoundland and Labrador) have moved to a *harmonized sales tax* (HST), which combines the federal goods and services tax (GST) and provincial sales tax (PST). The HST varies across provinces because each sets its own provincial sales tax rate. In general, the HST extends provincial taxes to services as well as goods, whereas the PST was only levied on goods. Despite the extension to many services previously not covered, the introduction of the HST is revenue-neutral once all the exemptions are included.

Elasticity and Tax Incidence

In Figure 6-5, *S* and *D* represent the pre-tax market for a certain domestic wine from the Niagara Peninsula. The no-tax equilibrium price and quantity are $8 per bottle and 15 million bottles. If the Ontario government levies a tax of $2 per bottle directly on the winery for every bottle sold, who actually pays it?

DIVISION OF BURDEN

Since the provincial government places the tax on the sellers (suppliers), the tax can be viewed as an addition to the cost of the product. Now sellers must get $2 more for each bottle to receive the same per-unit profit they were getting before the tax. While sellers are willing to offer, for example, 5 million bottles of untaxed wine at $4 per bottle, they must now receive $6 per bottle—$4 plus the $2 tax—to offer the same 5 million bottles. The tax shifts the supply curve upward (leftward) as shown in Figure 6-5, where S_t is the after-tax supply curve.

The after-tax equilibrium price is $9 per bottle, whereas the before-tax price was $8. So, in this case, half the $2 tax is paid by consumers as a higher price; the other half must be paid by producers in a lower after-tax per-unit revenue. That is, after paying the $2 tax per unit to the provincial government, producers receive $7, or $1 less than the $8 before-tax price. In this instance, consumers and producers share the burden of this tax equally; producers shift half the tax to consumers in a higher price and bear the other half themselves.

Note also that the equilibrium quantity decreases as a result of the tax levy and the higher price it imposes on consumers. In Figure 6-5 that decline in quantity is from 15 million bottles per month to 12.5 million bottles per month.

ELASTICITIES

If the elasticities of demand and supply were different from those shown in Figure 6-5, the incidence of tax would also be different. Two generalizations are relevant.

FIGURE 6-5   The Incidence of a Tax

A tax of a specified amount per unit levied on producers—here, $2 per unit—shifts the supply curve upward by the amount of the tax per unit: the vertical distance between *S* and S_t. This shift results in a higher price (here, $9) to the consumer and a lower after-tax price (here, $7) to the producer. Thus, consumers and producers share the burden of the tax in some proportion (here, equally at $2 per unit).

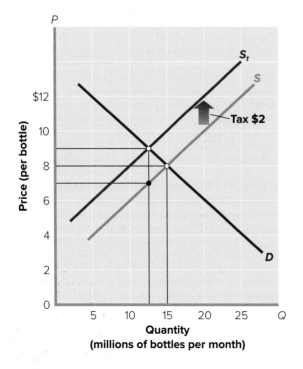

FIGURE 6-6   Demand Elasticity and the Incidence of a Tax

(a) If demand is elastic in the relevant price range, price rises modestly (P_1 to P_e) when a tax is levied. Hence, the producer bears most of the tax burden. (b) If demand is inelastic, the price to the buyer will increase substantially (P_1 to P_i) and most of the tax will be shifted to consumers.

| (a) Tax incidence and elastic demand | (b) Tax incidence and inelastic demand |

1. *With a specific supply, the more inelastic the demand for the product, the larger the portion of the tax shifted to consumers.* To verify this, sketch graphically the extreme cases where demand is perfectly elastic or perfectly inelastic. In the first case, the incidence of the tax is entirely on sellers; in the second, the tax is shifted entirely to consumers.

   Figure 6-6 contrasts the more usual cases where demand is either relatively elastic or relatively inelastic in the relevant price range. With elastic demand, shown in Figure 6-6a, a small portion of the tax ($P_e - P_1$) is shifted to consumers and most of the tax ($P_1 - P_a$) is paid by producers. With inelastic demand, shown in Figure 6-6b, most of the tax ($P_i - P_1$) is shifted to consumers and only a small amount ($P_1 - P_b$) is paid by producers. In both graphs the per-unit tax is represented by the vertical distance between S_t and S.

   Note also that the decline in equilibrium quantity (from Q_1 to Q_2 in Figure 6-6a and from Q_4 to Q_5 in Figure 6-6b) is smaller when demand is more inelastic. This is the basis of our previous applications of the elasticity concept: revenue-seeking legislatures place heavy sales taxes on liquor, cigarettes, and other products whose demands are thought to be inelastic. Since demand for these products is relatively inelastic, the tax does not reduce sales much, so the tax revenue stays high.

2. The second generalization is that, *with a specific demand, the more inelastic the supply, the larger the portion of the tax paid by producers.* When supply is elastic, as in Figure 6-7a, most of the tax ($P_2 - P_1$) is shifted to consumers, and only a small portion ($P_1 - P_3$) is paid by sellers. But when supply is inelastic, as in Figure 6-7b, the reverse is true: the major portion of the tax ($P_4 - P_6$) falls on sellers, and a relatively small amount ($P_5 - P_6$) is shifted to buyers. The equilibrium quantity also declines less with an inelastic supply than it does with an elastic supply.

   Gold is an example of a product with an inelastic supply, one where the burden of a tax would mainly fall on producers. Conversely, because the supply of baseballs is elastic, producers would pass on to consumers much of a tax on baseballs. You may want to reverse the analysis and assume that the government levies a (sales) tax on consumers.

Efficiency Loss of a Tax

We just observed that producers and consumers typically each bear part of a tax levied on producers. Let's now look more closely at the overall economic effect of the tax. Consider Figure 6-8, which is similar to Figure 6-7 but contains the additional detail we need for our discussion.

TAX REVENUES

In our example, a $2 tax on wine increases its market price from $8 to $9 per bottle and reduces the equilibrium quantity from 15 million bottles to 12.5 million. Government tax revenue is $25 million (= $2 × 12.5 million

FIGURE 6-7   Supply Elasticity and the Incidence of a Tax

(a) With an elastic supply, the sales tax results in a large price increase (P_1 to P_2), and the tax is therefore paid mainly by consumers. (b) If supply is inelastic, the price rise is small (P_4 to P_5), and sellers will have to bear most of the tax.

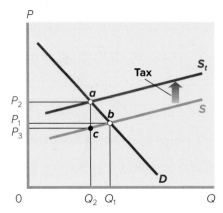

(a) Tax incidence and elastic supply

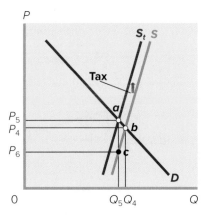

(b) Tax incidence and inelastic supply

bottles), an amount shown as the rectangle *efac* in Figure 6-8. The elasticities of supply and demand in this case are such that consumers and producers each pays half this total amount, or $12.5 million apiece (= $1 × 12.5 million bottles). The government uses this $25 million of tax revenue to provide public goods and services. So this transfer of dollars from consumers and producers to government involves no loss of well-being to society.

EFFICIENCY LOSS

The $2 tax on wine does more than require consumers and producers to pay $25 million of taxes; it also reduces the equilibrium amount of wine produced and consumed by 2.5 million bottles. The fact that consumers and producers demanded and supplied 2.5 million more bottles of wine before the tax means that those 2.5 million bottles provided benefits in excess of their production costs. This is clear from the following analysis.

Segment *ab* of demand curve *D* in Figure 6-8 indicates the willingness to pay—the marginal benefit—associated with each of the 2.5 million bottles consumed before (but not after) the tax. Segment *cb* of supply curve *S* reflects the marginal cost of each of the bottles of wine. For all but the very last one of these 2.5 million bottles, the marginal benefit (shown by a point on *ab*) exceeds the marginal cost (shown by a point on *cb*). Not producing these 2.5 million bottles of wine reduces well-being by an amount represented by the triangle *abc*. The area of this triangle identifies the **efficiency loss of a tax** (also called the *deadweight loss of a tax*). This loss is society's sacrifice of net benefit because the tax reduces production and consumption of the product below their levels of economic efficiency, where marginal benefit and marginal cost are equal.

ROLE OF ELASTICITIES

Most taxes create some degree of efficiency loss, but just how much depends on the supply and demand elasticities. Glancing back at Figure 6-6, we see that the efficiency loss area *abc* is greater in Figure 6.6a, where demand is relatively elastic, than in Figure 6.6b, where demand is relatively inelastic. Similarly, area *abc* is greater in Figure 6.7a than in Figure 6.7b, indicating a larger efficiency loss where supply is more elastic. Other things equal, the greater the elasticities of supply and demand, the greater the efficiency loss of a particular tax.

Two taxes yielding equal revenues do not necessarily impose equal costs on society. The government must keep this fact in mind in designing a tax system to finance beneficial public goods and services. In general, it should minimize the efficiency loss of the tax system in raising any specific dollar amount of tax revenue.

FIGURE 6-8 Efficiency Loss (or Deadweight Loss) of a Tax

The levy of a $2 tax per bottle of wine increases the price per bottle from $8 to $9 and reduces the equilibrium quantity from 15 million to 12.5 million. Tax revenue to the government is $25 million (area *efac*). The efficiency loss of the tax arises from the 2.5 million decline in output; the amount of that loss is shown as triangle *abc*.

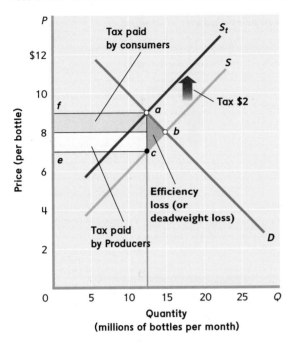

QUALIFICATIONS

We must acknowledge, however, that other tax goals may be as important as, or even more important than, minimizing efficiency losses from taxes. Here are two examples:

- **Redistributive Goals**   Government may wish to impose taxes as a way to redistribute income.

- **Reducing Negative Externalities**   Our analysis of the efficiency loss of a tax assumes no negative externalities arising from either the production or consumption of the product in question. Where such spillover costs occur, an excise tax on producers might actually improve allocative efficiency by reducing output and thus lessening the negative externality. For example, the $2 tax on wine in our example might be part of a broader set of taxes on alcoholic beverages. The government may have concluded that the consumption of these beverages produces certain negative externalities. Therefore, it might have purposely levied this $2 tax to shift the market supply curve in Figure 6-8 to increase the price of wine, decrease alcohol consumption, and reduce the amount of resources devoted to wine.

Some sales taxes that are intended to reduce the production and consumption of products with negative externalities are sometimes referred to as *sin taxes,* implying that governments are motivated to impose these taxes to discourage activities that are perceived to be harmful or sinful. Taxes on cigarettes and alcohol in particular are commonly referred to as sin taxes.

QUICK REVIEW 6.3

- Given fixed demand, more elastic supply shifts tax burdens to consumers; given fixed supply, more elastic demand shifts tax burdens to producers.

- Taxes imposed in markets raise the market equilibrium price, reduce the market equilibrium output, and normally generate efficiency losses.

The LAST WORD

Elasticity and Pricing Power: Why Different Consumers Pay Different Prices

Firms and nonprofit institutions often recognize and exploit differences in price elasticity of demand.

All the buyers of a product traded in a highly competitive market pay the same market price for the product, regardless of their individual price elasticities of demand. If the price rises, Jones may have an elastic demand and greatly reduce her purchases. Green may have a unit-elastic demand and reduce his purchases less than Jones. Lopez may have an inelastic demand and hardly curtail his purchases at all. But all three consumers will pay the single higher price regardless of their demand elasticities.

In later chapters we will find that not all sellers must passively accept a "one for all" price. Some firms have *market power* or *pricing power* that allows them to set their product prices in their best interests. For some goods and services, firms may find it advantageous to determine differences in price elasticity of demand and then charge different prices to different buyers.

It is extremely difficult to tailor prices to each customer on the basis of elasticity of demand, but it is relatively easy to observe differences in group elasticities. Consider airline tickets. Business travellers generally have inelastic demand for air travel. Because their time is highly valuable, they do not see slower modes of transportation as realistic substitutes. Also, their employers pay for their tickets as part of their business expenses. In contrast, leisure travellers tend to have elastic demand. They have the option to drive rather than fly, or simply not to travel at all. They also pay for their tickets out of their own pockets and thus are more sensitive to price.

Airlines recognize the difference between the groups in terms of price elasticity of demand and charge business travellers more than leisure travellers. To accomplish that, they have to dissuade business travellers from buying the less expensive round-trip tickets aimed at leisure travellers. One way to do this is by putting restrictions on the lower-priced tickets. For example, airlines make the tickets nonrefundable, require at least two-week advance purchase, and require Saturday-night stays. These restrictions chase off most business travellers, who engage in last-minute travel and want to be home for the weekend. As a result, a business traveller often pays hundreds of dollars more for a ticket than a leisure traveller on the same plane.

Discounts for children are another example of pricing based on group differences in price elasticity of demand. For many products, children have more elastic demands than adults because children have low budgets, often financed by their parents. Sellers recognize the elasticity difference and price accordingly. The barber spends as much time cutting a child's hair as an adult's but charges the child much less. A child takes up a full seat at the baseball game but pays a lower price than an adult. A child snowboarder occupies the same space on a chairlift as an adult snowboarder but qualifies for a discounted lift ticket.

Finally, consider pricing by colleges and universities. Price elasticities of demand for higher education are greater for prospective students from low-income families, who generally have more elastic demands for higher education than similar students from high-income families. This makes sense because tuition is a much larger proportion of household income for a low-income student or family than for his or her high-income counterpart. Desiring a diverse student body, universities charge different *net* prices (= tuition *minus* financial aid) to the two groups on the basis of elasticity of demand. High-income students pay full tuition, unless they receive merit-based scholarships. Low-income students receive considerable financial aid in addition to merit-based scholarships and, in effect, pay a lower net price.

© Tom Prettyman/PhotoEdit

It is common for schools to announce a large tuition increase and immediately cushion the news by emphasizing that they are also increasing financial aid. In effect, the school is increasing the tuition for students who have inelastic demand by the full amount and raising the net tuition of those with elastic demand by some lesser amount or not at all. Through this strategy, colleges and universities boost revenue to cover rising costs while maintaining affordability for a wide range of students.

There are a number of other examples of dual or multiple pricing. All relate directly to price elasticity of demand. We will revisit this topic in Chapter 11 when we discuss what economists call *price discrimination*—charging different prices to different customers for the same product.

Question

What is the purpose of charging different groups of customers different prices? Supplement the three broad examples in this Last Word with two examples of your own. (*Hint:* Think of price discounts based on group characteristics or time of purchase.)

Chapter Summary

LO6.1 Discuss price elasticity of demand and how it is calculated.

- Price elasticity of demand measures consumer response to price changes. If consumers are relatively sensitive to price changes, demand is elastic. If they are relatively unresponsive to price changes, demand is inelastic.

- The price elasticity coefficient E_d measures the degree of elasticity or inelasticity of demand. The coefficient is found by the formula

$$E_d = \frac{\text{percentage change in quantity demanded of product X}}{\text{percentage change in price of product X}}$$

The averages of prices and quantities under consideration are used as reference points in determining percentage changes in price and quantity. If E_d is greater than 1, demand is elastic. If E_d is less than 1, demand is inelastic. Unit elasticity is the special case in which E_d equals 1.

- Perfectly inelastic demand is graphed as a line parallel to the vertical axis; perfectly elastic demand is shown by a line above and parallel to the horizontal axis.

- Elasticity varies at different price ranges on a demand curve, tending to be elastic in the upper left segment and inelastic in the lower right segment. Elasticity cannot be judged by the steepness or flatness of a demand curve.

LO6.2 Explain the usefulness of the total-revenue test for price elasticity of demand.

- If total revenue changes in the opposite direction from prices, demand is elastic. If price and total revenue change in the same direction, demand is inelastic. Where demand is of unit elasticity, a change in prices leaves total revenue unchanged.

LO6.3 List the factors that affect price elasticity of demand and describe some applications of price elasticity of demand.

- The number of available substitutes, the size of an item's price relative to one's income, whether the product is a luxury or a necessity, and the time given to adjust are all determinants of elasticity of demand.

LO6.4 Describe price elasticity of supply and how it can be applied.

- The elasticity concept also applies to supply. The coefficient of price elasticity of supply is found by the formula

$$E_s = \frac{\text{percentage change in quantity supplied of product X}}{\text{percentage change in price of product X}}$$

The averages of the price and quantities under consideration are used as reference points for computing percentage changes. Elasticity of supply depends on the ease of shifting resources between alternative uses, which in turn varies directly with the time producers have to adjust to a particular price change.

LO6.5 Apply cross elasticity of demand and income elasticity of demand.

- Cross elasticity of demand indicates how sensitive the purchase of one product is to changes in the price of another product. The coefficient of cross elasticity of demand is found by the formula

$$E_{xy} = \frac{\text{percentage change in quantity demanded of product X}}{\text{percentage change in price of product Y}}$$

- Positive cross elasticity of demand identifies substitute goods; negative cross elasticity identifies complementary goods.

- Income elasticity of demand indicates the responsiveness of consumer purchases to a change in income. The coefficient of income elasticity of demand is found by the formula

$$E_i = \frac{\text{percentage change in quantity demanded of product X}}{\text{percentage change in income}}$$

The coefficient is positive for normal goods and negative for inferior goods.

- Industries selling products that have high income elasticity of demand coefficients are particularly hard hit by recessions. Those with products that have low or negative income elasticity of demand coefficients fare much better.

LO6.6 Explain the principles relating to tax shifting, tax incidence, and the efficiency losses caused by taxes.

- Sales taxes affect supply and, therefore, equilibrium price and quantity. The more inelastic the demand for a product, the greater the proportion of a sales tax shifted to consumers. The greater the inelasticity of supply, the larger the proportion of the tax paid by the seller.

- Taxation involves the loss of some output whose marginal benefit exceeds its marginal cost. The more elastic the supply and demand curves, the greater the efficiency loss (or deadweight loss) resulting from a particular tax.

Terms and Concepts

price elasticity of demand

midpoint formula

elastic demand

inelastic demand

unit elasticity

perfectly inelastic

perfectly elastic demand

total revenue (TR)

total-revenue test

price elasticity of supply

immediate market period
short run
long run
cross elasticity of demand

income elasticity of demand
tax incidence
efficiency loss of a tax

Discussion Questions

1. Explain why the choice between 1, 2, 3, 4, 5, 6, 7, and 8 movie tickets or 1000, 2000, 3000, 4000, 5000, 6000, 7000, and 8000 movie tickets makes no difference in determining elasticity in Table 6-1. [**LO6.1**]

2. What effect would a rule stating that university students must live in university dormitories have on the price elasticity of demand for dormitory space? What impact might this in turn have on room rates? [**LO6.1**]

3. The income elasticities of demand for movies, dental services, and clothing have been estimated to be +3.4, +1.0, and +0.5,

respectively. Interpret these coefficients. What does it mean if an income elasticity coefficient is negative? [**LO6.5**]

4. Research has found that an increase in the price of beer would reduce the amount of marijuana consumed. Is cross elasticity of demand between the two products positive or negative? Are these products substitutes or complements? What might be the logic behind this relationship? [**LO6.5**]

5. What is the tax incidence of a sales tax when demand is highly inelastic? Highly elastic? What effect does the elasticity of supply have on the incidence of a sales tax? [**LO6.6**]

Review Questions

1. Graph the accompanying demand data and then use the midpoint formula for E_d to determine price elasticity of demand for each of the four possible $1 price changes. What can you conclude about the relationship between the slope of a curve and its elasticity? Explain in a non-technical way why demand is elastic in the upper left segment of the demand curve and inelastic in the lower right segment. [**LO6.1**]

Product price	Quantity demanded
$5	1
4	2
3	3
2	4
1	5

2. What are the major determinants of price elasticity of demand? Use those determinants and your own reasoning in judging whether demand for each of the following products is probably elastic or inelastic: [**LO6.1**]

   a. Bottled water
   b. Toothpaste
   c. Crest toothpaste
   d. Ketchup
   e. Diamond bracelets
   f. Microsoft's Windows operating system

3. Calculate total-revenue data from the demand schedule in Review Question 1. Graph total revenue below your demand curve. Generalize about the relationship between price elasticity and total revenue. [**LO6.2**]

4. How would the following changes in price affect total revenue? That is, would total revenue increase, decrease, or remain unchanged? [**LO6.2**]

   a. Price falls and demand is inelastic.
   b. Price rises and demand is elastic.
   c. Price rises and supply is elastic.
   d. Price rises and supply is inelastic.
   e. Price rises and demand is inelastic.
   f. Price falls and demand is elastic.
   g. Price falls and demand is of unit elasticity.

5. In 2015, Paul Gauguin's painting *When Will You Marry* sold for $300 million. Portray this sale in a demand-and-supply diagram and comment on the elasticity of supply. Comedian George Carlin once mused, "If a painting can be forged well enough to fool some experts, why is the original so valuable?" Provide an answer. [**LO6.4**]

6. Suppose the cross elasticity of demand for products A and B is +3.6 and for products C and D is −5.4. What can you conclude about how products A and B are related? Products C and D? [**LO6.5**]

7. True or False? The incidence of property taxes that are levied on rented houses and apartments is high—meaning that they are paid almost entirely by the landlords, who are billed by the government for those taxes. [**LO6.6**]

Problems

1. Look at the demand curve in Figure 6-2a. Use the midpoint formula and points *a* and *b* to calculate the elasticity of demand for that range of the demand curve. Do the same for the demand curves in Figures 6-2b and 6-2c using, respectively, points *c* and *d* for Figure 6-2b and points *e* and *f* for Figure 6-2c. [**LO6.1**]

2. Investigate how demand elasticities are affected by increases in demand. Shift each of the demand curves in Figures 6-2a, 6-2b, and 6-2c to the right by 10 units. For example, point *a* in Figure 6-2a would shift to the right from location (10 units, $2) to (20 units, $2) while point *b* would shift to the right from location (40 units, $1) to (50 units, $1). After making these shifts, apply the midpoint formula to calculate the demand elasticities for the shifted points. Are they larger or smaller than the elasticities you calculated in Problem 1 for the original points? In terms of the midpoint formula, what explains the change in elasticities? [**LO6.1**]

3. Suppose that the total revenue received by a company selling basketballs is $600 when the price is set at $30 per basketball and $600 when the price is set at $20 per basketball. Without using the midpoint formula, can you tell whether demand is elastic, inelastic, or unit elastic over this price range? [**LO6.2**]

4. Danny "Dimes" Donahue is a neighbourhood's nine-year-old entrepreneur. His most recent venture is selling homemade brownies he bakes himself. At a price of $1.50 each, he sells 100. At $1 each, he sells 300. Is demand elastic or inelastic over this price range? If demand had the same elasticity for a price decline from $1 to $0.50 as it does for the decline from $1.50 to $1, would cutting the price from $1 to $0.50 increase or decrease Danny's total revenue? [**LO6.2**]

5. What is the formula for measuring the price elasticity of supply? Suppose the price of apples goes up from $20 to $22 a box. In direct response, Goldsboro Farms supplies 1200 boxes of apples instead of 1000 boxes. Compute the coefficient of price elasticity (midpoints approach) for Goldsboro's supply. Is its supply elastic or is it inelastic? [**LO6.4**]

6. **Advanced Analysis** Currently, at a price of $1 each, 100 popsicles are sold per day in the perpetually hot town of Rostin. Consider the elasticity of supply. In the short run, a price increase from $1 to $2 is unit elastic ($E_s = 1.0$). How many popsicles will be sold each day in the short run if the price rises to $2 each? In the long run, a price increase from $1 to $2 has an elasticity of supply of 1.50. How many popsicles will be sold per day in the long run if the price rises to $2 each? (*Hint:* Apply the midpoints approach to the elasticity of supply.) [**LO6.4**]

7. Lorena likes to play golf. How many times per year she plays depends on two things: (1) the price of playing a round of golf and (2) Lorena's income and the cost of other types of entertainment—in particular, how much it costs to see a movie instead of playing golf. The three demand schedules in the table below show how many rounds of golf per year Lorena will demand at each price in three different scenarios. In scenario D_1, Lorena's income is $50,000 per year and movies cost $9 each. In scenario D_2, Lorena's income is also $50,000 per year, but the price of seeing a movie rises to $11. And in scenario D_3, Lorena's income goes up to $70,000 per year while movies cost $11. [**LO6.5**]

	QUANTITY DEMANDED		
Price	D_1	D_2	D_3
35	25	15	30
20	40	20	50

a. Using the data under D_1 and D_2, calculate the cross elasticity of Lorena's demand for golf at all three prices. (To do this, apply the midpoints approach to the cross elasticity of demand.) Is the cross elasticity the same at all three prices? Are movies and golf substitute goods, complementary goods, or independent goods?

b. Using the data under D_2 and D_3, calculate the income elasticity of Lorena's demand for golf at all three prices. (To do this, apply the midpoints approach to the income elasticity of demand.) Is the income elasticity the same at all three prices? Is golf an inferior good?

8. **Advanced Analysis** Suppose the equation for the demand curve for some product X is $P = 8 + 0.6Q$ and the supply curve is $P = 2 + 0.4Q$. What are the equilibrium price and quantity? Now suppose an excise tax is imposed on X such that the new supply equation is $P = 4 + 0.4Q$. How much tax revenue will this excise tax yield the government? [**LO6.6**]

CHAPTER 7

Consumer Choice and Utility Maximization

LEARNING OBJECTIVES

LO7.1 Define and explain the relationship between total utility, marginal utility, and the law of diminishing marginal utility.

LO7.2 Describe how rational consumers maximize utility by comparing marginal-utility-to-price ratios for all products they could possibly purchase.

LO7.3 Explain how a demand curve can be derived by observing the outcomes of price changes in the utility-maximization model.

LO7.4 Discuss how the utility-maximization model helps highlight the income and substitution effects of a price change.

LO7.5 Give examples of several real-world phenomena that can be explained by applying the theory of consumer choice.

LOA7.1 (Appendix) Relate how the indifference curve model of consumer choice derives demand curves from budget lines, indifference curves, and utility maximization.

If you were to compare the shopping carts of almost any two consumers, you would observe striking differences. Why does Paula have potatoes, peaches, and Pepsi in her cart while Sam has sugar, saltines, and 7-Up in his? Why didn't Paula also buy pasta and plums? Why didn't Sam have soup and spaghetti on his grocery list?

In this chapter you will see how individual consumers allocate their income among the various goods and services available to them. Given a certain budget, how does a consumer decide which goods and services to buy? This chapter will develop a model to answer this question.

7.1   The Law of Diminishing Marginal Utility

LO7.1   **Define and explain the relationship between total utility, marginal utility, and the law of diminishing marginal utility.**

The simplest theory of consumer choice rests squarely on the **law of diminishing marginal utility**. This principle, first discussed in Chapter 3, is that added satisfaction declines as a consumer acquires additional units of a given product. Although consumer wants in general may be insatiable, wants for a particular item can be satisfied. In a specific span of time over which consumers' tastes remain unchanged, consumers can get as much of a particular good or service as they can afford. But the more of that product they obtain, the less they want still more of it.

Consider durable goods, for example. Consumers' desires for an automobile, when they have none, may be very strong, but the desire is less intense for a second car, and weaker and weaker for a third or fourth. Unless they are collectors, even the wealthiest families rarely have more than a half-dozen cars, although their income would allow them to purchase a whole fleet of vehicles.

Evidence indicates that consumers can fulfill specific wants with succeeding units of a product but that each added unit provides less utility than the previous unit purchased. Recall that a product has utility if it can satisfy a want: **utility** is want-satisfying power. The utility of a good or service is the satisfaction or pleasure one gets from consuming it. Keep in mind three characteristics of this concept.

1. *Utility* and *usefulness* are not synonymous. Paintings by Picasso may offer great utility to art connoisseurs but are useless functionally (other than for hiding a crack in a wall!).

2. Utility is subjective. The utility of a specific product may vary widely from person to person. A Céline Dion CD has tremendous utility for one of her fans, but no utility to someone who listens only to the Tragically Hip.

3. Utility is difficult to quantify. But, for purposes of illustration, we assume that people can measure satisfaction with units called *utils* (units of utility). For example, a particular consumer may get 100 utils of satisfaction from a smoothie, 10 utils of satisfaction from a candy bar, and 1 util of satisfaction from a stick of gum. These imaginary units of satisfaction are convenient for quantifying consumer behaviour for explanatory purposes.

Total Utility and Marginal Utility

Total utility and marginal utility are related but different ideas. The **total utility** is the total amount of satisfaction or pleasure a person derives from consuming some specific quantity—for example, ten units—of a good or service. The **marginal utility** is the *extra* satisfaction a consumer gets from one additional unit of that product, for example, from the eleventh unit. Alternatively, marginal utility is the change in total utility that results from the consumption of one more unit of a product.

Figure 7-1 (Key Graph) and its accompanying table demonstrate the relation between total utility and marginal utility. The curves reflect the data in the table. Column 2 shows the total utility at each level of consumption of tacos; column 3 shows the marginal utility—the change in total utility—that results from the consumption of each successive taco. Starting at the origin in Figure 7-1a, we observe that each of the first five units increases total utility (TU) but by a diminishing amount. Total utility reaches a maximum at the sixth unit and then declines. The marginal utility is also measured by the slope of the total utility curve.

So in Figure 7-1b marginal utility (MU) remains positive but diminishes through the first five units (because total utility increases at a declining rate). Marginal utility is zero for the sixth unit (because that unit doesn't change total utility). Marginal utility then becomes negative with the seventh unit as the diner becomes ill (because total utility is falling). Figure 7-1b and column 3 of the table reveal that each successive taco yields less extra utility, meaning fewer utils, than the preceding taco.[1] That is, the table and the graph illustrate the law of diminishing marginal utility.

---

[1] In Figure 6-1b we graphed marginal utility at half-units. For example, we graphed the marginal utility of 4 utils at 3½ units because the 4 utils refers to neither the third nor the fourth unit per se but to the *addition* or *subtraction* of the fourth unit.

KEY GRAPH

FIGURE 7-1   Total and Marginal Utility

Curves TU and MU are graphed from the data in the table. (a) As more of a product is consumed, total utility increases at a diminishing rate, reaches a maximum, and then declines. (b) Marginal utility, by definition, reflects the changes in total utility. Thus marginal utility diminishes with increased consumption, becomes zero when total utility is at a maximum, and is negative when total utility declines. As shown by the shaded rectangles in panels (a) and (b), marginal utility is the change in total utility associated with each additional taco. Or, alternatively, each new level of total utility is found by adding marginal utility to the preceding level of total utility.

(a) Total utility

(b) Marginal utility

(1)	(2)	(3)
Tacos consumed per meal	Total utility, utils	Marginal utility, utils
0	0	
		10
1	10	
		8
2	18	
		6
3	24	
		4
4	28	
		2
5	30	
		0
6	30	
		−2
7	28	

QUICK QUIZ

1. **Marginal utility**
   a. Is the extra output a firm obtains when it adds another unit of labour
   b. Explains why product supply curves slope upward
   c. Typically rises as successive units of a good are consumed
   d. Is the extra satisfaction from the consumption of one more unit of some good or service

2. **Marginal utility in Figure 7-1b is positive, but declining, when total utility in Figure 7-1a is positive and**
   a. Rising at an increasing rate
   b. Falling at an increasing rate
   c. Rising at a decreasing rate
   d. Falling at a decreasing rate

3. **When marginal utility is zero in panel (b), total utility in panel (a) is**
   a. Also zero
   b. Neither rising nor falling
   c. Negative
   d. Rising but at a declining rate

4. **Suppose the person represented by these graphs experienced a diminished taste for tacos. As a result the**
   a. TU curve would get steeper
   b. MU curve would get flatter
   c. TU and MU curves would shift downward
   d. MU curve, but not the TU curve, would collapse to the horizontal axis

Answers   1.d; 2.c; 3.b; 4.c

If successive units of a good yield smaller and smaller amounts of marginal utility, the consumer will buy additional units only if its price falls.

© Tacrafts/Dreamstime.com

Marginal Utility and Demand

The law of diminishing marginal utility explains why the demand curve for a given product slopes downward. If successive units of a good yield smaller and smaller amounts of marginal, or extra, utility, then the consumer will buy additional units of a product only if its price falls. The consumer for whom Figure 7-1 is relevant may buy two tacos at a price of $1 each, but because less marginal utility is obtained from additional tacos, the consumer will choose not to buy more at that price. The consumer would rather spend additional dollars on products that provide more (or equal) utility, not less. Therefore, additional tacos with less utility are not worth buying unless the price declines. (When marginal utility becomes negative, the restaurant would have to pay you to consume another taco!) Thus, diminishing marginal utility supports the idea that price must decrease for quantity demanded to increase. In other words, the law of diminishing marginal utility empowers the law of demand. Or, to put it yet another way, consumers behave in ways that make demand curves downsloping.

MATH 7.1   Law of Diminishing Marginal Utility

QUICK REVIEW 7.1

- The law of diminishing marginal utility indicates that gains in satisfaction become smaller as successive units of a specific product are consumed.

- Utility is the benefit or satisfaction a person receives from consuming a good or a service.

- Diminishing marginal utility provides a simple rationale for the law of demand.

7.2   The Theory of Consumer Choice

LO7.2   Describe how rational consumers maximize utility by comparing marginal-utility-to-price ratios for all products they could possibly purchase.

In addition to explaining the law of demand, the idea of diminishing marginal utility explains how consumers allocate their money income among the many goods and services available for purchase.

CHOOSING A LITTLE MORE OR LESS

Consumer Choice and the Budget Constraint

For simplicity, we will assume that the situation for the typical consumer has the following dimensions.

- *Rational Behaviour* The consumer is a rational person who tries to use his or her money income to get the greatest amount of satisfaction, or utility, from it. Consumers want to get the most for their money or, technically, to maximize their total utility. They engage in **rational behaviour**.

- *Preferences* Each consumer has clear-cut preferences for certain goods and services of those available in the market. Buyers also have a good idea of how much marginal utility they will get from successive units of the various products they purchase.

- *Budget Constraints* At any point in time the consumer has a fixed, limited amount of money income. Since each consumer supplies a finite amount of human and property resources to society, he or she earns only limited income. Thus, as noted in Chapter 1, every consumer faces a **budget constraint**, even consumers who can earn millions of dollars a year. Of course, those budget constraints are more severe for consumers with average incomes than for those with extraordinarily high incomes.

- *Prices* Goods are scarce relative to the demand for them, so every good carries a price tag. We assume those price tags are not affected by the amounts of specific goods each person buys. After all, each person's purchase is only a tiny part of total demand. Also, because the consumer has a limited number of dollars, he or she cannot buy everything wanted. This point drives home the reality of scarcity to each consumer.

So consumers must compromise and choose the most personally satisfying affordable combination of goods and services. Different individuals will choose different mixes.

Utility-Maximizing Rule

Of all the different combinations of goods and services a consumer can obtain within his or her budget, which specific combination will yield the maximum utility or satisfaction? *To maximize satisfaction, consumers should allocate their money income so that the last dollar spent on each product yields the same amount of extra (marginal) utility.* We call this the **utility-maximizing rule**. When the consumer has "balanced his or her margins" using this rule, **consumer equilibrium** is achieved and thus the consumer has no incentive to alter the expenditure pattern. The consumer is in equilibrium and would be worse off—total utility would decline—if any revision occurred in the bundle of goods purchased, providing no change occurs in taste, income, products, or prices.

A Numerical Example

An illustration will help explain the utility-maximizing rule. For simplicity we limit our example to two products, but the analysis also applies if there are more. Suppose consumer Holly is analyzing which combination of two products—apples and oranges—she should purchase with her fixed daily income of $10.

Holly's preferences for apples and oranges, their prices, and her income are the basic data determining the combination that will maximize her satisfaction. Table 7-1 summarizes those data, with column 2a showing the amounts of marginal utility Holly will get from each successive apple and column 3a showing the same thing for oranges. Both columns reflect the law of diminishing marginal utility, which is assumed to begin with the second unit of each product purchased.

MARGINAL UTILITY PER DOLLAR

To see how the utility-maximizing rule works, we must put the marginal utility information in columns 2a and 3a on a per-dollar-spent basis. Holly's choices are influenced not only by the extra utility that successive units of apples will yield, but also by how many dollars (and therefore how many oranges) she must give up to obtain additional apples.

The rational consumer compares the extra utility from each product with its added cost (that is, its price). Switching examples for a moment, suppose that you prefer a pizza whose marginal utility is, say, 36 utils to a movie whose marginal utility is 24 utils. But if the pizza's price is $12 and the movie costs only $6, you would choose the movie rather than the pizza! Why? Because the marginal utility per dollar spent would be 4 utils for the movie

TABLE 7-1	The Utility-Maximizing Combinations of Apples and Oranges Obtainable with an Income of $10*			
(1) **UNIT OF PRODUCT**	**(2)** **APPLE (PRODUCT A): PRICE = $1**		**(3)** **ORANGE (PRODUCT B): PRICE = $2**	
	(a) **Marginal utility,** **utils**	**(b)** **Marginal utility** **per dollar (MU/price)**	**(a)** **Marginal utility,** **utils**	**(b)** **Marginal utility per** **dollar (MU/price)**
First	10	10	24	12
Second	8	8	20	10
Third	7	7	18	9
Fourth	6	6	16	8
Fifth	5	5	12	6
Sixth	4	4	6	3
Seventh	3	3	4	2

*It is assumed in this table that the amount of marginal utility received from additional units of each of the two products is independent of the quantity of the other product. For example, the marginal-utility schedule for apples is independent of the number of oranges obtained by the consumer.

(= 24 utils ÷ $6) compared to only 3 utils for the pizza (= 36 utils ÷ $12). You could buy two movies for $12 and, assuming that the marginal utility of the second movie is, say, 16 utils, your total utility would be 40 utils. Clearly, 40 units of satisfaction from two movies are superior to 36 utils from the same $12 expenditure on one pizza.

To make the amounts of extra utility derived from differently priced goods comparable, marginal utilities must be put on a per-dollar-spent basis. We do this in columns 2b and 3b by dividing the marginal utility data of columns 2a and 3a by the prices of apples and oranges, $1 and $2, respectively.

DECISION-MAKING PROCESS

Table 7-1 shows Holly's preferences on a unit basis and a per-dollar basis, as well as the price tags of apples and oranges. With $10 to spend, in what order will Holly allocate her dollars on apples and oranges to achieve the highest amount of utility within the $10 limit imposed by her income? What specific combination of the two products will she purchase to get the most from her $10?

Concentrating on columns 2b and 3b in Table 7-1, we find that Holly should begin by spending $2 on the first orange, because its marginal utility per dollar of 12 utils per dollar is higher than the first apple's 10 utils per dollar. Now Holly finds herself indifferent about whether she should buy a second orange or the first apple because the marginal utility per dollar of both is 10 utils per dollar. So she buys both of them. Holly now has one apple and two oranges. Also, the last dollar she spent on each good yielded the same marginal utility per dollar (10 utils), but this combination of apples and oranges does not represent the maximum amount of utility that Holly can obtain. It cost her only $5 (= (1 × $1) + (2 × $2)), so she has $5 remaining, which she can spend to achieve a still higher level of total utility.

Examining columns 2b and 3b again, we find that Holly should spend the next $2 on a third orange because marginal utility per dollar for the third orange is 9 utils compared with 8 utils for the second apple. Now, with one apple and three oranges, she is again indifferent between a second apple and a fourth orange because both provide 8 utils per dollar. So Holly purchases one more of each. Now the last dollar spent on each product provides the same marginal utility per dollar (8 utils), and Holly's money income of $10 is exhausted.

The utility-maximizing combination of goods Holly can attain is two apples and four oranges. By summing marginal utility information from columns 2a and 3a, we find that Holly is getting 18 (= 10 + 8) utils of satisfaction from the two apples and 78 (= 24 + 20 + 18 + 16) utils of satisfaction from the four oranges. Her $10, optimally spent, yields 96 (= 18 + 78) utils of satisfaction.

Table 7-2 summarizes our step-by-step process for maximizing Holly's utility. Note that we have assumed Holly spends her entire income—she neither borrows nor saves. However, saving can be regarded as a "commodity" that yields utility and be incorporated into our analysis. In fact, we treat it that way in Problem 4 at the end of this chapter.

TABLE 7-2	Sequence of Purchases to Achieve Consumer Equilibrium, Using the Data in Table 7-1

Choice number	Potential choices	Marginal utility per dollar	Purchase decision	Income remaining
1	First apple First orange	10 12	First orange for $2	$8 = $10 − $2
2	First apple Second orange	10 10	First apple for $1 and second orange for $2	$5 = $8 − $3
3	Second apple Third orange	8 9	Third orange for $2	$3 = $5 − $2
4	Second apple Fourth orange	8 8	Second apple for $1 and fourth orange for $2	$0 = $3 − $3

INFERIOR OPTIONS

Holly can obtain other combinations of apples and oranges with $10, but none will yield as great a total utility as do two apples and four oranges. As an example, she can obtain four apples and three oranges for $10. But this combination yields only 93 utils, clearly inferior to the 96 utils she gets from two apples and four oranges. True, other combinations of apples and oranges exist (such as four apples and five oranges, or one apple and two oranges) in which the marginal utility of the last dollar spent is the same for both apples and oranges. All such combinations are either unobtainable with Holly's limited money income (such as four apples and five oranges) or do not exhaust her money income (such as one apple and two oranges), and therefore do not yield the maximum utility attainable.

WORKED PROBLEM 7.1   Consumer Choice

ALGEBRAIC RESTATEMENT

Economists generalize the utility-maximizing rule by saying that a consumer will maximize satisfaction by allocating money income so that the last dollar spent on product A, the last on product B, and so forth, yield equal amounts of marginal utility. The marginal utility per dollar spent on product A is indicated by the MU of product A

CONSIDER THIS

There's No Accounting for Taste

In 2015, the U.S. federal government started requiring restaurants to print calorie counts next to menu items. A similar requirement became law in Ontario in 2017 for all food-service chains with twenty or more locations in the province. The regulation was intended to help consumers make healthful choices. In particular, it was assumed that if they could see how many calories each item contained, consumers would consume fewer total calories. They would opt for salads instead of milkshakes.

© Kim Kulish/Corbis

But a funny thing happened when the new rules went into effect. Some people started consuming *more* calories. They did so because their preferences were not what policymakers

expected. Instead of trying to maximize the amount of healthfulness per dollar spent, they instead chose to maximize the number of calories per dollar spent. Their preferences were such that when it came to maximizing utility, what they wanted was the maximum number of calories, not the maximum amount of health. So when the new regulations provided them with calorie counts, they went for milkshakes instead of salads and double cheeseburgers instead of chicken skewers.

The lesson learned? Know what people are trying to maximize before you attempt to alter their behaviour.

divided by the price of product A (column 2b in Table 7-1), and the marginal utility per dollar spent on product B is indicated by the MU of product B divided by the price of product B (column 3b in Table 7-1). Our utility-maximizing rule merely requires that these ratios be equal for the last dollar spent on product A and the last dollar spent on product B. Algebraically,

$$\frac{\text{MU of product A}}{\text{price of A}} = \frac{\text{MU of product B}}{\text{price of B}}$$

Of course, the consumer must exhaust her available income. Table 7-1 shows us that the combination of two units of A (apples) and four of B (oranges) fulfills these conditions in that

$$\frac{8 \text{ utils}}{\$1} = \frac{16 \text{ utils}}{\$2}$$

and the consumer's $10 income is all spent.

If the equation is not fulfilled, then some reallocation of the consumer's expenditures between products A and B (from the low to the high marginal-utility-per-dollar product) will increase the consumer's total utility. For example, if the consumer spent $10 on four units of A (apples) and three of B (oranges), we would find that

$$\frac{\text{MU of A of 6 utils}}{\text{price of A of \$1}} < \frac{\text{MU of B of 18 utils}}{\text{price of B of \$2}}$$

Here the last dollar spent on A provides only 6 utils of satisfaction while the last dollar spent on B provides 9 utils (= 18 utils ÷ $2). So, the consumer can increase total satisfaction by purchasing more of B and less of A. As dollars are reallocated from A to B, the marginal utility per dollar of A will increase while the marginal utility per dollar of B will decrease. At some new combination of A and B the two will be equal, and consumer equilibrium will be achieved. Here, that combination is two units of A (apples) and four of B (oranges).

7.3 Utility Maximization and the Demand Curve

LO7.3   Explain how a demand curve can be derived by observing the outcomes of price changes in the utility-maximization model.

Once you understand the utility-maximizing rule, you can easily see why product price and quantity demanded are inversely related. Recall that the basic determinants of an individual's demand for a specific product are (1) preferences or tastes, (2) money income, and (3) the prices of other goods. The utility data in Table 7-1 reflect our consumer's preferences. We continue to suppose that her money income is $10. Concentrating on the construction of a simple demand curve for oranges, we assume that the price of apples, now representing all "other goods," is still $1.

MATH 7.2   Utility-Maximizing Rule

Deriving the Demand Schedule and Curve

We can derive a single consumer's demand schedule for oranges by considering alternative prices at which oranges might be sold and then determining the quantity the consumer will purchase. We already know one such price–quantity combination in the utility-maximizing example: Given tastes, income, and the prices of other goods, Holly will purchase four oranges at $2.

Now let's assume the price of oranges falls to $1. The marginal-utility-per-dollar data of column 3b in Table 7-1 will double because the price of oranges has been halved; the new data for column 3b are (by coincidence) identical to the data in column 3a. The doubling of the MU per dollar for each successive orange means that the purchase of two apples and four oranges is no longer an equilibrium combination. By applying the same reasoning we used previously, we now find that Holly's utility-maximizing combination is four apples and six oranges. As summarized in the table in Figure 7-2, Holly will purchase six oranges when the price of oranges is $1. Using the data in this table, we can sketch the downsloping demand curve D_B shown in Figure 7-2. This exercise, then, clearly links the utility-maximizing behaviour of a consumer and that person's demand curve for a particular product.

FIGURE 7-2   Deriving an Individual Demand Curve

The consumer represented by the data in the table maximizes utility by purchasing 4 oranges at a price of $2. The decline in the price of oranges to $1 disrupts the consumer's initial utility-maximizing equilibrium. The consumer restores equilibrium by purchasing 6 rather than 4 oranges. Thus, a simple price–quantity schedule emerges, which locates two points on a downsloping demand curve.

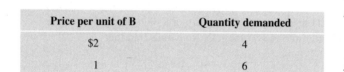

Price per unit of B	Quantity demanded
$2	4
1	6

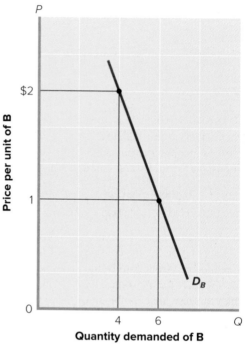

Quantity demanded of B

7.4   Income and Substitution Effects

LO7.4   Discuss how the utility-maximization model helps highlight the income and substitution effects of a price change.

Recall from Chapter 3 that the **income effect** is the impact that a change in the price of a product has on a consumer's real income and consequently on the quantity demanded of that good. In contrast, the **substitution effect** is the impact that a change in a product's price has on its relative expensiveness and consequently on the quantity demanded. Both effects help explain why a demand curve such as that in Figure 7-2 is downsloping.

Let's first look at the substitution effect. Recall that before the price of oranges declined, Holly was in equilibrium when purchasing two apples and four oranges because

$$\frac{\text{MU of apples of 8}}{\text{price of apples of \$1}} = \frac{\text{MU of oranges of 16}}{\text{price of oranges of \$2}}$$

But after the price of oranges declines from $2 to $1,

$$\frac{\text{MU of apples of 8}}{\text{price of apples of \$1}} < \frac{\textit{MU of oranges of 16}}{\textit{price of oranges of \$1}}$$

More simply, the last dollar spent on oranges now yields more utility (16 utils) than does the last dollar spent on apples (8 utils). This will lead Holly to switch, or substitute, purchases away from apples and toward oranges so as to restore consumer equilibrium. This substitution effect contributes to the inverse relationship between price and quantity that is found along her demand curve for oranges: When the price of oranges declines, the substitution effect causes Holly to buy more oranges.

What about the income effect? The decline in the price of oranges from $2 to $1 increases Holly's real income. Before the price decline, she wanted two apples and four oranges. But at the lower $1 price for oranges, Holly would have to spend only $6 rather than $10 on the same combination of goods. That means the lower price of oranges has freed up $4 Holly can spend on buying more apples, more oranges, or more of both. How many more will be determined by applying the utility-maximizing rule to the new situation. But it is quite likely that the increase in real income caused by the reduction in the price of oranges will cause Holly to end up buying more oranges than before the price reduction. Any such increase in orange purchases is referred to as the income effect of the reduction in the price of oranges and it, too, helps to explain why demand curves are downsloping: When the price of oranges falls, the income effect causes Holly to buy more oranges.

QUICK REVIEW 7.2

- The theory of consumer choice assumes that, with limited income and a set of product prices, consumers make rational choices on the basis of well-defined preferences.

- A consumer maximizes utility by allocating income so that the marginal utility per dollar spent is the same for every good purchased.

- A downsloping demand curve can be derived by changing the price of one product in the consumer-choice model and noting the change in the utility-maximizing quantity of that product demanded.

- By providing insights on the income effect and substitution effect of a price decline, the utility-maximization model helps explain why demand curves are downsloping.

7.5 Applications and Extensions

LO7.5 Give examples of several real-world phenomena that can be explained by applying the theory of consumer choice.

Many real-world phenomena can be explained by applying the theory of consumer choice.

iPads

Every so often a new product totally captures consumers' imaginations. One such product is Apple's iPad, which debuted in April 2010. Less than three years later, Apple sold its 100 millionth unit.

The swift ascendancy of the iPad resulted mainly from a leap in technology. It was the first touchscreen tablet computer and became a hit because it was much better for the consumption of digital media—music, pictures, videos, and many games—than existing laptop or desktop computers. Those larger machines still held the advantage if a consumer wanted to create content or edit documents, but for consuming digital content the iPad was far superior in the eyes of millions of consumers.

In the language of our analysis, Apple's introduction of the iPad severely disrupted consumer equilibrium. Consumers concluded en masse that iPads had a higher marginal-utility-to-price ratio (= MU/P) than the ratios for alternative products. Therefore, they shifted spending away from those other products and toward iPads as a way to increase total utility. Of course, for most people the marginal utility of a second or third iPad relative to price is quite low, so most consumers purchased only a single unit. But Apple continued to enhance the iPad, enticing some of the buyers of older models to buy new ones.

This example demonstrates a simple but important point: New products succeed by enhancing consumers' total utility. This "delivery of value" generates a revenue stream. If revenues exceed production costs, substantial profits can result—as they have for Apple.

The Diamond–Water Paradox

Early economists such as Adam Smith were puzzled that some essential goods had much lower prices than some unimportant goods. Why would water, essential to life, be priced below diamonds, which have much less usefulness? The paradox is resolved when we consider that water is in great supply relative to demand and thus has a very low price per litre. Diamonds, in contrast, are rare. Their supply is small relative to demand, and as a result, they have a very high price per carat.

Moreover, the marginal utility of the last unit of water consumed is very low. The reason follows from our utility-maximizing rule. Consumers (and producers) respond to the very low price of water by using a great deal of it for generating electricity, irrigating crops, heating buildings, watering lawns, quenching thirst, and so on. Consumption is expanded until marginal utility, which declines as more water is consumed, equals its low price. Conversely, relatively few diamonds are purchased because of their prohibitively high price, meaning that their marginal utility remains high. In equilibrium,

$$\frac{\text{MU of water (low)}}{\text{price of water (low)}} = \frac{\text{MU of diamonds (high)}}{\text{price of diamonds (high)}}$$

Although the marginal utility of the last unit of water consumed is low and the marginal utility of the last diamond purchased is high, the total utility of water is very high and the total utility of diamonds is quite low. The total utility derived from the consumption of water is large because of the enormous amounts of water consumed. Total utility is the sum of the marginal utilities of all the litres of water consumed, including the trillions of litres that have far higher marginal utilities than the last unit consumed. In contrast, the total utility derived from diamonds is low since their high price means relatively few are bought. Thus the diamond–water paradox is solved: Water has much more total utility (roughly, usefulness) than diamonds even though the price of diamonds greatly exceeds the price of water. These relative prices relate to marginal utility, not total utility.

Opportunity Cost and the Value of Time

The theory of consumer choice can be generalized to account for the economic value of *time*. Both consumption and production take time. Time is a valuable economic commodity; by using an hour in productive work, a person can earn $6, $10, $50, or more, depending on education and skills. By using that hour for leisure or in consumption activities, the individual incurs the opportunity cost of forgone income and sacrifices the $6, $10, or $50 that could have been earned by working.

Imagine a self-employed consumer in Victoria named Linden who is considering buying a round of golf and a concert ticket. The market price of the golf game is $30 and that of the ticket is $40, but the golf game takes more time than the concert. Suppose Linden spends four hours on the golf course but only two hours at the concert. If Linden's time is worth $10 per hour as evidenced by the $10 wage obtained by working, then the full price of the golf game is $70 (the $30 market price plus $40 worth of time), while the full price of the concert is $60 (the $40 market price plus $20 worth of time). We find that, contrary to what market prices alone indicate, the full price of the concert is really less than the full price of the golf game.

If we now assume that the marginal utilities derived from successive golf games and concerts are identical, traditional theory would indicate that Linden should consume more golf games than concerts because the market price of golf games ($30) is lower than that of concerts ($40). But when time is taken into account, the situation is reversed and golf games ($70) are more expensive than concerts ($60). So it is rational for Linden to consume more concerts than golf games.

Another example is the consumption of health care services. In Canada, government-sponsored insurance pays the full amount of a doctor's visit. The price the consumer pays is zero. But if we consider the time and cost of travelling to the doctor's office, and the waiting time in the office, the full price is considerably more than zero.

By accounting for the opportunity cost of a consumer's time, we can explain certain phenomena that are otherwise quite puzzling. It may be rational for the unskilled worker or retiree whose time has little market value to ride a bus from Halifax to Montreal, but the corporate executive, whose time is very valuable, will find it cheaper to fly, even though bus fare is only a fraction of plane fare. It is sensible for the retiree, living on a modest income and having ample time, to spend many hours shopping for bargains at the mall or taking long trips in a motor home. It is equally rational for the highly paid physician, working fifty-five hours per week, to buy a new personal computer over the Internet and take short vacations at expensive resorts.

People in poor nations often conclude that affluent Canadians are wasteful of food and other material goods but overly economical in their use of time. Canadians who visit developing countries may think that time is used casually or squandered, while material goods are very highly prized and carefully used. These differences are not a paradox or a case of radically different temperaments; the differences are primarily a rational reflection that the high productivity of labour in an industrially advanced society gives time a high market value, whereas the opposite is true in a low-income, developing country.

Cash and Noncash Gifts

Marginal utility analysis also helps us understand why people generally prefer cash gifts to noncash gifts costing the same amount. The reason is simply that the noncash gifts may not match the recipient's preferences and thus may not add as much as cash to total utility. Thought of differently, consumers know their own preferences better than the gift giver does, and the $100 cash gift provides more choices.

Look back at Table 7-1. Suppose Holly has zero earned income but is given the choice of a $2 cash gift or a noncash gift of two apples. Because two apples can be bought with $2, these two gifts are of equal monetary value, but by spending the $2 cash gift on the first orange Holly could obtain 24 utils. The noncash gift of the first two apples would yield only 18 (= 10 + 8) units of utility. The conclusion is that the noncash gift yields less utility to the beneficiary than the cash gift.

Since giving of noncash gifts is common, considerable value of those gifts is potentially lost because they do not match their recipients' tastes. For example, Uncle Fred may have paid $30 for the ski goggles he gave you for your birthday, but you would pay only $15 for them. Thus, a $15, or 50 percent, value loss is involved. Multiplied by billions of gifts a year, the total potential loss of value is huge.

But some of that loss is avoided by the creative ways individuals handle the problem. For example, newlyweds set up gift registries for their weddings to help match their wants to the noncash gifts received. Also, people obtain cash refunds or exchanges for gifts, so they can buy goods that provide more utility. And people have even been known to recycle gifts by giving them to someone else at a later time. All three actions support the proposition that individuals take actions to maximize their total utility.

The LAST WORD

Criminal Behaviour

Although economic analysis is not particularly relevant in explaining some crimes of passion and violence (for example, murder and rape), it does provide interesting insights on such property crimes as robbery, burglary, and auto theft.

© Digital Vision/Getty Images

The theory of rational consumer choice can be extended to provide some useful insights on criminal behaviour. Both the lawful consumer and the criminal try to maximize their total utility (or net benefit). For example, you can remove a textbook from the campus bookstore by either purchasing it or stealing it. If you *buy* the book, your action is legal; you have fully compensated the bookstore for the product. (The bookstore would rather have your money than the book.) If you *steal* the book, you have broken the law. Theft is outlawed because it imposes uncompensated costs on others. In this case, your action reduces the bookstore's revenue and profit and also may impose costs on other buyers who now must pay higher prices for their textbooks.

Why might someone engage in a criminal activity such as stealing? Just like the consumer who compares the marginal utility of a good with its price, the potential criminal compares the marginal benefit from his or her action with the "price" or cost. If the marginal benefit (to the criminal) exceeds the price or marginal cost (also to the criminal), the individual undertakes the criminal activity.

Most people, however, do not engage in theft, burglary, or fraud. Why not? The answer is that they perceive the personal price of engaging in these illegal activities to be too high relative to the marginal benefit. The price or marginal cost to the potential criminal has several facets. First, there are the guilt costs, which for many people are substantial. Such individuals would not steal from others even if there were no penalties for doing so. Their moral sense of right and wrong would entail too great a guilt cost relative to the benefit from the stolen good. Other types of costs include the direct cost of the criminal activity (supplies and tools) and the forgone income from legitimate activities (the opportunity cost to the criminal).

Unfortunately, guilt costs, direct costs, and forgone income are not sufficient to deter some people from stealing. So society imposes other costs, mainly fines and imprisonment, on lawbreakers. The potential of being fined increases the marginal cost to the criminal. The potential of being imprisoned boosts marginal cost still further. Most people highly value their personal freedom and lose considerable legitimate earnings while incarcerated. Given these types of costs, the potential criminal estimates the marginal cost and benefit of committing the crime. As a simple example, suppose that the direct cost and the opportunity cost of stealing an $80 textbook are both zero. The probability of getting caught is 10 percent and, if apprehended, there will be a $500 fine. The potential criminal will estimate the marginal cost of stealing the book as $50 (= $500 fine × 0.10 chance of apprehension). Someone who has a guilt cost of zero will choose to steal the book because the marginal benefit of $80 would exceed the marginal cost of $50. In contrast, someone having a guilt cost of, say, $40 will not steal the book. The marginal benefit of $80 will not be as great as the marginal cost of $90 (= $50 of penalty cost + $40 of guilt cost).

This perspective on illegal behaviour has some interesting implications. For example, other things equal, crime will rise (more of it will be "bought") when its price falls. This explains, for instance, why some people who do not steal from stores under normal circumstances participate in looting stores during riots, when the perceived marginal cost of being apprehended has substantially declined.

Another implication is that society can reduce unlawful behaviour by increasing the "price" of crime. It can nourish and increase guilt costs through family, educational, and religious efforts. It can increase the direct cost of crime by using more sophisticated security systems (locks, alarms, video surveillance) so that criminals will have to buy and use more sophisticated tools. It can undertake education and training initiatives to enhance the legitimate earnings of people who might otherwise engage in illegal activity. It can increase policing to raise the probability of being apprehended for crime. And it can impose greater penalties for those who are caught and convicted.

Question

In what way is criminal behaviour similar to consumer behaviour? Why do most people obtain goods via legal behaviour as opposed to illegal behaviour? What are society's main options for reducing illegal behaviour?

Chapter Summary

LO7.1   Define and explain the relationship between total utility, marginal utility, and the law of diminishing marginal utility.

- The law of diminishing marginal utility states that, beyond a certain quantity, additional units of a specific good will yield declining amounts of extra satisfaction to a consumer.

LO7.2   Describe how rational consumers maximize utility by comparing the marginal-utility-to-price ratios of all the products they could possibly purchase.

- The utility-maximizing model assumes that the typical consumer is rational and acts based on well-defined preferences. Because income is limited and goods have prices, consumers cannot purchase all the goods and services they might want. Consumers therefore select the attainable combination of goods that maximizes their utility or satisfaction.

- A consumer's utility is maximized when income is allocated so that the last dollar spent on each product purchased yields the same amount of extra satisfaction. Algebraically, the

utility-maximizing rule is fulfilled when the consumer's total income is spent and

$$\frac{\text{MU of product A}}{\text{price of A}} = \frac{\text{MU of product B}}{\text{price of B}}$$

LO7.3   Explain how a demand curve can be derived by observing the outcomes of price changes in the utility-maximization model.

- The utility-maximizing rule and the demand curve are logically consistent. Because marginal utility declines, a lower price is needed to induce the consumer to buy more of a particular product.

LO7.4   Discuss how the utility-maximization model helps highlight the income and substitution effects of a price change.

- The utility-maximization model illuminates the income and substitution effects of a price change. The income effect implies that a decline in the price of a product increases the consumer's real income and enables the consumer to buy more of that product with a fixed money income. The substitution effect implies that a lower price makes a product relatively more attractive and therefore increases the consumer's willingness to substitute it for other products.

LO7.5   **Give examples of several real-world phenomena that can be explained by applying the theory of consumer choice.**

- The theory of consumer choice can explain many real-world phenomena, including the rapid adoption of popular consumer goods like the iPad that feature disruptive technologies, and why people would often rather get cash as a gift than particular items or objects of the same monetary value.

Terms and Concepts

law of diminishing marginal utility
utility
total utility
marginal utility
rational behaviour

budget constraint
utility-maximizing rule
consumer equilibrium
income effect
substitution effect

Discussion Questions

1. Complete the following table and answer the questions. [LO7.1]

   a. At which rate is total utility increasing: a constant rate, a decreasing rate, or an increasing rate? How do you know?

   b. "A rational consumer will purchase only one unit of the product represented by these data, since that amount maximizes marginal utility." Do you agree? Explain why or why not.

   c. "It is possible that a rational consumer will not purchase any units of the product represented by these data." Do you agree? Explain why or why not.

Units consumed	Total utility	Marginal utility
0	0	10
1	10	8
2	—	—
3	25	—
4	30	3
5	—	—
6	34	

2. Mrs. Simpson buys loaves of bread and litres of milk each week at prices of $1 and $0.80, respectively. At present she is buying these two products in amounts such that the marginal utilities from the last units purchased of the two products are 80 and 70 utils, respectively. Is she buying the utility-maximizing combination of bread and milk? If not, how should she reallocate her expenditures between the two goods? [LO7.2]

3. How can time be incorporated into the theory of consumer choice? Explain the following observation: If you want to make millions of dollars, devise a product that saves Canadians lots of time. [LO7.2]

4. Explain what is meant by the following statements: [LO7.2]

   a. Before economic growth, there were too few goods; after growth, there is too little time.

   b. It is irrational for an individual to take the time to be completely rational in economic decision making.

   c. Telling your spouse where you would like to go out to eat for your birthday makes sense in terms of utility maximization.

5. In the past decade or so, there has been a dramatic expansion of small retail convenience stores (such as Mac's, 7-Eleven, etc.), even though their prices are generally much higher than prices in large supermarkets. What explains the success of the convenience stores? [LO7.2]

6. Many apartment-complex owners are installing water meters for each apartment and billing the occupants according to the amount of water they use, in contrast to the former procedure of having a central meter for the entire complex and dividing up the water expense as part of the rent. Where individual meters have been installed, water usage has declined 10–40 percent. Explain that drop, referring to price and marginal utility. [LO7.3]

7. Using the utility-maximizing rule as your point of reference, explain the income and substitution effects of an increase in the price of product B with no change in the price of product A. [LO7.4]

8. **Advanced Analysis** A mathematically "fair bet" is one in which a gambler bets, say, $100 for a 10 percent chance to win $1000 ($100 = 0.10 × $1000). Assuming diminishing marginal utility of dollars, explain why this is *not* a fair bet in terms of utility. Why is it an even less fair bet when the house takes a cut of each dollar bet? So is gambling irrational? [LO7.4]

9. Rank each of the following three gift possibilities in terms of how much utility they are likely to bring, and explain your reasoning. A store-specific gift card worth $15, a $15 item from that specific store, and $15 of cash that can be spent anywhere. [LO7.5]

Review Questions

1. True or False? The law of diminishing marginal utility predicts the consumption behaviour of addicts quite well.   [LO7.1]

2. Frank spends $75 on 10 magazines and 25 newspapers. The magazines cost $5 each and the newspapers cost $2.50 each. Suppose that his MU from the final magazine is 10 utils while his MU from the final newspaper is also 10 utils. According to the utility-maximizing rule, Frank should   [LO7.2]

   a. Reallocate spending from magazines to newspapers

   b. Reallocate spending from newspapers to magazines

   c. Be satisfied because he is already maximizing his total utility

   d. None of the above

3. Demand curves slope downward because, other things held equal,   [LO7.3]

   a. An increase in a product's price lowers MU

   b. A decrease in a product's price lowers MU

   c. A decrease in a product's price raises MU per dollar and makes consumers wish to purchase more units

   d. An increase in a product's price raises MU per dollar and makes consumers wish to purchase more units

4. Jermaine spends his money on cucumbers and lettuce. If the price of cucumbers falls, the MU per dollar of cucumbers will _____ and Jermaine will _____ cucumbers for lettuce. [LO7.4]

   a. Fall; substitute

   b. Rise; substitute

   c. Fall; supply

   d. Rise; demand

5. Tammy spends her money on lemonade and iced tea. If the price of lemonade falls, it is as though her income _____.   [LO7.4]

   a. Increases

   b. Decreases

   c. Stays the same

Problems

1. Miley's total utility from singing the same song over and over is 50 utils after one repetition, 90 utils after two repetitions, 70 utils after three repetitions, 20 utils after four repetitions, −50 utils after five repetitions, and −200 utils after six repetitions. Write down her marginal utility for each repetition. Once Miley's total utility begins to decrease, does each additional repetition of the song hurt more than the previous one or less than the previous one?   [LO7.1]

2. John likes Coca-Cola. After consuming one Coke, John has a total utility of 10 utils. After two Cokes, he has a total utility of 25 utils. After three Cokes, he has a total utility of 50 utils. Does John show decreasing or increasing marginal utility for Coke? Suppose that John has $3 in his pocket. If Cokes cost $1 each and John is willing to spend one of his dollars on purchasing a first can of Coke, would he spend his second dollar on a Coke, too? What about the third dollar? If John's marginal utility for Coke keeps on increasing no matter how many Cokes he drinks, would it be fair to say he is addicted to Coke?   [LO7.1]

3. Suppose that Omar's marginal utility for cups of coffee is constant at 1.5 utils per cup no matter how many cups he drinks.

On the other hand, his marginal utility per doughnut is 10 utils for the first doughnut he eats, 9 utils for the second, 8 utils for the third, and so on (that is, declining by 1 util per additional doughnut). In addition, suppose that coffee costs $1 per cup, doughnuts cost $1 each, and Omar has a budget that he can spend only on doughnuts, coffee, or both. How big would that budget have to be before he would spend a dollar buying a first cup of coffee?   [LO7.2]

4. Columns 1 through 4 in the following table show the marginal utility, measured in utils, that Ricardo would get by purchasing various amounts of products A, B, C, and D. Column 5 shows the marginal utility Ricardo gets from saving. Assume that the prices of A, B, C, and D are $18, $6, $4, and $24, respectively, and that Ricardo has an income of $106.   [LO7.2]

   a. What quantities of A, B, C, and D will Ricardo purchase in maximizing his utility?

   b. How many dollars will Ricardo choose to save?

   c. Check your answers by substituting them into the algebraic statement of the utility-maximizing rule.

COLUMN 1		COLUMN 2		COLUMN 3		COLUMN 4		COLUMN 5	
Units of A	MU	Units of B	MU	Units of C	MU	Units of D	MU	Number of dollars saved	MU
1	72	1	24	1	15	1	36	1	5
2	54	2	15	2	12	2	30	2	4
3	45	3	12	3	8	3	24	3	3
4	36	4	9	4	7	4	18	4	2
5	27	5	7	5	5	5	13	5	1
6	18	6	5	6	4	6	7	6	½
7	15	7	2	7	3½	7	4	7	¼
8	12	8	1	8	3	8	2	8	⅛

5. You are choosing between two goods, X and Y, and your marginal utility from each is as shown below. If your income is $9 and the prices of X and Y are $2 and $1, respectively, what quantities of each will you purchase to maximize utility? What total utility will you realize? Assume that, other things remaining unchanged, the price of X falls to $1. What quantities of X and Y will you now purchase? Using the two prices and quantities for X, derive a demand schedule (a table showing prices and quantities demanded) for X.   [**LO7.3**]

Units of X	MU$_X$	Units of Y	MU$_Y$
1	10	1	8
2	8	2	7
3	6	3	6
4	4	4	5
5	3	5	4
6	2	6	3

6. **Advanced Analysis** Let $MU_A = z = 10 - x$ and $MU_B = z = 21 - 2y$, where z is marginal utility per dollar measured in utils, x is the amount spent on product A, and y is the amount spent on product B. Assume that the consumer has $10 to spend on A and B—that is, $x + y = 10$. How is the $10 best allocated between A and B? How much utility will the marginal dollar yield?   [**LO7.3**]

7. Suppose that with a budget of $100, Deborah spends $60 on sushi and $40 on bagels when sushi costs $2 per piece and bagels cost $2 per bagel. But then, after the price of bagels falls to $1 per bagel, she spends $50 on sushi and $50 on bagels. How many pieces of sushi and how many bagels did Deborah consume before the price change? At the new prices, how much money would it have cost Deborah to buy those same quantities (the ones that she consumed before the price change)? Given that it used to take Deborah's entire $100 to buy those quantities, how big is the income effect caused by the reduction in the price of bagels?   [**LO7.4**]

A7.1 Indifference Curve Analysis

LOA7.1 Relate how the indifference curve model of consumer choice derives demand curves from budget lines, indifference curves, and utility maximization.

The utility-maximizing rule requires individuals to measure and compare utility, much as a business would measure and compare costs or revenues. Such *cardinal utility* is measured in units such as 1, 2, 3, 4, and so forth, and can be added, subtracted, multiplied, and divided, just like the cardinal numbers in mathematics. More importantly, cardinal utility allows us to precisely quantify the marginal utilities upon which the utility-maximizing rule depends. In fact, the marginal-utility theory of consumer demand that we explained in the body of this chapter rests squarely on the assumption that economists are able to measure cardinal utility. The reality, however, is that measuring cardinal utility is highly difficult, at best. (Can you, for instance, state exactly how many utils you are getting from reading this book right now, or how many utils you would get from watching a sunset?)

To avoid this measurement problem, economists have developed an alternative explanation of consumer choice and equilibrium in which such measurement is not required. In this more advanced analysis, the consumer must simply *rank* various combinations of goods in terms of preference. For instance, Sally can simply report that she *prefers* four units of A to six units of B without having to put number values on how much she likes either option. The model of consumer choice that is based on such *ordinal utility* rankings is called indifference curve analysis. It has two main elements: budget lines and indifference curves.

The Budget Line: What Is Attainable

We know from Chapter 1 that a **budget line** (or, more technically, a *budget constraint*) is a schedule or curve showing various combinations of two products a consumer can purchase with a specific money income. If the price of product A is $1.50 and the price of product B is $1, a consumer could purchase all the combinations of A and B shown in the table of Figure A7-1 with $12 of money income. At one extreme, the consumer might spend all the income on eight units of A and have nothing left to spend on B. Or, by giving up two units of A and thereby freeing $3, the consumer could have six units of A and three of B. At the other extreme, the consumer could buy twelve units of B at $1 each, spending his or her entire money income on B with nothing left to spend on A.

Figure A7-1 also shows the budget line graphically. Note that the graph is not restricted to whole units of A and B as is the table. Every point on the graph represents a possible combination of A and B, including fractional quantities. The slope

FIGURE A7-1 A Consumer's Budget Line

The budget line shows all the combinations of any two products that can be purchased given the prices of the products and the consumer's money income.

Units of A (price = $1.50)	Units of B (price = $1.00)	Total expenditure
8	0	$12 (= $12 + $0)
6	3	$12 (= $9 + $3)
4	6	$12 (= $6 + $6)
2	9	$12 (= $3 + $9)
0	12	$12 (= $0 + $12)

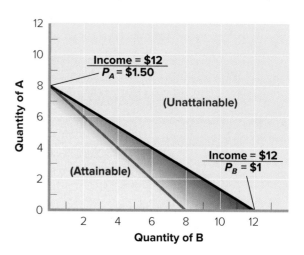

of the graphed budget line measures the ratio of the price of B to the price of A; more precisely, the absolute value of the slope is $P_B/P_A = \$1/\$1.50 = 2/3$. This is the mathematical way of saying that the consumer must forgo two units of A (measured on the vertical axis) to buy three units of B (measured on the horizontal axis). In moving down the budget or price line, two units of A (at \$1.50 each) must be given up to obtain three more units of B (at \$1 each). This yields a slope of 2/3.

Note that all combinations of A and B that lie on or inside the budget line are attainable from the consumer's \$12 of money income. He can afford to buy not only the combinations of A and B that lie along the budget line itself but also those that lie below it. He could, for instance, afford to buy two units of A and four units of B, thereby using up only \$7 (= \$3 spent on two units of A at a price of \$1.50 each + \$4 spent on four units of B at a price of \$1 each). That combination is clearly attainable because it would use up only half of the consumer's \$12 budget. But to achieve maximum utility, the consumer will want to spend the full \$12. The budget line shows all combinations that cost exactly the full \$12.

The budget line has two other significant characteristics:

1. **Income Changes** The location of the budget line varies with money income. An increase in money income shifts the budget line to the right; a decrease in money income shifts it to the left. To verify this, recalculate the table in Figure A7-1, assuming that money income is (a) \$24 and (b) \$6, and plot the new budget lines.

2. **Price Changes** A change in product prices also shifts the budget line. A decline in the prices of both products—the equivalent of an increase in real income—shifts the curve to the right. (You can verify this by recalculating the table in Figure A7-1 and replotting the graph, assuming that $P_A = \$0.75$ and $P_B = \$0.50$.) Conversely, an increase in the prices of A and B shifts the curve to the left. (Assume $P_A = \$3$ and $P_B = \$2$ and rework the table and the graph to substantiate this statement.)

Note what happens if P_B changes while P_A and money income remain constant. In particular, if P_B drops, say from \$1 to \$0.50, the lower end of the budget line fans outward to the right. Conversely, if P_B increases, say, from \$1 to \$1.50, the lower end of the line fans inward to the left as illustrated in Figure A7-1. In both instances the line remains anchored at eight units on the vertical axis because P_A has not changed.

Indifference Curves: What Is Preferred

Budget lines reflect objective market data, specifically income and prices. They reveal combinations of products A and B that can be purchased given current money income and prices.

Indifference curves, on the other hand, reflect subjective information about consumer preferences for A and B. An **indifference curve** shows all the combinations of two products A and B that will yield the same total satisfaction or total utility to a consumer. Figure A7-2 presents a hypothetical indifference curve for products A and B. The consumer's subjective preferences are such that he or she will realize the same total utility from each combination of A and B shown in the table or on the curve. The consumer will be indifferent (will not care) as to which combination is actually obtained.

Indifference curves have several important characteristics.

INDIFFERENCE CURVES ARE DOWNSLOPING

An indifference curve slopes downward because more of one product means less of the other if total utility is to remain unchanged. Suppose the consumer moves from one combination of A and B to another, say, from j to k in Figure A7-2. In

FIGURE A7-2   A Consumer's Indifference Curve

Every point on indifference curve I represents some combination of products A and B, and all those combinations are equally satisfactory to the consumer. That is, each combination of A and B on the curve yields the same total utility.

Combination	Units of A	Units of B
j	12	2
k	6	4
l	4	6
m	3	8

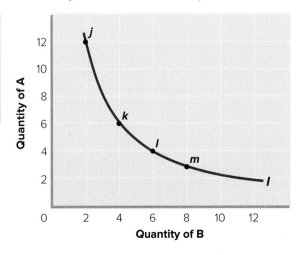

so doing, the consumer obtains more of product B, increasing total utility. But because total utility is the same everywhere on the curve, the consumer must give up some of the other product, A, to reduce total utility by a precisely offsetting amount. Thus more of B necessitates less of A, and the quantities of A and B are inversely related. A curve that reflects inversely related variables is downsloping.

INDIFFERENCE CURVES ARE CONVEX TO THE ORIGIN

Recall from the appendix to Chapter 1 that the slope of a curve at a particular point is measured by drawing a straight line that is tangent to that point and then measuring the *rise over run* of the straight line. If you drew such straight lines for several points on the curve in Figure A7-2, you would find that their slopes decline (in absolute terms) as you move down the curve. Technically, the slope of the indifference curve at each point measures the **marginal rate of substitution (MRS)** of the combination represented by that point. The slope or MRS shows the rate at which the consumer who possesses that combination must substitute one good for the other (say B for A) to remain equally satisfied. The diminishing slope of the indifference curve means that the willingness to substitute B for A diminishes as more of B is obtained.

MATH A7.1   The Marginal Rate of Substitution

The rationale for this convexity—that is, for a diminishing MRS—is that consumers' subjective willingness to substitute B for A (or A for B) will depend on the amounts of B and A they have to begin with. Consider Figure A7-2 again, beginning at point *j*. Here, in relative terms, the consumer has a substantial amount of A and very little of B. Within this combination, a unit of B is very valuable (that is, its marginal utility is high), while a unit of A is less valuable (its marginal utility is low). The consumer will then be willing to give up a substantial amount of A to get, say, 2 more units of B. In this case, the consumer is willing to forgo 6 units of A to get 2 more units of B; the MRS is 6/2, or 3, for the *j* segment of the curve.

But at point *k* the consumer has less A and more B. Here A is somewhat more valuable and B less valuable at the margin. In a move from point *k* to point *l*, the consumer is willing to give up only two units of A to get two more units of B, so the MRS is only 2/2, or 1. Having still less of A and more of B at point *l*, the consumer is willing to give up only one unit of A in return for two more units of B and the MRS falls to 1/2 between points *l* and *m*.[2]

In general, as the amount of B *increases*, the marginal utility of additional units of B *decreases*. Similarly, as the quantity of A *decreases*, its marginal utility *increases*. In Figure A7-2 we see

that in moving down the curve, the consumer will be willing to give up smaller and smaller amounts of A to offset acquiring each additional unit of B. The result is a curve with a diminishing slope, a curve that is convex to the origin. The MRS declines as one moves southeast along the indifference curve.

The Indifference Map

The single indifference curve of Figure A7-2 reflects some constant (but unspecified) level of total utility or satisfaction. It is possible and useful to sketch a whole series of indifference curves or an **indifference map**, as shown in Figure A7-3. Each curve reflects a different level of total utility and therefore never crosses another indifference curve. Specifically, each curve to the right of our original curve (labelled I_3 in Figure A7-3) reflects combinations of A and B that yield more utility than I_3. Each curve to the left of I_3 reflects less total utility than I_3. As we move out from the origin, each successive indifference curve represents a higher level of total utility. To demonstrate this fact, draw a line in a northeasterly direction from the origin; note that its points of intersection with successive curves entail larger amounts of both A and B and, therefore, higher levels of total utility.

Equilibrium at Tangency

Since the axes in Figures A7-1 and A7-3 are identical, we can superimpose a budget line on the consumer's indifference map, as shown in Figure A7-4. By definition, the budget line indicates all the combinations of A and B that the consumer can attain with his or her money income given the prices of A and B. Of these attainable combinations, the consumer will prefer that combination that yields the greatest satisfaction or utility. Specifically, the utility-maximizing combination will be the combination lying on the highest attainable indifference curve. It is called the consumer's **equilibrium position**.

In Figure A7-4 the consumer's equilibrium position is at point *X*, where the budget line is *tangent* to I_3. Why not point *Y*? Because *Y* is on a lower indifference curve, I_2. By moving down the budget line—by shifting dollars from purchases of A to purchases of B—the consumer can attain an indifference curve farther from the origin and thereby increase the total utility from the same income. Why not point *Z*? For the same reason as for *Y*: Point *Z* is on a lower indifference curve, I_1. By moving up the budget line—by reallocating dollars from B to A—the consumer can get on the higher indifference curve I_3 and increase total utility.

How about point *W* on indifference curve I_4? While it is true that *W* would yield a greater total utility than *X*, point *W*

---

[2] MRS declines continuously between *j* and *k*, *k* and *l*, and *l* and *m*. Our numerical values for MRS relate to the curve segments between points and are not the actual values of the MRS at each point. For example, the MRS *at* point *l* is 2/3.

FIGURE A7-3   An Indifference Map

An indifference map is a set of indifference curves. Curves farther from the origin indicate higher levels of total utility. Thus, any combination of products A and B represented by a point on I_4 has greater total utility than any combination of A and B and represented by a point on I_3, I_2, or I_1.

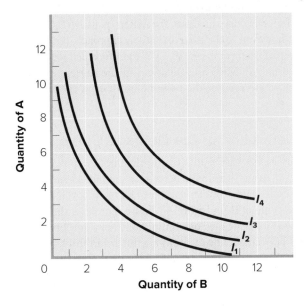

FIGURE A7-4   The Consumer's Equilibrium Position

The consumer's equilibrium position is represented by point X, where the black budget line is tangent to indifference curve I_3. The consumer buys four units of A at $1.50 per unit and six of B at $1 per unit with a $12 money income. Points Z and Y represent attainable combinations of A and B that yield less total utility, as is evidenced by the fact that they are on lower indifference curves. Point W would entail more utility than X, but it requires a greater income than the $12 represented by the budget line.

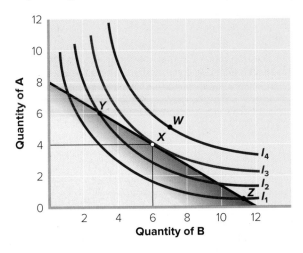

is beyond (outside) the budget line and, hence, is *not* attainable by the consumer. Point X represents the optimal *attainable* combination of products A and B. Note that, according to the definition of tangency, the slope of the highest attainable indifference curve equals the slope of the budget line. Because the slope of the indifference curve reflects the MRS (marginal rate of substitution) and the slope of the budget line is P_B/P_A, the consumer's optimal or equilibrium position is the point where

$$\text{MRS} = \frac{P_B}{P_A}$$

(You may benefit from trying to answer Appendix Discussion Question 3 right now.)

Equivalency at Equilibrium

As indicated at the beginning of this appendix, there is an important difference between the marginal utility theory of consumer demand and the indifference curve theory. The marginal utility theory assumes that utility is *numerically* measurable; that is, that the consumer can say how much extra utility he or she derives from each extra unit of A or B. The consumer needs that information to realize the utility-maximizing (equilibrium) position, as indicated by

$$\frac{\text{marginal utility of A}}{\text{price of A}} = \frac{\text{marginal utility of B}}{\text{price of B}}$$

The indifference curve approach imposes a less stringent requirement on the consumer, who needs only specify whether a particular combination of A and B will yield more, less, or the same amount of utility than some other combination of A and B. The consumer need only say, for example, that six units of A and seven of B will yield more (or less) satisfaction than four of A and nine of B. Indifference curve theory does not require that the consumer specify *how much* more (or less) satisfaction will be realized.

That said, it is a remarkable mathematical fact that both models of consumer behaviour will, in any given situation, point to exactly the same consumer equilibrium, and consequently exactly the same demand behaviour. This fact allows

us to combine the separate pieces of information that each theory gives us about equilibrium in order to deduce an interesting property about marginal utilities that must also hold true in equilibrium. To see this, note that when we compare the equilibrium situations in the two theories, we find that in the indifference curve analysis, the MRS equals P_B/P_A at equilibrium; however, in the marginal utility approach, the ratio of marginal utilities equals P_B/P_A. We therefore deduce that at equilibrium, the MRS is equivalent in the marginal utility approach to the ratio of the marginal utilities of the last purchased units of the two products.[3]

The Derivation of the Demand Curve

We noted earlier that with a fixed price for A, an increase in the price of B will cause the bottom of the budget line to fan inward to the left. We can use that fact to derive a demand curve for product B. In Figure A7-5a we reproduce the part of Figure A7-4 that shows our initial consumer equilibrium at point X. The budget line determining this equilibrium position assumes that money income is $12 and that $P_A = \$1.50$ and $P_B = \$1$. Let's see what happens to the equilibrium position when we increase P_B to $1.50 and hold constant both money income and the price of A.

The result is shown in Figure A7-5a. The budget line fans to the left, yielding a new equilibrium point X' where it is

[3] If we begin with the utility-maximizing rule, $MU_A/P_A = MU_B/P_B$, and then multiply through by P_B and divide through by MU_A, we obtain $P_B/P_A = MU_B/MU_A$. In indifference curve analysis we know that, at the equilibrium position, MRS = P_B/P_A. Hence, at equilibrium, MRS also equals MU_B/MU_A.

FIGURE A7-5   Deriving the Demand Curve

(a) When the price of product B is increased from $1 to $1.50, the equilibrium position moves from X to X', decreasing the quantity of product B demanded from six to three units. (b) The demand curve for product B is determined by plotting the $1–six-unit and $1.50–three-unit price–quantity combinations for product B.

(a) Two equilibrium positions

(b) The demand curve for product B

tangent to lower indifference curve I_2. At X' the consumer buys three units of B and five of A compared with four of A and six of B at X. Our interest is in B, and we now have sufficient information to locate two points on the demand curve for product B. We know that at equilibrium point X, the price of B is $1 and six units are purchased; at equilibrium point X', the price of B is $1.50 and three units are purchased.

These data are shown graphically in Figure A7-5b as points on the consumer's demand curve for B. Note that the horizontal axes of Figure A7-5a and A7-5b are identical; both measure the quantity demanded of B. We can therefore drop vertical reference lines from Figure A7-5a down to the horizontal axis of Figure A7-5b. On the vertical axis of Figure A7-5b we locate the two chosen prices of B. Knowing that these prices yield the relevant quantities demanded, we locate two points on the demand curve for B. By simple manipulation of the price of B in an indifference curve–budget line context, we have obtained a downsloping demand curve for B. We have thus again derived the law of demand assuming other things are equal, since only the price of B was changed (the price of A and the consumer's money income and tastes remained constant). In this case, we have

derived the demand curve without resorting to the questionable assumption that consumers can measure utility in units called utils. In this indifference-curve approach, consumers simply compare combinations of products A and B and determine which combination they prefer given their incomes and the prices of the two products.

Income and Substitution Effects

In the body of this chapter we noted that a change in price is composed of two effects. The *income effect* is the impact that a change in the price of a product has on a consumer's real income and the consequent effect on the quantity demanded of that good. In contrast, the *substitution effect* is the impact that a change in a product's price has on its relative expensiveness and consequently on the quantity demanded.

We can measure the magnitude of the income and substitution effects with the help of indifference curve analysis. Let's assume we have consumer Pam with a budget of $20 and that she consumes two normal goods, A and B. Good A is priced at $1 and good B at $2. In Figure A7-6a we can see that Pam can purchase a maximum of ten units of good B and a

FIGURE A7-6   Income and Substitution Effects of a Fall in Price

When the price of product B falls, Pam demands more of product B and less of product A. In panel (a) the fall in price of product B leads Pam to move to point Z on a higher indifference curve. The move from X to Z in panel (a) represents the increased quantity demanded of product B due to both the substitution effect and the income effect. In panel (b), if Pam's income is held constant (dashed line) the now-lower price of B leads her to demand more of it and she moves to point Y on indifference curve I_3. This rise in quantity demanded is the substitution effect due to the lower price of product B. The move from Y on indifference curve I_3 to Z on indifference curve I_4 represents the increased demand of product B due to the income effect as a result of the lower price of product B. At point Y the MRS is equal to the new price ratio.

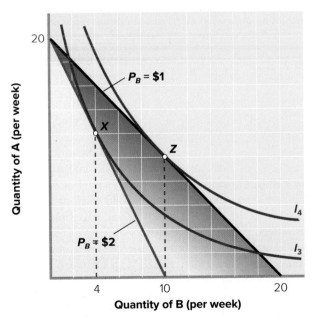

(a) Total effect of a price drop on quality demanded

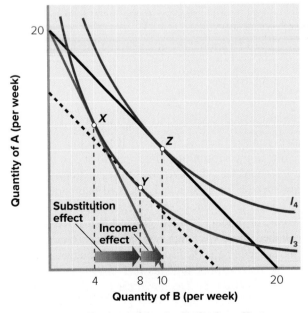

(b) The income and substitution effects

Indifference Maps and Topographical Maps

The familiar topographical map may help you understand the idea of indifference curves and indifference maps. Each line on a topographical map represents a particular elevation above sea level, say 1200 metres. Similarly, an indifference curve represents a particular level of total utility. When you move from one point on a specific elevation line to another, the elevation remains the same. So it is with an indifference curve. A move from one position to another on the curve leaves total utility unchanged. Neither elevation lines nor indifference curves can intersect. If they did, the meaning of each line or curve would be violated. An elevation line is an *equal-elevation line*; an indifference curve is an *equal-total-utility curve*.

Like the topographical map, an indifference map contains not just one line but a series of lines. That is, the

Courtesy of Maps a la carte, Inc.

topographical map may have elevation lines representing successively higher elevations of 500, 1000, 1500, 2000, and 2500 metres. Similarly, the indifference curves on the indifference map represent successively higher levels of total utility. The climber whose goal is to maximize elevation wants to get to the highest possible elevation line; the consumer desiring to maximize total utility wants to get to the highest possible indifference curve.

Finally, both topographical maps and indifference maps show only a few of the many such lines that could be drawn. The topographical map, for example, leaves out the elevation lines for 501 metres, 502 metres, 503 metres, and so on. The indifference map leaves out all the indifference curves that could be drawn between those that are displayed.

---

maximum of twenty units of good A. Given Pam's indifference curve and the relative prices of goods A and B, she is at equilibrium at point X on indifference curve I_3, consuming four units of good B.

Now let's assume that the price of good B drops to \$1. In Figure A7-6a you can see that when the price of good B drops from \$2 to \$1 Pam will be at a new equilibrium, at point Z, and on the higher indifference curve I_4. Pam now consumes more of good B (ten units, compared to four units previously) and less of good A.

The analysis so far has been similar to what we saw in Figure A7-5. But now we want to discover what part of Pam's increased purchase of good B from four to ten units was due to the substitution effect and what part was due to the income effect. To determine the substitution effect in Figure A7-6b we have added a dashed line parallel to the new budget constraint to see the extra amount Pam would consume of product B solely due to lower price. In reality the dashed line keeps Pam's real income constant. The slope of the dashed line is the same as the new budget constraint, meaning that the price ratio between product A and product B is 1 (as 10/10 = 1). The initial price ratio between products A and B was 2 (as 20/10 = 2). Thus, we are holding

Pam's income constant and keeping her on the original indifference curve to see how much of product B she will want at the lower price.

Holding Pam's income constant we find in Figure A7-6b that the drop in price of product B from \$2 to \$1 leads her to increase the purchase of product B by four units, moving her to point Y on indifference curve I_3. This is the substitution effect. Note that at point Y the MRS is equal to the new price ratio, which is 1.

The movement from point Y to point Z on indifference curve I_4 represents Pam's additional purchase of product B, in this case two additional units, due to the income effect brought about by the drop in the price of product B. So now we can see in Figure A7-6b that a price drop for product B will increase Pam's demand for product B by a total of six units. Of the six-unit increase in demand of product B, four units are attributable to the substitution effect and two units to the income effect.

If product B were an inferior good, the foregoing analysis would change somewhat. Recall from Chapter 6 that the consumption of an inferior good falls as income rises. Thus, the income effect would be negative for an inferior good.

APPENDIX   Summary

LOA7.1   Relate how the indifference curve model of consumer choice derives demand curves from budget lines, indifference curves, and utility maximization.

- The indifference curve approach to consumer behaviour is based on the consumer's budget line and indifference curves.

- The budget line shows all combinations of two products that the consumer can purchase given product prices and money income. A change in either product prices or money income moves the budget line.

- An indifference curve shows all combinations of two products that will yield the same total utility to a consumer. Indifference curves are downsloping and convex from the origin.

- An indifference map consists of a number of indifference curves; the farther from the origin, the higher the total utility associated with a curve.

- The consumer is in equilibrium (utility is maximized) at the point on the budget line that lies on the highest attainable indifference curve. At that point the budget line and indifference curve are tangent.

- Changing the price of one product shifts the budget line and determines a new equilibrium point. A downsloping demand curve can be determined by plotting the price–quantity combinations associated with two or more equilibrium points.

- A price change causes a change in the quantity demanded. The change in the quantity demanded is due to the substitution and income effects.

APPENDIX   Terms and Concepts

budget line
indifference curve
marginal rate of substitution (MRS)

indifference map
equilibrium position

APPENDIX   Discussion Questions

1. What information is embodied in a budget line? What shifts occur in the budget line when money income (a) increases and (b) decreases? What shifts occur in the budget line when the price of the product shown on the vertical axis (a) increases and (b) decreases?   [**LOA7.1**]

2. What information is contained in an indifference curve? Why are such curves (a) downsloping and (b) convex to the origin? Why does total utility increase as the consumer moves to indifference curves farther from the origin? Why can't indifference curves intersect?   [**LOA7.1**]

3. Using Figure A7-4, explain why the point of tangency of the budget line with an indifference curve is the consumer's equilibrium position. Explain why any point where the budget line intersects an indifference curve is not equilibrium. Also, explain the following statement: The consumer is in equilibrium where $MRS = P_B/P_A$.   [**LOA7.1**]

APPENDIX   Review Questions

1. Consider two bundles of coffee and chocolate and how Ted feels about them. The first bundle consists of two cups of coffee and two chocolate bars. The second bundle consists of one cup of coffee and three chocolate bars. If the first bundle gives Ted a total utility of 18 utils while the second bundle gives Ted a total utility of 19 bundles, could the two bundles be on the same indifference curve? Answer yes or no.   [**LOA7.1**]

2. Bill spends his money on flowers and cookies so as to maximize his total utility. Both flowers and cookies start off costing $2 each. At that price, Bill buys three flowers and two cookies.

When the price of flowers is lowered to $1, Bill buys eight flowers and one cookie. Which of the following statements about Bill's reaction to the price change is *not* true?   [**LOA7.1**]

a. Bill's budget line shifted outward when the price of flowers fell.

b. Bill moved to a higher indifference curve after the price of flowers fell.

c. Bill's demand curve for flowers shifted to the right.

d. Bill's attainable set was smaller before the price of flowers fell.

APPENDIX Problems

1. Assume that the data in the following table give an indifference curve for Mr. Chen. Graph this curve, putting A on the vertical axis and B on the horizontal axis. Assuming that the prices of A and B are $1.50 and $1, respectively, and that Mr. Chen has $24 to spend, add his budget line to your graph. What combination of A and B will Mr. Chen purchase? Does your answer meet the MRS = P_B/P_A rule for equilibrium? [**LOA7.1**]

Units of A	Units of B
16	6
12	8
8	2
4	24

2. Explain graphically how indifference analysis can be used to derive a demand curve. [**LOA7.1**]

3. Show the substitution and income effects of a decrease in the price of gasoline. Assume gasoline is a normal good. How would your result change if gasoline were an inferior good? [**LOA7.1**]

4. **Advanced Analysis** First, graphically illustrate a doubling of income without price changes in the indifference curve model. Next, on the same graph, show a situation in which the person whose indifference curves you are drawing buys considerably more of good B than A after the income increase. What can you conclude about the relative coefficients of income elasticity of demand for goods A and B (Chapter 6)? [**LOA7.1**]

PART 4 MICROECONOMICS OF PRODUCT MARKETS AND COMPETITION POLICY

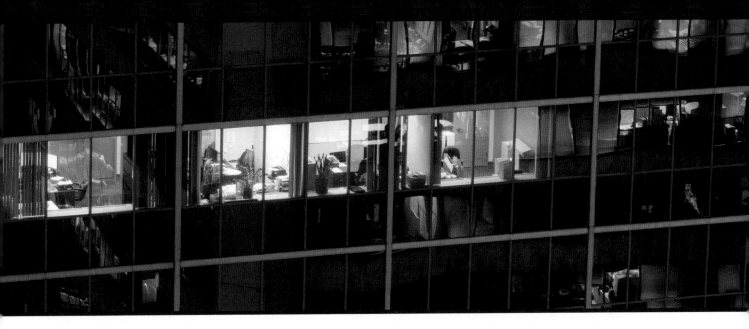

CHAPTER 8

The Firm and the Costs of Production

LEARNING OBJECTIVES

LO8.1   Explain why economic costs include both explicit (revealed and expressed) costs and implicit (present but not obvious) costs.

LO8.2   Relate the law of diminishing returns to a firm's short-run production costs.

LO8.3   Describe the distinctions between fixed and variable costs, and among total, average, and marginal costs.

LO8.4   Use economies of scale to link a firm's size and production costs in the long run.

LO8.5   Give business examples of short-run costs, economies of scale, and minimum efficient scale (MES).

Our attention now turns from the behaviour of consumers to the behaviour of producers. In market economies, a wide variety of firms, from family-owned businesses to large corporations, produce an even wider variety of goods and services. Every business requires inputs to produce its products. To acquire these, a firm makes monetary payments to factor owners (for example, workers) and incurs opportunity costs when using resources it already owns (for example, entrepreneurial talent). Those payments and opportunity costs together make up the firm's *costs of production*, which we discuss in this chapter.

Then in the next several chapters we bring product demand, product prices, and revenue back into the analysis and explain how firms compare revenues and costs to determine how much to produce. Our ultimate purpose is to show how those comparisons relate to economic efficiency.

8.1 Economic Costs

LO8.1   **Explain why economic costs include both explicit (revealed and expressed) costs and implicit (present but not obvious) costs.**

Firms face costs because the resources they need to produce their products are scarce and have alternative uses. Because of scarcity, firms wanting a particular resource have to bid it away from other firms. That process is costly for firms because it requires a payment to the resource owner. This reality causes economists to define an **economic cost** as the payment that must be made to obtain and retain the services of a resource. It is the income the firm must provide to resource suppliers to attract resources away from alternative uses.

 OPPORTUNITY COSTS

This section explains how firms incorporate opportunity costs to calculate economic costs. If you need a refresher on opportunity costs, a brief review of the section on opportunity costs in Chapter 1 might be useful before continuing with the rest of this section.

Explicit and Implicit Costs

To properly calculate a firm's economic costs, you must remember that each of the resources (factors of production) used by the firm have an opportunity cost. This is true for both the resources that a firm purchases from outsiders and the resources that it already owns.

As an example, consider a table-making firm that starts this month with $5000 in cash as well as ownership of a small oak forest from which it gets the oak that it turns into tables.

Suppose that during the month it spends the $5000 paying its workers. Clearly, the $5000 the firm spends purchasing labour comes at the opportunity cost of forgoing the best alternatives that could have been bought with that money. Less obvious, however, is the opportunity cost of the oak that the firm grows itself and that it uses to make tables. Suppose that the oak has a market value of $1500, meaning that our table-making firm could sell it to outsiders for $1500. This implies that using the oak to make tables has an opportunity cost of $1500. Choosing to convert the oak into tables means giving up the best alternatives that the firm could have purchased with the $1500.

As a result, keep in mind that *all* of the resources that a firm uses—whether purchased from outside or already owned—have opportunity costs and thus economic costs. Economists refer to these two types of economic costs as *explicit costs* and *implicit costs*:

- A firm's **explicit costs** are the monetary payments it makes to those from whom it must purchase resources that it does not own. Because these costs involve an obvious cash transaction, they are referred to as explicit costs. Be sure to remember that explicit costs are opportunity costs because every monetary payment used to purchase outside resources necessarily involves forgoing the best alternatives that could have been purchased with the money.

- A firm's **implicit costs** are the opportunity costs of using the resources that it already owns to make the firm's own product rather than selling those resources to outsiders for cash. Because these costs are present but not obvious, they are referred to as implicit costs.

A firm's economic costs are the sum of its explicit costs and its implicit costs:

Economic costs = explicit costs + implicit costs

The following example makes clear how both explicit costs and implicit costs affect firm profits and firm behaviour.

Accounting Profit and Normal Profit

Suppose that after many years working as a sales representative for a large T-shirt manufacturer, you decide to strike out on your own. After considering many potential business ventures, you decide to open a retail T-shirt shop. As we explained in Chapter 2, you will be providing two different economic resources to your new enterprise: labour and entrepreneurial ability. The part of your job that involves providing labour includes any of the routine tasks that are needed to help run the business—things like answering customer emails, taking inventory, and sweeping the floor. The part of your job that involves providing entrepreneurial ability includes any of the non-routine tasks involved with organizing the business and directing its strategy—such as deciding on whether to use Internet ads or in-person events to promote your business, whether to include children's clothing in your product mix, and how to decorate your store to maximize its appeal to potential customers.

You begin providing entrepreneurial ability to your new firm by making some initial organizational decisions. You decide to work full time at your new business, so you quit your old job that paid you $22,000 per year. You invest $20,000 of savings that have been earning $1000 per year. You decide that your new firm will occupy a small retail space that you own and that you had been previously renting out for $5000 per year. Finally, you decide to hire one clerk to help you in the store. She agrees to work for you for $18,000 per year.

After a year in business, you total up your accounts and find the following:

Total sales revenue	$120,000
Cost of T-shirts $40,000	
Clerk's salary 18,000	
Utilities 5,000	
Total (explicit) costs	63,000
Accounting profit	57,000

These numbers look very good. In particular, you are happy with your $57,000 **accounting profit**, the profit number that accountants calculate by subtracting total explicit costs from total sales revenue. This is the profit (or *net income*) that would appear on your accounting statement and that you would report to the government for tax purposes.

But don't celebrate yet! Your $57,000 accounting profit overstates the economic success of your business because it ignores your implicit costs. Success is not defined as "having a total sales revenue that exceeds total explicit costs." Rather, the true measure of success is doing as well as you possibly can—that is, making more money in your new venture selling T-shirts than you could pursuing any other business venture.

To figure out whether you are achieving that goal, you must take into account all of your opportunity costs—both your implicit costs and your explicit costs. Doing so will indicate whether your new business venture is earning more money than what you could have earned in any other business venture.

Costs of production exist because resources are scarce and have alternative uses.

To see how these calculations are made, let's continue with our example.

By providing your own financial capital, retail space, and labour, you incurred three different implicit costs during the year: $1000 of forgone interest, $5000 of forgone rent, and $22,000 of forgone wages. But don't forget that there is another implicit cost that you must also take into account—how much income you chose to forgo by applying your entrepreneurial abilities to your current retail T-shirt venture rather than applying them to other potential business ventures.

But what dollar value should we place on the size of the profits that you might have made if you had provided your entrepreneurial ability to one of those other ventures?

The answer is given by estimating a **normal profit**, the typical (or "normal") amount of accounting profit that you would most likely have earned in one of these other ventures. For the sake of argument, let us assume that with your particular set of skills and talents your entrepreneurial abilities would have on average yielded a normal profit of $5000 in one of the other potential ventures. Knowing that value, we can take all of your implicit costs properly into account by subtracting them from your accounting profit:

Accounting profit		$57,000
Forgone interest	$ 1,000	
Forgone rent	5,000	
Forgone wages	22,000	
Forgone entrepreneurial income	5,000	
Total implicit costs		33,000
Economic profit		24,000

Economic Profit

After subtracting your $33,000 of implicit costs from your accounting profit of $57,000, we are left with an *economic profit* of $24,000.

It is important to distinguish clearly between accounting profit and economic profit. Accounting profit is the result of subtracting only explicit costs from revenue:

Accounting profit = revenue − explicit costs

By contrast, **economic profit** is the result of subtracting all of your economic costs—both explicit costs and implicit costs—from revenue:

Economic profit = revenue − explicit costs − implicit costs

By subtracting *all* of your economic costs from your revenue, you determine how your current business venture compares with your best alternative business venture. In our example, the fact that you are generating an economic profit of $24,000 means that you are making $24,000 more than you could expect to make in your best alternative business venture.

By contrast, suppose that you had instead done poorly in business, so that this year your firm generated an economic loss (a negative economic profit) of $8000. This would mean that you were doing worse in your current venture than you could have done in your best alternative venture. You would, as a result, wish to switch to that alternative.

Generalizing this point, we see that there is a very important behavioural threshold at $0 of economic profit. If a firm is breaking even (that is, earning exactly $0 of economic profit), then its entrepreneurs know that they are doing exactly as well as they could expect to do in their best alternative business venture. They are earning enough to cover all their explicit and implicit costs, including the normal profit that they could expect to earn in other business ventures. Thus, they have no incentive to change. By contrast, anyone earning a positive economic profit knows they are doing better than they could in alternative ventures and will want to continue doing what they are doing or maybe even expand their business. And anyone earning an economic loss (a negative economic profit) knows that they could do better by switching to something else.

FIGURE 8-1   Economic Profit Versus Accounting Profit

Economic profit is equal to total revenue less economic costs. Economic costs are the sum of explicit and implicit costs and include a normal profit to the entrepreneur. Accounting profit is equal to total revenue less accounting (explicit) costs.

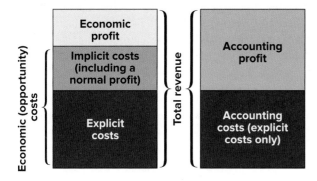

It is for this reason that economists focus on economic profits rather than accounting profits. Simply put, economic profits direct how resources are allocated in the economy. Entrepreneurs running economic losses close their current businesses, thereby liberating the land, labour, capital, and entrepreneurial ability that they had been using. These resources are freed up to be used by firms that are generating positive economic profits or are at least breaking even. Resources thus flow from producing goods and services with lower net benefits toward producing goods and services with higher net benefits. Allocative efficiency increases as firms are led by their profit signals to produce more of what consumers want the most.

WORKED PROBLEM 8.1   Economic Profit

Figure 8-1 shows the relationship among the various cost and profit concepts that we have just discussed. To test yourself, you might want to enter the cost numbers from our example in the appropriate blocks.

Short Run and Long Run

When the demand for a firm's product changes, the firm's profitability may depend on how quickly it can adjust the amounts of the various factors it employs. It can easily and quickly adjust the quantities employed of many resources such as hourly labour, raw materials, fuel, and power. It needs much more time, however, to adjust its *plant capacity*—the size of the factory building, the amount of machinery and equipment, and other capital resources. In some heavy industries, such as aircraft manufacturing, a firm such as Bombardier may need several years to alter plant capacity. Because of these differences in adjustment time, economists find it useful to distinguish between two conceptual periods: the *short run* and the *long run*. We will discover that costs differ in these two periods.

SHORT RUN: FIXED PLANT

In microeconomics, the **short run** is a period too brief for a firm to alter its plant capacity, yet long enough to permit a change in the degree to which the plant's current capacity is used. The firm's plant capacity is fixed in the short run. However, the firm can vary its output by applying larger or smaller amounts of labour, materials, and other inputs to that plant, using its existing plant capacity more or less intensively in the short run.

LONG RUN: VARIABLE PLANT

In microeconomics, the **long run** is a period long enough for a firm to adjust the quantities of all the factors that it employs, including plant capacity. For the industry, the long run also includes enough time for existing firms to dissolve and leave the industry or for new firms to be created and enter the industry. While the short run is a *fixed-plant* period, the long run is a *variable-plant* period.

ILLUSTRATION

If Bombardier hires 100 extra workers for one of its aircraft plants, or adds an entire shift of workers, we are speaking of the short run. If it adds a new production facility and installs more equipment, we are referring to the long run. The first situation is a short-run adjustment; the second is a long-run adjustment.

The short run and the long run are conceptual periods rather than calendar periods. In light-manufacturing industries, changes in plant capacity may be accomplished almost overnight. A small T-shirt manufacturer can increase its plant capacity in a matter of days by ordering and installing two or three new cutting tables and several extra sewing machines. But for heavy industry the long run is a different matter. Petro-Canada may need several years to construct a new oil refinery.

QUICK REVIEW 8.1

- Explicit costs are money payments a firm makes to outside suppliers of factors of production; implicit costs are the opportunity costs associated with a firm's use of inputs it owns.

- Normal profit is the implicit cost of entrepreneurship. Economic profit is total revenue less all explicit and implicit costs, including a normal profit.

- In the short run, a firm's plant capacity is fixed; in the long run, a firm can vary its plant size and firms can enter or leave the industry.

8.2 Short-Run Production Relationships

LO8.2   **Relate the law of diminishing returns to a firm's short-run production costs.**

A firm's costs of producing a specific output depend on the prices and the quantities of the resources (inputs) needed to produce that output. Factor supply and demand determine input prices. The technological aspects of production, specifically the relationships between inputs and output, determine the quantities of factors of production needed. Our focus will be on the *labour*–output relationship, given a fixed-plant capacity. But before examining that relationship, we need to define three terms:

1. The **total product (TP)** is the total quantity, or total output, of a particular good or service produced.

2. The **marginal product (MP)** is the extra output associated with adding a unit of variable input, in this case labour, to the production process. Thus

$$\text{Marginal product} = \frac{\text{change in total product}}{\text{change in labour input}}$$

3. The **average product (AP)**, also called *labour productivity*, is output per unit of labour input:

$$\text{Average product} = \frac{\text{total product}}{\text{units of labour}}$$

In the short run, a firm can for a time increase its output by adding units of labour to its fixed plant. But by how much will output rise when it adds more labour? And why do we say "for a time"?

Law of Diminishing Returns

The answers are provided in general terms by the **law of diminishing returns**, also called the *law of diminishing marginal product*. This law assumes that technology is fixed, so that the techniques of production do not change.

It states that as successive units of a variable factor (say labour) are added to a fixed factor (say capital or land), beyond some point the extra, or marginal, product that can be attributed to each additional unit of the variable factor will decline. For example, if additional workers are hired to work with a constant amount of capital equipment, output will eventually rise by smaller and smaller amounts as more workers are hired.

RATIONALE

Suppose a farmer in Ontario has a fixed supply of 80 hectares planted in corn. If the farmer does not cultivate the cornfields, the yield will be 40 bushels per hectare. If she cultivates the land once, output may rise to 50 bushels per hectare. A second cultivation may increase output to 57 bushels per hectare, a third to 61, and a fourth to 63. Succeeding cultivations would add less and less to the land's yield. If this were not so, the world's need for corn could be fulfilled by extremely intense cultivation of this single 80-hectare plot of land. Indeed, if diminishing returns did not occur, the world could be fed out of a flowerpot. Why not? Just keep adding more seed, fertilizer, and harvesters!

 CHOOSING A LITTLE MORE OR LESS

The law of diminishing returns also holds true in non-agricultural industries. Assume a wood shop is manufacturing chairs. It has a specific amount of equipment such as lathes, planers, saws, and sanders. If this shop hired just one or two workers, total output and productivity (output per worker) would be low. (Note that we assume all units of labour are of equal quality.) The workers would have to perform many different jobs, and the advantages of specialization would not be realized. Time would be lost switching from one job to another and machines would stand idle much of the time. In short, the plant would be understaffed and production would be inefficient because there would be too much capital relative to the amount of labour.

CONSIDER THIS

Diminishing Returns from Study

Here is a noneconomic example of the relationship between *inputs* and *output* may help you better understand the idea of diminishing returns. Suppose for an individual that

Total course learning = *f*(intelligence, quality of course materials, instructor effectiveness, class time, and study time)

where *f* means "function of" or "depends on." So this relationship supposes that total course learning depends on intelligence (however defined), the quality of course materials such as the textbook, the effectiveness of the instructor, the amount of class time, and the amount of personal study time outside the class.

For analytical purposes, let's assume that one's intelligence, the quality of course materials, the effectiveness of the instructor, and the amount of class time are *fixed*—meaning they do not change over the length of the course. Now let's add units of study time per day over the length of the course to "produce" greater course learning. The first hour of study time per day increases total course learning. Will the second hour enhance course learning by as much as

the first? By how much will the third, fourth, fifth . . . fifteenth hour of study per day contribute to total course learning relative to the *immediately previous hour*?

We think you will agree that diminish-

© BananaStock/JupiterImages RF

ing returns to course learning eventually will set in as successive hours of study are added each day. At some point the marginal product of an extra hour of study time will decline and, at some further point, become zero.

This is also true of production relationships within firms. As successive units of a variable input (say labour) are added to a fixed input (say capital), the marginal product of the variable input eventually declines. In short, diminishing returns will occur sooner or later. Total product eventually will rise at a diminishing rate, reach a maximum, and then decline.

The shop could eliminate those difficulties by hiring more workers. Then the equipment would be more fully used, and workers could specialize in doing a single job. Time would no longer be lost switching from job to job. As more workers were added, production would become more efficient and the marginal product of each successive worker would rise.

But the rise could not go on indefinitely. Beyond a certain point, adding more workers would cause overcrowding. Since workers would then have to wait in line to use the machinery, it would be underused. Total output would increase at a diminishing rate, because, given the fixed size of the plant, each worker would have less capital equipment to work with as more and more labour was hired. The marginal product of additional workers would decline because there would be more labour in proportion to the fixed amount of capital. Eventually, adding still more workers would cause so much congestion that marginal product would become negative and total product would decline. At the extreme, the addition of more and more labour would exhaust all the standing room and total product would fall to zero.

WORKED PROBLEM 8.2   Total, Marginal, and Average Product

TABULAR EXAMPLE

Table 8-1 is a numerical hypothetical illustration of the law of diminishing returns in a wood shop manufacturing chairs. Column 2 shows the total product, or total output, resulting from combining each level of a variable input (labour) in column 1 with a fixed amount of capital.

Column 3 shows the marginal product (MP), the change in total product associated with each additional unit of labour. Note that with no labour input, total product is zero; a plant with no workers will produce no output. The first three units of labour generate increasing marginal returns, with marginal products of ten, fifteen, and twenty units, respectively. But beginning with the fourth unit of labour, marginal product diminishes continually, becoming zero with the seventh unit of labour and negative with the eighth.

Average product, or output per labour unit, is shown in column 4. It is calculated by dividing total product (column 2) by the number of labour units needed to produce it (column 1). At five units of labour, for example, AP is 14 (= 70/5).

GRAPHICAL PORTRAYAL

Figure 8-2 (Key Graph) shows the diminishing returns data in Table 8-1 graphically and further clarifies the relationships between total, marginal, and average products. (Marginal product in Figure 8-2b is plotted halfway between the units of labour, since it applies to the addition of each labour unit.)

TABLE 8-1   Total, Marginal, and Average Product: The Law of Diminishing Returns

(1) Units of the variable factor (workers per day)	(2) Total product (TP) (chairs per day)	(3) Marginal product (MP) (chairs per additional worker) change in (2)/change in (1)		(4) Average product (AP) (chairs per worker) (2)/(1)
0	0	10	Increasing marginal returns	—
1	10	15		10.00
2	25	20		12.50
3	45	15		15.00
4	60	10	Diminishing marginal returns	15.00
5	70	5		14.00
6	75	0		12.50
7	75	−5	Negative marginal returns	10.71
8	70			8.75

KEY GRAPH

FIGURE 8-2   The Law of Diminishing Returns

(a) As a variable resource (labour) is added to fixed amounts of other resources (land or capital), the total product that results will eventually increase by diminishing amounts, reach a maximum, and then decline. (b) Marginal product is the change in total product associated with each new unit of labour. Average product is simply output per labour unit. Note that marginal product intersects average product at the maximum average product.

(a) Total product

(b) Marginal and average product

QUICK QUIZ

1. **Which of the following is an assumption underlying these figures?**
   a. Firms first hire highly skilled workers and then hire less skilled workers.
   b. Capital and labour are both variable, but labour increases more rapidly than capital.
   c. Consumers will buy all the output (total product) produced.
   d. Workers are of equal quality.

2. **Marginal product is**
   a. The change in total product divided by the change in the quantity of labour
   b. Total product divided by the quantity of labour
   c. Always positive
   d. Unrelated to total product

3. **Marginal product in panel (b) is zero when**
   a. Average product in panel (b) stops rising
   b. The slope of the marginal-product curve in panel (b) is zero
   c. Total product in panel (a) begins to rise at a diminishing rate
   d. The slope of the total-product curve in panel (a) is zero

4. **Average product in panel (b)**
   a. Rises when it is less than marginal product
   b. Is the change in total product divided by the change in the quantity of labour
   c. Can never exceed marginal product
   d. Falls whenever total product in panel (a) rises at a diminishing rate

Note first in Figure 8-2a that total product, TP, goes through three phases: it rises initially at an increasing rate, then it increases, but at a diminishing rate, and finally, after reaching a maximum, it declines.

Geometrically, marginal product—shown by the MP curve in Figure 8-2b—is the slope of the total product curve. Marginal product measures the change in total output of chairs associated with each succeeding unit of labour. Thus, the three phases of total product are also reflected in marginal product. Where total product is increasing at an increasing rate, marginal product is rising. Here, extra units of labour are adding larger and larger amounts to total product. Similarly, where total product is increasing but at a decreasing rate, marginal product is positive but falling. Each additional unit of labour adds fewer chairs than did the previous unit. When total product is at a maximum, marginal product is zero. When total product declines, marginal product becomes negative.

MATH 8.1   Marginal and Average Product

Average product, AP in Figure 8-2b, displays the same tendencies as marginal product. It increases, reaches a maximum, and then decreases as more units of labour are added to the fixed plant. But note the relationship between marginal product and average product: Where marginal product exceeds average product, average product rises. And where marginal product is less than average product, average product declines. It follows that marginal product intersects average product where average product is at a maximum.

This relationship is a mathematical necessity. If you add to a total a number that is larger than the current average of that total, the average must rise; if you add to a total a number that is smaller than the current average of that total, the average must fall. You raise your average examination grade only when your score on an additional (marginal) examination is greater than the average of all your past scores. You lower your average when your grade on an additional exam is below your current average. In our production example, when the amount an extra worker adds to total product exceeds the average product of all workers currently employed, average product will rise. Conversely, when the amount an extra worker adds to total product is less than the current average product, then average product will decrease.

The law of diminishing returns is reflected in the shapes of all three curves. But, as our definition of the law of diminishing returns indicates, we are most concerned with its effects on marginal product. The regions of increasing, diminishing, and negative marginal product (returns) are shown in Figure 8-2b.

8.3   Short-Run Production Costs

LO8.3   Describe the distinctions between fixed and variable costs, and among total, average, and marginal costs.

Production information such as that provided in Table 8-1 and Figures 8-2a and 8-2b must be coupled with prices of factors of production to determine the total and per-unit costs of producing various levels of output. We know that in the short run resources associated with the firm's plant are fixed. Other resources, however, are variable in the short run. As a result, short-run costs can be either fixed or variable.

Fixed, Variable, and Total Costs

Let's see what distinguishes fixed costs, variable costs, and total costs from one another.

FIXED COSTS

Costs that in total do not vary with changes in output are known as **fixed costs**. Fixed costs are associated with the very existence of a firm's plant and, therefore, must be paid even if its output is zero. Such costs as rental payments, interest on a firm's debts, and insurance premiums are generally fixed; they do not change even if a firm produces more. In column 2 in Table 8-2 we assume that the firm's total fixed cost is $100. By definition, this fixed cost is incurred at all levels of output, including zero. The firm cannot avoid paying these costs in the short run.

VARIABLE COSTS

Variable costs are those costs that change with the level of output. They include payments for materials, fuel, power, transportation services, most labour, and similar variable resources. In column 3 of Table 8-2 we find that

TABLE 8-2	Total-Cost, Average-Cost, and Marginal-Cost Schedules for an Individual Firm in the Short Run						
	TOTAL-COST DATA			**AVERAGE-COST DATA**			**MARGINAL COST**
(1) Total product (Q)	**(2)** Total fixed cost (TFC)	**(3)** Total variable cost (TVC)	**(4)** Total cost (TC) TC = TFC + TVC	**(5)** Average fixed cost (AFC) AFC = TFC/Q	**(6)** Average variable cost (AVC) AVC = TVC/Q	**(7)** Average total cost (ATC) ATC = TC/Q	**(8)** Marginal cost (MC) MC = change in TC/change in Q
(chairs per day)	(dollars per day)			(dollars per chair)			(dollars per additional chair)
0	$100	$ 0	$ 100				$ 90
1	100	90	190	$100.00	$90.00	$190.00	80
2	100	170	270	50.00	85.00	135.00	70
3	100	240	340	33.33	80.00	113.33	60
4	100	300	400	25.00	75.00	100.00	70
5	100	370	470	20.00	74.00	94.00	80
6	100	450	550	16.67	75.00	91.67	90
7	100	540	640	14.29	77.14	91.43	110
8	100	650	750	12.50	81.25	93.75	130
9	100	780	880	11.11	86.67	97.78	150
10	100	930	1,030	10.00	93.00	103.00	

the total of variable costs changes directly with output, but note that the increases in variable cost associated with succeeding one-unit increases in output are not equal. As production begins, variable cost will for a time increase by a decreasing amount; this is true through the fourth unit of output in Table 8-2. Beyond the fourth unit, however, variable cost rises by increasing amounts for succeeding units of output.

The reason lies in the shape of the marginal product curve. At first, as in Figure 8-2b, marginal product is increasing, so smaller and smaller increases in the amounts of variable inputs are needed to produce successive units of output. Thus, the variable cost of successive units of output decreases. But when, as diminishing returns are encountered, marginal product begins to decline, larger and larger additional amounts of variable inputs are needed to produce successive units of output. Total variable cost, therefore, increases by increasing amounts.

TOTAL COST

The **total cost** is the sum of the fixed costs and variable costs at each level of output:

TC = TFC + TVC

TC is shown in column 4 in Table 8-2. At zero units of output, total cost is equal to the firm's fixed cost. Then for each unit of the 10 units of production, total cost increases by the same amount as variable cost.

Figure 8-3 shows graphically the fixed-cost, variable-cost, and total-cost data given in Table 8-2. Observe that total variable cost, TVC, is measured vertically from the horizontal axis at each level of output. The amount of

FIGURE 8-3   Total Cost Is the Sum of Fixed Cost and Variable Cost

Total variable cost (TVC) changes with output. Total fixed cost (TFC) is independent of the level of output. The total cost (TC) at any output is the vertical sum of the fixed cost and variable cost at that output.

fixed cost, shown as TFC, is added vertically to the total variable cost curve to obtain the points on the total-cost curve, TC.

The distinction between fixed and variable costs is significant to the business manager. Variable costs can be controlled or altered in the short run by changing production levels. Fixed costs are beyond the business manager's current control; they are incurred in the short run and must be paid regardless of output level.

Per-Unit, or Average, Costs

Producers are certainly interested in their total costs, but they are equally concerned with per-unit, or average, costs. In particular, average-cost data are more meaningful for making comparisons with product price, which is always stated on a per-unit basis. Average fixed cost, average variable cost, and average total cost are shown in columns 5 to 7, Table 8-2.

AFC

The **average fixed cost (AFC)** for any output level is found by dividing total fixed cost (TFC) by that amount of output (Q). That is,

$$AFC = \frac{TFC}{Q}$$

Because the total fixed cost is, by definition, the same regardless of output, AFC must decline as output increases. As output rises, the total fixed cost is spread over a larger and larger output. When output is just one unit in Table 8-2, TFC and AFC are the same at $100. But at two units of output, the total fixed cost of $100 becomes $50 of AFC or fixed cost per unit; then it becomes $33.33 per unit as $100 is spread over three units, and $25 per unit when spread over four units. This process is sometimes referred to as *spreading the overhead*. Figure 8-4 shows that AFC graphs as a continuously declining curve as total output is increased.

$$AVC = \frac{TVC}{Q}$$

FIGURE 8-4   The Average-Cost Curves

AFC falls as a given amount of fixed costs is apportioned over a larger and larger output. AVC initially falls because of increasing marginal returns but then rises because of diminishing marginal returns. Average total cost (ATC) is the vertical sum of average variable cost (AVC) and average fixed cost (AFC).

AVC

The **average variable cost (AVC)** for any output level is calculated by dividing total variable cost (TVC) by that amount of output (Q):

$$AVC = \frac{TVC}{Q}$$

Due to increasing and then diminishing returns, AVC declines initially, reaches a minimum, and then increases again. A graph of AVC is a U-shaped curve, as shown in Figure 8-4.

Because total variable cost reflects the law of diminishing returns, so must AVC, which is derived from total variable cost. Marginal returns increase initially because it takes fewer and fewer additional variable inputs to produce each of the first four units of output. As a result, variable cost per unit declines. AVC hits a minimum with the fifth unit of output, and beyond that point AVC rises as diminishing returns require more variable inputs to produce each additional unit of output.

Rephrased, production is relatively inefficient—and therefore costly—at low levels of output. Because the firm's fixed plant is understaffed, average variable cost is relatively high. As output expands, however, greater specialization and better use of the firm's capital equipment yield more efficiency, and variable cost per unit of output declines. As still more variable resources are added, a point is reached where crowding causes diminishing returns to set in. Once diminishing returns start, each additional unit of input does not increase output by as much as preceding units did. This means that AVC eventually increases.

You can verify the U shape of the AVC curve by returning to Table 8-1. Assume the price of labour is $10 per unit. By dividing average product (output per labour unit) into $10 (price per labour unit), we determine the labour cost per unit of output. Because we have assumed labour to be the only variable input, the labour cost per unit of output is the variable cost per unit of output or AVC. When average product is initially low, AVC is high. As workers are added, average product rises and AVC falls. When average product is at its maximum, AVC is at its minimum. Then, as still more workers are added and average product declines, AVC rises. The hump of the average product curve is reflected in the U shape of the AVC curve. As you will soon see, the two are mirror images of each other.

ATC

The **average total cost (ATC)** for any output level is found by dividing the total cost (TC) by that output (Q) or by adding AFC and AVC at that output:

$$ATC = \frac{TC}{Q} = \frac{TFC}{Q} + \frac{TVC}{Q}$$
$$= AFC + AVC$$

Graphically, ATC can be found by adding vertically the AFC and AVC curves, as in Figure 8-4. Thus, the vertical distance between the ATC and AVC curves measures AFC at any level of output.

Marginal Cost

One final and crucial cost concept remains: The **marginal cost (MC)** is the extra, or additional, cost of producing one more unit of output. MC can be determined for each added unit of output by noting the change in total cost entailed by that unit's production:

$$MC = \frac{\text{change in TC}}{\text{change in } Q}$$

MATH 8.2 Marginal Cost as a Change in Cost

CALCULATIONS

In column 4 of Table 8-2, production of the first unit of output increases total cost from $100 to $190. Therefore, the additional, or marginal, cost of that first unit is $90 (column 8). The marginal cost of the second unit is $80 (= $270 − $190); the MC of the third is $70 (= $340 − $270); and so forth. The MC for each of the ten units of output is shown in column 8. MC can also be calculated from the total-variable-cost column, because the only difference between total cost and total variable cost is the constant amount of fixed costs ($100). Thus, the change in total cost and the change in total variable cost associated with each additional unit of output are always the same.

CONSIDER THIS

Ignoring Sunk Costs

It is a deep-seated human tendency to drag past costs—so called *sunk costs*—into marginal-benefit-versus-marginal-cost calculations. Doing so is known as the *sunk cost fallacy*.

As an example of this error, suppose a family that's on vacation stops at a roadside stand to buy some apples. After driving a bit, the family discovers that the apples are mushy and gross. Would it be logical for the father to insist that everyone eat the apples "because we paid a premium price for them"?

© Don Farrall/Getty Images RF

Absolutely not. In making a new decision, you should ignore all costs that are not affected by that new decision. The prior bad decision (in retrospect) to buy the apples should not dictate a subsequent decision for which marginal benefit is less than marginal cost.

Consider a business example. Suppose that a firm spends $1 million on R&D to bring out a new product, only to discover that the product sells very poorly. Should the firm continue to produce the product at a loss even when there is no realistic hope for future success? Obviously, it should not. In making this decision, the firm should realize that the amount it spent developing the product is irrelevant; it should stop production and cut its losses.

The emotional tendency that drives the sunk cost fallacy is the desire to get one's money's worth out of a past expenditure. But giving in to that emotion can lead to "throwing good money after bad," to use a common expression. Instead, you should ignore all past costs and focus solely on those that depend on the decision at hand.

CHOOSING A LITTLE MORE OR LESS

MARGINAL DECISIONS

Marginal costs are costs the firm can control directly and immediately. Specifically, MC designates all the additional cost incurred in producing the last unit of output. Thus, it also designates the cost that can be saved by not producing that last unit. Average-cost figures do not provide this information. For example, suppose the firm is undecided whether to produce three or four units of output. At four units, Table 8-2 indicates that ATC is $100. But the firm does not increase its total costs by $100 by producing the fourth unit, nor does it save $100 by not producing that unit. Rather, the change in costs is only $60, as the MC column in Table 8-2 reveals.

WORKED PROBLEM 8.3   Per-Unit Cost

A firm's decisions as to what output level to produce are typically decisions to produce a few more or a few less units. Marginal cost is the change in costs when one more or one less unit of output is produced. When coupled with marginal revenue, marginal cost allows a firm to determine whether it is profitable to expand or contract its production. The analysis in the next three chapters focuses on those marginal calculations.

GRAPHICAL PORTRAYAL

Marginal cost is shown graphically in Figure 8-5 (Key Graph). Marginal cost at first declines sharply, reaches a minimum, and then rises rather abruptly. This pattern reflects the fact that the variable costs, and therefore total cost, increase at first by decreasing amounts and then by increasing amounts (see columns 3 and 4, Table 8-2).

MATH 8.3   Productivity and Cost

MARGINAL COST AND MARGINAL PRODUCT

The shape of the marginal-cost curve is a consequence of the law of diminishing returns. Looking back at Table 8-1, we can see the relationship between marginal product and marginal cost. If all units of a variable factor (here, labour) are hired at the same price, the marginal cost of each extra unit of output will fall as long as the marginal product of each additional worker is rising, because marginal cost is the (constant) cost of an extra worker divided by his or her marginal product. Therefore, in Table 8-1, suppose that each worker can be hired for $10. Because the first worker's marginal product is ten units of output, and hiring this worker increases the firm's costs by $10, the marginal cost of each of these ten extra units of output is $1 (= $10 ÷ 10 units). The second worker also increases costs by $10, but the marginal product is 15, so the marginal cost of each of these fifteen extra units of output is $0.67 (= $10 ÷ 15 units). Similarly, the MC of each of the twenty extra units of output contributed by the third worker is $0.50 (= $10 ÷ 20 units). To generalize, as long as marginal product is rising, marginal cost will fall.

But with the fourth worker, diminishing returns set in and marginal cost begins to rise. For the fourth worker, marginal cost is $0.67 (= $10 ÷ 15 units); for the fifth worker, MC is $1 (= $10 ÷ 10 units); for the sixth, MC is $2 (= $10 ÷ 5 units), and so on. If the price (cost) of the variable resource remains constant, increasing marginal returns will be reflected in a declining marginal cost, and diminishing marginal returns in a rising marginal cost. The MC curve is a mirror image of the marginal-product curve. As you can see in Figure 8-6, when marginal product is rising, marginal cost is necessarily falling. When marginal product is at its maximum, marginal cost is at its minimum; when marginal product is falling, marginal cost is rising.

RELATION OF MC TO AVC AND ATC

Figure 8-5 shows that the marginal-cost curve MC intersects both the AVC and ATC curves at their minimum points. As noted earlier, this marginal-average relationship is a mathematical necessity, which a simple illustration will reveal. Suppose a Toronto Raptors basketball player scored an average of 20 points a game in the first three games he played. Now, whether his average rises or falls as a result of playing a fourth (marginal) game will depend

KEY GRAPH

FIGURE 8-5   The Relationship of the Marginal-Cost Curve to the Average-Total-Cost and Average-Variable-Cost Curves

The marginal-cost (MC) curve cuts through the average-total-cost (ATC) curve and the average-variable-cost (AVC) curve at their minimum points. When MC is below average total cost, ATC falls; when MC is above average total cost, ATC rises. Similarly, when MC is below average variable cost, AVC falls; when MC is above average variable cost, AVC rises.

QUICK QUIZ

1. **The marginal-cost curve first declines and then increases because of**
   a. Increasing, then diminishing, marginal utility
   b. The decline in the gap between ATC and AVC as output expands
   c. Increasing, then diminishing, marginal returns
   d. Constant marginal revenue

2. **The vertical distance between ATC and AVC measures**
   a. Marginal cost
   b. Total fixed cost
   c. Average fixed cost
   d. Economic profit per unit

3. **ATC is**
   a. AVC − AFC
   b. MC + AVC
   c. AFC + AVC
   d. (AFC + AVC) × Q

4. **When the marginal-cost curve lies**
   a. Above the ATC curve, ATC rises
   b. Above the AVC curve, ATC rises
   c. Below the AVC curve, total fixed cost increases
   d. Below the ATC curve, total fixed cost falls

Answers   1. c; 2. c; 3. c; 4. a

FIGURE 8-6   The Relationship Between Productivity Curves and Cost Curves

The marginal-cost (MC) curve and the average-variable-cost (AVC) curve in (b) are mirror images of the marginal-product (MP) and average-product (AP) curves in (a). Assuming that labour is the only variable input and that its price (the wage rate) is constant, then when MP is rising, MC is falling, and when MP is falling, MC is rising. Under the same assumptions, when AP is rising, AVC is falling, and when AP is falling, AVC is rising.

(a) Production curves

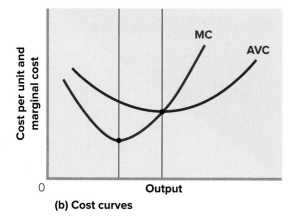

(b) Cost curves

on whether the additional points he scores in that game are fewer or more than his current 20-point average. If in the fourth game he scores fewer than 20 points—for example, 16—his total points will rise from 60 to 76 and his average will fall from 20 to 19 (= 76/4). Conversely, if in the fourth (marginal) game he scores more than 20 points—say 24—his total will increase from 60 to 84 and his average will rise from 20 to 21 (= 84/4).

So it is with costs. When the amount (the marginal cost) added to total cost is less than the current average total cost, ATC will fall. Conversely, when the marginal cost exceeds ATC, ATC will rise, which means that in Figure 8-5, as long as MC lies below ATC, ATC will fall, and whenever MC lies above ATC, ATC will rise. At the point of intersection, where MC equals ATC, ATC has just stopped falling but has not yet begun rising. This point, by definition, is the minimum point on the ATC curve. The marginal-cost curve intersects the average-total-cost curve at the ATC curve's minimum point.

Marginal cost can be defined as the addition either to total cost or to total variable cost resulting from one more unit of output; thus, this same rationale explains why the MC curve also crosses the AVC curve at the AVC curve's minimum point. No such relationship exists between the MC curve and the average-fixed-cost curve, because the two are not related; marginal cost includes only those costs that change with output, and fixed costs by definition are those that are independent of output.

MATH 8.4   Relation of MC to AVC and ATC

Shifts of Cost Curves

Changes in either technology or the prices of factors of production will change costs, and therefore the cost curves will shift. If fixed costs double from $100 to $200, the AFC curve in Figure 8-5 will shift upward. At each level of output, fixed costs would be higher. The ATC curve would also move upward, because AFC is a component of ATC. The positions of the AVC and MC curves would be unchanged, because their locations are based on the prices of variable rather than fixed factors of production. However, if the price of labour (wages) or some other variable input rises, AVC, ATC, and MC will rise, and those cost curves would all shift upward. The AFC curve would remain in place because fixed costs have not changed.

The discovery of a more efficient technology would increase the productivity of all inputs, and the AVC, ATC, and MC cost figures in Table 8-2 would all be lower. To illustrate, if labour is the only variable input, if wages are $10 per hour, and if the average product is ten units, then AVC would be $1. But if a technological improvement increases the average product of labour to twenty units, then AVC will decline to $0.50. More generally, an upward shift in the productivity curves shown in Figure 8-6a means a downward shift in the cost curves portrayed in Figure 8-6b.

QUICK REVIEW 8.2

- The law of diminishing returns indicates that, beyond some point, output will increase by diminishing amounts as more units of a variable factor (labour) are added to a fixed factor (capital).

- In the short run, the total cost of any level of output is the sum of fixed and variable costs (TC = TFC + TVC).

- Average fixed, average variable, and average total costs are fixed, variable, and total costs per unit of output; marginal cost is the extra cost of producing one more unit of output.

- Average fixed cost declines continuously as output increases; the average-variable-cost and average-total-cost curves are U-shaped, reflecting increasing and then diminishing returns; the marginal-cost curve falls but then rises, intersecting both the average-variable-cost curve and the average-total-cost curve at their minimum points.

8.4 Long-Run Production Costs

LO8.4   Use economies of scale to link a firm's size and production costs in the long run.

In the long run firms can undertake all desired input adjustments. The firm can alter its plant capacity; it can build a larger plant or revert to a smaller plant than that assumed in Table 8-2. The industry also can change its plant size; the long run allows sufficient time for new firms to enter or for existing firms to leave an industry. We will discuss the impact of the entry and exit of firms to and from an industry in the next chapter; here we are concerned only with changes in plant capacity made by a single firm. Let's express our analysis in terms of average total cost (ATC), making no distinction between fixed and variable costs because all inputs, and therefore all costs, are variable in the long run.

Firm Size and Costs

Suppose a single-plant manufacturer begins on a small scale and, as the result of successful operations, expands to successively larger plant sizes with larger output capacities. What happens to average total cost as this occurs? For a time, successively larger plants will reduce average total cost. However, eventually the building of a still larger plant will cause ATC to rise.

Figure 8-7 illustrates this situation for five possible plant sizes. ATC-1 is the short-run average-total-cost curve for the smallest of the five plants, and ATC-5 is the curve for the largest. Constructing larger plants will lower the minimum average total costs through plant size 3, but then larger plants will mean higher minimum average total costs.

The Long-Run Cost Curve

The vertical lines perpendicular to the output axis in Figure 8-7 indicate those outputs at which the firm should change plant size to realize the lowest attainable average total costs of production. These are the outputs at which

FIGURE 8-7   The Long-Run Average-Total-Cost Curve: Five Possible Plant Sizes

The long-run average-total-cost curve is made up of segments of the short-run cost curves (ATC-1, ATC-2, etc.) of the various-size plants from which the firm might choose. Each point on the planning curve shows the least unit cost attainable for any output when the firm has had time to make all desired changes in its plant size.

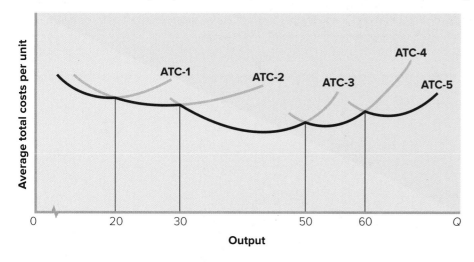

the per-unit costs for a larger plant drop below those for the current, smaller plant. For all outputs up to 20 units, the lowest average total costs are attainable with plant size 1. However, if the firm's volume of sales expands to between 20 and 30 units, it can achieve lower per-unit costs by constructing larger plant size 2. Although total cost will be higher at the expanded levels of production, the cost per unit of output will be less. For any output between 30 and 50 units, plant size 3 will yield the lowest average total costs. From 50 to 60 units of output, the firm must build plant size 4 to achieve the lowest unit costs. Lowest average total costs for any output over 60 units require construction of the still larger plant size 5.

Tracing these adjustments, we find that the long-run ATC curve for the enterprise is made up of segments of the short-run ATC curves for the various plant sizes that can be constructed. The long-run ATC curve shows the lowest average total cost at which *any output level* can be produced after the firm has had time to make all appropriate adjustments in its plant size. In Figure 8-7 the dark blue, uneven curve is the firm's long-run ATC curve or, as it is often called, the firm's *planning curve.*

In most lines of production, the choice of plant size is much wider than in our illustration. In many industries the number of possible plant sizes is virtually unlimited, and in time quite small changes in the volume of output will lead to changes in plant size. Graphically, this implies an unlimited number of short-run ATC curves, one for each output level, as suggested by Figure 8-8 (Key Graph). Then, rather than consisting of segments of short-run ATC curves as in Figure 8-7, the long-run ATC curve is made up of all the points of tangency of the unlimited number of short-run ATC curves from which the long-run ATC curve is derived. Therefore, the planning curve is smooth rather than bumpy. Each point on it tells us the minimum ATC of producing the corresponding level of output.

Economies and Diseconomies of Scale

We have assumed that for a time increasing plant sizes will lead to lower unit costs but that beyond some point successively larger plants will mean higher average total costs. That is, we have assumed that the long-run ATC curve is U-shaped. But why should this be? It turns out that the U shape is caused by economies and diseconomies of large-scale production, as we explain in a moment. But before we do, please understand that the U shape of the long-run average-total-cost curve *cannot* be the result of rising factor prices or the law of diminishing returns. First, our discussion assumes that factor prices are constant. Second, the law of diminishing returns does not apply to production in the long run. This is true because the law of diminishing returns deals only with situations in which a productive input is held constant. Under our definition of *long run*, all resources and inputs are variable.

KEY GRAPH

FIGURE 8-8 The Long-Run Average-Total-Cost Curve: Unlimited Number of Plant Sizes

If the number of possible plant sizes is very large, the long-run average-total-cost curve approximates a smooth curve. Economies of scale, followed by diseconomies of scale, cause the curve to be U-shaped.

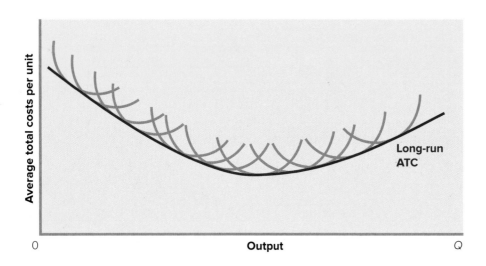

QUICK QUIZ

1. **The unlabelled light blue curves in this figure illustrate the**
   a. Long-run average-total-cost curves of various firms constituting the industry
   b. Short-run average-total-cost curves of various firms constituting the industry
   c. Short-run average-total-cost curves of various plant sizes available to a particular firm
   d. Short-run marginal-cost curves of various plant sizes available to a particular firm

2. **The unlabelled light blue curves in this figure derive their shapes from**
   a. Decreasing, then increasing, short-run returns
   b. Increasing, then decreasing, short-run returns
   c. Economies, then diseconomies, of scale
   d. Diseconomies, then economies, of scale

3. **The long-run ATC curve in this figure derives its shape from**
   a. Decreasing, then increasing, short-run returns
   b. Increasing, then decreasing, short-run returns
   c. Economies, then diseconomies, of scale
   d. Diseconomies, then economies, of scale

4. **The long-run ATC curve is often called the firm's**
   a. Planning curve
   b. Capital-expansion path
   c. Total-product curve
   d. Production possibilities curve

Answers 1. c; 2. b; 3. c; 4. a

ECONOMIES OF SCALE

Economies of scale, or economies of mass production, explain the downsloping part of the long-run ATC curve, as indicated in Figure 8-9, graphs (a), (b), and (c). As plant size increases, a number of factors will for a time lead to lower average costs of production.

FIGURE 8-9   Various Possible Long-Run Average-Total-Cost Curves

(a) Economies of scale are rather rapidly obtained as plant size rises, and diseconomies of scale are not encountered until a considerably large scale of output has been achieved. Thus, long-run average total cost is constant over a wide range of output. (b) Economies of scale are extensive, and diseconomies of scale occur only at very large outputs. Average total cost, therefore, declines over a broad range of output. (c) Economies of scale are exhausted quickly, followed immediately by diseconomies of scale. Minimum ATC thus occurs at a relatively low output.

(a)

(b)

(c)

Labour Specialization

Increased specialization in the use of labour becomes more achievable as a plant increases in size. Hiring more workers means jobs can be divided and subdivided. Each worker may now have just one task to perform instead of five or six. Workers can work full-time on those tasks for which they have special skills. By contrast, skilled machinists in a small plant may spend half their time performing unskilled tasks, leading to higher production costs.

Further, by working at fewer tasks, workers become even more proficient at those tasks. The jack-of-all-trades doing five or six jobs is not likely to be efficient in any of them. By concentrating on one task, the same worker may become highly efficient.

Finally, greater labour specialization eliminates the loss of time that accompanies each shift of a worker from one task to another.

Managerial Specialization

Large-scale production also means better use of, and greater specialization in, management. A supervisor who can handle twenty workers is underused in a small plant that employs only ten people. The production staff could be doubled with no increase in supervisory costs.

Small firms cannot use management specialists to their best advantage. For example, a sales specialist working in a small plant may have to spend some time on functions outside her area of expertise, for example, marketing, personnel, and finance. A larger scale of operations means that the marketing expert can supervise marketing full-time, while specialists perform other managerial functions. Greater efficiency and lower unit costs are the net result.

Efficient Capital

Small firms often cannot afford the most efficient equipment. In many lines of production such machinery is available only in very large and extremely expensive units. Effective use of such equipment demands a high volume of production, and that again requires large-scale producers.

In the automobile industry the most efficient fabrication method in North America employs robotics and elaborate assembly-line equipment. Effective use of this equipment demands an annual output of several hundred thousand automobiles. Only very-large-scale producers can afford to purchase and use this equipment efficiently. The small-scale producer is faced with a dilemma. Fabricating automobiles using other equipment is inefficient and therefore more costly per unit. But so too is buying and underutilizing the equipment used by the large manufacturers. Because it cannot spread the high equipment cost over very many units of output, the small-scale producer will be stuck with high costs per unit of output.

Other Factors

Many products have design and development costs, as well as other start-up costs, that must be incurred regardless of projected sales. These costs decline per unit as output is increased. Similarly, advertising costs decline per auto, per computer, per stereo system, and per box of detergent as more units are produced and sold. The firm's production and marketing expertise usually rises as it produces and sells more output. This *learning-by-doing* is a further source of economies of scale.

All these factors contribute to lower average total costs for the firm that is able to expand its scale of operations. Where economies of scale are possible, an increase in all inputs of, say, 10 percent will cause a more-than-proportionate increase in output of, say, 20 percent. The result will be a decline in ATC.

In many Canadian manufacturing industries, from automobile to aircraft production, economies of scale have been of great significance. Firms that have expanded their scale of operations to obtain economies of mass production have survived and flourished. Those unable to expand have become relatively high-cost producers, doomed to struggle to survive.

DISECONOMIES OF SCALE

In time the expansion of a firm may lead to diseconomies and, therefore, higher average total costs. The main factor causing **diseconomies of scale** is the difficulty of efficiently controlling and coordinating a firm's operations as it becomes a large-scale producer. In a small plant a single key executive may make all the basic decisions for the plant's operation. Because of the firm's small size, the executive is close to the production line, understands the firm's operations, and can make efficient decisions because the small plant size requires only a relatively small amount of information to be examined and understood in order to optimize production.

This neat picture changes as a firm grows. One person cannot assemble, digest, and understand all the information essential to decision making on a large scale. Authority must be delegated to many vice-presidents, second vice-presidents, and so forth. This expansion of the management hierarchy leads to problems of communication and cooperation, bureaucratic red tape, and the possibility that decisions will not be coordinated. At the same time, each new manager must be paid a salary. Thus declining efficiency in making and executing decisions goes hand in hand with rising average total costs as bureaucracy expands beyond a certain point.

Also, in massive production facilities workers may feel alienated from their employers and care little about working efficiently. Opportunities to shirk responsibilities, by avoiding work in favour of on-the-job leisure, may be greater in large plants than in small ones. Countering worker alienation and shirking may require additional supervision, which increases costs.

Where diseconomies of scale are operative, an increase in all inputs of, say, 10 percent will cause a less-than-proportionate increase in output of, say, 5 percent. As a consequence, ATC will increase. The rising portion of the long-run cost curves in Figure 8-9a illustrates diseconomies of scale.

CONSTANT RETURNS TO SCALE

In some industries a rather wide range of output may exist between the output at which economies of scale end and the output at which diseconomies of scale begin. That is, a range of **constant returns to scale** may exist over which long-run average cost does not change. The q_1–q_2 output range of Figure 8-9a is an example. Here a given percentage increase in all inputs of, say, 10 percent will cause a proportionate 10 percent increase in output. Thus, in this range ATC is constant.

Minimum Efficient Scale and Industry Structure

Economies and diseconomies of scale are an important determinant of an industry's structure. We now introduce the concept of **minimum efficient scale (MES)**, which is the lowest level of output at which a firm can minimize long-run average costs. In Figure 8-9a that level occurs at q_1 units of output. Because of the extended range of constant returns to scale, firms within the q_1 to q_2 range would be equally efficient, so we would not be surprised to find an industry with such cost conditions to be populated by firms of quite different sizes. The apparel, food processing, furniture, wood products, snowboard, and small-appliance industries are examples. With an extended range of constant returns to scale, relatively large and relatively small firms can coexist in an industry and be equally successful.

Compare this with Figure 8-9b, where economies of scale prevail over a wide range of output and diseconomies of scale appear only at very high levels of output. This pattern of declining long-run average total cost may occur over an extended range of output, as in the automobile, aluminum, steel, and other heavy industries. The same pattern holds in several of the new industries related to information technology, for example, computer microchips, operating system software, and Internet service provision.

Given consumer demand, efficient production will be achieved with a few large-scale producers. Small firms cannot realize the minimum efficient scale and will not be able to compete. In the extreme, economies of scale might extend beyond the market's size, resulting in what is termed **natural monopoly**, a relatively rare market situation in which average total cost is minimized when only one firm produces the particular good or service.

Where economies of scale are few and diseconomies come into play quickly, the minimum efficient size occurs at a low level of output, as shown in Figure 8-9c. In such industries a particular level of consumer demand will support a large number of relatively small producers. Many retail trades and some types of farming fall into this category. So do certain kinds of light manufacturing, such as the baking, clothing, and shoe industries. Fairly small firms are as efficient as, or more efficient than, large-scale producers in such industries.

Our point here is that the shape of the long-run average-total-cost curve is determined by technology and the economies and diseconomies of scale that result. The shape of the long-run ATC curve, in turn, can be significant in determining whether an industry has a relatively large number of small firms or is dominated by a few large producers—or lies somewhere in between.

But we must be cautious in our assessment, because industry structure does not depend on cost conditions alone. Government policies, the geographic size of markets, managerial strategy and skill, and other factors must be considered in explaining the structure of a particular industry.

QUICK REVIEW 8.3

- Most firms have U-shaped long-run average-total-cost curves, reflecting economies and then diseconomies of scale.

- Economies of scale are the consequence of greater specialization of labour and management, more efficient capital equipment, and spreading start-up costs over more units of output.

- Diseconomies of scale are caused by the problems of coordination and communication that arise in large firms.

- Minimum efficient scale is the lowest level of output at which a firm's long-run average total cost is at a minimum.

8.5 Applications and Illustrations

LO8.5 **Give business examples of short-run costs, economies of scale, and minimum efficient scale (MES).**

The business world offers many examples relating to short-run costs, economies of scale, and minimum efficient scale (MES). Here are just a few.

RISING GASOLINE PRICES

As we discussed in the appendix to Chapter 3, changes in supply and demand often lead to rapid increases in the price of gasoline. Because gasoline is used to power the vast majority of all motor vehicles, including those used by businesses, increases in the price of gasoline lead to increases in firms' short-run variable costs, marginal costs, and average total costs. In terms of our analysis, their AVC, MC, and ATC curves all shift upward when an increase in the price of gasoline increases production costs.

The extent of these upward shifts depends upon the relative importance of gasoline as a variable input in the various firms' individual production processes. Package-delivery companies like FedEx that use a lot of gasoline-powered vehicles will see substantial upward shifts while software companies like Open Text (an enterprise software company based in Waterloo, Ontario) that mainly deliver their products through Internet downloads, may see only very small upward shifts.

SUCCESSFUL START-UP FIRMS

The Canadian economy has greatly benefited over the past few decades from explosive growth of start-up firms. These firms typically reduce their costs by moving from higher to lower points on their short-run cost curves, and by shifts downward and to the right of their short-run cost curves via economies of scale.

A major source of lower average costs is the ability to spread huge product development and advertising costs over an increasing number of units of output. These firms also achieve economies of scale from learning-by-doing, through increased specialization of labour, management, and equipment. After starting up, such firms experience declining average total costs over the years or even decades it takes them to eventually reach their respective levels of MES.

THE DAILY NEWSPAPER

Daily newspapers have been going bankrupt in rapid succession over the past several years as both advertising dollars and news readership have shifted to the Internet. The falling circulation numbers have caused average fixed costs to skyrocket as newspapers are forced to spread their substantial fixed costs over fewer and fewer papers. The spike in average fixed costs has, in turn, forced newspapers to sharply increase their prices.

With readership continuing to fall, newspapers face an average-fixed-cost death spiral. The more they their raise prices, the less they will sell. But the less their sales, the higher their average fixed costs and thus the more they must raise their prices. As a result, printed newspapers could ultimately be a thing of the past, with both advertising and news delivery shifting almost entirely to the Internet.

THE VERSON STAMPING MACHINE

In 1996, Verson (a U.S. firm located in Chicago) introduced a 15-metre-tall metal-stamping machine that is the size of a house and weighs as much as 12 locomotives. This US$30 million machine, which cuts and sculpts raw sheets of steel into automobile hoods and fenders, enables automakers to make new parts in just 5 minutes compared with 8 hours for older stamping presses. A single machine is designed to make 5 million auto parts per year. To realize the cost saving from the machine, an auto manufacturer must have sufficient auto production to use all of these parts. When a firm is large enough to use this cost-saving piece of equipment, it achieves economies of scale.

AIRCRAFT AND CONCRETE PLANTS

Why are there only two plants in Canada (in Toronto and Montreal, both operated by Bombardier) that produce business and regional aircraft, but hundreds of plants that produce ready-mixed concrete? The simple answer is that MES is radically different in the two industries. Why is that? First, while economies of scale are extensive in

Economies and diseconomies of scale are important determinants of an industry's market structure.

assembling business and regional aircraft, they are very modest in mixing concrete. Manufacturing airplanes is a complex process that requires huge facilities, thousands of workers, and very expensive, specialized machinery. Economies of scale extend to huge plant sizes. But mixing portland cement, sand, gravel, and water to produce concrete requires only a handful of workers and relatively inexpensive equipment. Economies of scale are exhausted at a relatively small size.

The differing minimum efficient scales also derive from the vastly different sizes of the geographic markets. The market for business and regional airplanes is global, and aircraft manufacturers can deliver new airplanes anywhere in the world by flying them there. In contrast, the geographic market for a concrete plant is roughly the 75-kilometre radius that enables the concrete to be delivered before it sets up. So hundreds of small concrete plants locate close to their customers in small and large cities in Canada.

The LAST WORD

3-D Printers

© Timur Emek/Getty Images

3-D printers are poised to replace mass production with mass customization.

Both a billionaire and your Average Joe can buy a pocketknife for $10. They can also both buy an iPhone for $299 (on a contract with a cellular phone provider). And they can both purchase a new compact car for under $20,000.

The fact that all of these items are affordable to both a billionaire and your Average Joe is due to mass production and economies of scale. The iPhone, for instance, is one of the most complicated devices ever made. It contains cutting-edge technologies for graphics, voice recognition, battery length, screen durability, and many other features. Most of those technologies took hundreds of millions—if not billions—of dollars to develop and the factories that manufacture the iPhone and its

components themselves cost many billions of dollars to set up. Yet the iPhone is so inexpensive that Average Joes can afford to buy one.

That mass affordability is the result of mass production coupled with mass sales. Marginal costs are typically quite low with mass production. So if manufacturers can tap mass markets and sell their products in large numbers, they can achieve low per-unit costs by spreading the massive fixed costs (for developing the new technologies and setting up the factories) over many units. Doing so results in economies of scale, low average total costs per unit, and low prices that even average folks can afford.

Mass production and mass sales first became possible during the Industrial Revolution, which began in England during the late 1700s and then spread through most of the rest of the world during the next two centuries. The Industrial Revolution occurred when steam-powered engines became powerful enough to drive factory equipment, propel ships, and pull trains. Engineers and inventors used steam power to automate factories and initiate the low-cost mass production of consumer goods. That process only accelerated when, in the late 19th century, the so-called Second Industrial Revolution saw electricity harnessed to drive factories and provide lighting.

Mass sales, however, are not easy. They require large distribution networks, massive advertising budgets, and perhaps most importantly, cheap ways of shipping products from factories to consumers. Thus it was crucially important that transportation was also vastly improved during the first and second Industrial Revolutions. If not for better ships, smoother roads, and cheap transportation by railroad, transportation costs would have been so high that consumers would not have been able to afford mass-produced products shipped from distant factories.

Now, a new technology promises to deliver a Third Industrial Revolution that will feature not only low production costs but also zero transportation costs. Even better, both of those highly attractive features will be possible *even if you make only a single unit of a product*. In addition, each unit can be fully customized to a consumer's wants and needs. As a result, our world of affordable mass production may soon be replaced by a world of affordable mass customization.

The new technology is called additive manufacturing and it creates objects using computer-controlled devices known as 3-D printers. The 3-D (three-dimensional) printers contain a fine powder of metal or plastic particles that sit in a bin. A laser moves rapidly over the powder, the heat of its beam fusing small clumps of the powder together. Guided by a computerized blueprint, the rapidly moving laser can fuse a single layer of a complicated object together in just a few seconds.

The bin is then lowered a bit, another layer of powder is placed on top, and the laser again begins to shoot, this time fusing together both the previous layer and the current layer. Doing this over and over, one layer atop another, results in a solid object whose shape is limited only by the complexity of the blueprint. Any of the powder that is not struck by the laser and incorporated into the object is simply recycled for later use.

Because 3-D printers are inexpensive, they could potentially be located anywhere. Thus, there is no need to worry about transportation costs since objects could be manufactured by consumers in their own homes or in local workshops located only a short drive away. And because the powders are cheap and the machines only require a modest amount of electricity, anything that could be made using a 3-D printer would be inexpensive, even if you were only making a single unit.

The First Industrial Revolution delivered low prices by spreading massive fixed costs over many units. The Third Industrial Revolution is set to deliver even lower prices by eliminating two types of costs—the massive fixed costs necessary to set up large factories and the transportation costs needed to ship resources to factories and then finished goods to consumers.

One major cost might still remain, however. That is the cost of paying people to make the blueprints that drive the 3-D printers. But just as digital file sharing has pushed the price of recorded music towards zero, many analysts suspect that digital file sharing will also drive the price of blueprints very low. If so, the cost of manufactured goods may soon plunge to levels even lower than what has been achieved through mass production.

So far, only relatively simple objects can be made with 3-D printers. But some engineers see a day in the not-so-distant future when it may be possible to create even complicated devices like an iPhone using additive manufacturing. If so, people will simply download inexpensive blueprints, make a few changes to customize the product, and then "print" what they want.

Question

Does additive manufacturing rely on economies of scale to deliver low costs? What are two ways in which additive manufacturing lowers costs? Besides what's written in the Last Word, might there be another reason to expect 3-D blueprints to be inexpensive? (*Hint:* Think in terms of supply and demand.)

Chapter Summary

LO8.1 Explain why economic costs include both explicit (revealed and expressed) costs and implicit (present but not obvious) costs.

- The economic cost of using a resource to produce a good or service is the value or worth that the resource would have had in its best alternative use. Economic costs include explicit costs, which flow to resources owned and supplied by others, and implicit costs, which are payments for the use of self-owned

and self-employed resources. One implicit cost is a normal profit to the entrepreneur. Economic profit occurs when total revenue exceeds total cost (= explicit costs + implicit costs, including a normal profit).

- In the short run a firm's plant capacity is fixed. The firm can use its plant more or less intensively by adding or subtracting units of various factors of production, but it does not have sufficient time in the short run to alter plant size.

LO8.2   Relate the law of diminishing returns to a firm's short-run production costs.

- The law of diminishing returns describes what happens to output as a fixed plant is used more intensively; as successive units of a variable factor such as labour are added to a fixed plant, beyond some point the marginal product associated with each additional worker declines.

LO8.3   Describe the distinctions between fixed and variable costs, and among total, average, and marginal costs.

- Because some factors of production are fixed and others are variable, costs can be classified as fixed or variable in the short run. Fixed costs are independent of the level of output; variable costs vary with output. The total cost of any output is the sum of fixed and variable costs at that output.

- Average fixed costs, average variable costs, and average total costs are fixed, variable, and total costs per unit of output. Average fixed cost declines continuously as output increases because a fixed sum is being spread over an increasing number of units of production. A graph of average variable cost is U-shaped, reflecting the law of diminishing returns. Average total cost is the sum of average fixed and average variable costs; its graph is also U-shaped.

- Marginal cost is the extra cost of producing one more unit of output. It is the amount by which total cost and total variable cost change when one more or one fewer unit of output is produced. Graphically, the marginal cost curve intersects the ATC and AVC curves at their minimum points.

- Lower input prices shift cost curves downward, as does technological progress. Higher input prices shift cost curves upward.

LO8.4   Use economies of scale to link a firm's size and production costs in the long run.

- The long run is a period of time sufficiently long for a firm to vary the amounts of all inputs used, including plant size. In the long run all costs are variable. The long-run ATC, or planning, curve is composed of segments of the short-run ATC curves, and it represents the various plant sizes a firm can construct in the long run.

- The long-run ATC curve is generally U-shaped. Economies of scale are first encountered as a small firm expands. Greater specialization in the use of labour and management, the ability to use the most efficient equipment, and spreading start-up costs among more units of output all contribute to economies of scale. As the firm continues to grow, it will encounter diseconomies of scale stemming from the managerial complexities that accompany large-scale production. The output ranges over which economies and diseconomies of scale occur in an industry are often an important determinant of the structure of that industry.

- A firm's minimum efficient scale (MES) is the lowest level of output at which it can minimize its long-run average cost. In some industries, MES occurs at such low levels of output that numerous firms can populate the industry. In other industries, MES occurs at such high output levels that only a few firms can exist in the long run.

LO8.5   Give business examples of short-run costs, economies of scale, and minimum efficient scale (MES).

- Rising gasoline prices increase (shift upward) the AVC, ATC, and MC cost curves of firms like Canada Post that use gasoline as an input in their production processes.

- Many successful start-up firms experienced rapid growth and reduced costs, and shifted their cost curves down and to the right by spreading product-development and advertising costs over larger numbers of units as well as by exploiting the economies of scale that can be generated through learning-by-doing and increased specialization of labour, management, and equipment.

- Because minimum efficient scale (MES) is extremely large for commercial aircraft, Bombardier only has two production facilities in Canada. By contrast, MES is very small in concrete manufacturing, so there are thousands of concrete makers in Canada.

Terms and Concepts

economic cost
explicit costs
implicit costs
accounting profit
normal profit
economic profit
short run
long run
total product (TP)
marginal product (MP)
average product (AP)
law of diminishing returns

fixed costs
variable costs
total cost
average fixed cost (AFC)
average variable cost (AVC)
average total cost (ATC)
marginal cost (MC)
economies of scale
diseconomies of scale
constant returns to scale
minimum efficient scale (MES)
natural monopoly

Discussion Questions

1. Distinguish between explicit and implicit costs, giving examples of each. What are some explicit and implicit costs of attending college or university?   [**LO8.1**]

2. Distinguish between accounting profit, economic profit, and normal profit. Does accounting profit or economic profit determine how entrepreneurs allocate resources between different business ventures? Explain.   [**LO8.1**]

3. Complete the following table by calculating marginal product and average product from the data given.   [**LO8.2**]

Inputs of labour	Total product	Marginal product	Average product
0	0	_____	_____
1	15	_____	_____
2	34	_____	_____
3	51	_____	_____
4	65	_____	_____
5	74	_____	_____
6	80	_____	_____
7	83	_____	_____
8	82	_____	_____

   a. Plot the total, marginal, and average products and explain in detail the relationship between each pair of curves.

   b. Explain why marginal product first rises, then declines, and ultimately becomes negative.

   c. What bearing does the law of diminishing returns have on short-run costs? Be specific.

   d. When marginal product is rising, marginal cost is falling. And when marginal product is diminishing, marginal cost is rising. Explain and illustrate graphically.

4. Why can the distinction between fixed costs and variable costs be made in the short run? Explain the following statement: There are no fixed costs in the long run; all costs are variable. Then classify the following as fixed or variable costs.   [**LO8.3**]

   a. Advertising expenditures

   b. Fuel

   c. Interest on company-issued bonds

   d. Shipping charges

   e. Payments for raw materials

   f. Real estate taxes

   g. Executive salaries

   h. Insurance premiums

   i. Wage payments

   j. Depreciation and obsolescence charges

   k. Sales taxes

   l. Rental payments on leased office machinery

5. List several fixed and variable costs associated with owning and operating an automobile. Suppose you are considering whether to drive your car or fly 2000 kilometres for spring break. Which costs—fixed, variable, or both—would you take into account in making your decision? Would any implicit costs be relevant? Explain.   [**LO8.3**]

6. Use the concepts of economies and diseconomies of scale to explain the shape of a firm's long-run ATC curve. What is the concept of minimum efficient scale? What bearing can the shape of the long-run ATC curve have on the structure of an industry?   [**LO8.4**]

Review Questions

1. Linda sells 100 bottles of homemade ketchup for $10 each. The cost of the ingredients, the bottles, and the labels was $700. In addition, it took her 20 hours to make the ketchup and to do so she took time off from a job that paid her $20 per hour. Linda's accounting profit is _____ while her economic profit is _____.   [**LO8.1**]

   a. $700; $400

   b. $300; $100

   c. $300; negative $100

   d. $1000; negative $1100

2. Which of the following are short-run and which are long-run adjustments?   [**LO8.1**]

   a. Wendy's builds a new restaurant.

   b. Scotiabank hires 200 more workers.

   c. A farmer increases the amount of fertilizer used on her corn crop.

   d. An Alcan aluminum plant adds a third shift of workers.

3. A firm has $60 in fixed costs and variable costs as indicated in the table below. Complete the table; check your calculations by referring to Problem 4 at the end of Chapter 9.   [**LO8.3**]

Total product	Total fixed cost	Total variable cost	Total cost	Average fixed cost	Average variable cost	Average total cost	Marginal cost
0	$_____	$ 0	$_____			$_____	
1	_____	45	_____	$_____	$_____	_____	
2	_____	85	_____	_____	_____	_____	$_____
3	_____	120	_____	_____	_____	_____	_____
4	_____	150	_____	_____	_____	_____	_____
5	_____	185	_____	_____	_____	_____	_____
6	_____	225	_____	_____	_____	_____	_____
7	_____	270	_____	_____	_____	_____	_____
8	_____	325	_____	_____	_____	_____	_____
9	_____	390	_____	_____	_____	_____	_____
10	_____	465	_____	_____	_____	_____	_____

a. Graph total fixed cost, total variable cost, and total cost. Explain how the law of diminishing returns influences the shapes of the variable-cost and total-cost curves.

b. Graph AFC, AVC, ATC, and MC. Explain the derivation and shape of each of these four curves and their relationships to one another. Specifically, explain in non-technical terms why the MC curve intersects both the AVC and ATC curves at their minimum points.

c. Explain how the location of each curve graphed in question 3(b) would be altered if (1) total fixed cost had been $100 rather than $60 and (2) total variable cost had been $10 less at each level of output.

4. Indicate how each of the following would shift the (1) marginal-cost curve, (2) average-variable-cost curve, (3) average-fixed-cost curve, and (4) average-total-cost curve of a manufacturing firm. In each case specify the direction of the shift. [**LO8.3**]

   a. A reduction in business property taxes

   b. An increase in the nominal wages of production workers

   c. A decrease in the price of electricity

   d. An increase in insurance rates on plant and equipment

   e. An increase in transportation costs

5. True or False? The U shape of the long-run ATC curve is the result of diminishing returns. [**LO8.4**]

6. Suppose a firm has only three possible plant-size options, represented by the ATC curves shown in the figure below. What plant size will the firm choose in producing (a) 50, (b) 130, (c) 160, and (d) 250 units of output? Draw the firm's long-run average-cost curve on the diagram and describe this curve. [**LO8.4**]

Problems

1. Gomez runs a small pottery firm. He hires one helper at $12,000 per year, pays annual rent of $5000 for his shop, and spends $20,000 per year on materials. He has $40,000 of his own funds invested in equipment (pottery wheels, kilns, and so forth) that could earn him $4000 per year if alternatively invested. He has been offered $15,000 per year to work as a potter for a competitor. He estimates his entrepreneurial talents to be worth $3000 per year. Total annual revenue from pottery sales is $72,000. Calculate the accounting profit and the economic profit for Gomez's pottery firm. [**LO8.1**]

2. Imagine you have some workers and some hand-held computers that you can use to take inventory at a warehouse. There are diminishing returns to taking inventory. If one worker uses one computer, he can inventory 100 items per hour. Two workers can together inventory 150 items per hour. Three workers can together inventory 160 items per hour. And four or more workers can together inventory fewer than 160 items per hour. Computers cost $100 each and you must pay each worker $25 per hour. If you assign one worker per computer, what is the cost of inventorying a single item with one worker? What if you assign two workers per computer? Three? How many workers per computer should you assign if you wish to minimize the cost of inventorying a single item?   [**LO8.2**]

3. You are a newspaper publisher. You are in the middle of a one-year rental contract for your factory that requires you to pay $500,000 per month, and you have contractual labour obligations of $1 million per month that you can't get out of. You also have a marginal printing cost of $0.25 per paper as well as a marginal delivery cost of $0.10 per paper. If sales fall

by 20 percent from 1 million papers per month to 800,000 papers per month, what happens to the AFC per paper, to the MC per paper, and to the minimum amount that you must charge to break even on these costs?   [**LO8.3**]

4. There are economies of scale in ranching, especially with regard to fencing land. Suppose that barbed-wire fencing costs $10,000 per kilometre to set up. How much would it cost to fence a single property whose area is one square kilometre if that property also happens to be perfectly square, with sides that are each one kilometre long? How much would it cost to fence exactly four such properties, which together would contain four square kilometres of area? Now, consider how much it would cost to fence in four square kilometres of ranch land if, instead, it comes as a single large square that is two kilometres long on each side. Which is more costly—fencing in the four, one-square-kilometre properties or the single four-square-kilometre property?   [**LO8.4**]

CHAPTER 9

Perfect Competition in the Short Run

LEARNING OBJECTIVES

LO9.1 Give the names and the main characteristics of the four basic market models.

LO9.2 List the conditions required for perfectly competitive markets.

LO9.3 Explain how demand is seen by a perfectly competitive seller.

LO9.4 Convey how firms in perfect competition can use the total-revenue–total-cost approach to maximize profits or minimize losses in the short run.

LO9.5 Explain how perfectly competitive firms can use the marginal-revenue–marginal-cost approach to maximize profits or minimize losses in the short run.

LO9.6 Explain why a competitive firm's marginal cost curve is the same as its supply curve.

In Chapter 6 we examined the relationship between product demand and total revenue, and in Chapter 8 we discussed production costs. Now we want to connect revenues and costs to see how a business decides what price to charge and how much output to produce. A firm's decisions concerning price and production depend greatly on the market structure of the industry in which it operates. No "average" or "typical" industry exists. At one extreme is an industry in which a single producer dominates the market; at the other extreme are industries in which thousands of firms each produce a minute fraction of market supply. Between these extremes are many other types of industries.

Since we cannot examine each industry individually, we will focus on four basic *models* of **market structure**. Together, these models will help you to understand how price and output are determined in the many product markets in the economy. They also will help you evaluate the efficiency or inefficiency of those markets. Finally, these four models provide a crucial background for assessing public policies (such as anti-combines policy) relating to certain firms and industries.

9.1 Four Market Structures

LO9.1 **Give the names and the main characteristics of the four basic market models.**

Economists group industries into four distinct market structures: perfect competition, monopoly, monopolistic competition, and oligopoly. These four market models differ in several respects: the number of firms in the industry, whether those firms produce a standardized product or try to differentiate their products from those of other firms, and how easy or how difficult it is for firms to enter the industry.

Very briefly, the four models are as follows:

1. **Perfect competition** involves a very large number of firms producing a standardized product (that is, a product such as cotton for which each producer's output is virtually identical to that of every other producer). New firms can enter the industry very easily.

2. **Monopoly** is a market structure in which one firm is the sole seller of a product or service (for example, a local electrical utility). Since the entry of additional firms is blocked, one firm constitutes the entire industry. The monopolist produces a unique product, so product differentiation is not an issue.

3. **Monopolistic competition** is characterized by a relatively large number of sellers produce differentiated products (clothing, furniture, books). Present in this model is widespread *nonprice competition,* a selling strategy in which a firm does not try to distinguish its product on the basis of price but instead on attributes like design and quality (an approach called *product differentiation*). Entry to monopolistically competitive industries is quite easy.

4. **Oligopoly** involves only a few sellers of a standardized or differentiated product, so each firm is affected by the decisions of its rivals and must take those decisions into account when determining its own price and output.

Table 9-1 summarizes the characteristics of the four models for easy comparison and later reference. In discussing these four market models, we occasionally distinguish the characteristics of *perfect competition* from those of the three other basic market structures, which together we designate as **imperfect competition**.

TABLE 9-1	Characteristics of the Four Basic Market Models			
	MARKET MODEL			
CHARACTERISTIC	**Perfect competition**	**Monopolistic competition**	**Oligopoly**	**Monopoly**
Number of firms	A very large number	Many	Few	One
Type of product	Standardized	Differentiated	Standardized or differentiated	Unique; no close substitutes
Control over price	None	Some, but within rather narrow limits	Limited by mutual interdependence; considerable with collusion	Considerable
Conditions of entry	Very easy, no obstacles	Relatively easy	Significant obstacles	Blocked
Nonprice competition	None	Considerable emphasis on advertising, brand names, trademarks	Typically a great deal, particularly with product differentiation	Mostly public relations/advertising
Examples	Agriculture	Retail trade, dresses, shoes	Steel, automobiles, farm implements, many household appliances	Local utilities

9.2 Perfect Competition: Characteristics and Occurrence

LO9.2   List the conditions required for perfectly competitive markets.

Although perfect competition is relatively rare in the real world, this market model is highly relevant. A few industries more closely approximate perfect competition than any other market structure. In particular, we can learn much about markets for agricultural goods, fish products, foreign exchange, basic metals, and stock shares by studying the perfect competition model. Also, perfect competition is a meaningful starting point for any discussion of price and output determination. The operation of a competitive economy provides a standard, or norm, for evaluating the efficiency of the real-world economy. Let's take a fuller look at perfect competition, the focus of the remainder of this chapter. Perfect competition is characterized by

Firms in a perfectly competitive industry produce a standardized product.

- *Very Large Numbers* A basic feature of a perfectly competitive market is the presence of a large number of independently acting sellers offering their products in large national or international markets. None of the firms in a perfectly competitive market structure have market power. Some examples are the farm commodities market, the stock market, and the foreign exchange market.

- *Standardized Product* Firms in perfect competition produce a standardized (identical or homogeneous) product. As long as the price is the same, consumers will be indifferent about which seller to buy the product from. Buyers view the products of firms B, C, D, and E as perfect substitutes for the product of firm A. Because firms in a perfectly competitive industry sell standardized products, they make no attempt to differentiate their products and do not engage in other forms of nonprice competition. An example of a standardized product is organically grown apples.

- *Price-Takers* Individual firms in perfectly competitive markets do not exert control over product price. Each firm produces such a small fraction of total output that increasing or decreasing its output will not noticeably influence total supply or, therefore, product price. In short, the competitive firm is a **price-taker**: It cannot change the market price, but can only adjust to it. Asking a price higher than the market price would be futile; consumers will not buy from firm A at $2.05 per unit when its 9999 competitors are selling an identical product at $2 per unit. Conversely, because firm A can sell as much as it chooses at $2 per unit, it has no reason to charge a lower price, say, $1.95. Doing that would lower its profit. It should be noted that many firms in Canada exporting goods and services in the international market are, for all intents and purposes, price-takers.

- *Easy Entry and Exit* New firms can easily enter, and existing firms can easily leave, perfectly competitive industries in the long run. No significant legal, technological, financial, or other obstacles prohibit new firms from selling their output in any perfectly competitive market.

9.3 Demand for a Firm in Perfect Competition

LO9.3   Explain how demand is seen by a perfectly competitive seller.

We begin by examining demand from a perfectly competitive seller's viewpoint to see how it affects revenue. This seller might be a wheat farmer, a strawberry grower, or a foreign currency broker. Each firm in a perfectly competitive industry offers only a negligible fraction of total market supply, so it must accept the price determined by the market; it is a price-taker, not a price-maker.

© Daniel Koebe/Corbis

Although perfect competition is rare in the real world, by studying it we can learn much about markets such as the market for agricultural products.

PERFECTLY ELASTIC DEMAND

The demand schedule faced by the *individual firm* in a purely competitive industry is perfectly elastic at the market price, as demonstrated in Figure 9-1. As shown in column 1 of the table in Figure 9-1, the market price is $131. The firm cannot obtain a higher price by restricting its output, nor does it need to lower its price to increase its sales volume. Columns 1 and 2 show that the firm can produce and sell as many or as few units as it likes at the market price of $131.

We are *not* saying that *market* demand is perfectly elastic in a competitive market. Rather, market demand graphs as a downsloping curve. An entire industry (all firms producing a particular product) can affect price by changing industry output. For example, all firms, acting independently but simultaneously, can increase price by reducing output. But the individual competitive firm cannot do that, because its output represents such a small fraction of its industry's total output. For the individual competitive firm, the market price is therefore a fixed value at which it can sell as many or as few units as it cares to. Graphically, this implies that the individual competitive firm's demand curve will plot as a straight, horizontal line such as *D* in Figure 9-1.

Average, Total, and Marginal Revenue

The firm's demand schedule is also its average-revenue schedule. Price per unit to the purchaser is also revenue per unit, or average revenue, to the seller. To say that all buyers must pay $131 per unit is to say that the revenue per unit, or **average revenue** received by the seller, is $131. Price and average revenue are the same thing.

The **total revenue (TR)** for each sales level is found by multiplying price by the corresponding quantity the firm can sell (column 1 multiplied by column 2 in the table in Figure 9-1 yields column 3). In this case, total revenue increases by a constant amount, $131, for each additional unit of sales. Each unit sold adds exactly its constant price—no more and no less—to total revenue.

When a firm is pondering a change in its output, it considers how its total revenue will change as a result. **Marginal revenue** is the change in total revenue (or the extra revenue) that results from selling one more unit of output. In column 3 of the table in Figure 9-1, total revenue is zero when zero units are sold. The first unit of output sold increases total revenue from zero to $131, so marginal revenue for that unit is $131. The second unit sold increases total revenue from $131 to $262, and marginal revenue is again $131. Note in column 4 that marginal revenue is a constant $131, as is price. *In perfect competition, marginal revenue and price are equal.*

Figure 9-1 shows the perfectly competitive firm's total-revenue, demand, marginal-revenue, and average-revenue curves. Total revenue (TR) is a straight line that slopes upward to the right. Its slope is constant because each extra unit of sales increases TR by $131. The demand curve (*D*) is horizontal, indicating perfect price elasticity. The marginal-revenue curve (MR) coincides with the demand curve because the product price (and hence MR) is constant. The average revenue equals price and therefore also coincides with the demand curve.

FIGURE 9-1   The Demand and Revenue Curves for a Firm in Perfect Competition

FIRM'S DEMAND SCHEDULE		FIRM'S REVENUE DATA	
(1) Product price (*P*) (average revenue)	(2) Quantity demanded (*Q*)	(3) Total revenue (TR) (1) × (2)	(4) Marginal revenue (MR)
$131	0	$ 0	
			$131
131	1	131	
			131
131	2	262	
			131
131	3	393	
			131
131	4	524	
			131
131	5	655	
			131
131	6	786	
			131
131	7	917	
			131
131	8	1048	
			131
131	9	1179	
			131
131	10	1310	

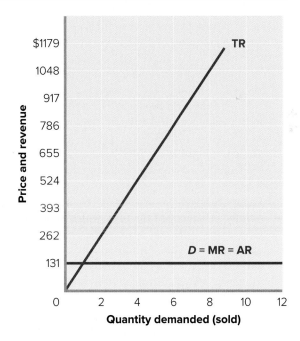

The demand curve (*D*) of a firm in a perfectly competitive industry is a horizontal line (perfectly elastic) because the firm can sell as much output as it wants at the market price (here, $131). Because each additional unit sold increases total revenue by the amount of the price, the firm's total-revenue curve (TR) is a straight upsloping line and its marginal-revenue curve (MR) coincides with the firm's demand curve. The average-revenue curve (AR) also coincides with the demand curve.

QUICK REVIEW 9.1

- In a perfectly competitive industry a large number of firms produce a standardized product and no significant barriers to entry exist.

- The demand of a competitive firm is perfectly elastic—horizontal on a graph—at the market price.

- Marginal revenue and average revenue for a competitive firm coincide with the firm's demand curve; total revenue rises by the product price for each additional unit sold.

9.4 Profit Maximization in the Short Run: Total-Revenue–Total-Cost Approach

LO9.4   Convey how firms in perfect competition can use the total-revenue–total-cost approach to maximize profits or minimize losses in the short run.

Since the firm in a perfectly competitive market structure is a price-taker, it cannot attempt to maximize its profit by raising or lowering the price it charges. With its price set by supply and demand in the overall market, the only variable that the firm can control is its output. As a result, the purely competitive firm attempts to maximize its economic profit (or minimize its economic loss) by adjusting its *output*. And in the short run, the firm has a fixed plant. Thus, it can adjust its output only through changes in the amount of variable inputs (materials, labour) it uses. It adjusts its variable inputs to achieve the output level that maximizes its profit or minimizes its loss.

There are two ways to determine the level of output at which a competitive firm will obtain maximum profit or minimum loss. One method is to compare total revenue and total cost; the other is to compare marginal revenue and marginal cost. Both approaches apply to all firms, whether they are perfectly competitive, monopolists, monopolistic competitors, or oligopolists.[1]

We begin by examining profit maximization using the total-revenue–total-cost approach. Confronted with the market price of its product, the competitive producer will ask the following: (1) Should we produce this product? (2) If so, in what amount? (3) What economic profit (or loss) will we realize?

WORKED PROBLEM 9.1   Profit Maximization: TR – TC Approach

Let's demonstrate how a firm in perfect competition answers these questions, given a particular set of cost data and a specific market price in Figure 9-2. Our cost data are total-fixed-cost, total-variable-cost, and total-cost data that reflect explicit and implicit costs, including a normal profit. Assuming that the market price is $131, the total revenue for each output level is found by multiplying output (total product) by price. Total-revenue data are in column 5. Then in column 6 we find the profit or loss at each output level by subtracting total cost, TC (column 4), from total revenue, TR (column 5).

Should the firm produce? Definitely. It can make a profit by doing so. How much should it produce? Nine units. Column 6 tells us that this is the output at which total economic profit is at a maximum. What economic profit (or loss) will the firm realize? A $299 economic profit—the difference between total revenue ($1179) and total cost ($880).

Figure 9-2a compares total revenue and total cost graphically for this profit-maximizing case. Observe again that the total-revenue curve for a firm in a perfectly competitive industry is a straight line. Total cost increases with output because more production requires more factors of production, but the *rate* of increase in total cost varies with the efficiency of the firm, which in turn varies with the amount of variable inputs that are being combined with the firm's current amount of capital (which is fixed in the short run). Stated slightly differently, the cost data reflect the law of diminishing returns, discussed in Chapter 8. From zero to four units of output, total cost increases at a decreasing rate as the firm temporarily experiences increasing returns. At higher levels of output, however, efficiency falls as crowding causes diminishing returns to set in. Once that happens, the firm's total cost goes up at an increasing rate because each additional unit of input yields less output than the previous unit.

Total revenue and total cost are equal where the two curves in Figure 9-2a intersect (at roughly two units of output). Total revenue covers all costs (including a normal profit, which is included in the cost curve) but there is no economic profit. For this reason economists call this output a **break-even point**: an output at which a firm makes a *normal profit* but not an economic profit. If we extended the data beyond ten units of output, another break-even point would occur where total cost would catch up with total revenue somewhere between thirteen and fourteen units of output in Figure 9-2a. Any output between the two break-even points identified in the figure will yield an economic profit. The firm achieves maximum profit, however, where the vertical distance between the total-revenue and total-cost curves is greatest. For our particular data, this is at nine units of output, where maximum profit is $299.

The profit-maximizing output is easier to see in Figure 9-2b, where total economic profit is graphed for each level of output. Where the total-revenue and total-cost curves intersect in Figure 9-2a, economic profit is zero, as

---

[1] To make sure you understand these two approaches, we will apply them both to output determination under perfect competition; but since we want to emphasize the marginal approach, we will limit our graphical application of the total-revenue approach to a situation in which the firm maximizes profits. We will then use the marginal approach to examine three cases: profit maximization, loss minimization, and shutdown.

FIGURE 9-2   Total-Revenue–Total-Cost Approach to Profit Maximization for a Firm in a Perfectly Competitive Industry

				PRICE: $131	
(1) Total product (output), Q	(2) Total fixed cost, TFC	(3) Total variable cost, TVC	(4) Total cost, TC	(5) Total revenue, TR	(6) Profit (+) or loss (−)
0	$ 100	$ 0	$ 100	$ 0	$−100
1	100	90	190	131	−59
2	100	170	270	262	−8
3	100	240	340	393	+53
4	100	300	400	524	+124
5	100	370	470	655	+185
6	100	450	550	786	+236
7	100	540	640	917	+277
8	100	650	750	1048	+298
9	**100**	**780**	**880**	**1179**	**+299**
10	100	930	1030	1310	+280

(a) The firm's profit is maximized at that output (nine units) where total revenue, TR, exceeds total cost, TC, by the maximum amount. (b) The vertical distance between TR and TC in (a) is plotted as a total-economic-profit curve. Maximum economic profit is $299 at nine units of output.

(a) Profit-maximizing case

(b) Total economic profit

shown by the total-profit line in Figure 9-2b. Where the vertical distance between TR and TC is greatest in the upper graph, economic profit is at its peak ($299), as shown in the lower graph. This firm will choose to produce nine units, since that output maximizes its profit.

9.5   Profit Maximization in the Short Run: Marginal-Revenue–Marginal-Cost Approach

 CHOOSING A LITTLE MORE OR LESS

LO9.5   Explain how perfectly competitive firms can use the marginal-revenue–marginal-cost approach to maximize profits or minimize losses in the short run.

In the second approach, the firm compares the amounts that each *additional* unit of output would add to total revenue and to total cost. In other words, the firm compares the *marginal revenue* (MR) and the *marginal cost* (MC) of each successive unit of output. Assuming that producing is preferable to shutting down, the firm will produce any unit of output whose marginal revenue exceeds its marginal cost because the firm would gain more in revenue from selling that unit than it would add to its costs by producing it. Conversely, if the marginal cost of a unit of output exceeds its marginal revenue, the firm will not produce that unit. Producing it would add more to costs than to revenue, and profit would decline or loss would increase.

In the initial stages of production, where output is relatively low, marginal revenue will usually (but not always) exceed marginal cost. So it is profitable to produce through this range of output. But at later stages of production, where output is relatively high, rising marginal costs will exceed marginal revenue. Obviously, a profit-maximizing firm will want to avoid output levels in that range. Separating these two production ranges is a unique point at which marginal revenue equals marginal cost. This point is the key to the output-determining rule: *In the short run, the firm will maximize profit or minimize loss by producing the output at which marginal revenue equals marginal cost (as long as producing is preferable to shutting down).* This profit-maximizing guide is known as the **MR = MC rule**.

Keep in mind these features of the MR = MC rule:

* For most sets of MR and MC data, MR and MC will be precisely equal at a fractional level of output. In such instances the firm should produce the last complete unit of output for which MR exceeds MC.

* The rule applies only if producing is preferable to shutting down. We will show shortly that if marginal revenue does not equal or exceed average variable cost, the firm will shut down rather than produce the MR = MC output.

* The rule is an accurate guide to profit maximization for all firms, whether they are perfectly competitive, monopolistic, monopolistically competitive, or oligopolistic.

* The rule can be restated as $P = MC$ when applied to a firm in a perfectly competitive industry. Because the demand schedule faced by a competitive seller is perfectly elastic at the going market price, product price and marginal revenue are equal. So under perfect competition (and only under perfect competition) we may substitute P for MR in the rule: *When producing is preferable to shutting down, the competitive firm should produce at that point where price equals marginal cost ($P = MC$).*

MATH 9.1   MR = MC

Now let's apply the MR = MC rule, first using the same price as in our total-revenue–total-cost approach to profit maximization. Then, by considering other prices, we will demonstrate two additional cases: loss minimization and shutdown. It is crucial that you understand the MR = MC analysis that follows, since it reappears in Chapters 10, 11, and 12.

PROFIT-MAXIMIZING CASE

The first five columns of the table in Figure 9-3 (Key Graph) are AFC, AVC, ATC, and MC data. It is the marginal-cost data of column 6 that we will compare with price (equals marginal revenue) for each unit of output. Suppose first that the market price, and therefore marginal revenue, is $131, as shown in column 7.

KEY GRAPH

FIGURE 9-3   Short-Run Profit Maximizing for a Firm in a Perfectly Competitive Industry

The MR = MC output enables the firm in a perfectly competitive industry to maximize profits or to minimize losses. In this case MR (= P in pure competition) and MC are equal at an output Q of nine units. There, P exceeds the average total cost A = $97.78, so the firm realizes an economic profit of P − A per unit. The total economic profit is represented by the grey rectangle and is 9 × (P − A).

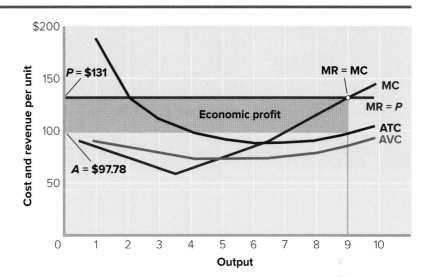

(1) Total product (output)	(2) Average fixed cost, AFC	(3) Average variable cost, AVC	(4) Average total cost, ATC	(5) Marginal cost, MC	(6) Price = marginal revenue, MR	(7) Total economic profit (+) or loss (−)
0						$−100
1	$ 100.00	$ 90.00	$ 190.00	$ 90	$ 131	−59
2	50.00	85.00	135.00	80	131	−8
3	33.33	80.00	113.33	70	131	+53
4	25.00	75.00	100.00	60	131	+124
5	20.00	74.00	94.00	70	131	+185
6	16.67	75.00	91.67	80	131	+236
7	14.29	77.14	91.43	90	131	+277
8	12.50	81.25	93.75	110	131	+298
9	**11.11**	**86.67**	**97.78**	**130**	**131**	**+299**
10	10.00	93.00	103.00	150	131	+280

QUICK QUIZ

1. **Curve MR is horizontal because**
   a. Product price falls as output increases
   b. The law of diminishing marginal utility is at work
   c. The market demand for this product is perfectly elastic
   d. The firm is a price-taker

2. **At a price of $131 and seven units of output**
   a. MR exceeds MC, and the firm should expand its output
   b. Total revenue is less than total cost
   c. AVC exceeds ATC
   d. The firm would earn only a normal profit

3. In maximizing profits at nine units of output, this firm is adhering to which of the following decision rules?

a. Produce where MR exceeds MC by the greatest amount.

b. Produce where *P* exceeds ATC by the greatest amount.

c. Produce where total revenue exceeds total cost by the greatest amount.

d. Produce where average fixed costs are zero.

4. Suppose price declined from $131 to $100. This firm's

a. Marginal-cost curve would shift downward

b. Economic profit would fall to zero

c. Profit-maximizing output would decline

d. Total cost would fall by more than its total revenue

Answers   1.d; 2.a; 3.c; 4.c

What is the profit-maximizing output? Each of the first nine units adds to the firm's profit and will be produced. The tenth unit, however, will not be produced. It would add more to cost ($150) than to revenue ($131). So nine units is the profit-maximizing output.

The economic profit realized by producing nine units can be calculated by subtracting total cost from total revenue. Multiplying price ($131) by output (9), we find that total revenue is $1179. From the average-total-cost data in column 4, we see that ATC is $97.78 at nine units of output. Multiplying $97.78 by 9 gives us total cost of $880.[2] The difference of $299 (= $1179 − $880) is the economic profit. Clearly, this firm will prefer to operate rather than shut down.

Perhaps an easier way to calculate the economic profit is to use this simple equation, in which *A* is average total cost:

$$\text{Profit} = (P - A) \times Q$$

WORKED PROBLEM 9.2   Profit Maximization: MR = MC Approach

So, by subtracting the average total cost ($97.78) from the product price ($131), we obtain a per-unit profit of $33.22. Multiplying that amount by nine units of output, we determine that the profit is $299. Take some time now to verify the numbers in column 7. You will find that any output other than that which adheres to the MR = MC rule will mean either profits below $299 or losses.

The graph in Figure 9-3 shows price (= MR) and marginal cost graphically. Price equals marginal cost at the profit-maximizing output of nine units. There the per-unit economic profit is $P - A$, where *P* is the market price and *A* is the average total cost for an output of nine units. The total economic profit is $9 \times (P - A)$, shown by the grey rectangular area.

Note that the firm wants to maximize its total profit, not its per-unit profit. Per-unit profit is greatest at seven units of output, where price exceeds average total cost by $39.57 (= $131 − $91.43). But by producing only seven units, the firm would not produce two additional units of output that would clearly contribute to total profit. The firm is happy to accept lower per-unit profits for additional units of output because they nonetheless add to total profit.

LOSS-MINIMIZING CASE

Now let's assume that the market price is $81 rather than $131. Should the firm still produce? If so, how much? What will be the resulting profit or loss? The answers, respectively, are "yes," "six units," and "a loss of $64."

---

[2] Most of the unit-cost data are rounded figures. Therefore, economic profits calculated from them will typically vary by a few cents from the profits determined in the total-revenue-total–cost approach. Here we simply ignore the few-cent differentials to make our answers consistent with the results of the total-revenue–total-cost approach.

FIGURE 9-4 **The Short-Run Loss-Minimizing Position of a Firm in a Perfectly Competitive Industry**

If price *P* exceeds the minimum AVC (here, $74 at *Q* = 5) but is less than ATC, the MR = MC output (here, six units) will permit the firm to minimize its losses. In this instance the loss is *A* − *P* per unit, where *A* is the average total cost at six units of output. The total loss is shown by the grey area and is equal to 6 × (*A* − *P*).

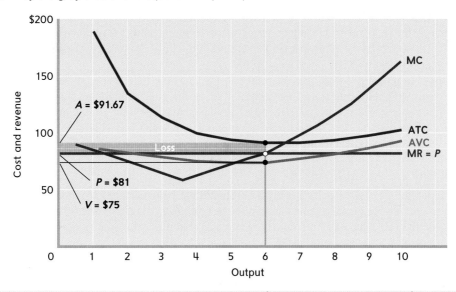

(1) Total product (output)	(2) Average fixed cost (AFC)	(3) Average variable cost (AVC)	(4) Average total cost (ATC)	(5) Marginal cost (MC)	(6) Loss-minimizing case $81 price = marginal revenue (MR)	(7) Profit (+) or loss (−), $81 price	(8) Shut-down case $71 price = marginal revenue (MR)	(9) Profit (+) or loss (−), $71 price
0						$−100		*$−100*
1	$100.00	$90.00	$190.00	$ 90	$81	−109	$71	−119
2	50.00	85.00	135.00	80	81	−108	71	−128
3	33.33	80.00	113.33	70	81	−97	71	−127
4	25.00	75.00	100.00	60	81	−76	71	−116
5	20.00	74.00	94.00	70	81	−65	71	−115
6	**16.67**	**75.00**	**91.67**	**80**	**81**	**−64**	71	−124
7	14.29	77.14	91.43	90	81	−73	71	−143
8	12.50	81.25	93.75	110	81	−102	71	−182
9	11.11	86.67	97.78	130	81	−151	71	−241
10	10.00	93.00	103.00	150	81	−220	71	−320

The first five columns of the table in Figure 9-4 are the same as the first five columns of the table in Figure 9-3. Column 6 of the table in Figure 9-4 shows the new price (equal to MR), $81. Comparing columns 5 and 6, we find that the first unit of output adds $90 to total cost but only $81 to total revenue. One might conclude: "Don't produce—close down!" But that would be hasty. For units two through six, price exceeds marginal cost. Each of these five units adds more to revenue than to cost and, as shown in column 7, they decrease the total loss. Together they more than compensate for the loss taken on the first unit. Beyond six units, however,

MC exceeds MR (= *P*). The firm should therefore produce six units. In general, the profit-seeking producer should always compare marginal revenue (or price under perfect competition) with the rising portion of the marginal-cost schedule or curve.

Will production be profitable? No, because at six units of output the average total cost of $91.67 exceeds the price of $81 by $10.67 per unit. If we multiply that by the six units of output, we find the firm's total loss is $64.

Then why produce? Because this loss is less than the firm's $100 of fixed costs, which is the $100 loss the firm would incur in the short run by closing down. The firm receives enough revenue per unit ($81) to cover its average variable costs of $75 and also provide $6 per unit, or a total of $36, to apply against fixed costs. Therefore, the firm's loss is only $64 (= $100 − $36), not $100.

This loss-minimizing case is also illustrated in the graph in Figure 9-4. Wherever price *P* exceeds average variable cost, AVC, the firm can pay part, but not all, of its fixed costs by producing. The loss is minimized by producing the output at which MC = MR (here, six units). At that output, each unit contributes *P* − *V* to covering fixed cost, where *V* is the AVC at six units of output. The per-unit loss is *A* − *P* = $10.67, and the total loss is 6 × (*A* − *P*), or $64, as shown by the grey area.

SHUTDOWN CASE

Suppose now that the market price is only $71. Should the firm produce? No, because at every output level the firm's average variable cost is greater than the price (compare columns 3 and 8 of the table in Figure 9-4). The smallest loss the firm can incur by producing is greater than the $100 fixed cost it will lose by shutting down (as shown by column 9). The best action is to shut down.

You can see this shutdown situation in Figure 9-5. Price comes closest to covering average variable costs at the MR (= *P*) = MC output of five units. But even here, price or revenue per unit would fall short of average variable cost by $3 (= $74 − $71). By producing at the MR (= *P*) = MC output, the firm would lose its $100 worth of fixed cost plus $15 ($3 of variable cost on each of the five units), for a total loss of $115. This compares unfavourably with the $100 fixed-cost loss the firm would incur by shutting down and producing no output. So it will make sense for the firm to shut down rather than produce at a $71 price—or at any price less than the minimum average variable cost of $74.

The shutdown case reminds us of the qualifier to our MR (= *P*) = MC rule. A competitive firm will maximize profit or minimize loss in the short run by producing that output at which MR (= *P*) = MC, *provided that market price exceeds minimum average variable cost.*

FIGURE 9-5   The Short-Run Shutdown Position of a Firm in Perfect Competition

If price *P* falls below the minimum AVC (here $74 at *Q* = 5), the competitive firm will minimize its losses in the short run by shutting down. There is no level of output at which the firm can produce and incur a loss smaller than its total fixed cost

CONSIDER THIS

The "Still There" Motel

Have you ever driven by a poorly maintained business facility and wondered why the owner doesn't either fix up the property or go out of business? The somewhat surprising answer is that it may be unprofitable to improve the facility, yet profitable to continue to operate it as it deteriorates. Seeing why will aid your understanding of fixed cost, variable cost, profit maximization, and shutdown points.

Consider the story of the Still There Motel, a one-storey motel on Old Highway North, Any Town, Canada. The owner of Still There built the motel on the basis of traffic patterns and competition that existed several decades ago. As more highways were built, Still There found itself located on a relatively vacant stretch of road. Also, it faced greatly heightened competition from new chain motels located closer to the main highway that crossed the province.

As demand and revenue fell, Still There moved from profitability to loss. At first its room rates and annual revenue were sufficient to cover its total variable costs and contribute

© Getty Images

some to the payment of fixed costs such as insurance and property taxes (or P > AVC; P < ATC). By staying open, Still There lost less than it would have if it had shut down. But since its total revenue did not cover its total costs (or P < ATC), the owner realized that something must be done in the long run. The owner decided to lower costs by reducing annual maintenance. In effect, the owner opted to allow the motel to deteriorate as a way of temporarily regaining profitability.

This renewed profitability of Still There cannot last, because in time no further reduction of maintenance costs will be possible. The deterioration of the motel structure will produce even lower room rates, and therefore even less total revenue. The owner of Still There knows that sooner or later total revenue will again fall below total cost (or P will again fall below ATC), even with an annual maintenance expense of zero. When that occurs, the owner will close down the business, tear down the structure, and sell the vacant property. But, in the meantime, the motel is still there—open, deteriorating, and profitable.

QUICK REVIEW 9.2

- A firm will choose to produce if it can at least break even and generate a normal profit.

- Profit is maximized, or loss minimized, at the output at which marginal revenue (or price in pure competition) equals marginal cost.

- If the market price is below the minimum average variable cost, the firm will minimize its losses by shutting down.

9.6   Marginal Cost and Short-Run Supply

LO9.6   Explain why a competitive firm's marginal cost curve is the same as its supply curve.

In the preceding section we simply selected three different prices and asked what quantity the profit-seeking competitive firm, faced with certain costs, would choose to offer in the market at each price. This set of product prices and corresponding quantities supplied constitutes part of the supply schedule for the competitive firm.

Table 9-2 summarizes the supply schedule data for those three prices ($131, $81, and $71) and four others. This table confirms the direct relationship between product price and quantity supplied that we identified in Chapter 3. Note first that the firm will not produce at price $61 or $71, because both are less than the $74 minimum AVC. Then note that quantity supplied increases as price increases. Observe finally that economic profit is higher at higher prices.

TABLE 9-2	The Supply Schedule of a Competitive Firm with the Cost Data in Figure 9-3	
Price	Quantity supplied	Maximum profit (+) or minimum loss (−)
$151	10	$+480
131	9	+299
111	8	+138
91	7	−3
81	6	−64
71	0	−100
61	0	−100

Generalized Depiction

Figure 9-6 (Key Graph) generalizes the MR = MC rule and the relationship between short-run production costs and the firm's supply behaviour. The ATC, AVC, and MC curves are shown, along with several marginal-revenue lines drawn at possible market prices. Let's observe quantity supplied at each of these prices.

- Price P_1 is below the firm's minimum average variable cost, so at this price the firm won't operate at all. Quantity supplied will be zero, as it will be at all other prices below P_2.

- Price P_2 is just equal to the minimum average variable cost. The firm will supply Q_2 units of output (where $MR_2 = MC$) and just cover its total variable cost. Its loss will equal its total fixed cost. (Actually, the firm would be indifferent as to shutting down or supplying Q_2 units of output, but we assume it produces.)

- At price P_3 the firm will supply Q_3 units of output to minimize its short-run losses. At any of the other prices between P_2 and P_4 the firm will also minimize its losses by producing and supplying the quantity at which MR $(= P) = MC$.

- The firm will just break even at price P_4, where it will supply Q_4 units of output (where $MR_4 = MC$), earning a normal profit but not an economic profit. Total revenue will just cover total cost, including a normal profit, because the revenue per unit ($MR_4 = P_4$) and the total cost per unit (ATC) are the same.

- At price P_5 the firm will earn an economic profit by producing and supplying Q_5 units of output. In fact, at any price above P_4 the firm will earn an economic profit by producing to the point where MR $(= P) = MC$.

Note that each of the MR $(= P) = MC$ intersection points labelled *b*, *c*, *d*, and *e* in Figure 9-6 indicates a possible product price (on the vertical axis) and the corresponding quantity that the firm would supply at that price (on the horizontal axis). Thus, points such as these are on the upsloping supply curve of the competitive firm. Note, too, that quantity supplied would be zero at any price below the minimum average variable cost (AVC). *We can conclude that the portion of the firm's marginal-cost curve lying above its average-variable-cost curve is its short-run supply curve.* In Figure 9-6, the solid segment of the marginal-cost curve MC is this firm's **short-run supply curve.** It tells us the amount of output the firm will supply at each price in a series of prices.

Table 9-3 summarizes the MR = MC approach to determining the competitive firm's profit-maximizing output level. It also shows the equivalent analysis in terms of total revenue and total cost.

Diminishing Returns, Production Costs, and Product Supply

We have now identified the links between the law of diminishing returns (Chapter 8), production costs, and product supply in the short run. Because of the law of diminishing returns, marginal cost eventually rises as more units of output are produced. And because marginal cost rises with output, a firm in a perfectly competitive industry must get successively higher prices to motivate it to produce additional units of output.

KEY GRAPH

FIGURE 9-6   The $P = MC$ Rule and the Competitive Firm's Short-Run Supply Curve

Application of the $P = MC$ rule, as modified by the shutdown case, reveals that the (solid) segment of the firm's MC curve that lies above AVC is the firm's short-run supply curve. More specifically, at price P_1, $P = MC$ at point a, but the firm will produce no output because P_1 is less than minimum AVC. At price P_2 the firm will operate at point b, where it produces Q_2 units and incurs a loss equal to its total fixed cost. At P_3 it operates at point c, where output is Q_3 and the loss is less than the total fixed cost. With the price of P_4, the firm operates at point d; in this case the firm earns a normal profit because at output Q_4 price equals ATC. At price P_5 the firm operates at point e and maximizes its economic profit by producing Q_5 units.

QUICK QUIZ

1. **Which of the following might increase product price from P_3 to P_5?**
   a. An improvement in production technology
   b. A decline in the price of a substitute good
   c. An increase in the price of a complementary good
   d. Rising incomes if the product is a normal good

2. **An increase in price from P_3 to P_5 would**
   a. Shift this firm's MC curve to the right
   b. Mean that MR_5 exceeds MC at Q_3 units, inducing the firm to expand output to Q_5
   c. Decrease this firm's average variable costs
   d. Enable this firm to obtain a normal, but not an economic, profit

3. **At P_4**
   a. This firm has no economic profit
   b. This firm will earn only a normal profit and thus will shut down
   c. MR_4 will be less than MC at the profit-maximizing output
   d. The profit-maximizing output will be Q_5

4. **Suppose P_4 is \$10, P_5 is \$15, Q_4 is 8 units, and Q_5 is 10 units. This firm's**
   a. Supply curve is elastic over the Q_4–Q_5 range of output
   b. Supply curve is inelastic over the Q_4–Q_5 range of output
   c. Total revenue will decline if price rises from P_4 to P_5
   d. Marginal-cost curve will shift downward if price falls from P_5 to P_4

Answers   1. d; 2. b; 3. a; 4. b

TABLE 9-3	Output Determination in Perfect Competition in the Short Run

Question	Answer
Should this firm produce?	Yes, if price is equal to, or greater than, minimum average variable cost. This means that the firm is profitable or that its losses are less than its fixed cost.
What quantity should this firm produce?	Produce where MR (= *P*) = MC; there, profit is maximized (TR exceeds TC by a maximum amount) or loss is minimized.
Will production result in economic profit?	Yes, if price exceeds average total cost (so that TR exceeds TC). No, if average total cost exceeds price (so that TC exceeds TR).

Viewed alternatively, higher product prices and marginal revenue encourage a purely competitive firm to expand output. As its output increases, the firm's marginal costs rise as a result of the law of diminishing returns. At some now greater output, the higher MC equals the new product price and MR. Profit once again is maximized, but at a greater total amount. Quantity supplied has increased in direct response to an increase in product price and the desire to maximize profit.

Changes in Supply

In Chapter 8 we saw that changes in such factors as the prices of variable inputs or in technology will shift the marginal-cost or short-run supply curve to a new location. All else equal, a wage increase, for example, would shift the supply curve in Figure 9-6 upward and to the left, which means a decrease in supply. Similarly, technological progress that increases the productivity of labour would shift the marginal-cost or supply curve downward to the right, representing an increase in supply.

Firm and Industry: Equilibrium Price

In the preceding section we established the competitive firm's short-run supply curve by applying the MR (= *P*) = MC rule. But which of the various possible prices will actually be the market equilibrium price? From Chapter 3 we know that the market equilibrium price is the price at which the total quantity supplied of the product equals the total quantity demanded. So to determine equilibrium price, we first need to obtain a total supply schedule and a total demand schedule. We find the total supply schedule by assuming a particular number of firms in the industry and supposing that each firm has the same individual supply schedule as the firm represented in Figure 9-6. Then we sum the quantities supplied at each price level to obtain the total (or market) supply schedule. Columns 1 and 3 in Table 9-4 repeat the supply schedule for the individual competitive firm, as

TABLE 9-4	Firm and Market Supply and Market Demand		

(1) Quantity supplied, single firm	(2) Total quantity supplied, 1000 firms	(3) Product price	(4) Total quantity demanded
10	10,000	$151	4,000
9	9,000	131	6,000
8	**8,000**	**111**	**8,000**
7	7,000	91	9,000
6	6,000	81	11,000
0	0	71	13,000
0	0	61	16,000

derived in Table 9-2. Suppose 1000 firms compete in this industry, all having the same total and unit costs as the single firm we discussed. This assumption allows us to calculate the market supply schedule (columns 2 and 3) by multiplying the quantity-supplied figures of the single firm (column 1) by 1000.

MARKET PRICE AND PROFITS

To determine the equilibrium price and output, these total-supply data must be compared with total-demand data. Let's assume that total demand is as shown in columns 3 and 4 in Table 9-4. By comparing the total quantity supplied and the total quantity demanded at the seven possible prices, we determine that the equilibrium price is $111 and the equilibrium quantity is 8000 units for the industry—eight units for each of the 1000 identical firms.

Will these conditions of market supply and demand make this a profitable industry? Multiplying product price ($111) by output (8 units), we find that the total revenue of each firm is $888. The total cost is $750, found by looking at column 4 of the table in Figure 9-2. The $138 difference is the economic profit of each firm. For the industry, total economic profit is $138,000. This, then, is a profitable industry.

Another way of calculating economic profit is to determine per-unit profit by subtracting average total cost ($93.75) from product price ($111) and multiplying the difference (per-unit profit of $17.25) by the firm's equilibrium level of output (8). Again we obtain an economic profit of $138 per firm and $138,000 for the industry.

Figure 9-7 shows this analysis graphically. The individual supply curves of each of the 1000 identical firms—one of which is shown as $s = MC$ in Figure 9-7a—are summed horizontally to get the total-supply curve $S = \Sigma MC$ of Figure 9-7b. Together with total-demand curve D, it determines the equilibrium price $111 and equilibrium quantity (for the industry) 8000 units. This equilibrium price is given and unalterable to the individual firm; that is, each firm's demand curve is perfectly elastic at the equilibrium price, as indicated by d in Figure 9-7a. Because the individual firm is a price-taker, the marginal-revenue curve coincides with the firm's demand curve d. This $111 price exceeds the average total cost at the firm's equilibrium $MR = MC$ output of eight units, so the firm earns an economic profit represented by the grey area in Figure 9-7a.

Assuming costs and market demand do not change, these diagrams reveal a genuine equilibrium in the short run. No shortages or surpluses occur in the market to cause price or total quantity to change. Nor can any one firm in the industry increase its profit by changing its output. Note, too, that higher unit and marginal costs on the one hand, or weaker market demand on the other, could change the situation so that Figure 9-7a resembles Figure 9-4 or Figure 9-5.

WORKED PROBLEM 9.3   Short-Run Competitive Equilibrium

FIGURE 9-7   Short-Run Competitive Equilibrium for a Firm and the Industry

The horizontal sum of the 1000 firms' individual supply curves (s) determines the industry supply curve (S). Given industry demand (D), the short-run equilibrium price and output for the industry are $111 and 8000 units. Taking the equilibrium price as given, the individual firm establishes its profit-maximizing output at eight units and, in this case, realizes the economic profit represented by the grey area.

(a) Single firm

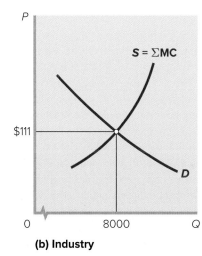

(b) Industry

FIRM VERSUS INDUSTRY

Figure 9-7 underscores a point made earlier: product price is a given fact to the *individual* competitive firm, but the supply plans of all competitive producers *as a group* are a basic determinant of product price. If we recall the fallacy of composition (see Last Word, Chapter 1), we find there is no inconsistency here. Although one firm, supplying a negligible fraction of total supply, cannot affect price, the industry supply curve does have an important bearing on price.

QUICK REVIEW 9.3

- A competitive firm's short-run supply curve is the portion of its marginal cost (MC) curve that lies above its average variable cost (AVC) curve.

- If price *P* is greater than minimum average variable cost, the firm will produce the amount of output where MR (= *P*) = MC in order to either maximize its profit (if price exceeds minimum ATC) or minimize its loss (if price lies between minimum AVC and minimum ATC).

- Market supply in a competitive industry is the horizontal sum of the individual supply curves of all of the firms in the industry. The market equilibrium price is determined by where the industry's market supply curve intersects the industry's market demand curve.

The LAST WORD

Fixed Costs: Digging Yourself Out of a Hole

For firms facing losses due to fixed costs, shutting down in the short run does not mean shutting down forever.

© iStockphoto

A firm with fixed costs starts each month standing at the bottom of a deep financial hole. The depth of that "money pit" is equal to the dollar value of all the payments that the firm is legally obligated to make even if it is producing nothing. These fixed costs include contractually guaranteed salaries, interest payments on loans, and equipment rental fees that are locked in by long-term contracts. As the firm stands at the bottom of this fixed-cost financial hole and stares upward looking for a way out, it has to ask itself: Will producing output make the hole even deeper?

Naturally, the firm hopes that producing output will generate positive cash flows that will offset its fixed costs and start filling in the hole. If those positive flows are large enough, they may completely offset the firm's fixed costs, fill up the hole, and allow

the firm to break even. And if they are just a bit larger, they will not only fill up the hole but also accumulate a nice little pile of profits above ground.

But those are just the firm's hopes. The firm's reality may be quite unpleasant. In particular, the firm may be facing a situation in which producing output would make its financial situation worse rather than better. As explained in this chapter, if the firm's price falls too low, then producing output will yield cash flows that are negative rather than positive because revenues will be less than variable costs. If that happens, producing output will lose money for the firm so that the firm would be better off shutting down production rather than producing output. By shutting down, it will lose only its fixed costs. By shutting down, its financial hole won't get even deeper.

A crucial thing to understand, however, is that the low prices that cause firms to shut down production are often temporary—so that shutdowns are also often temporary. Just because a firm shuts down at a given moment to prevent its financial hole from getting any deeper does not mean that the firm will go out of business forever. On the contrary, many industries are characterized by firms that regularly switch production on and off depending upon the market price they can get for their output and, consequently, whether producing output will generate positive or negative cash flows.

Oil production is a good example. Different wells have different variable production costs. If the price of oil drops below a given well's variable costs, then it would be better to halt production on that well and just lose the value of its fixed costs rather than pumping oil whose variable cost exceeds the revenue that it generates when sold.

Seasonal resorts are another good example of turning production on and off depending on the price. The demand for hotel rooms near ski resorts in Quebec, for instance, is much higher during the winter ski season than it is during the summer. As a result, the market price of hotel rooms falls so low during the summer that many inns and resorts close during the warmer months. They have all sorts of fixed costs, but it makes more sense for them to shut down rather than remain open because operating in the summer would cost more in variable costs than it would generate in revenues. It is better to lose only their fixed costs. Similarly, mills in northwestern Ontario experience temporary shutdowns due to fluctuating demand for pulp, paper,

and lumber. Numerous other examples of temporary shutdowns occur during recessions, the occasional economy-wide economic slowdowns during which demand declines for nearly all goods and services. The 2008–2009 recession in Canada, for instance, saw many manufacturing companies temporarily shut down and "mothball" their production facilities. The recession witnessed the mothballing of electric generating plants, factories that make fibre optic cable, automobile factories, and chemical plants. Many other firms also shut down production to wait out the recession—so many, in fact, that there was a mini-boom for consulting firms that specialized in helping firms mothball their factories (the main problem being how to properly store idle machinery so that it will work again when it is eventually brought back into service).

Firms that mothball factories or equipment during a recession do so expecting to eventually turn them back on. But the lengths of recessions vary, as do the specific circumstances of individual firms. So while many firms shut down in the short run with the expectation of reopening as soon as their particular business conditions improve, sometimes their business conditions do not improve. Sometimes the only way to terminate fixed costs is to terminate the firm.

Question

If a firm's current revenues are less than its current variable costs, when should it shut down? If it decides to shut down, should we expect that decision to be final? Explain using an example that is not in the textbook.

Chapter Summary

LO9.1   Give the names and the main characteristics of the four basic market models.

- Economists group industries into four models based on their market structures: (1) perfect competition, (2) monopoly, (3) monopolistic competition, and (4) oligopoly.

LO9.2   List the conditions required for perfectly competitive markets.

- A perfectly competitive industry consists of a large number of independent firms producing a standardized product. Perfect competition assumes that firms and factors of production are mobile among different industries.

LO9.3   Explain how demand is seen by a perfectly competitive seller.

- In a competitive industry, no single firm can influence market price, which means that the firm's demand curve is perfectly elastic and price equals marginal revenue.

LO9.4   Convey how firms in perfect competition can use the total-revenue–total-cost approach to maximize profits or minimize losses in the short run.

- We can analyze short-run profit maximization by a competitive firm by comparing total revenue and total cost or by applying marginal analysis. A firm maximizes its short-run profit by producing the output at which total revenue exceeds total cost by the greatest amount.

LO9.5   Explain how perfectly competitive firms can use the marginal-revenue–marginal-cost approach to maximize profits or minimize losses in the short run.

- Provided price exceeds minimum average variable cost, a competitive firm maximizes profit or minimizes loss in the short run by producing the output at which price or marginal revenue equals marginal cost.

- If price is less than average variable cost, the firm minimizes its loss by shutting down. If price is greater than average variable cost but is less than average total cost, the firm minimizes its loss by producing the $P = MC$ output. If price also exceeds average total cost, the firm maximizes its economic profit at the $P = MC$ output.

LO9.6   Explain why a competitive firm's marginal cost curve is the same as its supply curve.

- Applying the MR (= *P*) = MC rule at various possible market prices leads to the conclusion that the segment of the firm's short-run marginal-cost curve that lies above the firm's average-variable-cost curve is its short-run supply curve.

- A competitive firm shuts down production at least temporarily if price is less than minimum average variable cost because in those situations producing any amount of output will always result in variable costs exceeding revenues. Shutting down therefore results in a smaller loss because the firm will only lose its fixed cost whereas, if it operated, it would lose its fixed cost plus whatever money is lost due to variable costs exceeding revenues.

- Competitive firms choose to operate rather than shut down whenever price is greater than average variable cost but less than average total cost because in those situations revenues will always exceed variable costs. The amount by which revenues exceed variable costs can be used to help pay down some of the firm's fixed costs. Thus, the firm loses less money by operating (and paying down some of its fixed costs) than it would if it shut down (in which case it would suffer a loss equal to the full amount of its fixed costs).

Terms and Concepts

market structure
perfect competition
monopoly
monopolistic competition
oligopoly
imperfect competition
price-taker

average revenue
total revenue (TR)
marginal revenue
break-even point
MR = MC rule
short-run supply curve

Discussion Questions

1. Briefly state the basic characteristics of perfect competition, monopoly, monopolistic competition, and oligopoly. Under which of these market classifications does each of the following most accurately fit? (a) a supermarket in your home town, (b) the steel industry, (c) a Saskatchewan wheat farm, (d) the chartered bank in which you have or your family has an account, (e) the automobile industry. In each case, justify your classification.   [**LO9.1**]

2. Strictly speaking, perfect competition is relatively rare. Then why study it?   [**LO9.2**]

3. "Even if a firm is losing money, it may be better to stay in business in the short run." Is this statement ever true? Under what condition(s)?   [**LO9.5**]

4. Consider a firm that has no fixed costs and that is currently losing money. Are there any situations in which it would want to stay open for business in the short run? If a firm has no fixed costs, is it sensible to speak of the firm distinguishing between the short run and the long run?   [**LO9.5**]

5. Why is the equality of marginal revenue and marginal cost essential for profit maximization in all market structures? Explain why price can be substituted for marginal revenue in the MR = MC rule when an industry is perfectly competitive.   [**LO9.5**]

6. "That segment of a competitive firm's marginal-cost curve that lies above its average variable-cost curve constitutes the short-run supply curve for the firm." Explain using a graph and words.   [**LO9.6**]

Review Questions

1. Suppose that the paper clip industry is perfectly competitive. Also assume that the market price for paper clips is 2 cents per paper clip. The demand curve faced by each firm in the industry is   [**LO9.3**]

   a. A horizontal line at 2 cents per paper clip

   b. A vertical line at 2 cents per paper clip

   c. The same as the market demand curve for paper clips

   d. Always higher than the firm's MC curve

2. Use the following demand schedule to determine total revenue and marginal revenue for each possible level of sales: [**LO9.3**]

Product price	Quantity demanded	Marginal revenue	Total revenue
$2	0	$_____	$_____
2	1	_____	_____
2	2	_____	_____
2	3	_____	_____
2	4	_____	_____
2	5		_____

a. What can you conclude about the structure of the industry in which this firm is operating? Explain.

b. Graph the demand, total-revenue, and marginal-revenue curves for this firm.

c. Why do the demand and marginal-revenue curves coincide?

d. "Marginal revenue is the change in total revenue associated with additional units of output." Explain in words and graphically, using the data in the table.

3. A perfectly competitive firm whose goal is to maximize profit will choose to produce the amount of output at which [**LO9.4**]

a. TR and TC are equal

b. TR exceeds TC by as much as possible

c. TC exceeds TR by as much as possible

d. None of the above

4. If it is possible for a perfectly competitive firm to do better financially by producing rather than shutting down, then it should produce the amount of output at which [**LO9.5**]

a. MR < MC

b. MR = MC

c. MR > MC

d. None of the above

5. A perfectly competitive firm that makes car batteries has a fixed cost of $10,000 per month. The market price at which it can sell its output is $100 per battery. The firm's minimum AVC is $105 per battery. The firm is currently producing 500 batteries a month (the output level at which MR = MC). This firm is making a _____ and should _____ production. [**LO9.5**]

a. Profit; increase

b. Profit; shut down

c. Loss; increase

d. Loss; shut down

6. Consider a profit-maximizing firm in a competitive industry. For each of the following situations, indicate whether the firm should shut down production or produce where MR = MC. [**LO9.5**]

a. P < minimum AVC

b. P > minimum ATC

c. Minimum AVC < P < minimum ATC

Problems

1. A perfectly competitive firm finds that the market price for its product is $20. It has a fixed cost of $100 and a variable cost of $10 per unit for the first 50 units and then $25 per unit for all successive units. Does price exceed average variable cost for the first 50 units? What about for the first 100 units? What is the marginal cost per unit for the first 50 units? What about for units 51 and higher? For each of the first 50 units, does MR exceed MC? What about for units 51 and higher? What output level will yield the largest possible profit for this perfectly competitive firm? (*Hint:* Draw a graph similar to Figure 9-2 using data for this firm.) [**LO9.5**]

2. A wheat farmer in a perfectly competitive industry can sell any wheat he grows for $10 per bushel. His five hectares of land show diminishing returns because some are better suited for wheat production than others. The first hectare can produce 1000 bushels of wheat, the second hectare 900, the third 800, and so on. Draw a table with multiple columns to help you answer the following questions. [**LO9.5**]

a. How many bushels will each of the farmer's five hectares produce?

b. How much revenue will each hectare generate?

c. What are the TR and MR for each hectare?

d. If the marginal cost of planting and harvesting a hectare is $7000 per hectare for each of the five hectares, how many hectares should the farmer plant and harvest?

3. Karen runs a print shop that makes posters for large companies. It is a very competitive business. The market price is currently $1 per poster. She has fixed costs of $250. Her variable costs are $1000 for the first thousand posters, $800 for the second thousand, and then $750 for each additional thousand posters. What is her AFC per poster (not per thousand!) if she prints 1000 posters? 2000? 10,000? What is her ATC per poster if she prints 1000? 2000? 10,000? If the market price fell to 70 cents per poster, would there be *any* output level at which Karen would *not* shut down production immediately? [**LO9.5**]

4. Assume that the following cost data are for a firm in perfect competition: [**LO9.5**]

Total product	Average fixed cost	Average variable cost	Average total cost	Marginal cost
0				$45
1	$60.00	$45.00	$105.00	40
2	30.00	42.50	72.50	35
3	20.00	40.00	60.00	30
4	15.00	37.50	52.50	35
5	12.00	37.00	49.00	40
6	10.00	37.50	47.50	45
7	8.57	38.57	47.14	55
8	7.50	40.63	48.13	65
9	6.67	43.33	50.00	75
10	6.00	46.50	52.50	

a. At a product price of $56, will this firm produce in the short run? If it preferable to produce, what will be the profit-maximizing or loss-minimizing output? What economic profit or loss will the firm realize per unit of output?

b. Answer the questions in part (a) assuming product price is $41.

c. Answer the questions in part (a) assuming product price is $32.

d. In the table below, complete the short-run supply schedule for the firm (columns 1 and 2) and indicate the profit or loss incurred at each output (column 3).

(1) Price	(2) Quantity supplied, single firm	(3) Profit (+) or loss (−)	(4) Quantity supplied, 1500 firms
$26	___	$ ___	___
32	___	___	___
38	___	___	___
41	___	___	___
46	___	___	___
56	___	___	___
66	___	___	___

e. Now assume that there are 1500 identical firms in this competitive industry; that is, there are 1500 firms, each of which has the cost data shown in the table. Complete the industry supply schedule (column 4).

f. Suppose the market demand data for the product are as follows:

Price	Total quantity demanded
$26	17,000
32	15,000
38	13,500
41	12,000
46	10,500
56	9,500
66	8,000

What will be the equilibrium price? What will be the equilibrium output for the industry? For each firm? What will profit or loss be per unit? Per firm? Will this industry expand or contract in the long run?

CHAPTER 10

Perfect Competition in the Long Run

LEARNING OBJECTIVES

LO10.1   Explain how the long run differs from the short run in perfect competition.

LO10.2   Describe how profits and losses drive the long-run adjustment process of perfect competition.

LO10.3   Explain the differences between constant-cost, increasing-cost, and decreasing-cost industries.

LO10.4   Show how long-run equilibrium in perfect competition produces an efficient allocation of resources.

LO10.5   Discuss creative destruction and the profit incentives for innovation.

The previous chapter discussed how perfect competition operates in the short run, the time period during which the individual firms in an industry are stuck with their current plant sizes and fixed-cost commitments. As you know, firms in perfect competition shut down production if prices are too low, or if prices are high enough, produce where MR = MC to minimize their losses or maximize their profits. Whether they make a profit or a loss depends on how high the market price is relative to their costs.

But profits and losses clearly cannot be the end of the perfect competition story because one of the key characteristics of perfect competition is the freedom of firms to enter or exit the industry. We know from Chapter 2 that profits attract entry and losses prompt exit.

In this chapter, we are keenly interested in how entry and exit relate to allocative and productive efficiency. We are also interested in how continuing competition leads to new products and new business methods replacing older products and older business methods through a process aptly referred to as *creative destruction*.

10.1 The Long Run Versus the Short Run in Perfect Competition

LO10.1 **Explain how the long run differs from the short run in perfect competition.**

The entry and exit of firms in our market models can only take place in the long run. In the short run, the industry is composed of a specific number of firms, each with a plant size that is fixed and unalterable in the short run. Firms may shut down, in the sense that they can produce zero units of output in the short run, but they do not have sufficient time to liquidate their assets and go out of business.

In the long run, by contrast, the firms already in an industry have sufficient time to either expand or contract their capacities. More important, the number of firms in the industry may either increase or decrease as new firms enter or existing firms leave.

The length of time constituting the long run varies substantially by industry, however, so you should not fix in your mind any specific number of years, months, or days. Instead, focus your attention on the incentives provided by profits and losses for the entry and exit of firms within any perfectly competitive industry and, later in the chapter, on how those incentives lead to productive and allocative efficiency. The time horizons are far less important than the process by which profits and losses guide business managers toward the efficient use of society's resources.

Profit Maximization in the Long Run

The first part of the perfect competition story (Chapter 9) was about profit, loss, and shut-down in the short run. The rest of the story (this chapter) is about entry and exit, and their impacts on industry size and allocative and productive efficiency in the long run.

To tell the rest of story well, we need to return to our graphical analysis and examine profit-maximization by firms in perfect competition in the long run. Three assumptions, none of which affect our conclusions, will keep things simple:

1. *Entry and Exit Only* The only long-run adjustment in our graphical analysis is caused by the entry or exit of firms. Moreover, we ignore all short-run adjustments to concentrate on the effects of the long-run adjustments.

2. *Identical Costs* All firms in the industry have identical cost curves. This assumption allows us to discuss a representative firm, knowing that all other firms in the industry are similarly affected by any long-run adjustments that occur. Using a representative firm allows us to simplify and better understand the perfectly competitive market structure.

3. *Constant-Cost Industry* The industry is a constant-cost industry, which means that the entry or exit of firms does not affect resource prices or, consequently, shift the average-total-cost or marginal-cost curves of individual firms.

10.2 The Long-Run Adjustment Process in Perfect Competition

LO10.2 **Describe how profits and losses drive the long-run adjustment process of perfect competition.**

The basic conclusion we want to explain is this: After all long-run adjustments in a perfectly competitive industry, product price will be exactly equal to, and production will occur at, each firm's minimum average total cost.

This conclusion follows from two basic facts: (1) firms seek profits and avoid losses and (2) under perfect competition, firms are free to enter and leave an industry. If market price in the short run exceeds average total cost, the resulting economic profit will attract new firms to the industry. But this industry expansion will increase supply until price is brought back down to equality with minimum average total cost in the long run. Conversely, if price in the short run is less than average total cost, the resulting loss will cause firms to leave the industry in the long run. As they leave, total supply will decline, bringing the price back up to equality with minimum average total cost.

Long-Run Equilibrium

Consider the average firm in a perfectly competitive industry that is initially in long-run equilibrium. This firm is represented in Figure 10-1a, where MR = MC, and price and minimum average total cost are equal at $50.

FIGURE 10-1   Temporary Profits and the Re-establishment of Long-Run Equilibrium in a Representative Firm and the Industry

A favourable shift in demand (D_1 to D_2) will upset the original industry equilibrium and produce economic profits. But those profits will entice new firms to enter the industry, increasing supply (S_1 to S_2) and lowering product price until economic profits are once again zero.

(a) Single firm

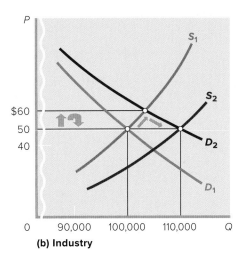

(b) Industry

Economic profit here is zero; the industry is in equilibrium and there is no tendency for firms to enter or to leave. The existing firms are earning normal profits, which means that their accounting profits are equal to those that the owners of these firms could expect to receive on average in other industries. It is because their current profits are the same as they could expect to earn elsewhere that there is no tendency for firms to enter or leave the industry. The $50 market price is determined in Figure 10-1b by market demand D_1 and supply S_1. (S_1 is a short-run supply curve; we will develop the long-run industry supply curve in our discussion.) And remember that normal profits earned by these firms are considered an opportunity cost, and are therefore included in the firms' cost curves.

As shown on the quantity axes of the two graphs, equilibrium output in the industry is 100,000, while equilibrium output for the single firm is 100. If all firms in the industry are identical, there must be 1000 firms (= 100,000/100).

ENTRY ELIMINATES ECONOMIC PROFITS

Let's upset the long-run equilibrium in Figure 10-1 and see what happens. Suppose a change in consumer tastes increases product demand from D_1 to D_2. Price will rise to $60, as determined at the intersection of D_2 and S_1, and the firm's marginal-revenue curve will shift upward to $60. This $60 price exceeds the firm's average total cost of $50 at output 100, creating an economic profit of $10 per unit. This economic profit will lure new firms into the industry. Some entrants will be newly created firms; others will shift from less prosperous industries.

As firms enter, the market supply of the product increases, pushing the product price below $60. Economic profits persist, and entry continues until short-run supply increases to S_2. Market price falls to $50, as does marginal revenue for the firm. Price and minimum average total cost are again equal at $50. The economic profits caused by the boost in demand have disappeared because the firms that remain are earning only a normal profit (zero economic profit). Entry ceases and a new long-run equilibrium is reached.

Observe in Figure 10-1 that total quantity supplied is now 110,000 units and each firm is producing 100 units. Now 1100 firms rather than the original 1000 populate the industry. Economic profits have attracted 100 more firms.

EXIT ELIMINATES LOSSES

Now let's consider a shift in the opposite direction. We begin in Figure 10-2b with curves S_1 and D_1 setting the same initial long-run equilibrium situation as in our previous analysis, including the $50 price.

FIGURE 10-2   Temporary Losses and the Re-establishment of Long-Run Equilibrium in a Representative Firm and the Industry

An unfavourable shift in demand (D_1 to D_3) will upset the original industry equilibrium and produce losses, but those losses will cause firms to leave the industry, decreasing supply (S_1 to S_3) and increasing product price until all losses have disappeared.

(a) Single firm

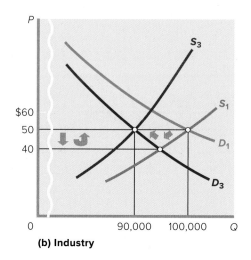

(b) Industry

Suppose consumer demand declines from D_1 to D_3. This decline forces the market price and marginal revenue down to \$40, making production unprofitable at the minimum ATC of \$50. In time the resulting economic losses will induce firms to leave the industry. Their owners will seek a normal profit elsewhere rather than accept the below-normal profits (loss) now confronting them. Other firms will simply go out of business. As this exodus of firms proceeds, however, industry supply in the long run decreases, pushing the price up from \$40 toward \$50. Losses continue and more firms leave the industry until the supply curve shifts to S_3. Once this happens, price is again \$50, just equal to the minimum average total cost. Losses have been eliminated so that the firms that remain are earning only a normal profit (zero economic profit). Since this is no better or worse than entrepreneurs could expect to earn in other business ventures, there is no longer any incentive to exit the industry. Long-run equilibrium is restored.

In Figure 10-2b, total quantity supplied is now 90,000 units and each firm is producing 10 units. Only 900 firms, not the original 1000, populate the industry. Losses have forced 100 firms out.

You may have noted that we have sidestepped the question of which firms will leave the industry when losses occur by assuming that all firms have identical cost curves. In the real world, of course, managerial talents differ. Even if resource prices and technology are the same for all firms, less skillfully managed firms tend to incur higher costs and therefore are the first to leave an industry when demand declines. Similarly, firms with less productive labour forces or higher transportation costs will be higher-cost producers and likely candidates to quit an industry when demand decreases.

We have now reached an intermediate goal: Our analysis verifies that competition, reflected in the entry and exit of firms, eliminates economic profits or losses by adjusting price to equal minimum long-run average total cost. In addition, this competition forces firms to select output levels at which average total cost is minimized.

10.3 Long-Run Supply Curves

LO10.3   Explain the differences between constant-cost, increasing-cost, and decreasing-cost industries.

Although our analysis has dealt with the long run, we have noted that the market supply curves in Figures 10-1b and 10-2b are short-run curves. What then is the character of the **long-run supply curve** of a competitive industry? The analysis points us toward an answer. The crucial factor here is the effect, if any, that changes in the number of firms in the industry will have on costs of the individual firms in the industry.

Long-Run Supply for a Constant-Cost Industry

In our analysis of long-run competitive equilibrium we assumed that the industry under discussion was a **constant-cost industry**, which means that industry expansion or contraction will not affect resource prices or production costs. Graphically, it means that the entry or exit of firms does not shift the long-run ATC curves of individual firms. This is the case when the industry's demand for factors of production is small in relation to the total demand for those resources; the industry can expand or contract without significantly affecting factor prices and costs.

What does the long-run supply curve of a constant-cost industry look like? The answer is contained in our previous analysis. There we saw that the entry and exit of firms changes industry output but always brings the product price back to its original level, where it is just equal to the constant minimum ATC. Specifically, we discovered that the industry would supply 90,000, 100,000, or 110,000 units of output, all at a price of $50 per unit. In other words, the long-run supply of a constant-cost industry is perfectly elastic.

This is demonstrated graphically in Figure 10-3, which uses data from Figures 10-1 and 10-2. Suppose industry demand is originally D_1, industry output is Q_1 (100,000 units), and product price is P_1 ($50). This situation, from Figure 10-1, is one of long-run equilibrium. We saw that when demand increases to D_2, upsetting this equilibrium, the resulting economic profits attract new firms. Because this is a constant-cost industry, entry continues and industry output expands until the price is driven back down to the level of the unchanged minimum ATC, which is at price P_2 ($50) and output Q_2 (110,000).

From Figure 10-2, we saw that a decline in market demand from D_1 to D_3 causes an exit of firms and ultimately restores equilibrium at price P_3 ($50) and output Q_3 (90,000 units). The points Z_1, Z_2, and Z_3 in Figure 10-3 represent these three price–quantity combinations. A line or curve connecting all such points shows the various price–quantity combinations that firms would produce if they had enough time to make all desired adjustments to changes in demand. This line or curve is the industry's long-run supply curve. In a constant-cost industry this curve (straight line) is horizontal, as in Figure 10-3, thus representing perfectly elastic supply.

Long-Run Supply for an Increasing-Cost Industry

Constant-cost industries are a special case. Most industries would fall into the **increasing-cost industry** category, in which firms' ATC curves shift upward as the industry expands and downward as the industry contracts. Usually the entry of new firms will increase factor prices, particularly in industries using specialized inputs whose long-run supplies do not readily increase in response to increases in factor demand. Higher input prices result in higher long-run average total costs for all firms in the industry. These higher costs cause upward shifts in each firm's long-run ATC curve.

FIGURE 10-3   The Long-Run Supply Curve for a Constant-Cost Industry

In a constant-cost industry, the entry and exit of firms does not affect resource prices, or, therefore, unit costs. So an increase in demand (D_1 to D_2) raises industry output (Q_1 to Q_2) but not price ($50). Similarly, a decrease in demand (D_1 to D_3) reduces output (Q_1 to Q_3) but not price. Thus the long-run industry supply curve (S) is horizontal through points Z_1, Z_2, and Z_3.

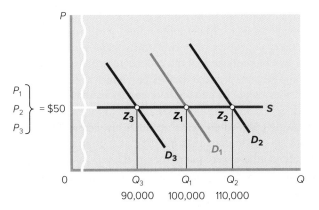

FIGURE 10-4   The Long-Run Supply Curve for an Increasing-Cost Industry

In an increasing-cost industry, the entry of new firms in response to an increase in demand (D_3 to D_1 to D_2) will bid up resource prices and thereby increase unit costs. As a result, an increased industry output (Q_3 to Q_1 to Q_2) will be forthcoming only at higher prices ($45 < $50 < $55). The long-run industry supply curve (S) therefore slopes upward through points Y_3, Y_1, and, Y_2.

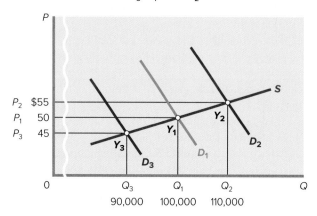

Thus, when an increase in product demand results in economic profits and attracts new firms to an increasing-cost industry, a two-way squeeze works to eliminate those profits. As before, the entry of new firms increases market supply and lowers the market price, but now the entire ATC curve shifts upward. The overall result is a higher-than-original equilibrium price. The industry produces a larger output at a higher product price because the industry expansion has increased factor prices and the minimum average total cost.

Since greater output will be supplied at a higher price, the long-run industry supply curve is upsloping. Instead of supplying 90,000, 100,000, or 110,000 units at the same price of $50, an increasing-cost industry might supply 90,000 units at $45, 100,000 units at $50, and 110,000 units at $55. A higher price is required to induce more production, because costs per unit of output increase as production rises.

Figure 9-4 nicely illustrates the situation. Original market demand is D_1 and industry price and output are P_1 ($50) and Q_1 (100,000 units), respectively, at equilibrium point Y_1. An increase in demand to D_2 upsets this equilibrium and leads to economic profits. New firms enter the industry, increasing both market supply and production costs of individual firms. A new price is established at point Y_2, where P_2 is $55 and Q_2 is 110,000 units.

Conversely, a decline in demand from D_1 to D_3 makes production unprofitable and causes firms to leave the industry. The resulting decline in factor prices reduces the minimum average total cost of production for firms that stay. A new equilibrium price is established at some level below the original price—say at point Y_3, where P_3 is $45 and Q_3 is 90,000 units. Connecting these three equilibrium positions, we derive the upsloping long-run supply curve S in Figure 10-4.

Long-Run Supply for a Decreasing-Cost Industry

In a **decreasing-cost industry**, a firm experiences lower costs as the industry expands. For example, as demand for personal computers increased, new manufacturers entered the personal computer industry and greatly increased the input demand for the components used to build them (memory chips, hard drives, monitors, and operating software). The expanded production of those components enabled the producers of those items to achieve substantial economies of scale. The decreased production costs of the components reduced their prices, which greatly lowered the computer manufacturers' average costs of production. The supply of personal computers increased by more than demand, and the price of personal computers declined.

Unfortunately, however, the industries that show decreasing costs when output expands also show increasing costs if output contracts. A good example is the Canadian shoe-manufacturing industry as it contracted due to foreign competition. Back when the industry was doing well and there were many shoe-making firms, the cost of specialized technicians who repair shoe-making machinery could be spread across many firms. This was because the repairmen worked as independent contractors going from one firm's factory to another firm's factory on a daily basis as various pieces of equipment at different factories needed repairs. But as the demand for Canadian-made

FIGURE 10-5   The Long-Run Supply Curve for a Decreasing-Cost Industry

In a decreasing-cost industry the entry of new firms in response to an increase in demand (D_3 to D_1 to D_2) will lead to decreased input prices and consequently decreased unit costs. As a result, an increase in industry output (Q_3 to Q_1 to Q_2) will be accompanied by lower prices ($55 > $50 > $45). The long-run industry supply curve (S) therefore slopes downward through points X_3, X_1, and X_2.

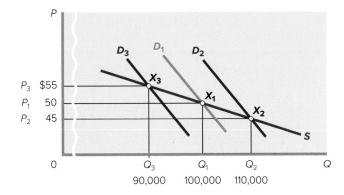

footwear fell over time, there were fewer and fewer factories, so that the cost of a repairperson had to be spread over fewer and fewer firms. Thus, costs per firm and per unit of output increased.

Figure 10-5 illustrates the situation. Original market demand is D_1 and industry price and output are P_1 ($50) and Q_1 (100,000 units), respectively at equilibrium point X_1. An increase in demand to D_2 upsets this equilibrium and leads to economic profits. New firms enter the industry, increasing market supply but decreasing the production costs of individual firms. A new price is established at point X_2, where P_2 is $45 and Q_2 is 110,000 units.

Conversely, a decline in demand from D_1 to D_3 makes production unprofitable and causes firms to leave the industry. The resulting increase in input prices increases the minimum average total cost of production for the firms that remain. A new equilibrium price is established at some level above the original price—say at point X_3, where P_3 is $55 and Q_3 is 90,000 units. Connecting these three equilibrium positions in Figure 10-5, we derive the downsloping long-run supply curve S for this decreasing-cost industry.

QUICK REVIEW 10.1

- In perfect competition, entrepreneurs remove resources from industries and firms that are generating economic losses in order to transfer them to industries and firms that are generating economic profits.

- In the long run, the entry of firms into an industry will compete away any economic profits, and the exit of firms will eliminate economic losses, so price and minimum

average total cost are equal. Entry and exit cease when the firms in the industry return to making a normal profit (zero economic profit).

- The long-run supply curves of constant-, increasing-, and decreasing-cost industries are horizontal, upsloping, and downsloping, respectively.

10.4 Perfect Competition and Efficiency

LO10.4   Show how long-run equilibrium in perfect competition produces an efficient allocation of resources.

Figure 10-6 (Key Graph) demonstrates the efficiency characteristics of the individual firms (Figure 10-6a) and the market (Figure 10-6b) after long-run adjustments in perfect competition. Assuming a constant- or increasing-cost industry, the final long-run equilibrium positions of all firms have the same basic efficiency characteristics. As shown in Figure 10-6a, price (and marginal revenue) will settle where it is equal to minimum average total cost: P (and MR) = minimum ATC. Moreover, since the marginal-cost curve intersects the average-total-cost

KEY GRAPH

FIGURE 10-6   Long-Run Equilibrium: A Competitive Firm and Market

(a) The equality of price (*P*), marginal cost (MC), and minimum average total cost (ATC) at output Q_f indicates that the firm is achieving productive efficiency and allocative efficiency. It is using the most efficient technology, charging the lowest price, and producing the greatest output consistent with its costs. It is receiving only a normal profit, which is incorporated into the ATC curve. The equality of price and marginal cost indicates that society is allocating its scarce resources in accordance with consumer preferences. (b) In the perfectly competitive market, allocative efficiency occurs at the market equilibrium output Q_e. The sum of consumer surplus (green area) and producer surplus (blue area) is maximized.

(a) Single firm

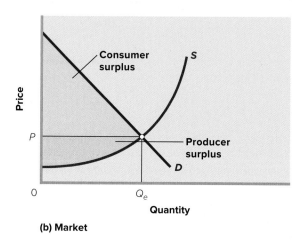

(b) Market

QUICK QUIZ

1. **We know the firm is a price-taker because**
    a. Its MC curve slopes upward
    b. Its ATC curve is U-shaped
    c. Its MR curve is horizontal
    d. MC and ATC are equal at the profit-maximizing output

2. **At this firm's profit-maximizing output**
    a. Total revenue equals total cost
    b. It is earning an economic profit
    c. Allocative, but not necessarily productive, efficiency is achieved
    d. Productive, but not necessarily allocative, efficiency is achieved

3. **The equality of *P*, MC, and minimum ATC**
    a. Occurs only in constant-cost industries
    b. Encourages entry of new firms
    c. Means that the "right goods" are being produced in the "right ways"
    c. Results in a zero accounting profit

4. **When *P* = MC = lowest ATC for individual firms, in the market**
    a. Consumer surplus necessarily exceeds producer surplus
    b. Consumer surplus plus producer surplus is at a maximum
    c. Producer surplus necessarily exceeds consumer surplus
    d. Supply and demand are identical

Answers   1.c; 2.a; 3.c; 4.b

curve at its minimum point, marginal cost and average total cost are equal: MC = minimum ATC. So in long-run equilibrium a triple equality occurs: P (and MR) = MC = minimum ATC. Thus, in long-run equilibrium, each firm produces at the output level Q_f that is associated with this triple equality.[1]

The triple equality tells us two very important things about long-run equilibrium. First, it tells us that although a competitive firm may realize economic profit or loss in the short run, it will earn only a normal profit by producing in accordance with the MR (= P) = MC rule in the long run. Second, the triple equality tells us that in long-run equilibrium, the profit-maximizing decision rule that leads each firm to produce the quantity at which P = MR also implies that each firm will produce at the output level Q_f that is associated with the minimum point on each identical firm's ATC curve.

This is very important, because it suggests that perfect competition leads to the most efficient possible use of society's resources. Indeed, subject only to Chapter 4's qualifications relating to public goods and externalities, an idealized perfectly competitive economy composed of constant- or increasing-cost industries will generate both productive efficiency and allocative efficiency.

Productive Efficiency: *P* = Minimum ATC

Productive efficiency requires that goods be produced in the least costly way. In the long run, perfect competition forces firms to produce at the minimum average total cost of production and to charge a price that is just consistent with that cost. This is true because firms that do not use the best available (least cost) production methods and combinations of inputs will not survive.

To see why, suppose that Figure 10-6 has to do with perfect competition in the cucumber industry. In the final equilibrium position shown in Figure 10-6a, suppose each firm in the cucumber industry is producing 100 units (say truckloads) of cucumbers by using $5000 (equal to average total cost of $50 × 100 units) of resources. If any firm produced that same amount of output at any higher total cost—say $7000—it would be wasting resources because all of the other firms in the industry are able to produce that same amount of output using only $5000 of resources. Society would be faced with a net loss of $2000 worth of alternative products. But this cannot happen in perfect competition; this firm would incur a loss of $2000, requiring it to either reduce its costs or go out of business.

Note, too, that consumers benefit from productive efficiency by paying the lowest product price possible under the prevailing technology and cost conditions. And the firm receives only a normal profit, which is part of its economic costs and thus incorporated in its ATC curve.

Allocative Efficiency: *P* = MC

Long-run equilibrium in pure competition guarantees productive efficiency, such that output will be produced in the least costly way. But productive efficiency by itself does not guarantee that anyone will want to buy the items that are being produced in the least-cost manner. For all we know, consumers might prefer that the resources used to produce those items be redirected toward producing other products instead.

Fortunately, long-run equilibrium in pure competition also guarantees **allocative efficiency** so that we can be certain that society's scarce resources are directed toward producing the goods and services that people most want to consume. Stated formally, allocative efficiency occurs when it is impossible to produce any net gains for society by altering the combination of goods and services that are produced from society's limited supply of resources.

To understand how perfect competition leads to allocative efficiency, recall the concept of opportunity cost while looking at Figure 10-6b, where Q_e total units are being produced in equilibrium by the firms in a purely competitive industry. For every unit up to Q_e, market demand curve D lies above market supply curve S. Recall from Chapter 4 what this means in terms of marginal benefits and marginal costs.

MATH 10.1 Allocative Efficiency

- For each unit of output on the horizontal axis, the point directly above it on demand curve D shows how many dollars' worth of other goods and services consumers are willing to give up to obtain that unit of output. Consequently, the demand curve shows the dollar value of the marginal benefit that consumers place on each unit.

---

[1] This triple equality does not hold for decreasing-cost industries because MC always remains below ATC if average costs are decreasing. We will discuss this situation of "natural monopoly" in Chapter 11.

- For each unit of output on the horizontal axis, the point directly above it on supply curve S shows how many dollars' worth of other products have to be sacrificed in order to direct the underlying resources toward producing each unit of this product. Consequently, the supply curve S shows the dollar value of the marginal opportunity cost of each unit.

Keeping these definitions in mind, the fact that the demand curve lies above the supply curve for every unit up to Q_e means that marginal benefit exceeds marginal cost for every one of these units. Stated slightly differently, producing and consuming these units brings net benefits because consumers are willing to give up more of other goods to obtain these units than must actually be forgone to produce them. Furthermore, because the supply curve includes the opportunity cost of the other goods that must be given up when resources are directed to producing these units, we can be certain that consumers prefer to have the necessary resources directed toward producing these units rather than anything else. In other words, allocative efficiency has been achieved because redirecting the necessary resources toward producing anything else would make people less happy.

The fact that perfect competition yields allocative efficiency can also be understood by looking at the situation facing each individual firm in long-run equilibrium. To see this, take the market equilibrium price P that is determined in Figure 10-6b and sees how it affects the behaviour of the individual firm shown in Figure 10-6a. This profit-maximizing firm takes P as fixed and produces Q_f units, the output level at which $P = \text{MC}$.

By comparing the horizontal line at P with the upsloping MC curve, it is clear that for every unit up to Q_f the price at which each unit can be sold exceeds the marginal cost of producing it. That is equivalent to saying that these units are worth more to consumers than they cost to make. Why? Because consumers are willing to forgo P dollars' worth of other goods and services when they pay P dollars for these units, but at the same time the firm only has to use less than P dollars' worth of resources to produce them. Thus, if these units are produced and consumed, there are net benefits and society comes out ahead. And, as with our previous analysis, allocative efficiency is also achieved because by spending their P dollars per unit on these units rather than anything else, consumers are indicating that they would rather have the necessary resources directed toward producing these units rather than anything else.

Maximum Consumer and Producer Surplus

We confirm the existence of allocative efficiency in Figure 10-6b, where we see that perfect competition maximizes the sum of the "benefit surpluses" to consumers and producers. Recall from Chapter 4 that **consumer surplus** is the difference between the maximum prices that consumers are willing to pay for a product (as shown by the demand curve) and the market price of the product. In Figure 10-6b, consumer surplus is the green triangle, which is the sum of the vertical distances between the demand curve and equilibrium price. In contrast, **producer surplus** is the difference between the minimum prices that producers are willing to accept for a product (as shown by the supply curve) and the market price of the product. Producer surplus is the sum of the vertical distances between the equilibrium price and supply curve. Here producer surplus is the blue area.

At the equilibrium quantity Q_e the combined amount of consumer surplus and producer surplus is maximized. Allocative efficiency occurs because, at Q_e, marginal benefit, reflected by points on the demand curve, equals marginal cost, reflected by points on the supply curve. Alternatively, the maximum willingness of consumers to pay for unit Q_e equals the minimum acceptable price of that unit to producers. At any output less than Q_e the sum of consumer and producer surplus—the combined size of the green and blue areas—would be less than that shown. At any output greater than Q_e, an efficiency loss would subtract from the combined consumer and producer surplus shown by the green and blue areas.

After long-run adjustments, perfect competition produces allocative efficiency. It yields a level of output at which $P = \text{MC} = \text{lowest ATC}$, marginal benefit = marginal cost, maximum willingness to pay for the last unit = minimum acceptable price for that unit, and combined consumer and producer surplus are maximized.

Dynamic Adjustments

A further attribute of perfectly competitive markets is their ability to restore the efficiency just described when disrupted by changes in the economy. A change in consumer tastes, resource supplies, or technology will automatically set in motion the appropriate realignments of resources. For example, suppose that cucumbers and pickles become dramatically more popular. First, the demand for cucumbers will increase in the market, increasing the price of cucumbers. So at current output the price of cucumbers will exceed their marginal cost. At this point efficiency will be lost, but the higher price will create economic profits in the cucumber industry and stimulate its expansion. The profitability of cucumbers will permit the industry to bid resources away from now less pressing uses, say, watermelons. Expansion of the industry will end only when the supply of cucumbers has expanded such that the price of cucumbers and their marginal cost are equal—that is, when allocative efficiency has been restored.

Similarly, a change in a production technique or in the supply of a particular resource—for example, the field labourers who pick cucumbers—will upset an existing price–marginal cost equality by either raising or lowering marginal cost. The resulting inequality of MC and P will cause producers, in either pursuing profit or avoiding loss, to reallocate resources until product supply is such that price once again equals marginal cost. In so doing, they will correct any inefficiency in the allocation of resources that the original change may have temporarily imposed on the economy.

The "Invisible Hand" Revisited

Finally, the highly efficient allocation of resources that a perfectly competitive economy promotes comes about because businesses and resource suppliers seek to further their self-interest. For private goods with no externalities (Chapter 4), the invisible hand is at work (Chapter 2). The competitive system not only maximizes profits for individual producers but at the same time creates a pattern of resource allocation that maximizes consumer satisfaction. The invisible hand thus organizes the private interests of producers in a way that is fully in sync with society's interest in using scarce resources efficiently. Striving to obtain profit (and avoid losses) produces highly desirable economic outcomes.

10.5 Technological Advance and Competition

LO10.5   Discuss creative destruction and the profit incentives for innovation.

In explaining the model of perfect competition, we assumed for simplicity that all the firms in an industry had the same cost curves. Competition, as a result, only involved entrepreneurs entering and exiting industries in response to changes in profits caused by changes in the market price. This form of competition is important, but it is just a game of copycat because firms entering an industry simply duplicate the production methods and cost curves of existing firms in order to duplicate their above-normal profits. In this type of competition, there is no dynamism and no innovation, just more of the same.

By contrast, the most dynamic and interesting parts of competition are the fights between firms over the creation of new production technologies and new products. Firms have a strong profit incentive to develop improved ways of making existing products as well as creating totally new products. To put that incentive in context, recall one fact that you just learned about long-run equilibrium in perfect competition. When each firm in a perfectly competitive industry has the same productive technology and therefore the same cost structure for producing output, entry and exit assure that in the long run every firm will make the same normal profit.

Entrepreneurs, of course, would like to earn more than a normal profit. As a result, they are constantly attempting two different strategies for increasing their profits. The first involves attempting to lower the production costs of existing products through better technology or improved business organization. Because perfect competition implies that individual firms cannot affect the market price, anything that lowers an innovating firm's production costs will result in higher profits since the innovating firm's revenues per unit (which are equal to the market price per unit) will stay the same while its costs per unit fall due to its improved production technology.

The second strategy for earning a rate of return greater than a normal profit is to try to develop a totally new product that is popular with consumers. If a firm is first to market with a popular new product, it will face no competition, as it is the only producer. As long as the product remains popular and the firm remains the only producer, it will be able to charge prices that are higher than production costs, thereby allowing it to earn above-normal profits. (We say much more about this in Chapter 11, which covers monopoly.)

Notably, however, any advantages that innovative firms gain either by lowering the production costs of existing products or by introducing entirely new products will not normally persist. An innovative entrepreneur may put some of her current rivals out of business, but there are always other entrepreneurs with new ideas so that very soon it may be *her* firm that is going out of business due to innovations made by others. The Consider This box here shows just how rapidly new firms are created and destroyed.

CONSIDER THIS

Running a Company Is Hard Business

The life expectancy of a Canadian business is just 10.2 years. About 9.5 percent of Canadian firms go out of business each year. In addition, 22 percent of start-up firms go bankrupt within two years, 53 percent within five years, and nearly 65 percent within ten years.

These numbers testify to the ability of competition to quickly dispose of firms that have high production costs or unpopular products. In a competitive environment, such firms quickly prove unprofitable and are shut down by their owners. For example, BlackBerry, once one of Canada's outstanding successes, has recently lost market share

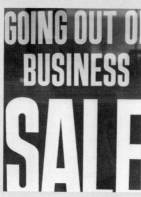

© Katrin Thomas/Getty Images

due to the relentless competition from Apple's iPhone and cellphones running Google's Android operating system.

Balancing out the dying firms are start-ups that hope to use the resources freed up by the closed firms to deliver better products or lower costs. In a typical year, more than 65,000 new businesses are started in Canada. Most of these new firms will themselves eventually fall victim to creative destruction and the pressures of competition, but it's also possible that one of them will be the next Apple, Canadian Tires, or Tim Hortons.

Creative Destruction

The innovations that firms achieve thanks to competition are considered by many economists to be the driving force behind economic growth and rising living standards. The transformative effects of competition are often referred to as **creative destruction** to capture the idea that the creation of new products and new production methods destroys the market positions of firms committed to existing products and old ways of doing business. In addition, just the *threat* that a rival may soon come out with a new technology or product can cause other firms to innovate and thereby replace or rectify their old ways of doing business. As argued many years ago by Harvard economist Joseph Schumpeter, the most important type of competition is

> . . . competition from the new commodity, the new technology, the new source of supply, the new type of business organization—competition which commands a decisive cost or quality advantage and which strikes not at the margins of profits of the existing firms but at their foundation and their very lives. This kind of competition is . . . so . . . important that it becomes a matter of comparative indifference whether competition in the ordinary [short-run or long-run] sense functions more or less promptly . . . competition of the kind we now have in mind acts not only when in being but also when it is merely an ever-present threat. It disciplines before it attacks. The businessman feels himself to be in a competitive situation even if he is alone in his field.[2]

There are many examples of creative destruction. In the 1800s wagons, ships, and barges were the only means of transporting freight until the railroads broke up their monopoly; the dominant market position of the railroads was, in turn, undermined by trucks and, later, by airplanes. Movies brought new competition to live theatre, at one time the "only show in town." But movies were later challenged by broadcast television, which was then challenged by cable TV. Both are now challenged by Netflix, Amazon Instant Video, and other online video-on-demand services. Cassettes replaced records before being supplanted in turn by compact discs. Then compact discs were done in by iPods and MP3 players, which in turn were done in by the availability of smartphones to play music—including music streamed (instead of purchased) via services like Spotify and Pandora. Electronic communications—including faxes and emails—have greatly affected Canada Post. And online retailers like Amazon.com have stolen substantial business from bricks-and-mortar retailers.

The "creative" part of creative destruction leads to new products and lower-cost production methods that are of great benefit to society because they allow for a more efficient use of society's scarce resources. Keep in mind, however, that the "destruction" part of creative destruction can be very hard on workers in the industries being

---

[2] Joseph A. Schumpeter, *Capitalism, Socialism, and Democracy*, 3rd ed. (New York: Harper & Row, 1950, pp. 84–85).

displaced by new technologies. A worker at a CD-making factory may see her job eliminated as consumers switch to online music downloads. Canada Post cut hundreds of jobs in 2011 partly due to the impact that email has had on the demand for postal services. We need fewer and fewer postal workers every year thanks to email and texting. And many jobs in retail have been eliminated due to competition with Amazon.com and other online retailers.

Normally, the process of creative destruction goes slowly enough that workers at firms being downsized can transition smoothly to jobs in firms that are expanding. But sometimes the change is too swift for all of them to find new jobs easily. And in other instances, such as a town with only one major employer—like a rural coal-mining town or a small town with a large auto factory—the loss of that one major employer can be devastating because there are not enough other firms in the local area to employ the workers laid off by the major employer.

While the net effects of creative destruction are indisputably positive—including ongoing economic growth and rising living standards—creative destruction involves costs as well as benefits. And while the benefits are widespread, the costs tend to be borne almost entirely by the relatively few workers in declining industries who are not positioned to make easy transitions to new jobs.

The LAST WORD

A Patent Failure?

Patents may hinder creative destruction. If so, should we consider abolishing patents?

Patents give inventors the sole legal right to market and sell their new ideas for a period of twenty years. So when considering the pluses and minuses of the patent system, it is important to begin with the fact that the possibility of obtaining a patent gives inventors a strong financial incentive to bear the research and development (R&D) costs necessary to come up with innovative solutions to old problems.

At the same time, however, the patent system also gives patent holders the ability to stifle the creative energies of other inventors by suing or threating to sue any individual or firm that they believe is infringing on their patent by producing or utilizing their invention without permission. The problem is most acute for products like cellphones that incorporate thousands of different technologies into a single product. That's because each of those technologies might possibly infringe on one or more patents. If so, a single lawsuit filed over just one of those patents could halt the production and sale of the entire product. The alleged infringement may be totally unintentional or a matter of honest dispute. But if a patent holder believes that some part of the phone is infringing on his patent, he can threaten to sue the manufacturer and demand the shutdown of all production unless he receives royalty payments in compensation.

Consider Microsoft, which thirty years ago was a successful innovator thanks to its Windows operating system. Over the past ten years, however, its Windows-based cellphones have been a failure. Yet it threatened to shut down the production of all Android phones because the Android software used in operating those extremely popular phones happens to incorporate the ability to schedule a meeting. That is a feature that most Android users don't even know about. But it is a functionality over which Microsoft holds a patent for mobile devices. So to avoid a lawsuit that could have shut down the production of all

Android phones, Android's parent company, Google, is now paying Microsoft a licensing fee on each and every Android phone. Similarly, in 2012 Nokia, the Finnish mobile phone maker, settled a patent dispute with BlackBerry, which will now pay ongoing fees to Nokia.

That situation is problematic for creative destruction because the patent system is being used to help an old company that hasn't had a successful product in many years to effectively tax and benefit from the successful innovations of a young rival. That ability to tax is a form of life support that allows stodgy old firms to survive longer than they should against innovative rivals and the pressures of creative destruction.

Even worse, companies known as "patent trolls" have been created to buy up patents simply for the chance to sue other companies and collect royalties. The patent trolls invent nothing and produce nothing. But they are free under the current system to make billions of dollars every year by suing innovative companies.

In response, some economists have begun to argue that the net benefits of the patent system have been overstated and that innovation might proceed faster in in certain industries if patents were abolished. Their key insight is that the net benefits of patents depend upon how easy it is for rivals to successfully copy and market an innovative product.

Consider pharmaceuticals. Once the chemical formula for a new drug becomes known, it is very easy for rivals to make chemically identical versions that will be easy to market because they will be just as effective as the version sold by the firm that invented the drug. At the same time, competition is so fierce in the pharmaceutical industry that without patent protection the price of the new drug would be driven down almost immediately to its marginal production cost. That is highly problematic, because the market price would be too low to ever recoup the large R&D costs necessary to identify and develop effective new medications. Thus, without patent protection, R&D would cease and no new drugs would be developed.

So for industries like pharmaceuticals that have easy-to-copy products, patents should continue to exist because they are the only way to provide the financial incentive necessary to get firms to invest the R&D monies that must be spent if you want innovation and creative destruction.

Things are very different, however, for complicated consumer products that are made up of thousands of separate technologies that are each difficult to copy and market. As an example, even if Apple's rivals obtained the blueprints for the iPhone, it would still be extremely costly for them to build the factories necessary to make copies. And even if they did that, they would still have to convince consumers that their copycat iPhones were as good as the original. Thus, unlike pharmaceuticals, patents are not necessary to provide the firms that produce complicated consumer goods with an incentive to develop new products and invest in R&D.

On the other hand, society would likely see great benefits if patents were eliminated for complicated consumer goods like cellphones and automobiles. Creative destruction would likely increase, as innovative companies would no longer fear patent-infringement lawsuits and old rivals could no longer delay their own demise by taxing innovators.

As a result, some economists now argue that patents should only be available for industries with simple products that are easy to copy and market. For industries with complicated products that are hard to copy and market, patents should be eliminated.

© Seattle Times/McClatchy-Tribune/Getty Images

Question

How can patents speed up the process of creative destruction? How can patents slow down the process of creative destruction? How do differences in manufacturing costs affect which industries would be most likely to be affected by the removal of patents?

Chapter Summary

LO10.1 Explain how the long run differs from the short run in perfect competition.

- In the short run when plant and equipment are fixed, the firms in a perfectly competitive industry may earn profits or suffer losses. In the long run when plant and equipment are adjustable, profits will attract new entrants while losses will cause existing firms to leave the industry.

LO10.2 Describe how profits and losses drive the long-run adjustment process of perfect competition.

- The entry or exit of firms will change industry supply. Entry or exit will continue until the market price determined by industry supply interacting with market demand generates a normal profit for firms in the industry. With firms earning a normal profit, there will be no incentive to either enter or exit the industry. This situation constitutes long-run equilibrium in a purely competitive industry.

- Entry and exit help to improve resource allocation. Firms that exit an industry due to low profits release their resources to be used more profitably in other industries. Firms that enter an industry chasing higher profits bring with them resources that were less profitably used in other industries. Both processes increase allocative efficiency.

- In the long run, the market price of a product will equal the minimum average total cost of production. At a higher price, economic profits will cause firms to enter the industry until those profits have been competed away. At a lower price, losses will force the exit of firms from the industry until the product price rises to equal average total cost.

LO10.3 Explain the differences between constant-cost, increasing-cost, and decreasing-cost industries.

- The long-run supply curve is horizontal for a constant-cost industry, uploping for an increasing-cost industry, and dowsloping for a decreasing-cost industry.

LO10.4   Show how long-run equilibrium in perfect competition produces an efficient allocation of resources.

- The long-run equality of price and minimum average total cost means that competitive firms will use the most efficient technology and charge the lowest price consistent with their production costs. That is, the firms will achieve productive efficiency.

- The long-run equality of price and marginal cost implies that resources will be allocated in accordance with consumer tastes. Allocative efficiency will occur. In the market, the combined amount of consumer surplus and producer surplus will be at a maximum.

- The competitive price system will reallocate resources in response to a change in consumer tastes, in technology, or in

factor supplies and will thereby maintain allocative efficiency over time.

LO10.5   Discuss creative destruction and the profit incentives for innovation.

- Competition involves never-ending attempts by entrepreneurs and managers to earn above-normal profits either by creating new products or by developing lower-cost production methods for existing products. These efforts cause creative destruction, the financial undoing of the market positions of firms committed to existing products and old ways of doing business by new firms with new products and innovative ways of doing business.

Terms and Concepts

long-run supply curve
constant-cost industry
increasing-cost industry
decreasing-cost industry
productive efficiency

allocative efficiency
consumer surplus
producer surplus
creative destruction

Discussion Questions

1. Explain how the long run differs from the short run in perfect competition.   [**LO10.1**]

2. Relate opportunity costs to why profits encourage entry into perfectly competitive industries and how losses encourage exit from perfectly competitive industries.   [**LO10.2**]

3. How do the entry and exit of firms in a perfectly competitive industry affect resource flows and long-run profits and losses?   [**LO10.2**]

4. In long-run equilibrium, P = minimum ATC = MC. Of what significance for economic efficiency is the equality of P and minimum ATC? The equality of P and MC? Distinguish between

productive efficiency and allocative efficiency in your answer.   [**LO10.4**]

5. The basic model of perfect competition reviewed in this chapter finds that in the long run all firms in a perfectly competitive industry will earn normal profits. If all firms will only earn a normal profit in the long run, why would any firms bother to develop new products or lower-cost production methods? Explain.   [**LO10.5**]

6. "Ninety percent of new products fail within two years—so you shouldn't be so eager to innovate." Do you agree? Explain why or why not.   [**LO10.5**]

Review Questions

1. When discussing perfect competition, the term *long run* refers to a period of time long enough to allow   [**LO10.1**]

   a. Firms already in an industry to either expand or contract their capacities

   b. New firms to enter or existing firms to leave

   c. Both (a) and (b)

   d. None of the above

2. Suppose that the pen-making industry is perfectly competitive. Also suppose that each current firm and any potential

firms that might enter the industry all have identical cost curves, with minimum ATC = $1.25 per pen. If the market equilibrium price of pens is currently $1.50, what would you expect it to be in the long run?   [**LO10.2**]

   a. $0.25

   b. $1

   c. $1.25

   d. $1.50

3. Suppose that as the output of mobile phones increases, the cost of touch screens and other component parts decreases. If the mobile phone industry features perfect competition, we would expect the long-run supply curve for mobile phones to be [**LO10.3**]

   a. Upsloping

   b. Downsloping

   c. Horizontal

   d. U-shaped

4. Using diagrams for both the industry and a representative firm, illustrate competitive long-run equilibrium. Assuming constant costs, employ these diagrams to show how (a) an increase and (b) a decrease in market demand will upset that long-run equilibrium. Trace graphically and describe in words the adjustment processes by which long-run equilibrium is restored. Now rework your analysis for increasing-cost and decreasing-cost industries, and compare the three long-run supply curves. [**LO10.3**]

5. Suppose that firms in a perfectly competitive industry producing cashews discover that *P* exceeds MC. Is their combined output of cashews too little, too much, or just right to achieve allocative efficiency? In the long run, what will happen to the supply of cashews and the price of cashews? Use a supply and demand diagram to show how that response will change the combined amount of consumer surplus and producer surplus in the market for cashews. [**LO10.4**]

Problems

1. A firm in a perfectly competitive industry has a typical cost structure. The normal rate of profit in the economy is 5 percent. This firm is earning $5.50 on every $50 invested by its founders. What is its percentage rate of return? Is it earning an economic profit? If so, how large? Will this industry see entry or exit? What will be the rate of return earned by firms in this industry once the industry reaches long-run equilibrium? [**LO10.2**]

2. A firm in a perfectly competitive industry is currently producing 1000 units per day at a total cost of $450. If it produced 800 units per day, its total cost would be $300, and if it produced 500 units per day, its total cost would be $275. What is the firm's ATC per unit at these three levels of production? If every firm in this industry has the same cost structure, is the industry in long run competitive equilibrium? From what you know about these firms' cost structures, what is the highest possible price per unit that could exist as the market price in long-run equilibrium? If that price ends up being the market price and if the normal rate of profit is 10 percent, how big will each firm's accounting profit per unit be? [**LO10.4**]

3. There are 300 farms in the perfectly competitive local dairy market. Of the 300 dairy farms, 298 have a cost structure that generates profits of $24 for every $300 invested. What is their percentage rate of return? The other two dairies have a cost structure that generates profits of $22 for every $200 invested. What is their percentage rate of return? Assuming that the normal rate of profit in the economy is 10 percent, will there be entry or exit? Will the change in the number of farms affect the two farms that earn $22 for every $200 invested? What will be the rate of return earned by most farms in the industry in long-run equilibrium? If farms can copy each other's technology, what will be the rate of return eventually earned by all farms? [**LO10.4**]

CHAPTER 11

Monopoly

LEARNING OBJECTIVES

LO11.1	**List the characteristics of monopoly.**
LO11.2	**List and explain the barriers to entry that shield monopolies from competition.**
LO11.3	**Explain how demand is seen by a monopolist.**
LO11.4	**Explain how a monopolist sets its maximizing output and price.**
LO11.5	**Discuss the economic effects of monopoly.**
LO11.6	**Describe why a monopolist might prefer to charge different prices in different markets.**
LO11.7	**Distinguish between the monopoly price, the socially optimal price, and the fair-return price of a government-regulated monopoly.**

We turn now from perfect competition to monopoly, which is at the opposite end of the spectrum of market structures listed in Table 9-1. You deal with monopolies more often than you might think. If you see the logo for Microsoft's Windows on your computer, you are dealing with a monopoly (or, at least, near-monopoly). When you purchase certain prescription drugs, you may be buying monopolized products. When you make a local telephone call, turn on your lights, or subscribe to cable TV, you may be patronizing a monopoly, depending on your location.

What precisely do we mean by monopoly and what conditions allow it to arise and survive? How does a monopolist determine its profit-maximizing price and output? Does a monopolist achieve the efficiencies associated with perfect competition? If not, what, if anything, should the government do about it? A simplified model of monopoly will help us answer these questions. It is the first of three models of imperfect competition.

11.1 Characteristics of Monopoly

LO11.1 List the characteristics of monopoly.

A **monopoly** exists when a single firm is the sole producer of a product or service for which there are no close substitutes. Here are the main characteristics of monopoly.

- *Single Seller* A monopoly is an industry in which a single firm is the sole producer or seller of a specific good or the sole supplier of a service.
- *No Close Substitutes* A monopoly's product is unique in that there are no close substitutes.
- *Price-Maker* The monopolist controls the total quantity supplied and thus has considerable control over price; it is a *price-maker*. The monopolist confronts the usual downsloping product demand curve. It can change its product price by changing the quantity of the product it produces. The monopolist will use this power whenever it is advantageous to do so.
- *Blocked Entry* A monopolist has no competitors because certain barriers keep potential competitors from entering the industry. Those barriers may be economic, technological, legal, or of some other type, but entry is totally blocked in monopoly.
- *Nonprice Competition* The product produced by a monopolist may be either standardized (as with natural gas and electricity) or differentiated (as with Microsoft's Windows software or Frisbees). Monopolists that have standardized products engage mainly in public relations advertising, whereas those with differentiated products sometimes advertise their products' attributes.

Examples of Monopoly

Examples of a single-price *pure* monopoly are relatively rare in Canada, but many examples of less pure forms exist. In many cities, government-owned or government-regulated public utilities—natural gas and electric companies, the water company, the cable TV company, and the local telephone company—may be monopolies or virtually so. For example, Toronto Hydro is the sole supplier of electricity in that urban market. In some Canadian markets, competition has been introduced for some of these traditional monopolies. Many urban areas now have more than one gas supplier to choose from, and rapid technological change has dramatically altered the delivery of communications services, effectively eliminating what was a virtual monopoly by Bell Canada. In some urban markets, such as Toronto and Montreal, Rogers Cable Communications, Telus, and other, smaller operators now compete with Bell Canada in the local telephone market. Wireless telephone services by Telus, Virgin, Chatr, Wind, Koodo, and Rogers have further eroded Bell's monopoly position in local markets. The telecom industry has gone from a virtual monopoly to an oligopolistic market structure. Ontario and Alberta have moved toward deregulating their electricity markets, although the public furor that this has caused has delayed full deregulation.

Many near-monopolies also exist in which a single firm has the bulk of sales in a specific market. Intel, for example, produces 80 percent of the central microprocessors used in personal computers. Microsoft's Windows operating system is on some 90 percent of home and business computers; Wham-O, through its Frisbee brand, sells

A monopoly exists when a single firm is the sole producer of a product or service for which no close substitutes exist.

© Ingram Publishing

90 percent of plastic throwing disks. Google executes nearly 70 percent of all Internet searches and consequently controls nearly 75 percent of all the revenue generated by search ads in Canada.

Professional sports teams are, in a sense, monopolies because they are the sole suppliers of specific services in large geographic areas. With a few exceptions, a single major-league team in each sport serves each large Canadian city. If you want to see a live Major League Baseball game in Toronto, you must patronize the Blue Jays. Other geographic monopolies exist. For example, a small town may be served by only one airline or railroad. In a small, isolated community, the local barber shop, dry cleaner, or grocery store may approximate a monopoly. And in the skies above, airlines control the only Internet access that is available to the passengers flying on their planes.

Of course, some competition almost always exists. Satellite television is a substitute for cable, and amateur softball is a substitute for professional baseball. The Apple operating system can substitute for Windows, and so on. But such substitutes are typically either more costly or in some way less appealing.

Dual Objectives of the Study of Monopoly

Monopoly is worth studying both for its own sake and because it provides insights about the more common market structures of monopolistic competition and oligopoly (see Chapter 12 and Chapter 13). These two market structures combine, in differing degrees, characteristics of perfect competition and monopoly.

11.2 Barriers to Entry

LO11.2   List and explain the barriers to entry that shield monopolies from competition.

The factors that prohibit firms from entering an industry are called **barriers to entry**. In monopoly, strong barriers to entry effectively block all potential competition. Somewhat weaker barriers may permit oligopoly, a market structure dominated by a few firms. Still weaker barriers may permit the entry of a fairly large number of competing firms, giving rise to monopolistic competition. The absence of any effective entry barriers permits the entry of a very large number of firms, which provides the basis of perfect competition. So barriers to entry are pertinent not only to the extreme case of monopoly but also to other market structures in which there are monopoly-like characteristics or monopoly-like behaviours.

We now discuss the four most prominent barriers to entry.

ECONOMIES OF SCALE

Modern technology in some industries is such that economies of scale—declining average total cost with added firm size—are extensive. In such cases, a firm's long-run average-cost schedule will decline over a wide range of output. Given market demand, only a few large firms or, in the extreme, only a single large firm can achieve low average total costs.

Figure 11-1 indicates economies of scale over a wide range of outputs. If total consumer demand is within that output range, then only a single producer can satisfy demand at least cost. Note, for example, that a monopolist can produce 200 units at a per-unit cost of $10 and a total cost of $2000. If there are two firms in the industry and each produces 100 units, the unit cost is $15 and total cost rises to $3000 (= 200 units × $15). A still more competitive situation with four firms each producing 50 units would boost unit and total cost to $20 and $4000, respectively. Thus we conclude that when long-run average total cost (ATC) is declining, only a single producer, a monopolist, can produce any amount of output at minimum total cost.

If a monopoly exists in such an industry, economies of scale will serve as an entry barrier and will protect the monopolist from competition. New firms that try to enter the industry as small-scale producers cannot realize the cost economies of the monopolist and therefore cannot obtain the normal profits necessary for survival or growth. A new firm might try to enter the industry as a large-scale producer so as to achieve the necessary economies of scale. But the massive expense of the plant facilities along with customer loyalty to the existing product would make the entry highly risky. Therefore, the new and untried enterprise would find it difficult to secure financing for its venture. In most cases the risks and financial obstacles to starting big are prohibitive, which explains why efforts to enter such industries as those manufacturing automobiles, computer operating software, commercial aircraft, and household laundry equipment are rare.

FIGURE 11-1   Economies of Scale: The Natural Monopoly Case

A declining long-run average-total-cost curve over a wide range of output quantities indicates extensive economies of scale. A single monopoly firm can produce, say, 200 units of output at lower cost ($10 each) than could two or more firms that had a combined output of 200 units.

A monopoly firm is referred to as a *natural monopoly* if the market demand curve intersects the long-run ATC curve at any point where average total costs are declining. If a natural monopoly were to set its price where market demand intersects long-run ATC, its price would be lower than if the industry were more competitive. But it will probably set a higher price. A monopolist may, instead, set its price far above ATC and obtain substantial economic profit. In that event, the cost advantage of a natural monopolist would accrue to the monopolist as profit and not as lower prices to consumers. That is why the government regulates some natural monopolies, specifying the price they may charge. We will say more about that later.

LEGAL BARRIERS TO ENTRY: PATENTS AND LICENCES

Government also creates legal barriers to entry by awarding patents and licences.

- *Patents*   A *patent* is the exclusive right of an inventor to use, or to allow another to use, her or his invention. Patent laws protect the inventor from rivals who would use the invention without having shared in the effort and expense of developing it. Patents thus provide the inventor with a monopoly position for the life of the patent. The world's nations have agreed on a uniform patent length of twenty years from the time of application. Patents have figured prominently in the growth of modern-day giants such as IBM, Microsoft, Pfizer, Xerox, Bombardier, General Electric, and BlackBerry.

- *Research and Development (R&D)*   is what leads to most patentable inventions and products. Firms that gain monopoly power through their own research or by purchasing the patents of others can use patents to strengthen their market position. The profit from one patent can finance the research required to develop new patentable products. In the pharmaceutical industry, patents on prescription drugs have produced large monopoly profits that have helped finance the discovery of new patentable medicines. So monopoly power achieved through patents may well be self-sustaining, even though patents eventually expire and generic drugs then compete with the original brand. (Chapter 10's Last Word has more on the costs and benefits of patents.)

- *Licences*   The government may also limit entry into an industry or occupation through *licensing*. At the national level, the Canadian Radio-television and Telecommunications Commission (CRTC) licenses a controlled number of radio and television stations in each geographic area. In many large cities, one of a limited number of municipal licences is required to drive a taxicab. The restriction of the supply of cabs creates economic profit for cab owners and drivers. New cabs cannot enter the industry to force prices and profit lower. In a few instances the government might license itself to provide some product and thereby create a public monopoly. For example, in some provinces only province-owned retail outlets can sell liquor. Similarly, many provinces have licensed themselves to run lotteries.

OWNERSHIP OR CONTROL OF ESSENTIAL RESOURCES

A monopolist can use private property as an obstacle to potential rivals. For example, a firm that owns or controls a resource essential to the production process can prohibit the entry of rival firms. At one time the International Nickel Company of Canada (now called Vale Canada Limited) controlled 90 percent of the world's known nickel reserves. A municipal sand and gravel firm may own all the nearby deposits of sand and gravel. And it is very difficult for new professional sports leagues to be created because existing leagues have contracts with the best players and long-term leases on the major stadiums and arenas.

PRICING AND OTHER STRATEGIC BARRIERS TO ENTRY

Even if a firm is not protected from entry by, say, extensive economies of scale or ownership of essential resources, entry may effectively be blocked by the way the monopolist responds when rivals attempt to enter the industry. Confronted with a new entrant, the monopolist may create an entry barrier by slashing prices, stepping up advertising, or taking other strategic action to make it difficult for the entrant to succeed.

A prominent example of entry deterrence is the case of American Express, which in 2015 was found guilty of an unlawful restraint of trade because it prohibited any merchant who had signed up to accept American Express credit cards from promoting rival credit cards—such as Visa and Mastercard—to their customers.

11.3 Monopoly Demand

LO11.3   Explain how demand is seen by a monopolist.

Now that we have explained the sources of monopoly, we will build a model of monopoly so that we can analyze its price and output decisions. Let's start by making three assumptions:

1. Economies of scale, patents, or resource ownership secure the monopolist's status.

2. Government does not regulate the firm.

3. The firm is a single-price monopolist; it charges the same price for all units of output.

The crucial difference between a monopolist and a seller in perfect competition lies on the demand side of the market. The seller in a competitive market faces a perfectly elastic demand at the price determined by market supply and demand. It is a *price-taker* that can sell as much or as little as it wants at the going market price. Each additional unit sold will add the amount of the constant product price to the firm's total revenue. That means that marginal revenue for the competitive seller is constant and equal to product price.

The demand curve for the monopolist (and for any imperfectly competitive seller) is quite different from that of a firm in perfect competition. Because the monopolist *is* the industry, its demand curve is *the market demand curve*, which is downsloping. Columns 1 and 2 in Table 11-1 illustrate this. Note that quantity demanded increases as price decreases.

In Figure 9-7 we drew separate demand curves for the perfectly competitive industry and for a single firm in such an industry; only a single demand curve is needed in a monopoly because the firm and the industry are one and the same. We have graphed part of the demand data in Table 11-1 as demand curve *D* in Figure 11-2. This is the monopolist's demand curve *and* the market demand curve. The downsloping demand curve has three implications that are essential to understanding the monopoly model.

1. MARGINAL REVENUE IS LESS THAN PRICE

With a fixed downsloping demand curve, the monopolist can increase sales only by charging a lower price. Consequently, marginal revenue is less than price (average revenue) for every level of output except the first. Why? The lower price of the extra unit of output also applies to all prior units of output. Each additional unit of output sold increases total revenue by an amount equal to its own price less the sum of the price cuts that apply to all prior units of output.

Figure 11-2 confirms this point. There we have highlighted two price–quantity combinations from the monopolist's demand curve. The monopolist can sell one more unit at $132 than it can at $142 and that way get an additional $132 of revenue (the light blue area). But to sell that fourth unit for $132, the monopolist must also sell the first three units at $132 rather than $142. This $10 reduction in revenue on three units results in a $30 revenue loss

TABLE 11-1   Revenue and Cost Data of a Monopolist

	REVENUE DATA				COST DATA		
(1) Quantity of output (Q)	(2) Price (average revenue) (P)	(3) Total revenue (TR = P × Q)	(4) Marginal revenue $MR = \dfrac{\Delta TR}{\Delta Q}$	(5) Average total cost (ATC)	(6) Total cost Q × ATC (TC)	(7) Marginal cost (MC)	(8) Profit (+) or loss (−)
0	$172	$ 0			$ 100		$−100
1	162	162	$162	$190.00	190	$ 90	−28
2	152	304	142	135.00	270	80	+34
3	142	426	122	113.33	340	70	+86
4	132	528	102	100.00	400	60	+128
5	**122**	**610**	**82**	**94.00**	**470**	**70**	**+140**
6	112	672	62	91.67	550	80	+122
7	102	714	42	91.43	640	90	+74
8	92	736	22	93.75	750	110	−14
9	82	738	2	97.78	880	130	−142
10	72	720	−18	103.00	1030	150	−310

(the pink area). Thus, the net difference in total revenue from selling a fourth unit is $102: the $132 gain from the fourth unit minus the $30 forgone on the first three units ($10 per unit × 3 units = $30). This net gain of $102—the marginal revenue of the fourth unit—is clearly less than the $132 price of the fourth unit.

Column 4 in Table 11-1 shows that marginal revenue is always less than the corresponding product price in column 2, except for the first unit of output. Because marginal revenue is the change in total revenue associated

FIGURE 11-2   Price and Marginal Revenue in Monopoly

A monopolist with a downsloping demand curve such as *D* must set a lower price to sell more output. Here, by charging $132 rather than $142, the monopolist sells an extra unit (the fourth unit) and gains $132 from that sale. But from this gain must be subtracted $30, which reflects the $10 less the monopolist charged for each of the first three units. Thus, the marginal revenue of the fourth unit is $102 (= $132 − $30), considerably less than its $132 price.

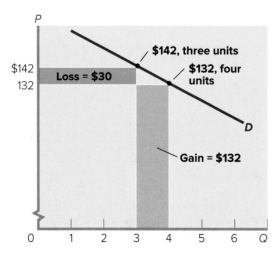

with each *additional* unit of output, the declining amounts of marginal revenue in column 4 mean that total revenue increases at a diminishing rate (as shown in column 3).

We show the relationship between the monopolist's marginal-revenue curve and total-revenue curve in Figure 11-3. For this figure, we extended the demand and revenue data of columns 1 through 4 in Table 11-1, assuming that each successive $10 price cut increases sales by one unit. For example, the monopolist can sell eleven units at $62, 12 units at $52, and so on.

Note that the monopolist's MR curve lies below the demand curve, indicating that marginal revenue is less than price at every output quantity but the very first unit. Observe also the special relationship between total revenue (Figure 11-3b) and marginal revenue (Figure 11-3a). Because marginal revenue is the change in total revenue, marginal revenue is positive while total revenue is increasing. When total revenue reaches its maximum, marginal revenue is zero. When total revenue is diminishing, marginal revenue is negative.

FIGURE 11-3   Demand, Marginal Revenue, and Total Revenue for a Monopolist

(a) Because an imperfectly competitive firm must lower its price on all units sold in order to increase its sales, the marginal-revenue curve (MR) lies below its downsloping demand curve (D). The elastic and inelastic regions of demand are highlighted. (b) Total revenue (TR) increases at a decreasing rate, reaches maximum, and then declines. Note that in the elastic region, TR is increasing and hence MR is positive. When TR reaches its maximum, MR is zero. In the inelastic region of demand, TR is declining, so MR is negative.

(a) Demand and marginal-revenue curves

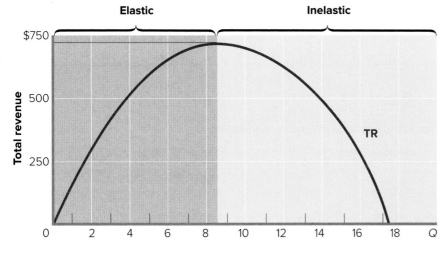

(b) Total-revenue curve

2. THE MONOPOLIST IS A PRICE-MAKER

All firms in imperfectly competitive market structures—whether monopoly, oligopoly, or monopolistic competition—face downsloping demand curves. As a result, any change in quantity produced causes a movement along their respective demand curves and a change in the price they can charge for their respective products. Economists summarize this fact by saying that firms with downsloping demand curves are *price-makers.*

This is most evident in monopoly, where an industry consists of a single monopoly firm so that total industry output is exactly equal to whatever the single monopoly firm chooses to produce. As we just mentioned, the monopolist faces a downsloping demand curve in which each amount of output is associated with some unique price. Thus, in deciding on the quantity of output to produce, the monopolist is also indirectly determining the price it will charge. Through control of output, it can make the price. From columns 1 and 2 in Table 11-1 we find that the monopolist can charge a price of $72 if it produces ten units, a price of $82 if it produces 9 units, and so forth.

MATH 11.1   Monopoly and Elasticity of Demand

3. THE MONOPOLIST SETS PRICES IN THE ELASTIC REGION OF DEMAND

The total-revenue test for price elasticity of demand is the basis for our third implication. Recall from Chapter 4 that the total-revenue test reveals that when demand is elastic, a decline in price will increase total revenue. Similarly, when demand is inelastic, a decline in price will *reduce* total revenue. Beginning at the top of demand curve *D* in Figure 11-3a, observe that as the price declines from $172 to approximately $82, total revenue increases (and marginal revenue, therefore, is positive), which means that demand is elastic in this price range. Conversely, for price declines below $82, total revenue decreases (marginal revenue is negative), which indicates that demand is inelastic there.

The implication is that a profit-maximizing monopolist will always want to avoid the inelastic segment of its demand curve in favour of some price–quantity combination in the elastic region. Here's why: To get into the inelastic region, the monopolist must lower price and increase output. In the inelastic region a lower price means less total revenue. And increased output always means increased total cost. Less total revenue and higher total cost yield lower profit.

QUICK REVIEW 11.1

- A monopolist is the sole supplier of a product or service for which no close substitutes exist.

- A monopoly survives because of entry barriers such as economies of scale, patents and licences, the ownership of essential resources, and strategic actions to exclude rivals.

- The monopolist's demand curve is downsloping, and its marginal-revenue curve lies below its demand curve.

- The downsloping demand curve means that the monopolist is a price-maker.

- The monopolist will operate in the elastic region of demand since it can increase total revenue and reduce total cost by reducing output.

11.4 Output and Price Determination

LO11.4   **Explain how a monopolist sets its maximizing output and price.**

At what specific price–quantity combination will a profit-maximizing monopolist choose to operate? To answer this question, we must add production costs to our analysis.

Cost Data

On the cost side, we will assume that, although the firm is a monopolist in the product market, it hires factors of production in competitive markets and employs the same technology, and therefore has the same cost structure as the perfectly competitive firm that we studied in Chapters 8 and 9. By using the same cost data that we developed in Chapter 7, and applied to the competitive firm in Chapters 8 and 9, we will be able to directly compare the price and output decisions of a monopoly with those of a firm in perfect competition. This will help us demonstrate that the price and output differences between a monopolist and a firm in perfect competition are not the result of two different sets of costs. Columns 5 through 7 in Table 11-1 reproduce the relevant cost data from Table 8-2.

MR = MC Rule

A monopolist seeking to maximize total profit will employ the same rationale as a profit-seeking firm in a competitive industry. It will produce another unit of output as long as that unit adds more to total revenue than it adds to total cost. The firm will increase output up to the output at which marginal revenue equals marginal cost (MR = MC).

A comparison of columns 4 and 7 in Table 11-1 indicates that the profit-maximizing output is five units, because the fifth unit is the last unit of output whose marginal revenue exceeds its marginal cost. What price will the monopolist charge? The demand schedule shown as columns 1 and 2 in Table 11-1 indicates there is only one price at which five units can be sold: $122.

This analysis is shown in Figure 11-4 (Key Graph), where we have graphed the demand, marginal-revenue, average-total-cost, and marginal-cost data of Table 11-1. The profit-maximizing output occurs at five units of output (Q_m) where the marginal-revenue (MR) and marginal-cost (MC) curves intersect (MR = MC).

To find the price the monopolist will charge, we extend a vertical line from Q_m up to the demand curve D. The price P_m at which Q_m units can be sold is $122, which is in this case the profit-maximizing price. So the monopolist sets the quantity at Q_m to charge its profit-maximizing price of $122.

WORKED PROBLEM 11.1 Monopoly Price and Output

Columns 2 and 5 in Table 11-1 show that, at five units of output, the product price ($122) exceeds the average total cost ($94). The monopolist thus earns an economic profit of $28 per unit and the total economic profit is $140 (= 5 units × $28). In Figure 11-4, per-unit profit is $P_m - A$, where A is the average total cost of producing Q_m units. Total economic profit—the blue rectangle—is found by multiplying this per-unit profit by the profit-maximizing output Q_m.

Another way we can determine the profit-maximizing output is by comparing total revenue and total cost at each level of production and choosing the output with the greatest positive difference. Use columns 3 and 6 in Table 11-1 to verify our conclusion that five units is the profit-maximizing output. Graphing total revenue and total cost also shows the greatest difference (the maximum profit) at five units of output. Table 11-2 summarizes the process for determining the profit-maximizing output, the profit-maximizing price, and economic profit in monopoly.

No Monopoly Supply Curve

Recall that for firms in perfect competition MR equals P and the supply curve of a firm is determined by applying the MR (= P) = MC profit-maximizing rule. The supply curve for each firm is the portion of the firm's MC curve that lies above the average-variable-cost curve (see Figure 9-6).

At first glance we would suspect that the monopolist's marginal-cost curve would also be its supply curve, but that is *not* the case. *The monopolist has no supply curve.* Like the competitive firm, the monopolist equates marginal revenue and marginal cost to determine output, but for the monopolist marginal revenue is less than price. Because the monopolist does not equate marginal cost to price, it is possible for different demand conditions to bring about different prices for the same output. To understand this point, refer to Figure 11-4 and pencil in a new, steeper marginal-revenue curve that intersects the marginal-cost curve at the same point as does the present marginal-revenue curve. Then draw in a new demand curve that is roughly consistent with your new marginal-revenue curve. With the new curves, the same MR = MC output of five units now means a higher profit-maximizing price. So we conclude that there is no supply curve for the monopolist.

Misconceptions About Monopoly Pricing

Our analysis exposes two fallacies about the behaviour of a monopolist.

- *Not the Highest Price* Because a monopolist can manipulate output and price, people often believe it will charge the highest price it can get. That is incorrect. Prices above P_m in Figure 11-4 yield less than maximum total profit. The monopolist seeks maximum total profit, not maximum price. Prices above P_m would reduce sales and total revenue by more than a decrease in total cost.

KEY GRAPH

FIGURE 11-4 Profit Maximization by a Monopolist

The monopolist maximizes profit by producing the MR = MC output, here $Q_m = 5$ units. Then, as shown by the demand curve, it will charge price $P_m = \$122$. Average total cost will be $A = \$94$, meaning that per-unit profit is $P_m - A$ and total profit is $5 \times (P_m - A)$. Total economic profit is thus represented by the grey rectangle.

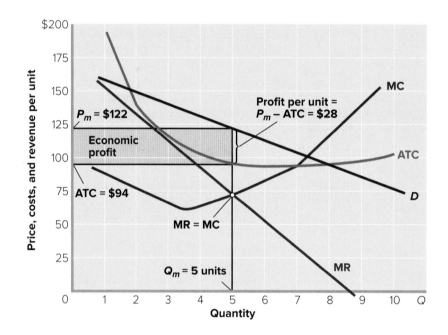

QUICK QUIZ

1. **The MR curve lies below the demand curve in this figure because**
   a. The demand curve is linear (a straight line)
   b. The demand curve is highly inelastic throughout its full length
   c. The demand curve is highly elastic throughout its full length
   d. The gain in revenue from an extra unit of output is less than the price charged for that unit of output

2. **The area labelled "Economic profit" can be found by multiplying the difference between *P* and ATC by quantity. It also can be found by**
   a. Dividing profit per unit by quantity
   b. Subtracting total cost from total revenue
   c. Multiplying the coefficient of demand elasticity by quantity

   d. Multiplying the difference between *P* and MC by quantity

3. **This monopolist**
   a. Charges the highest price it can get
   b. Earns only a normal profit in the long run
   c. Restricts output to create an insurmountable entry barrier
   d. Restricts output to increase its price and total economic profit

4. **At this monopolist's profit-maximizing output**
   a. Price equals marginal revenue
   b. Price equals marginal cost
   c. Price exceeds marginal cost
   d. Profit per unit is maximized

TABLE 11-2	**Steps for Graphically Determining the Profit-Maximizing Price and Economic Profit (If Any) in Monopoly**
Step 1	Determine the profit-maximizing output by finding where MR = MC.
Step 2	Determine the profit-maximizing price by extending a vertical line upward from the output determined in step 1 to the monopolist's demand curve.
Step 3	Determine the monopolist's economic profit using one of two methods.
Method 1	Find profit per unit by subtracting the average total cost of the profit-maximizing output from the profit-maximizing price. Then multiply the difference by the profit-maximizing output to determine economic profit (if any).
Method 2	Find total cost by multiplying the average total cost of the profit-maximizing output by that output. Find total revenue by multiplying the profit-maximizing output by the profit-maximizing price. Then subtract total cost from total revenue to determine economic profit (if any).

- *Total, Not Unit, Profit* The monopolist seeks maximum total profit, not maximum unit profit. In Figure 11-4 a comparison of the vertical distance between average total cost and price at various possible outputs indicates that per-unit profit is greater at a point slightly to the left of the profit-maximizing output Q_m. This is shown in Table 11-1 where the per-unit profit at four units of output is $32 (= $132 − $100) compared with $28 (= $122 − $94) at the profit-maximizing output of five units. Here the monopolist accepts a lower-than-maximum per-unit profit because additional sales more than compensate for the lower unit profit. A monopolist prefers to sell five units at a profit of $28 per unit (for a total profit of $140) than four units at a profit of $32 per unit (for a total profit of only $128).

Possibility of Losses by a Monopolist

The likelihood of economic profit is greater for a monopolist than for a firm in perfect competition; in the long run only a normal profit is possible in a perfectly competitive industry, whereas barriers to entry mean that for the monopolist economic profits can persist. In monopoly there are no new entrants to increase supply, drive down price, and eliminate economic profit.

But monopoly does not *guarantee* profit. The monopolist is not immune to changes in tastes that reduce the demand for its product. Nor is it immune to upward-shifting cost curves caused by escalating prices of factors of production. If the demand and cost situation faced by the monopolist is far less favourable than that in Figure 11-4, the monopolist will incur losses in the short run. Consider the monopoly enterprise shown in Figure 11-5. Despite

FIGURE 11-5 The Loss-Minimizing Position of a Monopolist

If demand D is weak and costs are high, the monopolist may be unable to make a profit. Because P_m exceeds V (AVC), the average variable cost at the MR = MC output Q_m, the monopolist will minimize losses in the short run by producing at that output. The loss per unit is A (ATC) − P_m, and the total loss is indicated by the pink rectangle.

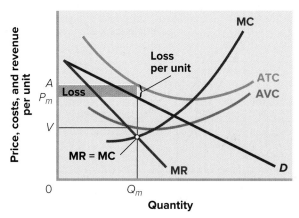

its dominance in the market (as, say, a seller of home sewing machines), it suffers a loss, as shown, because of weak demand and relatively high costs. Yet it will continue to operate because its total loss is less than its fixed cost. More precisely, at output Q_m the monopolist's price P_m exceeds its average variable cost V. Its loss per unit is $A - P_m$, and the total loss is shown by the pink rectangle.

Like a firm in perfect competition, the monopolist will not operate at a loss in the long run. Faced with continuing losses, in the long run the firm's owners will move their resources to other industries that offer better profit opportunities. A monopolist such as the one depicted in Figure 11-5 must obtain a minimum of a normal profit in the long run or it will go out of business.

11.5 Economic Effects of Monopoly

LO11.5 Discuss the economic effects of monopoly.

Let's now evaluate monopoly from the standpoint of society as a whole. The standard reference for this evaluation is the long-run efficiency in a perfectly competitive market, identified by the triple equality $P = MC = $ minimum ATC.

Price, Output, and Efficiency

Figure 11-6 graphically contrasts the price, output, and efficiency outcomes of monopoly and a perfectly competitive *industry*. Recall that in perfect competition at the equilibrium price–output combination both productive efficiency and allocative efficiency are achieved. *Productive efficiency* is achieved because competitive pressures force firms to operate where average total cost is at a minimum, Q_c. Product price is at the lowest level consistent with minimum average total cost. Also, *allocative efficiency* is achieved because production occurs up to that output at which price (the measure of a product's value or marginal benefit to society) equals marginal cost (the worth of the alternative products forgone by society in producing any given commodity). In short, $P = MC = $ minimum ATC.

Now let's suppose that this industry becomes a monopoly (Figure 11-6b) as a result of one firm acquiring all its competitors. We also assume that no changes in costs or market demand result from this dramatic change in the industry structure. Thousands of formerly competing firms are now a single monopolist.

FIGURE 11-6 Inefficiency of Monopoly Relative to a Perfectly Competitive Industry

(a) In a perfectly competitive industry, entry and exit of firms ensures that price (P_c) equals marginal cost (MC) and that the minimum average-total-cost output (Q_c) is produced. Both productive efficiency ($P = $ minimum ATC) and allocative efficiency ($P = MC$) are obtained. (b) In monopoly, the MR curve lies below the demand curve. The monopolist maximizes profit at output Q_m, where MR = MC, and charges price P_m. Thus, output is lower (Q_m rather than Q_c) and price is higher (P_m rather than P_c) than they would be in a perfectly competitive industry. Monopoly is inefficient, since output is less than that required for achieving minimum ATC (here at Q_c) and because the monopolist's price exceeds MC. Monopoly creates an efficiency loss (here of triangle *abc*). There is also a transfer of income from consumers to the monopoly (here of rectangle P_cP_mbd).

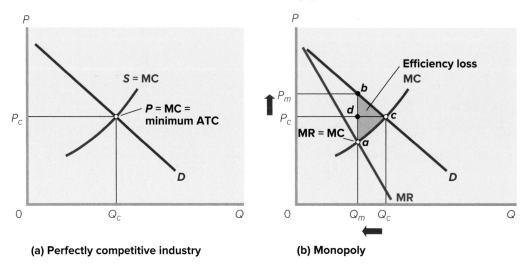

(a) Perfectly competitive industry   **(b) Monopoly**

The competitive market supply curve *S* has become the marginal-cost curve (MC) of the monopolist. (Since the monopolist does not have a supply curve as such, we have removed the *S* label.) The important change, however, is on the demand side. From the viewpoint of each individual competitive firm, demand was perfectly elastic, and marginal revenue was therefore equal to the market equilibrium price P_c. So each firm equated its marginal revenue of P_c dollars per unit with its individual marginal cost curve to maximize profits. But market demand and individual demand are the same to the monopolist. The firm *is* the industry, and thus the monopolist sees the downsloping demand curve *D* shown in Figure 11-6b.

This means that marginal revenue is less than price, and that graphically the MR curve lies below demand curve *D*. In using the MR = MC rule, the monopolist selects output Q_m and price P_m. A comparison of both graphs in Figure 11-6 reveals that the monopolist finds it profitable to sell a smaller output at a higher price than would prevail in a competitive industry.

Monopoly yields neither productive nor allocative efficiency. The lack of productive efficiency can be understood most directly by noting that the monopolist's output Q_m is less than Q_c, the output at which average total cost is lowest. In addition, the monopoly price P_m is higher than the competitive price P_c that we know in long-run equilibrium in pure competition equals minimum average total cost. Thus, the monopoly price exceeds minimum average total cost, thereby demonstrating in another way that the monopoly will not be productively efficient.

The monopolist's underproduction also implies allocative inefficiency. One way to see this is to note that at the monopoly output level Q_m, the monopoly price P_m that consumers are willing to pay exceeds the marginal cost of production. This means that consumers value additional units of this product more highly than they do the alternative products that could be produced from the resources that would be necessary to make more units of the monopolist's product.

The monopolist's allocative inefficiency can also be understood by noting that for every unit between Q_m and Q_c, marginal benefit exceeds marginal cost because the demand curve lies above the supply curve. By choosing not to produce these units, the monopolist reduces allocative efficiency because the resources that should have been used to make these units will be redirected instead toward producing items that bring lower net benefits to society. The total dollar value of this efficiency loss) is equal to the area of the blue triangle labelled *abc* in Figure 11-6b.

Monopoly and Deadweight Loss

In Figure 11-7 we have once again put a perfectly competitive industry alongside a monopoly to compare them. We have indicated the extent of consumer and producer surplus in each of the market structures. Recall from Chapter 10 that in a perfectly competitive market structure, equilibrium price P_c (= MC = minimum ATC) will create the

FIGURE 11-7   Monopoly and Deadweight Loss

(a) In perfect competition the long-run equilibrium price (P_c) and quantity (Q_c) maximize the sum of consumer surplus and producer surplus. (b) A monopolist restricts output to Q_m and increases price to P_m. Although the monopolist gains, a deadweight loss is created as a result of the lower consumer surplus brought about by the fall in output and rise in price.

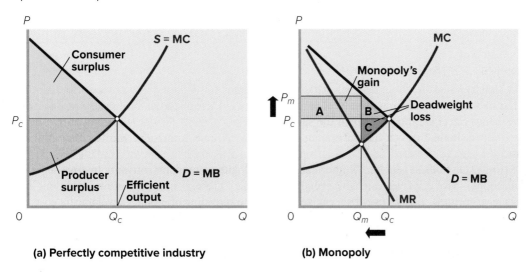

(a) Perfectly competitive industry   **(b) Monopoly**

maximum amount of consumer surplus and producer surplus, as indicated in Figure 11-7a. We also noted that in perfect competition marginal benefit equals marginal cost (MB = MC) at the equilibrium price and quantity, ensuring allocative efficiency.

In a monopoly, represented in Figure 11-7b, the output is lower than in a perfectly competitive market structure, and the profit-maximizing price P_m is above P_c, so consumers pay a price above the firm's (and the industry's) MC. At the lower output Q_m, the sum of consumer surplus and producer surplus has been reduced, compared to the perfect-competition scenario. The net loss of consumer surplus and producer surplus is referred to as **deadweight loss** of monopoly, and is indicated by the area covered by triangles B and C. At output Q_m, marginal benefit is greater than marginal cost (MB > MC), indicating that the monopolist is not producing as much output as consumers would like. Thus, allocative efficiency is not achieved.

Figure 11-7b shows that there has been a redistribution of resources from the consumer to the monopolist. The higher price results in a gain for the monopolist, represented by the grey area A. Consumers lose the consumer surplus represented by areas A and B, while the monopolist loses the producer surplus represented by area C, but gains area A. The monopolist will enjoy a net gain if its gain (area A) is larger than its loss of producer surplus (area C). The monopolist's gain is the difference between the monopoly price (P_m) and the equilibrium price in perfect competition (P_c) multiplied by the quantity sold (Q_m).

Income Transfer

In general, a monopoly transfers income from consumers to the owners of the monopoly. The income is received by the owners as revenue. Because a monopoly has market power, it can charge a higher price than would a perfectly competitive firm with the same costs. So the monopoly in effect levies a "private tax" on consumers. This private tax can often generate substantial economic profits that can persist because entry to the industry is blocked.

The transfer from consumers to the monopolist is evident in Figure 11-6b. For the Q_m units of output demanded, consumers pay price P_m rather than the price P_c that they would pay to a pure competitor. The total amount of income transferred from consumers to the monopolist is $P_m - P_c$ multiplied by the number of units sold, Q_m. So the total transfer is the dollar amount of rectangle $P_c P_m bd$. What the consumer loses, the monopolist gains. In contrast, the efficiency loss *abc* is a *deadweight loss*—society totally loses the net benefits of the Q_c minus Q_m units that are not produced.

Cost Complications

Our evaluation of monopoly has led us to conclude that, given identical costs, a monopolist will charge a higher price, produce a smaller output, and allocate economic resources less efficiently than a perfectly competitive industry. These inferior results are rooted in the entry barriers characterizing monopoly.

But costs may not be the same for a firm in a perfectly competitive industry and a monopolist. The unit cost incurred by a monopolist may be either larger or smaller than that incurred by a firm in a competitive industry. There are four reasons why costs may differ: (1) economies of scale, (2) a phenomenon called *X-inefficiency*, (3) the need for monopoly-preserving expenditures, and (4) the very-long-run perspective, which allows for technological advance.

ECONOMIES OF SCALE ONCE AGAIN

Where economies of scale are extensive, market demand may not be sufficient to support a large number of competing firms, each producing at minimum efficient scale. In such cases, an industry of one or two firms will have a lower average total cost than the same industry made up of numerous competitive firms. At the extreme, only a single firm—a natural monopoly—might be able to achieve the lowest long-run average total cost.

Some firms whose business is in new information technologies—computer software, Internet service, wireless communications—have displayed extensive economies of scale. As these firms have grown, their long-run average total costs have declined. Greater use of specialized inputs, the spreading of product development costs, and learning by doing all have produced economies of scale. Also, *simultaneous consumption* and *network effects* have reduced costs.

A product's ability to satisfy a large number of consumers at the same time is called **simultaneous consumption** (or *non-rivalrous consumption*). Dell Computer Corporation needs to produce a personal computer for each customer, but Microsoft needs to produce its Windows program only once. Then, at very low marginal cost, Microsoft delivers its program online or by disc to millions of consumers. A similarly low cost of delivering product to additional customers is true for Internet service providers, such as Rogers and Bell Canada, music producers, and wireless communications firms such as BlackBerry and Telus. Because marginal costs are so low, the average total cost of output declines as more customers are added.

Increases in the value of a product to each user, including existing users, as the total number of users rises are known as **network effects**. Good examples are computer software, cellphones, and websites like Facebook where the content is provided by users. When others have Internet service and devices to access it, you can conveniently send email messages to them. When they have similar software, you can easily pass around attachments like spreadsheets and photos. The more people are connected to the product, the more its benefits to each person are magnified.

Such network effects may drive a market toward monopoly, because consumers tend to choose standard products that everyone else is using. The focused demand for these products permits their producers to grow rapidly and thus achieve economies of scale. Smaller firms, which have either higher-cost "right" products or "wrong" products, get acquired or go out of business.

Economists generally agree that some new information firms have not yet exhausted their economies of scale, but it is questionable whether such firms are truly natural monopolies. Most firms eventually achieve their minimum efficient scale at less than the full size of the market. That means competition among firms is possible.

But even if natural monopoly develops, it's unlikely the monopolist will pass cost reductions along to consumers. So, with perhaps a handful of exceptions, economies of scale do not change the general conclusion that monopoly industries are inefficient relative to competitive industries.

X-INEFFICIENCY

In constructing all the average-total-cost curves used in this book, we have assumed that the firm uses the most efficient technology. This assumption is only natural because firms cannot maximize profits unless they are minimizing costs. **X-inefficiency** occurs when a firm produces output at a higher cost than is necessary to produce it. In Figure 11-8, X-inefficiency is represented by operation at points X and X' above the lowest-cost ATC curve. At these points, per-unit costs are ATC_X (as opposed to ATC_1) for output Q_1 and $ATC_{X'}$ (as opposed to ATC_2) for output Q_2. Producing at any point above the average-total-cost curve in Figure 11-8 reflects inefficiency or bad management by the firm.

FIGURE 11-8   X-Inefficiency

The average-total-cost curve (ATC) is assumed to reflect the minimum cost of producing each particular unit of output. Any point above this lowest-cost ATC curve, such as X or X', implies X-inefficiency: operation at greater than lowest cost for a particular level of output.

Why does X-inefficiency occur if it reduces profits? The answer is that managers of a firm may have goals such as expanding power, an easier work life, avoiding business risk, or giving jobs to incompetent relatives, all which conflict with cost minimization. Or X-inefficiency may arise because a firm's workers are poorly motivated or ineffectively supervised. Or a firm may simply become lethargic and inert, relying on rules of thumb in decision making as opposed to relevant calculations of costs and revenues.

For our purposes the relevant question is whether a monopolist suffers more X-inefficiency than competitive firms do. There is evidence that it does. Firms in competitive industries are continually under pressure from rivals, forcing them to be internally efficient to survive. But monopolists are sheltered from such competitive forces by entry barriers. That lack of pressure may lead to X-inefficiency.

RENT-SEEKING EXPENDITURES

A **rent-seeking behaviour** is an activity designed to transfer income or wealth to a particular firm or resource supplier at someone else's, or even society's, expense. We have seen that a monopolist can obtain an economic profit even in the long run. Therefore, it is no surprise that a firm may go to great expense to acquire or maintain a monopoly granted by government through legislation or an exclusive licence. Such rent-seeking expenditures add nothing to the firm's output, but they clearly increase its costs. Taken alone, rent seeking implies that monopoly has even higher costs and even less efficiency than suggested in Figure 11-6b.

TECHNOLOGICAL ADVANCE

In the very long run, firms can reduce their costs through the discovery and implementation of new technology. If monopolists are more likely than competitive firms to develop more efficient production techniques over time, the inefficiency of monopoly might be overstated. Because research and development (R&D) is the topic of Chapter 19, we will provide only a brief assessment here.

The general view of economists is that a monopolist will not be technologically progressive. Although its economic profit provides ample means to finance research and development, it has little incentive to implement new techniques (or products). Because of its sheltered market position, the monopolist can afford to be complacent and lethargic. There simply is no major penalty for not being innovative.

One caveat: Research and technological advance can be a barrier to entry. Thus, the monopolist may continuously seek technological advance to avoid falling prey to new rivals. In this case, technological advance is essential to maintaining monopoly. But it is potential competition—not the monopoly market structure—that drives this technological advance. By assumption, no such competition exists in the monopoly model; entry is completely blocked.

Assessment and Policy Options

Monopoly is of legitimate concern because the monopolist can charge higher-than-competitive prices that result in an underallocation of resources. Monopolists can stifle innovation, foster X-inefficiency, and engage in rent-seeking behaviour. Even when their costs are low because of economies of scale, monopolists are unlikely to charge a price that reflects those low costs. The cost savings may simply accrue to the monopoly as greater economic profit.

Fortunately, however, monopoly is not widespread in the Canadian economy. Barriers to entry are seldom completely successful. Although research and technological advance may strengthen the market position of a monopoly, technology may also undermine monopoly power. Over time, the creation of new technologies may work to destroy monopoly positions. For example, the development of courier delivery, fax machines, and email has eroded the monopoly power of Canada Post Corporation. Similarly, cable television monopolies are now challenged by satellite TV and by new technologies that permit the transmission of audio and video over the Internet.

Patents eventually expire—and even before they do, the development of new and distinct products can undermine existing patent advantages. New sources of monopolized resources can be found, and competition from foreign firms may emerge (see Global Perspective 11.1). Finally, if a monopoly is sufficiently fearful of future competition from new products, it may keep its prices relatively low to discourage rivals from developing such products. If so, consumers may pay nearly competitive prices even though present competition is lacking.

So what should a government do about monopoly when it arises in the real world? The government needs to look carefully at monopoly on a case-by-case basis. Three general policy options are available:

1. If the monopoly is achieved and sustained through anticompetitive actions, creates substantial economic inefficiency, and appears to be long lasting, the government can file charges against the monopoly under Canada's

11.1 GLOBAL PERSPECTIVE

Competition from Foreign Multinational Corporations

Competition from foreign multinational corporations diminishes the market power of firms in Canada. Here are just a few of the hundreds of foreign multinational corporations that compete strongly with Canadian firms in certain Canadian markets.

Company (Country)	Main Products
Bayer (Germany)	chemicals
Daimler (Germany)	automobiles
Michelin (France)	tires
Lenovo (China)	electronics
Nestlé (Switzerland)	food products
Walmart (U.S.A.)	general merchandiser
Panasonic (Japan)	electronics
Exxon (U.S.A.)	gasoline
Apple (U.S.A.)	wireless phones
Samsung (South Korea)	electronics
Toyota (Japan)	automobiles

Source: Compiled from the Fortune 500 listing of the world's largest firms, "*Fortune* Global 500," 2016, www.fortune.com.

anticombines laws. If found guilty of monopoly abuse, the firm can either be prohibited from engaging in certain business activities or be broken into two or more competing firms.

2. If the monopoly is a natural monopoly, it may be allowed to continue expanding. If no competition emerges from new products, the government may then decide to regulate its prices and operations.

3. If the monopoly appears to be unsustainable because of emerging new technology, society can simply choose to ignore it. In such cases, society simply lets the process of creative destruction (discussed in Chapter 10) do its work. In Chapter 19, we discuss in detail the likelihood that real-world monopolies will collapse due to creative destruction and competition brought on by new technologies.

QUICK REVIEW 11.2

- The monopolist maximizes profit (or minimizes loss) at the output where MR = MC and charges the price that corresponds to that output on its demand curve.

- The monopolist has no supply curve, since any of several prices can be associated with a specific quantity of output supplied.

- Assuming identical costs, a monopolist will be less efficient than a perfectly competitive industry because it will fail to produce units of output for which marginal benefits exceed marginal costs.

- The inefficiency brought about by monopoly is referred to as deadweight loss.

- The inefficiencies of monopoly may be offset or lessened by economies of scale and, less likely, by technological progress, but may be intensified by the presence of X-inefficiency and rent-seeking expenditures.

11.6 Price Discrimination

LO11.6   Describe why a monopolist might prefer to charge different prices in different markets.

We have assumed in this chapter that the monopolist charges a single price to all buyers. But under certain conditions the monopolist can increase its profit by charging different prices to different buyers. In so doing, the monopolist is engaging in **price discrimination**, the practice of selling a product or service at more than one price when the price differences are not justified by cost differences. Price discrimination can take three forms:

- Charging each customer in a single market the maximum price she or he is willing to pay.

- Charging each customer one price for the first set of units purchased and a lower price for subsequent units purchased.

- Charging some customers one price and other customers another price.

Conditions

The opportunity to engage in price discrimination is not readily available to all sellers. Price discrimination is possible when the following conditions are met:

- *Monopoly Power*   The seller must be a monopolist with some ability to control output and price.

- *Market Segregation*   The seller must be able to segregate buyers into distinct classes, each of which has a different willingness or ability to pay for the product. This separation of buyers is usually based on different price elasticities of demand, as the examples that follow will make clear.

- *No Resale*   The original purchaser cannot resell the product or service. If buyers in the low-price segment of the market could easily resell in the high-price segment, the monopolist's price-discrimination strategy would create competition in the high-price segment. This competition would reduce the price in the high-price segment and undermine the monopolist's price-discrimination policy. This suggests that service industries such as transportation or legal and medical services, where resale is impossible, are good candidates for price discrimination.

Examples of Price Discrimination

Price discrimination is widely practised in the Canadian economy. For example, we noted in Chapter 6's Last Word that airlines, such as Air Canada, charge high fares to travelling executives, whose demand for travel is inelastic, and offer lower highly restricted, nonrefundable fares to attract vacationers and others whose demands are more elastic.

Movie theatres and golf courses vary their charges on the basis of time (higher rates in the evening and on weekends when demand is strong) and age (ability to pay). Railways vary the rate charged per tonne-kilometre of freight according to the market value of the product being shipped; the shipper of ten tonnes of television sets or costume jewellery is charged more than the shipper of ten tonnes of gravel or coal.

Issuing discount coupons redeemable at purchase is a form of price discrimination. It enables firms to give price discounts to their most price-sensitive customers who have elastic demand. Less price-sensitive consumers who have less elastic demand are not as likely to take the time to clip and redeem coupons. The firm thus makes a larger profit than if it had used a single-price, no-coupon strategy.

Price discrimination can often occur in international trade. A Russian aluminum producer, for example, might sell aluminum for less in Canada than in Russia. In Canada, this seller faces an elastic demand because several substitute suppliers are available. But in Russia, where the manufacturer dominates the market and trade barriers impede imports, consumers have fewer choices and thus demand is less elastic. (See the Consider This box for another example of price discrimination.)

Graphical Analysis

Figure 11-9 demonstrates graphically the most common form of price discrimination—charging different prices to different classes of buyers. The two side-to-side graphs are for a monopolist selling its product—say software—in two segregated parts of the market. Figure 11-9a illustrates demand for software by small-business customers; Figure 11-9b illustrates demand for software by students. Student versions of the software are identical to the

CONSIDER THIS

Price Discrimination at the Ballpark

A professional baseball team such as the Toronto Blue Jays earns substantial revenues through ticket sales. To maximize profit they offer significantly lower ticket prices for youths (whose demand is elastic) than for adults (whose demand is inelastic). This discount may be as much as 50 percent.

© Stephen Dunn/Getty Images

If this type of price discrimination increases revenue and profit, why don't teams also price discriminate at the concession stands? Why don't they offer half-price hot dogs, soft drinks, and peanuts to children?

The answer involves the three requirements for successful price discrimination. All three requirements are met for game tickets: (1) the team has monopoly power; (2) it can segregate ticket buyers by age group, each group having a different elasticity of demand; and (3) youths cannot resell their discounted tickets to adults.

It's a different situation at the concession stands. Specifically, the third condition is *not* met. If the team had dual prices, it could not prevent the exchange or resale of the concession goods from youths to adults. Many adults would send youths to buy food and soft drinks for them: "Here's some money, Billy. Go buy six hot dogs." In this case, price discrimination would reduce, not increase, team profit. Thus, youths and adults are charged the same high prices at the concession stands. (These prices are high relative to those for the same goods at the local convenience store because the stadium sellers have a captive audience and thus considerable monopoly power.)

versions sold to businesses but are available (one per person) only to customers with a student ID. Presumably, students have lower ability to pay for the software and are charged a discounted price.

The demand curve D_b in graph (a) indicates a relatively inelastic demand for the product on the part of business customers. The demand curve D_s, located in the right-hand graph, reflects the more elastic demand of students. The marginal revenue curves (MR_b and MR_s) lie below their respective demand curves, reflecting the demand–marginal revenue relationship previously described.

FIGURE 11-9   Price Discrimination to Different Groups of Buyers

The price-discriminating monopolist represented here maximizes its total profit by dividing the market into two segments based on differences in elasticity of demand. It then produces and sells the MR = MC output in each market segment. (For visual clarity, average total cost [ATC] is assumed to be constant. Therefore MC equals ATC at all output levels.) (a) The price-discriminating monopolist charges a high price (here, P_b) to small-business customers because they have a relatively inelastic demand curve for the product. (b) The firm charges a low price (here, P_s) to students because their demand curve is relatively elastic. The firm's total profit from using price discrimination (here, the sum of the two grey rectangles) exceeds the profit (not shown) that would have occurred if the monopolist had charged the same price to all customers.

(a) Small businesses

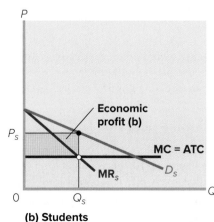

(b) Students

For visual clarity we have assumed that average total cost (ATC) is constant. Therefore, marginal cost (MC) equals ATC at all quantities of output. These costs are the same for both versions of the software and therefore appear as the identical straight lines labelled MC = ATC.

What price will the monopolist charge each set of customers? Using the MR = MC rule for profit maximization, the firm will offer Q_b units of the software for sale to small businesses. It can sell that profit-maximizing output by charging price P_b. Again using the MR = MC rule, the monopolist will offer Q_s units of software to students. To sell those Q_s units, the firm will charge students the lower price P_s.

Firms engage in price discrimination because it enhances their profit. The numbers (not shown) behind the curves in Figure 11-9 would clearly reveal that the sum of the two profit rectangles shown in colour exceeds the single profit rectangle the firm would obtain from a single monopoly price. How do consumers fare? In this case, students clearly benefit by paying a lower price than they would if the firm charged a single monopoly price; in contrast, the price discrimination results in a higher price for business customers. Therefore, compared to the single-price situation, students buy more of the software and small businesses buy less.

WORKED PROBLEM 11.2   Price Discrimination

Such price discrimination is widespread in the economy and is illegal only when it is part of a firm's strategy to lessen or eliminate competition. We will discuss illegal price discrimination in Chapter 13 where we discuss anti-combines policy.

11.7 Regulated Monopoly

   THE ROLE OF GOVERNMENTS

LO11.7   **Distinguish between the monopoly price, the socially optimal price, and the fair-return price of a government-regulated monopoly.**

Natural monopolies traditionally have been subject to *rate regulation* (price regulation), although the recent trend has been to deregulate those parts of the industries where competition seems possible. For example, long-distance phone service, natural gas distribution, wireless communication, cable television, and long-distance electricity transmission have been, to one degree or another, deregulated over the past several decades. And regulators in some provinces are beginning to allow new entrants to compete with local telephone and electricity providers. Nevertheless, provincial and local regulatory commissions still regulate the prices that most local natural gas distributors, regional telephone companies, and local electricity suppliers can charge. These locally regulated monopolies are commonly called "public utilities."

Let's consider the regulation of a local natural monopoly. Our example will be a single firm that is the only seller of natural gas in the town of Springfield. Figure 11-10 shows the demand and long-run cost curves facing our firm. Because of extensive economies of scale, the demand curve cuts the natural monopolist's long-run average-total-cost curve at a point where that curve is still falling. It would be inefficient to have several firms in this industry because each firm's lowest average total cost would be substantially higher than that of a single firm. So efficient, lowest-cost production requires a single seller.

We know by application of the MR = MC rule that Q_m and P_m are the profit-maximizing output and price that an unregulated monopolist would choose. Because price exceeds average total cost at output Q_m, the monopolist enjoys a substantial economic profit. Furthermore, price exceeds marginal cost, indicating an underallocation of resources to this product or service. Can government regulation bring about better results from society's point of view?

Socially Optimal Price: $P = MC$

One sensible goal for regulators would be to get the monopoly to produce the allocatively efficient output level. For our monopolist in Figure 11-10, this is output level Q_r, determined by where the demand curve D intersects the MC curve. Q_r is the allocatively efficient output level because for each unit of output up to Q_r, the demand curve lies above the MC curve, indicating that for all of these units marginal benefits exceed marginal costs.

FIGURE 11-10 Regulated Monopoly

The socially optimal price P_r, found where D and MC intersect, will result in an efficient allocation of resources but may entail losses to the monopoly. The fair-return price P_f will allow the monopolist to break even but will not fully correct the underallocation of resources.

But how can the regulatory commission actually motivate the monopoly to produce this output level? The trick is to set the regulated price P_r at a level such that the monopoly will be led by its profit-maximizing rule to voluntarily produce the allocatively efficiently level of output. To see how this works, note that because the monopoly will receive the regulated price P_r for all units that it sells, P_r becomes the monopoly's marginal revenue per unit. Thus, the monopoly's MR curve becomes the horizontal black line moving to the right from price P_r on the vertical axis.

The monopoly will at this point follow its usual rule for maximizing profits or minimizing losses: It will produce where marginal revenue equals marginal cost. As a result, the monopoly will produce where the horizontal MR ($= P_r$) line intersects the MC curve at point r. That is, the monopoly will end up producing the socially optimal output Q_r not because it is socially minded but because Q_r happens to be the output that either maximizes profits or minimizes losses when the firm is forced by the regulators to sell all units at the regulated price P_r.

The regulated price P_r that achieves allocative efficiency is called the **socially optimal price**. Because it is determined by where the MC curve intersects the demand curve, this type of regulation is often summarized by the equation $P = MC$.

Fair-Return Price: $P = ATC$

The socially optimal price suffers from a potentially fatal problem. P_r may be so low that average total costs are not covered, as is the case in Figure 11-10. In such situations, forcing the socially optimal price on the regulated monopoly would result in short-run losses and long-run exit. In our example, Springfield would be left without a gas company and its citizens without gas.

What can be done to rectify this problem? One option is to provide a public subsidy to cover the loss that the socially optimal price would entail. Another possibility is to condone price discrimination, allow the monopoly to charge some customers prices above P_r, and hope that the additional revenue that the monopoly gains from price discrimination will be enough to permit it to break even.

In practice, regulatory commissions in Canada have often pursued a third option that abandons the goal of producing every unit for which marginal benefits exceed marginal costs but which guarantees that regulated monopolies will be able to break even and continue in operation. Under this third option, regulators set a regulated price that is high enough for monopolists to break even and continue in operation. This price has come to be referred to as a **fair-return price** because the regulatory agencies must permit regulated utility owners to enjoy a "fair return" on their investments.

In practice, a fair return is equal to a normal profit. That is, a fair return is an accounting profit equal in size to what the owners of the monopoly would on average receive if they entered another type of business.

The regulator determines the fair-return price P_f by where the average total cost curve intersects the demand curve at point f. As we will explain, setting the regulated price at this level will cause the monopoly to produce Q_f

units while guaranteeing that it will break even and not wish to exit the industry. To see why the monopoly will voluntarily produce Q_f units, note that because the monopoly will receive P_f dollars for each unit it sells, its marginal revenue per unit becomes P_f dollars so that the horizontal line moving rightward from P_f on the vertical axis becomes the regulated monopoly's MR curve. Because this horizontal MR curve is always higher than the monopoly's MC curve, it is obvious that marginal revenues will exceed marginal costs for every possible level of output shown in Figure 11-10. Thus, the monopoly should be willing to supply whatever quantity of output is demanded by consumers at the regulated price P_f. That quantity is, of course, given by the demand curve. At price P_f, consumers will demand exactly Q_f units. Thus, by setting the regulated price at P_f, the regulator gets the monopoly to voluntarily supply exactly Q_f units.

Even better, the regulator also guarantees that the monopoly firm will earn exactly a normal profit. This can be seen in Figure 11-10 by noting that the rectangle $0afb$ is equal to both the monopoly's total cost and its total revenue. Its economic profit is therefore equal to zero, implying that it must be earning a normal accounting profit for its owners.

We will make one final point about allocative efficiency. By choosing the fair return price P_f, the regulator leads the monopoly to produce Q_f units. This is less than the socially optimal quantity Q_r, but still more than the Q_m units that the monopolist would produce if left unregulated. So while fair-return pricing does not lead to full allocative efficiency, it is still an improvement on what the monopoly would do if left to its own devices.

Dilemma of Regulation

Comparing results of the socially optimal price ($P = $ MC) and the fair-return price ($P = $ ATC) suggests a policy dilemma, sometimes termed the *dilemma of regulation*. When its price is set to achieve the most efficient allocation of resources ($P = $ MC), the regulated monopoly is likely to suffer losses. Survival of the firm would depend on permanent public subsidies from tax revenues. Conversely, although a fair-return price ($P = $ ATC) allows the monopolist to cover costs, it only partially resolves the underallocation of resources that the unregulated monopoly price would foster. Despite this dilemma, regulation can improve on the results of monopoly from the social point of view. Price regulation (even at the fair-return price) can simultaneously reduce price, increase output, and reduce the economic profit of monopolies.

That said, we need to provide an important caution: Fair-price regulation of monopoly looks rather simple in theory but is amazingly complex in practice. In the actual economy, rate regulation is accompanied by large, expensive rate-setting bureaucracies and maze-like sets of procedures. Also, rate decisions require extensive public input via letters and thorough public hearings. Rate decisions are subject to lengthy legal challenges. Further, because regulatory commissions must set prices sufficiently above costs to create fair returns, regulated monopolists have little incentive to minimize average total costs. When these costs creep up, the regulatory commissions must set higher prices.

Regulated firms therefore are noted for higher-than-competitive wages, more managers and staff than necessary, nicer-than-typical office buildings, and other forms of X-inefficiency. These inefficiencies help explain the trend of federal, provincial, and municipal governments to abandon price regulation where the possibility of competition looks promising.

QUICK REVIEW 11.3

- Price discrimination occurs when a firm sells a product at different prices that are not based on cost differences.

- The conditions necessary for price discrimination are (1) monopoly power, (2) the ability to segregate buyers based on demand elasticities, and (3) the inability of buyers to resell the product.

- Compared with single pricing by a monopolist, perfect price discrimination results in greater profit and greater output. Many consumers pay higher prices, but other buyers pay prices below the single price.

- Monopoly price can be reduced and output increased through government regulation.

- The socially optimal price ($P = $ MC) achieves allocative efficiency but may result in losses; the fair-return price ($P = $ ATC) yields a normal profit but falls short of allocative efficiency.

The LAST WORD

Personalized Pricing

© Miss Ty/Shutterstock.com

The perils of online price discrimination.

Internet retailers collect vast amounts of data about their customers. They know what you buy, who your friends are, what posts you like on Facebook, what websites you visit, and—by connecting that information with other data—how old you are, where you live, your credit history, and so on.

This huge collection of "Big Data" can be used by retailers with monopoly power to engage in an individually tailored form of price discrimination known as personalized pricing. As discussed in this chapter, price discrimination involves selling the same product to different buyers at different prices when the price differences are not justified by cost differences.

Traditionally, price discrimination has operated at the group level with, for example, senior citizens getting discounts at restaurants and children under the age of twelve getting discounts on movie tickets. Groups with relatively inelastic demand get charged higher prices while groups with relatively elastic demand get charged lower prices.

The trick behind personalized pricing is that online retailers now have the ability to set individualized prices for most patrons. When that is possible, a firm with monopoly power can set the very lowest price for the person with the most elastic demand, a slightly higher price for the person with the next-most-elastic demand, and so on all the way up to the highest price being presented to the person with the most *in*elastic demand.

By proceeding in this manner, the monopoly seller can attempt to set a price for each individual that is just below his or her reservation price. Doing so allows the monopoly seller to squeeze out as much revenue as possible from each customer while still leaving him or her with a bit of consumer surplus (and thus with a motive to still buy the product).

For an offline example of how personalized pricing works, think of car dealerships, where the final price paid by a buyer is usually the result of a negotiation. In particular, keep in mind that a car salesperson will negotiate much more aggressively if you

drive up in a fancy BMW rather than an average Hyundai. He or she will try to tailor the final price to your perceived ability to pay. Big Data allows the same tactic to be used online. The more online retailers know about your buying habits, background, and preferences, the more they can attempt to set a price that will maximize what they can get from you.

But personalized pricing has its limits. Most importantly, very few firms actually have any substantial monopoly power. As just one example, car dealers have to compete with each other. So a dealership that is driving too hard a bargain will drive customers toward rival dealers. That competitive pressure is probably even stronger online, where search engines and vast digital retail sites like eBay and Amazon often list multiple competing sellers for every item.

But even if a seller were to have monopoly power online, it would still confront another problem. Even with Big Data, it is hard for sellers to figure out what each potential buyer's reservation price is. So even if a firm with monopoly power wished to attempt personalized pricing, it probably wouldn't ever be able to figure out how to set a customized price for each individual.

On the other hand, online shoppers give up all their advantages if they fail to comparison-shop. If they treat the first seller they deal with as the only one, they are implicitly giving that seller monopoly power over them. In those situations, online merchants can run wild with personalized pricing. For example, in 2014, the U.S. company Allstate Insurance admitted to Wisconsin insurance regulators that its personalized pricing computer algorithms had presented essentially identical online customers with insurance prices that varied massively, in some cases by more than 800 percent. In many instances, the differences were driven by factors as trivial as one customer having a birthdate of January 12, 1968, and another having one of April 9, 1968.

Allstate customers who failed to shop around left themselves open to paying much more than they had to. Online shopping is speedy and convenient—but it still pays to shop around.

Question

Using Big Data to set personalized prices cannot be done with 100 percent precision. What would happen if personalized prices were set higher than customers' reservation prices? Would this possibility reduce the incentive to set the highest possible personalized prices? How can consumers protect themselves from personalized prices?

Chapter Summary

LO11.1   List the characteristics of monopoly.

- A monopolist is the sole producer of a commodity for which there are no close substitutes.

LO11.2   List and explain the barriers to entry that shield monopolies from competition.

- The existence of monopoly and other imperfectly competitive market structures is explained by barriers to entry, in the form of (a) economies of scale, (b) patents and licences, (c) ownership or control of essential factors of production, and (d) pricing and other strategic behaviour.

LO11.3   Explain how demand is seen by a monopolist.

- The monopolist's market situation differs from that of a competitive firm in that the monopolist's demand curve is downsloping, causing the marginal-revenue curve to lie below the demand curve. Like the competitive seller, the monopolist will maximize profit by equating marginal revenue and marginal cost. Barriers to entry may permit a monopolist to acquire economic profit even in the long run. However, (a) the monopolist does not charge the highest price it can get, (b) the price that yields maximum total profit to the monopolist rarely coincides with the price that yields maximum unit profit, (c) high costs and a weak demand may prevent the monopolist from realizing any profit at all, and (d) the monopolist avoids the inelastic region of its demand curve.

LO11.4   Explain how a monopolist sets its maximizing output and price.

- The monopolist maximizes profit (or minimizes loss) at the output where MR = MC and charges the price that corresponds to that output on its demand curve.

- With the same costs, the monopolist will find it profitable to restrict output and charge a higher price than would sellers in a purely competitive industry. This restriction of output causes resources to be misallocated, as is shown by the fact that price exceeds marginal cost in monopolized markets.

LO11.5   Discuss the economic effects of monopoly.

- Monopoly transfers income from consumers to monopolists because a monopolist can charge a higher price than would a perfectly competitive firm with the same costs. So monopolists in effect levy a "private tax" on consumers, and if demand is strong enough, obtain substantial economic profits.

- The costs monopolists and competitive producers face may not be the same. On the one hand, economies of scale may make lower unit costs available to monopolists but not to competitors, and monopoly may be more likely than perfect competition to reduce costs via technological advance because of the monopolist's ability to realize economic profit, which can be used to finance research. On the other hand, X-inefficiency is more common among monopolists than among competitive firms. Also, monopolists may make costly expenditures to maintain monopoly privileges that are conferred by government. Finally, the blocked entry of rival firms weakens the monopolist's incentive to be technologically progressive.

- The inefficiency of monopoly can be measured using the concepts of consumer surplus and producer surplus. The efficiency loss associated with monopoly is called deadweight loss.

LO11.6   Describe why a monopolist might prefer to charge different prices in different markets.

- A monopolist can increase its profit by practising price discrimination, provided (a) it can segregate buyers on the basis of elasticities of demand and (b) its product or service cannot be readily transferred between the segregated markets.

LO11.7   Distinguish between the monopoly price, the socially optimal price, and the fair-return price of a government-regulated monopoly.

- Price regulation can be invoked to wholly or partially eliminate the tendency of monopolists to underallocate resources and to earn economic profits. The socially optimal price is determined where the demand and marginal-cost curves intersect; the fair-return price is determined where the demand and average-total-cost curves intersect.

Terms and Concepts

monopoly
barriers to entry
deadweight loss
simultaneous consumption
network effects

X-inefficiency
rent-seeking behaviour
price discrimination
socially optimal price
fair-return price

Discussion Questions

1. "No firm is completely sheltered from rivals; all firms compete for consumer dollars. If that is so, then monopoly does not exist." Do you agree? Explain. How might you use Chapter 6's concept of cross elasticity of demand to judge whether monopoly exists?   [**LO11.1**]

2. Discuss the major barriers to entry into an industry. Explain how each barrier can foster either monopoly or oligopoly. Which barriers, if any, do you believe give rise to monopoly that is socially justifiable?   [**LO11.2**]

3. How does the demand curve faced by a monopolistic seller differ from that confronting a perfectly competitive firm? Why does it differ? Of what significance is the difference? Why is the monopolist's demand curve not perfectly inelastic?   [**LO11.3**]

4. Assume that a monopolist and a perfectly competitive firm have the same unit costs. Contrast the two with respect to (a) price, (b) output, (c) profits, (d) allocation of resources, and (e) impact on income transfers. Since both monopolists and competitive firms follow the MC = MR rule in maximizing profits, how do you account for the different results? Why might the costs of a perfectly competitive firm and a monopolist be different? What are the implications of such a cost difference?   [**LO11.5**]

5. Critically evaluate and explain the following statements: [**LO11.5**]

   a. Because they can control product price, monopolists are always assured of profitable production by simply charging the highest price consumers will pay.

   b. The monopolist seeks the output that will yield the greatest per-unit profit.

   c. An excess of price over marginal cost is the market's way of signalling the need for more production of a good.

   d. The more profitable a firm, the greater its monopoly power.

   e. The monopolist has a pricing policy; the competitive producer does not.

   f. With respect to resource allocation, the interests of the seller and of society coincide in a perfectly competitive market but conflict in a monopolized market.

6. Assume a monopolistic publisher has agreed to pay an author 10 percent of the total revenue from the sales of a text. Will the author and the publisher want to charge the same price for the text? Explain.   [**LO11.5**]

7. U.S. pharmaceutical companies charge different prices for prescription drugs to buyers in different nations, including Canada, depending on elasticity of demand and government-imposed price ceilings. Explain why these companies, for profit reasons, oppose laws allowing the re-importation of drugs to the United States.   [**LO11.6**]

8. Explain in words and graphically how price (rate) regulation may improve the performance of monopolies. In your answer distinguish between (a) socially optimal (marginal-cost) pricing and (b) fair-return (average-total-cost) pricing. What is the "dilemma of regulation"?   [**LO11.7**]

9. It has been proposed that natural monopolists should be allowed to determine their profit-maximizing outputs and prices and then government should tax their profits away and distribute them to consumers in proportion to their purchases from the monopoly. Is this proposal as socially desirable as requiring monopolists to equate price with marginal cost or average total cost?   [**LO11.7**]

Review Questions

1. Which of the following could explain why a firm is a monopoly? Select *one or more* answers from the choices shown.   [**LO11.2**]

   a. Patents

   b. Economies of scale

   c. Inelastic demand

   d. Government licenses

   e. Downsloping market demand

2. The MR curve of a perfectly competitive firm is horizontal. The MR curve of a monopoly firm is   [**LO11.3**]

   a. Also horizontal

   b. Upsloping

   c. Downsloping

   d. It depends

3. Use the demand schedule that follows to calculate total revenue and marginal revenue at each quantity. Plot the demand, total-revenue, and marginal-revenue curves, and explain the relationships among them. Explain why the marginal revenue of the fourth unit of output is $3.50, even though its price is $5. Use Chapter 6's total-revenue test for price elasticity to designate the elastic and inelastic segments of your graphed demand curve. What generalization can you make about the relationship between marginal revenue and elasticity of demand? Suppose the marginal cost of successive units of output were zero. What output would the profit-seeking firm produce? Finally, use your analysis to explain why a monopolist

would never produce in the inelastic region of demand. [**LO11.3**]

Price (P)	Quantity demanded (Q)	Price (P)	Quantity demanded (Q)
$7.00	0	$4.50	5
6.50	1	4.00	6
6.00	2	3.50	7
5.50	3	3.00	8
5.00	4	2.50	9

4. How often do *perfectly competitive* firms engage in price discrimination?   [**LO11.6**]

   a. Never

   b. Rarely

   c. Often

   d. Always

5. Suppose that a monopolist can segregate his buyers into two different groups to which he can charge two different prices.

In order to maximize profit, the monopolist should charge a higher price to the group that has   [**LO11.6**]

   a. The higher elasticity of demand

   b. The lower elasticity of demand

   c. Richer members

6. The socially optimal price (P = MC) is socially optimal because   [**LO11.7**]

   a. It reduces the monopolist's profit

   b. It yields a normal profit

   c. It minimizes ATC

   d. It achieves allocative efficiency

7. The main problem with imposing the socially optimal price (P = MC) on a monopoly is that the socially optimal price is that it   [**LO11.7**]

   a. May be so low that the regulated monopoly can't break even

   b. May cause the regulated monopoly to engage in price discrimination

   c. May be higher than the monopoly price

Problems

1. Suppose a monopolist is faced with the demand schedule shown below and the same cost data as the competitive producer discussed in Problem 4 at the end of Chapter 9. Calculate the missing total-revenue and marginal-revenue amounts, and determine the profit-maximizing price and profit-maximizing output for this monopolist. What is the monopolist's profit? Verify your answer graphically and by comparing total revenue and total cost.   [**LO11.4**]

Price	Quantity demanded	Total revenue	Marginal revenue
$115	0	$____	$____
100	1	____	____
83	2	____	____
71	3	____	____
63	4	____	____
55	5	____	____
48	6	____	____
42	7	____	____
37	8	____	____
33	9	____	____
29	10	____	

2. Suppose that a price-discriminating monopolist has segregated its market into two groups of buyers. The first group is described by the demand and revenue data that you developed for Problem 1. The demand and revenue data for the second group of buyers is shown in the table below. Assume that MC is $13 in both markets and MC = ATC at all output levels. What price will the firm charge in each market? Based solely on these two prices, which market has the higher price elasticity of demand? What will be this monopolist's total economic profit?   [**LO11.6**]

Price	Quantity demanded	Total revenue	Marginal revenue
$71	0	$ 0	
			$63
63	1	63	
			47
55	2	110	
			34
48	3	144	
			24
42	4	168	
			17
37	5	185	
			13
33	6	198	
			5
29	7	203	

3. Assume that the most efficient production technology available for making vitamin pills has the cost structure given in the

following table. Note that output is measured as the number of bottles of vitamins produced per day and that costs included a normal profit.   [**LO11.6**]

Output	TC	MC
25,000	$100,000	$0.50
50,000	150,000	1.00
75,000	187,500	2.50
100,000	275,500	3.00

a. What is ATC per unit for each level of output listed in the table?

b. Is this a decreasing-cost industry? (Answer yes or no.)

c. Suppose that the market price for a bottle of vitamins is $1.33 and that at that price the total market quantity demanded is 75,000,000 bottles. How many firms will there be in this industry?

d. Suppose that, instead, the market quantity demanded at a price of $1.33 is only 75,000 bottles. How many firms do you expect there to be in this industry?

e. Review your answers to parts (b), (c), and (d). Does the level of demand determine this industry's market structure?

4. A new production technology for making vitamins is invented by a university professor who decides not to patent it. Thus, it is available for anybody to copy and put into use. The TC per bottle for production up to 100,000 bottles per day is given in the following table.   [**LO11.6**]

Output	TC
25,000	$50,000
50,000	70,000
75,000	75,000
100,000	80,000

a. What is ATC for each level of output listed in the table?

b. Suppose that for each 25,000 bottle per day increase in production above 100,000 bottles per day, TC increases by $5000 (so that, for instance, 125,000 bottles per day would generate total costs of $85,000 and 150,000 bottles per day would generate total costs of $90,000). Is this a decreasing-cost industry?

c. Suppose that the price of a bottle of vitamins is $1.33 and at that price the total quantity demanded by consumers is 75,000,000 bottles. How many firms will there be in this industry?

d. Suppose that, instead, the market quantity demanded at a price of $1.33 is only 75,000. How many firms do you expect there to be in this industry?

e. Review your answers to parts (b), (c), and (d). Does the level of demand determine this industry's market structure?

f. Compare your answer to part (d) of this question with your answer to part (d) of Problem 3. Do both production technologies show constant returns to scale?

5. Suppose you have been tasked with regulating a single monopoly firm that sells 50-kilogram bags of concrete. The firm has fixed costs of $10 million per year and a variable cost of $1 per bag no matter how many bags are produced. [**LO11.7**]

a. If this firm kept on increasing its output level, would ATC per bag ever increase? Is this a decreasing-cost industry?

b. If you wished to regulate this monopoly by charging the socially optimal price, what price would you charge? At that price, what would be the size of the firm's profit or loss? Would the firm want to exit the industry?

c. You find out that if you set the price at $2 per bag, consumers will demand 10 million bags. How big will the firm's profit or loss be at that price?

d. If consumers instead demanded 20 million bags at a price of $2 per bag, how big would the firm's profit or loss be?

e. Suppose demand is perfectly inelastic at 20 million bags, so that consumers demand 20 million bags no matter what the price. What price should you charge if you want the firm to earn only fair rate of return? Assume, as always, that TC includes a normal profit.

CHAPTER 12

Monopolistic Competition

LEARNING OBJECTIVES

LO12.1	List the characteristics of monopolistic competition.
LO12.2	Explain why monopolistic competitors earn only a normal profit in the long run.
LO12.3	Explain why monopolistic competition delivers neither productive nor allocative efficiency.
LO12.4	Relate how the ability of monopolistic competition to deliver product differentiation helps to compensate for its failure to deliver economic efficiency.

In Canada, most industries have a market structure that falls somewhere between the two poles of perfect competition and monopoly. To begin with, most real-world industries have fewer than the large number of producers required for perfect competition but more than the single producer that defines monopoly. In addition, most firms in most industries have both distinguishable rather than standardized products and some discretion over the prices they charge. As a result, competition often occurs on the basis of price, quality, location, service, and advertising. Finally, entry to most real-world industries ranges from easy to very difficult but is rarely completely blocked.

This chapter examines the first of two models that more closely approximate these widespread industry structures. In this chapter, you will discover that *monopolistic competition* mixes a small amount of monopoly power with a large amount of competition. In Chapter 13, you will see how *oligopoly* blends a large amount of monopoly power with both considerable rivalry among existing firms and the threat of increased future competition due to foreign firms and new technologies. (You should quickly review Table 9-1 at this point.)

12.1 Monopolistic Competition

LO12.1 List the characteristics of monopolistic competition.

Let's begin by examining **monopolistic competition**, which is characterized by (1) a relatively large number of sellers, (2) differentiated products (often promoted by heavy advertising), and (3) easy entry to, and exit from, the industry. The first and third characteristics provide the "competitive" aspect of monopolistic competition; the second characteristic provides the "monopolistic" aspect. In general, however, monopolistically competitive industries are more competitive than they are monopolistic.

Relatively Large Number of Sellers

Monopolistic competition is characterized by a fairly large number of firms—say 25, 35, 60, or 70—not by the hundreds or thousands of firms in perfect competition. Consequently, monopolistic competition involves:

- *Small Market Shares*   Each firm has a comparatively small percentage of the total market and consequently has limited control over market price.

- *No Collusion*   The presence of a relatively large number of firms makes collusion by a group of firms to restrict output and set prices unlikely.

- *Independent Action*   With many firms in an industry, there is little interdependence among them; each firm can determine its own pricing policy without considering the possible reactions of rival firms. A single firm may realize a modest increase in sales by cutting its price, but the effect of that action on competitors' sales will be nearly imperceptible and will probably not trigger a response.

Differentiated Products

In contrast to perfect competition, in which there is a standardized product, monopolistic competition is distinguished by **product differentiation**. Firms in monopolistic competition turn out variations of a particular product. They produce products with slightly different physical characteristics, offer varying degrees of customer service, provide varying amounts of location convenience, or proclaim special qualities, real or imagined, for their products.

Let's examine these aspects of product differentiation in more detail.

PRODUCT ATTRIBUTES

Product differentiation may take the form of physical or qualitative differences in the products themselves. Real differences in functional features, materials, design, and quality of work are vital aspects of product differentiation. Personal computers, for example, differ in terms of storage capacity, speed, graphic displays, and included software. There are dozens of competing textbooks covering the principles of economics that differ in content, organization, presentation and readability, pedagogical aids, and graphics and design. Most cities have a variety of retail stores selling men's and women's clothing that differ greatly in styling, materials, and quality of work.

SERVICE

Service and the conditions surrounding the sale of a product are also forms of product differentiation. One grocery store may stress the helpfulness of its clerks who bag your groceries and carry them to your car. A warehouse supermarket may leave bagging and carrying to its customers but feature lower prices. Customers may prefer one-day over three-day dry cleaning of equal quality. The prestige appeal of a store, the courteousness and helpfulness of clerks, the firm's reputation for servicing or exchanging its products, and the credit it makes available are all service aspects of product differentiation. Similarly, one pizza place may feature thin-crust, Neapolitan-style pizza, while another may tout its thick-crust, Chicago-style pizza.

LOCATION

Products may also be differentiated through the location and accessibility of the stores that sell them. Small convenience stores manage to compete with large supermarkets, even though these minimarts have a more limited range of products and charge higher prices. They compete mainly on the basis of location—being close to customers and situated on busy streets. A motel's proximity to a main highway gives it a locational advantage that may allow it to charge a higher room rate than nearby motels in less convenient locations.

BRAND NAMES AND PACKAGING

Product differentiation may also be created through the use of brand names and trademarks, packaging, and celebrity connections. Most nonsteroidal anti-inflammatory drug tablets are very much alike, but many headache sufferers believe that one brand—for example, Advil, Tylenol, or Bayer's Aspirin—is superior and worth a higher price than a generic substitute. A celebrity's name associated with watches, perfume, or athletic shoes may enhance the appeal of those products for some buyers. Many customers prefer one style of ballpoint pen to another. Packaging that touts "natural spring" bottled water may attract additional customers.

Product differentiation may also be created through the use of brand names and trademarks, packaging, and celebrity connections.

© The McGraw Hill Companies Inc./
Bob Coyle, photographer

SOME CONTROL OVER PRICE

Despite the relatively large number of firms, monopolistic competitors do have some control over their product prices because of product differentiation. If consumers prefer the products of specific sellers, then within limits they will pay more to satisfy their preferences. But the control a firm in monopolistic competition has over price is quite limited, since there are numerous potential substitutes for its product.

Easy Entry and Exit

Entry into industries characterized by a monopolistic competition market structure is relatively easy compared to oligopoly or monopoly. Because firms are typically small, both absolutely and relatively, economies of scale are few and capital requirements are low. However, compared with perfect competition, financial barriers may result from the need to develop and advertise a different product from one's rivals. Some firms may have trade secrets relating to their products or hold trademarks on their brand names, making it difficult and costly for other firms to imitate them.

Exit from industries in monopolistic competition is easier still. Nothing prevents an unprofitable firm from holding a going-out-of-business sale and shutting down.

Advertising

The expense and effort involved in product differentiation would be wasted if consumers were not made aware of product differences. Thus, firms in monopolistic competition advertise their products, often heavily. The goal of product differentiation and advertising—so-called **nonprice competition**—is to make price less of a factor in consumer purchases and make product differences a greater factor. If successful, the firm's demand curve will shift to the right and will become less elastic.

Monopolistically Competitive Industries

Figure 12-1 lists several manufacturing industries that approximate monopolistic competition. Economists measure the degree of industry concentration—the extent to which the largest firms account for the bulk of the industry's output—to identify monopolistic competitive (versus oligopolistic) industries. Two such measures are the four-firm concentration ratio and the Herfindahl index.

A **four-firm concentration ratio**, expressed as a percentage, is the ratio of the output (sales) of the four largest firms in an industry relative to total industry sales.

$$\text{Four-firm concentration ratio} = \frac{\text{output of four largest firms}}{\text{total output in the industry}}$$

Four-firm concentration ratios are very low in perfectly competitive industries in which there are hundreds or even thousands of firms each with a tiny market share. In contrast, four-firm ratios are high in oligopoly and

FIGURE 12-1   Percentage of Output Produced by the Four Largest Firms in Selected Low-Concentration Sectors*

Several Canadian manufacturing industries approximate monopolistic competition, with a relatively large number of sellers producing differentiated products. There is easy entry into the industry and firms often differentiate their products through advertising.

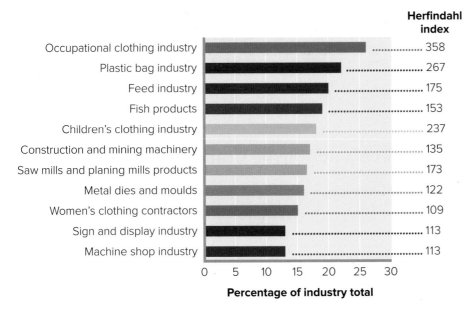

Herfindahl index

Industry	Herfindahl index
Occupational clothing industry	358
Plastic bag industry	267
Feed industry	175
Fish products	153
Children's clothing industry	237
Construction and mining machinery	135
Saw mills and planing mills products	173
Metal dies and moulds	122
Women's clothing contractors	109
Sign and display industry	113
Machine shop industry	113

Percentage of industry total

Source: Statistics Canada, *Industrial Organization and Concentration in Manufacturing, Mining and Logging Industries*, Catalogue No. 31C0024.

*As measured by dollar value of shipments.

monopoly. Industries in which the largest four firms account for 40 percent or more of the market are generally considered to be oligopolies. If the largest four firms account for less than 40 percent, they are likely to be monopolistically competitive. Observe that the concentration ratios in Figure 12-1 range from 13 to 27 percent.

Published concentration ratios such as those in Figure 12-1 are helpful in categorizing industries, but must be used cautiously because the market shares (percentage of total sales) are national in scope. As a result, some industries with low national concentration ratios are in fact substantially concentrated if one focuses on local markets. For example, the four-firm concentration ratio for ready-mix concrete (not shown) is usually low, suggesting a monopolistically competitive industry. But the sheer bulk of ready-mix concrete and the fact that it sets up as it dries limits the relevant market to a specific town, city, or metropolitan area. In most of these local markets only a few firms compete, not the numerous firms needed for monopolistic competition.

Figure 12-1 lists a second measure of concentration: the **Herfindahl index**. This index is the sum of the squared percentage market shares of all firms in the industry. In equation form,

$$\text{Herfindahl index} = (\%S_1)^2 + (\%S_2)^2 + (\%S_3)^2 + \cdots + (\%S_n)^2$$

where $\%S_1$ is the percentage market share of firm 1, $\%S_2$ is the percentage market share of firm 2, and so on for each firm in the industry. By squaring the percentage market shares of all firms in the industry, the Herfindahl index purposely gives much greater weight to larger, and thus more powerful, firms than to smaller ones. For a perfectly competitive industry, the index would approach zero, since each firm's market share—$\%S$ in the equation—is extremely small. In the case of a single-firm industry, the index would be at its maximum of 10,000 (= 100^2), indicating an industry with complete monopoly power.

We will discover later in the Chapter 13 that the Herfindahl index is important for assessing oligopolistic industries. But for now the relevant generalization is that the lower the Herfindahl index, the greater the likelihood an industry is monopolistically competitive rather than oligopolistic. Note that in Figure 12-1 the Herfindahl index values (computed for the top four firms, not all the industry firms) are decidedly closer to the bottom limit—0—than to the top limit—10,000.

The numbers in Figure 12-1 are for manufacturing industries. In Canada the least concentrated are machine shops, with a Herfindahl index of only 113. The shops serve manufacturers by making the various parts required for machines—for example, dies that are then used to stamp metal and plastic forms that are in turn used in a myriad of end products. Many machine shops provide custom service. Windsor, Ontario, where there are major automotive plants, boasts some 60 machine shops. Vancouver has over 100 machine shops, while Halifax has only about 30.

In addition, many retail establishments in metropolitan areas fall into the category of monopolistic competition, including grocery stores, gas stations, hair salons, dry cleaners, clothing stores, and restaurants. For example, Canada has some 80,800 commercial food services units. Of this total, about 36,400 are full-service and 32,000 limited-service restaurants. Of the remainder, about 6500 are contract and social caterers and 6100 are drinking places. While chain restaurants, such as McDonald's, make up 36 percent of Canada's restaurants, the remaining 64 percent are independent brands, meaning small restaurants that serve a local population. Also, many providers of professional services such as legal assistance, real estate sales, and basic bookkeeping are monopolistic competitors.

12.2 Price and Output in Monopolistic Competition

LO12.2   Explain why monopolistic competitors earn only a normal profit in the long run.

How does a firm in monopolistic competition decide on its price and output? To explain, we initially assume that each firm in the industry is producing a specific differentiated product and engaging in a particular amount of advertising. Later we'll see how changes in the product and in the amount of advertising modify our conclusions.

The Firm's Demand Curve

Our explanation is based on Figure 12-2 (Key Graph), which shows that the demand curve of each firm is highly, but not perfectly, elastic. It is precisely this feature that distinguishes monopolistic competition from both monopoly and perfect competition. The demand is more elastic than the demand faced by a monopolist because the firm in monopolistic competition has many competitors producing close substitutes. The monopolist has no rivals at all. Yet there are two reasons why the demand curve of a firm in monopolistic competition is not perfectly elastic, as is the case in perfect competition. First, it has fewer rivals; second, its products are differentiated, so they are not perfect substitutes.

The price elasticity of demand faced by the firm in monopolistic competition depends on the number of rivals and the degree of product differentiation. The larger the number of rivals and the weaker the product differentiation, the greater the price elasticity of each firm's demand, that is, the closer monopolistic competition will be to perfect competition.

The Short Run: Profit or Loss

In the short run, monopolistically competitive firms maximize profit or minimize loss using exactly the same strategy as pure competitors and monopolists: They produce the level of output at which marginal revenue equals marginal cost (MR = MC). Thus, the monopolistically competitive firm in Figure 12-2a produces output Q_1, where MR = MC. As shown by demand curve D_1, the firm then can charge price P_1. It realizes an economic profit, shown by the grey area $[= (P_1 - A_1) \times Q_1]$.

But with less favourable demand or costs, the firm may incur a loss in the short run. This possibility is shown in Figure 12-2b, where the firm's best strategy is to minimize its loss. It does so by producing output Q_2 (where MR = MC) and, as determined by demand curve D_2, by charging price P_2. Because price P_2 is less than average total cost A_2, the firm incurs a per-unit loss of $A_2 - P_2$ and a total loss represented by the pink area $[= (A_2 - P_2) \times Q_2]$.

The Long Run: Only a Normal Profit

In the long run, firms will enter a profitable monopolistically competitive industry and exit an unprofitable one. So a firm in monopolistic competition will earn only a normal profit in the long run. (Remember that the cost curves include both explicit and implicit costs, including a normal profit.)

FIGURE 12-2   A Monopolistically Competitive Firm: Short Run and Long Run

The firm in monopolistic competition maximizes profit or minimizes loss by producing the output at which MR = MC. The economic profit shown in (a) will induce new firms to enter, eventually eliminating economic profit. The loss shown in (b) will cause an exit of firms until normal profit is restored. After such entry and exit, the price will settle in (c) to where it just equals average total cost at the MR = MC output. At this price P_3 and output Q_3, the firm in monopolistic competition earns only a normal profit, and the industry is in long-run equilibrium.

(a) Short-run profits

(b) Short-run losses

(c) Long-run equilibrium

PROFITS: FIRMS ENTER

In the case of short-run profit in Figure 12-2a, economic profits attract new rivals because entry to the industry is relatively easy. As new firms enter, the demand curve faced by the typical firm shifts to the left (falls) because each firm has a smaller share of total demand. This decline in the firm's demand reduces its economic profit. When entry of new firms has reduced demand to the extent that the demand curve is tangent to the average-total-cost curve at the profit-maximizing output, the firm is just making a normal profit. This situation is shown in Figure 12-2c, where demand is D_3 and the firm's long-run equilibrium output is Q_3. As Figure 12-2c indicates, any greater or lesser output will entail an average total cost that exceeds product price P_3, meaning a loss for the firm. At the tangency point between the demand curve and ATC, total revenue equals total costs. With the economic profit gone, no further incentive exists for additional firms to enter.

LOSSES: FIRMS LEAVE

When the industry suffers short-run losses, as in Figure 12-2b, some firms will exit in the long run. Faced with fewer substitute products and with an expanded share of total demand, the surviving firms will see their demand curves shift to the right (rise), as to D_3. Their losses will disappear and give way to normal profits, shown in Figure 12-2b. (For simplicity we have assumed constant costs; shifts in the cost curves as firms enter or leave would complicate our discussion slightly but would not alter our conclusions.)

COMPLICATIONS

The representative firm in the monopolistic competition model earns only a normal profit in the long run. That outcome may not always occur for the following reasons:

- Some firms may achieve sufficient product differentiation that other firms cannot duplicate their products, even over time. For example, one hotel in a major city may have the best location for business and tourist activities. Or a firm may have developed a well-known brand name that gives it a slight but very long-lasting advantage over imitators. Such firms may have sufficient monopoly power to realize modest economic profits even in the long run.

- Entry to some monopolistically competitive industries may not be easy. Because of product differentiation, greater financial barriers to entry are likely to exist than if the product were standardized. This suggests some monopoly power, with small economic profits continuing even in the long run.

All things considered, however, the outcome that yields only a normal profit—the long-run equilibrium—shown in Figure 12-2c is a reasonable approximation of reality.

QUICK REVIEW 12.1

- Monopolistic competition involves a relatively large number of firms operating in a noncollusive way and producing differentiated products with easy industry entry and exit.

- In the short run, a monopolistic competitor will maximize profit or minimize loss by producing the level of output at which marginal revenue equals marginal cost.

- In the long run, easy entry and exit of firms causes monopolistic competitors to earn only a normal profit.

12.3 Monopolistic Competition and Efficiency

LO12.3 Explain why monopolistic competition delivers neither productive nor allocative efficiency.

We know from Chapter 10 that economic efficiency requires each firm to produce the amount of output at which $P = MC = $ minimum ATC. The equality of price and minimum average total cost yields *productive efficiency*. The good is being produced in the least costly way, and the price is just sufficient to cover average total cost, including a normal profit. The equality of price and marginal cost also yields *allocative efficiency*. The right amount of output is being produced, and thus the right amount of society's scarce resources is being devoted to this specific use.

How efficient is monopolistic competition, as measured against this triple equality? In particular, do monopolistically competitive firms produce the efficient output level associated with $P = MC = $ minimum ATC?

NEITHER PRODUCTIVE NOR ALLOCATIVE EFFICIENCY

In monopolistic competition, neither productive nor allocative efficiency is achieved in long-run equilibrium. Figure 12-3, which includes an enlargement of part of Figure 12-2c, clearly shows this. First note that the profit-maximizing price P_3 slightly exceeds the lowest average total cost, A_4. In producing the profit-maximizing output Q_3, the firm's average total cost therefore is slightly higher than optimal from society's perspective—productive efficiency is not achieved. Also note that the profit-maximizing price P_3 exceeds marginal cost (here M_3), meaning that monopolistic competition causes an underallocation of resources. To measure the size of this inefficiency, note that the allocatively optimal amount of output is determined by point c, where demand curve D intersects the MC curve. So for all units between Q_3 and the level of output associated with point c, marginal benefits exceed marginal costs. Consequently, by producing only Q_3 units, this monopolistic competitor creates an efficiency loss (deadweight loss) equal in size to area acd. The total efficiency loss for the industry as a whole will be the sum of the individual efficiency losses generated by each of the firms in the industry.

EXCESS CAPACITY

In monopolistic competition, the gap between the minimum-ATC output and the profit-maximizing output identifies **excess capacity**: plant or equipment that is underused because firms are producing less than the minimum-ATC output. This gap is shown as the distance between Q_4 and Q_3 in Figure 12-3. Note in the figure that the minimum ATC is at point b. If each monopolistic competitor could profitably produce at this point on its ATC curve, the lower average total cost would enable a lower price than P_3. More importantly, if each firm produced at b rather than at a, fewer firms would be needed to produce the industry output. But because monopolistically competitive firms produce at a in long-run equilibrium, monopolistically competitive industries are overpopulated with firms, each operating below its optimal capacity. This situation is typified by many kinds of retail establishments. For example, many cities have an abundance of small motels and restaurants that operate well below half capacity.

FIGURE 12-3   The Inefficiency of Monopolistic Competition

In long-run equilibrium a firm in monopolistic competition achieves neither productive nor allocative efficiency. Productive efficiency is not realized because production occurs where the average total cost A_3 exceeds the minimum average total cost A_4. Allocative efficiency is not achieved because the product price P_3 exceeds the marginal cost M_3. The results are an underallocation of resources as well as an efficiency loss and excess production capacity at every firm in the industry. This firm's efficiency loss is area acd and its excess production capacity is $Q_3 - Q_4$.

12.4 Product Variety

LO12.4   Relate how the ability of monopolistic competition to deliver product differentiation helps to compensate for its failure to deliver economic efficiency.

The situation portrayed in Figures 12-2c and 12-3 is not very satisfying to firms in monopolistic competition, since it allows only a normal profit. But the profit-realizing firm of Figure 12-2a need not stand by and watch new competitors eliminate its profit by imitating its product, matching its customer service, and copying its advertising. Each firm has a product that is distinguishable in some way from those of the other producers. So the firm can attempt to stay ahead of competitors and sustain its profit through further product differentiation and more effective advertising. By developing or improving its product, it may be able to postpone, at least for a while, the outcome of Figure 12-2c.

Although product differentiation and advertising add to the firm's costs, they can also increase the demand for its product. If demand increases by more than enough to compensate for the added costs, the firm will have improved its profit position. As Figure 12-3 suggests, the firm has little or no prospect of increasing profit by price cutting. So why not engage in nonprice competition?

Benefits of Product Variety

The product variety and product improvement that accompany the drive to maintain above-normal profit in monopolistic competition are a benefit for society—they may offset the cost of the inefficiency associated with monopolistic competition. Consumers have a wide diversity of tastes: some like hip-hop bands, others punk; some like contemporary furniture, others traditional. If a product is differentiated, at any time the consumer will be offered a wide range of types, styles, brands, and quality gradations of that product. Compared with perfect competition, this provides an advantage to the consumer. The range of choice is widened, and producers more fully meet the wide variation in consumer tastes.

CONSIDER THIS

The Spice of Life

The Wendy's hamburger chain debuted a hilarious TV commercial in 1987. The commercial depicts a Soviet communist fashion show. A woman walks down the runway in a drab grey factory uniform. The emcee shouts out, "Day wear!" Then she marches down the runway again in the same uniform but holding a flashlight. The emcee shouts out, "Evening wear!" She then marches out in the same uniform again but holding an inflatable beach ball. "Swimwear!"

Communist central planners didn't care about product differentiation. They typically made one design of a given product to be able to mass-produce it at the lowest possible cost. The result was a society of painful sameness.

The commercial hammered home a single idea—that we should embrace the fact that the food produced by Wendy's was different from that produced by its main rivals, McDonald's and Burger King. Unlike the communist central planning of the old Soviet Union, the free market system of the Canada allows for huge amounts of product differentiation. If "variety is the spice of life," Canadian capitalism is extremely well seasoned.

Source: Wendy's, "Soviet Fashion Show," 1987.

© Chuck Nacke/Alamy Stock Photo

In fact, it should be stressed that product differentiation creates a trade-off between consumer choice and productive efficiency. The stronger the product differentiation, the greater the excess capacity and, therefore, the greater the productive inefficiency. But the greater the product differentiation, the more likely that the firms will satisfy the great diversity of consumer tastes. The greater the excess capacity problem, the wider the range of consumer choice.

Further Complexity

Finally, the ability to engage in nonprice competition makes the firm's situation in monopolistic competition more complex than Figure 12-3 indicates. That figure assumes a given (unchanging) product and a given level of advertising expenditures. But we know that, in practice, product attributes, and advertising are not fixed. The firm in monopolistic competition juggles three factors—price, product, and advertising—in seeking maximum profit. It must determine what variety of product, selling at what price, and supplemented by what level of advertising will result in the greatest profit. This complex situation is not easily expressed in a simple economic model. At best, we can say that each possible combination of price, product, and advertising poses a different demand and cost (production cost plus advertising cost) situation for the firm, and that only one combination yields the maximum profit. In practice, this optimal combination cannot be readily forecast but must be found by trial and error.

QUICK REVIEW 12.2

- The long-run equilibrium output for a firm in monopolistic competition is such that price exceeds the minimum average total cost (implying that consumers do not get the product at the lowest price attainable) and price exceeds marginal cost (indicating that resources are underallocated to the product).

- The efficiency loss associated with monopolistic competition is greatly muted by the benefits consumers receive from product variety.

The LAST WORD

Higher Wages, More McRestaurants

© Sorbis/Shutterstock.com

In the monopolistically competitive restaurant market, higher wages favour big chain restaurants over small, "mom and pop" operations.

Restaurants are monopolistic competitors. Because each one has a unique location, it has some monopoly power. Additional bits of monopoly power are generated by product differentiation. Restaurants can differ on menu items, decor, speed of service, price, drive-through convenience, and a wide variety of additional characteristics.

Restaurants also differ in their production methods. Compare a McDonald's hamburger restaurant with a small "mom and pop" hamburger stand. The McDonald's will have a huge amount of specialized equipment. There will be special machines for frying, microwaving, making milkshakes, dispensing beverages into cups automatically, and of course cooking the hamburgers.

There will also in most cases be touchscreen computers for taking walk-up orders; wireless headsets for taking drive-through orders; and a fully computerized register system for keeping track of cash, credit, and debit transactions. And there will be a dining area, often tastefully decorated in modern styles at substantial expense. All these things imply that a McDonald's restaurant is capital intensive. It uses a large amount of capital equipment to produce and serve a hamburger.

By contrast, a small mom-and-pop hamburger stand will typically have only the bare minimum in terms of cooking equipment—a grill, a fryer, an unautomated beverage dispenser, and a refrigerator. Seating will be plain. The decor will be inexpensive and probably out of style. The stand will use relatively little capital to produce and serve a hamburger.

In a monopolistically competitive restaurant market, equilibrium can often include both highly capitalized chain stores like McDonald's and lightly capitalized mom-and-pop operations. As long as both types of restaurant can make zero economic profits, each type will have representatives in the local restaurant market.

Economists have recently discovered, however, that wage increases can tilt the local restaurant market in favour of highly capitalized chain stores. In particular, increases in the minimum wage tend to reduce the proportion of mom-and-pop restaurants.

This happens because increases in the minimum wage have a relatively small impact on the cost curves of highly capitalized chain restaurants. While it is true that a highly capitalized McDonald's *does* hire minimum-wage workers, the fact that it uses so much capital to produce hamburgers means that a large fraction of its costs derive from machinery and equipment. So

when the minimum wage goes up, only a relatively minor part of its production costs go up.

By contrast, mom-and-pop restaurants use relatively little capital combined with lots of labour. After all, if you don't have much in the way of machinery and specialized equipment, you need to have lots of labour to make up for the lack of capital. So when the minimum wage is increased, the cost curves of mom and pop stores shift upward by more than the cost curves of highly capitalized chain restaurants. In both cases, economic profits will turn negative—but they will become much more negative at the mom-and-pop restaurants, which are heavily reliant on labour.

The result is a greater tendency on the part of mom-and-pop restaurants to exit the industry. Both types of restaurant will see exits. But when a new equilibrium is eventually reestablished, there will be a higher proportion of highly capitalized chain restaurants and a lower proportion of labour-intensive mom-and-pop restaurants.

Higher minimum wages are often promoted as a way to help low-wage workers. But they generate an unintended consequence in the restaurant market, where they favour big chain stores over small local operations. Voters and politicians need to be aware that this happens when they consider raising the minimum wage.

Question

What would you expect to happen to the proportion of big chain restaurants relative to mom-and-pop restaurants in a town that lowered its minimum wage? Will the proportion change due to exits or entrances? Which type of restaurant will see more in the way of exits or entrances? Why?

Chapter Summary

LO12.1   List the characteristics of monopolistic competition.

- The distinguishing features of monopolistic competition are (a) enough firms are in the industry to ensure each firm has only limited control over price, mutual interdependence is absent, and collusion is nearly impossible; (b) products are characterized by real or perceived differences so that economic rivalry entails both price and nonprice competition; and (c) entry to the industry is relatively easy. Many aspects of retailing, and some manufacturing industries in which economies of scale are few, approximate monopolistic competition.

- The four-firm concentration ratio measures the percentage of total industry output accounted for by the largest four firms. The Herfindahl index sums the squares of the market shares of all firms in the industry.

LO12.2   Explain why monopolistic competitors earn only a normal profit in the long run.

- Monopolistically competitive firms may earn economic profits or incur losses in the short run. The easy entry and exit of firms results in only normal profits in the long run.

LO12.3   Explain why monopolistic competition delivers neither productive nor allocative efficiency.

- The long-run equilibrium position of the monopolistically competitive producer is less socially desirable than that of the perfect competitor. Under monopolistic competition, price exceeds marginal cost, suggesting an underallocation of resources to the product, and price exceeds minimum average total cost, indicating that consumers do not get the product at the lowest price that cost conditions might allow.

LO12.4 Relate how the ability of monopolistic competition to deliver product differentiation helps to compensate for its failure to deliver economic efficiency.

- Nonprice competition provides a means by which monopolistically competitive firms can offset the long-run tendency for economic profit to fall to zero. Through product differentiation, product development, and advertising, a firm may strive to increase the demand for its product more than enough to cover the added cost of such nonprice competition. Consumers benefit from the wide diversity of product choice that monopolistic competition provides.

- In practice, the monopolistic competitor seeks the specific combination of price, product, and advertising that will maximize profit.

Terms and Concepts

monopolistic competition
product differentiation
nonprice competition

four-firm concentration ratio
Herfindahl index
excess capacity

Discussion Questions

1. How does monopolistic competition differ from perfect competition in its basic characteristics? From monopoly? Explain fully what product differentiation may involve. Explain how the entry of firms into its industry affects the demand curve facing a monopolistic competitor and how that, in turn, affects its economic profit. [**LO12.1**]

2. Compare the elasticity of a monopolistic competitor's demand with that of a perfectly competitive firm and a monopolist. Assuming identical long-run costs, compare graphically the prices and outputs that would result in the long run under perfect competition and under monopolistic competition. Contrast the two market structures in terms of productive and allocative efficiency. Explain the following statement: Monopolistically competitive industries are characterized by too many firms, each of which produces too little. [**LO12.2**]

3. "Monopolistic competition is monopolistic up to the point at which consumers become willing to buy close-substitute products and competitive beyond that point." Explain. [**LO12.2**]

4. "Competition in quality and service may be just as effective as price competition in giving buyers more for their money." Do you agree? Why? Explain why monopolistically competitive firms frequently prefer nonprice competition to price competition. [**LO12.2**]

5. Critically evaluate and explain the following statements: [**LO12.2**]

   a. "In monopolistically competitive industries, economic profits are competed away in the long run; hence, there is no valid reason to criticize the performance and efficiency of such industries."

   b. "In the long run, monopolistic competition leads to a monopolistic price but not to monopolistic profits."

Review Questions

1. There are 10 firms in an industry, and each firm has a market share of 10 percent. The industry's Herfindahl index is [**LO12.1**]

   a. 10

   b. 100

   c. 1000

   d. 10,000

2. In the small town of Geneva, there are 5 firms that make watches. The firms' respective output levels are 30 watches per year, 20 watches per year, 20 watches per year, 20 watches per year, and 10 watches per year. The four-firm concentration ratio for the town's watch-making industry is [**LO12.1**]

   a. 5

   b. 70

   c. 90

   d. 100

3. Which of the following best describes the efficiency of monopolistically competitive firms? [**LO12.3**]

   a. Allocatively efficient but productively inefficient

   b. Allocatively inefficient but productively efficient

   c. Both allocatively efficient and productively efficient

   d. Neither allocatively efficient nor productively efficient

Problems

1. Suppose that a small town has seven burger shops whose respective shares of the local hamburger market are (as percentages of all hamburgers sold) 23, 22, 18, 12, 11, 8, and 6 percent. What is the four-firm concentration ratio of the hamburger industry in this town? What is the Herfindahl index for the hamburger industry in this town? If the top three sellers combined to form a single firm, what would happen to the four-firm concentration ratio and to the Herfindahl index? [**LO12.1**]

2. Suppose that the most popular car dealer in your area sells 10 percent of all vehicles. If all other car dealers sell either the same number of vehicles or fewer, what is the largest value that the Herfindahl index could possibly take for car dealers in your area? In that same situation, what would the four-firm concentration ratio be? [**LO12.1**]

3. Suppose that an monopolistically competitive restaurant is currently serving 230 meals per day (the output where MR = MC). At that output level, ATC per meal is $10 and consumers are willing to pay $12 per meal. What is the size of this firm's profit or loss? Will there be entry or exit? Will this restaurant's demand curve shift left or right? In long-run equilibrium, suppose that this restaurant charges $11 per meal for 180 meals and that the marginal cost of the 180th meal is $8. What is the size of the firm's profit? Suppose that the allocatively efficient output level in long-run equilibrium is 200 meals. Is the deadweight loss for this firm greater than or less than $60? [**LO12.1**]

CHAPTER 13

Oligopoly and Strategic Behaviour

LEARNING OBJECTIVES

LO13.1	**Describe the characteristics of oligopoly.**
LO13.2	**Discuss how game theory relates to oligopoly.**
LO13.3	**Explain the two main models of oligopoly pricing and output: collusive pricing and price leadership.**
LO13.4	**Contrast the potential positive and potential negative effects of advertising.**
LO13.5	**Discuss the efficiency of oligopoly from society's standpoint and whether it is more or less efficient than monopoly.**
LO13.6	**Utilize additional game-theory terminology and demonstrate how to find Nash equilibriums in both simultaneous and sequential games.**

In Canada, most industries have a market structure that falls somewhere between the two poles of perfect competition and monopoly. To begin with, most real-world industries have fewer than the large number of producers required for perfect competition but more than the single producer that defines monopoly. In addition, most firms in most industries have both distinguishable rather than standardized products as well as some discretion over the prices they charge. As a result, competition often occurs on the basis of price, quality, location, service, and advertising. Finally, entry to most real-world industries ranges from easy to very difficult but is rarely completely blocked.

This chapter examines the second of two models that more closely approximate these widespread industry structures. While the monopolistic competition model of Chapter 12 mixes a small amount of monopoly power with a large amount of competition, the oligopoly model covered in this chapter blends a large amount of monopoly power with both considerable rivalry among existing firms and the threat of increased future competition due to foreign firms and new technologies. (You should quickly review Table 9-1 at this point.)

13.1 Oligopoly

LO13.1 Describe the characteristics of oligopoly.

In terms of competitiveness, the spectrum of market structures reaches from perfect competition to monopolistic competition, to oligopoly, to monopoly (review Table 9-1). We now direct our attention to **oligopoly**, a market structure dominated by a few large producers of a homogeneous or differentiated product. Because of their small number, oligopolists have considerable control over their prices, but each must consider the possible reaction of rivals to its own pricing, output, and advertising decisions.

A Few Large Producers

The phrase "a few large producers" is necessarily vague, because the market model of oligopoly covers much ground, ranging between monopoly and monopolistic competition. Oligopoly encompasses the Canadian steel industry, in which two firms dominate an entire national market, and the situation in which four or five much smaller auto parts stores enjoy roughly equal shares of the market in a medium-sized town. Generally, however, when you hear a term such as Big Three, Big Four, or Big Six, you can be sure it refers to an oligopolistic industry.

Homogeneous or Differentiated Products

An oligopoly may be either a **homogeneous oligopoly** or a **differentiated oligopoly**, depending on whether the firms in the oligopoly produce standardized or differentiated products. Many industrial industries (steel, zinc, copper, aluminum, lead, cement, industrial alcohol) make virtually standardized products and so are homogeneous oligopolies. Many consumer goods industries (automobiles, tires, household appliances, electronics equipment, breakfast cereals, cigarettes, sporting goods) are differentiated oligopolies.

An example of a differentiated oligopoly in Canada is the media and telecommunications sector. It is dominated by Rogers Communications, which provides cable, Internet, and wireless services, has a sizeable magazine publishing arm, and owns the Toronto Blue Jays baseball tea. Another major player in the Canadian media telecommunication sector is BCE Inc., which controls Bell Canada and owns satellite broadcaster Bell ExpressVu, television stations, and *The Globe and Mail*. This type of oligopoly typically engages in considerable nonprice competition supported by heavy advertising.

Control over Price, but Mutual Interdependence

Because firms are few in oligopolistic industries, each is a price-maker; like the monopolist, it can set its price and output levels to maximize its profit. But unlike the monopolist, which has no rivals, the oligopolist must consider how its rivals will react to any change in its price, output, product characteristics, or advertising. Oligopoly is thus characterized by *strategic behaviour* and *mutual interdependence*. By **strategic behaviour** we simply mean self-interested behaviour that takes into account the reactions of others. Firms develop and implement price, quality, location, service, and advertising strategies to grow their business and expand their profits. But because rivals are few, there is **mutual interdependence**: a situation in which each firm's profit depends not just on its own price and sales strategies but also on the other firms in its highly concentrated industry. So oligopolistic firms base their decisions on how they think their rivals will react. For example, in deciding whether to increase the price of its cosmetics, L'Oréal will try to predict the response of other major cosmetics producers, such as Clinique. In deciding on its advertising strategy, Burger King will take into consideration how McDonald's might react.

Entry Barriers

The same barriers to entry that create monopoly also contribute to the creation of oligopoly. Economies of scale are important entry barriers in a number of oligopolistic industries, such as the aircraft, rubber, and cement industries. In those industries, three or four firms might each have sufficient sales to achieve economies of scale, but new firms would have such a small market share that they could not do so. They would then be high-cost producers, and as such they could not survive. A closely related barrier is the large expenditure for capital—the cost of obtaining necessary plant and equipment—required for entering certain industries. The automobile, commercial aircraft, and

CONSIDER THIS

Creative Strategic Behaviour

The following story, offered tongue in cheek, illustrates a localized market that exhibits some characteristics of oligopoly, including strategic behaviour.

Tracy Proudfoot's Native Canadian Arts and Crafts store is located in the centre of a small tourist town that borders on a national park. In the business's early days, Tracy had a mini-monopoly. Business was brisk and prices and profits were high.

© Richard Cummins/Corbis

But, to Tracy's chagrin, two copycat shops opened up right next door, one on either side of hers. Worse yet, they named their shops to take advantage of Tracy's advertising: One was Native Arts and Crafts, the other Indian Arts and Crafts. These new sellers drew business away from Tracy's store, forcing her to lower her prices. The three adjacent stores in the small, isolated town constituted a localized oligopoly for Native Canadian arts and crafts.

Tracy began to think strategically about ways to boost profit. She decided to distinguish her shop from those on either side by offering a greater mix of high-quality, expensive products and fewer inexpensive "souvenir" items. The tactic worked for a while, but the other stores eventually imitated her product mix.

Then, one of the two competitors escalated things by hanging up a large sign proclaiming "We Sell for Less!" Shortly thereafter, the other also put up a large sign proclaiming "We Won't Be Undersold!"

Not to be outdone, Tracy hung up a colourful sign of her own: "Main Entrance."

Clearly, competitive market forces demand creative strategic responses by firms.

petroleum-refining industries, for example, are all characterized by very high capital requirements. In Canada, the domestic automobile industry is dominated by Ford, General Motors, and Fiat Chrysler, whose plants are concentrated in Ontario and Quebec; Quebec's Bombardier is one of the world's largest manufacturers of small short-haul passenger planes, such as the Dash 8; and Suncor Energy is Canada's largest oil refiner, as well as a major international player in the oil and gas sector.

Ownership and control of raw materials helps explain why oligopoly exists in many mining industries, including gold, silver, and copper. In the computer, chemicals, consumer electronics, and pharmaceutical industries, patents have served as entry barriers. Oligopolists can also preclude the entry of new competitors through preemptive and retaliatory pricing and advertising strategies.

Mergers

Some oligopolies have emerged mainly through the growth of the dominant firms in a given industry (breakfast cereals, chewing gum, candy bars). But for other industries the route to oligopoly has been through mergers (examples are steel, in its early history, and, more recently, airlines, banking, and entertainment). The merging (combining) of two or more competing firms may substantially increase their market share, which in turn may allow the new firm to achieve greater economies of scale. Another motive underlying the "urge to merge" is the desire for monopoly power. The larger firm that results from a merger has greater control over market supply and thus the price of its product. Also, since it is a larger buyer of inputs, it may be able to demand and obtain lower prices (costs) on its production inputs.

Oligopolistic Industries

Figure 13-1 shows the Herfindahl index—the percentage of total industry sales accounted for by the four largest firms—for a number of oligopolistic industries. For example, the four largest Canadian producers of tobacco products manufacture more than 90 percent of all cigarettes produced in Canada. (In fact, the domestic tobacco market is largely controlled by the *three* largest Canadian companies: Imperial Tobacco Ltd., owned by Imasco Ltd.; Rothmans, Benson & Hedges Inc.; and JTI-MacDonald Ltd.)

FIGURE 13-1   Percentage of Output Produced by the Four Largest Firms in Selected High-Concentration Industries*

A concentration ratio reveals the percentage of total output produced and sold by an industry's four largest firms. The Herfindahl index is the sum of the squared percentage market shares of all the firms in the industry. The higher the Herfindahl index, the greater the market power within an industry. The tobacco industry is the most concentrated sector in Canada.

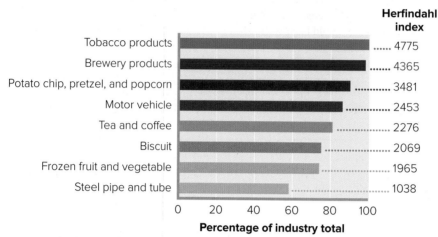

*As measured by dollar value of shipments.

Source: Statistics Canada, *Industrial Organization and Concentration in Manufacturing, Mining and Logging Industries.* Catalogue No. 31C0024.

When the four largest firms in an industry control 40 percent or more of the market (as in Figure 13-1), that industry is considered oligopolistic. Using this benchmark, about one-half of all Canadian manufacturing industries are oligopolies. Although concentration ratios help identify oligopoly, they have four shortcomings.

Localized Markets

We have already noted that concentration ratios relate to the nation as a whole, whereas the markets for some products are highly localized because of high transportation costs. Local oligopolies can exist even though national concentration ratios are low.

Interindustry Competition

Concentration ratios are based on somewhat arbitrary definitions of industries. In some cases, they disguise significant **interindustry competition**—competition between two products associated with different industries. The high concentration ratio for the steel pipe and tube industry shown in Figure 13-1 understates the competition in that industry, because copper and plastic tubing compete with steel tubing in many applications.

World Trade

The data in Figure 13-1 only take account of output in Canada and may overstate concentration because they do not account for the **import competition** of foreign suppliers. The automobile industry is a good example. Although Figure 13-1 shows that three firms produce almost 90 percent of the domestic output of those goods, it ignores the fact that a large portion of the automobiles and auto tires bought in Canada are imports. Many of the world's largest corporations are foreign, and many of them do business in Canada.

Dominant Firms

The four-firm concentration ratio does not reveal the extent to which one or two firms dominate an industry. Suppose that in industry X one firm produces the entire industry output. In a second industry, Y, four firms compete, each with 25 percent of the market. The concentration ratio is 100 percent for both these industries. But industry X is a pure monopoly, while industry Y is an oligopoly that may be experiencing significant economic rivalry. Most economists would agree that monopoly power (or market power) is substantially greater in industry X than in industry Y, a fact disguised by their identical 100 percent concentration ratios.

The Herfindahl index addresses this problem. Recall from section 12.1 that this index is the sum of the squared percentage market shares of all firms in the industry. Again, in equation form,

$$\text{Herfindahl index} = (\%S_1)^2 + (\%S_2)^2 + (\%S_3)^2 + \cdots + (\%S_n)^2$$

where $\%S_1$ is the percentage market share of firm 1, $\%S_2$ is the percentage market share of firm 2, and so on for each firm in the industry. Also remember that by squaring the percentage market shares of all firms in the industry, the Herfindahl index gives much greater weight to larger, and thus more powerful, firms than to smaller ones. In the case of the single-firm industry, X, the index would be at its maximum of 100^2 or 10,000, indicating an industry with complete monopoly power. For our four-firm industry, Y, the index would be $25^2 + 25^2 + 25^2 + 25^2$, or 2500, indicating much less market power.

The larger the Herfindahl index, the greater the market power within an industry. Note in Figure 13-1 that the four-firm concentration ratios for the tobacco products industry and the brewery products industry are similar. But the Herfindahl index of 4775 for the tobacco products industry suggests greater market power than the 4365 index for the brewery products industry, although both are highly concentrated. The automotive industry is dominated by General Motors and Ford, but it has become less concentrated with the establishment of North American manufacturing plants by the Japanese giants Toyota and Honda. The baked-goods industry in Canada is dominated by Weston Bakeries, owned by George Weston Limited. Among its many products are bread, rolls, cookies, and frozen baked goods. Also, contrast the much larger Herfindahl indexes in Figure 13-1 with those for the low-concentration industries in Figure 12-1.

WORKED PROBLEM 13.1   Measures of Industry Concentration

13.2 Oligopoly Pricing Behaviour: A Game Theory Overview

LO13.2   **Discuss how game theory relates to oligopoly.**

Oligopoly pricing behaviour has the characteristics of certain games of strategy, such as poker, chess, and bridge. The best way to play such a game depends on the way one's opponent plays. Players (and oligopolists) must plan their actions according to the actions and expected reactions of rivals. The study of how people behave in strategic situations is called **game theory**. We will use a simple game theory model to analyze the pricing behaviour of oligopolists. Game theory was first developed in the 1920s and expanded rapidly during World War II in response to the military need to develop formal ways of thinking about strategy.

Basic Concepts

Any interaction in which individuals or firms must make choices and in which the final outcome depends on what each individual or firm chooses to do is termed a *game*. Games have four basic components: (1) the players, (2) the rules, (3) the possible strategies, and (4) the payoffs. Games may be *cooperative*, meaning players in the game make specific agreements that are binding on the parties, or *non-cooperative*, where agreements among the players are not possible.

- *Players*   Each participant is referred to as a player. The players may be individuals, as in a chess game; firms, usually in imperfectly competitive markets; or countries, involved in a regional conflict. Game theory assumes players can choose among a set of possible actions. The players (decision makers) are rational in that they pursue well-defined objectives. For individuals, the primary objective is utility maximization; for firms, it is profit maximization. Players are assumed to reason strategically, meaning they take into account other players' knowledge and expectations. Games can have any number of players, but for simplicity we will focus on two-player games. We assume that each player chooses a course of action that will yield the greatest benefit for himself or herself.

- *Rules*   Games generally have clearly defined rules that players must follow in pursuing their strategies and goals, for example the rules chess players follow as they choose their moves. The rules of a game may also be viewed as *constraints* that players face as they make choices.

- *Strategies* A possible course of action for a player in a game is called a strategy. Usually players can choose among a number of strategies, while considering the likely response from other players in the game. We will focus on possible strategies in cooperative (collusive) and non-cooperative (non-collusive) games in a two-firm oligopoly.

- *Payoffs* Players in a game seek the best possible outcomes for themselves. The final returns to each player are called *payoffs*. Payoffs may be large, small, or even negative. In some instances, referred to as *zero-sum games,* one player may gain exactly what the other player loses. *Positive-sum games* offer positive payoffs to all players.

EQUILIBRIUM

Recall from Chapter 3 that competitive markets bring about equilibrium price and quantity for specific products or services. There is no unique equilibrium outcome in game theory. This is because outcomes depend not only on what one player may do, but also on how the other players in the game decide to react to any given initial move by the player making the first move.

Prisoner's Dilemma

To illustrate game theory in action, we'll look at the **prisoner's dilemma,** first introduced in the 1940s by Canadian economist A. W. Tucke. The prisoner's dilemma is a type of game between two prisoners that shows the difficulty of cooperating when the two cannot communicate with each other, even when it is in their best interests to cooperate. Let's take a look at an example.

Two individuals, Al and Bill, are caught by police in the act of breaking into a warehouse containing valuable carpets. On the way to headquarters, the police investigators run a check on other crimes in the area and discover that two men closely matching Al's and Bill's physical profiles stole $2 million worth of diamonds just six months earlier, in a robbery for which the police have no leads or witnesses. (Al and Bill did, indeed, steal the diamonds.) In hopes of getting a confession, police investigators decide to interrogate Al and Bill in different rooms so they can't communicate with each other. The game has been set in motion.

The police investigators inform Al and Bill that they are now suspects in the diamond robbery. Since they were caught red-handed trying to break into the carpet warehouse, Al and Bill know they will each get the mandatory two-year jail sentence for that crime alone. If both confess to the diamond robbery each will get four years for both crimes. But if one confesses and the other does not, the one who confesses will receive one year and the one who does not will get twelve.

What are the options for Al and Bill given the "rules" for this game? Figure 13-2 sets out the *payoff matrix* for Al and Bill. Four combinations are possible, and each of the four combinations is represented by a lettered cell. If both confess, they will each get four years in jail (cell A). If neither confesses, each will get only two years (cell D).

FIGURE 13-2 Prisoner's Dilemma Payoff Matrix

Al and Bill each have two possible strategies. Each lettered cell of this four-cell payoff matrix represents the jail terms, in years, that both Al and Bill would receive under various conditions.

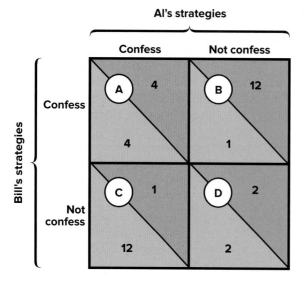

If Bill confesses, but Al does not, he gets one year and Al gets twelve (cell B). Alternatively, if Al confesses, but Bill does not, Al gets one year and Bill goes to the slammer for twelve years (cell C).

Recall that a player in a game will choose a strategy on the basis of what he or she expects the other players will do. If both Al and Bill expect the other to deny they participated in the diamond robbery, neither will confess. Both know this, but neither can be sure the other will deny participating in the robbery. If they were allowed to communicate with each other, they could cooperate (collude) to minimize their jail sentences. But they can't communicate, which means that they are in a non-cooperative game. The dilemma is that they should cooperate to minimize jail time, but if one confesses and the other does not, the latter will face a heavier penalty.

Given the uncertainty of what the other will do, confessing is the best strategy for both Al and Bill in this game. The risk of a much higher jail term is too great for either Al or Bill to consider denying involvement in the diamond robbery. By not confessing, the best that either one can hope for is a one-year jail term, but the possibility exists for a twelve-year term. If both Al and Bill confess, the worst-case scenario is a four-year jail sentence. You should be able to see that the *dominant strategy* for both Al and Bill is to confess.

Strategies in a Two-Firm Oligopoly

Let's now apply the game theory model to a two-firm oligopoly, also known as a *duopoly*. We assume a two-firm oligopoly producing athletic shoes. Each firm—let's call them RareAir and Uptown—has a choice of two pricing strategies: price high or price low. The profit each firm earns will depend on the strategy it chooses and the strategy its rival chooses. Note that we assume that the two companies do not talk to each other. Discussing pricing strategy could lead to a conviction for price fixing under existing laws.

Four possible combinations of strategies are possible for the two firms, and a lettered cell in Figure 13-2 represents each combination, also called the payoff matrix. For example, cell C represents a low-price strategy for Uptown along with a high-price strategy for RareAir. Cell C shows that if Uptown adopts a low-price strategy and RareAir a high-price strategy, then Uptown will earn $15 million (green portion) and RareAir will earn $6 million (tan portion).

Mutual Interdependence Revisited

The data in Figure 13-3 are hypothetical, but their relationships are typical of real situations. Recall that oligopolistic firms can increase their profits, and influence their rivals' profits, by changing their pricing strategies. Each firm's profit depends on its own pricing strategy and that of its rivals. This mutual interdependence of oligopolists is the most obvious point demonstrated by Figure 13-3. If Uptown adopts a high-price strategy, its profit will be $12 million, provided that RareAir also employs a high-price strategy (cell A). But if RareAir uses a low-price strategy against Uptown's high-price strategy (cell B), RareAir will increase its market share and boost its profit from $12 million to $15 million. RareAir's higher profit will come at the expense of Uptown, whose profit will fall from $12 million to $6 million. Uptown's high-price strategy is a good strategy only if RareAir also employs a high-price strategy.

Collusion

Figure 13-3 also suggests that oligopolists can often benefit from **collusion**—that is, cooperation with rivals. To see the benefits of collusion, first suppose that both firms in Figure 13-3 are acting independently and following high-price strategies. Each realizes a $12 million profit (cell A).

Note that either RareAir or Uptown could increase its profit by switching to a low-price strategy (cell B or C). The low-price firm would increase its profit to $15 million, and the high-price firm's profit would fall to $6 million. The high-price firm would be better off if it, too, adopted a low-price policy. Doing so would increase its profit from $6 million to $8 million (cell D). The effect of all this independent strategy shifting would be to reduce both firms' profits from $12 million (cell A) to $8 million (cell D).

In real situations, too, independent action by oligopolists may lead to competitive low-price strategies: Independent oligopolists compete with respect to price, which leads to lower prices and lower profits. This is clearly beneficial to consumers but not to the oligopolists' profits.

How might oligopolists avoid the low-profit outcome of cell D? The answer is that they might collude, rather than establish prices competitively or independently. In our example, the two firms might agree to establish and maintain a high-price policy. Each will increase its profit from $8 million (cell D) to $12 million (cell A).

Incentive to Cheat

The payoff matrix also explains why an oligopolist might be strongly tempted to cheat on a collusive agreement. Suppose Uptown and RareAir agree to maintain high-price policies, with each earning $12 million in profit

KEY GRAPH

FIGURE 13-3   Profit Payoff for a Two-Firm Oligopoly (in millions)

Each firm has two possible pricing strategies. RareAir's strategies are shown in the top margin, and Uptown's in the left margin. Each lettered cell of this four-cell payoff matrix represents one combination of a RareAir strategy and an Uptown strategy and shows the profit, in millions of dollars, that combination would earn for each firm.

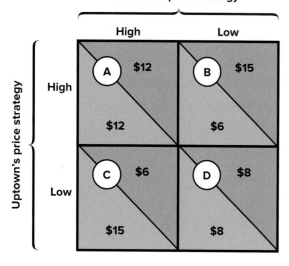

(cell A). Both are tempted to cheat on this collusive pricing agreement, because either firm can increase its profit to $15 million by lowering its price.

For instance, if Uptown secretly cheats and sells at the low price while RareAir keeps on charging the high price, the payoff would move from cell A to cell C so that Uptown's profit would rise to $15 million while RareAir's profit would fall to $6 million. On the other hand, if RareAir cheats and sets a low price while Uptown keeps the agreement and charges the high price, the payoff matrix would move from cell A to cell B so that RareAir would get $15 million while Uptown would get only $6 million.

As you can see, cheating is both very lucrative to the cheater and very costly to the firm that gets cheated on. As a result, both firms will probably cheat so that the game will settle back to cell D, with each firm using its low-price strategy.

QUICK REVIEW 13.1

- An oligopoly is made up of relatively few firms producing either homogeneous or differentiated products; these firms are mutually interdependent.

- Barriers to entry such as scale economies, control of patents or strategic resources, or the ability to engage in retaliatory pricing characterize oligopolies. Oligopolies may result from internal growth of firms, mergers, or both.

- The four-firm concentration ratio shows the percentage of an industry's sales accounted for by its four largest firms; the Herfindahl index measures the degree of market

power in an industry by summing the squares of the percentage market shares held by the individual firms in the industry.

- The prisoner's dilemma is a type of game that shows the difficulty of cooperating when the participants cannot communicate with each other.

- Game theory reveals that (1) oligopolies are mutually inter-dependent in their pricing policies, (2) collusion enhances oligopoly profits, and (3) there is a temptation for oligopolists to cheat on a collusive agreement.

13.3 The Incentives and Obstacles to Collusion: Two Oligopoly Strategies

LO13.3 Explain the two main models of oligopoly pricing and output: collusive pricing and price leadership.

To gain further insight into oligopolistic pricing and output behaviour, we will examine two distinct pricing strategies: (1) collusive pricing and (2) price leadership. Why not a simple single model as in our discussions of the other market structures? There are two reasons:

1. *Diversity of Oligopolies* Oligopoly has a greater range and diversity of market situations than other market structures, including the *tight* oligopoly, in which two or three firms dominate an entire market, and the *loose* oligopoly, in which six or seven firms share, say, 70–80 percent of a market while a competitive fringe of firms shares the remainder. Oligopoly includes both differentiated and standardized products. It includes cases in which firms act in collusion and those in which they act independently. The diversity of oligopoly makes it impossible to explain all oligopolistic behaviours with a single market model.

2. *Complications of Interdependence* The mutual interdependence of oligopolistic firms is what complicates matters. Because firms cannot predict the reactions of their rivals with certainty, they cannot estimate their own demand and marginal-revenue data. Without such data, firms cannot determine their profit-maximizing price and output.

Despite these analytical difficulties, two interrelated characteristics of oligopolistic pricing have been observed. First, prices change less frequently under oligopoly than under perfect competition, monopolistic competition, and, in some instances, monopoly. Second, when oligopolists do change prices, firms are likely to change their prices together, suggesting a tendency to act in concert, or collusively, in setting and changing prices (as we mentioned in the preceding section). The diversity of oligopolies and the presence of mutual interdependence are reflected in the models that follow.

Cartels and Other Collusion: Cooperative Strategies

Our game theory model demonstrates that one possible outcome of an oligopoly market structure is collusion. Collusion occurs whenever firms in an industry reach an agreement to fix prices, divide up the market, or otherwise restrict competition among themselves. The danger of non-collusive oligopolies is that a **price war** may break out, especially during a general business recession. Then each firm finds that, because of unsold goods and excess capacity, it can reduce per-unit costs by increasing market share. The possibility also exists that a new firm may surmount entry barriers and initiate aggressive price cutting to gain a foothold in the market. In addition, the oligopoly's tendency toward rigid prices may adversely affect profits if general inflationary pressures increase costs. But by controlling price through collusion, oligopolists may be able to reduce uncertainty, increase profits, and perhaps even prohibit the entry of new rivals.

PRICE AND OUTPUT

Assume that three oligopolistic firms (Gypsum, Sheetrock, and GSR) produce homogeneous products. All three firms have identical cost curves. Each firm's demand curve is indeterminate unless we know how its rivals will react to any price change. Therefore, we suppose each firm assumes that its two rivals will match either a price cut or a price increase. And, since they have identical cost data, and the same demand and thus marginal-revenue data, we can say that Figure 13-4 represents the position of each of our three oligopolistic firms.

What price and output combination should, say, Gypsum select? If Gypsum were a monopolist, the answer would be clear: Establish output at Q_0, where marginal revenue equals marginal cost, charge the corresponding price P_0, and enjoy the maximum profit attainable. However, Gypsum does have two rivals selling identical products, and if Gypsum's assumption that its rivals will match its price of P_0 proves to be incorrect, the consequences could be disastrous for Gypsum. Specifically, if Sheetrock and GSR actually charge prices below P_0, Gypsum's demand curve D will shift sharply to the left as its potential customers turn to its rivals, which are now selling the same product at a lower price. Of course, Gypsum can retaliate by cutting its price too, but this will move all three firms down their demand curves, lowering their profits. It may even drive them to a point where average total cost exceeds price and losses are incurred.

FIGURE 13-4   Collusion and Joint-Profit Maximization

If oligopolistic firms face identical or highly similar demand and cost conditions, they may collude to limit their joint output and to set a single, common price. Thus each firm acts as if it were a monopolist, setting output at Q_0 and charging price P_0. This price and output combination maximizes each oligopolist's profit (grey area) and thus their joint profit.

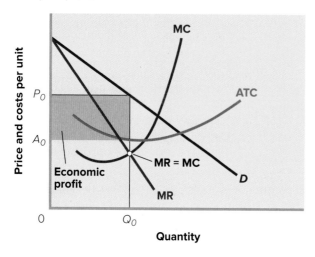

So the question becomes, will Sheetrock and GSR want to charge a price below P_0? Under our assumptions, and recognizing that Gypsum has little choice but to match any price they may set below P_0, the answer is no. Faced with the same demand and cost circumstances, Sheetrock and GSR will find it in their interest to produce Q_0 and charge P_0. This is a curious situation; each firm finds it most profitable to charge the same price, P_0, but only if its rivals also do so! How can the three firms ensure the price P_0 and quantity Q_0 solution in which each is keenly interested? How can they avoid the less profitable outcomes associated with either higher or lower prices?

The answer is evident: They could collude. They could get together, talk it over, and agree to charge the same price, P_0. In addition to reducing the possibility of price wars, this will give each firm the maximum profit. (But it will also subject them to anticombines prosecution if they get caught!) For society, the result will be the same as would occur if the industry were a monopoly composed of three identical plants.

OVERT COLLUSION: THE OPEC CARTEL

Collusion may assume a variety of forms. The most comprehensive form of collusion is the **cartel**, a group of producers that typically creates a formal written agreement specifying how much each member will produce and charge. Output must be controlled to maintain the agreed-on price. The collusion is *overt*, or open to view.

Undoubtedly the most significant international cartel is the Organization of the Petroleum Exporting Countries (OPEC), comprising twelve oil-producing nations (see Global Perspective 13.1). OPEC produces 34 percent of the world's oil and supplies 34 percent of all oil traded internationally. OPEC has in some cases been able to drastically alter oil prices by increasing or decreasing supply. In 1973, for instance, it caused the price of oil to more than triple by getting its members to restrict output. And again, in the late 1990s, it caused oil prices to rise from $11 per barrel to $34 per barrel over a 15-month period.

But it should be kept in mind that most increases in the price of oil are not caused by OPEC. Between 2005 and 2008, for example, oil prices went from $40 per barrel to $140 per barrel due to rapidly rising demand from China and supply uncertainties related to armed conflict in the Middle East. But as the recession that began in December 2008 took hold, demand slumped and oil prices collapsed back to about $40 per barrel. OPEC was largely a non-factor in this rise and fall. In 2014, the combination of the slowdown of the world economy and increasing supply from the U.S. helped bring the price of a barrel from around $100 to $55 by the end of the year, and it was still around the same price by the end of 2017. But in those cases where OPEC can effectively enforce its production agreements, there is little doubt that it can still hold the price of oil substantially above the marginal cost of production.

COVERT COLLUSION: EXAMPLES

Cartels are illegal in Canada, and hence any collusion that exists is *covert*, or secret. Yet there are examples, found in evidence from anticombines (antimonopoly) cases. One example of covert collusion is the 2013 case of the food

13.1 GLOBAL PERSPECTIVE

The 14 OPEC Nations' Daily Oil Production Agreement as of December 2015

The OPEC nations produce about 34 percent of the world's oil and 34 percent of the oil sold in the world market.

OPEC Country	Barrels of Oil
Saudi Arabia	10,088,000
Iraq	4,309,000
UAE	2,895,000
Iran	2,882,000
Kuwait	2,708,000
Venezuela	2,348,000
Nigeria	1,789,000
Angola	1,751,000
Algeria	1,103,000
Indonesia	693,000
Qatar	674,000
Ecuador	551,000
Libya	394,000
Gabon	219,000

Source: OPEC, *OPEC Monthly Oil Market Report*, January 2016.

giants Nestlé and Mars, and independent wholesale distributors attempting to fix the price of chocolates in Canada. Hershey Canada, an alleged co-conspirator, cooperated with Competition Bureau officials in the investigation and pleaded guilty in exchange for leniency. The former president of Nestlé Canada was also charged. The price-fixing scheme dated as far back as 2007.

On a more international scale, in 2011 U.S.-based Whirlpool, Japan-headquartered Panasonic, the Danish firm Danfoss, and the Italian company Appliance Components were fined over $200 million for attempting to run an international cartel that could rig the worldwide prices of refrigerator compressors. In 2012, several Japanese autoparts makers pleaded guilty to rigging the bids that they submitted to a major carmaker. The conspirators employed measures to keep their conduct secret, including using code names and instructing participants to destroy evidence of collusion.

In many other instances collusion is more subtle. Unwritten, informal understandings (historically called "gentlemen's agreements") are frequently made at cocktail parties, on golf courses, through phone calls, or at trade association meetings. In such agreements, executives reach verbal or even tacit (unspoken) understandings on product price, leaving market shares to be decided by nonprice competition. Although these agreements, too, violate anticombines (antitrust) laws—and can result in severe personal and corporate penalties—the elusive character of informal understandings makes them more difficult to detect.

OBSTACLES TO COLLUSION

Normally, cartels and similar collusive arrangements are difficult to establish and maintain, for several reasons:

- *Demand and Cost Differences* When oligopolists face different costs and demand curves, it is difficult for them to agree on a price. Even with highly standardized products, firms usually have somewhat different market shares and operate with differing degrees of productive efficiency. Thus, it is unlikely that even homogeneous oligopolists would have the same demand and cost curves.

In either case, differences in costs and demand mean that the profit-maximizing price will differ among firms; no single price will be readily acceptable to all, as we assumed was true in Figure 13-4. So price collusion depends on compromises and concessions that are not always easy to obtain, and hence they act as obstacles to collusion.

- *Number of Firms* Other things equal, the larger the number of firms, the more difficult it is to create a cartel or other form of price collusion. Agreement on price by three or four producers that control an entire market may be relatively easy to accomplish, but such agreement is more difficult to achieve where there are, say, ten firms, each with roughly 10 percent of the market, or where the Big Three have 70 percent of the market while a competitive fringe of eight to ten smaller firms battle for the remainder.

- *Cheating* As the game theory model makes clear, there is a temptation for collusive oligopolists to engage in secret price cutting to increase sales and profit. The difficulty with such cheating is that buyers who are paying a high price for a product may become aware of the lower-priced sales and demand similar treatment. Or buyers receiving a price concession from one producer may use the concession as a wedge to get even larger price concessions from a rival producer. Buyers' attempts to play producers against one another may precipitate price wars among the producers. Although secret price concessions are potentially profitable, they threaten collusive oligopolies over time. Collusion is more likely to succeed when cheating is easy to detect and punish. Then the conspirators are less likely to cheat on the price agreement.

- *Recession* Long-lasting recession usually serves as an enemy of collusion, because slumping markets increase average total cost. In technical terms, as the oligopolists' demand and marginal revenue curves shift to the left in Figure 13-4 in response to a recession, each firm moves leftward and upward to a higher operating point on its average-total-cost curve. Firms find they have substantial excess production capacity, sales are down, unit costs are up, and profits are being squeezed. Under such conditions, businesses may feel they can avoid serious profit reductions (or even losses) by cutting price and thus gaining sales at the expense of rivals.

- *Potential Entry* The greater prices and profits that result from collusion may attract new entrants, including foreign firms. Since that would increase market supply and reduce prices and profits, successful collusion requires that colluding oligopolists block the entry of new producers.

- *Legal Obstacles: Competition Policy* Canadian anticombines laws prohibit cartels and price-fixing collusion, so less obvious means of price control have evolved in Canada.

Price Leadership Model: Another Cooperative Strategy

One type of implicit understanding by which oligopolists can coordinate prices is called **price leadership**. A practice evolves whereby the dominant firm initiates price changes and all other firms more or less automatically follow the leader. Many industries, including cement, newsprint, glass containers, steel, beer, fertilizer, cigarettes, and tin, practise or have recently practised price leadership.

LEADERSHIP TACTICS

An examination of price leadership in a variety of industries suggests that the price leader is likely to use the following strategies.

- *Infrequent Price Changes* Because price changes always carry the risk that rivals will not follow the lead, price adjustments are made only infrequently, when cost and demand conditions have been altered significantly.

- *Communications* The price leader often communicates impending price adjustments to the industry through speeches by major executives, trade publication interviews, or press releases. By publicizing the need to raise prices, the price leader seeks agreement among its competitors regarding the actual increase.

- *Limit Pricing* The price leader does not always choose the price that maximizes short-run profits for the industry because the industry may want to discourage new firms from entering. To discourage new competitors and to maintain the current oligopolistic structure of the industry, the price leader may keep price below the short-run profit-maximizing level. The strategy of establishing a price that blocks the entry of new firms is called limit pricing.

BREAKDOWNS IN PRICE LEADERSHIP: PRICE WARS

Price leadership in oligopoly occasionally breaks down, and sometimes results in a price war. An example of price leadership temporarily breaking down occurred in the breakfast cereal industry, in which Kellogg traditionally had been the price leader. General Mills countered Kellogg's leadership in 1995 by reducing the prices of its cereals by 11 percent. In 1996 Post responded with a 20 percent price cut, which Kellogg then followed. Not to be outdone, Post reduced its prices by another 11 percent.

As another example, in October 2009 with the Christmas shopping season just getting under way, U.S.-based Walmart, the world's largest retailer, cut its price on ten highly anticipated new books to just $10 each. Within hours, Amazon.com matched the price. Walmart then retaliated by cutting its price for the books to just $9 each. Amazon.com matched that—at which point Walmart went to $8.99! Then, out of nowhere, Target, another large U.S. department store, jumped in at $8.98, a price that Amazon.com and Walmart immediately matched. And that is where the price finally came to rest—a level so low that each company was losing money on every book sold.

Most price wars eventually run their course. After a period of low or negative profits, they again cede price leadership to one of the industry's leading firms. That firm then begins to raise prices, and the other firms willingly follow suit.

QUICK REVIEW 13.2

- Cartels agree on production limits and set a common price to maximize the joint profit of their members as if each were a subsidiary of a single monopoly.

- Collusion among oligopolists is difficult because of (1) demand and cost differences among sellers, (2) the complexity of output coordination among producers, (3) the potential for cheating, (4) a tendency for agreements to break down during recessions, (5) the potential entry of new firms, and (6) competition laws.

- Price leadership involves an informal understanding among oligopolists to match any price change initiated by a designated firm (often the industry's dominant firm).

13.4 Oligopoly and Advertising

LO13.4   Contrast the potential positive and potential negative effects of advertising.

We have noted that oligopolists would rather not compete on the basis of price and may become involved in price collusion. Nonetheless, each firm's share of the total market is typically determined through product development and advertising, for two reasons:

1. Product improvements and successful advertising can produce more permanent gains in market share because they cannot be duplicated as quickly and completely as price reductions.

2. Oligopolists have sufficient financial resources to engage in product development and advertising. For most oligopolists, the economic profits earned in the past can help finance current advertising and product development.

In recent years, Canadian advertising has exceeded $9 billion annually, and worldwide advertising has reached almost $550 billion. Advertising is prevalent in both monopolistic competition and oligopoly.

Advertising may affect prices, competition, and efficiency both positively and negatively, depending on the circumstances. While our focus here is on advertising by oligopolists, the analysis is equally applicable to advertising by firms in monopolistic competition.

Positive Effects of Advertising

To make rational (efficient) decisions, consumers need information about product characteristics and prices. Media advertising may be a low-cost means for consumers to obtain that information. Suppose you are in the market for a high-quality camera and there is no advertising for such a product in newspapers or magazines or on the Internet. To make a rational choice, you may have to spend several days visiting stores to determine the prices and features of various brands. This search has both direct costs (gasoline, parking fees) and indirect costs (the value of your time). By providing information about the available options, advertising reduces your search time and minimizes these costs.

By providing information about the various competing goods that are available, advertising diminishes monopoly power. In fact, advertising is frequently associated with the introduction of new products designed to compete with existing brands. Could Toyota and Honda have so strongly challenged North American auto producers without advertising? Could FedEx have sliced market share away from UPS and Canada Post without advertising?

Viewed this way, advertising is an efficiency-enhancing activity. It is a relatively inexpensive means of providing useful information to consumers and thus lowering their search costs. By enhancing competition, advertising results in greater economic efficiency. By facilitating the introduction of new products, advertising speeds up technological progress. And by increasing output, advertising can reduce long-run average total cost by enabling firms to obtain economies of scale.

Potential Negative Effects of Advertising

Not all the effects of advertising are positive. Much advertising is designed simply to persuade consumers in favour of the advertiser's product. A television commercial showing that a popular personality drinks a particular brand of soft drink conveys little or no information to consumers about price or quality. Indeed, in some cases advertising may well persuade consumers to pay high prices for much-acclaimed but inferior products, forgoing better but unadvertised products selling at lower prices. For example, *Consumer Reports* recently found that heavily advertised premium motor oils and fancy additives provide no better engine performance and longevity than do cheaper brands.

Firms often establish substantial brand-name loyalty and thus achieve monopoly power via their advertising (see Global Perspective 13.2). As a consequence, they are able to increase their sales, expand their market share, and enjoy greater profits. Larger profit permits still more advertising and further enlargement of the firm's market share and profit. In time, consumers may lose the advantages of competitive markets and face the disadvantages of monopolized markets. Moreover, new entrants to the industry need to incur large advertising costs to establish their products in the marketplace; thus, advertising costs may be a barrier to entry.

Advertising may also be self-cancelling. The advertising campaign of one fast-food hamburger chain may be offset by equally costly campaigns waged by rivals, so each firm's demand actually remains unchanged. Few, if any,

13.2 GLOBAL PERSPECTIVE

The World's Top Ten Brand Names, 2015

Here are the world's top ten brands, based on four criteria: the brand's market share within its category, the brand's world appeal across age groups and nationalities, the loyalty of customers to the brand, and the ability of the brand to "stretch" to products beyond the original product.

World's Top 10 Brands

- Apple
- Google
- Coca-Cola
- Microsoft
- IBM
- Toyota
- Samsung
- General Electric
- McDonald's
- Amazon

Source: Interbrand, "100 Best Global Brands, 2015," www.interbrand.com.

extra burgers will be purchased, and each firm's market share will stay the same. But because of the advertising, the cost and hence the price of hamburgers will be higher. But because of the advertising, all firms will experience higher costs and either their profits will fall or, through successful price leadership, their product prices will rise.

When advertising either leads to increased monopoly power or is self-cancelling, economic inefficiency results.

13.5 Oligopoly and Efficiency

LO13.5   Discuss the efficiency of oligopoly from society's standpoint and whether it is more or less efficient than monopoly.

Is oligopoly, then, an efficient market structure from society's standpoint? How do the price and output decisions of the oligopolist measure up to the triple equality $P = MC = $ minimum ATC that occurs in perfect competition?

PRODUCTIVE AND ALLOCATIVE EFFICIENCY

Many economists believe that the outcome of some oligopolistic markets is approximately as shown in Figure 13-4. This view is bolstered by evidence that many oligopolists sustain sizable economic profits year after year. In that case, the oligopolist's production occurs where price exceeds marginal cost and average total cost. Moreover, production is below the output at which average total cost is minimized. In this view, neither productive efficiency ($P = $ minimum ATC) nor allocative efficiency ($P = MC$) is likely to occur under oligopoly.

A few observers assert that oligopoly is actually less desirable than monopoly, because government usually regulates monopoly to guard against abuses of monopoly power. Informal collusion among oligopolists may yield price and output results similar to those under monopoly yet give the outward appearance of competition involving independent firms.

QUALIFICATIONS

We should note, however, three qualifications to this view:

- *Increased Foreign Competition* In recent decades foreign competition has increased rivalry in a number of oligopolistic industries—steel, automobiles, video games, electric shavers, outboard motors, and copy machines, for example. This has helped to break down such cozy arrangements as price leadership and to stimulate much more competitive pricing.

- *Limit Pricing* Recall that some oligopolists may purposely keep prices below the short-run profit-maximizing level in order to bolster entry barriers. In essence, consumers and society may get some of the benefits of competition—prices closer to marginal cost and minimum average total cost—even without the competition that free entry would provide.

- *Technological Advance* Over time, oligopolistic industries may foster more rapid product development and greater improvement of production techniques than would be possible if they were perfectly competitive. Oligopolists have large economic profits from which they can fund expensive research and development (R&D). Moreover, the existence of barriers to entry may give the oligopolist some assurance that it will reap the rewards of successful R&D. Thus, the short-run economic inefficiencies of oligopolists may be partly or wholly offset by the oligopolists' contributions to better products, lower prices, and lower costs over time.

QUICK REVIEW 13.3

- Oligopolists emphasize nonprice competition because (a) advertising and product variations are harder to match than price changes and (b) oligopolists frequently have ample resources to fund nonprice competition.

- Advertising can help reduce monopoly power by presenting consumers with useful information about existing products and by helping to introduce new products.

- Advertising can hurt consumers and competition by promoting monopoly power and creating entry barriers.

13.6 Game Theory and Strategic Behaviour

LO13.6   Utilize additional game-theory terminology and demonstrate how to find Nash equilibriums in both simultaneous and sequential games.

We have seen that game theory is helpful in explaining mutual interdependence and strategic behaviour by oligopolists. This appendix provides additional oligopoly-based applications of game theory.

Consider Figure 13-5, which lists strategies and outcomes for two fictitious producers of the computer memory chips referred to as DRAMs (dynamic random access memory circuits). Chipco is the single producer of these chips in Canada and Dramco is the only producer in China. Each firm has two alternative strategies: an international strategy in which it competes directly against the other firm in both countries and a national strategy in which it confines its sales to its home country.

The game and payoff matrix shown in Figure 13-5 is a **one-time game,** because the firms select their optimal strategy in a single time period without regard to possible interactions in subsequent time periods. The game is also a **simultaneous game,** because the firms choose their strategies at the same time, and a **positive-sum game,** a game in which the sum of the two firms' outcomes (here, profits) is positive. (In contrast, the net gain in a **zero-sum game** is zero because one firm's gain must equal the other firm's loss, and the net gain in a **negative-sum game** is negative.) In some positive-sum games, both firms may have positive outcomes. That is the case in Figure 13-5.

To determine optimal strategies, Chipco looks across the two rows in the payoff matrix (green portion of cells in millions of dollars) and Dramco looks down the two columns (tan portion of cells). These payoffs indicate that both firms have a **dominant strategy**—an option that is better than any alternative option *regardless of what the other firm does.* To see this, notice that Chipco's international strategy will give it a higher profit than its national strategy—regardless of whether Dramco chooses to utilize an international or a national strategy. An international strategy will produce an $11 million profit for Chipco (green portion of cell A) if Dramco also uses an international strategy, while a national strategy will result in a $20 million profit for Chipco (green portion of cell B) if Dramco uses a national strategy. Chipco's possible $11 million and $20 million outcomes are clearly better than the $5 million (cell C) and $17 million (cell D) outcomes it could receive if it chose to pursue a national strategy. Chipco's international strategy is, consequently, its dominant strategy. Using similar logic, Dramco also concludes that its international strategy is its dominant strategy.

FIGURE 13-5   One-Time Game

In this single-period, positive-sum game, Chipco's international strategy is its dominant strategy—the alternative that is superior to any other strategy regardless of whatever Dramco does. Similarly, Dramco's international strategy is also its dominant strategy. With both firms choosing international strategies, the outcome of the game is cell A, where each firm receives an $11 million profit. Cell A is a Nash equilibrium because neither firm will independently want to move away from it given the other firm's strategy.

In this particular case, the outcome (cell A) of the two dominant strategies is the game's **Nash equilibrium**—an outcome from which neither rival wants to deviate.[1] At the Nash equilibrium, both rivals see their current strategy as optimal *given the other firm's strategic choice*. The Nash equilibrium is the only outcome in the payoff matrix in Figure 13-5 that, once achieved, is stable and therefore will persist.[2]

Credible and Empty Threats

In looking for optimal strategies, Chipco and Dramco both note that they could increase their profit from $11 million to $17 million if they could agree to jointly pursue national strategies (cell D) instead of independently pursuing international strategies (cell A). Presumably the national strategies would leave the firms as pure monopolists in their domestic economies, with each able to set higher prices and obtain greater profits as a result. But if this territorial agreement were put in place, both firms would have an incentive to cheat on the agreement by secretly selling DRAMs in each other's countries. That would temporarily move the game to either cell B or cell C. Once discovered, however, such cheating would undermine the territorial agreement and return the game to the Nash equilibrium (cell A).

Now let's add a new twist—a credible threat—to the game shown in Figure 13-5. A **credible threat** is a statement of coercion (a threat!) that is believable by the other firm. Suppose that Chipco is the low-cost producer of DRAMs because of its superior technology. Also, suppose that Chipco approaches Dramco saying that Chipco intends to use its national strategy and expects Dramco to do the same. If Dramco decides against the national strategy or agrees to the strategy and then later cheats on the agreement, Chipco will immediately drop its price to an ultra-low level equal to its average total cost (ATC). Both firms know that Chipco's ATC price is below Dramco's ATC. Although Chipco will see its economic profit fall to zero, Dramco will suffer an economic loss and possibly go out of business.

If Chipco's threat is credible, the two firms represented in Figure 13-5 will abandon the Nash equilibrium (cell A) to deploy their national strategies and achieve highly profitable cell D. In game theory, credible threats such as this can help establish and maintain collusive agreements. A strong "enforcer" can help prevent cheating and maintain the group discipline needed for cartels, price-fixing conspiracies, and territorial understandings to successfully generate high profits.

But credible threats are difficult to achieve in the actual economy. For example, Dramco might rightly wonder why Chipco had not previously driven it out of business through an ultra-low price strategy. Is Chipco fearful of the Canadian Competition Bureau, which enforces anticombines laws?

If Dramco does not wish to participate in the proposed scheme, it might counter Chipco's threat with its own: Forget that you ever talked to us and we will not take this illegal "offer" to the Competition Bureau. Dramco can make this threat because strict laws are in place against attempts to restrain trade through price fixing and territorial agreements.

So Dramco may view Chipco's threat as simply an **empty threat**—a statement of coercion that is not believable by the threatened firm. If so, the Nash equilibrium will prevail, with both firms pursuing an international strategy.

Repeated Games and Reciprocity Strategies

The Chipco–Dramco game was a one-time game, but many strategic situations are repeated by the same oligopolists over and over. For example, Coca-Cola and Pepsi face mutual interdependence on pricing, advertising, and product development year after year, decade after decade. The same is true for Boeing and Airbus, Walmart and Target, Toyota and General Motors, Labatt and Molson, Nike and Adidas, and numerous other dominant pairs.

In a **repeated game**—a game that recurs more than once—the optimal strategy may be to cooperate and refrain from competing as hard as possible, so long as the other firm reciprocates by also not competing as hard as possible.[3] To see how this works, consider two hypothetical producers of soft drinks: 2Cool and ThirstQ. If 2Cool competes hard with ThirstQ in today's situation, in which ThirstQ would like 2Cool to take things easy, ThirstQ will most like retaliate against 2Cool in any subsequent situation where the circumstances are reversed. In contrast, if ThirstQ cooperates with 2Cool in game 1, ThirstQ can expect 2Cool to reciprocate in game 2 of their repeated

---

[1] The Nash equilibrium is named for its discoverer, John F. Nash. Nash's life and Nobel Prize are the subject of the motion picture *A Beautiful Mind*, produced by Ron Howard and starring Russell Crowe.

[2] Dominant strategies in games are not required for Nash equilibriums to exist.

[3] We are assuming either an infinitely repeated game or a game of unknown time horizon. Games with a known ending date undermine reciprocity strategies.

FIGURE 13-6 A Repeated Game with Reciprocity

(a) In the first payoff matrix, 2Cool introduces its new Cool Cola with a large promotional advertising budget, but its rival ThirstQ maintains its normal advertising budget even though it could counter 2Cool with a large advertising budget of its own and drive the outcome from cell B to cell A. ThirstQ forgoes this $2 million of extra profit because it knows that it will soon be introducing its own new product (Quench It). (b) In the second payoff matrix, ThirstQ introduces Quench It with a large promotional advertising budget. Cool2 reciprocates ThirstQ's earlier accommodation by not matching ThirstQ's promotional advertising budget and instead allowing the outcome of the repeated game to be cell C. The profit of both 2Cool and ThirstQ is therefore larger over the two periods than if each firm had aggressively countered the other's single-period strategy.

(a) 2Cool introduces Cool Cola   **(b) ThirstQ introduces Quench It**

interaction. Both firms know full well the negative long-run consequences of ever refusing to cooperate. So the cooperation continues, not only in game 2, but in games 3, 4, 5, and beyond.

Figure 13-6 shows side-by-side payoff matrixes for the two games. In Figure 13-6a, 2Cool and ThirstQ face a situation in which 2Cool is introducing a new cola called Cool Cola and has two advertising options: a high promotional budget to introduce the new product and a normal advertising budget. ThirstQ has the same two options: a high promotional budget to try to counter 2Cool's product introduction and a normal advertising budget.

The analysis is now familiar to you. The dominant strategies for both firms are their large promotional advertising budgets, and the Nash equilibrium is cell A. Both firms could do better at cell D if each agreed to use normal advertising budgets. But 2Cool could do better still. It could achieve the $16 million of profit in cell B, but only if ThirstQ holds its advertising budget to its normal level during the introduction of Cool Cola.

ThirstQ might voluntarily do just that! It knows that game 2 (Figure 13-6b) is forthcoming, in which it will be introducing its new product, Quench It. By leaving its advertising budget at its normal level during 2Cool's introduction of Cool Cola, thereby sacrificing profit of $2 million (= $10 million in cell A − $8 million in cell B), it can expect ThirstQ to reciprocate in the subsequent game in which ThirstQ introduces Quench It.

Without formally colluding—and risking anticombines penalties—game 1 ends at cell B and repeated game 2 ends at cell C. Using reciprocity, 2Cool's total profit of $26 million (= $16 million in game 1 + $10 million in game 2) exceeds the $21 million (= $10 million + $11 million) it would have earned without the reciprocity. ThirstQ similarly benefits. To check your understanding, confirm this fact using the numbers in the two matrixes.

First-Mover Advantages and Pre-emption of Entry

The games we have highlighted thus far have been games in which two firms simultaneously select their optimal strategies. But in some actual economic circumstances, firms apply strategies sequentially: One firm moves first

FIGURE 13-7   A First-Mover Advantage and the Pre-emption of Entry

In this game in which strategies are pursued sequentially, the firm that moves first can take advantage of the particular situation represented in which only a single firm can exist profitably in some geographical market. Here, we suppose that Big Box moves first with its "build" strategy to achieve the $12 million profit outcome in cell C. Huge Box then will find that it will lose money if it also builds in this market because that will result in a $5 million loss, as shown in cell A.

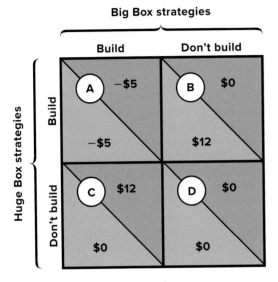

and commits to a strategy to which a rival firm must subsequently respond. In such a **sequential game**, the final outcome may depend upon which firm moves first, since the first mover may have the opportunity to establish a Nash equilibrium that works in its favour.

Consider Figure 13-7, which identifies a zero-sum game in which two large retailers—let's call them Big Box and Huge Box—are each considering building a large retail store in a small rural city. As indicated in the figure, each firm has two strategies: "Build" and "Don't build." The payoff matrix reflects that the city is not large enough to support two big box retailers profitably. If both retailers simultaneously build, the outcome will be cell A and each firm will lose $5 million. If neither firm builds the outcome will be cell D with both firms securing zero profit. If only Big Box builds, the outcome will be cell B and Big Box will profit handsomely at $12 million. If Huge Box builds but Big Box stays out, the outcome will be cell C and Huge Box will secure the $12 million profit. Either cell B or cell C is the possible Nash equilibrium. At either cell, both firms will have selected their best option in view of the strategy taken by the other firm.

The payoff matrix in Figure 13-7 clearly reveals that whoever builds first will pre-empt the other retailer from entering the market. An extremely large **first-mover advantage** exists in this particular game. Suppose that a well-thought-out strategy and adequate financing leave Big Box better prepared than Huge Box to move quickly to build a large retail store in this city. By exploiting its first-mover advantage, Big Box pre-empts Huge Box's entry to this market.

Many actual firms have used variations of this first-mover strategy to a greater or lesser extent to pre-empt major rivals, or at least greatly slow their entry. Examples are Canadian Tire, The Bay, Walmart, Home Depot, Costco, Starbucks, and many more. The strategy is highly risky, however, because it requires the commitment of huge amounts of investment funds to saturate the market and preclude entry by other firms. Also, to be the first mover in places that are being transformed from rural land into urban areas, firms may need to build their stores many months prior to the time when the area in question becomes developed enough to provide significant business. That may mean losses until the market grows sufficiently for profitability. Some firms like Walmart have become huge, profitable international enterprises by using a first-mover strategy. Other firms, such as Krispy Kreme Donuts, have lost millions of dollars because their extremely rapid expansion turned out to be unprofitable in many of their outlets when the expected customers never materialized.

QUICK REVIEW 13.4

- Positive-sum, zero-sum, and negative-sum games have combined payoffs across all players that sum to, respectively, something positive, zero, and something negative. Positive-sum games correspond to "win-win" situations; zero-sum games to "I win–you lose" situations; and negative-sum games to "we both lose" situations.

- A dominant strategy for a firm in a two-firm game is a strategy that leads to better outcomes for the firm no matter what the other firm does.

- A Nash equilibrium occurs when both firms are simultaneously playing dominant strategies, so that neither firm has any incentive to alter its behaviour.

- Reciprocity can improve outcomes in repeated games.

Extensive Form Representation of Sequential Games

Summarizing a game using a payoff matrix is referred to as displaying the game in *strategic form*, because the rows and columns of the matrix represent each firm's strategy choices (such as build or don't build in Figure 13-7). But sequential games can also be displayed in an alternative format called extensive form in which an extensive (spread out) "game tree" is used to display not only which strategy choices are available but the order in which decisions are made, starting with the first mover.

Figure 13-8 presents the extensive form representation of the first-mover game that was displayed in strategic form in Figure 13-7. As you will recall, Big Box (BB) gets to move first and then Huge Box (HB) gets to move second. There are three circular **decision nodes**, labelled BB, HB_1, and HB_2. Node BB represents the two choices that Big Box has as first mover. It can either choose Build or Don't Build. If it chooses Build, we follow the upsloping path from node BB. But if Big Box chooses Don't Build, we take the downsloping path from node BB.

The upsloping path leads to decision node HB_1 while the downsloping path leads to decision node HB_2. HB_1 represents the decision that Huge Box will have to face as second mover if Big Box has chosen Build in the first

FIGURE 13-8   Extensive Form Representation of First-Mover Advantage and the Pre-emption of Entry

Here we display the game shown in Figure 13-7 in extensive form (game-tree format) rather than in strategic form (payoff-matrix format). The extensive form allows us to study the sequence in which decisions are made, moving left to right. Big Box (BB) moves first at decision node BB. Its decision about Build or Don't Build will lead, respectively, to either node HB_1 or node HB_2. Huge Box moves second from either HB_1 or HB_2 (depending upon what Big Box did at node BB). Huge Box's decision at HB_1 or HB_2 will lead to one of the four terminal nodes: A, C, B, and D (which correspond to the identically labelled cells in Figure 13-7). The bold line segments indicate the subgame perfect Nash equilibrium path that shows how the game will be played out if each company always does what is most profitable for itself given what it knows about the profit incentives facing its rival.

stage. HB$_2$ represents the choice that Huge Box will have to face as second mover if Big Box has chosen Don't Build in the first stage. In either case, Huge Box must choose either Build or Don't Build. Those choices lead to the **terminal nodes** A, C, B, and D, which correspond to the identically labelled cells in the strategic form representation shown in Figure 13-7.

Associated with each terminal node is a pair of numbers representing the profits that will be earned by each firm if the sequential decisions made by Big Box and Huge Box lead to that particular terminal node. The profits are presented as a pair of numbers in the format: (Big Box profit, Huge Box profit). As an example, the profits of the two firms at terminal node C are $12 million for Big Box and $0 for Huge Box.

In Figure 13-8, two segments of the game tree have been drawn bolder to make them stand out: the upsloping segment that begins at BB and the downsloping segment that begins at HB$_1$. These lines represent the Nash equilibrium of the game. The way you determine the Nash equilibrium when a game is displayed in extensive form is by using a two-stage process called **backward induction** that first divides the overall game tree into nested "subgames" before working backwards from right to left—from the profits shown at each terminal node on the right to the preceding decisions that are necessary to end up at any particular terminal node.

To see how this works, notice that the upsloping and downsloping choices that emanate from decision node HB$_1$ form a **subgame** (or mini-game) within the overall game. Starting from HB$_1$, Huge Box can choose either Build or Don't Build. If we look at the payouts from those two choices, we see that Huge Box would prefer Don't Build so that it will receive a profit of $0 at terminal node C rather than a loss of −$5 million at terminal node A. So in the subgame that starts at decision node HB$_1$, Huge Box would prefer Don't Build. By contrast, in the subgame that starts at decision node HB$_2$, Huge box would prefer Build over Don't Build because choosing Build would lead to a profit of $12 million while choosing Don't Build would lead to a profit of $0.

We now know that if Huge Box ends up at decision node HB$_1$ it will choose Don't Build, so that the overall game will end at terminal node C. We also know that if Huge Box ends up at decision node HB$_2$ it will choose Build, thus forcing the overall game to end up at terminal node B. Those facts will be known perfectly well not only to us but to the managers of Big Box as well. So when Big Box makes its choice as the first mover at decision node BB, it will know that choosing Build will definitely lead to terminal node C because Huge Box will definitely choose Don't Build if it finds itself at decision node HB$_1$. Big Box will also understand that if it chooses Don't Build at decision node BB, the game will end up at terminal node B because Huge Box will definitely choose Build if it finds itself at decision node HB$_2$.

Thus, from Big Box's perspective, choosing Build will lead to the profits associated with C while choosing Don't Build will lead to the profits associated with B. Thus, Big Box's optimal decision at decision node BB comes down to seeing whether it will profit more highly at C than at B. If we compare Big Box's profits at C and B, we find that Big Box would prefer to end up at C rather than B because its profit at C would be $12 million while its profit at B would be $0. As a result, Big Box will choose Build at decision node BB. That choice leads upward to decision node HB$_1$, where Huge Box will definitely choose Don't Build. And that decision, in turn, will lead to both firms receiving the profits associated with terminal node C.

The two bold segments of the game tree show the path that results from those sequential decisions. It is a Nash equilibrium from which neither party has an incentive to deviate because by working backward from right to left through each of the subgames we have made sure that both firms will be making rational (profit-maximizing) choices at every decision node. Thus, when the game is played out in proper sequence from left to right, neither firm will want to deviate from the decisions indicated by the bold path. Economists sometimes refer to the bold path as the **subgame perfect Nash equilibrium** because the process of backward induction used to find the bold path relies on both firms having perfect information about (i.e., a complete understanding of) the decisions that will be made in each subgame.

Note that the subgame perfect Nash equilibrium path shown in Figure 13-8 implies the same outcome with regard to preemption of entry as we discovered when we studied the same game in strategic form in Figure 13-7. Along the bold equilibrium path, Big Box will choose Build as first mover and Huge Box will chose Don't Build as second mover. As a result, Big Box will be able to preempt Huge Box from entering the local market.

A Leader–Follower (Stackelberg Duopoly) Game

Extensive form representation and backward induction can also be used to solve for situations in which a leader (first mover) firm cannot preempt a follower firm from entering its industry. The subgame perfect Nash equilibrium involves both firms entering the industry and producing positive levels of output.

As an example, let us consider a duopoly (two-firm) automobile manufacturing industry in which both firms have to make sequential decisions about factory size and output levels. In other duopoly models, both firms move simultaneously. But in this section we are assuming a Stackelberg duopoly model in which the two competitors move sequentially.

In this sequential model, an established truck maker that has political connections will get to move first and decide how big a factory it will build. Its rival will then move second and determine how big its factory will be. Both firms are aware that the more the two firms produce and supply in total, the lower will be the market price of trucks. So there is a trade-off between building higher-capacity factories on the one hand and getting less revenue per truck on the other hand.

In this strategic situation, the leader firm's choice of factory size must attempt to rationally anticipate what the follower firm's factory-size choice will be. As an example, if the leader firm anticipates that the follower firm will end up building a huge factory, the leader firm may want to build a small factory to keep total output low enough that the market price of trucks does not collapse.

In Figure 13-9, the leader firm chooses first, at decision node L. Its choices are to either set up a smaller factory that can produce 5000 trucks per year or a larger factory that can produce 10,000 trucks per year. If the leader firm chooses the smaller factory, the upward-sloping option will lead to decision node F_1, where the follower firm can either choose to set up a factory that will produce 7000 trucks per year or one that can produce 12,000 trucks per year. Note that when starting at decision node F_1, both of the follower firm's factory-size options will produce more vehicles per year than the 5000 trucks per year that the leader firm would have had to have chosen at decision node L to have moved the game to decision node F_1. This reflects the fact that the follower firm would take the leader firm's decision to produce only 5000 cars per year as an opportunity to become the larger player in the two-firm industry. The only question for the follower firm at decision node F_1 is to decide on how much larger it will want its output of trucks to be.

By contrast, if the leader firm chooses to build the larger factory at decision node L, the game will follow the downsloping path to decision node F_2, where the follower firm can either choose to set up a factory that will produce 5000 cars per year or a factory that will produce 7000 cars per year. In this case, the follower firm is resigned to being the smaller firm in the industry, since both options will produce fewer cars per year than the 10,000 that the leader would have had to have chosen for the game to have ended up at decision node F_2.

We can now use subgames and backward induction to solve for the subgame perfect Nash equilibrium, which is indicated in Figure 13-8 by the bold segments of the game tree. As before, we solve the game tree backward, from

FIGURE 13-9 Extensive Form Representation of Leader–Follower (Stackelberg Duopoly) Game

There is a Leader firm and a Follower firm that sequentially must decide on their respective factory sizes. The Leader firm moves first at decision node L. The Follower firm moves second, starting from either decision node F_1 or decision node F_2 (depending on the Leader firm's decision at decision node L). Each firm wishes to make as much money as possible, but knows that there is a trade-off between producing more cars and reducing the market price per vehicle. Moving from right to left, backward induction indicates that the subgame perfect Nash equilibrium corresponds to the path indicated by the bold line segments.

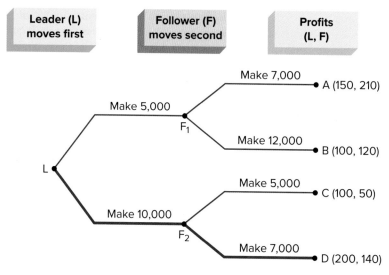

right to left. Consider first the subgame that begins at decision node F_1. There, the follower firm will want to choose to produce 7000 cars per year because the $210 million profit it would obtain from doing so will be nearly double the $120 million profit it would obtain if it chose to produce 12,000 cars per year. Next, consider the subgame that begins at decision node F_2. There, the follower firm will want to produce 7000 cars per year rather than 5000 cars per year because the former will generate a profit of $140 million per year while the latter would generate a profit of only $50 million per year.

The leader firm can now take into account at decision node L how the follower firm will behave if the game ends up at either decision node F_1 or decision node F_2. If the leader firm chooses to produce 5000 cars per year at decision node L, the follower firm will choose to produce 7000 cars at decision node F_1, thereby leading to terminal node A and a payoff of $150 million for the leader firm. By contrast, if the leader firm chooses to produce 10,000 cars per year at decision node L, the follower firm will choose to produce 7000 cars per year at decision node F_2, thereby leading to terminal node D and a payoff of $200 million for the leader firm.

The leader firm can see that it would be better off ending up at terminal node D rather than at terminal node A. It will consequently choose to build a factory that can produce 10,000 cars per year. The subgame perfect Nash equilibrium therefore consists of the line segment that leads downward from decision node L followed by the line segment that leads downward from decision node F_2. Along that path, neither firm has any reason to change its behaviour given the perfect (complete) knowledge it possesses about both its own incentives and those of the other firm.

Note that there is no preemption of entry in this game. Both firms produce, but at different levels of output. The leader firm produces more and the follower firm produces less. This intuition can be generalized from duopoly industries with just two firms to oligopoly industries with several firms. The leader goes first but the profit possibilities at the various terminal nodes imply a subgame perfect Nash equilibrium in which additional firms enter the industry as followers. The followers produce less than the leader but are still able to survive and carry on. Examples include microchips, where Intel was the leader and several other firms such as AMD became followers, and smartphones, where Apple was the leader and several other firms such as Samsung, LG, and Google became followers.

Please note, however, that once entry has occurred and competition is possible, it may be the case that one or more of the follower firms may come to dominate the industry, pushing aside the leader firm that once held sway. This happened with televisions. Early leaders such as Sylvania got pushed aside in the 1980s by Japanese brands such as Sony before Korean brands such as Samsung came to dominate in the 2000s.

The LAST WORD

Internet Oligopolies

© Anatolii Babii/Alamy Stock Photo

A few big companies dominate the Internet—and act as highly competitive oligopolists.

The Internet only became accessible to the average person in the mid 1990s. Over the past ten years, it has evolved into a medium dominated by a few major firms, chief among them Google, Facebook, and Amazon. Other major players are Microsoft and Apple.

A key characteristic of each of these firms is that it holds a near-monopoly in a particular part of the tech business. Google dominates search. Facebook holds sway in social networking. Amazon rules the roost in online shopping. Microsoft holds a near-monopoly on PC operating systems and business-productivity software. And Apple became the world's most valuable company in 2012 by being the planet's most profitable manufacturer of computers, mobile phones, and tablets—all of which run on Apple's own operating software. As of the start of 2015, it was still the most valuable company in the world.

But instead of just trying to maintain dominance in its own sector, each of these Internet titans has used the profits generated by its own near-monopoly to try to steal business from one or more of the other titans. The result has been intense oligopolistic competition between a few well-funded rivals.

Consider search. Google's nearly 70 percent share of the search market creates massive amounts of advertising revenue for Google. In fact, Google's 2014 ad revenues in Canada of approximately $4 billion exceeded the ad revenues received by all magazines and newspapers combined. So it may not be surprising that Microsoft created its Bing search engine to compete with Google. As of late 2014, Bing held almost 20 percent of the search market. Along with Yahoo, which held 10 percent, Bing maintains competitive pressure on Google, forcing ad rates lower.

Facebook is by far the largest social networking website, with more than one billion total users and 700 million regular users. But in 2011 Google succeeded in creating a large enough social network to challenge Facebook. Google did so by encouraging the users of its various free services—such as Gmail and YouTube—to join the Google+ social network. By late 2014, Google+ had some 540 million total users and 300 million regular users—enough to compete credibly with Facebook.

Google+ was important for Google because Facebook had been encouraging advertisers to switch from using Google search ads to using Facebook banner ads that could be targeted at specific types of Facebook users (such as "25-to-30-year-old males who live in Vancouver and own pets"). Google can now counter by offering its own social network on which advertisers can place those sorts of targeted ads.

Google has also challenged Apple by releasing its very popular Android operating system for mobile devices to compete with the iOS operating system that Apple uses on both its iPhone cell phones and its iPad tablet computers. By doing so, Google reduced the threat that Apple could at some point in the future substantially reduce Google's search revenues by directing searches done on Apple devices to a proprietary search engine of Apple's own design.

Apple's dominance in smartphones and tablets has also been challenged by some of the other Internet titans. In addition to licensing the Android operating system to any manufacturer who wanted to use it on their own cellphones or tablets, Google launched its own line of Nexus mobile devices to compete with Apple's iPhone and iPad. Also seeking to challenge Apple in mobile devices, Microsoft updated its Windows operating system to handle phones and tablets, launched its Surface line of tablets to compete with the iPad, and attempted to compete with the iPhone by marketing its own Windows Phone as well as by purchasing long-time cellphone maker Nokia.

Microsoft's fundamental problem is that smartphone and tablet sales are rising rapidly while PC sales are falling quickly. So unless Microsoft can generate revenues from smartphones, tablets, or search, it will suffer an inexorable decline as the PC sector continues to shrink.

Amazon has also made forays outside of the online retail sector that it dominates. The foray best known to the general public is its Kindle line of tablet computers, which compete directly with the tablets made by Apple, Google, Microsoft, and the various manufacturers that use Google's Android operating system. But behind the scenes, Amazon has also become a major competitor to Google and Microsoft in providing businesses with online "cloud computing" services that run on the massive servers that Amazon, Google, and Microsoft must maintain for their core businesses (like search). So in cloud computing, too, we see oligopoly competition resulting from Internet titans branching out of their own dominant sectors to compete with each other.

There's a simple reason for their aggressive competition. When a near-monopoly already dominates its own sector, its only chance for major profit growth is to invade a rival's sector.

Question

Why have tech firms with near-monopolies in their own sectors sought to compete with tech firms that have extremely strong, near-monopoly positions in other sectors?

Chapter Summary

LO13.1 Describe the characteristics of oligopoly.

- Oligopolistic industries are characterized by the presence of few firms, each having a significant fraction of the market. Firms thus situated are mutually interdependent: The behaviour of any one firm directly affects, and is affected by, the actions of rivals. Products may be either virtually uniform or significantly differentiated. Various barriers to entry, including economies of scale, underlie and maintain oligopoly.

- High concentration ratios are an indication of oligopoly (monopoly) power. By giving more weight to larger firms, the Herfindahl index is designed to measure market dominance in an industry.

LO13.2 Discuss how game theory relates to oligopoly.

- The prisoner's dilemma is a type of game that shows the difficulty of cooperating when the participants cannot communicate with one another.

- Game theory (a) shows the interdependence of the pricing policy of oligopolists, (b) reveals the tendency of oligopolists to collude, and (c) explains the temptation of oligopolists to cheat on collusive arrangements.

LO13.3   Explain the two main models of oligopoly pricing and output: collusive pricing and price leadership.

- The uncertainties inherent in oligopoly promote collusion. Collusive oligopolists such as cartels maximize joint profits—that is, they behave like pure monopolists. Demand and cost differences, a large number of firms, cheating through secret price concessions, recessions, and the anticombines laws are all obstacles to collusive oligopoly.

- Price leadership is an informal means of collusion whereby one firm, usually the largest or most efficient, initiates price changes and the other firms in the industry follow the leader.

- Market shares in oligopolistic industries are usually determined based on product development and advertising. Oligopolists emphasize nonprice competition because (a) advertising and product variations are harder for rivals to match and (b) oligopolists frequently have ample resources to finance nonprice competition.

LO13.4   Contrast the potential positive and potential negative effects of advertising.

- Advertising may affect prices, competition, and efficiency either positively or negatively. Positive effects are that it can provide consumers with low-cost information about competing products, help introduce new competing products into concentrated industries, and generally reduce monopoly power and its attendant inefficiencies. Negative effects include that it can promote monopoly power via persuasion and the creation of entry barriers. Moreover, when used by rivals advertising can be self-cancelling because it boosts costs and increases economic inefficiency while accomplishing little else.

LO13.5   Discuss the efficiency of oligopoly from society's standpoint and whether it is more or less efficient than monopoly.

- Neither productive nor allocative efficiency is realized in oligopolistic markets, but oligopoly may be superior to perfect competition in promoting research and development and technological progress.

- Table 9-1 provides a concise review of the characteristics of monopolistic competition and oligopoly as they compare to those of perfect competition and price war monopoly.

LO13.6   Utilize additional game-theory terminology and demonstrate how to find Nash equilibriums in both simultaneous and sequential games.

- Positive-sum games are games in which the payoffs to the firms sum to a positive number; zero-sum games are games in which the payoffs sum to zero; and negative-sum games are games in which the payoffs sum to less than zero. Positive-sum games allow for "win-win" opportunities, whereas zero-sum games always feature "I win–you lose" outcomes. Games can be either one-time games or repeated games. Decisions in games may be made either simultaneously or sequentially.

- When two firms are playing a strategic game, a firm is said to have a dominant strategy if there is an option that leads to better outcomes for the firm no matter what the other firm does. Not all games have dominant strategies. The Nash equilibrium is an outcome from which neither firm wants to deviate because both firms see their current strategy as optimal given the other firm's chosen strategy. The Nash equilibrium is stable and persistent. Attempts by the firms to rig games to achieve some other outcome are difficult to accomplish and maintain, although credible threats can sometimes work. In contrast, empty threats accomplish nothing and leave the outcome at the Nash equilibrium.

- Reciprocity can improve outcomes for firms participating in repeated games. In such games, one firm avoids taking advantage of the other firm because it knows that the other firm can take advantage of it in subsequent games. This reciprocity increases firm profits relative to what they would have been without reciprocity.

- Two possible Nash equilibriums can exist in sequential games with first-mover advantages. Which one occurs depends on which firm moves first since that firm can preempt the other firm, making it unprofitable for the other firm to match the choice made by the firm that moves first. Several real-world firms, including Walmart, have successfully used first-mover advantages to saturate markets and preempt entry by rivals.

- Sequential games can be represented as game trees in extensive form. In extensive form, the order of decisions made by players is displayed in sequence from left to right. The game can be solved for a subgame perfect Nash equilibrium by using backward induction to examine each of the overall game's nested subgames from right to left.

Terms and Concepts

oligopoly	price war
homogeneous oligopoly	cartel
differentiated oligopoly	price leadership
strategic behaviour	one-time game
mutual interdependence	simultaneous game
interindustry competition	positive-sum game
import competition	zero-sum game
game theory	negative-sum game
prisoner's dilemma	dominant strategy
collusion	Nash equilibrium

credible threat
empty threat
repeated game
sequential game
first-mover advantage

decision node
terminal node
backward induction
subgame
subgame perfect Nash equilibrium

Discussion Questions

1. Why do oligopolies exist? List five or six oligopolists whose products you own or regularly purchase. What distinguishes oligopoly from monopolistic competition? **[LO13.1]**

2. Answer the following questions, which relate to measures of concentration: **[LO13.1]**

   a. What is the meaning of a four-firm concentration ratio of 60 percent? 90 percent? What are the shortcomings of concentration ratios as measures of monopoly power?

   b. Suppose that the five firms in industry A have annual sales of 30, 30, 20, 10, and 10 percent of total industry sales. For the five firms in industry B the figures are 60, 25, 5, 5, and 5 percent. Calculate the Herfindahl index for each industry and compare their likely competitiveness.

3. Explain the general meaning of the following payoff matrix for oligopolists X and Y. All profit figures are in thousands. **[LO13.2]**

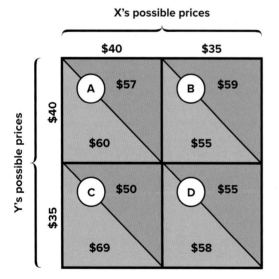

a. Use the payoff matrix to explain the mutual interdependence that characterizes oligopolistic industries.

b. Assuming no collusion between C and D, what is the likely pricing outcome?

c. In view of your answer to part (b), explain why price collusion is mutually profitable. Why might there be a temptation to cheat on the collusive agreement?

4. Why might price collusion occur in oligopolistic industries? Assess the economic desirability of collusive pricing. What are the main obstacles to collusion? Speculate why price leadership is legal in Canada, whereas price fixing is not. **[LO13.3]**

5. Why is there so much advertising in monopolistic competition and oligopoly? How does such advertising help consumers and promote efficiency? Why might it be excessive at times? **[LO13.4]**

6. **Advanced Analysis** Construct a game theory matrix involving two firms and their decisions on high versus low advertising budgets and the effects of each decision on profits. Show a circumstance in which both firms select high advertising budgets even though both would be more profitable with low advertising budgets. Why won't they unilaterally cut their advertising budgets? **[LO13.4]**

7. Is the game shown in Figure 13-3 a zero-sum game or a positive-sum game? How can you tell? Are there dominant strategies in this game? If so, what are they? What cell represents a Nash equilibrium and why? Explain why it is so difficult for Uptown and RareAir to achieve and maintain a more favourable cell than the Nash equilibrium in this single-period pricing game. **[LO13.6]**

8. Refer to the payoff matrix in Discussion Question 3. First, assume this is a one-time game. Explain how the $60/$57 outcome might be achieved through a credible threat. Next, assume this is a repeated game, not a one-time game, such that the interaction between the two firms occurs indefinitely. Why might collusion with a credible threat not be necessary to achieve the $60/$57 outcome? **[LO13.6]**

9. Refer to the payoff matrix below. **[LO13.6]**

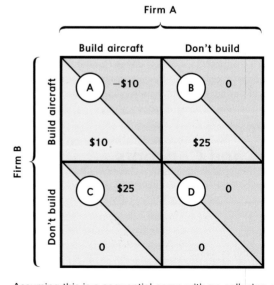

Assuming this is a sequential game with no collusion, what is the outcome if firm A moves first to build a new type of commercial aircraft? Explain why first-mover strategies in the real world are only as good as the profit projections on which they are based. How could a supposed "win" from moving first turn out to be a big loss, whereas the "loss" of being pre-empted might turn out to be a blessing in disguise?

10. **Advanced Analysis** Suppose you are playing a game in which you and one other person each picks a number between 1 and 100, with the person closest to some randomly selected number between 1 and 100 winning the jackpot. (Ask your instructor to fund the jackpot.) Your opponent picks first. What number do you expect her to choose? Why? What

number would you then pick? Why are the two numbers so close? How might this example relate to why Home Depot and Rona, Shoppers Drug Mart and Rexall, McDonald's and Burger King, and other major pairs of rivals locate so close to each other in many well-defined geographical markets that are large enough for both firms to be profitable?   [**LO13.6**]

11. Are the subgames of a sequential game visible when the entire game is presented in strategic form? Explain.   [**LO13.6**]

12. Can backward induction be readily applied when a sequential game is presented as a payoff matrix? Discuss.   [**LO13.6**]

Review Questions

1. Which of the following apply to oligopoly industries? Select *one or more* answers from the choices shown.   [**LO13.1**]

   a. A few large producers

   b. Many small producers

   c. Strategic behaviour

   d. Price taking

2. Consider an oligopoly industry whose firms have identical demand and cost conditions. If the firms decide to collude, then they will want to collectively produce the amount of output that would be produced by   [**LO13.3**]

   a. A monopolistic competitor

   b. A perfect competitor

   c. A monopolist

   d. None of the above

3. In an oligopoly, each firm's share of the total market is typically determined by   [**LO13.4**]

   a. Scarcity and competition

   b. Payoff matrices

   c. Homogeneous products and import competition

   d. Product development and advertising

4. Some analysts consider oligopolies to be potentially less efficient than monopoly firms because at least monopoly firms tend to be regulated. Arguments in favour of a more benign view of oligopolies include: [**LO13.5**]

   a. Oligopolies are self-regulating.

   b. Oligopolies can be kept in line by foreign competition.

   c. Oligopolistic industries may promote technological progress.

   d. Oligopolies may engage in limit pricing to keep out potential entrants.

5. Collusive agreements can be established and maintained by   [**LO13.6**]

   a. Credible threats

   b. One-time games

   c. Empty threats

   d. First-mover advantage

6. True or False? Potential rivals may be more likely to collude if they view themselves as playing a repeated game rather than a one-time game.   [**LO13.6**]

7. Property developers who build shopping malls like to have them "anchored" with the outlets of one or more famous national retail chains, like Hudson's Bay Company or Canadian Tire. Having such anchors is obviously good for the mall developers because anchor stores bring a lot of foot traffic that can help generate sales for smaller stores that lack well-known national brands. But what's in it for the national retail chains? Why become an anchor? Choose the best answer from the following list.   [**LO13.6**]

   a. The anchor stores want to make a credible threat against the developer.

   b. The anchor stores may feel there is a first-mover advantage to becoming one of only a few anchor stores at a new mall.

   c. The property developers are making empty threats to smaller stores.

   d. The smaller stores face a negative-sum game.

8. Look back at Figure 13-7. Suppose that the payouts at terminal node B change to (13, 12) while everything else in the game stays the same. The new subgame perfect Nash equilibrium will consist of the two line segments   [**LO13.6**]

   a. Build at BB followed by Build at HB_1

   b. Build at BB followed by Don't Build at HB_1

   c. Don't Build at BB followed by Build at HB_2

   d. Don't Build at BB followed by Don't Build at HB_2

9. Look back at Figure 13-8. Suppose that the two firms switch places—the firm that was the follower now gets to go first while the firm that was the leader now has to go second. The new subgame perfect Nash equilibrium will lead to terminal node   [**LO13.6**]

   a. A

   b. B

   c. C

   d. D

Problems

1. Consider a "punishment" variation of the two-firm oligopoly situation shown in Figure 13-3. Suppose that if one firm sets a low price while the other sets a high price, the firm setting the high price can fine the firm setting the low price. Suppose that whenever a fine is imposed, X dollars are taken from the low-price firm and given to the high-price firm. What is the smallest amount that the fine X can be such that both firms will want to always set the high price?   [**LO13.6**]

2. Consider whether the promises and threats made toward each other by duopolists and oligopolists are always credible (believable). Look back at Figure 13-3. Imagine that the two firms will play this game twice in sequence and that each firm claims the following policy. Each says that if both it and the other firm choose the high price in the first game, it will also choose the high price in the second game (as a reward to the other firm for cooperating in the first game).   [**LO13.6**]

   a. As a first step toward thinking about whether this policy is credible, consider the situation facing both firms in the second game. If each firm bases its decision on what to do in the second game entirely on the payouts facing the firms in the second game, which strategy will each firm choose in the second game?

   b. Now move backward in time one step. Imagine that it is the start of the first game and each firm must decide what to do during the first game. Given your answer to part (a), is the publicly stated policy credible? (*Hint:* No matter what happens in the first game, what will both firms do in the second game?)

   c. Given your answers to (a) and (b), what strategy will each firm choose in the first game?

3. Examine the following game tree. Fred and Sally are planning on running competing restaurants. Each must decide whether to rent space or buy space. Fred goes first at decision node F. Sally goes second at either decision node S_1 or decision node S_2 (depending on what Fred chose to do at decision node F). Note that the payoff to Sally at terminal node A is X.   [**LO13.6**]

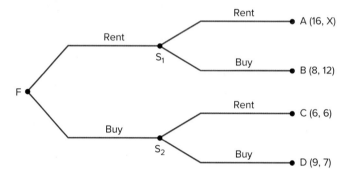

   a. If X < 12, what terminal node will the subgame perfect Nash equilibrium path lead to?

   b. If X > 12, what terminal node will the subgame perfect Nash equilibrium path lead to?

   c. Suppose that X = 11 and that it is now possible for Fred to make a side payment of value V to Sally that will boost her payout at terminal node A from X = 11 to X = 11 + V. What is the minimum amount that V can be such that the subgame perfect Nash equilibrium path will lead to terminal node A? Assume that V can take on only discrete units (0, 1, 2, 3, etc.).

CHAPTER 14

Technology, R&D, and Efficiency

LEARNING OBJECTIVES

LO14.1 Differentiate among invention, innovation, and technological diffusion.

LO14.2 Explain how entrepreneurs and other innovators further technological advance.

LO14.3 Summarize how a firm determines its optimal amount of research and development (R&D).

LO14.4 Discuss how technological change can increase profits by raising revenues or lowering costs.

LO14.5 Relate why firms can benefit from their innovation even though rivals have an incentive to imitate it.

LO14.6 Discuss the role of market structure in promoting technological advance.

LO14.7 Show how technological advance enhances productive efficiency and allocative efficiency.

- "Just Do It." In 1968 two U.S. entrepreneurs from Oregon developed a lightweight sport shoe and formed a new company called Nike, incorporating a "swoosh" logo (designed by a graduate student for $35). Today, Nike sells $24 billion worth of goods annually.

- "Leap Ahead." In 1967 neither Intel nor its product existed. Today it is the world's largest producer of microprocessors for personal computers, with about $54 billion of annual sales.

- "Save Money, Live Better." Expanding from a single store in 1962 to about 7000 worldwide today, Walmart's annual revenue ($444 billion) exceeds that of General Motors or IBM.

Nike, Intel, and Walmart owe much of their success to **technological advance**, broadly defined as new and better goods and services or new and better ways of producing or distributing them. Nike and Intel pioneered innovative new products, and Walmart developed creative ways to manage inventories and distribute goods.

Multiply these examples—perhaps on a smaller scale—by thousands in the economy! The pursuit of technological advance is a major competitive activity among firms. In this chapter, we examine some of the microeconomics of that activity.

14.1 Invention, Innovation, and Diffusion

LO14.1 Differentiate among invention, innovation, and technological diffusion.

For economists, technological advance occurs over a theoretical time period called the *very long run*, which can be as short as a few months or as long as many years. Compare the concept of the very long run with the two shorter-duration time concepts that we developed while discussing our four market models (perfect competition, monopolistic competition, oligopoly, and monopoly). In the short run, technology and plant and equipment are fixed. In the long run, technology is constant but firms can change their plant sizes and are free to enter or exit industries. In contrast, the **very long run** is a period in which technology can change and in which firms can develop and offer entirely new products.

In Chapter 1 we saw that technological advance shifts an economy's production possibilities curve outward, enabling the economy to obtain more goods and services. Technological advance is a three-step process of invention, innovation, and diffusion.

Invention

The basis of technological advance is **invention**: the conception of a new product or process combined with the first proof that it will work. Invention is a process of imagination, ingenious thinking, and experimentation. The result of the process is called *an* invention. The prototypes (basic working models) of the telephone, the automobile, and the microchip were inventions.

Invention usually is based on scientific knowledge and is the product of individuals, working either on their own or as members of corporate research and development (R&D) teams. Later on you will see how governments encourage invention by providing the inventor with a **patent**, an exclusive right to sell any new and useful process, machine, or product for a set period of time. In recent years, the United States has had more patents than any other country, about 17,000, followed by Canada at the number two position at almost 5000 patents. In 2015, the top ten firms in terms of securing the most U.S. patents were household names such as IBM (7355 patents), Samsung (5072), Canon (4134), Qualcomm (2900), Google (2835), Toshiba (2627), Sony (2455), LG (2242), Intel (2048), and Microsoft (1956). Numbers like these, of course, do not reveal the quality of the patents; some are much more significant than others. Patents have a worldwide duration of twenty years from the time of application for the patent.

Innovation

Innovation draws directly on invention. While invention is the discovery and first proof of workability, **innovation** is the first successful commercial introduction of a new product, the first use of a new method, or the creation of a new form of business enterprise. Innovation is of two types: **product innovation**, which refers to new and improved products or services; and **process innovation**, which refers to new and improved methods of production or distribution.

Unlike inventions, innovations cannot be patented. Nevertheless, innovation is a major factor in competition, since it sometimes enables a firm to leapfrog competitors by rendering their products or processes obsolete. For example, personal computers coupled with software for word processing pushed some major typewriter manufacturers into obscurity. More recently, innovations in hardware retailing (by large warehouse stores such as Canadian Tire, Home Depot and Lowe's) have threatened the existence of smaller, more traditional hardware stores.

But innovation need not weaken or destroy existing firms. Aware that new products and processes may threaten their survival, existing firms have a powerful incentive to engage continuously in R&D of their own. Innovative products and processes often enable such firms to maintain or increase their profits. The introduction of disposable contact lenses by Johnson & Johnson, scientific calculators by Hewlett-Packard, and smartphones by BlackBerry are good examples. Thus, innovation can either diminish or strengthen market power.

Diffusion

Diffusion is the spread of an innovation to other products or processes through imitation or copying. To take advantage of new profit opportunities or to slow the erosion of profit, both new and existing firms emulate the successful innovations of others. Alamo, the car rental company, greatly increased its auto rentals by offering customers unlimited mileage, and Hertz, Avis, Budget, and others eventually followed. Chrysler profitably introduced a luxury version of its Jeep Grand Cherokee; other manufacturers, including Acura, Mercedes, and Lexus, countered with luxury sport-utility vehicles of their own. In 2007 Apple introduced the iPhone, a palm-sized telephone that was also a music player, camera, Internet browser, and mini personal computer. BlackBerry, Nokia, Samsung, and Palm soon brought out similar products.

Other recent examples: Early successful cholesterol-reducing drugs (statins) such as Bristol-Myers Squibb's Pravachol were soon followed by chemically distinct but similar statins such as Merck's Zocor and Pfizer's Lipitor. Early video game consoles such as those by Atari eventually gave rise to more popular consoles by Nintendo (Wii), Sony (PlayStation), and Microsoft (Xbox). Facebook, LinkedIn, Pinterest, and Instagram mimicked the social networking innovation pioneered by Classmates.com.

In each of these cases, other firms incorporated the innovation into their own businesses and products through imitation, modification, and extension. The original innovation thus became commonplace and mainly of historical interest.

Though less dramatic than invention and innovation, diffusion is a critical element of technological change.

R&D Expenditures

As related to *businesses*, the term "research and development" is used loosely to include direct efforts toward invention, innovation, and diffusion. However, *government* also engages in R&D, particularly R&D having to do with national defense. In 2015 *total* Canadian R&D expenditures (business *plus* government) were about $35 billion. Relative to GDP, the amount was about 1.75 percent, which is below the OECD average of 2.4 percent. In contrast, U.S. R&D expenditures (business *plus* government) were about $400 billion. Relative to GDP

14.1 GLOBAL PERSPECTIVE

Total R&D Expenditures as a Percentage of GDP, Selected Nations

Relative R&D spending varies across leading industrial nations. From a microeconomic perspective, R&D helps promote economic efficiency; from a macroeconomic perspective, R&D helps promote economic growth.

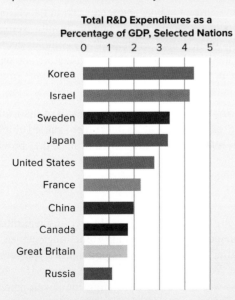

Total R&D Expenditures as a Percentage of GDP, Selected Nations

Source: National Science Foundation, www.nsf.gov, and *OECD Factbook 2014: Economic, Environmental and Social Statistics*, www.oecd.org. Latest available data.

that amount was about 2.8 percent. As shown in Global Perspective 14.1, Canada's performance is a relatively low percentage of GDP compared to that of several other nations.

Modern View of Technological Advance

For decades most economists regarded technological advance as a random *external* force to which the economy adjusted. Advances in scientific and technological knowledge were seen as unforeseeable, lucky events unrelated to anything going on in the economy. But when they occurred from time to time, they paved the way for major new products (automobiles, airplanes) and major new production processes (assembly lines). Firms and industries incorporated a new technology into their products or processes to enhance or maintain their profits. After integrating the new technology, they settled back into new long-run equilibrium positions. Although they agreed with modern economists that technological advance was vitally important to the economy, economists of that era believed that the development of new technologies was rooted in the independent advance of science, which is largely external to the market system.

Most contemporary economists have a different view. They see capitalism itself as the driving force behind technological advance. Invention, innovation, and diffusion occur in response to incentives within the economy, meaning that technological advance is *internal* to capitalism. Specifically, technological advance arises from intense rivalry among individuals and firms that motivates them to seek and exploit new profit opportunities or to expand existing opportunities. That rivalry occurs both among existing firms and between existing firms and newly created firms. Moreover, many advances in "pure" scientific knowledge are motivated, at least in part, by the prospect of commercial applicability and eventual profit. In the modern view, entrepreneurs and other innovators are at the heart of technological advance.

14.2 Role of Entrepreneurs and Other Innovators

LO14.2 Explain how entrepreneurs and other innovators further technological advance.

It will be helpful to distinguish between "entrepreneurs" and "other innovators":

- *Entrepreneurs* Recall that the entrepreneur is an initiator, innovator, and risk bearer. His or her entrepreneurial ability is the productive resource that combines the other productive resources of land, labour, and capital in new and unique ways to produce new goods and services. In the past, a single individual, for example Andrew Carnegie in steel, Henry Ford in automobiles, or Levi Strauss in blue jeans, carried out the entrepreneurial role. Such advances as air conditioning, the ballpoint pen, cellophane, the jet engine, insulin, xerography, and the helicopter all have an individualistic heritage. But in today's more technologically complex economy, entrepreneurship is just as likely to be carried out by entrepreneurial teams. Such teams may include only two or three people working "as their own bosses" on some new product idea or it may consist of larger groups of entrepreneurs who have pooled their financial resources to pursue a business idea.

- *Other Innovators* This designation includes other key people involved in the pursuit of innovation who do not bear personal financial risk. Among them are key executives, scientists, and other salaried employees engaged in commercial R&D activities. (They are sometimes referred to as *intrapreneurs*, since they provide the spirit of entrepreneurship within existing firms.)

Forming Start-ups

Entrepreneurs often form small new companies called **start-ups** that focus on creating and introducing a new product or employing a new production or distribution technique. Two twenty-somethings named Steve Jobs and Steve Wozniak formed a start-up in the mid-1970s, after months of tinkering on a prototype personal computer that they had built in a garage during their free time. When neither of their employers—Hewlett-Packard and Atari, the developer of Pong (the first video game)—was interested in funding the development of their new computer, they founded their own company: Apple. Other examples of successful start-ups are Amgen, a biotechnology firm specializing in new medical treatments; BlackBerry (the Waterloo-based company formerly known as Research In Motion), one of the first smartphone vendors specializing in secure communication and mobile productivity; Second Cup, a seller of gourmet coffee; Amazon, an Internet retailer; and Google, an Internet search provider.

Innovating Within Existing Firms

Innovators are also at work within existing corporations, large and small. Such innovators are salaried workers, although many firms have pay systems that provide them with substantial bonuses or profit shares. Examples of firms known for their skillful internal innovators are BlackBerry, which became phenomenally successful with its push email devices and services; 3M Corporation, the U.S. developer of Scotch tape; Post-it Brand, maker of note stickers; Thinsulate insulation; and General Electric, the developer of innovative major kitchen appliances, medical imaging machines, and jet aircraft engines. R&D work in major corporations has produced significant technological improvements in such products as television sets, telephones, home appliances, automobiles, automobile tires, and sporting equipment.

Some large firms, aware that excessive bureaucracy can stifle creative thinking and technological advance, have separated part of their R&D and manufacturing divisions to form new, more flexible, innovative firms. Three significant examples of such "spin-off firms" are Lucent Technologies (now Alcatel-Lucent), a telephone equipment and R&D firm created by the U.S. telephone company AT&T; Imation, a high-technology firm spun off from 3M Corporation; and Yum! Brands, which operates restaurant chains Taco Bell, KFC, and Pizza Hut, and was spun off from Pepsi.

Anticipating the Future

In 1949 a writer for *Popular Mechanics* magazine boldly predicted, "Computers in the future may weigh no more than 1.5 tons." Today's notebook computers weigh just a little over 1 kilogram, and an iPhone just a little over 100 grams.

Anticipating the future is difficult, but that is what innovators try to do. Those with strong anticipatory ability and determination have a knack for introducing new and improved products or services at just the right time.

The rewards for success are both monetary and nonmonetary. Product innovation and development are creative endeavors, with such intangible rewards as personal satisfaction. Also, many people simply enjoy participating in the competitive "contest." Of course, the "winners" can reap huge monetary rewards in the form of economic profits, stock appreciation, or large bonuses. Extreme examples are Bill Gates and Paul Allen, who founded Microsoft in 1975, and had net worth in 2016 of $75.4 billion and $18.1 billion, respectively, mainly in the form of Microsoft stock.

Past successes often give entrepreneurs and innovative firms access to resources for further innovations that anticipate consumer wants. Although they may not succeed a second time, the market tends to entrust the production of goods and services to businesses that have consistently succeeded in filling consumer wants. And the market does not care whether these "winning" entrepreneurs and innovative firms are Canadian, American, Brazilian, Japanese, German, or Swiss. Entrepreneurship and innovation are global in scope.

Exploiting University and Government Scientific Research

Government and university labs have been the scene of many technological breakthroughs, including hybrid seeds, nuclear energy, satellite communications, the computer mouse, genetic engineering, and the Internet. Entire high-tech industries such as computers and biotechnology have their roots in major research universities and government laboratories. And nations with strong scientific communities tend to have the most technologically progressive firms and industries.

Also, firms increasingly help fund university research that relates to their products. Business funding of R&D at universities has grown rapidly. Today, the separation between university scientists and innovators is narrowing; scientists and universities increasingly realize that their work may have commercial value and are teaming up with innovators to share in the potential profit.

A few firms, of course, find it profitable to conduct basic scientific research on their own. New knowledge can give them a head start in creating an invention or a new product. This is particularly true in the pharmaceutical industry, where it is not uncommon for firms to parlay new scientific knowledge generated in their corporate labs into new, patentable drugs.

QUICK REVIEW 14.1

- Broadly defined, technological advance means new or improved products and services, and new or improved production and distribution processes.

- Invention is the *discovery* of a new product or method; innovation is the *successful commercial application* of some invention; and diffusion is the *widespread adoption* of the innovation.

- Many economists view technological advance as mainly a response to profit opportunities arising within a capitalist economy.

- Technological advance is fostered by entrepreneurs and other innovators and is supported by the scientific research of universities and government-sponsored laboratories.

14.3 A Firm's Optimal Amount of R&D

LO14.3 Summarize how a firm determines its optimal amount of research and development (R&D).

How does a firm decide on its optimal amount of research and development? That amount depends on the firm's perception of the marginal benefit and marginal cost of R&D activity. The decision rule here flows from basic economics: To earn the greatest profit, expand a particular activity until its marginal benefit (MB) equals its marginal cost (MC). A firm that sees the marginal benefit of a particular R&D activity, say innovation, as exceeding the marginal cost should expand that activity. In contrast, an activity whose marginal benefit promises to be less than its marginal cost should be cut back. But the R&D spending decision is complex, since it involves a present sacrifice for a future expected gain. While the cost of R&D is immediate, the expected benefits occur at some future time and are highly uncertain. So estimating those benefits is often more art than science. Nevertheless, the MB = MC way of thinking remains relevant for analyzing R&D decisions.

Interest-Rate Cost of Funds

Firms have several ways of obtaining the funds they need to finance R&D activities:

- *Bank Loans* Some firms are able to obtain a loan from a bank or other financial institution. The cost of using the funds is the interest paid to the lender. The marginal cost is the cost per extra dollar borrowed, which is simply the market interest rate for borrowed funds.

- *Bonds* Bonds are financial contracts through which a borrower (typically a firm or a government) is obligated to pay the owner of a bond both the principal and interest due on a loan on dates specified in the bond contract. Established, profitable firms may be able to borrow funds for R&D by issuing bonds and selling them in the bond market. In this case, the cost is the interest paid to the lenders—the bondholders. Again the marginal cost of using the funds is the interest rate.

- *Retained Earnings* A large, well-established firm may be able to draw on its own corporate savings to finance R&D. Typically, such a firm retains part of its profit rather than paying it all out as dividends to the firm's shareholders (owners). Some of the undistributed profit, called *retained earnings*, can be used to finance R&D activity. The marginal cost of using retained earnings for R&D is an opportunity cost—the rate of interest that those funds could have earned as deposits in a financial institution.

- *Venture Capital* A small start-up firm may be able to attract venture capital to finance its R&D projects. Venture capital is financial capital, or simply money, not real capital. **Venture capital** consists of that part of household saving used to finance high-risk business ventures in exchange for shares of the profit if the ventures succeed. The marginal cost of venture capital is the share of expected profit that the firm will have to pay to those who provided the money. This can be stated as a percentage of the venture capital, so it is essentially an interest rate.

- *Personal Savings* Finally, individual entrepreneurs might draw on their own savings to finance the R&D for a new venture. The marginal cost of the financing is the forgone interest rate.

FIGURE 14-1 **The Interest-Rate Cost-of-Funds Schedule and Curve**

As it relates to R&D, a firm's interest-rate cost-of-funds schedule (the table) and curve (the graph) show the interest rate the firm must pay to obtain any particular amount of funds to finance R&D. Curve i indicates the firm can finance as little or as much R&D as it wants at a constant 8 percent rate of interest.

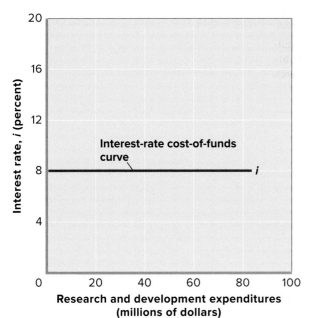

R&D, millions	Interest-rate cost of funds, %
$10	8
20	8
30	8
40	8
50	8
60	8
70	8
80	8

Thus, whatever the source of the R&D funds, we can state the marginal cost of these funds as an interest rate i. For simplicity, let's assume that this interest rate is the same no matter how much financing is required. Further, we assume that a certain firm called MedTech must pay an interest rate of 8 percent for the least expensive funding available to it. Then a graph of the marginal cost of each funding amount for this firm is a horizontal line at the 8 percent interest rate, as shown in Figure 14-1. Such a graph is called an **interest-rate cost-of-funds curve**. This one tells us that MedTech can borrow any amount of money at the 8 percent interest rate. The table accompanying the graph contains the data used to construct the graph and tells us much the same thing.

With these data in hand, MedTech wants to determine how much R&D it should finance in the coming year.

Expected Rate of Return

A firm's marginal benefit from R&D is its expected profit (or return) from the last (marginal) dollar spent on R&D. That is, the R&D is expected to result in a new product or production method that will increase revenue, reduce production costs, or both (in ways we will soon explain). This return is expected, not certain—there is risk in R&D decisions. Let's suppose that after considering such risks, MedTech anticipates that an R&D expenditure of $1 million will result in a new product that will yield a one-time added profit of $1.2 million a year later. As a result, the expected rate of return r on the $1 million R&D expenditure (after the $1 million has been repaid) is 20 percent (= $200,000/$1,000,000). This is the marginal benefit of the first $1 million of R&D. (Stretching the return over several years complicates the computation of r, but it does not alter the basic analysis.)

MedTech can use this same method to estimate the expected rates of return for R&D expenditures of $2 million, $3 million, $4 million, and so on. Suppose those marginal rates of return are the ones indicated in the table in Figure 14-2, where they are also graphed as the **expected-rate-of-return curve**. This curve shows the expected rate of return, which is the marginal benefit of each dollar of expenditure on R&D. The curve slopes downward because of diminishing returns to R&D expenditures. A firm will direct its initial R&D expenditures to the highest expected-rate-of-return activities and then use additional funding for activities with successively lower expected rates of return. That is, the firm will experience lower and lower expected rates of return as it expands its R&D spending.

FIGURE 14-2   The Expected-Rate-of-Return Schedule and Curve

As they relate to R&D, a firm's expected-rate-of-return schedule (the table) and curve (the graph) show the firm's expected gain in profit, as a percentage of R&D spending, for each level of R&D spending. Curve *r* slopes downward because the firm assesses its potential R&D projects in descending order of expected rates of return.

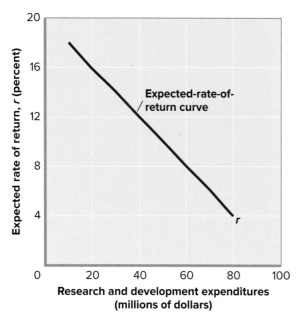

R&D, millions	Expected rate of return, %
$10	18
20	16
30	14
40	12
50	10
60	8
70	6
80	4

Optimal R&D Expenditures

Figure 14-3 combines the interest-rate cost-of-funds curve (Figure 14-1) and the expected-rate-of-return curve (Figure 14-2). The curves intersect at MedTech's **optimal amount of R&D**, which is $60 million. This amount can also be determined from the table as the amount of funding for which the expected rate of return and the interest cost of borrowing are equal (here, 8 percent).

Both the curve and the table in Figure 14-3 tell us that at $60 million of R&D expenditures, the marginal benefit and the marginal cost of the last dollar spent on R&D are equal. MedTech should undertake all R&D expenditures up to $60 million since those outlays yield a higher marginal benefit or expected rate of return, *r*, than the 8 percent marginal cost or interest-rate cost of borrowing, *i*. But it should not undertake R&D expenditures beyond $60 million; for these outlays, *r* (marginal benefit) is less than *i* (marginal cost). Only at $60 million do we have $r = i$, telling us that MedTech will spend $60 million on R&D.

Our analysis reinforces three important points:

- *Optimal Versus Affordable R&D* From earlier discussions we know there can be too much, as well as too little, of a "good thing." So it is with R&D and technological advance. Figure 14-3 shows that R&D expenditures make sense to a firm only as long as the expected return from the outlay equals or exceeds the cost of obtaining the funds needed to finance it. Many R&D expenditures may be affordable but not worthwhile because their marginal benefit is likely to be less than their marginal cost.

- *Expected, Not Guaranteed, Returns* The outcomes from R&D are expected, not guaranteed. With 20-20 hindsight, a firm can always look back and decide whether a particular expenditure for R&D was worthwhile. But that assessment is irrelevant to the original decision. At the time of the decision, the expenditure was thought to be worthwhile on the basis of existing information and expectations. Some R&D decisions may be more like an informed gamble than the typical business decision. Invention and innovation, in particular, carry with them a great deal of risk. For every successful outcome, there are scores of costly disappointments.

- *Adjustments* Firms adjust their R&D expenditures when expected rates of return on various projects change (when curves such as *r* in Figure 14-3 shift).

FIGURE 14-3   A Firm's Optimal Level of R&D Expenditures

The firm's optimal level of R&D expenditures ($60 million) occurs where its expected rate of return equals the interest-rate cost of funds, as shown in both the table and the graph. At $60 million of R&D spending, the firm has taken advantage of all R&D opportunities for which the expected rate of return, *r*, exceeds or equals the 8 percent interest cost of borrowing, *i*.

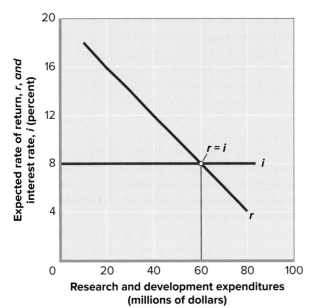

Expected rate of return, %	R&D, millions	Interest-rate cost-of-funds, %
18	$10	8
16	20	8
14	30	8
12	40	8
10	50	8
8	**60**	**8**
6	70	8
4	80	8

14.4 Increased Profit via Innovation

LO14.4   Discuss how technological change can increase profits by raising revenues or lowering costs.

In discussing how a firm determines its optimal amount of R&D spending, we sidestepped the question of how technological change can increase a firm's profit. Although the answer may seem obvious—by increasing revenue or reducing production costs—insights can be gained by exploring these two possibilities in some detail.

Increased Revenue via Product Innovation

Firms here and abroad have profitably introduced hundreds of new products in the past two or three decades. Examples include roller blades, microwave popcorn, cordless drills, digital cameras, camcorders, and high-definition TVs. Other new products are snowboards, cellular phones, tablet computers, and automobile air bags. All these items reflect technological advance in the form of product innovation.

How do such new products gain consumer acceptance? As you know from Chapter 7, to maximize their satisfaction, consumers purchase products that have the highest marginal utility per dollar. They determine which products to buy in view of their limited money incomes by comparing the ratios of MU/price for the various goods. They first select the unit of the good with the highest MU/price ratio, then the one with the next highest, and so on, until their incomes are used up.

The first five columns of Table 14-1 repeat some of the information in Table 7-1. Before the introduction of new product C, the consumer maximized the total utility she could get from $10 of income by buying 2 units of A at $1 per unit and 4 units of B at $2 per unit. Her total budget of $10 was thus fully expended, with $2 spent on A and $8 on B. As shown in columns 2b and 3b, the marginal utility per dollar spent on the last unit of each product was 8 (= 8/$1 = 16/$2). The total utility, derived from columns 2a and 3a, was 96 utils (= 10 + 8 from the first 2 units of A plus 24 + 20 + 18 + 16 from the first 4 units of B). (If you are uncertain about this outcome, please review the discussion of Table 7-1.)

TABLE 14-1	Utility Maximization with the Introduction of a New Product (Income = $10)*					
(1) **UNIT OF** **PRODUCT**	**(2)** **PRODUCT A: Price = $1**		**(3)** **PRODUCT B: Price = $2**		**(4)** **NEW PRODUCT C: Price = $4**	
	(a) **Marginal** **utility,** **utils**	**(b)** **Marginal** **utility** **per dollar** **(MU/price)**	**(a)** **Marginal** **utility,** **utils**	**(b)** **Marginal** **utility** **per dollar** **(MU/price)**	**(a)** **Marginal** **utility,** **utils**	**(b)** **Marginal utility** **per dollar** **(MU/price)**
First	10	10	24	12	52	13
Second	8	8	20	10	48	12
Third	7	7	18	9	44	11
Fourth	6	6	16	8	36	9
Fifth	5	5	12	6	32	8

*It is assumed in this table that the amount of marginal utility received from additional units of each of the three products is independent of the quantity purchased of the other products. For example, the marginal-utility schedule for product C is independent of the amount of A and B purchased by the consumer.

Now suppose an innovative firm offers new product C (columns 4a and 4b in Table 14-1), priced at $4 per unit. Note that the first unit of C has a higher marginal utility per dollar (13) than any unit of A or B and that the second unit of C and the first unit of B have equal MU/price ratios of 12. To maximize satisfaction, the consumer now buys 2 units of C at $4 per unit, 1 unit of B at $2 per unit, and zero units of A. Our consumer has spent all of her $10 income ($8 on C and $2 on B), and the MU/price ratios of the last units of B and C are equal at 12. But as determined via columns 3a and 4a, the consumer's total utility is now 124 utils (= 24 from the first unit of B plus 52 + 48 from the first 2 units of C).

Total utility has increased by 28 utils (= 124 utils − 96 utils), and that is why product C was purchased. Consumers will buy a new product only if it increases the total utility they obtain from their limited incomes.

From the innovating firm's perspective, these "dollar votes" represent new product demand that yields increased revenue. When per-unit revenue exceeds per-unit cost, the product innovation creates per-unit profit. Total profit rises by the per-unit profit multiplied by the number of units sold. As a percentage of the original R&D expenditure, the rise in total profit is the return on that R&D expenditure. It was the basis for the expected-rate-of-return curve *r* in Figure 14-3.

Other, related points:

- *Importance of Price* Consumer acceptance of a new product depends on both its marginal utility and its price. (Confirm that the consumer represented in Table 14-1 would buy zero units of new product C if its price were $8 rather than $4.) To be successful, a new product must not only deliver utility to consumers but do so at an acceptable price.

- *Unsuccessful New Products* For every successful new product, hundreds do not succeed; the expected return that motivates product innovation is not always realized. Examples of colossal flops are Ford's Edsel automobile, quadraphonic stereo, New Coke by Coca-Cola, and Kodak disc cameras. Less dramatic failures include the hundreds of dot-com firms that have gone out of business since the late 1990s. In each case, millions of dollars of R&D and promotion expense ultimately resulted in loss, not profit.

- *Product Improvements* Most product innovation consists of incremental improvements to existing products rather than radical inventions. Examples: more fuel-efficient automobile engines, new varieties of pizza, lighter-weight shafts for golf clubs, more flavorful bubble gum, "rock shocks" for mountain bikes, and clothing made of wrinkle-free fabrics.

Reduced Cost via Process Innovation

The introduction of better methods of producing products—process innovation—is also a path toward enhanced profit and a positive return on R&D expenditures. Suppose a firm introduces a new and better production process, such as assembling its product by teams rather than by a standard assembly line. Alternatively, suppose this firm

FIGURE 14-4   Process Innovation, Total Product, and Average Total Cost

(a) Process innovation shifts a firm's total-product curve upward from TP_1 to TP_2, meaning that with a given amount of capital the firm can produce more output at each level of labor input. As shown, with 1000 units of labour it can produce 2500 rather than 2000 units of output. (b) The upward shift in the total-product curve results in a downward shift in the firm's average-total-cost curve, from ATC_1 to ATC_2. This means the firm can produce any particular unit of output at a lower average total cost than it could previously. For example, the original 2000 units can be produced at less than $4 per unit, versus $5 per unit originally. Or 2500 units can now be produced at $4 per unit.

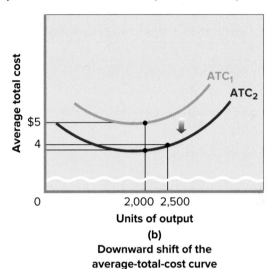

(a) Upward shift of the total-product curve

(b) Downward shift of the average-total-cost curve

replaces old equipment with more productive equipment embodying a technological advance. In either case, the innovation yields an upward shift in the firm's total-product curve from TP_1 to TP_2 in Figure 14-4a. As a result, more units of output can now be produced at each level of resource usage. Note from the figure, for example, that this firm can now produce 2500 units of output, rather than 2000 units, when using 1000 units of labour. So its average product has increased from 2 (= 2000 units of output/1000 units of labour) to 2.5 (= 2500 units of output/1000 units of labour).

The result is a downward shift in the firm's average-total-cost curve, from ATC_1 to ATC_2 in Figure 14-4b. To understand why, let's assume this firm pays $1000 for the use of its capital and $9 for each unit of labour. Since it uses 1000 units of labour, its labour cost is $9000 (= $9 × 1000); its capital cost is $1000; and thus its total cost is $10,000. When its output increases from 2000 to 2500 units as a result of the process innovation, its total cost remains $10,000. So its average total cost declines from $5 (= $10,000/2000) to $4 (= $10,000/2500). Alternatively, the firm could produce the original 2000 units of output with fewer units of labour at an even lower average total cost.

This reduction in average total cost enhances the firm's profit. As a percentage of the R&D expenditure that fostered it, this extra profit is the expected return *r* that was the basis for the rate-of-return curve in Figure 14-3. In this case, the expected increase in profit arose from the prospect of lower production costs through process innovation.

Example: Computer-based inventory control systems, such as those pioneered by Walmart, enabled innovators to reduce the number of people needed to keep track of inventories. The new systems also enabled firms to keep goods arriving "just in time," reducing the cost of storing inventories. The consequence? Significant increases in sales per worker, declines in average total cost, and increased profit.

14.5 Imitation and R&D Incentives

LO14.5   Relate why firms can benefit from their innovation even though rivals have an incentive to imitate it.

Our analysis of product and process innovation explains how technological advance enhances a firm's profit. But it also hints at a potential **imitation problem**: A firm's rivals may be able to imitate its new product or process, greatly reducing the originator's profit from its R&D effort. As just one example, in the 1980s North American auto firms took apart Japanese Honda Accords, piece by piece, to discover the secrets of their high quality. This *reverse engineering*—a procedure that ironically had been perfected by the Japanese—helped the domestic firms incorporate innovative features into their own cars. This type of imitation is perfectly legitimate and fully anticipated; it is often the main path to widespread diffusion of an innovation.

In fact, a dominant firm that is making large profits from its existing products may let smaller firms in the industry incur the high costs of product innovation while it closely monitors their successes and failures. The dominant firm then moves quickly to imitate any successful new product; its goal is to become the second firm to embrace the innovation. In using this so-called **fast-second strategy**, the dominant firm counts on its own product-improvement abilities, marketing prowess, or economies of scale to prevail.

Examples abound: Royal Crown introduced the first diet cola, but Diet Coke and Diet Pepsi dominate diet-cola sales today. In the U.S., Meister Brau introduced the first low-calorie beer, but Miller popularized the product with its Miller Lite. Gillette moved quickly with its own stainless-steel razor blade only after a smaller firm, Wilkinson, introduced this product innovation. Creative Technology (the maker of Sound Blaster audio cards for personal computers) introduced the first miniature MP3 player, but Apple popularized the product with its iPod before incorporating a music player into its iPhone smartphone.

Benefits of Being First

Imitation and the fast-second strategy raise an important question: What incentive is there for any firm to bear the expenses and risks of innovation if competitors can imitate its new or improved product? Why not let others bear the costs and risks of product development and then just imitate the successful innovations? Although we have seen that this may be a plausible strategy in some situations, there are several protections for, and potential advantages to, taking the lead.

PATENTS

Some technological breakthroughs, specifically inventions, can be patented. Once patented, they cannot be legally imitated for two decades from time of patent application. The purpose of patents is, in fact, to reduce imitation and its negative effect on the incentive for engaging in R&D. Example: Polaroid's patent of its instant camera enabled it to earn high economic profits for many years. When Kodak "cloned" the camera, Polaroid won a patent-infringement lawsuit against its rival. Kodak not only had to stop producing its version but also had to buy back the Kodak instant cameras it had sold and pay millions of dollars in damages to Polaroid.

There are hundreds of other examples of long-run profits based on U.S. patents; they involve products from prescription drugs to pop-top cans to weed trimmers. As shown in Global Perspective 14.2, Canadian citizens and firms hold the seventh-highest number of U.S. patents along with American citizens and firms.

COPYRIGHTS AND TRADEMARKS

Copyrights protect publishers of books, computer software, movies, videos, and musical compositions from having their works copied. *Trademarks* give the original innovators of products the exclusive right to use a particular product name ("M&Ms," "Barbie" dolls, "Wheaties"). By reducing the problem of direct copying, these legal protections increase the incentive for product innovation. They have been strengthened worldwide through recent international trade agreements.

BRAND-NAME RECOGNITION

Along with trademark protection, brand-name recognition may give the original innovator a major marketing advantage for years or even decades. Consumers often identify a new product with the firm that first introduced and popularized it in the mass market. Examples: Levi's blue jeans, Kleenex soft tissues, Johnson & Johnson's Band-Aids, Gatorade sports drink, and Kellogg's Corn Flakes.

TRADE SECRETS AND LEARNING BY DOING

Some innovations involve trade secrets, without which competitors cannot imitate the product or process. Example: Coca-Cola has successfully kept its formula for Coke a secret from potential rivals. Many other firms have perfected special production techniques known only to them. In a related advantage, a firm's head start with a new product often allows it to achieve substantial cost reductions through learning by doing. The innovator's lower cost may enable it to continue to profit even after imitators have entered the market.

14.2 GLOBAL PERSPECTIVE

Distribution of U.S. Patents, by Foreign Nation

Foreign citizens, corporations, and governments hold 42 percent of U.S. patents. The top ten foreign countries in terms of U.S. patent holdings since 1963 are listed below, with the number of U.S. patents (through 2014) in parentheses.

Top 10 Foreign Countries

- Japan (1,014,977)
- Germany (347,875)
- Taiwan (150,121)
- South Korea (146,153)
- United Kingdom (133,063)
- France (132,840)
- Canada (116,413)
- Italy (59,058)
- Switzerland (54,294)
- Netherlands (47,556)

Source: U.S. Patent and Trademark Office, www.uspto.gov.

TIME LAGS

Time lags between innovation and diffusion often enable innovating firms to realize a substantial economic profit. It takes time for an imitator to gain knowledge of the properties of a new innovation. And once it has that knowledge, the imitator must design a substitute product, gear up a factory for its production, and conduct a marketing campaign. Various entry barriers, such as large financial requirements, economies of scale, and price cutting, may extend the time lag between innovation and imitation. In practice, it may take years or even decades before rival firms can successfully imitate a profitable new product and cut into the market share of the innovator. In the meantime, the innovator continues to profit.

PROFITABLE BUYOUTS

A final advantage of being first arises from the possibility of a buyout (outright purchase) of the innovating firm by a larger firm. Here, the innovative entrepreneurs take their rewards immediately, as cash or as shares in the purchasing firm, rather than waiting for perhaps uncertain long-run profits from their own production and marketing efforts.

Examples: When Minnetonka's Softsoap became a huge success, it sold its product to Colgate-Palmolive. More recently, Swiss conglomerate Nestlé bought out Chef America, the highly successful maker of Hot Pockets frozen meat-and-cheese sandwiches. Such buyouts are legal as long as they do not substantially lessen competition in the affected industry. For this to be the case, there must be other strong competitors in the market. That was not true, for example, when Microsoft tried to buy out Intuit (maker of Quicken, the best-selling financial software). That buyout was disallowed because Intuit and Microsoft were the two main suppliers of financial software for personal computers.

In short, despite the imitation problem, significant protections and advantages enable most innovating firms to profit from their R&D efforts, as implied by the continuing high levels of R&D spending by firms year after year. The high levels of spending simply would not continue if imitation consistently and severely depressed rates of return on R&D expenditures.

CONSIDER THIS

Trade Secrets

Trade secrets have long played an important role in maintaining returns from research and development (R&D). Long before Coca-Cola's secret formula or Colonel Sanders' secret herbs and spices, legend has it that the Roman citizen Erasmo (*c*. A.D. 130) had a secret ingredient for violin strings.* As the demand for his new product grew, he falsely identified his strings as *catgut*, when they were actually made of sheep intestines. Why the deception? At the time, it was considered to be extremely bad luck to kill a cat. By identifying his strings as catgut, he hoped

© Don Farrall/Getty Images RF

that nobody would imitate his product and reduce his monopoly profit. Moreover, his product name would help him preserve his valuable trade secret.

*We found this anecdote in Dennis W. Carleton and Jeffrey Perloff, *Modern Industrial Organization*, 2nd ed. (New York: HarperCollins, 1994), p. 139. Their source, in turn, was L. Boyd, *San Francisco Chronicle*, October 27, 1984, p. 35.

QUICK REVIEW 14.2

- A firm's optimal R&D expenditure is the amount at which the expected rate of return (marginal benefit) from the R&D expenditure just equals the interest-rate cost of borrowing (marginal cost) required to finance it.

- Product innovation can entice consumers to substitute a new product for existing products to increase their total utility, thereby increasing the innovating firm's revenue and profit.

- Process innovation can lower a firm's production costs and increase its profit by increasing total product and decreasing average total cost.

- A firm faces reduced profitability from R&D if competitors can successfully imitate its new product or process. Nevertheless, there are significant potential protections and benefits to being first, including patents, copyrights, and trademarks; brand-name recognition; trade secrets; cost reductions from learning by doing; and major time lags between innovation and imitation.

14.6 Role of Market Structure

LO14.6   Discuss the role of market structure in promoting technological advance.

In view of our discussion of market structures in the previous four chapters, asking whether some particular market structure or firm size is best suited to technological progress is logical. Is a highly competitive industry consisting of thousands of relatively small firms likely to produce faster technological progress than a monopoly? Or is perhaps an intermediate market structure like oligopoly the most likely to produce rapid technological progress?

Market Structure and Technological Advance

As a first step toward answering these questions, we survey the strengths and shortcomings of our four market models as related to technological advance.

PERFECT COMPETITION

Does a firm in perfect competition have a strong incentive and strong ability to undertake R&D? On the positive side, strong competition provides a reason for such firms to innovate; competitive firms tend to be less complacent than monopolists. If a firm in perfect competition does not seize the initiative, one or more rivals may introduce a new product or cost-reducing production technique that could drive it from the market. As a matter of short-term profit and long-term survival, the individual firm in perfect competition is under continual pressure to improve products and lower costs through innovation. Also, where there are many competing firms, there is less chance that an idea for improving a product or process will be overlooked by a single firm.

On the negative side, the expected rate of return on R&D may be low or even negative for a firm in perfect competition. Because of easy entry, its profit rewards from innovation may quickly be competed away by existing or entering firms that also produce the new product or adopt the new technology. Also, the small size of competitive firms and the fact that they earn only a normal profit in the long run lead to serious questions as to whether they can finance substantial R&D programs. Observers have noted that the high rate of technological advance in the highly competitive agricultural industry, for example, has come not from the R&D of individual farmers but from government-sponsored research and from the development of fertilizers, hybrid seed, and farm implements by oligopolistic firms.

MONOPOLISTIC COMPETITION

Like firms in perfect competition, firms in monopolistic competition cannot afford to become complacent. But unlike firms in perfect competition, which sell standardized products, monopolistic competitors have a strong profit incentive to engage in product innovation. This incentive to differentiate products from those of competitors stems from the fact that sufficiently novel products may create monopoly power and thus economic profit. There are many examples of innovative firms (McDonald's, Starbucks, BlackBerry) that started out as monopolistic competitors in localized markets but soon gained considerable national market power, with the attendant economic profit.

For the typical firm, however, the shortcomings of monopolistic competition in relation to technological advance are the same as those of perfect competition. Most monopolistic competitors remain small, which limits their ability to secure inexpensive financing for R&D. In addition, monopolistic competitors find it difficult to extract large profits from technological advances. Any economic profits from innovation are usually temporary because entry to monopolistically competitive industries is relatively easy. In the long run, new entrants with similar goods reduce the demand for the innovator's product, leaving the innovator with only a normal profit. Monopolistic competitors therefore usually have relatively low expected rates of return on R&D expenditures.

OLIGOPOLY

Many of the characteristics of oligopoly are conducive to technological advance. First, the large size of oligopolists enables them to finance the often-large R&D costs associated with major product or process innovation. In particular, the typical oligopolist realizes an ongoing economic profit, a part of which is retained. This undistributed profit serves as a major source of readily available, relatively low-cost funding for R&D. Moreover, the existence of barriers to entry gives the oligopolist some assurance that it can maintain any economic profit it gains from innovation. Then, too, the large sales volume of the oligopolist enables it to spread the cost of specialized R&D equipment and teams of specialized researchers over a great many units of output. Finally, the broad scope of R&D activity within oligopolistic firms helps them offset the inevitable R&D "misses" with more-than-compensating R&D "hits." Thus, oligopolists clearly have the means and incentive to innovate.

But there is also a negative side to R&D in oligopoly. In many instances, the oligopolist's incentive to innovate may be far less than we have just implied because oligopoly tends to breed complacency. An oligopolist may reason that introducing costly new technology and producing new products makes little sense when it currently is earning a sizable economic profit without them. The oligopolist wants to maximize its profit by exploiting fully all its capital assets. Why rush to develop a new product (say batteries for electric automobiles) when that product's success will render obsolete much of the firm's current equipment designed to produce its existing product (say gasoline engines)? It is not difficult to cite oligopolistic industries in which the largest firms' interest in R&D has been quite modest. Examples: the steel, cigarette, and aluminum industries.

MONOPOLY

In general, the monopolist has little incentive to engage in R&D; it maintains its high profit through entry barriers that, in theory, are complete. The only incentive for the monopolist to engage in R&D is defensive: to reduce the risk of being blindsided by some new product or production process that destroys its monopoly. If such a product is out there to be discovered, the monopolist may have an incentive to find it. By so doing, it can either exploit the new product or process for continued monopoly profit or suppress the product until the monopolist has extracted the maximum profit from its current capital assets. But, in general, economists agree that monopoly is the market structure least conducive to innovation.

Inverted-U Theory of R&D

Analysis like this has led some experts on technological progress to postulate a so-called **inverted-U theory of R&D**, which deals with the relationship between market structure and technological advance. This theory is illustrated in Figure 14-5, which relates R&D spending as a percentage of a firm's sales (vertical axis) to the industry's four-firm concentration ratio (horizontal axis). The "inverted-U" shape of the curve suggests that R&D effort is at best weak in both very-low-concentration industries (perfect competition) and very-high-concentration industries (monopoly). Starting from the lowest concentrations, R&D spending as a percentage of sales rises with concentration until a concentration ratio of 50 percent or so is reached, meaning that the four largest firms account for about one-half the total industry output. Beyond that, relative R&D spending decreases as concentration rises.

The logic of the inverted-U theory follows from our discussion. Firms in industries with very low concentration ratios are mainly competitive firms. They are small, and this makes it difficult for them to finance R&D. Moreover, entry to these industries is easy, making it difficult to sustain economic profit from innovations that are not supported by patents. As a result, firms in these industries spend little on R&D relative to their sales. At the other end (far right) of the curve, where concentration is exceptionally high, monopoly profit is already high and innovation will not add much more profit. Furthermore, innovation typically requires costly retooling of very large factories, which will cut into whatever additional profit is realized. As a result, the expected rate of return from R&D is quite low, as are expenditures for R&D relative to sales. Finally, the lack of rivals makes the monopolist quite complacent about R&D.

The optimal industry structure for R&D is one in which expected returns on R&D spending are high and funds to finance it are readily available and inexpensive. From our discussion, those factors seem to occur in industries where a few firms are absolutely and relatively large but where the concentration ratio is not so high as to prohibit vigorous competition by smaller rivals. Rivalry among the larger oligopolistic firms and competition between the larger and the smaller firms then provide a strong incentive for R&D. The inverted-U theory of R&D, as represented by Figure 14-5, also points toward this "loose" oligopoly as the optimal structure for R&D spending.

Market Structure and Technological Advance: The Evidence

Various industry studies and cross-industry studies collectively support the inverted-U theory of R&D.[1] Other things equal, the optimal market structure for technological advance seems to be an industry in which there is a mix of large oligopolistic firms (a 40 to 60 percent concentration ratio), with several highly innovative smaller firms.

FIGURE 14-5   The Inverted-U Theory of R&D Expenditures

The inverted-U theory suggests that R&D expenditures as a percentage of sales rise with industry concentration until the four-firm concentration ratio reaches about 50 percent. Further increases in industry concentration are associated with lower relative R&D expenditures.

[1] One such study is that by Philippe Aghion et al., "Competition and Innovation: An Inverted-U Relationship," *Quarterly Journal of Economics*, May 2005, pp. 701–728.

But our "other things equal" qualification is quite important here. Whether a particular industry is highly technical may well be a more important determinant of R&D than its structure. While some concentrated industries (electronics, aircraft, and petroleum) devote large quantities of resources to R&D and are very innovative, others (cigarettes, aluminum, gypsum products) are not. The level of R&D spending within an industry seems to depend as much on its technical character and "technological opportunities" as on its market structure. There may simply be more opportunities to innovate in the computer and pharmaceutical industries, for example, than in the brick-making and coal-mining industries.

Conclusion: The inverted-U curve shown in Figure 14-5 is a useful depiction of the general relationship between R&D spending and market structure, other things equal.

14.7 Technological Advance and Efficiency

LO14.7 Show how technological advance enhances productive efficiency and allocative efficiency.

Technological advance contributes significantly to economic efficiency. New and better processes and products enable society to produce more output, as well as a higher-valued mix of output.

Productive Efficiency

Technological advance as embodied in process innovation improves *productive efficiency* by increasing the productivity of inputs (as indicated in Figure 14-4a) and by reducing average total costs (as in Figure 14-4b). In other words, it enables society to produce the same amount of a particular good or service while using fewer scarce resources, thereby freeing the unused resources to produce other goods and services. Or if society desires more of the now less expensive good, process innovation enables it to have that greater quantity without sacrificing other goods. Viewed either way, process innovation enhances productive efficiency: It reduces society's per-unit cost of whatever mix of goods and services it chooses. It is thus an important means of shifting an economy's production possibilities curve rightward.

Allocative Efficiency

Technological advance as embodied in *product* (or service) innovation enhances allocative efficiency by giving society a more preferred mix of goods and services. Recall from our earlier discussion that consumers buy a new product rather than an old product only when buying the new one increases the total utility obtained from their limited incomes. Obviously, then, a popular new product—and the new mix of products it implies—creates a higher level of total utility for society.

In terms of markets, the demand for the new product rises and the demand for the old product declines. The high economic profit engendered by the new product attracts resources away from less valued uses and to the production of the new product. In theory, such shifting of resources continues until the price of the new product equals its marginal cost.

There is a caveat here, however. Innovation (either product or process) can create monopoly power through patents or through the many advantages of being first. When new monopoly power results from an innovation, society may lose part of the improved efficiency it otherwise would have gained from that innovation. The reason is that the profit-maximizing monopolist restricts output to keep its product price above marginal cost. For example, Microsoft's innovative Windows product has resulted in dominance in the market for operating systems for personal computers. Microsoft's substantial monopoly power permits it to charge prices that are well above marginal cost and minimum average total cost.

Creative Destruction

Although innovation can create monopoly power, it also can reduce or eliminate it. By increasing competition where it previously was weak, innovation can push prices down toward marginal cost. For example, Intel's microprocessor enabled the use of personal computers, and their ease of production eventually diminished IBM's monopoly power in the sale of computer hardware. More recently, Google's Android operating system has provided some promising competition for Microsoft Windows.

At the extreme, innovation may cause *creative destruction*, the phenomenon discussed in Chapter 10 whereby the market positions of firms committed to existing products and old ways of doing business are destroyed by the creation and spread of new products and new production methods.

According to early proponents like MIT economist Joseph Schumpeter, creative destruction is such a powerful force that it will automatically displace any monopolist that no longer delivers superior performance. But many contemporary economists think this notion reflects more wishful thinking than fact. In this view, the idea that creative destruction is automatic

> neglects the ability of powerful established firms to erect private storm shelters—or lobby government to build public storm shelters for them—in order to shield themselves from the Schumpeterian gales of creative destruction. It ignores the difference between the legal freedom of entry and the economic reality deterring the entry of potential newcomers into concentrated industries.[2]

That is, some dominant firms may be able to use strategies such as selective price cutting, buyouts, and massive advertising to block entry and competition from even the most innovative new firms and existing rivals. Moreover, politically active dominant firms have been known to persuade government to give them tax breaks, subsidies, and tariff protection that strengthen their market power.

In short, while innovation in general enhances economic efficiency, in some cases it may lead to entrenched monopoly power. Further innovation may eventually destroy that monopoly power, but the process of creative destruction is neither automatic nor inevitable. On the other hand, the possession of monopoly power does not necessarily preclude rapid technological advance, innovation, or efficiency.

The LAST WORD

Research and Development Spending in Canada

The Canadian Press/Fred Chartrand

Gross domestic expenditures on research and development (GERD) in Canada is low compared to that of many other countries.

Science Minister Kirsty Duncan looks into a microscope at the stem cell research lab after announcing $2.2 million funding for stem cell research at the Ottawa Hospital, Thursday, November 24, 2016.

In 2015 Canada's gross domestic expenditures on research and development (GERD) totalled just under $34 billion. About 54 percent of that was represented by the business enterprise sector, followed by higher education sector at 37 percent. The federal and provincial governments and the private nonprofit sectors accounted for the remaining 9 percent.

---

[2] Walter Adams and James Brock, *The Structure of American Industry*, 10th ed. (Upper Saddle River, NJ: Prentice Hall, 2001), pp. 363–64.

Ontario accounts for the largest share of Canadian GERD spending at approximately 44 percent of the total, followed by Quebec at 26 percent and Alberta at 11 percent.

R&D spending in Canada in 2015 was concentrated on natural science and engineering and on the social sciences and the humanities. The natural sciences and engineering accounted for the bulk of R&D spending, at 90 percent of GERD, of which well over half was attributable to the business enterprise sector. In the social sciences and the humanities 91 percent of the R&D expenditures were carried out by the higher education sector.

In the past, government research spending has been helpful to long-term economic growth, because most of it flows to basic scientific research, which produces fundamental discoveries that in turn generate widespread applications. It should be noted, however, that basic scientific research typically generates ideas that are years—if not decades—away from commercialization.

As a result, private firms concentrate their R&D efforts on more developed technologies that are closer to commercialization. That strategy minimizes the risk that their spending will fail to yield profitable products. But it also means that only a small percentage of private R&D spending goes toward basic scientific research.

Many economists consider that low percentage of R&D spending by governments in Canada as indicating a misallocation of resources, since productivity-enhancing research activities can help raise future consumption.

Question

Explain why businesses don't devote more of their R&D spending toward basic scientific research.

Sources: Statistics Canada, "Spending on Research and Development, 2016," *The Daily*, June 23, 2017.

Chapter Summary

LO14.1 Differentiate among invention, innovation, and technological diffusion.

- Technological advance is evidenced by new and improved goods and services and new and improved production or distribution processes. In economists' models, technological advance occurs only in the *very long run*.

- Invention is the discovery of a product or process through the use of imagination, ingenuity, and experimentation. Innovation is the first successful commercial introduction of a new product, the first use of a new method, or the creation of a new form of business enterprise. Diffusion is the spread of an earlier innovation among competing firms. Firms channel a majority of their R&D expenditures to innovation and imitation, rather than to basic scientific research and invention.

LO14.2 Explain how entrepreneurs and other innovators further technological advance.

- Historically, most economists viewed technological advance as a random, external force to which the economy adjusted. Many contemporary economists see technological advance as occurring in response to profit incentives within the economy and thus as an integral part of capitalism.

- Entrepreneurs and other innovators try to anticipate the future. They play a central role in technological advance by initiating changes in products and processes. Entrepreneurs often form start-up firms that focus on creating and introducing new products. Sometimes, innovators work in the R&D labs of major corporations. Entrepreneurs and innovative firms often rely heavily on the basic research done by university and government scientists.

LO14.3 Summarize how a firm determines its optimal amount of research and development (R&D).

- A firm's optimal amount of R&D spending occurs where its expected return (marginal benefit) from R&D equals its interest-rate cost of funds (marginal cost) to finance R&D. Entrepreneurs and firms use several sources to finance R&D, including (a) bank loans, (b) bonds, (c) venture capital (funds given in return for a share of the profits if the business succeeds), (d) undistributed corporate profits (retained earnings), and (e) personal savings.

LO14.4 Discuss how technological change can increase profits by raising revenues or lowering costs.

- Process innovation can lower a firm's production costs by improving its internal production techniques. Such improvement increases the firm's total product, thereby lowering its average total cost and increasing its profit. The added profit provides a positive rate of return on the R&D spending that produced the process innovation.

LO14.5 Relate why firms can benefit from their innovation even though rivals have an incentive to imitate it.

- Product innovation, the introduction of new products, succeeds when it provides consumers with a higher marginal utility per dollar spent than do existing products. The new product enables consumers to obtain greater total utility from a given income. From the firm's perspective, product innovation increases net revenue sufficiently to yield a positive rate of return on the R&D spending that produced the innovation.

- Imitation poses a potential problem for innovators, since it threatens their returns on R&D expenditures. Some dominant firms use a fast-second strategy, letting smaller firms initiate new products and then quickly imitating the successes. Nevertheless, there are significant protections and potential benefits for firms that take the lead with R&D and innovation, including

(a) patent protection, (b) copyrights and trademarks, (c) lasting brand-name recognition, (d) benefits from trade secrets and learning by doing, (e) high economic profits during the time lag between a product's introduction and its imitation, and (f) the possibility of lucrative buyout offers from larger firms.

LO14.6 Discuss the role of market structure in promoting technological advance.

- Each of the four basic market structures has potential strengths and weaknesses regarding the likelihood of R&D and innovation. The inverted-U theory of R&D holds that a firm's R&D spending as a percentage of its sales rises with its industry four-firm concentration ratio, reaches a peak at a 50 percent concentration ratio, and then declines as concentration increases further. Empirical evidence is not clear-cut, but it lends general support to this theory. For any specific industry, however, the technological opportunities that are available may count more than market structure in determining R&D spending and innovation.

LO14.7 Show how technological advance enhances productive efficiency and allocative efficiency.

- In general, technological advance enhances both productive and allocative efficiency. But in some situations patents and the advantages of being first with an innovation can increase monopoly power. While in some cases creative destruction eventually destroys monopolies, most economists doubt that this process is either automatic or inevitable.

Terms and Concepts

technological advance
very long run
invention
patent
innovation
product innovation
process innovation
diffusion
entrepreneurs

start-ups
venture capital
interest-rate cost-of-funds curve
expected-rate-of-return curve
optimal amount of R&D
imitation problem
fast-second strategy
inverted-U theory of R&D

Discussion Questions

The following and additional problems can be found in ≣ connect

1. What is meant by technological advance, as broadly defined? How does technological advance enter into the definition of the very long run? Which of the following are examples of technological advance, and which are not: an improved production process; entry of a firm into a profitable perfectly competitive industry; the imitation of a new production process by another firm; an increase in a firm's advertising expenditures?   [LO14.1]

2. Contrast the older and the modern views of technological advance as they relate to the economy. What is the role of entrepreneurs and other innovators in technological advance? How does research by universities and government affect innovators and technological advance? Why do you think some university researchers are becoming more like entrepreneurs and less like "pure scientists"?   [LO14.2]

3. Consider the effect that corporate profit taxes have on investing. Look back at Figure 14-3. Suppose that the *r* line is the rate of return a firm earns before taxes. If corporate profit taxes are imposed, the firm's after-tax returns will be lower (and the higher the tax rate, the lower the after-tax returns). If the firm's decisions about R&D spending are based on comparing after-tax returns with the interest-rate cost of funds, how will increased corporate profit taxes affect R&D spending? Does this effect modify your views on corporate profit taxes? Discuss.   [LO14.3]

4. Answer the following lettered questions on the basis of the information in this table: [LO14.3]

Amount of R&D, millions	Expected rate of return on R&D, %
$10	16
20	14
30	12
40	10
50	8
60	6

a. If the interest-rate cost of funds is 8 percent, what will be the optimal amount of R&D spending for this firm?

b. Explain why $20 million of R&D spending will not be optimal.

c. Why won't $60 million be optimal either?

5. Explain: "The success of a new product depends not only on its marginal utility but also on its price." [**LO14.4**]

6. Learning how to use software takes time. So once customers have learned to use a particular software package, it is easier to sell them software upgrades than to convince them to switch to new software. What implications does this have for expected rates of return on R&D spending for software firms developing upgrades versus firms developing imitative products? [**LO14.5**]

7. Why might a firm making a large economic profit from its existing product employ a fast-second strategy in relationship to new or improved products? What risks does it run in pursuing this strategy? What incentive does a firm have to engage in R&D when rivals can imitate its new product? [**LO14.5**]

8. Do you think the overall level of R&D would increase or decrease over the next 20 to 30 years if the lengths of new patents were extended from 20 years to, say, "forever"? What if the duration were reduced from 20 years to 3? [**LO14.5**]

9. Make a case that neither perfect competition nor monopoly is conducive to a great deal of R&D spending and innovation. Why might oligopoly be more favourable to R&D spending and innovation than either perfect competition or monopoly? What is the inverted-U theory of R&D, and how does it relate to your answers to these questions? [**LO14.6**]

10. Evaluate: "Society does not need laws outlawing monopolization and monopoly. Inevitably, monopoly causes its own self-destruction, since its high profit is the lure for other firms or entrepreneurs to develop substitute products." [**LO14.7**]

Review Questions

1. Listed below are several possible actions by firms. Write "INV" beside those that reflect invention, "INN" beside those that reflect innovation, and "DIF" beside those that reflect diffusion. [**LO14.1**]

   a. An auto manufacturer adds "heated seats" as a standard feature in its luxury cars to keep pace with a rival firm whose luxury cars already have this feature.

   b. A television production company pioneers the first music video channel.

   c. A firm develops and patents a working model of a self-erasing whiteboard for classrooms.

   d. A lightbulb firm is the first to produce and market lighting fixtures with LEDs (light-emitting diodes).

   e. A rival toy maker introduces a new Jezebel doll to compete with Mattel's Barbie doll.

2. A firm is considering three possible one-year investments, which we will name X, Y, and Z.

   - Investment X would cost $10 million now and would return $11 million next year, for a net gain of $1 million.

   - Investment Y would cost $100 million now and would return $105 million next year, for a net gain of $5 million.

   - Investment Z would cost $1 million now and would return $1.2 million next year, for a net gain of $200,000.

   The firm currently has $150 million of cash on hand that it can loan out at 15 percent interest. Which of the three possible investments should it undertake? [**LO14.3**]

   a. X only

   b. Y only

   c. Z only

   d. X and Y

   e. X and Z

   f. X, Y, and Z

3. An additional unit of Old Product X will bring Cindy an MU of 15 utils, an additional unit of New Product Y will bring Cindy an MU of 30 utils, and an additional unit of New Product Z will bring Cindy an MU of 40 utils. If a unit of Old Product X costs $10, a unit of New Product Y costs $30, and a unit of New Product Z costs $20, which product will Cindy prefer to spend her money on? [**LO14.4**]

   a. Old Product X

   b. New Product Y

   c. New Product Z

   d. More information is required

4. The inverted-U theory suggests that R&D expenditures as a percentage of sales _____ with industry concentration after the four-firm concentration ratio exceeds about 50 percent. [**LO14.6**]

   a. Rise

   b. Fall

   c. Fluctuate

   d. Flatline

5. Which statement about market structure and innovation is true? [**LO14.7**]

   a. Innovation helps only dominant firms.

   b. Innovation keeps new firms from ever catching up with leading firms.

   c. Innovation often leads to creative destruction and the replacement of established firms by new firms.

   d. Innovation always leads to entrenched monopoly power.

Problems

1. Suppose a firm expects that a $20 million expenditure on R&D in the current year will result in a new product that can be sold next year. Selling that product next year would increase the firm's revenue next year by $30 million and its costs next year by $29 million.   [**LO14.3**]

   a. What is the expected rate of return on this R&D expenditure?

   b. Suppose the firm can get a bank loan at 6 percent interest to finance its $20 million R&D project. Will the firm undertake the project?

   c. Now suppose the interest-rate cost of borrowing, in effect, falls to 4 percent because the firm decides to use its own retained earnings to finance the R&D. Will this lower interest rate change the firm's R&D decision?

   d. Now suppose that the firm has savings of $20 million—enough money to fund the R&D expenditure without borrowing. If the firm has the chance to invest this money either in the R&D project or in government bonds that pay 3.5 percent per year, which should it do?

   e. What if the government bonds were paying 6.5 percent per year?

2. A firm faces the following costs: total cost of capital = $1000; price paid for labour = $12 per labour unit; and price paid for raw materials = $4 per raw-material unit.   [**LO14.4**]

   a. Suppose the firm can produce 5000 units of output this year by combining its fixed capital with 100 units of labour and 450 units of raw materials. What are the total cost and average total cost of producing the 5000 units?

   b. Now assume the firm improves its production process so that it can produce 6000 units of output this year by combining its fixed capital with 100 units of labour and 450 units of raw materials. What are the total cost and average total cost of producing the 6000 units?

   c. If units of output can always be sold for $1 each, by how much does the firm's profit increase after it improves its production process?

   d. Suppose that implementing the improved production process would require a one-time cost of $1100. If the firm only considers this year's profit, would it implement the improved production process? What if it considers its profit not just this year but in future years as well?

CHAPTER 15

Competition Policy and Regulation

LEARNING OBJECTIVES

LO15.1 Describe what industrial concentration is and how governments combat it.

LO15.2 Identify and explain the economic principles and difficulties relating to the setting of prices (rates) charged by so-called natural monopolies.

LO15.3 Discuss the nature of *social regulation*, its benefits and costs, and its optimal level.

In this chapter we look at three sets of government policies toward business: competition policy, industrial regulation, and social regulation. *Competition policy* consists of the laws and government actions designed to prevent monopoly and promote competition. *Industrial regulation* pertains to government regulation of firms' prices (or rates) within selected industries. *Social regulation* is government regulation of the conditions under which goods are produced, the physical characteristics of goods, and the impact of the production and consumption of goods on society.

15.1 Industrial Concentration

LO15.1 Describe what industrial concentration is and how governments combat it.

In Chapter 11 we developed and applied a strict definition of monopoly. A *monopoly* is a one-firm industry—a unique product is being produced entirely by a single firm and entry to the industry is totally blocked.

In this chapter we will use the term *industrial concentration* to include monopoly and markets in which much potential monopoly power exists. Industrial concentration occurs whenever a single firm or a small number of firms control the major portion of an industry's output. One, two, or three firms dominate, potentially resulting in higher-than-competitive prices and profits. This definition, which is closer to how the general public understands the monopoly problem, includes many industries we have previously designated as oligopolies.

Industrial concentration in this chapter thus refers to industries in which firms are large in absolute terms and in relation to the total market. Examples in Canada are the wireless mobile communications industry, in which Rogers

Communications, BCE Inc., and Telus Corporation dominate; the petro-chemical industry, which Dow Chemical Canada, Imperial Oil (Exxon), and Petro-Canada dominate; the aluminum industry, which industrial giant Rio Tinto Alcan dominates; and the steel industry, which two large producers, ArcelorMittal Dofasco and U.S. Steel Canada, dominate.

 THE ROLE OF GOVERNMENTS

Competition Policy

The underlying purpose of **competition policy** is to prevent industrial concentration or monopolization, to promote competition, and to achieve allocative efficiency. Although all economists would agree that these are praiseworthy goals, conflicting opinions exist about the effectiveness of Canadian competition law.

The main economic case against monopoly is familiar to you from Chapter 11. Monopolists produce less output and charge higher prices than if their industries were competitive. With perfect competition, each competitive firm maximizes profit by producing the output level at which $P = MC$. That output level generates allocative efficiency and this equality represents an efficient allocation of resources because P measures the marginal benefit to society of an extra unit of output, while marginal cost (MC) reflects the cost of an extra unit. When $P = MC$, society cannot gain by producing one more or one fewer unit of the product. In contrast, a monopolist maximizes profit by producing the lower output level at which marginal revenue (rather than price) equals marginal cost. At this $MR = MC$ point, price exceeds marginal cost, meaning that by producing extra units society would obtain more benefit than it would incur cost. There is an underallocation of resources to the monopolized product, and so the economic well-being of society is less than it would be with greater competition.

But an efficiency loss isn't the only consequence of the monopolist's higher-than-competitive price. The higher price also transfers income from consumers to the monopolist. This transfer causes significant resentment, because it results purely from the monopolist's ability to restrict output and cannot be justified on the basis of increased production costs. Consumers consequently express their ire to elected officials to "do something about the situation."

Responding to that pressure, government officials concluded in the late 1800s and early 1900s that monopolized industries lacked enough of the beneficial market forces that help to protect consumers in competitive industries, achieve fair competition, and achieve allocative efficiency. So the government instituted two alternative means of control as substitutes for, or supplements to, market forces:

- *Regulatory Agencies* In the few markets where the nature of the product or technology creates a *natural monopoly*, the government established public regulatory agencies to control such firms.

- *Competition Law* In most other markets, government control took the form of laws designed to inhibit or prevent the growth of monopoly.

We will shortly review the anticombines legislation that constitutes the basic law of the land with respect to corporate size and concentration. Before we do, let's examine merger types.

Merger Types

Mergers of firms are one of the main causes of industrial concentration. There are three basic types of mergers. A **horizontal merger** occurs between two competitors selling similar products in the same market. Examples of horizontal mergers would be the buyout of Eaton's by Sears, Air Canada's merger with Canadian Airlines, and Best Buy's merger with Future Shop. A **vertical merger** occurs between firms at different stages of the production process. Vertical mergers involve firms having buyer–seller relationships. Examples of mergers of this type are PepsiCo's mergers with Pizza Hut, Taco Bell, and Kentucky Fried Chicken; PepsiCo supplies soft drinks to each of these fast-food outlets. A **conglomerate merger** is officially defined as any merger that is not horizontal or vertical; in general, it is the combination of firms in different industries or firms operating in different geographical areas. Conglomerate mergers can extend the line of products sold, or combine totally unrelated companies. An example of a conglomerate is Power Corporation of Canada, headquartered in Montreal. Among its holdings are Great-West Life Co. Inc., a life insurance subsidiary, and Power Broadcast Inc., a subsidiary that owns newspapers and radio stations. In Europe, Power Corporation has investments in major communications, industrial, energy, utility, financial services, and food companies.

Competition Law

The basis of competition policy (sometimes referred to as *anticombines* policy) in Canada is the Competition Act, passed in 1986. It replaced the Combines Investigation Act, which had been in force in different forms since 1910.

The Competition Act is administered and enforced by the federal Competition Bureau, which promotes and maintains fair competition in Canada. One of its main innovations was that uncompetitive market structures (monopoly and oligopoly) and mergers, previously covered by criminal law, came under the jurisdiction of civil law, making it easier to prosecute mergers and monopolies not deemed to be in the public interest. Price fixing, however, is still handled in the criminal courts, where the standard of evidence is "beyond a reasonable doubt." Those sections of the Competition Act now under the jurisdiction of civil law are adjudicated by the federal **Competition Tribunal**. The tribunal is made up of judges of the Federal Court and laypersons, with a judge as chairperson. It must be emphasized that the Competition Act does not directly prohibit monopoly; a firm can legally have 100 percent of the market as long as it does not abuse its position.

Merger Guidelines

The federal government has established merger guidelines based on the concentration ratio. Recall from Chapter 12 that this measure of concentration is the sum of the squared percentage market shares of the firms within an industry. An industry of only four firms, each with a 25 percent market share, has a Herfindahl index of 2500 ($= 25^2 + 25^2 + 25^2 + 25^2$). In perfect competition, where each firm's market share is minuscule, the index approaches 0 ($= 0^2 + 0^2 + \cdots + 0^2$). In monopoly, the index for that single firm is 10,000 ($= 100^2$).

The Competition Bureau's main concern in the case of a horizontal merger is unilateral market power of the new merged entity as well as the combined market power of the four largest firms in the sector. It is likely to challenge a horizontal merger if the postmerger Herfindahl index would be high (above 1800) and if the merger has substantially increased the index (added 100 or more points). However, other factors, such as economies of scale, the degree of foreign competition, and the ease of entry of new firms, are also considered. Furthermore, horizontal mergers are usually allowed if one of the merging firms is suffering major continuing losses (one reason why Air Canada was allowed to acquire Canadian Airlines in 1999).

Most *vertical mergers* escape anticombines prosecution, because they do not substantially lessen competition in either of the two markets. However, a vertical merger between large firms in a highly concentrated industry might be challenged.

Conglomerate mergers are generally permitted. If an auto manufacturer acquires a blue jeans producer no anticombines action is likely, since neither firm has increased its own market share as a result. That means the Herfindahl index remains unchanged in each industry.

PRICE FIXING

Price fixing among firms is dealt with strictly. Evidence of price fixing, even by small firms, will bring the action of the Competition Tribunal, as will other collusive activities, such as scheming to rig bids on government contracts or dividing up sales in a market. To gain a conviction the government or other party making the charge need show only that there was a conspiracy to fix prices, rig bids, or divide up markets, not that the conspiracy succeeded or caused serious damage to other parties.

PRICE DISCRIMINATION

Price discrimination is a common business practice that rarely reduces competition and therefore is rarely challenged by the Competition Tribunal. The exception occurs when a firm engages in price discrimination as part of a strategy to block entry or drive out competitors.

TYING CONTRACTS

The Competition Tribunal strictly enforces the prohibition of tying contracts, particularly when practised by dominant firms. A **tying contract** is a requirement imposed by a seller that a buyer purchase another (or other) of its products as a condition for buying a desired product.

RECENT CASES

The Competition Act is designed to achieve economic efficiency and to be adaptable to changing market conditions and international trade. Only those mergers resulting in an unacceptable lessening of competition can be prohibited or modified by the competition tribunal. Mergers that result in efficiency gains through capturing economies of scale have generally been allowed. For example, in April 2003, the Competition Bureau reported it would not challenge the merger of certain assets of the coal businesses of Fording Inc., Teck Cominco Ltd., Luscar Ltd., and Consol Energy Inc., in the thermal coal, metallurgical coal, and coal terminal port businesses in Canada.

The Competition Bureau recommended against chartered bank mergers in 1998, when the Royal Bank of Canada and the Bank of Montreal announced their intention to merge. Soon after, the Canadian Imperial Bank of Commerce and the Toronto-Dominion Bank also decided to merge. The banks argued that they needed to merge to capture economies of scale and be able to compete internationally. The Competition Bureau was not convinced by the banks' argument, citing fears that competition would be greatly curtailed in smaller centres for both consumers and small and medium-sized firms. The Bureau noted that even if more foreign banks were allowed to compete in the Canadian market, the large established network of branches of the Canadian banks provided a large barrier to entry for any new competitor. The Royal Bank of Canada and the Bank of Montreal were, however, successful in merging the processing of their credit card operations.

In May 2005 the Competition Bureau announced that Mitsubishi Corporation, Japan's largest trading company, pleaded guilty to charges of attempting to maintain the international price of graphite electrodes, used mainly in electric arc furnace steel production. Mitsubishi Corporation was fined $1,000,000 by the Federal Court of Canada under the price maintenance provision of the act. Earlier in 2005 Robert J. Hart and Company, with headquarters in the United Kingdom, was fined $50,000 in the same graphite electrodes price maintenance scheme. In 2008 and 2010 a total of 38 individuals and 14 companies were accused of fixing the price of gas at the pumps in Victoriaville, Thetford Mines, Magog, and Sherbrooke, all in the province of Quebec. Fines totalling almost $3 million were imposed and some of the individuals charged received prison sentences.

The antitrust agency for the European Union (EU) has generally been more aggressive than Canada in prosecuting monopolists. For example, in 2004 the EU fined Microsoft $600 million for monopolization and required it to share its computer coding with other firms that supplied Windows applications (such as media players). The purpose of the code-sharing requirement was to enable competitors to compete on an equal footing against Microsoft's own application software. Microsoft was fined a further $1.3 billion by the EU in 2008 for failing to quickly and fully comply with the 2004 remedy ordering Microsoft to share its computer code.

The U.S. has also prosecuted several international price fixing schemes. For example:

- Between 2008 and 2010, five manufacturers of liquid crystal displays—LG, Sharp, Hitachi, Chi Mei Optoelectronics, and Chunghwa Picture Tubes—were fined a total of over $860 million for fixing the prices of the displays they sold to computer maker Dell Inc.

- In 2009, three international cargo airlines—Cargolux of Luxembourg, Nippon Cargo of Japan, and Asiana Airlines of South Korea—were fined $214 million for conspiring to fix international airline cargo rates.

- In 2012, nine Japanese, German, and Swedish auto-parts makers were fined a total of $790 million for conspiring to fix the prices of automobile heater control panels. Eleven corporate officers received jail sentences ranging from one to two years.

- In 2013 Apple was convicted along with five publishers—Harper Collins, Penguin, Simon & Schuster, Hachette, and Macmillan—of horizontal price fixing in the market for eBooks to be sold on Apple's iBook store. Apple was ordered to pay $450 million in reparations to those harmed by the scheme, which raised prices 20 percent on Apple's online book store.

ISSUES OF ENFORCEMENT: TRADE-OFFS AMONG GOALS

Promoting competition is only one of society's goals, and strict enforcement of competition laws may sometimes conflict with some other goal.

Occasionally, new technologies combine to create new products and services. A current example is the meshing of computer and communications technologies relating to the Internet. This interactive network has improved the communications capabilities of households, businesses, and governments across the globe.

Should the government strictly enforce competition laws to block some of those mergers, specifically ones that produce dominant firms and threaten to reduce competition? Or should the government temporarily suspend

CONSIDER THIS

Gas Price Fixing in Quebec

Canadian consumers are suspicious of gas prices. When the price of gas increases, they often suspect "rigging" by the oil companies. Often the price of gasoline goes up just before long summer holiday weekends, right when consumers are driving their cars more. The higher price of gasoline may reflect the forces of supply and demand. But sometimes the consumers' suspicions turn out to be correct. In 2008 the Competition Bureau began an investigation of the price of gasoline in the province of Quebec. Subsequently, it brought charges against a number of companies and individuals, some of whom were convicted while other cases were still in court as of the writing of this text. In 2012 the Competition Bureau brought charges of alleged price fixing against one of Canada's largest oil distributors, Irving Oil, including the manager of the company for the province of Quebec. Irving Oil is a family-owned company headquartered in Saint John, New Brunswick, which operates service stations in Quebec and eastern Canada. Altogether some fifteen companies and forty-five

© Photopal604 | Dreamstime.com

individuals were charged in the price-fixing scheme in the province of Quebec.

For an update of the Competition Bureau's activities, go to www.competitionbureau.gc.ca/eic/site/cb-bc.nsf/eng/home.

competition rules to encourage the restructuring of industries and speed the expansion of this new technology? Hastening the advance of Internet-related technologies might also increase Canadian exports of electronic services.

Each of these enforcement trade-offs, by itself, triggers controversy. Some argue that the gains from competition policy must be weighed against the effects of the policy on conflicting objectives. Others contend that selective enforcement of competition laws dangerously interferes with the market process. Obviously, different policymakers and different administrations may view such considerations and trade-offs differently.

QUICK REVIEW 15.1

- Industrial concentration exists where a single firm or a small number of firms control the major portion of an industry's output.

- Three types of mergers can occur: horizontal, vertical, and conglomerate.

- The Competition Act, passed in 1986, allows mergers that bring about significant efficiency gains.

15.2 Industrial Regulation

LO15.2 **Identify and explain the economic principles and difficulties relating to the setting of prices (rates) charged by so-called natural monopolies.**

Competition policy assumes that society will benefit if monopoly is prevented from evolving or if it is dissolved where it already exists. We now return to the special situation in which there is an economic reason for an industry to be organized monopolistically.

THE ROLE OF GOVERNMENTS

Natural Monopoly

A **natural monopoly** exists when economies of scale are so extensive that a single firm can supply the entire market at a lower unit cost than could a number of competing firms. Clear-cut circumstances of natural monopoly are relatively rare, but such conditions exist for many public utilities, such as local electricity and water. As we discussed in Chapter 11, large-scale operations are necessary in some cases to obtain low unit costs and a low product price. Where natural monopoly exists, competition does not enhance efficiency. If the market were divided among many producers, economies of scale would not be achieved and unit costs and prices would increase.

There are two possible alternatives for promoting better economic outcomes where natural monopoly exists: public ownership and public regulation.

Public ownership, or some approximation of it, has been established in a few instances, such as Canada Post, water supply systems, and garbage collection at the local level. But *public regulation*, or what economists call *industrial regulation*, has been the preferred option in Canada. In this type of regulation, government commissions regulate the prices (usually called rates) charged by natural monopolists so as to prevent these from taking advantage of their market power to increase prices not warranted by their costs.

The economic objective of industrial regulation is reflected in the **public interest theory of regulation**. In that theory, industrial regulation is necessary to keep a natural monopoly from charging monopoly prices and thus harming consumers and society. The goal of such regulation is to garner for society at least part of the cost reductions associated with natural monopoly while avoiding the restrictions of output and high prices that come with unregulated monopoly. If competition is impractical, society should allow or even encourage a monopoly but regulate its prices. Regulation should then be structured so that ratepayers benefit from the economies of scale—the lower per-unit costs—that natural monopolists are able to achieve.

In practice, regulators seek to establish rates that will cover production costs and yield a fair return to the enterprise. The goal is to set price equal to average total cost so that the regulated firm receives a normal profit, as described in Chapter 11's section 11.5. In particular, you should carefully review Figure 11-10.

Problems with Industrial Regulation

There is considerable disagreement on the effectiveness of industrial regulation. Let's examine two criticisms.

COSTS AND INEFFICIENCY

An unregulated firm has a strong incentive to reduce its costs at each level of output, because that will increase its profit. The regulatory commission, however, confines the regulated firm to a normal profit or a fair return on the value of its assets. If a regulated firm lowers its operating costs, the rising profit eventually will lead the regulatory commission to require the firm to lower its rates and return its profits to normal. The regulated firm, therefore, has no incentive to reduce its operating costs.

Worse yet, higher costs do not result in lower profit. Because the regulatory commissions must allow the public utility a fair return, the regulated monopolist can simply pass higher production costs to consumers by charging higher rates. A regulated firm may reason that it might as well have high salaries for its workers, luxurious working conditions for management, and the like, since the return is the same in percentage terms whether costs are minimized or not. So, although a natural monopoly reduces costs through economies of scale, industrial regulation fosters considerable X-inefficiency (refer to Figure 11-8). Because of the absence of competition, the potential cost savings from natural monopoly may never actually materialize.

PERPETUATING MONOPOLY

A second general problem with industrial regulation is that it sometimes perpetuates monopoly long after the conditions of natural monopoly have ended.

Technological change often creates the potential for competition in all or at least some portions of the regulated industry, as when trucks began competing with railroads, when transmission of voice and data by microwave and satellites began competing with transmission over telephone wires, when satellite TV began competing with cable TV, and when cellphones began competing with landlines.

But, spurred by the firms they regulate, commissions often protect the regulated firms from new competition by either blocking entry or extending regulation to competitors. Industrial regulation therefore may perpetuate a monopoly that is no longer a natural monopoly and would otherwise erode. Ordinary monopoly, protected by government, may supplant natural monopoly. If so, the regulated prices may exceed those that would occur with competition. The beneficiaries of outdated regulation are the regulated firms and their employees. The losers are consumers and the potential entrants.

Legal Cartel Theory

In Chapter 13, we noted that a *cartel* is formed when a group of previously competing firms make a formal agreement to cease competing. They either control the price of a product by establishing the amounts of output that each cartel member will produce or they divide up the overall market for the product geographically so that each firm becomes a monopolist within its assigned region.

Privately organized cartels are illegal in Canada. But, in some cases, government regulations can have effects on prices and competition very similar to cartels. Thus, firms may seek to be regulated if they believe that regulation will reduce competition and raise prices in the same way a private cartel would. In essence, they see regulation as a way of creating a legal, publicly sanctioned cartel.

This possibility is known as the **legal cartel theory of regulation**. In place of socially minded officials forcing regulation on natural monopolies to protect consumers, holders of this view see practical politicians as supplying regulation to local, regional, and national firms that fear the impact of competition on their profits or even on their long-term survival. These firms desire regulation because it yields a legal monopoly that can guarantee a profit. Specifically, the regulatory commission performs such functions as blocking entry, or, where there are several firms, dividing up the market much as an illegal cartel does (for example, before airline deregulation, the federal government assigned routes to specific airlines). The commission may also restrict potential competition by enlarging the cartel.

While private cartels are illegal, unstable, and often break down, the special attraction of a government-sponsored cartel under the guise of regulation is that it endures. The legal cartel theory of regulation suggests that regulation is a form of regulatory capture that results from the rent-seeking activities of private firms and the desire of politicians to be responsive in order to win re-election.

Occupational licensing is a labour-market application of the legal cartel theory. Certain occupational groups—dentists, barbers, hairstylists, dietitians, lawyers—demand stringent licensing on the grounds that it protects the public from charlatans and quacks, but skeptics say the real reason may be to limit entry into the occupational group so that practitioners can receive monopoly incomes.

Deregulation

Beginning in the 1970s, the legal cartel theory, evidence of inefficiency in regulated industries, and the contention that the government was regulating potentially competitive industries all contributed to a wave of deregulation. Since then, Parliament and most provincial legislatures have passed legislation that has deregulated in varying degrees the airline, trucking, banking, railroad, natural gas, electricity, and television broadcasting industries. Deregulation has also occurred in the telecommunications industry. Bell Canada now competes with other carriers, such as Rogers Home Phone, in the local and long-distance markets. It also competes with cellular companies, such as Telus. Deregulation in the 1970s and 1980s was one of the most extensive experiments in economic policy to take place during the past fifty years.

The overwhelming consensus among economists is that deregulation has produced large net benefits for consumers and society. Most of the gains from deregulation have occurred in three industries: airlines, railroads, and trucking. Airfares (adjusted for inflation) have declined by about one-third, and airline safety has improved. Railroad and trucking freight rates (again, adjusted for inflation) have dropped by about one-half.

Significant efficiency gains have occurred in long-distance telecommunications, and slight efficiency gains have been made in cable television, stock brokerage services, and the natural gas industry. Deregulation has unleashed a wave of technological advances that have resulted in such new and improved products and services as fax machines, cellphones, fibre-optic cable, microwave systems in communications, and the Internet.

This success has led to further calls for deregulation. The latest industry to begin the process is electricity, led by Alberta and Ontario. Deregulation is now occurring at the wholesale level, where firms are free to build generating facilities and sell electricity at market prices.

However, the financial crisis that spread from the U.S. to most economies around the world has had many questioning deregulation of the financial industry in recent decades. As a consequence, in many countries, including Canada, governments and central banks are taking a closer look at their financial sectors to ensure that financial entities do not take on excessive risk. They are putting regulations in place to minimize contagion in the event of financial problems in one of the major economies, such as that of the United States. Recent sovereign-debt problems in some of the European economies, which has put at risk some large European banks, has further strengthened the view that suitable regulations of the financial sector are needed.

QUICK REVIEW 15.2

- Natural monopoly occurs where economies of scale are so extensive that only a single firm can produce the product at minimum average total cost.

- The public interest theory of regulation says that government must regulate natural monopolies to prevent abuses arising from monopoly power. Regulated firms, however, have less incentive than competitive firms to reduce costs; that is, regulated firms tend to be X-inefficient.

- The legal cartel theory of regulation suggests that some firms seek government regulation to reduce price competition and ensure stable profits.

- Deregulation initiated by government in the past three decades has yielded large annual efficiency gains for society.

15.3 Social Regulation

LO15.3   Discuss the nature of *social regulation*, its benefits and costs, and its optimal level.

The industrial regulation discussed in the preceding section has focused on the regulation of prices (or rates) in natural monopolies. But in the early 1960s, a new type of regulation began to emerge. A concept known as *social regulation* is concerned with the conditions under which goods and services are produced, the impact of production on society, and the physical qualities of the goods themselves.

 THE ROLE OF GOVERNMENTS

Distinguishing Features

Social regulation differs from industrial regulation in several ways.

First, social regulation is often applied across the board to all industries and directly affects more producers than does industrial regulation. For instance, while the industrial regulation by the Air Transport Committee of the National Transport Agency of Canada controls only the air transport industry, the rules and regulations of the Canada Labour (Safety) Code and its provincial counterparts apply to every employer.

Second, social regulation intrudes into the day-to-day production process to a greater extent than industrial regulation. While industrial regulation focuses on rates, costs, and profits, social regulation often dictates the design of products, the conditions of employment, and the nature of the production process. For example, rather than specifying safety standards for vehicles, the *Motor Vehicle Safety Act* includes six standards limiting motor vehicle exhaust and noise emission.

Finally, social regulation has expanded rapidly during the same period in which industrial regulation has waned. Under this social regulation, firms must provide reasonable accommodations for qualified workers and job applicants with disabilities. Also, sellers must provide reasonable access for customers with disabilities. As much of our society had achieved a fairly affluent standard of living by the 1960s, attention shifted to improvement in the nonmaterial quality of life. That focus called for safer products, less pollution, improved working conditions, and greater equality of economic opportunity.

The Optimal Level of Social Regulation

While economists agree on the need for social regulation, they disagree on whether the current level of such regulation is optimal. Recall that an activity should be expanded so long as its marginal benefit (MB) exceeds its marginal cost (MC). If the MB of social regulation exceeds its MC, there is too little social regulation; if MC exceeds MB, there is too much social regulation. Unfortunately, the marginal costs and benefits of social regulation are not always easy to measure and therefore may be illusory. So, ideology about the proper size and role of government often drives the debate over social regulation as much as, or perhaps more than, economic cost–benefit analysis.

IN SUPPORT OF SOCIAL REGULATION

Defenders of social regulation say that it has achieved notable successes and, overall, has greatly enhanced society's well-being. They point out that social regulation confronts serious and substantial problems. Hundreds of workers die annually in job-related accidents and many thousands of workers suffer injuries that force them to miss a day or more of work. Air pollution continues to cloud major Canadian cities, imposing large costs in terms of reduced property values and increased health care expense. Numerous children and adults die each year because of poorly designed or manufactured products (for example, car tires) or tainted food (for example, *E. coli* in food products). Discrimination against some ethnic minorities, persons with disabilities, and older workers reduces their earnings and imposes heavy costs on society.

Proponents of social regulation acknowledge that social regulation is costly, but they correctly point out that a high price for something does not necessarily mean that it should not be purchased. They say that the appropriate economic test should be not whether the costs of social regulation are high or low but whether the benefits of social regulation exceed the costs. After decades of neglect, they further assert, society cannot expect to cleanse the environment, enhance the safety of the workplace, and promote economic opportunity for all without incurring substantial costs. So statements about the huge costs of social regulation are irrelevant, say defenders, since the benefits are even greater. The public often underestimates those benefits, since they are more difficult to measure than costs and often become apparent only after some time has passed (for example, the benefits of reducing global warming).

Proponents of social regulation point to its many specific benefits. It is estimated that highway fatalities would be 40 percent greater annually in the absence of auto safety features mandated through regulation. Compliance with child safety seat and seatbelt laws has significantly reduced the auto fatality rate for small children. The national air quality standards set by law have been reached in nearly all parts of the nation for sulphur dioxide, nitrogen dioxide, and lead. Recent studies clearly link cleaner air, other things equal, with increases in the values of homes. Employment equity regulations have increased the labour demand for ethnic minorities and females. The use of childproof lids has resulted in a 90 percent decline in child deaths caused by accidental swallowing of poisonous substances.

Some defenders of social regulation say many areas remain in which greater regulation would generate net benefits to society. For example, some call for greater regulation of the meat, poultry, and seafood industries to improve food safety. Others say that more regulation is needed to ensure that violent movies, CDs, and video games are not marketed to children.

Advocates of social regulation claim that the benefits of such regulation are well worth the considerable costs. The costs are simply the price we must pay to create a hospitable, sustainable, and just society.

CRITICISMS OF SOCIAL REGULATION

Critics of social regulation contend that, in many instances, it has been expanded to the point where the marginal costs exceed the marginal benefits. In this view, society would achieve net benefits by cutting back on meddlesome social regulation. Critics say that many social regulation laws are poorly written, making regulatory objectives and standards difficult to understand. As a result, regulators pursue goals well beyond the original intent of the legislation. Businesses complain that regulators often press for additional increments of improvement, unmindful of costs.

Also, opponents of social regulation say that the regulatory agencies may attract overzealous workers who are hostile toward the market system and believe too fervently in regulation. For example, some staff members of government agencies may view large corporations as "bad guys" who regularly cause pollution, provide inadequate safety for workers, deceive their customers, and generally abuse their power in the community. Such biases can lead to seemingly never-ending calls for more regulation, rather than objective assessments of the costs and benefits of added regulation.

Two Reminders

The debate over the proper amount of social regulation will surely continue. By helping determine costs and benefits, economic analysis can lead to more informed discussion and to better decisions. In this regard, we leave both ardent supporters and opponents of social regulation with pertinent reminders.

THERE IS NO FREE LUNCH

Fervent supporters of social regulation need to remember that there is no free lunch. Social regulation can produce higher prices, stifle innovation, and reduce competition.

Social regulation raises product prices in two ways. It does so directly because compliance costs normally get passed on to consumers, and it does so indirectly by reducing labour productivity. Resources invested in making workplaces accessible to workers with disabilities, for example, are not available for investment in new machinery designed to increase output per worker. Where the wage rate is fixed, a drop in labour productivity increases the marginal and average total costs of production. In effect, the supply curve for the product shifts leftward, causing the price of the product to rise.

Social regulation may have a negative impact on the rate of innovation. Technological advance may be stifled by, say, the fear that a new plant will not meet Environment Canada's guidelines or that a new medicine will require years of testing before being approved by the federal government.

Social regulation may weaken competition, since it usually places a relatively greater burden on small firms than on large ones. The costs of complying with social regulation are, in effect, fixed costs. Because smaller firms produce less output over which to distribute those costs, their compliance costs per unit of output put them at a competitive disadvantage with their larger rivals. Social regulation is more likely to force smaller firms out of business, thus contributing to the increased concentration of industry.

LESS GOVERNMENT IS NOT ALWAYS BETTER THAN MORE

On the opposite side of the issue, passionate opponents of social regulation need to remember that less government is not always better than more government. Although the market system is a powerful engine for producing goods and services and generating income, it has its flaws. Through appropriate amounts of social regulation, government can clearly increase economic efficiency and thus society's well-being. Ironically, by taking the rough edges off of capitalism, social regulation may be a strong pro-capitalism force. Properly conceived and executed, social regulation helps maintain political support for the market system. Such support could quickly wane if there were a steady stream of reports of unsafe workplaces, unsafe products, employment discrimination, choking pollution, deceived loan customers, and the like. Social regulation helps the market system deliver not only goods and services but also a "good society."

QUICK REVIEW 15.3

- Social regulation is concerned with the conditions under which goods and services are produced, the effects of production on society, and the physical characteristics of the goods themselves.

- Defenders of social regulation point to the benefits arising from policies that keep dangerous products from the marketplace, reduce workplace injuries and deaths,

contribute to clean air and water, and reduce employment discrimination.

- Critics of social regulation say uneconomical policy goals, inadequate information, unintended side effects, and overzealous personnel create excessive regulation, for which regulatory costs exceed regulatory benefits.

The **LAST WORD**

Antitrust Online

The Internet has presented antitrust authorities with both old and new causes for concern.

grzegorz knec/Alamy Stock Photo

The Airline Tariff Publishing case in the U.S. was the first important example of how digital communication platforms could be used by businesses to engage in price-fixing. In the late 1980s, U.S. airlines began to post both current and future prices for airline tickets on a centralized computer system known as the Airline Tariff Publishing Company. The system was set up so that travel agents could comparison-shop for their clients. But the airlines used the system's ability to list start dates and end dates for ticket purchases as a way of colluding.

As an example, suppose that American Airlines and Delta Airlines had both been charging $200 for a one-way ticket between New York and Chicago. American could then post a higher price of $250 for the route with the stipulation that nobody could start buying tickets at that price until the next month. Delta could then respond by also saying that it would start selling tickets at the higher price next month. In that way, the two airlines could tacitly coordinate their price setting ahead of time so as to collude on a major price increase.

The antitrust authorities at the U.S. Department of Justice stopped this practice in 1994 by getting the airlines to agree to the behavioural remedy that any fare changes would have to become immediately available to consumers. Airlines could no longer use suggested future prices as a way of signalling each other about how to collude.

The monopoly power gained during the 1990s and early 2000s by online giants such as Microsoft and Google has also led to business practices that have raised the ire of antitrust authorities in all countries. Microsoft, for example, was fined $2.7 billion after being convicted in 2000 of using the near-monopoly (95 percent market share) dominance of its Windows operating system software to coerce computer makers into favouring Microsoft's Internet Explorer web browser over rival browsers such as Netscape Navigator.

More recently, Google was indicted in 2015 by European Union antitrust officials for allegedly using its 90 percent share of the market for Internet searches in Europe to favour its Google Shopping price-comparison service over such services run by rival firms. For example, if a person in Germany types "prices for used iPhones" into Google's search bar, the top of the search results page will feature images of several used iPhones for sale on Google Shopping. By contrast, anyone wanting comparison prices for used iPhones listed on other price-comparison sites will have to click on links farther down on the search-results page to get to those other sites and their respective lists of used iPhone prices. Google was convicted and slapped with a US$2.7 billion fine for this practice in June 2017.

The most recent threat to competition spawned by the Internet is the rise of collusion via pieces of software that use pricing algorithms (automatically applied rules for setting prices) to constantly adjust a company's the online prices in response to seeing what rival firms are charging for similar products. The problem for regulators is that the pricing algorithms of different firms might end up interacting in ways that collusively raise prices for consumers. This is especially true for pieces of software that use artificial intelligence to learn how to achieve pre-set goals. Two such pieces of software could each be programmed to try to maximize profits and, as they interacted with each other, "realize" that the best way to do so is by coordinating rather than competing.

That possibility is especially challenging because, given the way antitrust laws are currently written, firms can be prosecuted for collusion only if they make an anticompetitive "agreement" with each other. If the algorithms come to collude on their own, there is no such agreement to prosecute. In fact, the behaviour of the two pieces of software could just as easily be interpreted as independent parallel conduct rather than coordination, since they don't even directly communicate with each other. And, in addition, should asking a piece of software to try to figure out how to maximize profits be illegal just by itself?

These issues are still very much up in the air, but they are being faced squarely by regulators. In the U.S. the first prosecution against the collusive use of algorithmic pricing software was started in 2015. To combat collusion online, the Office of Technology Research and Investigation was established as part of the Federal Trade Commission's Bureau of Consumer Protection that same year.

Question

On what basis were U.S. airlines found guilty of violating antitrust laws in the Airline Tariff Publishing case? What was the remedy? By contrast, why might it be hard to prosecute algorithmic collusion, which also uses prices posted electronically?

Chapter Summary

LO15.1 Describe what industrial concentration is and how governments combat it.

- There are three types of mergers: horizontal, vertical, and conglomerate.

- The Competition Act was passed in 1986, supplanting the Combines Investigation Act.

LO15.2 Identify and explain the economic principles and difficulties relating to the setting of prices (rates) charged by so-called natural monopolies.

- The objective of industrial regulation is to protect the public from the market power of natural monopolies by regulating prices and quality of service.

- Critics of industrial regulation contend that it can lead to inefficiency and rising costs, and that in many instances it constitutes a legal cartel for the regulated firms. Legislation passed in the late 1970s and the 1980s has brought about varying degrees of deregulation in the airline, trucking, banking, railroad, and television broadcasting industries. Studies indicate that deregulation is producing sizable annual gains to society through lower prices, lower costs, and increased output. The latest Canadian industries to begin the deregulation process are telecommunications, electricity, and natural gas.

LO15.3 Discuss the nature of *social regulation*, its benefits and costs, and its optimal level.

- Social regulation is concerned with product safety, working conditions, and the effects of production on society. While industrial regulation is on the wane, social regulation continues to expand. The optimal amount of social regulation occurs where MB = MC.

- People who support social regulation point to its numerous specific successes and assert that it has greatly enhanced society's well-being. Critics contend that businesses are excessively regulated to the point where marginal costs exceed marginal benefits. They also say that social regulation often produces unintended and costly side effects.

Terms and Concepts

competition policy
social regulation
horizontal merger
vertical merger
conglomerate merger

Competition Tribunal
tying contract
public interest theory of regulation
legal cartel theory of regulation

Discussion Questions

1. Both competition policy and industrial policy deal with monopoly. What distinguishes their approaches? How does government decide to use one form of remedy rather than the other? **[LO15.1]**

2. Explain how strict enforcement of competition laws might conflict with (a) promoting exports to achieve a balance of trade and (b) encouraging new technologies. Do you see any dangers in using selective competition enforcement as part of a broader policy to increase exports? **[LO15.1]**

3. How would you expect competition authorities to react to **[LO15.1]**

   a. A proposed merger of Ford and General Motors

   b. Evidence of secret meetings by contractors to rig bids for highway construction projects

   c. A proposed merger of a large shoe manufacturer and a chain of retail shoe stores

   d. A proposed merger of a small life insurance company and a regional candy manufacturer

   e. An automobile rental firm that charges higher rates for last-minute rentals than for rentals reserved weeks in advance

4. Suppose a proposed merger of firms would simultaneously lessen competition and reduce unit costs through economies of scale. Do you think such a merger should be allowed? **[LO15.1]**

5. In the 1980s, PepsiCo Inc., which then had 28 percent of the soft-drink market, proposed to acquire the 7-Up Company. Shortly thereafter the Coca-Cola Company, with 39 percent of the market, indicated it wanted to acquire the Dr. Pepper Company; 7-Up and Dr. Pepper each controlled about 7 percent of the market. In your judgment, was the government's decision to block these mergers appropriate? **[LO15.1]**

6. "The competition laws serve to penalize efficiently managed firms." Do you agree? Why or why not? **[LO15.2]**

7. "The social desirability of any particular firm should be judged not on the basis of its market share but on the basis of its conduct and performance." Make a counterargument, referring to the monopoly model in your statement. **[LO15.2]**

8. What types of industry, if any, should be subjected to industrial regulation? What specific problems are entailed by industrial regulation? **[LO15.2]**

9. In view of the problems involved in regulating natural monopolies, compare socially optimal (marginal-cost) pricing and fair-return pricing by referring again to Figure 11-10. Assuming that a government subsidy might be used to cover any loss resulting from marginal-cost pricing, which pricing policy would you favour? Why? What problems might such a subsidy entail? **[LO15.2]**

10. How does social regulation differ from industrial regulation? What types of benefits and costs are associated with social regulation? **[LO15.3]**

11. Use economic analysis to explain why the optimal amount of product safety may be less than the amount that would totally eliminate risks of accidents and deaths. Use automobiles as an example. **[LO15.3]**

Review Questions

1. How would you expect the Competition Bureau to react to each of the following? **[LO15.1]**

   a. A proposed merger of Ford and General Motors

   b. Evidence of secret meetings by contractors to rig bids for highway construction projects

   c. A proposed merger of a large shoe manufacturer and a chain of retail shoe stores

   d. A proposed merger of a small life-insurance company and a regional candy manufacturer

   e. An automobile rental firm that charges higher rates for last-minute rentals than for rentals reserved weeks in advance

2. When confronted with a natural monopoly that restricts output and charges monopoly prices, the two methods that governments have for promoting better outcomes are **[LO15.2]**

   a. Public ownership and public regulation

   b. Sole proprietorships and public goods

   c. Anticombines law and horizontal mergers

   d. Creative destruction and laissez-faire

3. Which of the following is the correct name for the idea that certain firms prefer government regulation because regulation shields them from the pressures of competition and, in effect, guarantees them a regulated profit? **[LO15.2]**

   a. The public interest theory of regulation

   b. The structuralists' theory of monopoly

   c. The legal cartel theory of regulation

   d. The public regulation theory of natural monopoly

4. True or False? Economists believe that social regulation is an exception to the MB = MC rule because social regulation should, in every case, extend as far as possible in order to ensure safe products, less pollution, and improved working conditions. **[LO15.3]**

Problems

1. Carrot Computers and its competitors purchase touch screens for their handheld computers from several suppliers. The six makers of touch screens have market shares of 19 percent, 18 percent, 14 percent, 16 percent, 20 percent, and 13 percent. [**LO15.2**]

    a. What is the Herfindahl index for the touch screen manufacturing industry?

    b. By how much would a proposed merger between the two smallest touch-screen makers increase the Herfindahl index? Would the government be likely to challenge that proposed merger?

    c. If Carrot Computers horizontally merges with its competitor, Blueberry Handhelds, by how much would the Herfindahl index change for the touch-screen industry?

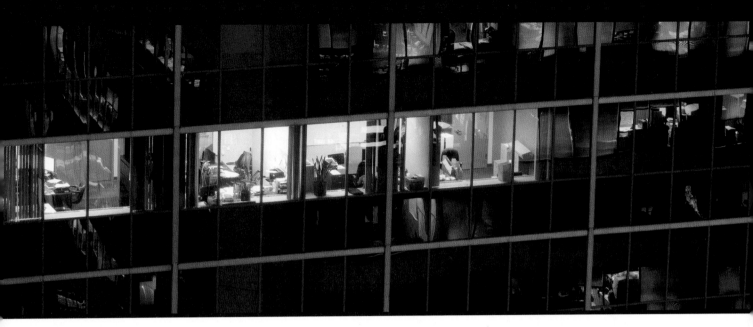

CHAPTER 16

The Demand for Factors of Production

LEARNING OBJECTIVES

LO16.1	Explain the significance of factor pricing.
LO16.2	Convey how the marginal revenue productivity of a factor relates to a firm's demand for that factor.
LO16.3	List the causes that increase or decrease factor demand.
LO16.4	Discuss the determinants of elasticity of factor demand.
LO16.5	Determine how a competitive firm selects its optimal combination of factors.
LO16.6	Explain the marginal productivity theory of income distribution.

When you finish your education, you will probably be looking for a job. But why would someone want to hire you? The answer, of course, is that you have much to offer. Employers have a demand for educated, productive workers like you.

We need to learn more about the demand for labour and other factors. That's why, we now turn from the pricing and production of *goods and services* to the pricing and employment of *resources*, or *factors of production*. Although firms come in various sizes and operate under highly different market conditions, they each have a demand for factors of production. They obtain those resources from households—the owners of land, labour, capital, and entrepreneurial resources. So, referring to the circular flow model (Figure 2-2), we shift our attention from the bottom loop of the diagram (which shows that firms supply products and services that households want) to the top loop (which shows the demand for factors of production that households supply).

This chapter looks at the *demand* for factors of production. Although the discussion concentrates on labour, the principles we develop also apply to land, capital, and entrepreneurial ability. In Chapter 17 we will combine factor (labour) demand with labour *supply* to analyze wage rates. Then, in Chapter 18, we will use factor demand and factor supply to examine the prices of, and returns to, other productive factors.

16.1 Significance of Factor Pricing

LO16.1   Explain the significance of factor pricing.

As you saw in Chapter 2, the circular flow diagram has two main markets: the product market and the factor market. Up to this point, we have concentrated on supply and demand in the product market, where the prices of goods and services are determined. But to produce goods and services, we need factors of production: labour, land, capital, and entrepreneurial resources. As we also noted in Chapter 2, all factors of production are provided by households to firms. We now turn to the determination of supply and demand in the factor market.

Studying factor pricing is important for several reasons:

- *Money-Income Determination* Factor prices are a major determinant of household income. The expenditures that firms make in acquiring factors of production flow as wage, rent, interest, and profit incomes to households.

- *Cost Minimization* To the firm, factor prices are costs, and to realize maximum profit the firm must produce the profit-maximizing output with the most efficient (least costly) combination of resources. Factor prices determine the quantities of land, labour, capital, and entrepreneurial ability that will be combined in producing each good or service.

- *Resource Allocation* Just as product prices allocate finished goods and services to consumers, factor prices allocate inputs among industries and firms. In a dynamic economy, where technology and tastes often change, the efficient allocation of resources over time means a continuous shift of factors of production from one use to another. Changes in factor prices are a major determinant of those shifts.

- *Policy Issues* There are many policy issues surrounding the factor market: To what extent should government redistribute income through taxes and transfers? Should government do anything to discourage "excess" pay to corporate executives? Should it increase the legal minimum wage? Does it make sense to provide subsidies to farmers? Should it encourage or restrict labour unions? The facts and debates relating to these policy questions are based on factor pricing.

16.2 Marginal Productivity Theory of Factor Demand

LO16.2   Convey how the marginal revenue productivity of a factor relates to a firm's demand for that factor.

In discussing factor demand, we will first assume that a firm sells its output in a perfectly competitive product market and hires a certain factor in a perfectly competitive factor market. This assumption keeps things simple and is consistent with the model of a competitive factor market that we will develop in Chapter 17. In a competitive *product market* the firm is a price-taker and can dispose of as much output as it chooses at the market price. The firm sells such a negligible fraction of total output that it exerts no influence on product price. Similarly, in the competitive *factor market*, the firm is a wage-taker. It hires such a negligible fraction of the total supply of the factor that it cannot influence its price.

CHOOSING A LITTLE MORE OR LESS

FACTOR DEMAND AS A DERIVED DEMAND

Factor demand is the starting point for any discussion of factor prices. Factor demand is a schedule or a curve showing the amounts of a factor that buyers are willing and able to purchase at various prices over some period of time. Crucially, factor demand is a **derived demand**, meaning that the demand for a factor is derived from the demand for the products that the factor helps to produce. This is true because factors usually do not directly satisfy customer wants but do so indirectly through their use in producing goods and services. No one wants to consume a hectare of land, a tractor, or the labour services of a farmer, but households do want to consume the food products that these factors help produce.

MARGINAL REVENUE PRODUCT (MRP)

Because resource demand is derived from product demand, the strength of the demand for any factor of production will depend on (a) the productivity of the factor and (b) the price of the good it helps to produce.

Other things equal, a factor that is highly productive in turning out a highly valued commodity will be in great demand, while a relatively unproductive factor that is capable of producing only a slightly valued commodity will be in little demand. And no demand whatsoever will exist for a factor of production that is phenomenally efficient in producing something that no one wants to buy.

- *Productivity* Table 16-1 shows the roles of productivity and product price in determining demand for factors of production. Here, we assume that a firm adds a single variable factor, labour, to its fixed plant. Columns 1 and 2 give the number of units of the factor employed and the resulting total product (output). Column 3 shows the **marginal product (MP)**, or additional output, from each additional factor unit. Columns 1 through 3 remind us that the law of diminishing returns applies here, causing the marginal product of labour to fall beyond some point. For simplicity, we assume that diminishing marginal returns begin after the first worker hired.

- *Product Price* The derived demand for a factor depends also on the price of the product it produces. Column 4 in Table 16-1 adds this price information. Product price is constant, in this case at $2, because the product market is competitive. The firm is a price-taker and can sell units of output only at this market price. Multiplying column 2 by column 4 gives us the total-revenue data of column 5. From these total-revenue data we can compute **marginal revenue product (MRP)**, the change in total revenue resulting from the use of each additional unit of a factor (labour, in this case). In equation form,

$$\text{Marginal revenue product} = \frac{\text{change in total revenue}}{\text{unit change in factor quantity}}$$

The MRPs are listed in column 6 in Table 16-1.

RULE FOR EMPLOYING FACTORS: MRP = MFC

The MRP schedule, shown as columns 1 and 6, is the firm's demand schedule for labour. To understand why, you must first know the rule that guides a profit-seeking firm in hiring any factor of production: To maximize profit, a firm will hire additional units of a specific factor as long as each successive unit adds more to the firm's total revenue than it adds to total cost.

The demand for factors is derived from the products or services that those factors help produce.

TABLE 16-1	The Demand for Labour: Perfect Competition in the Sale of the Product				
(1) Units of a factor	(2) Total product (output)	(3) Marginal product, MP	(4) Product price	(5) Total revenue, or (2) × (4)	(6) Marginal revenue product, MRP
0	0		$2	$ 0	
		7			$14
1	7		2	14	
		6			12
2	13		2	26	
		5			10
3	18		2	36	
		4			8
4	22		2	44	
		3			6
5	25		2	50	
		2			4
6	27		2	54	
		1			2
7	28		2	56	

We have seen that MRP measures how much each successive unit of a factor adds to total revenue. The amount that each additional unit of a factor adds to the firm's total (factor) cost is called its **marginal factor cost (MFC)**. In equation form,

$$\text{Marginal factor cost} = \frac{\text{change in total (factor) cost}}{\text{unit change in factor quantity}}$$

We can restate our rule for hiring factors as follows: It will be profitable for a firm to hire additional units of a factor up to the point at which that factor's MRP is equal to its MFC. For example, as the rule applies to labour, if the number of workers a firm is currently hiring is such that the MRP of the last worker exceeds his or her MFC, the firm can increase profit by hiring more workers. But if the number being hired is such that the MFC of the last worker exceeds his or her MRP, the firm is hiring workers who are not paying their way, and it can increase its profit by laying off some workers. You may have recognized that this **MRP = MFC rule** is similar to the MR = MC profit-maximizing rule employed throughout our discussion of price and output determination. The rationale of the two rules is the same, but the point of reference is now *inputs* of a factor of production, not *outputs* of a product.

MATH 16.1   MRP = MFC Rule

MRP AS A FACTOR DEMAND SCHEDULE

Let's continue with our focus on labour, knowing that the analysis also applies to other factors. In a perfectly competitive labour market, supply and demand establish the wage rate. Because each firm hires such a small fraction of market supply, it cannot influence the market wage rate; it is a wage-taker, not a wage-maker. This means that for each additional unit of labour hired, each firm's total factor cost increases by exactly the amount of the constant market wage rate. More specifically, the MFC of labour exactly equals the market wage rate. Thus, factor price (the market wage rate) and factor cost (marginal factor cost) are equal for a firm that hires labour in a competitive labour market. As a result, the MRP = MFC rule tells us that, in perfect competition, the firm will hire workers up to the point at which the market *wage rate* (its MFC) is equal to its MRP.

In terms of the data in columns 1 and 6 in Table 16-1, if the market wage rate is, say, $13.95, the firm will hire only one worker, because only the hiring of the first worker results in an increase in profits. To see this, note that for the first worker MRP (= $14) exceeds MFC (= $13.95). Thus, hiring the first worker is profitable. For each successive worker, however, MFC (= $13.95) exceeds MRP (= $12 or less), indicating that it will not be profitable to hire any of those workers. If the wage rate is $11.95, by the same reasoning we discover that it will pay the firm to hire both the first and second workers. Similarly, if the wage rate is $9.95, three workers will be hired; if $7.95,

FIGURE 16-1   The Perfectly Competitive Seller's Demand for a Factor

The MRP curve is the factor demand curve; each of its points relates a particular factor price (= MRP when profit is maximized) with a corresponding quantity of the factor demanded. Under perfect competition, product price is constant; therefore, the downslope of the D = MRP curve is due solely to the decline in the factor's marginal product (law of diminishing marginal returns).

four; if $5.95, five; and so forth. Here is the key generalization: The MRP schedule constitutes the firm's demand for labour, because each point on this schedule (or curve) indicates the number of workers the firm would hire at each possible wage rate.

In Figure 16-1, we show the D = MRP curve based on the data in Table 16-1. The perfectly competitive firm's factor demand curve identifies an inverse relationship between the wage rate and the quantity of labour demanded, other things equal. The curve slopes downward because of diminishing marginal returns.[1]

FACTOR DEMAND UNDER IMPERFECT PRODUCT MARKET COMPETITION

Factor demand (here, labour demand) is more complex when the firm is selling its product in an imperfectly competitive market, one in which the firm is a price-maker. That is because imperfect competitors (monopolists, oligopolists, and monopolistic competitors) face downsloping product demand curves. As a result, whenever an imperfect competitor's product demand curve is fixed in place, the only way to increase sales is by setting a lower price (and thereby moving down along the fixed demand curve).

The productivity data in Table 16-1 are retained in columns 1 to 3 in Table 16-2. But in Table 16-2 we show in column 4 that product price must be lowered to sell the marginal product of each successive worker. The MRP of the perfectly competitive seller of Table 16-1 falls for only one reason: Marginal product diminishes. The MRP of the imperfectly competitive seller of Table 16-2 falls for two reasons: Marginal product diminishes *and* product price falls as output increases.

We emphasize that the lower price accompanying each increase in output (total product) applies not only to the marginal product of each successive worker but also to *all prior output*. Note that the second worker's marginal product is six units. These six units can be sold for $2.40 each, or, as a group, for $14.40. But $14.40 is not the MRP of the second worker. To sell these six units, the firm must take a 20-cent price cut on the seven units produced by the first worker—units that otherwise could have been sold for $2.60 each. Thus, the MRP of the second worker is only $13 (= $14.40 − (7 × 20 cents)), as shown.

Similarly, the third worker adds five units to total product, and these units are worth $2.20 each, or $11 total. But to sell these five units the firm must take a 20-cent price cut on the thirteen units produced by the first two workers. So the third worker's MRP is only $8.40 [= $11.00 − (13 × 20 cents)]. The numbers in column 6 reflect such calculations.

In Figure 16-2 we graph the MRP data from Table 16-2 and label it D = MRP (imperfect competition). The broken-line factor demand curve, in contrast, is that of the perfectly competitive seller represented in

---

[1] Note that we plot the points in Figure 16-1 halfway between succeeding numbers of factor units, because MRP is associated with the addition of one more unit. Thus, for example, we plot the MRP of the second unit ($12) not at 1 or 2, but at 1.5. This smoothing enables us to sketch a continuously downsloping curve rather than one that moves downward in discrete steps (like a staircase) as each new unit of labour is hired.

TABLE 16-2	**The Demand for Labour: Imperfect Competition in the Sale of the Product**				
(1) Units of a factor	**(2)** Total product (output)	**(3)** Marginal product, MP	**(4)** Product price	**(5)** Total revenue, or (2) × (4)	**(6)** Marginal revenue product, MRP
0	0		$2.80	$ 0	
		7			$18.20
1	7		2.60	18.20	
		6			13.00
2	13		2.40	31.20	
		5			8.40
3	18		2.20	39.60	
		4			4.40
4	22		2.00	44.00	
		3			2.25
5	25		1.85	46.25	
		2			1.00
6	27		1.75	47.25	
		1			−1.05
7	28		1.65	46.20	

Figure 16-1. A comparison of the two curves demonstrates that, other things equal, the factor demand curve of an imperfectly competitive seller is less elastic than that of a perfectly competitive seller. Consider the effects of an identical percentage decline in the wage rate (factor price) from $11 to $6 in Figure 16-2. Comparison of the two curves reveals that the firm in imperfect competition does not expand the quantity of labour by as large a percentage as does the firm in perfect competition (broken curve).

It is not surprising that the imperfectly competitive producer is less responsive to factor price cuts than the perfectly competitive producer. When factor prices fall, MC per unit declines for imperfectly competitive firms as well as perfectly competitive firms. Because both types of firms maximize profits by producing where MR = MC, the decline in MC will cause both types of firms to produce more. But the effect will be muted for imperfectly competitive firms

FIGURE 16-2   The Imperfectly Competitive Seller's Demand Curve for a Factor

An imperfectly competitive seller's factor demand curve *D* (solid) slopes downward because both marginal product and product price fall as factor employment and output rise. This downward slope is greater than that for a perfectly competitive seller (dashed factor demand curve) because the perfect competitor can sell the added output at a constant price.

Quantity of a factor demanded

because their downsloping demand curves cause them also to face downsloping MR curves—so that for each additional unit sold, MR declines. By contrast, MR is constant (and equal to the market equilibrium price P) for competitive firms, so that they do not have to worry about MR per unit falling as they produce more units. As a result, competitive firms increase production by a larger amount than imperfectly competitive firms whenever resource prices fall.

WORKED PROBLEM 16.1 Factor Demand

MARKET DEMAND FOR A FACTOR

The total, or market, demand curve for a specific resource shows the various total amounts of the resource that firms will purchase or hire at various resource prices, other things equal. Recall that the total, or market, demand curve for a *product* is found by summing horizontally the demand curves of all individual buyers in the market. The market demand curve for a particular *factor* is derived the same way—by summing horizontally the individual demand or MRP curves for all firms employing that factor.

QUICK REVIEW 16.1

- To maximize profit a firm will purchase or hire a factor of production in an amount at which the factor's marginal revenue product equals its marginal factor cost (MRP = MFC).

- Application of the MRP = MFC rule to a firm's MRP curve demonstrates that the MRP curve is the firm's factor demand curve. In a perfectly competitive factor market, factor price (the wage rate) equals MFC.

- The factor demand curve of a firm in perfect competition is downsloping solely because the marginal product of the factor diminishes; the factor demand curve of a firm in imperfect competition is downsloping because marginal product diminishes and product price falls as output is increased.

16.3 Determinants of Factor Demand

LO16.3   List the causes that increase or decrease factor demand.

What will shift the factor demand curve? The fact that factor demand is derived from *product demand* and depends on *factor productivity* suggests two things that can shift factor demand. Also, our analysis of how changes in the prices of other products can shift a product's demand curve (Chapter 3) suggests another reason: changes in *the prices of other factors of production*.

Changes in Product Demand

Other things equal, an increase in the demand for a product that uses a particular factor will increase the demand for that factor of production, whereas a decrease in product demand will decrease the resource demand.

Let's see how this works. The first thing to recall is that a change in the demand for a product will change its price. In Table 16-1, let's assume that an increase in product demand boosts the product price from $2 to $3. You should calculate the new factor demand schedule (columns 1 and 6), and plot it in Figure 16-1 to verify that the new factor demand curve lies to the right of the old demand curve. Similarly, a decline in the product demand (and price) will shift the factor demand curve to the left.

For example, assuming no offsetting change in supply, a decrease in the demand for new houses will drive down house prices. Those lower prices will decrease the MRP of construction workers, and therefore the demand for construction workers will fall. The factor demand curve such as in Figure 16-1 or Figure 16-2 will shift to the left.

Changes in Productivity

Other things equal, an increase in the productivity of a factor of production will increase the demand for that factor. If we doubled the MP data of column 3 in Table 16-1, the MRP data of column 6 would also double, indicating a rightward shift of the factor demand curve.

CONSIDER THIS

Superstars

In what economist Robert Frank calls "winner-take-all markets," a few highly talented performers have huge earnings relative to the average performers in the market. Because consumers and firms seek out the best performers, small differences in talent or popularity get magnified into huge differences in pay.

In winner-take-all markets, consumer spending gets channelled toward a few performers. The media then hypes these new stars, which further increases the public's awareness of their talents. More consumers then buy the stars' products, and superstars emerge. The high earnings of superstars result from the high revenues they generate from their work. Consider Beyoncé Knowles. If she sold only a few thousand CDs and attracted only a few hundred fans to each concert, the

© PRNewsFoto/Diamond Information Center

revenue she would produce—her marginal revenue product—would be quite modest. So, too, would be her earnings.

Some consumers have anointed Justin Bieber king of pop culture. The demand for his CDs and concerts is extraordinarily high. He sells millions of CDs, not thousands, and draws thousands to his concerts, not hundreds. His high net earnings derive from his extraordinarily high marginal revenue product.

So it is for the other superstars in winner-take-all markets. Influenced by media hype but coerced by no one, consumers direct their spending toward a select few. The high marginal revenue product that results means strong demand for these stars' services. And because top talent (by definition) is very limited, superstars receive amazingly high earnings.

The productivity of any factor may be altered over the long run in several ways:

- *Quantities of Other Factors* The marginal productivity of any factor will vary with the quantities of the other factors used with it. The greater the amount of capital and land resources used with, say, labour, the greater will labour's marginal productivity and, thus, labour demand.

- *Technological Advance* Technological improvements that increase the quality of other factors, such as capital, have the same effect. The better the quality of capital, the greater the productivity of labour used with it. Office workers employed with a specific amount of real capital in the form of computers are more productive than office workers with the same amount of real capital embodied in typewriters and filing cabinets.

- *Quality of the Variable Factor* Improvements in the quality of the variable factor, such as labour, will increase its marginal productivity and therefore its demand.

All these considerations help explain why the average level of (real) wages is higher in industrially advanced nations (for example, Canada, the United States, Germany, Japan, and France) than in developing nations (for example, Nicaragua, Ethiopia, Angola, and Cambodia). Workers in industrially advanced nations are generally healthier, better educated, and better trained than are workers in developing countries. Also, in most industries, workers in industrially advanced nations work with a larger and more efficient stock of capital goods and more abundant natural resources. This increase in productivity creates a strong demand for labour. On the supply side of the market, labour is relatively scarce compared with that in most developing nations. A strong demand and a relatively scarce supply of labour result in high wage rates in the industrially advanced nations.

Changes in the Prices of Other Factors

Changes in the prices of other factors of production may change the demand for a specific factor. For example, a change in the price of capital may change the demand for labour. The direction of the change in labour demand will depend on whether labour and capital are substitutes or complements in production.

SUBSTITUTE FACTORS OF PRODUCTION

Suppose the technology in a certain production process is such that labour and capital can be substituted. A firm can produce a specific amount of output using a relatively small amount of labour and a relatively large amount of capital, or vice versa. Now assume that the price of machinery (capital) falls. The effect on the demand for labour will be the net result of two opposed effects: the substitution effect and the output effect.

- *Substitution Effect* The decline in the price of machinery prompts the firm to substitute machinery for labour. This substitution allows the firm to produce its output at a lower cost. So, at the fixed wage rate, smaller quantities of labour are now employed. This **substitution effect** decreases the demand for labour. More generally, the substitution effect indicates that a firm will purchase more of an input whose relative price has declined and, conversely, use less of an output whose relative price has increased.

- *Output Effect* Because the price of machinery has fallen, the costs of producing various outputs must also decline. With lower costs, the firm finds it profitable to produce and sell a greater output. The greater output increases the demand for all factors of production, including labour. So this **output effect** increases the demand for labour. More generally, the output effect means that the firm will purchase more of one particular input when the price of the other input falls and less of that particular input when the price of the other input rises.

- *Net Effect* The substitution and output effects are both present when the price of an input changes. The net change in factor demand depends on the relative sizes of the two effects. For example, if the substitution effect outweighs the output effect, a decrease in the price of capital decreases the demand for labour. If the output effect exceeds the substitution effect, a decrease in the price of capital increases the demand for labour.

COMPLEMENTARY FACTORS OF PRODUCTION

Recall from Chapter 3 that certain products, such as computers and software, are complementary goods; they go together and are jointly demanded. Factors of production can also be complementary; an increase in the quantity of one of them used in the production process requires an increase in the amount used of the other, and vice versa. Suppose a small design firm does computer-assisted design (CAD) with relatively expensive personal computers as its basic piece of capital equipment. Each computer requires a single design engineer to operate it; the machine is not automated—it will not run itself—and a second engineer would have nothing to do.

Now assume that a technological advance in the production of these computers substantially reduces their price. No substitution effect can occur, because labour and capital must be used in *fixed proportions*, one person for one machine. Capital cannot be substituted for labour. But there is an output effect. Other things equal, the reduction in the price of capital goods means lower production costs. It will therefore be profitable to produce a larger output. In doing so, the firm will use both more capital and more labour. When labour and capital are complementary, a decline in the price of capital increases the demand for labour through the output effect.

We have cast our analysis of substitute factors and complementary factors mainly in terms of a decline in the price of capital. In Table 16-3 we summarize the effects of an *increase* in the price of capital on the demand for labour; study it carefully.

TABLE 16-3	The Effect of an Increase in the Price of Capital on the Demand for Labour, D_L		
(1) **RELATIONSHIP** **OF INPUTS**	**(2)** **INCREASE IN THE PRICE OF CAPITAL**		
	(a) **Substitution effect**	**(b)** **Output effect**	**(c)** **Combined effect**
Substitutes in production	Labour substituted for capital	Production costs up, output down, and less of both capital and labour used	D_L increases if the substitution effect exceeds the output effect; D_L decreases if the output effect exceeds the substitution effect
Complements in production	No substitution of labour for capital	Production costs up, output down, and less of both capital and labour used	D_L decreases (since only the output effect applies)

TABLE 16-4	Determinants of Labour Demand: Factors That Shift the Labour Demand Curve
Determinant	**Examples**
Changes in product demand	Gambling increases in popularity, increasing the demand for workers at casinos.
	Consumers decrease their demand for leather coats, decreasing the demand for tanners.
	The federal government reduces spending on the military, reducing the demand for military personnel.
Changes in productivity	An increase in the skill levels of physicians increases the demand for their services.
	Computer-assisted graphic design increases the productivity of, and demand for, graphic artists.
Changes in the price of another factor	An increase in the price of electricity increases the cost of producing aluminum and reduces the demand for aluminum workers.
	The price of security equipment used by businesses to protect against illegal entry falls, decreasing the demand for night guards.
	The price of cellphone equipment decreases, reducing the cost of cellphone service, which in turn increases the demand for cellphone assemblers.

Now that we have discussed the full list of the determinants of labour demand, let's again review their effects. Stated in terms of the labour resource, the demand for labour will increase (the labour demand curve will shift rightward) when

- The demand for the product produced by that labour *increases*
- The productivity (MP) of labour *increases*
- The price of a substitute input *decreases*, provided the output effect exceeds the substitution effect
- The price of a substitute input *increases*, provided the substitution effect exceeds the output effect
- The price of a complementary input *decreases*

Be sure that you can reverse these effects to explain a *decrease* in labour demand. Table 16-4 provides several illustrations of the determinants of labour demand, listed by the categories of determinants we have discussed. You will benefit from giving them a close look.

16.4 Elasticity of Factor Demand

LO16.4 Discuss the determinants of elasticity of factor demand.

The employment changes we have just discussed result from shifts of factor demand curves. Such changes in demand must be distinguished from changes in the quantity demanded of a factor of production caused by a change in the price of the specific factor. Such a change is not caused by a shift of the demand curve but rather by a movement from one point to another on a fixed factor demand curve. For example, we note that an increase in the wage rate from $5 to $7 will reduce the quantity of labour demanded from five to four units. This is a change in the *quantity of labour demanded* as distinct from a *change in demand for labour*.

The sensitivity of factor quantity to changes in factor prices along a fixed factor demand curve is measured by the **elasticity of factor demand**. In coefficient form,

$$E_{fd} = \frac{\text{percentage change in factor quantity demanded}}{\text{percentage change in factor price}}$$

When E_{fd} is greater than 1, factor demand is elastic; when E_{fd} is less than 1, factor demand is inelastic; and when E_{fd} equals 1, factor demand is unit elastic. What determines the elasticity of factor demand? Several determinants are at work.

EASE OF FACTOR SUBSTITUTABILITY

The degree to which resources are substitutable is a fundamental determinant of elasticity. More specifically, the greater the substitutability of other factors, the more elastic is the demand for a particular factor. As an example, the high degree to which computerized voice recognition systems are substitutable for human beings implies that the demand for human beings answering phone calls at call centres is quite elastic. In contrast, there are few good substitutes for physicians, so demand for them is less elastic or even inelastic. If a furniture manufacturer finds that several types of wood are equally satisfactory in making coffee tables, a rise in the price of any one type of wood may cause a sharp drop in the amount demanded as the producer substitutes one of the other woods. At the other extreme, no reasonable substitutes may exist; bauxite is absolutely essential in the production of aluminum. Thus the demand for bauxite by aluminum producers is inelastic.

Time can play a role in the ease of input substitution. For example, a firm's truck drivers may obtain a substantial wage increase with little or no immediate decline in employment. But over time, as the firm's trucks wear out and are replaced, that wage increase may motivate the company to purchase larger trucks so they can deliver the same total output with fewer drivers.

ELASTICITY OF PRODUCT DEMAND

The elasticity of demand for any factor depends on the elasticity of demand for the product that it helps produce. Other things equal, the greater the elasticity of product demand, the greater the elasticity of factor demand. The derived nature of factor demand leads us to expect this relationship. A small rise in the price of a product with great elasticity of demand will sharply reduce output, bringing about relatively large declines in the amounts of various factors of production demanded; the demand for the factor is elastic. But if the demand for the product is inelastic, the increase in the amount of the product demanded will be small, as will be the increases in the quantity of labour demanded. This suggests an inelastic demand for labour.

Remember that the factor demand curve in Figure 16-1 is more elastic than the factor demand curve shown in Figure 16-2. The difference arises because in Figure 16-1 we assume a perfectly elastic product demand curve, whereas Figure 16-2 is based on a downsloping or less than perfectly elastic product demand curve.

RATIO OF FACTOR COST TO TOTAL COST

The larger the proportion of total production costs accounted for by a factor of production, the greater the elasticity of demand for that factor. For example, if labour cost is the only production cost, a 20 percent increase in wage rates will shift all the firm's cost curves upward by the full 20 percent. If product demand is elastic, this substantial increase in wage costs will cause a relatively large decline in sales and a sharp decline in the amount of labour demanded. So labour demand is highly elastic. But if labour cost is only 50 percent of production cost, a 20 percent increase in wage rates will increase costs by only 10 percent. With the same elasticity of product demand, this will cause a relatively small decline in sales and therefore in the amount of labour demanded. In this case the demand for labor is much less elastic.

QUICK REVIEW 16.2

- A factor demand curve will shift because of changes in product demand, changes in the productivity of the factor, and changes in the prices of other inputs.

- If factors A and B are substitutable, a decline in the price of A will decrease the demand for B provided the substitution effect exceeds the output effect. If the output effect exceeds the substitution effect, the demand for B will increase.

- If factors C and D are complements, a decline in the price of C will increase the demand for D.

- Elasticity of factor demand measures the extent to which producers change the quantity of a factor they hire when its price changes.

- For any particular factor, the elasticity of factor demand will be less the smaller the number of substitutes, the smaller the elasticity of product demand, and the smaller the proportion of total cost accounted for by the factor.

16.5 Optimal Combination of Factors*

LO16.5 **Determine how a competitive firm selects its optimal combination of factors.**

So far our main focus has been on one variable input, labour. But in the long run, firms can vary the amounts of all the factors of production they use. That's why we need to consider what combination of factors a firm will choose when *all* its inputs are variable. While our analysis is based on two factors, it can be extended to any number of inputs.

We will consider two interrelated questions:

1. What combination of factors will minimize costs at a specific level of output?

2. What combination of factors will maximize profit?

 CHOOSING A LITTLE MORE OR LESS

The Least-Cost Rule

A firm is producing a specific output with the **least-cost combination of factors** when the last dollar spent on each factor yields the same marginal product. To see how this rule maximizes profits in a more concrete setting, consider firms that are competitive buyers in resource markets. Because each firm is too small to affect resource prices, each firm's marginal factor costs will equal market factor prices and each firm will be able to hire as many or as few units as it would like of any and all factors at their respective market prices. Thus, if there are just two factors, labour and capital, a competitive firm will minimize its total cost of a specific output when

$$\frac{\text{marginal product of labour (MP}_L)}{\text{price of labour }(P_L)} = \frac{\text{marginal product of capital (MP}_C)}{\text{price of capital }(P_C)} \qquad (1)$$

Throughout, we will refer to the marginal products of labour and capital as MP_L and MP_C, respectively, and symbolize the price of labour by P_L and the price of capital by P_C.

MATH 16.2   The Least-Cost Rule

A concrete example shows why fulfilling the condition in equation (1) leads to least-cost production. Assume that the price of both capital and labour is \$1 per unit, but that Siam Soups is currently employed in such amounts that the marginal product of labour is 10 and the marginal product of capital is 5. Our equation immediately tells us that this is not the least costly combination of resources.

$$\frac{MP_L = 10}{P_L = \$1} > \frac{MP_C = 5}{P_C = \$1}$$

Suppose Siam spends \$1 less on capital and shifts that dollar to labour. It loses five units of output produced by the last dollar's worth of capital, but it gains ten units of output from the extra dollar's worth of labour. Net output increases by 5 (= 10 − 5) units for the same total cost. More such shifting of dollars from capital to labour will push the firm *down* along its MP curve for labour and *up* along its MP curve for capital, increasing output and moving the firm toward a position of equilibrium where equation (1) is fulfilled. At that equilibrium position, the MP per dollar for the last unit of both labour and capital might be, for example, 7. And Siam will be producing a greater output for the same (original) cost.

Whenever the same total resource cost can result in a greater total output, the cost per unit—and therefore the total cost of any specific level of output—can be reduced. The cost of producing any specific output can be reduced as long as equation (1) does not hold. But when dollars have been shifted between capital and labour to the point where equation (1) holds, no additional changes in the use of capital and labour will reduce costs further. Siam is now producing that output using the least-cost combination of capital and labour.

The cost of producing any specific output can be reduced as long as equation one does not hold. But when dollars have been shifted between capital and labour to the point where equation one holds, no additional changes

Note to Instructors: We consider this section optional; it can be skipped without loss of continuity, or deferred until after the discussion of wage determination in Chapter 17.

in the use of capital and labour will reduce costs further. Siam will be producing that output using the least-cost combination of capital and labour.

All the long-run cost curves developed in Chapter 8 and used thereafter assume that the least-cost combination of inputs has been realized at each level of output. Any firm that combines resources in violation of the least-cost rule would have a higher-than-necessary average total cost at each level of output. That is, it would incur *X-inefficiency*, as discussed in Figure 11-7.

The producer's least-cost rule is analogous to the consumer's utility-maximizing rule described in Chapter 7. In achieving the utility-maximizing combination of goods, the consumer considers both his or her preferences as reflected in diminishing-marginal-utility data and the prices of the various products. Similarly, in achieving the cost-minimizing combination of resources, the producer considers both the marginal-product data and the prices (costs) of the various resources.

The Profit-Maximizing Rule

Minimizing cost is not sufficient for maximizing profit. A firm can produce any level of output in the least costly way by applying equation (1), but only one unique level of output can maximize profit. Our earlier analysis of product markets showed that this profit-maximizing output occurs where marginal revenue equals marginal cost (MR = MC). Near the beginning of this chapter, we determined that we could write this profit-maximizing condition as MRP = MFC as it relates to factor inputs.

MATH 16.3   The Profit-Maximizing Rule

In a perfectly competitive factor market, the marginal factor cost (MFC) is exactly equal to the factor price, P. Thus, for any competitive factor market, we have as our profit-maximizing equation

$$\text{MRP(factor)} = P\text{(factor)}$$

This condition must hold for every variable factor—and in the long run all factors are variable. In competitive markets, a firm will therefore achieve its **profit-maximizing combination of factors** when each factor is employed to the point at which its marginal revenue product equals its price. For two factors, labour and capital, we need both $P_L = \text{MRP}_L$ and $P_C = \text{MRP}_C$.

We can combine these conditions by dividing both sides of each equation by their respective prices and equating the results, to get

$$\frac{\text{MRP}_L}{P_L} = \frac{\text{MRP}_C}{P_C} = 1 \qquad (2)$$

Note in equation (2) that it is not sufficient that the MRPs of the two factors be *proportionate* to their prices; the MRPs must be *equal* to their prices and the ratios, therefore, equal to 1. For example, if $\text{MRP}_L = \$15$, $P_L = \$5$, $\text{MRP}_C = \$9$, and $P_C = \$3$, Siam is underemploying both capital and labour even though the ratios of MRP to resource price are identical for both factors. The firm can expand its profit by hiring additional amounts of both capital and labour until it moves down their downsloping MRP curves to the points at which $\text{MRP}_L = \$5$ and $\text{MRP}_C = \$3$. The ratios will then be 5/5 and 3/3 and equal to 1.

WORKED PROBLEM 16.2   Optimal Combination of Resources

The profit-maximizing position in equation (2) includes the cost-minimizing condition of equation (1). That is, if a firm is maximizing profit according to equation (2), then it must be using the least-cost combination of inputs to do so. However, the converse is not true: A firm operating at least cost according to equation (1) may not be operating at the output that maximizes its profit.

Numerical Illustration

A numerical illustration will help you understand the least-cost and profit-maximizing rules. In columns 2, 3, 2′, and 3′ in Table 16-5, we show the total products and marginal products for various amounts of labour and capital that are assumed to be the only inputs Siam needs in producing some product, say soup. Both inputs are subject to diminishing returns.

TABLE 16-5	Data for Finding the Least-Cost and Profit-Maximizing Combination of Labour and Capital, Siam's Soup*								
LABOUR (PRICE = $8)					**CAPITAL (PRICE = $12)**				
(1) Quantity	(2) Total product (output)	(3) Marginal product	(4) Total revenue	(5) Marginal revenue product	(1′) Quantity	(2′) Total product (output)	(3′) Marginal product	(4′) Total revenue	(5′) Marginal revenue product
0	0		$0		0	0		$ 0	
		12		$24			13		$26
1	12		24		1	13		26	
		10		20			9		18
2	22		44		2	22		44	
		6		12			6		**12**
3	28		56		**3**	28		56	
		5		10			4		8
4	33		66		4	32		64	
		4		**8**			3		6
5	37		74		5	35		70	
		3		6			2		4
6	40		80		6	37		74	
		2		4			1		2
7	42		84		7	38		76	

*To simplify, it is assumed in this table that the productivity of each factor is independent of the quantity of the other. For example, the total and marginal product of labour is assumed not to vary with the quantity of capital employed.

We also assume that labour and capital are supplied in competitive factor markets at $8 and $12, respectively, and that Siam's soup sells competitively at $2 per unit. For both labour and capital, we can determine the total revenue associated with each input level by multiplying total product by the $2 product price. These data are shown in columns 4 and 4′. They enable us to calculate the marginal revenue product of each successive input of labour and capital as shown in columns 5 and 5′, respectively.

PRODUCING AT LEAST COST

What is the least-cost combination of labour and capital to use in producing, say, fifty units of output? The answer, which we can obtain by trial and error, is three units of labour and two units of capital. Columns 2 and 2′ indicate that this combination of labour and capital does, indeed, result in the required 50 (= 28 + 22) units of output. Now, note from columns 3 and 3′ that hiring three units of labour gives us $MP_L/P_L = 6/8 = 3/4$, and hiring two units of capital gives us $MP_C/P_C = 9/12 = 3/4$. So equation (1) is fulfilled. How can we verify that costs are actually minimized? First, we see that the total cost of employing three units of labour and two of capital is $48 (= (3 × $8) + (2 × $12)).

Other combinations of labour and capital will also yield fifty units of output, but at a higher cost than $48. For example, five units of labour and one unit of capital will produce 50 (= 37 + 13) units, but total cost is higher at $52 (= (5 × $8) + (1 × $12)). This result comes as no surprise, because five units of labour and one unit of capital violate the least-cost rule—$MP_L/P_L = 4/8$, $MP_C/P_C = 13/12$. Only the combination (three units of labour and two units of capital) that minimizes total cost will satisfy equation (1). All other combinations capable of producing fifty units of output violate the cost-minimizing rule, and therefore cost more than $48.

MAXIMIZING PROFIT

Will fifty units of output maximize Siam's profit? No, because the profit-maximizing terms of equation (2) are not satisfied when the firm employs three units of labour and two of capital. To maximize profit, each input should be employed until its price equals its marginal revenue product. But for three units of labour, labour's MRP in column 5 is $12 while its price is only $8; the firm could increase its profit by hiring more labour. Similarly, for two units of capital, we see in column 5′ that capital's MRP is $18 and its price is only $12. This result indicates that more capital should also be employed. By producing only fifty units of output (even though they are produced at least cost), labour and capital are being used in less-than-profit-maximizing amounts. The firm needs to expand its employment of labour and capital, thereby increasing its output.

Table 16-5 shows that the MRPs of labour and capital are equal to their prices, so that equation (2) is fulfilled when Siam is employing five units of labour and three units of capital. This is the profit-maximizing combination of inputs.[2] The firm's total cost will be $76, made up of $40 (= 5 × $8) of labour and $36 (= 3 × $12) of capital. Total revenue will be $130, found either by multiplying the total output of 65 (= 37 + 28) by the $2 product price or by summing the total revenues attributable to labour ($74) and to capital ($56). The difference between total revenue and total cost in this instance is $54 (= $130 − $76). Experiment with other combinations of labour and capital to demonstrate that they yield an economic profit of less than $54.

Note that the profit-maximizing combination of five units of labour and three units of capital is also a least-cost combination for this particular level of output. Using these factor amounts satisfies the least-cost requirement of equation (1) in that $MP_L/P_L = 4/8 = 1/2$ and $MP_C/P_C = 6/12 = 1/2$.

16.6 Marginal Productivity Theory of Income Distribution

LO16.6 Explain the marginal productivity theory of income distribution.

Our discussion of factor pricing is the cornerstone of the controversial view that fairness and economic justice are two of the outcomes of a competitive market economy. Table 16-5 demonstrates, in effect, that workers receive income payments (wages) equal to the marginal contributions they make to their employers' outputs and revenues. In other words, workers are paid according to the value of the labour services that they contribute to production. Similarly, owners of the other factors of production receive income based on the value of the factors they supply in the production process.

In this **marginal productivity theory of income distribution**, income is distributed according to the contribution to society's output. So, if you are willing to accept the proposition "To each according to the value of what he or she creates," income payments based on marginal revenue product provide a fair and equitable distribution of society's income.

This sounds reasonable, but you need to be aware of serious criticisms of this theory of income distribution.

- *Inequality* Critics argue that the distribution of income resulting from payment according to marginal productivity may be highly unequal, because productive factors are very unequally distributed in the first place. Aside from their differences in mental and physical attributes, individuals encounter substantially different opportunities to enhance their productivity through education and training. Some people may not be able to participate in production at all because of mental or physical disabilities, and they would obtain no income under a system of distribution based solely on marginal productivity. Ownership of property resources is also highly unequal. Many owners of land and capital resources obtain their property by inheritance rather than through their own productive effort. Hence, income from inherited property resources conflicts with the "To each according to the values of what he or she creates" idea. This reasoning, say critics, calls for progressive taxation and government spending programs that modify the income distributions made strictly according to marginal productivity.

- *Market Imperfections* The marginal productivity theory of income distribution rests on the assumptions of competitive markets. But, as we will see in Chapter 17, not all labour markets are highly competitive. Employers in some labour markets exert their wage-setting power to pay less-than-competitive wages. And some workers, through labour unions, professional associations, and occupational licensing laws, wield wage-setting power to increase their wages in selling their services. In addition, discrimination in the labour market can distort earnings patterns. In short, because of real-world market imperfections, wage rates and other factor prices are not always based solely on contributions to output.

QUICK REVIEW 16.3

- Any specific level of output will be produced with the least-costly combination of variable factors when the marginal product per dollar's worth of each input is the same.

- A firm is employing the profit-maximizing combination of factors when each factor is used to the point where its marginal revenue product equals its price.

- The marginal productivity theory of income distribution holds that all factors are paid according to their marginal contributions to output.

---

[2] Because we are dealing with discrete (non-fractional) units of the two outputs here, the use of four units of labour and two units of capital is equally profitable. The fifth unit of labour's MRP and its price (cost) are equal at $8, so that the fifth labour unit neither adds to nor subtracts from the firm's profit; similarly, the third unit of capital has no effect on profit.

The LAST WORD

Labour and Capital: Substitutes or Complements?

Automatic banking machines (ABMs) have complemented some types of labour while substituting for other types of labour.

As you have learned from this chapter, a firm achieves its least-cost combination of inputs when the last dollar it spends on each input makes the same contribution to total output. This raises an interesting real-world question: What happens when technological advance makes available a new, highly productive capital good for which MP/*P* is greater than it is for other inputs, say a particular type of labour?

The answer is that the least-cost mix of factors abruptly changes and the firm responds accordingly. If the new capital is a substitute for labour (rather than a complement), the firm replaces the particular type of labour with the new capital. But if the new capital is a complement for a particular type of labour, the firm will add additional amounts of that type of labour.

Consider bank tellers. One of their core functions, before ABMs became common in the 1980s, was to handle deposits and withdrawals of cash. Bank tellers had several other tasks that they needed to handle, but one particular type of labour they supplied was handling cash transactions. The task of handling cash transactions can, however, be equally well-managed by ABMs—but at one-quarter the cost. Naturally, banks responded to that cost advantage by installing more ABMs.

That might make you think that ABMs displaced tellers, because it would seem natural in this scenario that ABMs were a substitute for bank tellers. But the data tell a different story! According to the Canadian Banking Association, the number of people it employs has increased by over 20 percent in the last decade, to about 275,000, while the number of ABMs has also increased. This means that over that entire time period, ABM machines must have been to some extent a complement to the labour provided by bank tellers.

To understand what happened, you have to keep in mind that bank tellers can be put to work doing many different tasks. Only one of those many possible tasks is handling cash. So while it is true that ABMs were indeed a substitute for bank tellers in terms of cash handling, ABMs did not offer a cheaper alternative for the other tasks that bank tellers could engage in. Thus, while there was a strong tendency for ABMs to substitute for the labour involved in handling cash, ABMs could not substitute for other bank teller activities.

In fact, ABMs ended up becoming a complement for those other activities. Canada's chartered banks realized that bank tellers could be trained in more complex tasks like selling financial products and helping to issue home mortgages. Once banks figured out these new ways to employ tellers, ABMs turned from a substitute for bank teller labour into a complement for bank teller labour. By freeing human beings from having to handle cash transactions, ABMs acted as a complement for other types of human labour, such as selling financial products.

We can generalize from the history of ABMs. Capital is, overall, a complement for human labour, not a substitute. Certain types of human labour are substituted away as new technologies arrive, but humans end up being complemented by capital as they perform other tasks. Some types of work will disappear and the government may need to help displaced workers train for new jobs. But the newly deployed capital will end up increasing wages, because it will increase the overall demand for human labour.

Question

To save money, some fast-food chains are now having their customers place their orders at computer kiosks. Will the kiosks necessarily reduce the total number of workers employed in the fast-food industry?

Chapter Summary

LO16.1   Explain the significance of factor pricing.

- Factor prices help determine money incomes, and they simultaneously ration factors of production to various industries and firms.

LO16.2   Convey how the marginal revenue productivity of a factor relates to a firm's demand for that factor.

- The demand for any factor is derived from the product it helps produce. That means the demand for a factor will depend on its productivity and on the market value (price) of the good it is used to produce.

- Marginal revenue product is the extra revenue a firm obtains when it employs one more unit of a factor. The MRP curve for any factor is the demand curve for that factor, because the firm equates factor price and MRP in determining its profit-maximizing level of factor employment. Thus, each point on the MRP curve indicates how many factor units the firm will hire at a specific factor price.

- The firm's demand curve for a factor slopes downward, because the marginal product of additional units declines in accordance with the law of diminishing returns. When a firm is selling in an imperfectly competitive market, the factor demand curve falls for a second reason: Product price must be reduced for the firm to sell a larger output. We can derive the market demand curve for a factor by summing horizontally the demand curves of all the firms hiring that factor.

LO16.3   List the causes that increase or decrease factor demand.

- The demand curve for a factor will shift as the result of (a) a change in the demand for, and therefore the price of, the product the factor is producing; (b) changes in the productivity of the factor; and (c) changes in the prices of other factors.

- If factors A and B are substitutable for each other, a decline in the price of A will decrease the demand for B provided the substitution effect is greater than the output effect. But if the output effect *exceeds* the substitution effect, a decline in the price of A will increase the demand for B.

- If factors C and D are complementary or jointly demanded, there is only an output effect; a change in the price of C will change the demand for D in the opposite direction.

LO16.4   Discuss the determinants of elasticity of factor demand.

- The elasticity of demand for a factor measures the responsiveness of producers to a change in the factor's price. The coefficient of the elasticity of factor demand is

$$E_{fd} = \frac{\text{percentage change in factor quantity demanded}}{\text{percentage change in factor price}}$$

When E_{fd} is greater than 1, factor demand is elastic; when E_{fd} is less than 1, factor demand is inelastic; and when E_{fd} equals 1, factor demand is unit elastic.

- The elasticity of demand for a factor will be greater (a) the greater the ease of substituting other resources for labour, (b) the greater the elasticity of demand for the product, and (c) the larger the proportion of total production costs attributable to the factor.

LO16.5   Determine how a competitive firm selects its optimal combination of factors.

- Any specific level of output will be produced with the least costly combination of variable factors when the marginal product per dollar's worth of each input is the same—that is, when

$$\frac{\text{MP of labour}}{\text{price of labour}} = \frac{\text{MP of capital}}{\text{price of capital}}$$

- A firm is employing the profit-maximizing combination of factors when each factor is used to the point where its marginal revenue product equals its price. In terms of labour and capital, that occurs when the MRP of labour equals the price of labour and the MRP of capital equals the price of capital—that is, when

$$\frac{\text{MRP of labour}}{\text{price of labour}} = \frac{\text{MRP of capital}}{\text{price of capital}} = 1$$

LO16.6   Explain the marginal productivity theory of income distribution.

- The marginal productivity theory of income distribution holds that factors are paid according to their marginal contribution to output. Critics say that such an income distribution is too unequal and real-world market imperfections result in pay above and below marginal contributions to output.

Terms and Concepts

derived demand
marginal product (MP)
marginal revenue product (MRP)
marginal factor cost (MFC)
MRP = MFC rule
substitution effect

output effect
elasticity of factor demand
least-cost combination of factors
profit-maximizing combination of factors
marginal productivity theory of income distribution

Discussion Questions

1. What is the significance of factor pricing? Explain how the determinants of factor demand differ from those underlying product demand. Explain the meaning and significance of the fact that the demand for a factor is a derived demand. Why do factor demand curves slope downward? [**LO16.1**]

2. In 2009 General Motors (GM) announced that it would reduce employment by 21,000 workers. What does this decision reveal about how it viewed its marginal revenue product (MRP) and marginal factor cost (MFC)? Why didn't GM reduce employment by more than 21,000 workers? By fewer than 21,000 workers? [**LO16.3**]

3. What are the determinants of the elasticity of factor demand? What effect will each of the following have on the elasticity or the location of the demand for factor C, which is being used to produce commodity X? Where there is any uncertainty as to the outcome, specify the causes of that uncertainty. [**LO16.4**]

   a. An increase in the demand for product X

   b. An increase in the price of substitute factor D

   c. An increase in the number of factors substitutable for C in producing X

   d. A technological improvement in the capital equipment with which factor C is combined

   e. A decline in the price of complementary factor E

   f. A decline in the elasticity of demand for product X due to a decline in the competitiveness of product market X

4. In each of the following four cases, MRP_L and MRP_C refer to the marginal revenue products of labour and capital, respectively, and P_L and P_C refer to their prices. Indicate in each case whether the conditions are consistent with maximum profits for the firm. If not, state which factor(s) should be used in larger amounts and which factor(s) should be used in smaller amounts. [**LO16.5**]

   a. $MRP_L = \$8$; $P_L = \$4$; $MRP_C = \$8$; $P_C = \$4$

   b. $MRP_L = \$10$; $P_L = \$12$; $MRP_C = \$14$; $P_C = \$9$

   c. $MRP_L = \$6$; $P_L = \$6$; $MRP_C = \$12$; $P_C = \$12$

   d. $MRP_L = \$22$; $P_L = \$26$; $MRP_C = \$16$; $P_C = \$19$

5. Florida citrus growers say that the recent crackdown on illegal immigration is increasing the market wage rates necessary to get their oranges picked. Some are turning to $100,000-to-$300,000 mechanical harvesters known as "trunk, shake, and catch" pickers, which vigorously shake oranges from the trees. If widely adopted, what will be the effect on the demand for human orange pickers? What does that imply about the relative strengths of the substitution and output effects? [**LO16.5**]

Review Questions

1. Cindy is a baker and runs a large cupcake shop. She has already hired 11 employees and is thinking of hiring a 12th. Cindy estimates that a 12th worker would cost her $100 per day in wages and benefits while increasing her total revenue from $2600 per day to $2750 per day. Should Cindy hire a 12th worker? [**LO16.2**]

   a. Yes

   b. No

   c. You need more information to figure this out

2. Complete the following labour demand table for a firm that is hiring labour competitively and selling its product in a competitive market. [**LO16.2**]

Units of labour	Total product	Marginal product	Product price	Total revenue	Marginal revenue product
0	0	_____	$2	$_____	$_____
1	17	_____	2	_____	_____
2	31	_____	2	_____	_____
3	43	_____	2	_____	_____
4	53	_____	2	_____	_____
5	60	_____	2	_____	_____
6	65	_____	2	_____	

   a. How many workers will the firm hire if the market wage rate is $27.95? $19.95? Explain why the firm will not hire a larger or smaller number of units of labour at each of these wage rates.

   b. Show in schedule form and graphically the labour demand curve of this firm.

   c. Now again determine the firm's demand curve for labour, assuming that it is selling in an imperfectly competitive market and that, although it can sell 17 units at $2.20 per unit, it must lower product price by $0.05 to sell the marginal product of each successive labour unit. Compare this demand curve with that derived in part (b). Which curve is more elastic? Explain.

3. Alice runs a shoemaking factory that uses both labour and capital to make shoes. Which of the following would shift the factory's demand for capital? Select *one or more* answers from the choices shown. [**LO16.3**]

   a. Many consumers decide to walk barefoot all the time.

   b. New shoemaking machines are twice as efficient as older machines.

   c. The wages that the factory has to pay its workers rise due to an economy-wide labour shortage.

4. FreshLeaf is a commercial salad maker that produces "salad in a bag" that is sold at many local supermarkets. Its customers like lettuce but don't care so much what type of lettuce is

included in each bag of salad, so you would expect FreshLeaf's demand for iceberg lettuce to be [LO16.4]

a. Elastic

b. Inelastic

c. Unit elastic

d. All of the above

5. Suppose the productivity of capital and the productivity of labour are as shown in the table that follows. The output of these factors sells in a perfectly competitive market for $1 per unit. Both capital and labour are hired under perfectly competitive conditions at $3 and $1, respectively. [LO16.5]

Units of capital	MP of capital	Units of labour	MP of labour
0		0	
	24		11
1		1	
	21		9
2		2	
	18		8
3		3	
	15		7
4		4	
	9		6
5		5	
	6		4
6		6	
	3		1
7		7	
	1		½
8		8	

a. What is the least-cost combination of labour and capital the firm should employ in producing 80 units of output? Explain.

b. What is the profit-maximizing combination of labour and capital the firm should use? Explain. What is the resulting level of output? What is the economic profit? Is this the least costly way of producing the profit maximizing output?

6. A software company in Silicon Valley uses programmers (labour) and computers (capital) to produce apps for mobile devices. The firm estimates that when it comes to labour, $MP_L = 5$ apps per month while $P_L = \$1000$ per month. And when it comes to capital, $MP_C = 8$ apps per month while $P_C = \$1000$ per month. If the company wants to maximize its profits, it should [LO16.5]

a. Increase labour while decreasing capital

b. Decrease labour while increasing capital

c. Keep the current amounts of capital and labour just as they are

d. None of the above

Problems

1. A delivery company is considering adding another vehicle to its delivery fleet, all the vehicles of which are rented for $100 per day. Assume that the additional vehicle would be capable of delivering 1500 packages per day and that each package that is delivered brings in ten cents ($0.10) in revenue. Also assume that adding the delivery vehicle would not affect any other costs. [LO16.2]

a. What is the MRP? What is the MFC? Should the firm add this delivery vehicle?

b. Now suppose that the cost of renting a vehicle doubles to $200 per day. What are the MRP and MFC? Should the firm add a delivery vehicle under these circumstances?

c. Next suppose that the cost of renting a vehicle falls back down to $100 per day, but due to extremely congested freeways an additional vehicle would only be able to deliver 750 packages per day. What are the MRP and MFC in this situation? Would adding a vehicle under these circumstances increase the firm's profits?

2. Suppose that marginal product tripled while product price fell by one-half in Table 16-1. What would be the new MRP values in the table? What would be the net impact on the location of the factor demand curve in Figure 16-1? [LO16.2]

3. Suppose a monopoly firm finds that its MR is $50 for the first unit sold each day, $49 for the second unit sold each day, $48 for the third unit sold each day, and so on. Further suppose that the first worker hired produces 5 units per day, the second 4 units per day, the third 3 units per day, and so on. [LO16.3]

a. What is the firm's MRP for each of the first 5 workers?

b. Suppose that the monopolist is subjected to rate regulation and the regulator stipulates that it must charge exactly $40 per unit for all units sold. At that price, what is the firm's MRP for each of the first 5 workers?

c. If the daily wage paid to workers is $170 per day, how many workers will the unregulated monopoly demand? How many will the regulated monopoly demand? Looking at those figures, will the regulated or the unregulated monopoly demand more workers at that wage?

d. If the daily wage paid to workers falls to $77 per day, how many workers will the unregulated monopoly demand? How many will the regulated monopoly demand? Looking at those figures, will the regulated or the unregulated monopoly demand more workers at that wage?

    e. Comparing your answers to parts (c) and (d), does regulating a monopoly's output price *always* increase its demand for resources?

4. Consider a small landscaping company run by Mr. Viemeister. He is considering increasing his firm's capacity. If he adds 1 more worker, the firm's total monthly revenue will increase from $50,000 to $58,000. If he adds 1 more tractor, monthly revenue will increase from $50,000 to $62,000. Additional workers each cost $4000 per month while an additional tractor would also cost $6000 per month.　**[LO16.5]**

    a. What is the marginal product of labour? The marginal product of capital?

    b. What is the ratio of the marginal product of labour to the price of labour (MP_L/P_L)? What is the ratio of the marginal product of capital to the price of capital (MP_K/P_K)?

    c. Is the firm using the least costly combination of inputs?

    d. Does adding an additional worker or adding an additional tractor yield a larger increase in total revenue for each dollar spent?

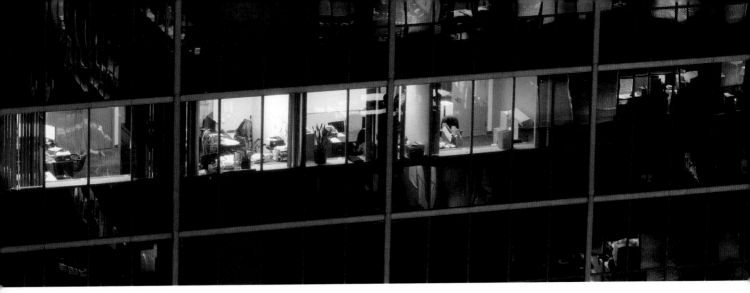

CHAPTER 17

Wage Determination

Over 18 million Canadians go to work every day. We work at an amazing variety of jobs for thousands of different firms for considerable differences in pay. What determines our hourly wage or annual salary? Why is the salary for, say, a top major league baseball player $18 million or more a year, whereas the pay for a first-rate schoolteacher is $95,000? Why are starting salaries for university graduates who major in engineering and accounting so much higher than for graduates majoring in journalism and sociology?

Having explored the major factors that underlie labour demand, we now bring *labour supply* into our analysis to help answer these questions. Generally, labour supply and labour demand interact to determine the hourly wage rate or annual salary in each occupation. Collectively, those wages and salaries make up about 70 percent of all income paid to Canadian resource suppliers.

17.1 Labour, Wages, and Earnings

LO17.1   Explain why labour productivity and real hourly compensation track so closely over time.

Economists use the term *labour* broadly to apply to (1) blue-collar and white-collar workers of all varieties; (2) professionals such as lawyers, physicians, dentists, and teachers; and (3) owners of small businesses, including barbers, plumbers, and a host of retailers who provide labour as they operate their own business.

Wages are the price that employers pay for labour. Wages take the form not only of direct money payments such as hourly pay, annual salaries, bonuses, royalties, and commissions, but also fringe benefits, such as paid vacations and dental insurance. We will use the term *wages* to mean all such payments and benefits converted to an hourly basis. That will remind us that the **wage rate** is a price paid per unit of labour services, in this case an hour of work. It will also let us distinguish between the wage rate and labour earnings, the latter being determined by multiplying the number of hours worked per week, per month, or per year by the hourly wage or wage rate.

We must also distinguish between nominal wages and real wages. A **nominal wage** is the amount of money received per hour, per day, and so on. A **real wage** is the quantity of goods and services a worker can obtain with nominal wages; real wages reveal the purchasing power of nominal wages.

Your real wage depends on your nominal wage and the prices of the goods and services you purchase. Suppose you receive a 5 percent increase in your nominal wage during a certain year, but in that same year the price level increases by 3 percent. Then your real wage has increased by 2 percent (= 5 percent *minus* 3 percent). Unless otherwise indicated, we will discuss only *real* wages.

General Level of Wages

Wages differ across nations, regions, occupations, and individuals. Wage rates are much higher in Canada than in China or India. Wages are slightly higher in central Canada and the west than in the east. Plumbers are paid less than NHL hockey players, and lawyer Adam may earn twice as much as lawyer Bharti for the same number of hours of work. The average wages earned by workers also differ by gender, race, and ethnic background.

Wages are the price that employers pay for labour.

© Dream Pictures/Shannon Faulk/
Blend Images/Corbis

The general level of wages includes a wide range of different wage rates. It includes the wages of bakers, barbers, brickmasons, and brain surgeons. By averaging such wages, we can more easily compare wages among regions and among nations.

As Global Perspective 17.1 suggests, the general level of real wages in Canada, especially in the skilled trades, is relatively high—although not the highest in the world.

The explanation for the high real wages in Canada and other industrially advanced economies (referred to hereafter as advanced economies) is that the demand for labour in these nations is relatively large compared to the supply of labour.

Role of Productivity

We know from Chapter 16 that the demand for labour, or for any other factor, depends on its productivity. Generally, the greater the productivity of labour, the greater the demand for it. If the total supply of labour is fixed, the demand for labour will be stronger, and the average level of real wages will be higher. The demand for labour in Canada and the other major advanced economies is large because labour in these countries is highly productive. There are several reasons for that high productivity:

- *Plentiful Capital* Workers in the advanced economies have access to large amounts of physical capital (machinery and buildings). The total physical capital per worker in Canada is one of the highest in the world.

- *Access to Abundant Natural Resources* In advanced economies, natural resources are abundant in relation to the size of the labour force. Some of those resources are available domestically and others are imported

17.1 GLOBAL PERSPECTIVE

Hourly Wages of Production Workers, Selected Nations

Wage differences are pronounced worldwide. These data indicate that hourly compensation in Canada is not as high as in some European nations. It is important to note, however, that the prices of goods and services vary greatly among nations, and the process of converting foreign wages into dollars may not accurately reflect such variations.

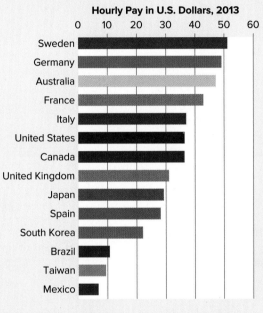

Hourly Pay in U.S. Dollars, 2013

Sweden, Germany, Australia, France, Italy, United States, Canada, United Kingdom, Japan, Spain, South Korea, Brazil, Taiwan, Mexico

Source: The Conference Board, www.conference-board.org.

from abroad. Canada, for example, is richly endowed with arable land, mineral resources, and sources of energy for industry.

- *Advanced Technology* The level of technological progress is generally high in advanced economies. Not only do workers in these economies have more capital equipment to work with, but that equipment is also technologically superior to the equipment available to the vast majority of workers worldwide. Work methods in the advanced economies are also steadily being improved through scientific study and research.

- *Labour Quality* The health, education, and training of workers in advanced economies are generally superior to those of workers in developing nations. Thus, even with the same quantity and quality of natural and capital resources, workers in advanced economies tend to be more productive than many of their counterparts elsewhere.

- *Other Factors* Less obvious factors also underlie the high productivity in some of the advanced economies. In Canada, for example, such factors include (1) the efficiency and flexibility of management; (2) business, social, and political environments that emphasize production and productivity; (3) access to a large market, which enables firms to engage in mass production; and (4) increased specialization of production made possible by free trade agreements with other nations.

Real Wages and Productivity

Figure 17-1 shows the close long-run relationship between output per hour of work and real hourly earnings in Canada. Because real income and real output are two ways of viewing the same thing, real income (earnings) per worker can increase only at about the same rate as output per worker. When workers produce more real output per hour, more real income is available to distribute to them for each hour worked.

FIGURE 17-1   Output per Hour and Real Hourly Compensation in Canada

Over a long time period, output per hour of work and real hourly compensation are closely related.

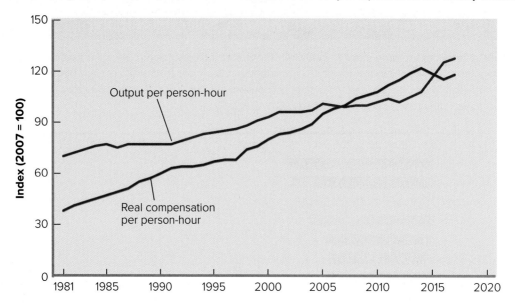

Source: Adapted from Statistics Canada CANSIM database, http://www5.statcan.gc.ca/cansim/a47, Table 383-0012.

However, suppliers of land, capital, and entrepreneurial talent also share in the income from production. Real wages, therefore, do not always rise in lockstep with gains in productivity over short spans of time. But over long periods, productivity and real wages tend to rise together.

Long-Run Trend of Real Wages

Basic supply-and-demand analysis helps explain the long-term trend of real-wage growth in Canada. The nation's labour force has grown significantly over the decades. But, as a result of the productivity-increasing factors we have mentioned, increases in labour demand have outstripped increases in labour supply. Figure 17-2 shows several such increases in labour supply and labour demand. The result has been a long-run increase in wage rates and employment. For example, real hourly compensation in Canada has roughly doubled since 1960. Over that same period, employment has increased by about 12 million workers.

FIGURE 17-2   The Long-Run Trend of Real Wages in Canada

The productivity of Canadian labour has increased substantially over the long run, causing the demand for labour, *D*, to shift to the right more rapidly than increases in the supply of labour, *S*. The result has been increases in real wages.

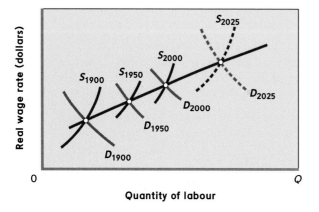

17.2 A Perfectly Competitive Labour Market

LO17.2   Show how wages rates and employment are determined in a competitive labour market.

Average levels of wages disguise the great variation of wage rates among and within occupations. What determines the wage rate paid for a specific type of labour? Demand and supply analysis is again revealing. Let's begin by examining labour demand and labour supply in a **perfectly competitive labour market**. In this type of market,

- Numerous firms compete with one another in hiring a specific type of labour.

- Many qualified workers with identical skills supply that type of labour.

- Individual firms and individual workers are wage-takers, since neither can exert any control over the market wage rate.

   CHOOSING A LITTLE MORE OR LESS

Market Demand for Labour

Suppose 200 firms demand a particular type of labour, say carpenters. These firms need not be in the same industry; firms producing wood-framed furniture, wooden windows and doors, houses and apartment buildings, and wooden cabinets might all demand carpenters at one time or another. To find the total, or market, labour demand curve for a particular labour service, we sum horizontally the labour demand curves (the marginal revenue product curves) of the individual firms, as indicated in Figure 17-3 (Key Graph). The horizontal summing of the 200 labour demand curves like d in Figure 17-3b yields the market labour demand curve D in Figure 17-3a.

Market Supply of Labour

On the supply side of a perfectly competitive labour market, we assume that no union is present and that workers individually compete for available jobs. Keep in mind that the supply of labour come from households, and thus the labour supply curves presented are those seen by firms. The supply curve for each type of labour slopes upward, indicating that employers as a group must pay higher wage rates to obtain more workers. They must do this to bid workers away from other industries, occupations, and localities. Within limits, workers have alternative job opportunities. For example, they may work in other industries in the same locality, they may work in their present occupations in different cities or provinces, or they may work in other occupations.

Firms that want to hire these workers (here, carpenters) must pay higher wage rates to attract them away from the alternative job opportunities available to them. They must also pay higher wages to induce people who are not currently in the labour force—perhaps doing household activities or enjoying leisure—to seek employment. In short, assuming that wages are constant in other labour markets, higher wages in a particular labour market entice more workers to offer their labour services in that market—a fact confirmed by the upsloping market supply of labour curve S in Figure 17-3a.

Labour Market Equilibrium

The intersection of the market labour demand curve and the market labour supply curve determines the equilibrium wage rate and level of employment in purely competitive labour markets. In Figure 17-3a the equilibrium wage rate is W_c ($10), and the number of workers hired is Q_c (1000). To the individual firm the market wage rate W_c is given. Each of the many firms employs such a small fraction of the total available supply of this type of labour that no single firm can influence the wage rate. As shown by the horizontal line s in Figure 17-3b, the supply of this labour is perfectly elastic to the individual firm.

Each individual firm will maximize its profit (or minimize loss) by hiring this type of labour up to the point at which marginal revenue product is equal to marginal factor cost. This is merely an application of the MRP = MFC rule we developed in Chapter 16.

KEY GRAPH

FIGURE 17-3 Labour Supply and Labour Demand in a Perfectly Competitive Labour Market and a Single Competitive Firm

In a perfectly competitive labour market (a) market labour supply S and market labour demand D determine the equilibrium wage rate W_c and the equilibrium number of workers Q_c. Each individual competitive firm (b) takes this competitive wage W_c as given. Thus, the individual firm's labour supply curve S = MFC is perfectly elastic at the going wage rate W_c. Its labour demand curve is its MRP curve (here labelled "mrp"). The firm maximizes its profit by hiring workers up to where MRP = MFC. Area $0abc$ represents both the firm's total revenue and its total cost. The green area is its total wage cost; the blue area is its non-labour costs, including a normal profit—that is, the firm's payments to the suppliers of land, capital, and entrepreneurship.

(a) Labour market   **(b) Single firm**

QUICK QUIZ

1. The supply of labour curve S slopes upward in graph (a) because
   a. The law of diminishing marginal utility applies
   b. The law of diminishing returns applies
   c. Workers can afford to buy more leisure when the wage rate increases
   d. Higher wages are needed to attract workers away from other labour markets, household activities, and leisure

2. This firm's labour demand curve d in graph (b) slopes downward because
   a. The law of diminishing marginal utility applies
   b. The law of diminishing returns applies
   c. The firm must lower its price to sell additional units of its product
   d. The firm is a competitive employer, not a monopsonist

3. In employing five workers, the firm represented in graph (b)
   a. Has a total wage cost of $6000
   b. Is adhering to the general principle of undertaking all actions for which the marginal benefit exceeds the marginal cost
   c. Uses less labour than would be ideal from society's perspective
   d. Experiences increasing marginal returns

4. A rightward shift of the labour supply curve in graph (a) would shift curve
   a. d = mrp leftward in graph (b)
   b. d = mrp rightward in graph (b)
   c. s = MFC upward in graph (b)
   d. s = MFC downward in graph (b)

TABLE 17-1	The Supply of Labour: Perfect Competition in the Hire of Labour		
(1) Units of labour	(2) Wage rate	(3) Total labour cost (wage bill)	(4) Marginal factor (labour) cost
0	$10	$ 0	
1	10	10	$10
2	10	20	10
3	10	30	10
4	10	40	10
5	10	50	10
6	10	60	10

As Table 17-1 indicates, when an individual competitive firm faces the market price for a resource, that resource's marginal factor cost (MFC) is constant and is equal to the market price for each and every unit that the competitive firm may choose to purchase. Note that MFC is constant at $10 and matches the $10 wage rate. Each additional worker hired adds precisely his or her own wage rate ($10 in this case) to the firm's total resource cost. So the firm in a perfectly competitive labour market maximizes its profit by hiring workers up to the point at which its wage rate equals MRP. In Figure 17-3b this firm will hire Q_c (five) workers, paying each worker the market wage rate, W_c ($10). The other 199 firms (not shown) that are hiring workers in this labour market will also each employ five workers and pay $10 per hour.

To determine a firm's total revenue from employing a particular number of labour units, we sum the MRPs of those units. For example, if a firm employs three labour units with marginal revenue products of $14, $13, and

CONSIDER THIS

Fringe Benefits Versus Take-Home Pay

Figure 17-2 shows that total compensation has risen significantly over the past several decades. Not shown in that figure, however, is the fact that the amount of take-home pay received by middle-class Canadian workers has increased by much less. One contributing factor has been the rise of fringe benefits.

To see why fringe benefits matter, recall that throughout this chapter we have defined the wage as the total price that employers pay to obtain labour and compensate workers for providing it. Under our definition, wages are the sum of take-home pay (such as hourly pay and annual salaries) and fringe benefits (such as paid vacations, dental insurance, and pensions).

So now consider an equilibrium wage, such as W_c in Figure 17-3. If workers want higher fringe benefits, they can

© numbeos/E-plus/Getty Images RF

have them—but only if the take-home pay falls by an equal amount. With the equilibrium wage fixed by supply and demand, the only way workers can get more fringe benefits is by accepting lower take-home pay.

This is an important point to understand, because in recent decades workers have received an increasing fraction of their total compensation in the form of fringe benefits. Those benefits are costly, and in a competitive labour market each $1 increase in fringe benefits means $1 less for the paycheque.

That trade-off helps explain why take-home pay has increased by less than total compensation in recent decades. With a rising fraction of total compensation flowing toward fringe benefits, the increase in take-home pay was much less than the overall increase in total compensation.

$12, respectively, then the firm's total revenue is $39 (= $14 + $13 + $12). In Figure 17-3b, where we are not restricted to whole units of labour, total revenue is represented by area $0abc$ under the MRP curve to the left of Q_c. What area represents the firm's total cost, including a normal profit? For Q_c units, the same area—$0abc$. The green rectangle represents the firm's total wage cost ($0Q_c \times 0W_c$). The blue triangle (total revenue minus total wage cost) represents the firm's non-labour costs—its explicit and implicit payments to land, capital, and entrepreneurship. Thus, in this case, total cost (wages plus other income payments) equals total revenue. This firm and others like it are earning only a normal profit. Figure 17-3b represents a long-run equilibrium for a firm that is selling its product in a perfectly competitive product market and hiring its labour in a perfectly competitive labour market.

17.3 Monopsony Model

LO17.3   Demonstrate how monopsony (a market with a single employer) can reduce wages below competitive levels.

In the perfectly competitive labour market described in the preceding section, each employer hires too small an amount of labour to influence the wage rate. The situation is quite different when the labour market is a **monopsony**, a market structure in which there is only a single buyer. Labour market monopsony has the following characteristics:

- There is only a single buyer of a particular type of labour.

- The workers providing this type of labour have few employment options other than working for the monopsony either because they are geographically immobile or because finding alternative employment would mean having to acquire new skills.

- The firm is a wage-maker, because the wage rate it must pay varies directly with the number of workers it employs.

As is true of monopoly power, there are various degrees of monopsony power. In a perfect monopsony such power is at its maximum because only a single employer exists in the labour market. The best real-world examples are probably the labour markets in some towns that depend almost entirely on one major firm. For example, a copper-mining concern may be almost the only source of employment in a remote British Columbia town, and a textile mill in Quebec's Eastern Townships, a paper mill in Gatineau, or a fish processor in Newfoundland may provide most of the employment in its locale.

In other cases three or four firms may each hire a large portion of the supply of labour in a certain market and, therefore, have some monopsony power. If they tacitly or openly act in concert in hiring labour, they greatly enhance their monopsony power.

Upsloping Labour Supply to a Firm

When a firm hires most of the available supply of a certain type of labour, its decision to employ more or fewer workers affects the wage rate it pays to those workers. If a firm is large in relation to the size of the labour market, it will have to pay a higher wage rate to obtain more labour. Suppose that there is only one employer of a particular type of labour in a certain geographic area. In this monopsony situation, the labour supply curve for the *firm* and the total labour supply curve for the *labour market* are identical. The monopsonist's supply curve—represented by curve S in Figure 17-4—is upsloping because the firm must pay higher wage rates if it wants to attract and hire additional workers. This same curve is also the monopsonist's average-cost-of-labour curve. Each point on curve S indicates the wage rate (cost) per worker that must be paid to attract the corresponding number of workers.

MFC Higher Than the Wage Rate

When a monopsonist pays a higher wage to attract an additional worker, it must pay that higher wage to all the workers it is currently employing at a lower wage. If not, labour morale will deteriorate, and the employer will

When a firm hires most of the available supply of a particular type of labour, its decision to hire more or fewer workers affects the wage rate it pays to those workers.

© Alistair Berg/Photodisc/Getty Images

be plagued with labour unrest because of wage-rate differences for the same job. Paying a uniform wage to all workers means that the cost of an extra worker—the marginal factor (labour) cost (MFC)—is the sum of that worker's wage rate and the amount necessary to bring the wage rate of all current workers up to the new wage level.

Table 17-2 illustrates this point. One worker can be hired at a wage rate of $6, but hiring a second worker forces the firm to pay a higher wage rate of $7. The marginal factor (labour) cost of the second worker is $8—the $7 paid to the second worker plus a $1 raise for the first worker. From another viewpoint, total labour cost is now $14 (= 2 × $7), up from $6 (= 1 × $6). So the MFC of the second worker is $8 (= $14 − $6), not just the $7 wage rate paid to that worker. Similarly, the marginal labour cost of the third worker is $10—the $8 that must be paid to attract this worker from alternative employment, plus $1 raises, from $7 to $8, for the first two workers.

Here is the key point: Because the monopsonist is the only employer in the labour market, its marginal resource (labour) cost exceeds the wage rate. Graphically, the monopsonist's MFC curve lies above the average-cost-of-labour curve, or labour supply curve S, as is clearly shown in Figure 17-4.

Equilibrium Wage and Employment

How many units of labour will the monopsonist hire and what wage rate will it pay? To maximize profit, the monopsonist will employ the quantity of labour Q_m in Figure 17-4, because at that quantity MFC and MRP are

FIGURE 17-4   The Wage Rate and Level of Employment in a Monopsonistic Labour Market

In a monopsonistic labour market, the employer's marginal factor (labour) cost curve (MFC) lies above the labour supply curve, S. Equating MFC with MRP at point b, the monopsonist hires Q_m workers (compared with Q_c under competition). As indicated by point c on S, it pays only wage rate W_m (compared with the competitive wage W_c).

TABLE 17-2	The Supply of Labour: Monopsony in Hiring Labour

(1) Units of labour	(2) Wage rate	(3) Total labour cost (wage bill)	(4) Marginal factor (labour) cost
0	$ 5	$ 0	
			$ 6
1	6	6	
			8
2	7	14	
			10
3	8	24	
			12
4	9	36	
			14
5	10	50	
			16
6	11	66	

equal (point b).[1] The monopsonist next determines how much it must pay to attract these Q_m workers. From the supply curve S, specifically point c, it sees that it must pay wage rate W_m. Clearly, it need not pay a wage equal to MRP; it can attract and hire exactly the number of workers it wants (Q_m) with wage rate W_m. And that is the wage rate it will pay.

Contrast these results with those that would prevail in a competitive labour market. With competition in the hiring of labour, the level of employment would be greater (at Q_c) and the wage rate would be higher (at W_c). Other things equal, the monopsonist maximizes its profit by hiring a smaller number of workers and thereby paying a less-than-competitive wage rate. Society obtains a smaller output, and workers receive a wage rate that is less by bc than their marginal revenue product. Just as a monopolist finds it profitable to restrict product output to realize an above-competitive price for its goods, the monopsonist finds it profitable to restrict employment to reduce wage rates below those that would occur under competitive conditions.

WORKED PROBLEM 17.1 Labour Markets: Competition and Monopsony

Examples of Monopsony Power

Fortunately, monopsonistic labour markets are uncommon in the Canadian economy. In most labour markets, several employers compete for workers, particularly for workers who are occupationally and geographically mobile. Also, in a potential monopsony in a local labour market, unions have often sprung up to counteract that power by forcing firms to negotiate wages. Nevertheless, there is evidence of monopsony power in such diverse labour markets as the markets for nurses, professional athletes, public-school teachers, newspaper employees, and some building trades workers.

---

[1] The fact that MFC exceeds factor price when factors are hired or purchased under imperfectly competitive (monopsonistic) conditions calls for adjustments in Chapter 16's least-cost and profit-maximizing rules for hiring factors. (See equations (1) and (2) in section 16.5, Optimal Combination of Factors.) Specifically, we must substitute MFC for resource price in the denominators of our two equations. That is, with imperfect competition in the hiring of both labour and capital, equation (1) becomes

$$\frac{MP_L}{MFC_L} = \frac{MP_C}{MFC_C} \tag{1}$$

and equation (2) is restated as

$$\frac{MRP_L}{MFC_L} = \frac{MRP_C}{MFC_C} = 1 \tag{2}$$

In fact, equations (1) and (2) can be regarded as special cases of (1′) and (2′) in which firms happen to be hiring under perfectly competitive conditions and factor price is, therefore, equal to, and can be substituted for, marginal factor cost.

QUICK REVIEW 17.1

- Real wages have increased over time in Canada because labour demand has increased relative to labour supply.

- Over the long term, real wages per worker have increased at approximately the same rate as worker productivity.

- The competitive employer is a wage-taker and employs workers at the point where the wage rate (= MFC) equals MRP.

- The labour supply curve for a monopsonist is upsloping, causing MFC to exceed the wage rate for each worker. Other things equal, the monopsonist, hiring where MFC = MRP, will employ fewer workers and pay a lower wage rate than would a perfectly competitive employer.

17.4 Unions and the Labour Market: Three Models

LO17.4   Discuss how unions increase wage rates by pursuing the demand-enhancement model, the craft union model, or the industrial union model.

Our assumption thus far has been that workers compete with one another in selling their labour services. But in some labour markets, workers unionize and sell their labour services collectively.

When a union is formed in an otherwise competitive labour market, it usually bargains with a relatively large number of employers. It has many goals, the most important of which is to raise wage rates. It can pursue that objective in several ways.

Demand-Enhancement Model

Unions recognize that their ability to influence the demand for labour is limited. But, from the union's viewpoint, increasing the demand for union labour is highly desirable. As Figure 17-5 shows, an increase in the demand for union labour will create a higher union wage along with more jobs. Unions can increase the demand for their labour by increasing the demand for the goods or services they help produce. Political lobby is the main tool for increasing the demand for union-produced goods or services. For example, construction unions lobby for new highways, mass-transit systems, and stadium projects. Teachers' unions and associations push for increased public spending on education. Unions in the steel sector and forest-products sector lobby for tariffs and quotas on imports of steel and lumber, respectively. Such trade restrictions shift the demand for labour away from foreign countries and toward unionized Canadian labour.

Unions can also increase the demand for union labour by altering the price of other inputs. For example, although union members are generally paid significantly more than the minimum wage, unions have strongly supported increases in the minimum wage. The purpose may be to raise the price of low-wage, non-union labour, which in some cases is substitutable for union labour. A higher minimum wage for non-union workers will discourage employers from substituting such workers for union workers and thereby increase the demand for union members.

Similarly, unions have sometimes sought to increase the demand for their labour by supporting policy that reduces or holds down the price of complementary factors of production. For example, unions that represent workers who transport fruit and vegetables may support legislation that allows low-wage foreign agricultural workers to work in Canada temporarily. Where union labour and other resources are complementary, a price decrease for the other factors will increase the demand for union labour through the output effect (Chapter 16).

Exclusive or Craft Union Model

Unions can also boost wage rates by reducing the supply of labour, and over the years organized labour has favoured policies to do just that. The Canadian Labour Congress, an umbrella organization representing 3.3 million workers, has supported legislation that has (1) restricted permanent immigration, (2) reduced child labour, (3) encouraged compulsory retirement, and (4) enforced a shorter workweek.

FIGURE 17-5   Unions and Demand Enhancement

When unions can increase the demand for union labour (say from D_1 to D_2), they can realize higher wage rates (W_c to W_u) and more jobs (Q_c to Q_u).

Moreover, certain types of workers have adopted techniques designed to restrict the number of workers who can join their union. This is especially true of *craft unions*, whose members possess a particular skill, such as carpenters, brickmasons, or plumbers. Craft unions have frequently forced employers to agree to hire only union members, thereby gaining virtually complete control of the labour supply. Then, by following restrictive membership policies—for example, long apprenticeships, very high initiation fees, and limits on the number of new members admitted—they artificially restrict labour supply. As indicated in Figure 17-6, such practices result in higher wage rates and constitute what is called **exclusive unionism**. By excluding workers from unions and therefore from the labour supply, craft unions succeed in elevating wage rates.

Another means of restricting the supply of specific kinds of labour is **occupational licensing**. Here a group of workers in a given occupation pressure provincial or municipal governments to pass a law that says some occupational group (for example, barbers, physicians, plumbers, car mechanics, or pest controllers) can practise their trade only if they meet certain requirements. Those requirements might include level of education, amount of work experience, the passing of an examination, and personal characteristics (for example, "good moral

FIGURE 17-6   Exclusive or Craft Unionism

By reducing the supply of labour (say from S_1 to S_2) through the use of restrictive membership policies, exclusive unions achieve higher wage rates (W_c to W_u). However, restriction of the labour supply also reduces the number of workers employed (Q_c to Q_u).

character"). Members of the licensed occupation typically dominate the licensing board that administers such laws. The result is self-regulation, which often leads to policies that serve only to restrict entry to the occupation and reduce the labour supply.

The expressed purpose of licensing is to protect consumers from incompetent practitioners—surely a worthy goal. But such licensing also results in above-competitive wages and earnings for those in the licensed occupation (Figure 17-6). Moreover, licensing often includes a residency requirement, which inhibits the interprovincial movement of qualified workers. Some 300 occupations are now licensed in Canada.

Inclusive or Industrial Union Model

Instead of trying to limit their membership, however, most unions seek to organize all available workers. This is especially true of the *industrial unions*, such as the Canadian Auto Workers and the United Steelworkers. Such unions seek as members all available unskilled, semiskilled, and skilled workers in an industry. It makes sense for a union to be exclusive when its members are skilled craft workers for whom the employer has few substitutes. But it does not make sense for a union to be exclusive when trying to organize unskilled and semi-skilled workers. To break a strike, employers could then easily substitute unskilled or semi-skilled non-union workers for the unskilled or semi-skilled union workers.

By contrast, an industrial union that includes virtually all available workers in its membership can put firms under great pressure to agree to its wage demands. Because of its legal right to strike, such a union can threaten to deprive firms of their entire labour supply; an actual strike can do just that. Further, with virtually all available workers in the union, it will be difficult in the short run for new non-union firms to emerge and thereby undermine what the union is demanding from existing firms.

We illustrate such **inclusive unionism** in Figure 17-7. Initially, the competitive equilibrium wage rate is W_c and the level of employment is Q_c. Now suppose an industrial union is formed that demands a higher, above-equilibrium wage rate of, say, W_u. That rate would create a perfectly elastic labour supply over the range ae in Figure 17-7. If firms wanted to hire any workers in this range, they would have to pay the union-imposed wage rate. If they decide against meeting this wage demand, the union will supply no labour at all, and the firms will be faced with a strike. If firms decide it is better to pay the higher wage rate than to suffer a strike, they will cut back on employment from Q_c to Q_u.

By agreeing to the union's W_u wage demand, individual employers become wage-takers. Because labour supply is perfectly elastic over range ae, the marginal resource (labour) cost is equal to the wage rate W_u over this range. The Q_u level of employment is the result of employers equating this MFC (now equal to the wage rate) with MRP, according to our profit-maximizing rule.

FIGURE 17-7   Inclusive or Industrial Unionism

By organizing virtually all available workers to control the supply of labour, inclusive industrial unions may impose a wage rate, such as W_u, which is above the competitive wage rate W_c. The effect is to change the labour supply curve from S to aeS. At wage rate W_u, employers will cut employment from Q_c to Q_u.

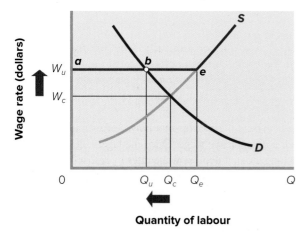

Quantity of labour

Note from point e on labour supply curve S that Q_e workers desire employment at wage W_u. But, as indicated by point b on labour demand curve D, only Q_u workers are employed. The result is a surplus of labour of $Q_e - Q_u$ (also shown by distance eb). In a perfectly competitive labour market without the union, the effect of a surplus of unemployed workers would be lower wages. Specifically, the wage rate would fall to the equilibrium level, W_c, where the quantity of labour supplied equals the quantity of labour demanded (each Q_c). But this drop in wages does not happen because workers are acting collectively through their union. Individual workers cannot offer to work for less than W_u nor can employers pay less than that.

Wage Increases and Job Loss

Have Canadian unions been successful in raising the wages of their members? Evidence suggests that union members on average achieve a 15 percent wage advantage over non-union workers.

As Figures 17-6 and 17-7 show, the effect of wage-raising actions by both exclusive and inclusive unionism is to reduce employment in unionized firms. A union's success in achieving above-equilibrium wage rates thus tends to be accompanied by a decline in the number of workers employed. That result acts as a restraining influence on union wage demands. A union cannot expect to maintain solidarity within its ranks if it seeks a wage rate so high that 20 to 30 percent of its members lose their jobs.

17.5 Bilateral Monopoly Model

LO17.5 **Explain why wages and employment are determined by collective bargaining in a situation of bilateral monopoly.**

Suppose a strong industrial union is formed in a monopsonist labour market rather than a competitive market, creating a combination of the monopsony model and the inclusive unionism model. Economists call the result **bilateral monopoly** because there is a single seller and a single buyer. The union is a monopolistic "seller" of labour that controls labour supply and can influence wage rates, but it faces a monopsonistic "buyer" of labour that can also affect wages by altering its employment. This is not an uncommon case, particularly in less-pure forms in which a single union confronts two, three, or four large employers, such as steel, automobiles, construction equipment, and professional sports.

Indeterminate Outcome of Bilateral Monopoly

We show this situation in Figure 17-8, where Figure 17-7 is superimposed onto Figure 17-4. The monopsonistic employer will seek the below-competitive-equilibrium wage rate W_m, and the union will press for some above-competitive-equilibrium wage rate such as W_u. Which will be the outcome? We cannot say with certainty, because the bilateral monopoly model does not explain what will happen at the collective bargaining table. We can expect the wage outcome to lie somewhere between W_m and W_u. Beyond that, about all we can say is that the party with the greater bargaining power and the more effective negotiating strategy will probably get a wage closer to the one it seeks.

Desirability of Bilateral Monopoly

The wage and employment outcomes in this situation might be more economically desirable than the term "bilateral monopoly" implies. The monopoly on one side of the market might in effect cancel out the monopoly on the other side, yielding competitive or near-competitive results. If either the union or management prevailed in this market—that is, if the actual wage rate were either W_u or W_m—employment would be restricted to Q_m (where MRP = MFC), which is below the competitive level.

But now suppose the monopoly power of the union roughly offsets the monopsony power of management, and the union and management agree on wage rate W_c, which is the competitive wage. Once management accepts this wage rate, its incentive to restrict employment disappears; no longer can it depress wage rates by restricting employment. Instead, management hires at the most profitable resource quantity, where the bargained wage rate W_c (which is now the firm's MFC) is equal to the MRP. It hires Q_c workers. Thus, with monopoly on both sides of the labour market, the resulting wage rate and level of employment may be closer to competitive levels than would be the case if monopoly existed on only one side of the market.

FIGURE 17-8   Bilateral Monopoly in the Labour Market

A monopsonist seeks to hire Q_m workers (where MFC = MRP) and pay wage rate W_m corresponding to Q_m labour on labour supply curve S. The inclusive union it faces seeks the above-equilibrium wage rate W_u. The actual outcome cannot be predicted by economic theory. It will result from bargaining between the two parties.

QUICK REVIEW 17.2

- In the demand-enhancement union model, a union increases the wage rate by increasing labour demand through actions that increase product demand, or alter the prices of related inputs.

- In the exclusive (craft) union model, a union increases wage rates by artificially restricting labour supply, through, say, long apprenticeships or occupational licensing.

- In the inclusive (industrial) union model, a union raises the wage rate by gaining control over a firm's labour supply and threatening to withhold labour via a strike unless a negotiated wage is obtained.

- Bilateral monopoly occurs in a labour market where a monopsonist bargains with an inclusive, or industrial, union. Wage and employment outcomes are determined by collective bargaining in this situation.

17.6 The Minimum Wage Controversy

LO17.6   Discuss how minimum wage laws affect labour markets.

In Canada both the federal and provincial governments have enacted **minimum wage** legislation, but it is the provincial laws that cover most workers. The provincial minimum wage ranges from $10.85 per hour in Nova Scotia to $15 per hour in Alberta and Ontario. The purpose of the minimum wage is to provide a "wage floor" that will help less-skilled workers earn enough income to escape poverty.

Case Against the Minimum Wage

Critics, reasoning in terms of Figure 17-7, contend that an above-equilibrium minimum wage (say W_u) will cause employers to hire fewer workers. In other words, increasing the minimum wage leads to a decrease in the number of people employed at that wage. Downsloping labour demand curves are a reality. The higher labour costs may even force some firms out of business. Then, some of the poor, low-wage workers whom the minimum wage was designed to help will find themselves out of work. Critics point out that a worker who is *unemployed* at a minimum wage of $15 per hour is clearly worse off than if *employed* at a market wage rate of, say, $13 per hour.

A second criticism of the minimum wage is that it is "poorly targeted" to reduce household poverty. Critics point out that much of the benefit of the minimum wage accrues to workers, including many teenagers, who do not live in impoverished households.

Case for the Minimum Wage

Advocates of the minimum wage say that critics analyze its impact in an unrealistic context. Figure 17-7, advocates claim, assumes a competitive, static market. But in a less competitive, low-pay labour market where employers possess some monopsony power (Figure 17-8), the minimum wage can increase wage rates without causing significant unemployment. Indeed, a higher minimum wage may even produce more jobs by eliminating the motive that monopsonistic firms have for restricting employment. For example, a minimum wage floor of W_c in Figure 17-8 would change the firm's labour supply curve to $W_c aS$ and prompt the firm to increase its employment from Q_m workers to Q_c workers.

Moreover, even if the labour market is competitive, the higher wage rate might prompt firms to find more productive tasks for low-paid workers, thereby raising their productivity. Alternatively, the minimum wage may reduce *labour turnover* (the rate at which workers voluntarily quit). With fewer low-productive trainees, the *average* productivity of the firm's workers would rise. In either case, the alleged negative employment effects of the minimum wage might not occur.

Evidence and Conclusions

Which view is correct? Unfortunately, there is no clear answer. All economists agree that firms will not hire workers who cost more per hour in *real* terms than the value of their hourly output. So some minimum real wage is sufficiently high—say, $20 an hour—that it would severely reduce employment. Consider $30 an hour, as an absurd example. Because the majority of Canadian workers earned less than $20 per hour in 2018, a minimum wage of $30 per hour would render the majority of them unemployable because the minimum wage that they would have to be paid by potential employers would far exceed their marginal revenue products.

Remember that a minimum wage will only cause unemployment in labour markets where the minimum wage is higher than the equilibrium wage. Because the average provincial minimum wage of about $12 per hour is much lower than the average hourly wage of about $27 that was earned by Canadian workers in 2017, any unemployment caused by the $12 per hour minimum wage is most likely to fall on low-skilled workers who earn low wages due to their low productivity. These workers are mostly teenagers, adults who did not complete high school, and immigrants with low levels of education and poor English proficiency. For members of such groups, recent research suggests that a 10 percent increase in the minimum wage will cause a 1–3 percent decline in employment. However, estimates of the employment effect of minimum wage laws vary from study to study so that significant controversy remains.

The overall effect of the minimum wage is thus uncertain. On the one hand, the employment and unemployment effects of the minimum wage do not appear to be as great as many critics fear. On the other hand, because a large part of its effect is dissipated on families not experiencing poverty, the minimum wage is not as strong an antipoverty tool as many supporters contend.

Voting patterns and surveys make it clear, however, that the minimum wage has strong political support. Perhaps this stems from two realities: (1) More workers are believed to be helped than hurt by the minimum wage and (2) the minimum wage gives society some assurance that employers are not "taking undue advantage" of vulnerable, low-skilled workers.

17.7 Wage Differentials

LO17.7   List the major causes of wage differentials.

Hourly real wage rates and annual salaries differ greatly among occupations. In Table 17-3 we list average weekly wages for several industries to illustrate such occupational **wage differentials**. For example, observe that construction workers on average earn one-third more than those workers in the health and social service industry. Large wage differentials also exist within some of the occupations listed (not shown). For example, although average wages for retail salespersons are relatively low, some top salespersons selling on commission make several times the average wages for their occupation.

What explains wage differentials such as these? Once again, the forces of demand and supply are revealing. As we demonstrate in Figure 17-9, wage differentials can arise on either the supply or demand side of labour markets.

TABLE 17-3	Average Weekly Wages in Selected Industries, October 2014
Industry	**Average weekly earnings (including overtime)**
All industries	**$ 983.00**
Mining, and oil and gas extraction	2050.19
Construction	1239.70
Finance, insurance, and real estate	1326.57
Manufacturing	1097.69
Logging and forestry	1101.71
Transportation and warehousing	1040.70
Educational and related services	1050.58
Real estate services	997.80
Health and social services	892.24

Source: Data from Statistics Canada. http://www.statcan.gc.ca/tables-tableaux/sum-som/l01/cst01/labor93a-eng.htm. Accessed December 27, 2017.

Figures 17-9a and 17-9b represent labour markets for two occupational groups that have identical *labour supply curves*. The labour market in panel (a) has a relatively high equilibrium wage (W_a) because labour demand is very strong. The labour market in panel (b) has an equilibrium wage that is relatively low (W_b) since labour demand is weak. Clearly, the wage differential between occupations (a) and (b) results solely from differences in the magnitude of labour demand.

Contrast that situation with Figure 17-9c and 17-9d, where the *labour demand curves* are identical. In the labour market in panel (c), the equilibrium wage is relatively high (W_c) because labour supply is low. In the labour market in panel (d) labour supply is highly abundant, so the equilibrium wage (W_d) is relatively low. The wage differential between (c) and (d) results solely from the differences in the magnitude of the labour supply.

Although Figure 17-9 provides a good starting point for understanding wage differentials, we need to know *why* demand and supply conditions differ in various labour markets.

Marginal Revenue Productivity

The strength of labour demand—how far to the right the labour demand curve is located—differs greatly among occupations because of differences in how much various occupational groups contribute to their employers' revenue. This revenue contribution, in turn, depends on the workers' productivity and the strength of the demand for the products they are helping to produce. Where labour is highly productive and product demand is strong, labour demand also is strong and, other things equal, pay is high. Top professional athletes, for example, are highly productive at sports entertainment, for which millions of people are willing to pay billions of dollars over the course of a season. Because the **marginal revenue productivity** of these players is so high, they are in very high demand by sports teams. This high demand leads to their extremely high salaries (as in Figure 17-9a). In contrast, most workers generate much more modest revenue for their employers. This results in much lower demand for their labour and, consequently, much lower wages (as in Figure 17-9b).

Noncompeting Groups

On the supply side of the labour market, workers are not homogeneous; they differ in their mental and physical capabilities and in their education and training. At any given time the labour force is made up of many **noncompeting groups** of workers, each representing several occupations for which the members of a particular group qualify. In some groups qualified workers are relatively few, whereas in others they are highly abundant. Workers in one group do not qualify for the occupations of other groups.

FIGURE 17-9   Labour Demand, Labour Supply, and Wage Differentials

Wage differentials in labour markets are caused by varying supply and demand conditions. (a) and (b) Because the labour supply curves S_a and S_b are identical in the labour markets depicted in the two top graphs, differences in demand are the sole cause of the the $W_a - W_b$ wage differential. (c) and (d) Because the labour demand curves D_c and D_d are identical in the bottom two graphs, the $W_c - W_d$ wage differential results solely from differences in labour supply.

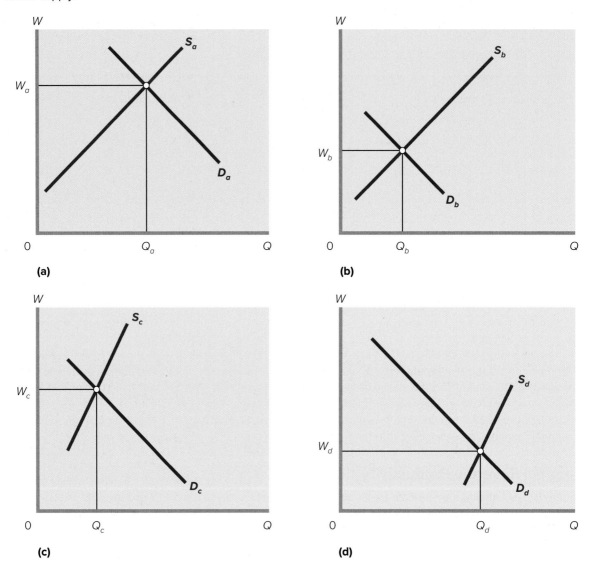

ABILITY

Only a few workers have the ability or physical attributes to be brain surgeons, concert violinists, top fashion models, research scientists, or professional athletes. Because the supply of these particular types of labour is very small in relation to labour demand, their wages are high, as in Figure 17-9c. The members of these and similar groups do not compete with one another or with other skilled or semi-skilled workers. The violinist does not compete with the surgeon, nor does the surgeon compete with the professional athlete or the fashion model.

The concept of noncompeting groups can be applied to various subgroups and even to individuals in a particular group. An especially skilled violinist can command a higher salary than colleagues who play the same instrument. A handful of top corporate executives earn ten to twenty times as much as the average chief

CONSIDER THIS

My Entire Life

Human capital is the accumulation of outcomes of prior investments in education, training, and other factors that increase productivity and earnings. It is the stock of knowledge, know-how, and skills that enables individuals to be productive and thus earn income. A valuable stock of human capital, together with a strong demand for one's services, can add up to a large capacity to earn income. For some people, high earnings have little to do with actual hours of work and much to do

with their tremendous skill, which reflects their accumulated stock of human capital.

The point is demonstrated in the following story: It is said that a tourist once spotted the famous Spanish artist Pablo Picasso (1881–1973) in a Paris café. The tourist asked him if he would do a sketch of his wife for pay. Picasso sketched the wife in a matter of minutes and said, "That will be 10,000 francs [roughly $2000]." Hearing the high price, the tourist became irritated, saying, "But that took you only a few minutes."

"No," replied Picasso, "it took me my entire life!"

Source: Reunion des Musées Nationaux/Art Resource, NY © Estate of Pablo Picasso/Artists Right Society (ARS), New York.

executive officer. In each of these cases, the supply of top talent is highly limited, since less talented colleagues are only imperfect substitutes.

EDUCATION AND TRAINING

Another source of wage differentials is differing amounts of **human capital**, which is the personal stock of knowledge, know-how, and skills that enables a person to be productive and thus to earn income. Such stocks result from investments in human capital. Like expenditures on machinery and equipment, productivity-enhancing expenditures on education or training are investments. In both cases, people incur *present costs* with the intention that those expenditures will lead to a greater flow of *future earnings*.

Although education yields higher incomes, it carries substantial costs. A college or university education involves not only direct costs (tuition, fees, books) but also indirect or opportunity costs (forgone earnings). Does the higher pay received by better-educated workers compensate for these costs? The answer is yes. Rates of return are estimated to be 10–13 percent for investments in secondary education and 8–12 percent for investments in college and university education. One generally accepted estimate is that each year of schooling raises a worker's wage by about 8 percent.

Compensating Differences

If the workers in a particular noncompeting group are equally capable of performing several different jobs, you might expect the wage rates to be identical for all these jobs. Not so. A group of high-school graduates may be equally capable of becoming sales clerks or construction workers, but these jobs pay different wages. In virtually all locales, construction labourers receive much higher wages than sales clerks. These wage differentials are called **compensating differences**, because they must be paid to compensate for nonmonetary differences in various jobs.

The construction job involves dirty working conditions, the hazard of accidents, and irregular employment. The retail sales job means clean clothing, pleasant, air-conditioned surroundings, and less fear of injury or layoff. Other things equal, it is easy to see why some workers would rather pick up a credit card than a shovel. So labour supply is less for construction firms, as in Figure 17-9c, than for retail shops, as in Figure 17-9d. Construction firms must pay higher wages than retailers to compensate for the unattractive aspects of construction jobs.

Such compensating differences spring up throughout the economy. Other things equal, jobs having high risk of injury or death pay more than comparable, safer jobs. Jobs lacking employer-paid health insurance, pensions, and vacation time pay more than comparable jobs that provide these fringe benefits. Jobs with more flexible hours pay less than jobs with rigid work-hour requirements. Jobs with greater risk of unemployment pay more than comparable jobs with little unemployment risk. Entry-level jobs in occupations that provide very poor prospects for pay advancement pay more than entry-level jobs that have clearly defined "job ladders."

These and other compensating differences play an important role in allocating society's scarce labour resources. If very few workers want to be garbage collectors, society must pay high wages to attract garbage collectors. If many more people want to be sales clerks than are needed, society need not pay them as much as garbage collectors to get those services performed.

Market Imperfections

Differences in marginal revenue productivity, amounts of human capital, and nonmonetary aspects of jobs explain most of the wage differentials in the economy. But other persistent differentials result from various market imperfections that impede workers moving from lower-paying jobs to higher-paying jobs.

- *Lack of Job Information* Workers may simply be unaware of job opportunities and wage rates in other geographic areas and in other jobs for which they qualify. Consequently, the flow of qualified labour from lower-paying to higher-paying jobs may not be sufficient to equalize wages within occupations.

- *Geographic Immobility* Many workers are reluctant to move to new places, to leave friends, relatives, and associates, to force their children to change schools, to sell their houses, or to incur the costs and inconveniences of adjusting to a new job and a new community. As Adam Smith noted more than two centuries ago, "A [person] is of all sorts of luggage the most difficult to be transported." The reluctance of workers to move creates persistent geographic wage differentials within the same occupation. Some economists point out that Canada's employment insurance program contributes to labour immobility.

- *Unions and Government Restraints* Wage differentials may be reinforced by artificial restrictions on mobility imposed by unions and government. We have noted that craft unions keep their wages high by restricting membership. Thus, the low-paid non-union carpenter of Edmonton, Alberta, may be willing to move to Vancouver in the pursuit of higher wages, but her chances of succeeding are slim. She may be unable to get a union card, and no card means no job. Similarly, an optometrist or lawyer qualified to practise in one province may not meet the licensing requirements of other provinces, so his ability to move is limited. Other artificial barriers involve pension plans and seniority rights that might be jeopardized by moving from one job to another.

- *Discrimination* Despite legislation to combat the stuation, discrimination results in lower wages being paid to women and visible-minority workers than to white males doing virtually identical work. Also, women and minorities may be crowded into certain low-paying occupations, driving down wages there and raising them elsewhere. If discrimination keeps qualified women and minorities from taking the higher-paying jobs, differences in pay will persist.

All four considerations—differences in marginal revenue productivity, noncompeting groups, compensating differences, and market imperfections—come into play in explaining actual real wage differentials. For example, the differential between the wages of a physician and those of a construction worker can be explained based on marginal revenue productivity and noncompeting groups. Physicians generate considerable revenue because of their high productivity and the strong willingness of consumers (via provincial governments) to pay for health care. Physicians also fall into a noncompeting group where, because of stringent training requirements, only a relatively few persons qualify. So the supply of labour is small in relation to demand.

In construction work, where training requirements are much less significant, the supply of labour is great relative to demand. So wages are much lower for construction workers than for physicians. However, if not for the unpleasantness of the construction worker's job and the fact that his or her craft union observes restrictive membership policies, the differential would be even greater than it is.

17.8 Pay for Performance

LO17.8   Identify the types, benefits, and costs of pay-for-performance plans.

The models of wage determination we have described in this chapter assume that worker pay is always a standard amount for each hour's work, for example $15 per hour. But pay schemes are often more complex than that in both composition and purpose. For instance, many workers receive annual salaries rather than hourly pay. Many workers also receive fringe benefits: dental insurance, life insurance, paid vacations, paid sick-leave days, pension contributions, and so on. Finally, some pay plans are designed to elicit a desired level of performance from workers. This last aspect of pay plans requires further elaboration.

The Principal–Agent Problem

The **principal–agent problem** is usually associated with the possible differences in the interests of corporate shareholders (principals) and the executives (agents) they hire. But this problem extends to all paid employees. Firms hire workers to help produce the goods and services the firms sell for a profit. Workers are the firms' agents; they are hired to advance the interest (profit) of the firms. The principals are the firms; they hire agents to advance their goals. Firms and workers have one interest in common: They both want the firm to survive and thrive. That will ensure profit for the firm and continued employment and wages for the workers.

But the interests of the firm and of the workers are not identical. A principal–agent problem arises when those interests diverge. Workers may seek to increase their utility by shirking on the job, that is, by providing less than the agreed-on effort or by taking unauthorized breaks. The night security guard in a warehouse may leave work early or spend time reading a novel rather than making the assigned rounds. A salaried manager may spend time away from the office visiting friends rather than attending to company business.

Firms (principals) have a profit incentive to reduce or eliminate shirking. One option is to monitor workers, but monitoring is difficult and costly. Hiring another worker to supervise or monitor the security guard might double the cost of maintaining a secure warehouse. Another way of resolving the principal–agent problem is through some sort of **incentive pay plan** that ties worker compensation more closely to output or performance. Such incentive pay schemes include piece rates, commissions and royalties, bonuses and profit sharing, and efficiency wages.

PIECE RATES

Piece rates are compensation paid according to the number of units of output a worker produces. If a principal pays fruit pickers by the bushel or typists by the page, it need not be concerned with shirking or with monitoring costs.

COMMISSIONS OR ROYALTIES

Unlike piece rates, commissions and royalties tie compensation to the value of sales. Employees who sell products or services—including real estate agents, insurance agents, stockbrokers, and retail salespersons—commonly receive *commissions* that are computed as a percentage of the monetary value of their sales. Recording artists and authors are paid *royalties*, computed as a certain percentage of sales revenues from their works. These types of compensation link the financial interests of the salespeople or artists and authors to the profit interest of the firms.

BONUSES, STOCK OPTIONS, AND PROFIT SHARING

Bonuses are payments in addition to one's annual salary that are based on some factor such as the performance of the individual worker, or of a group of workers, or of the firm itself. A professional baseball player may receive a bonus based on a high batting average, the number of home runs hit, or the number of runs batted in. A business manager may receive a bonus based on the profitability of her or his unit. *Stock options* allow workers to buy shares of their employer's stock at a fixed price. If the firm does well and its stock prices rise, the workers' stock holdings rise in value. Such options are part of the compensation packages of top corporate officials, as well as many workers in relatively new high-technology firms. *Profit-sharing plans* allocate a percentage of a firm's profit to its employees. Such plans have in recent years resulted in large annual payments to many Canadian workers.

EFFICIENCY WAGES

The rationale behind *efficiency wages* is that employers will enjoy greater effort from their workers by paying them above-equilibrium wage rates. Glance back at Figure 17-3, which shows a competitive labour market in which the equilibrium wage rate is $10. What if an employer decides to pay an above-equilibrium wage of $12 per hour? Rather than putting the firm at a cost disadvantage compared with rival firms paying only $10, the higher wage might improve worker effort and productivity so that unit labour costs actually fall. For example, if each worker produces ten units of output per hour at the $12 wage rate compared with only six units at the $10 wage rate, unit labour costs for the high-wage firm will be only $1.20 (= $12/10) compared to $1.67 (= $10/6) for firms paying the equilibrium wage.

An above-equilibrium wage may enhance worker efficiency in several ways. It enables the firm to attract higher-quality workers. It lifts worker morale. And it lowers turnover, resulting in a more experienced workforce, greater worker productivity, and lower recruitment and training costs. Because the opportunity cost of losing a higher-higher-wage job is greater, workers are more likely to put forth their best efforts with less supervision and monitoring. In fact, efficiency wage payments have proved effective for many employers.

Addenda: The Negative Side Effects of Pay for Performance

Although pay for performance may help to overcome the principal–agent problem and enhance worker productivity, such plans may have negative side effects and so require careful design. Here are a few examples:

- The rapid production pace that piece rates encourage may result in poor product quality and may compromise the safety of workers. Such outcomes can be costly to the firm over the long run.

- Commissions may cause some salespeople to engage in questionable or even fraudulent sales practices, such as making exaggerated claims about products or recommending unneeded repairs. Such practices may lead to private lawsuits or government legal action.

- Bonuses based on personal performance may disrupt the close cooperation needed for maximum team production. A professional hockey player who receives a bonus for goals scored may be reluctant to pass the puck to teammates.

- Since profit sharing is usually tied to the performance of the entire firm, less energetic workers can free-ride by obtaining their profit share based on the hard work of others.

- Stock options may prompt some unscrupulous executives to manipulate the cost and revenue streams of their firms to create a false appearance of rapidly rising profit. When the firm's stock value rises, the executives exercise their stock options at inflated share prices and reap a personal fortune.

- There may be a downside to the reduced turnover resulting from above-market wages. Firms that pay efficiency wages have fewer opportunities to hire new workers and suffer the loss of the creative energy that new workers often bring to the workplace.

QUICK REVIEW 17.3

- Proponents of the minimum wage argue that it is needed to assist the working poor and to counter monopsony where it might exist; critics say that it is poorly targeted to reduce poverty and that it reduces employment.

- Wage differentials are generally attributable to the forces of supply and demand, influenced by differences in workers' marginal revenue productivity, workers' education and skills, and nonmonetary differences in jobs. Several labour market imperfections also play a role.

- As it applies to labour, the principal–agent problem is one of workers pursuing their own interests to the detriment of the employer's profit objective.

- Pay-for-performance plans (piece rates, commissions, royalties, bonuses, stock options, and profit sharing) are designed to improve worker productivity by overcoming the principal–agent problem.

Are Top Executives in Canada Overpaid?

© Peter Weber/Getty Images

The multimillion-dollar pay of major corporate CEOs has drawn considerable criticism.

THE FIVE HIGHEST-PAID CANADIAN CEOs, 2017*

Name	Company	Total pay (in millions)
1. Michael Pearson	Valeant Pharmaceuticals Inc.	$182.9
2. Donald J. Walker	Magna International	$ 26.1
3. Hunter Harrison	Canadian Pacific Railways Ltd.	$ 19.9
4. Steve Hudson	Element Financial	$ 19.3
5. Mark Barrenechea	Open Text	$ 18.0

Top executives of Canadian corporations typically receive total annual pay (salary, bonuses, and stock options) in the millions of dollars. As shown in the table, each of the five highest-paid Canadian executives earned more than $18 million in 2017. The highest-paid CEO earned over $180 million!

CEO pay in Canada is not only exceptionally high relative to the average pay of Canadian managers and workers, but is also the second-highest CEO pay among industrialized countries (surpassed only by CEO pay in the U.S.). Mark Lore of Walmart, who was among the highest-paid CEOs in the U.S. in 2016, was paid US$236.9 million; Tim Cooke, of Apple, received a total of US$150 million.

Is high CEO pay simply the outcome of labour supply and labour demand, as is the pay for star athletes and entertainers? Does it reflect marginal revenue productivity—that is, the contributions by CEOs to their company's output and revenue?

Observers who answer affirmatively point out that decisions made by the CEOs of large corporations affect the productivity of every employee in the organization. Good decisions enhance productivity throughout the organization and increase revenue; bad decisions reduce productivity and revenue. Only executives who have consistently made good business decisions attain the top positions in large corporations. Because the supply of these people is highly limited and their marginal revenue productivity is enormous, top CEOs command huge salaries and performance bonuses.

Also, some economists note that CEO pay in Canada may be like the prizes professional golfers and tennis players receive for winning tournaments. These valuable prizes are designed to promote the productivity of all those who aspire to achieve them. In corporations the top prizes go to the winners of the "contests" among managers to attain, at least eventually, the CEO positions. Thus high CEO pay does not derive solely from the CEO's direct productivity. Instead, it may exist because the high pay creates incentives that raise the productivity of scores of other corporate executives who seek to achieve the top position. In this view, high CEO pay is still based on high productivity.

Critics of existing CEO pay acknowledge that CEOs deserve substantially higher salaries than ordinary workers or typical managers, but they question pay packages that run into the millions of dollars. They reject the "tournament pay" idea on the grounds that corporations require cooperative team effort by managers and executives, not the type of high-stakes competition promoted by "winner take most" pay. They believe that corporations, although owned by their shareholders, are controlled by corporate boards and professional executives. Because many board members are present or past CEOs of other corporations, they often exaggerate CEO importance, and consequently overpay their own CEOs, at the expense of the firm's shareholders.

In summary, defenders of CEO pay say that high pay is justified by the direct or indirect marginal revenue contribution of CEOs. Like it or not, CEO pay is market-determined pay. In contrast, critics say that multimillion-dollar CEO pay bears little relationship to marginal revenue productivity and is unfair to ordinary shareholders. It is clear from our discussion that these issues remain unsettled.

Source for salary data: "Canada's Top 100 Highest-Paid CEOs," *Canadian Business*, January 2, 2018, http://www.canadianbusiness.com/lists-and-rankings/richest-people/canada-100-highest-paid-ceos. Accessed December 27, 2017.

Question

Do you think exceptionally high pay to CEOs is economically justified? Why or why not?

Chapter Summary

LO17.1   Explain why labour productivity and real hourly compensation track so closely over time.

- The term *labour* encompasses all people who work for pay. The wage rate is the price paid per unit of time for labour. Labour earnings comprise total pay and are found by multiplying the number of hours worked by the hourly wage rate. The nominal wage rate is the amount of money received per unit of time; the real wage rate is the purchasing power of the nominal wage.

- The long-run growth of real hourly earnings—the average real wage—roughly matches that of productivity, with both increasing over the long run.

- Global comparisons suggest that real wages in Canada are relatively high, but not the highest internationally. High real wages in the advanced industrial countries stem largely from high labour productivity.

LO17.2   Show how wages rates and employment are determined in a competitive labour market.

- Specific wage rates depend on the structure of the particular labour market. In a competitive labour market, the equilibrium wage rate and level of employment are determined at the intersection of the labour supply curve and labour demand curve. For the individual firm, the market wage rate establishes a horizontal labour supply curve, meaning that the wage rate equals the firm's constant marginal resource cost. The firm hires workers to the point where its MRP equals this MFC.

LO17.3   Demonstrate how monopsony (a market with a single employer) can reduce wages below competitive levels.

- Under monopsony the MFC curve lies above the factor supply curve because the monopsonist must bid up the wage rate to hire extra workers and must pay that higher wage rate to all workers. The monopsonist hires fewer workers than are hired under competitive conditions, pays less-than-competitive wage rates (has lower labour costs), and thus obtains greater profit.

LO17.4   Discuss how unions increase wage rates by pursuing the demand-enhancement model, the craft union model, or the industrial union model.

- A union may raise competitive wage rates by (a) increasing the derived demand for labour, (b) restricting the supply of labour through exclusive unionism, or (c) directly enforcing an above-equilibrium wage rate through inclusive unionism.

LO17.5   Explain why wages and employment are determined by collective bargaining in a situation of bilateral monopoly.

- In many industries the labour market takes the form of bilateral monopoly, in which a strong union sells labour to a monopsonistic employer. The wage-rate outcome of this labour market model depends on union and employer bargaining power.

LO17.6   Discuss how minimum wage laws affect labour markets.

- On average, unionized workers realize wage rates 15 percent higher than those of comparable non-union workers.

- Economists disagree about the desirability of the minimum wage as an antipoverty mechanism. While it causes unemployment for some low-income workers, it raises the incomes of those who retain their jobs.

LO17.7   List the major causes of wage differentials.

- Wage differentials are largely explainable in terms of (a) marginal revenue productivity of various groups of workers; (b) noncompeting groups arising from differences in the capacities and education of different groups of workers; (c) compensating differences, that is, wage differences that must be paid to offset nonmonetary differences in jobs; and (d) market imperfections in the form of lack of job information, geographical immobility, union and government restraints, and discrimination.

LO17.8   Identify the types, benefits, and costs of pay-for-performance plans.

- As it applies to labour, the principal–agent problem arises when workers provide less than the expected effort. Firms may combat this by monitoring workers or by creating incentive pay schemes that link worker compensation to performance.

Terms and Concepts

wage rate
nominal wage
real wage
perfectly competitive labour market
monopsony
exclusive unionism
occupational licensing
inclusive unionism
bilateral monopoly

minimum wage
wage differentials
marginal revenue productivity
noncompeting groups
human capital
compensating differences
principal–agent problem
incentive pay plan

Discussion Questions

1. Explain why the general level of wages is high in Canada and other industrially advanced countries. What is the single most important factor underlying the long-run increase in average real-wage rates in Canada?   [**LO17.1**]

2. Why is a firm in a perfectly competitive labour market a wage-taker? What would happen if that firm decided to pay less than the going market wage rate?   [**LO17.2**]

3. Describe wage determination in a labour market in which workers are unorganized and many firms actively compete for the services of labour. Show this situation graphically, using W_1 to indicate the equilibrium wage rate and Q_1 to show the number of workers hired by the firms as a group. Show the labour supply curve of the individual firm and compare it with that of the total market. Why are there differences? In the diagram representing the firm, identify total revenue, total wage cost, and revenue available for the payment of non-labour resources.   [**LO17.2**]

4. Suppose the formerly competing firms in question 3 form an employers' association that hires labour as a monopsonist would. Describe verbally the effect on wage rates and employment. Adjust the graph you drew for question 3, showing the monopsonistic wage rate and employment level as W_2 and Q_2, respectively. Using this monopsony model, explain why hospital administrators sometimes

complain about a shortage of nurses. How might such a shortage be corrected?   [**LO17.3**]

5. Assume a monopsonistic employer is paying a wage rate of Wm and hiring Q_m workers, as indicated in Figure 17-8. Now suppose an industrial union is formed that forces the employer to accept a wage rate of W_c. Explain verbally and graphically why in this instance the higher wage rate will be accompanied by an increase in the number of workers hired.   [**LO17.5**]

6. Have you ever worked for the minimum wage? If so, for how long? Would you favour increasing the minimum wage by a dollar? By two dollars? By five dollars? Explain your reasoning.   [**LO17.6**]

7. "Many of the lowest-paid people in society—for example, short-order cooks—also have relatively poor working conditions. Hence, the notion of compensating wage differentials is disproved." Do you agree? Explain.   [**LO17.7**]

8. What is meant by *investment in human capital*? Use this concept to explain (a) wage differentials and (b) the long-run rise of real wage rates in Canada.   [**LO17.7**]

9. What is the principal–agent problem? Have you ever worked in a setting where this problem arose? If so, do you think increased monitoring would have eliminated the problem? Why don't firms simply hire more supervisors to eliminate shirking?   [**LO17.8**]

Review Questions

1. Brenda owns a construction company that employs bricklayers and other skilled tradesmen. Her firm's MRP for bricklayers is $22.25 per hour for each of the first seven bricklayers, $18.50 for an eighth brick layer, and $17.75 for a ninth bricklayer. Given that she is a price-taker when hiring bricklayers, how many bricklayers will she hire if the market equilibrium wage for bricklayers is $18 per hour?   [**LO17.2**]

   a. Zero

   b. Seven

   c. Eight

   d. Nine

   e. More information is required to answer this question

2. Because a perfectly competitive employer's MFC curve is _____, it will hire _____ workers than would a monoposony employer with the same MRP curve.   [**LO17.3**]

   a. Upsloping; more

   b. Upsloping; fewer

   c. Flat; more

   d. Flat; fewer

   e. Downsloping; more

   f. Downsloping; fewer

3. True or False? When a labour market consists of a single monopsony buyer of labour interacting with a single monopoly seller of labour (such as a trade union), the resulting quantity of labour that is hired will always be inefficiently low.   [**LO17.3**]

4. The market equilibrium wage is currently $12 per hour among hairdressers. At that wage, 17,323 hairdressers are currently employed in the province. The provincial legislature then sets a minimum wage of $11.50 per hour for hairdressers. If there are no changes to either the demand or supply for hairdressers when that minimum wage is imposed, the number of hairdressers employed in the province will be   [**LO17.6**]

   a. Fewer than 17,323

   b. Still 17,323

   c. More than 17,323

   d. This is a bilateral monopsony so you can't tell

5. On average, 50-year-old workers are paid several times more than workers in their teens and twenties. Which of the following options is the most likely explanation for that huge difference in average earnings?   [**LO17.7**]

   a. Older workers have more human capital and higher MRPs.

   b. Employers engage in widespread discrimination against younger workers.

   c. Young people lack information about the existence of the high-paying jobs occupied by older workers.

   d. Older workers receive compensating differences because they do jobs that are more risky than the jobs done by younger workers.

6. Manny owns a local fast-food franchise. Angel runs it for him. So in this situation, Manny is the _____ and Angel is the _____.   [**LO17.8**]

   a. Free rider; entrepreneur

   b. Agent; principal

   c. Principal; agent

   d. Producer; consumer

7. A principal is worried that her agent may not do what she wants. As a solution, she should consider   [**LO17.8**]

   a. Commissions

   b. Bonuses

   c. Profit sharing

   d. All of the above

Problems

1. Workers are compensated by firms with *benefits* in addition to wages and salaries. The most prominent benefit offered by many firms is health insurance. Suppose that, in 2000, workers at one steel plant were paid $20 per hour and in addition received health benefits at the rate of $4 per hour. Also suppose that, by 2010, workers at that plant were paid $21 per hour but received $9 in health insurance benefits.   [**LO17.1**]

   a. By what percentage did total compensation (wages plus benefits) change at this plant from 2000 to 2010? What was the approximate average annual percentage change in total compensation?

   b. By what percentage did wages change at this plant from 2000 to 2010? What was the approximate average annual percentage change in wages?

   c. If workers value a dollar of health benefits as much as they value a dollar of wages, by what total percentage will they feel that their incomes have risen over this time period? What if they only consider wages when calculating their incomes?

   d. Is it possible for workers to feel as though their wages are stagnating even if total compensation is rising?

2. Complete the following labour supply table for a firm hiring labour competitively: [**LO17.2**]

Units of labour	Wage rate	Total labour cost	Marginal factor (labour) cost
0	$14	$_____	
1	14	_____	$_____
2	14	_____	_____
3	14	_____	_____
4	14	_____	_____
5	14	_____	_____
6	14	_____	_____

   a. Show graphically the labour supply and marginal factor (labour) cost curves for this firm. Are the curves the same or different? If they are different, which one is higher?

   b. Plot the labour demand data of Review Question 2 in Chapter 16 on the graph used in part (a) above. What are the equilibrium wage rate and level of employment?

3. Assume a firm is a monopsonist that can hire its first worker for $6 but must increase the wage rate by $3 to attract each successive worker (so that the second worker must be paid $9, the third $12, and so on).   [**LO17.3**]

   a. Draw the firm's labour supply and marginal resource cost curves. Are the curves the same or different? If they are different, which one is higher?

   b. On the same graph, plot the labour demand data of Review Question 2 in Chapter 16. What are the equilibrium wage rate and level of employment?

   c. Compare these answers with those you found in Problem 2. By how much does the monoposonist reduce wages below the competitive wage? By how much does the monopsonist reduce employment below the competitive level?

4. Suppose that low-skill workers employed in clearing wood-land can each clear one hectare per month if they are each equipped with a shovel, a machete, and a chainsaw. Clearing one hectare brings in $1000 in revenue. Each worker's equipment costs the worker's employer $150 per month to rent and each worker toils 40 hours per week for four weeks each month.   [**LO17.6**]

   a. What is the marginal revenue product of hiring one low-skill worker to clear woodland for one month?

   b. How much revenue per hour does each worker bring in?

   c. If the minimum wage were $6.20, would the revenue per hour in part (b) exceed the minimum wage? If so, by how much per hour?

   d. Now consider the employer's total costs. These include the equipment costs as well as a normal profit of $50 per acre. If the firm pays workers the minimum wage of $6.20 per hour, what will the firm's economic profit or loss be per acre?

   e. At what value would the minimum wage have to be set so that the firm would make zero economic profit from employing an additional low-skilled worker to clear wood-land?

5. Suppose that a car dealership wishes to see if efficiency wages will help improve its salespeople's productivity. Currently, each salesperson sells an average of one car per day while being paid $20 per hour for an eight-hour day.   [**LO17.8**]

   a. What is the current labour cost per car sold?

   b. Suppose when the dealer raises the price of labour to $30 per hour the average number of cars sold by a salesperson increases to two per day. What is now the labour cost per car sold? By how much is it higher or lower than it was before? Has the efficiency of labour expenditures by the firm (cars sold per dollar of wages paid to salespeople) increased or decreased?

   c. Suppose that if the wage is raised a second time to $40 per hour the number of cars sold rises to an average of 2.5 per day. What is now the labour cost per car sold?

   d. If the firm's goal is to maximize the efficiency of its labour expenditures, which of the three hourly salary rates should it use: $20 per hour, $30 per hour, or $40 per hour?

   e. By contrast, which salary maximizes the productivity of the car dealer's workers (cars sold per worker per day)?

CHAPTER 18

Rent, Interest, and Profit

In Chapter 17, we focused on the wages and salaries paid by firms to obtain labour. Here our attention is focused on the rent, interest, and profit paid by firms to obtain, respectively, land, capital, and entrepreneurship. Our analysis will provide answers to numerous practical questions, including:

- How are *land prices* and *land rents* established, and why do they differ from property to property? For example, why can a hectare of land in the middle of Toronto or Vancouver sell for more than $100 million, while a hectare in northern Ontario may fetch no more than $500?

- What determines *interest rates* and causes them to change? For instance, why were interest rates on three-month guaranteed investment certificates (GICs) 1.3 percent in January 2003, 5.4 percent in June 2006, and only about 1 percent in January 2018? How does interest compound over time, and how does that compounding relate to the present value and future value of a particular sum of money?

- What are the sources of *profits* and *losses*, and why do they vary? For example, why did the Royal Bank of Canada earn a net income of almost $11.5 billion in 2016 while General Motors went bankrupt and needed a government bailout after losing nearly $75 billion between 2007 and 2009?

18.1 Economic Rent

LO18.1 Explain the nature of economic rent and how it is determined.

To most people, *rent* means the money they must pay for the use of an apartment or a room. To the business executive, *rent* is a payment made for the use of a factory building, machine, or warehouse facility owned by others. Such definitions of rent can be confusing and ambiguous, however. On-campus residence rent, for example, may include other payments as well: interest on money the university borrowed to finance the residence, wages for maintenance services, utility payments, and so on.

Economists use *rent* in a much narrower sense. **Economic rent** is the price paid for the use of land and other natural resources that are completely fixed in total supply. As you will see, this fixed overall supply distinguishes rent payments from wage, interest, and profit payments.

Let's examine this idea and some of its implications through supply and demand analysis. We first assume that all land is of the same quality, meaning that each arable (tillable) hectare of land is as productive as every other hectare. We assume, too, that all land has a single use, for example, producing wheat. And we suppose that land is leased in a competitive market in which many producers are demanding land and many landowners are offering land in the market.

In Figure 18-1, curve S represents the supply of arable land available in the economy as a whole, and curve D_2 represents the demand of producers for use of that land. As with all economic resources, the demand for land is a derived demand, meaning that the demand for land is derived from the demand for the products that land helps to produce. Demand curves such as D_2 reflect the marginal revenue product (MRP = MP × P) of land. The curve slopes downward because of diminishing returns (MP declines) and because, for producers as a group, additional units of land result in greater output and lower output prices (P is less).

Perfectly Inelastic Supply

The unique feature of our analysis is on the supply side. For all practical purposes, the supply of land is perfectly inelastic (in both the short run and the long run), as reflected in supply curve S. Land has no production cost; it is a "free and non-reproducible gift of nature." The economy has only so much land, and that's that. Of course, within limits, any parcel of land can be made more usable by clearing, drainage, and irrigation. But these are capital improvements and not changes in the amount of land itself.

FIGURE 18-1 The Determination of Land Rent

Because the supply S of land (and other natural resources) is perfectly inelastic, demand is the sole active determinant of land rent. An increase in demand from D_2 to D_1 or a decrease in demand from D_2 to D_3 will cause a considerable change in rent: from R_2 to R_1 in the first instance and from R_2 to R_3 in the second. But the amount of land supplied will remain at L_0. If demand is very low (D_4) relative to supply, land will be a free good, commanding no rent.

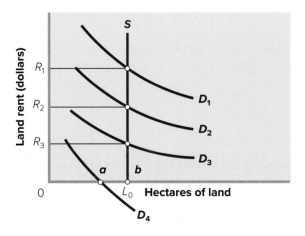

Equilibrium Rent and Changes in Demand

Since the supply of land is fixed, demand is the only determinant of land rent. In this case, supply is passive. And what determines the demand for land? The factors we discussed in Chapter 16 do: the price of the products produced on the land, the productivity of land (which depends in part on the quantity and quality of the factors of production with which land is combined), and the prices of the other factors that are combined with land.

If demand is D_2, as we have suggested, the equilibrium rent will be R_2. The quantity of land L_0 that producers wish to rent will equal the quantity of land available (also L_0). But if the demand for land in Figure 18-1 increased from D_2 to D_1, land rent would rise from R_2 to R_1. If the demand for land declined from D_2 to D_3, land rent would fall from R_2 to R_3. Finally, if the demand for land were only D_4, land rent would be zero. In this situation, land would be a *free good*—a good for which demand is so low relative to supply that there is an excess supply of it even if the market price is zero. In Figure 18-1, we show this excess supply as distance $b - a$ at a rent of zero. This essentially was the situation in the free-land era of Canadian history.

The ideas underlying Figure 18-1 help answer one of our chapter-opening questions. Land prices and rents are very high in central Toronto and Vancouver because the demand for that land is tremendous; it is capable of producing exceptionally high revenue from offices, hotel lodging, and entertainment. In contrast, the demand for isolated land in northern Manitoba is highly limited because very little revenue can be generated from its use. (It is an entirely different matter, of course, if gold can be mined from the land!)

Productivity Differences and Rent Differences

So far, we have assumed that all land is equally productive. That assumption is unrealistic, because land varies widely in terms of productivity. As an example, differences in rainfall, soil quality, and other factors imply that while land in Manitoba is excellently suited to wheat production, the plains of British Columbia are much less well suited, and those of the Yukon are practically useless. Such productivity differences are reflected in resource demands and economic rents. Competitive bidding by producers will establish a high rent for highly productive Manitoba land; less productive British Columbia land will command a lower rent, and the tundra of the Northwest Territories will command no rent at all.

This process whereby differences in productivity lead to differences in rents can be understood graphically if we look at Figure 18-1 from a slightly different perspective. As before, assume that land can only be used for wheat production. But this time assume that there are four different plots of land. Each plot is of the same size L_0 but differs in productivity so that different marginal revenue products emerge when each plot of land is combined with identical amounts of labour, capital, and entrepreneurial talent.

These differences in marginal revenue products lead to four different demand curves: D_1, D_2, D_3, and D_4. D_1 is the highest demand curve because plot 1 has the highest productivity. D_4 is the lowest demand curve because plot 4 has the lowest productivity. When combined with supply curve S, the different demand curves yield different equilibrium rents: R_1, R_2, R_3, and R_4. The differences in rents mirror the differences in productivity so that plot 1 commands the highest rent while plot 4 is so poor in quality that, given supply S, farmers won't pay anything to use it. It will be a free good, because it is not sufficiently scarce in relation to demand for it to command a price above zero.

As a final point, be aware that location itself can affect productivity and rent. Other things equal, renters will pay more for a unit of land that is strategically located with respect to materials, transportation, labour, and customers than they will for a unit of land whose location is remote from these things. Examples include the enormously high land prices near major ski resorts and the high price of land that contains oil beneath it.

Land Rent: A Surplus Payment

The supply of land is perfectly inelastic both in total and with respect to individual parcels of land. Whether land prices rise or fall, a nation will have the same total area to work with and individual plots of land will stay the same size.

The perfectly inelastic supply of land must be contrasted with the relatively elastic supply of non-land resources. Consider capital, which includes apartment buildings, fibre optic networks, and machinery. When the prices of these and other capital goods rise, entrepreneurs respond by increasing the production of capital goods. Conversely, a decline in capital goods prices results in reduced production of capital goods. As a result, the supply curves of non-land resources are normally upward sloping, so that the prices paid to such resources provide an **incentive function**. A high price provides an incentive to offer more of the resource, whereas a low price prompts resource suppliers to offer less.

Not so with unimproved land. Rent serves no incentive function, because both the total area of land in a nation as well as the sizes of individual plots of land will always stay exactly the same no matter what land prices are. As a result, economists consider land rents to be *surplus payments* that are not necessary to ensure that land is made available for economic use. From this perspective, the sum of all the land rents paid across a nation constitutes a giant surplus payment because it has no effect on the total supply of land in the nation. And in the same way, the individual land rents paid on particular plots of land are also surplus payments because they likewise have no effect on the sizes of those individual plots.

Land Ownership: Fairness Versus Allocative Efficiency

If land is a gift of nature, costs nothing to produce, and would be available even without rental payments, why should rent be paid to those who just happen to be landowners? Socialists have long argued that all land rents are unearned incomes, because the act of owning land and renting it out to others produces nothing of value in and of itself. They urge that land should be nationalized (owned by the state) so that any payment for its use can be put to work by the government to further the well-being of the entire population.

Opponents of land nationalization argue that private land ownership allows Adam Smith's invisible hand to work its magic in terms of allocating scarce land resources to their best possible uses. In a nation where land is privately owned and rents are charged for the use of land, individuals and firms are forced to consider opportunity costs when deciding whether to secure the use of a particular piece of land. This gives them an incentive to allocate each piece of land to its highest-value use. In particular, renters will only allocate land to uses that generate enough revenue to both pay the rent and cover all other costs, including a normal profit.

Private land ownership and having to pay market-determined land rents also aids economic growth and development, because, as consumer tastes change and as new technologies are developed, the best uses to which particular pieces of land can be put also change. These changing opportunity costs are reflected in land rents, whose changing values help to reallocate land from lower-value to higher-value uses as the economy evolves. Thus, the often-heard remark, "The land was just too valuable for its previous use."

By contrast, if land were nationalized, government planners would have a very difficult time assigning each piece of land to its best possible use and adjusting its use with changing circumstances without the guidance about opportunity costs provided by market-determined rents.

Along those lines, it is important to be clear that, while economic rents are surplus payments when viewed from the perspective of society as a whole, they are most definitely costs to individual people and individual firms. To see why this is true, recall that because land is a free gift of nature, there is no cost to society as a whole for obtaining the current supply of land. Thus, economic rents are, from the perspective of society, surplus payments, because they have no effect on land supply. But individuals must pay economic rents because such rents determine how society's fixed supply of land is allocated among competing potential uses. Those who are willing and able to pay the market rent get to use the land, while those who are unwilling or unable to pay the market rent do not. Put slightly differently: Economic rents do not cause land to be supplied—they cause land to be directed.

QUICK REVIEW 18.1

- Rent is the price paid for unimproved land whose supply is perfectly inelastic.

- Differences in rent arise from differences in land productivity and location.

- Rent is socially useful because it puts an opportunity cost on land parcels, thereby helping to allocate each parcel of land to its best possible use.

18.2 Interest

LO18.2   Define interest and explain how interest rates vary based on risk, maturity, loan size, and taxability.

Interest is the price paid for the use of money. It can be thought of as the amount of money that a borrower must pay a lender for the use of the lender's money over some period of time. As an example, a borrower might be required to pay $100 of interest for the use of $1000 for one year.

Because borrowers pay for loans of money with money, interest can be stated as a percentage of the amount of money borrowed rather than as a dollar amount. This is very useful because it is far less clumsy to say that interest is "12 percent annually" than to say that interest is "$120 per year per $1000."

Stating interest as a percentage also makes it much easier to compare the interest paid on loans involving different amounts of money. By expressing interest as a percentage, we can immediately compare an interest payment of, say, $432 per year per $2880 with one of $1800 per year per $12,000. Both interest payments are 15 percent per year, which is not obvious from the actual dollar figures.

And to make things even simpler, an interest payment of 15 percent per year can also be referred to as a 15 percent interest rate.

Money Is Not a Resource

When considering why borrowers are willing to pay interest for the right to use borrowed money, it is very important to remember that money is not itself an economic resource. Whether money comes in the form of coins, paper currency, or chequing accounts, you cannot directly produce any goods and services with it.

Thus, borrowers do not value money for its own sake. Rather, they value money because of what it can purchase. Individuals and households are willing to pay interest to borrow for consumption spending because they would prefer to consume certain goods and services sooner rather than later. And businesses are willing to pay interest because they can use the money they borrow to expand their businesses and increase their profits. In particular, borrowed money can be used to fund the acquisition of capital goods such as computers, machinery, and warehouses.

Interest Rates and Interest Income

The interest rate on money loans determines the *interest income* earned by households for providing capital to firms. This is true because firms have the choice of either leasing capital from households or purchasing their own capital. Because businesses have this option, households wishing to lease their capital to businesses cannot charge more for the use of their capital than businesses would have to pay in terms of interest payments to borrow the money needed to purchase their own capital. As an example, consider a custom T-shirt shop that needs a $10,000 embroidering machine to expand production. If the owners of the shop can borrow the money to buy such a machine at an interest rate of 8 percent per year, then anyone wishing to lease them an identical machine could charge them no more than $800 per year for it (since $800 is how much per year the shop would have to pay in interest to borrow $10,000 at an 8 percent interest rate).

Range of Interest Rates

For convenience, economists often speak in terms of a single interest rate. However, there are actually a number of interest rates in the economy. Table 18-1 lists several interest rates often referred to in the media. In January 2018, these rates ranged from 1.00 percent to 19.99 percent. Why the differences?

- **Risk** Loans to different borrowers for different purposes carry varying degrees of risk. The greater the chance that a borrower will not repay his loan, the higher the interest rate the lender will charge to compensate for that risk.

- **Maturity** The time length of a loan or its *maturity* (when it needs to be paid back) also affects the interest rate. Other things equal, longer-term loans usually command higher interest rates than shorter-term loans. This is true because one function of interest rates is to compensate lenders for the inconvenience and potential financial sacrifices involved with forgoing alternative uses of their money until their loans are repaid. Longer-term loans must offer higher interest rates to compensate lenders for having to forgo alternative opportunities for longer periods of time.

TABLE 18-1	Selected Interest Rates, January 2018
Type of interest rate	**Annual percentage**
10-year Government of Canada bond	2.20
5-year Government of Canada bond	1.60
3-year Government of Canada bond	1.35
91-day Treasury Bill (Government of Canada)	1.00
5-year closed mortgage	5.00
Prime rate (rate charged by banks to their best corporate customers)	3.20
Overnight lending rate	1.00
Visa interest rate	19.99

Source: Adapted from Bank of Canada, https://www.bankofcanada.ca/rates/interest-rates.

- *Loan Size* If there are two loans of equal maturity and risk, the interest rate on the smaller of the two loans usually will be higher. The administrative costs of issuing a large loan and a small loan are about the same in dollars, but the cost is greater *as a percentage* of the smaller loan.

Pure Rate of Interest

When economists and financial specialists talk of "the" interest rate, they typically have in mind the **pure rate of interest**. This is the hypothetical interest rate that would serve purely and solely to compensate lenders for their willingness to patiently forgo alternative consumption and investment opportunities until their money is repaid.

The pure rate of interest is best approximated by the interest rates of long-term, virtually riskless securities such as the 30-year Government of Canada bond. The interest paid by such bonds can be thought of as being made purely and solely for the use of money over an extended time period because such bonds involve minimal risk and negligible administrative costs. In January 2018 the pure rate of interest in Canada was 2.2 percent.

18.3 Loanable Funds Theory of Interest

LO18.3 Explain the loanable funds theory of interest rates.

Because macroeconomics deals with the entire economy, it typically focuses on the pure rate of interest and assumes that it is determined by the total supply and demand for money in the economy. But because our present focus is on microeconomics, we will concentrate on a more micro-based theory of interest rates. By doing so, we will be able to explain why the interest rates on different types of loans vary so greatly, as in Table 18-1.

The **loanable funds theory of interest** explains the interest rate on any particular type of loan in terms of the supply of and demand for *funds available for lending* in the loanable funds market that exists for that particular type of loan. As Figure 18-2 (Key Graph) shows, the equilibrium interest rate (here, 8 percent) on a particular type of loan is the rate at which the quantities of loanable funds supplied and demanded are equal for that type of loan.

To gain a deeper understanding of the loanable funds theory of interest, let's focus on a simplified lending market. First, assume that, for a particular type of loan, households or consumers are the sole suppliers of loanable funds while businesses are the sole demanders of loanable funds. Also assume that lending occurs directly between households and businesses so that there are no financial institutions acting as intermediaries.

SUPPLY OF LOANABLE FUNDS

The supply of loanable funds in our simplified lending market is represented by curve *S* in Figure 18-2. Its upward slope indicates that households will make available a larger quantity of funds at high interest rates than at low

KEY GRAPH

FIGURE 18-2 The Market for Loanable Funds

The upsloping supply curve *S* for loanable funds reflects the idea that at higher interest rates households will defer more of their present consumption (save more), making more funds available for lending. The downsloping demand curve *D* for loanable funds indicates that businesses will borrow more at lower interest rates than at higher interest rates. At the equilibrium interest rate (here, 8 percent), the quantities of loanable funds loaned and borrowed are equal (here, F_0 each).

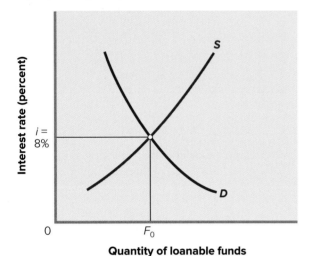

interest rates. Most people prefer to use their income to purchase desirable goods and services *today*, rather than to delay purchases to sometime in the *future*. For people to delay consumption and increase their saving, they must be compensated by an interest payment. The larger the amount of that payment, the greater the deferral of household consumption and thus the greater the amount of money made available for loans.

DEMAND FOR LOANABLE FUNDS

Businesses borrow loanable funds primarily to add to their stocks of capital goods, such as new plants or warehouses, machinery, and equipment. Assume that a firm wants to buy a machine that will increase output and sales such that the firm's total revenue will rise by $110 for the year. Also assume that the machine costs $100 and has a useful life of just one year. Comparing the $10 earned with the $100 cost of the machine, we find that the expected rate of return on this investment is 10 percent ($= \$10/\$100$) for one year.

To determine whether the investment would be profitable and whether it should be made, the firm must compare the interest rate—the price of loanable funds—with the 10 percent expected rate of return. If funds can be borrowed at some rate less than the rate of return, say, at 8 percent, as in Figure 18-2, then the investment is profitable and should be made. But if funds can be borrowed only at an interest rate above the 10 percent rate of return, say, at 14 percent, the investment is unprofitable and should not be made.

Why is the demand for loanable funds downsloping, as in Figure 18-2? At higher interest rates, fewer investment projects will be profitable and therefore a smaller quantity of loanable funds will be demanded. At lower interest rates, more investment projects will be profitable, and therefore more loanable funds will be demanded. Indeed, as we have just seen, it is profitable to purchase the $100 machine if funds can be borrowed at 8 percent but not if the firm must borrow at 14 percent.

Extending the Model

There is a loanable funds market for nearly every type of loan in the economy. The best known are the markets for corporate and government bonds. But there are also loanable funds markets for student loans, home mortgages, and car loans. Each type of loan ends up with its own equilibrium interest rate determined by the demand for and supply of loanable funds in its particular market.

We now extend the simple loanable funds model to make it more realistic and better able to capture the diversity of these many lending markets.

Financial Institutions

Households rarely directly lend their savings to the businesses that are borrowing funds for investment. Instead, they place their savings in chartered banks (and other financial institutions). The banks pay interest to savers to attract loanable funds and in turn lend those funds to businesses. Businesses borrow the funds from the banks, paying them interest for the use of the money. Financial institutions profit by charging borrowers higher interest rates than the interest rates they pay savers. Both interest rates, however, are based on the supply of and demand for loanable funds in their respective markets.

Changes in Supply

Anything that causes households to be thriftier will prompt them to save more at each interest rate, shifting the supply curve rightward. For example, if interest earned on savings were to be suddenly exempt from taxation, we would expect the supply of loanable funds to increase and the equilibrium interest rate to decrease. In 2009 the federal government introduced the Tax Free Savings Account (TFSA), which exempts up to $5500 a year in a savings account from taxation. This policy has given many Canadians an incentive to save more of their income.

Conversely, a decline in thriftiness would shift the supply-of-loanable-funds curve leftward and increase the equilibrium interest rate. For example, if the government expanded social insurance to cover more fully the costs of hospitalization, prescription drugs, and retirement living, the incentive of households to save might diminish.

Changes in Demand

On the demand side, anything that increases the rate of return on potential investments will increase the demand for loanable funds. Let's return to our earlier example, where a firm would receive additional revenue of $110 by purchasing a $100 machine and, therefore, would realize a 10 percent return on investment. What factors might increase or decrease the rate of return? Suppose a technological advance raised the productivity of the machine so that the firm's total revenue increased by $120 rather than $110. The rate of return would then be 20 percent, not 10 percent. Before the technological advance, the firm would have demanded zero loanable funds at, say, an interest rate of 14 percent, but now it will demand $100 of loanable funds at that interest rate, meaning that the demand curve for loanable funds has shifted to the right.

Similarly, an increase in consumer demand for the firm's product will increase the price of its product. So even though the productivity of the machine is unchanged, its potential revenue will rise from $110 to, say, $120, increasing the firm's rate of return from 10 to 20 percent. Again, the firm will be willing to borrow more than previously at our presumed 8 or 14 percent interest rate, implying that the demand curve for loanable funds has shifted rightward. This shift in demand increases the equilibrium interest rate.

Conversely, a decline in the productivity or in the price of the firm's product would shift the demand curve for loanable funds leftward, reducing the equilibrium interest rate.

Other Participants

We must recognize that participation in many loanable funds markets may go well beyond our simplification of households as suppliers of funds and businesses as demanders of funds. For example, while households are suppliers of loanable funds, many are also demanders of such funds. Households borrow to finance expensive purchases such as housing, automobiles, furniture, and household appliances. Governments also are on the demand side of a loanable funds market when they borrow to finance budgetary deficits. And businesses that have revenues in excess of their current expenditures may offer some of those revenues in various loanable funds markets. Thus, like households, businesses operate on both the supply and the demand sides of the various loanable funds markets.

Finally, in addition to gathering and making available the savings of households, banks and other financial institutions also increase funds through the lending process and decrease funds when the money that is used to pay off loans is retained by the banks rather than being loaned out again to other borrowers. The Bank of Canada (the nation's central bank) controls the amount of this bank activity and thus influences a wide variety of interest rates.

This fact helps answer one of our chapter-opening questions: Why did the interest rate on a one-year GIC drop from 3.3 percent in 2007 to 1.0 percent in 2011? There are two reasons: (1) the demand for loanable funds decreased because businesses did not need to purchase more capital goods and (2) the Bank of Canada, in an effort to stimulate aggregate expenditures, took monetary actions that increased the supply of loanable funds.

18.4 Time Value of Money

LO18.4 Demonstrate how interest rates relate to the time value of money.

Interest is central to understanding the **time value of money**—the idea that a specific amount of money is more valuable to a person the sooner it is obtained. To see where money's time value comes from, suppose that you could choose between being paid $1000 today or $1000 in a year. The fact that $1000 received today can be invested at interest and grow into more than $1000 in a year implies that it is better to receive $1000 today than $1000 in a year. By how much is it better? By the amount of interest that can be gained over the course of the year. The higher the interest rate, the greater the time value of money.

In addition to giving money its time value, the fact that money can be invested to earn interest also implies a way in which a given amount of money today can be thought of as being equivalent to a larger amount of money in the future and how a future amount of money can be thought of as being equivalent to a smaller amount of money today. We explore this idea next.

COMPOUND INTEREST

The total interest that cumulates over time on money placed into an interest-bearing account is called **compound interest**. Table 18-2 helps explain compound interest, as well as the related ideas of future value and present value. Suppose that Max places $1000 in an interest-bearing account at 10 percent interest intending to let the principal (the initial deposit) and interest compound for three years. The first row of each column shows the beginning period sum; the second column shows the yearly computation as to how that sum grows, given a particular interest rate. That growth is found by multiplying the dollar amount by $1 + i,$ where i is the interest rate expressed as a decimal.

In year 1 the 10 percent interest rate increases the money in the account from $1000 to $1100 (= $1000 × 1.10). So, as shown in column 3, total interest is $100. Column 4 again lists the $1100, but reinforces that it consists of the original principal plus total interest. Similarly, in year 2, the $1100 now in the account grows to $1210 (= $1100 × 1.10) because $110 of new interest accrues on the $1100. At the end of year 2, the principal remains $1000, but the total interest is $210, and the total amount in the account is $1210. Interest in year 3 is $121 and total interest rises to $331. After this $331 of total interest is added to the $1000 principal, the accumulation is $1331. As shown in Column 3, compound interest builds and builds over time.

FUTURE VALUE AND PRESENT VALUE

Now note from Table 18-2 that we can look at the time value of money in two distinct ways. The **future value** is the amount to which some current amount of money will grow as interest compounds over time. In our table, the future value (FV) of $1000 today at 10 percent interest is $1331 three years from now. Future value is always forward looking.

But we can just as easily look backward from the end value of $1331 and ask how much that amount is worth today, given the 10 percent interest rate. The **present value** is today's value of some amount of money to be

TABLE 18-2	Compound Interest, Future Value, and Present Value, 10 Percent Interest Rate		
(1) **Beginning period value**	**(2)** **Computation**	**(3)** **Total interest**	**(4)** **End period value**
$1000 (year 1)	$1000 × 1.10 = $1100	$100	$1100 (= $1000 + $100)
$1100 (year 2)	$1100 × 1.10 = $1210	$210 (= $100 + $110)	$1210 (= $1000 + $210)
$1210 (year 2)	$1210 × 1.10 = $1331	$331 (= $100 +$110 +$121)	$1331 (= $1000 + $331)

CONSIDER THIS

That Is Interest

The following story told by economist Irving Fisher (1867–1947) helps illustrate the time value of money.*

While giving him a treatment, a masseur told Fisher he was a socialist and believed "interest is the basis of capitalism, and is robbery."

After the massage, Fisher asked, "How much do I owe you?" The masseur replied, "Thirty dollars."

"Very well," said Fisher, "I will give you a note payable a hundred years hence. I suppose you have no objections to taking this note without any interest. At the end of that time, you, or perhaps your grandchildren, can redeem it."

© Matthew Borkoski Photography/ Getty Image

"But I cannot afford to wait that long," said the masseur.

"I thought you said that interest was robbery. If interest is robbery, you ought to be willing to wait indefinitely for the money. If you are willing to wait ten years, how much would you require?"

"Well, I would have to get more than thirty dollars."

His point now made, Fisher replied, "That is interest."

*Irving Fisher, as quoted in Irving Norton Fisher, *My Father Irving Fisher* (New York: Comet, 1956), p. 77.

received in the future. In terms of the table, the present value (PV) of $1331 is $1000. Here, FV is "discounted" by three years at 10 percent to remove all interest compounding and that way obtain PV. (We explain the discounting procedure in our chapter on financial economics in *Macroeconomics*.)[1]

With any positive real interest rate, a person would prefer to receive $1000 today rather than $1000 at some time in the future. The higher the interest rate, the greater is the *future value* of a specific amount of money today. To confirm, substitute a 20 percent interest rate for the 10 percent rate in Table 18-2 and rework the analysis. Finally, you should know that the analysis presented in the table is extendable to any number of years.

The time value of money is an important concept. For example, we will use it in Chapter 19B, which deals with natural resource and energy economics. Also, we will discuss present discounted value in much more detail in our chapter on financial economics in *Macroeconomics*. Our simple goal in this chapter is to stress that *money has time value because of the potential for compound interest.*

18.5 Role of Interest Rates

> **LO18.5** Explain the role of interest rates in allocating capital, allocating R&D spending, and helping to determine the economy's total output of goods and services.

We have already explained that interest rates on money loans determine the interest incomes earned by the owners of capital goods. This fact implies that interest rates are the crucial prices determining both the *level* and *composition* of new investments in capital goods as well as the amount of research and development (R&D) spending in the economy.

INTEREST AND TOTAL OUTPUT

Lower equilibrium interest rates encourage businesses to borrow more for investment, other things equal. As a result, total spending in the economy rises, and so does total output if the economy has unused resources.

---

[1] For readers interested in the mathematics: $FV = PV(1 + i)^t$ and $PV = FV/(1 + i)^t$ where i is the interest rate and t is time, here the number of years of compounding.

Conversely, higher equilibrium interest rates discourage businesses from borrowing for investment, which reduces investment and total spending. Such a decrease in spending may be desirable if an economy is experiencing inflation.

Central banks often manage interest rates to try to expand investment and output on the one hand, or to reduce investment and inflation on the other. Central banks affect the interest rates by changing the supply of money. Increases in the money supply increase the supply of loanable funds, causing the equilibrium interest rate to fall. This boosts investment spending and expands the economy. In contrast, decreases in the money supply decrease the supply of loanable funds, boosting the equilibrium interest rate. As a result, investment is constrained and so is the economy.

INTEREST AND THE ALLOCATION OF CAPITAL

Prices are rationing devices. Interest rates are prices. Thus, when it comes to allocating capital in the economy, the interest rates charged on investment loans ration the available supply of loanable investment funds to investment projects that have expected rates of return at or above the interest rate cost of the borrowed funds.

If, say, the computer industry expects to earn a return of 12 percent on the money it invests in physical capital and it can secure the required funds at an interest rate of 8 percent, it can borrow and expand its physical capital. If the expected rate of return on additional capital in the steel industry is only 6 percent, that industry will find it unprofitable to expand its capital stock at 8 percent interest. The interest rate allocates money, and ultimately physical capital, to those industries in which it will be most productive and, therefore, most profitable. Such an allocation of capital goods benefits society.

INTEREST AND R&D SPENDING

In Chapter 14, we pointed out that, similarly to an investment decision, a decision on how much to spend on R&D depends on the cost of borrowing funds in relationship to the expected rate of return. Other things equal, the lower the interest rate and thus the lower the cost of borrowing funds for R&D, the greater the amount of R&D spending that is potentially profitable. Low interest rates encourage R&D spending; high interest rates discourage it.

Also, the interest rate allocates R&D funds to those firms and industries for which the expected rate of return on R&D is the greatest. Ace Microcircuits may have an expected rate of return of 16 percent on an R&D project, while Glow Paints has only a 2 percent expected rate of return on an R&D project. With the interest rate at 8 percent, loanable funds will flow to Ace, not to Glow. Society will benefit by having R&D spending allocated to projects that have sufficiently high expected rates of return to justify using scarce resources for R&D rather than for other purposes.

NOMINAL AND REAL INTEREST RATES

This discussion of the role of interest in investment decisions and in R&D decisions assumes that there is no inflation. If inflation exists, we must distinguish between nominal and real interest rates, just as we needed to distinguish between nominal and real wages in Chapter 17. The **nominal interest rate** is the rate of interest expressed in dollars of current value. The **real interest rate** is the rate of interest expressed in purchasing power—dollars of inflation-adjusted value.

Example: Suppose the nominal interest rate and the rate of inflation are both 10 percent. If you borrow $100, you must pay back $110 a year from now. However, because of 10 percent inflation, each of these 110 dollars will be worth 10 percent less. Thus, the real value or purchasing power of your $110 at the end of the year is only $100. In inflation-adjusted dollars you are borrowing $100 and at year's end you are paying back $100. While the nominal interest rate is 10 percent, the real interest rate is zero. We determine the real interest rate by subtracting the 10 percent inflation rate from the 10 percent nominal interest rate. It is the real interest rate, not the nominal rate, that affects investment and R&D decisions.

For a comparison of nominal interest rates on bank loans in selected countries, see Global Perspective 18.1. Note that some countries now have negative nominal interest rates, meaning that a saver will get back less than the amount she invested. Negative nominal interest rates are the result of deliberate central bank monetary policies intended to get people to consume more. The central banks are hoping that consumers will save less and consume more when savings earns a negative return due to negative rates.

18.1 GLOBAL PERSPECTIVE

Short-Term Nominal Interest Rates, Selected Nations

These data show the short-term nominal interest rates (those on three-month loans) in various countries in 2015. Because these are nominal rates, much of the variation reflects differences in rates of inflation, but differences in central bank monetary policies and default risk also influence the variation.

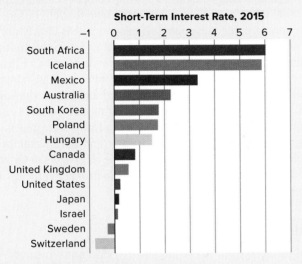

Short-Term Interest Rate, 2015

South Africa, Iceland, Mexico, Australia, South Korea, Poland, Hungary, Canada, United Kingdom, United States, Japan, Israel, Sweden, Switzerland

Source: "OECD Economic Outlook," Organisation for Economic Co-operation and Development, www.oecd.org. Used with permission.

QUICK REVIEW 18.2

- Interest is the price paid for the use of money and determines the interest income earned by households for providing capital to firms.

- The range of interest rates is influenced by risk, maturity, and loan size.

- In the loanable funds model, the equilibrium interest rate is determined by the demand for and supply of loanable funds.

- The time value of money is the idea that $1 can be converted into more than $1 of future value through

compound interest, therefore $1 to be received sometime in the future has less than $1 of present value.

- Interest rates on investment loans affect the total level of investment and, therefore, the levels of total spending and total output; they also affect allocation of money and real capital to specific industries and firms. Similarly, interest rates also affect the level and composition of R&D spending.

18.6 Economic Profit

LO18.6 Relate why economic profits occur, and how profits, along with losses, allocate resources among alternative uses.

Recall from previous chapters that economists define profit narrowly. To accountants, profit is what remains of a firm's total revenue after it has paid individuals and other firms for the materials, capital, and labour they have supplied to the firm. To the economist, these *accounting profits* overstate profit. The reason is that the accountant's view of profit considers only **explicit costs**: payments made by the firm to outsiders. It ignores **implicit costs**: the monetary income the firm sacrifices when it uses resources that it owns, rather than supplying those resources to the market. The economist considers implicit costs to be opportunity costs that must be accounted for in determining profit. The economic (pure) profit is what remains after all costs—both explicit and implicit, the latter including a normal profit—have been subtracted from a firm's total revenue. Economic profit may be either positive or negative (a loss).

Entrepreneurship and Profit

Economic profit flows to individuals to motivate them to provide the economic resource known as entrepreneurship. For illustration, let's suppose that two entrepreneurs establish a start-up company called Upside and that they are the only owners. They do not incorporate or borrow and instead use their own funds to finance the firm.

As discussed in previous chapters, the resource that these entrepreneurs provide is clearly not labour. Typical workers simply complete assigned tasks and engage in routine activities. For their labour inputs, they are compensated with wages and salaries. Entrepreneurs, by contrast, make non-routine decisions that involve substantial financial risk. Among other things, they (1) decide their firm's strategy for combining land, labour, and capital to produce a good or service; (2) decide whether and how to develop new products and new production processes; and (3) personally bear the financial risks associated with the success or failure of their respective firms.

With regard to bearing those financial risks, it is crucial to understand that a firm's entrepreneurs are its *residual claimants*, meaning that they only receive whatever residual revenue—if any—remains after all the other factors of production have been paid. As residual claimants, the entrepreneurs at Upside receive whatever accounting profit or accounting loss the firm generates. Thus, the financial risks of running the firm are borne by its two entrepreneurs. If Upside loses money, it loses *their* money.

Insurable and Uninsurable Risks

As residual claimants, entrepreneurs face financial risks. These fall into two categories: insurable risks are those risks for which it is possible to buy insurance from an insurance company, while uninsurable risks are those risks for which it is not possible to buy insurance from an insurance company.

Individuals and firms who purchase insurance policies (contracts) from an insurance company are referred to as policyholders. In exchange for an annual premium (fee), the policyholders obtain the insurance company's guarantee to reimburse them for any financial losses caused by any of the risks covered under the insurance contract. In order to be able to keep that promise, the insurance company must be able to collect enough in premiums from its policyholders in the present to be able to fully reimburse the ones who eventually suffer losses in the future. This is only possible with risks like fire, flood, theft, accident, and death whose frequencies of occurrence can be predicted with relative accuracy. Risks whose frequencies of occurrence cannot be predicted with accuracy are uninsurable.

Sources of Uninsurable Risks

Because insurance is available for insurable risks, entrepreneurs only have to deal with uninsurable risks whose frequency of occurrence cannot be predicted with any accuracy. In practice, these are the result of uncontrollable and unpredictable changes in demand and supply that either reduce revenues or increase costs. These uninsurable risks fall into four main categories:

- *Changes in the General Economic Environment* An economy-wide downturn in business (a recession), can lead to greatly reduced demand, sales, and revenues, and thus to business losses. An otherwise prosperous firm may experience substantial losses through no fault of its own.

- *Changes in the Structure of the Economy* Consumer tastes, technology, resource availability, and prices change unpredictably in the real world, bringing changes in production costs and revenues. For example, Air Canada may earn an economic profit one year, but may sustain substantial losses the next year as the result of a significant increase in the price of jet fuel.

- *Changes in Government Policy* A newly instituted regulation, the removal of a tariff, or a change in national defence policy may significantly alter the cost and revenue data of the affected industry and firms.

- *New Products or Production Methods Pioneered by Rivals* Any firm can suddenly find itself losing sales and revenue to popular new products brought out by rivals. Similarly, a firm may suddenly find itself having to sell its product at a loss if rival firms cut their prices after figuring out a lower-cost way to make the same product.

Profit as Compensation for Bearing Uninsurable Risks

Economists list entrepreneurship as its own economic resource—separate from land, labour, and capital—because it is not possible to run a business without somebody being willing to undertake and live with uninsurable risks. Entrepreneurs are rewarded with profit precisely to compensate them for personally taking on the uninsurable risks of running a business. Indeed, their willingness to bear those uninsurable risks means that the providers of the firm's other resource inputs (of land, labour, and capital) can almost completely ignore those risks.

To see why this is true, again consider our start-up company, Upside, and suppose that its two entrepreneurs used $100,000 of their own money to fund the firm. If revenues ever run below costs, the entrepreneurs will use that pile of money to cover the losses and make sure that the firm's workers and other resource suppliers get paid on time and in full. The resource suppliers are shielded from the losses because the entrepreneurs have taken it upon themselves to bear the firm's uninsurable financial risks. In such situations, no bill is sent to the workers or other resource suppliers asking them to help make up the firm's losses. The entrepreneurs, who took on the firm's uninsurable risks, are "on the hook."

The entrepreneurs' compensation for providing entrepreneurship and shielding the other resource suppliers from uninsurable risk is the opportunity to run the business and keep the firm's profits if things go well. Thus, entrepreneurship boils down to a simple bargain: In exchange for making sure that everyone else gets paid if things go wrong, the entrepreneur gets to receive the firm's profits if things go right.

Sources of Economic Profit

For bearing a firm's uninsurable risks, its entrepreneurs receive control of the firm. This allows them to try to make as much profit as possible in exchange for taking on those risks. Along those lines, there are three main ways in which entrepreneurs can generate economic profits (that is, accounting profits that exceed normal profits):

- *Create Popular New Products* If an entrepreneur can develop a popular new product at a sufficiently low cost, his firm will be able to generate economic profits until competitors bring out competing products.

- *Reduce Production Costs Below Rivals' Costs* Entrepreneurs who implement more-efficient production methods for existing products can generate economic profits until their efficiency gains are matched or exceeded by competitors.

- *Create and Maintain a Profitable Monopoly* Entrepreneurs who possess a monopoly for their product may be able to generate economic rent by restricting their outputs and raising their prices. And such economic profits may persist if entry to the industry is blocked. But remember from Chapter 11 that having a monopoly does not guarantee that a monopoly will be profitable. If demand is weak relative to production costs, monopolies can and will go bankrupt.

By reallocating resources toward the production of popular new products that consumers prefer to old products, entrepreneurs improve allocative efficiency. By reducing production costs, they improve productive efficiency. Thus, with the important exception of monopoly, the entrepreneur's pursuit of profit clearly benefits society.

With monopolies, though, things are very different because a monopoly's profit cannot be justified as rewarding its entrepreneurs for personally taking on a firm's financial risks or for making perceptive business decisions that enhance productive or allocative efficiency. As a result, governments use anticombines laws to impede monopolies from forming, or if they arise, break them up or restrict their business behaviours. In some instances, governments also regulate away their excessive profits.

Profit Rations Entrepreneurship

Even if a firm is making an accounting profit, its entrepreneurs may decide to quit and go into another line of business. This is because they will want their accounting profit to be at least as large as the typical accounting profit that their risk taking and decision making could on average be expected to earn in other business ventures. This typical accounting profit is known as their **normal profit**.

Because entrepreneurs will be comparing their current accounting profit with the normal profit that they could be making elsewhere, profit can be thought of as the "price" that allocates the scarce resource of entrepreneurship to different possible economic activities. Just as wages must be paid to attract and retain labour, profits must be paid to attract and retain entrepreneurial talent. And just as higher wages attract workers, higher profits attract entrepreneurs.

CONSIDER THIS

Profits and Efficiency

Entrepreneurs focus on a single number: profit. That might make you think that entrepreneurs will end up neglecting the other aspects of their business. But a wonderful thing about the market system is that the only way for a firm to maximize profit is by paying close attention to *every* aspect of its operations.

This is true because entrepreneurs have to make many simultaneous decisions about how to spend their firm's limited budget. Should they allocate a little more money to research and development? Should they reduce spending on advertising? How about allocating more money for bonuses?

The only way to give one activity more resources is to give another activity fewer resources. If an entrepreneur wishes to maximize her firm's overall profit, she will have to get all of these marginal decisions right, and simultaneously. She will also

© AFP Getty Images

have to find the correct allocation of the firm's limited resources across all possible tasks so that MB = MC for each budget item. So while profit is just a single number, focusing on profit forces entrepreneurs to be efficient in every aspect of her firm's operations.

Profit also helps to allocate resources among alternative lines of production. Entrepreneurs seek profit and avoid losses. Economic profit in an industry is a signal that society wants that particular industry to expand. It attracts factors of production from industries that are not profitable. But the rewards of profit are more than an inducement for an industry to expand; they also attract the financing needed for expansion. In contrast, continuing losses penalize firms or industries that fail to adjust their productive efforts to match wants. Such losses signal society's desire for the afflicted industries to contract.

Entrepreneurs, Profits, and Corporate Stockholders

In the actual economy, economic profits are distributed widely beyond the entrepreneurs who first start new businesses. The corporate structure of business enterprise has allowed millions of individuals to purchase ownership shares in corporations and therefore to share in the risks and rewards of ownership.

Some of these people participate in the for-profit economy by purchasing the stock of individual firms or by investing in mutual funds that, in turn, buy corporate stock. Millions of additional people share in the profits of corporations through the financial investments of their pension funds. But at their core, all of the profits that are shared with these direct and indirect corporate shareholders are made possible in the first place by the activities of entrepreneurs. For instance, without Mike Lazaridis and Jim Balsillie, there would have been no Research In

© Royalty Free/Corbis

Innovation, one dynamic feature of a market economy, occurs at the initiative of the entrepreneur.

Motion (RIM) corporation (now BlackBerry Limited)—and, consequently, no RIM profits (dividends) to distribute to the millions of owners of RIM stock in the past. (In recent years BlackBerry has lost much of its lustre as it lost market share to rivals.)

Many millions of people wish to own corporate stock and thereby share in the risks and rewards of business, which reflects the fact that economic profit is the main energizer of the market economy. It influences both the level of economic output and the allocation of resources among alternative uses. The expectation of economic profit motivates firms to innovate. Innovation stimulates new investment, increasing total output and employment.

QUICK REVIEW 18.3

- Pure or economic profit is what remains after all explicit and implicit costs (including a normal profit) are subtracted from a firm's total revenue.

- As residual claimants, entrepreneurs receive accounting profit. They earn economic profit if their accounting profit exceeds the normal profit they could earn as entrepreneurs elsewhere.

- Economic profit has three sources: the bearing of uninsurable risk, the uncertainty of innovation, and monopoly power.

- The corporate structure of business enables millions of individuals to share in the risks and rewards of enterprise.

- Profit and profit expectations affect the levels of investment, total spending, and domestic output; profit and loss also allocate resources among alternative uses.

The LAST WORD

Determining the Price of Credit

© Royalty Free/Corbis

A variety of lending practices may cause the effective interest rate to be quite different from what it appears to be.

Borrowing and lending—receiving and granting credit—are a way of life. Individuals receive credit when they negotiate a mortgage loan and when they use their credit cards. Individuals make loans when they open a savings account in a chartered bank or buy a bond.

It is sometimes difficult to determine exactly how much interest we pay and receive when we borrow and lend. Let's suppose that you borrow $10,000, which you agree to repay with $1000 of interest at the end of one year. In this instance, the interest rate is 10 percent per year. To determine the interest rate i, we compare the interest paid with the amount borrowed:

$$i = \frac{\$1000}{\$10,000} = 10\%$$

But in some cases a lender—say, a bank—will discount the interest payment from the loan amount at the time the loan is made. Thus, instead of giving the borrower $10,000, the bank discounts the $1000 interest payment in advance, giving the borrower only $9000. This increases the interest rate:

$$i = \frac{\$1000}{\$9000} = 11\%$$

While the absolute amount of interest paid is the same, in this second case the borrower has only $9000 available for the year.

An even more subtle point is that, to simplify their calculations, some financial institutions assume a 360-day year (twelve 30-day months), which means the borrower has the use of the lender's funds for five fewer days than the normal year. This use of a short year also increases the actual interest rate paid by the borrower.

The interest rate paid may change dramatically if a loan is repaid in installments. Suppose a bank lends you $10,000 and charges interest in the amount of $1000 to be paid at the end of the year. But the loan contract requires that you repay the $10,000 loan in twelve equal monthly installments. As a result, the average amount of the loan outstanding during the year is only $5000. Therefore

$$i = \frac{\$1000}{\$5000} = 20\%$$

Here interest is paid on the total amount of the loan ($10,000) rather than on the outstanding balance (which averages $5000 for the year), making for a much higher interest rate.

Another factor that influences the effective interest rate is whether interest is compounded. Suppose you deposit $10,000 in a savings account that pays a 10 percent interest rate compounded semi-annually. In other words, interest is paid on your loan to the bank twice a year. At the end of the first six months, $500 of interest (10 percent of $10,000 for half a year) is added to your account. At the end of the year, interest is calculated on $10,500 so that the second interest payment is $525 (10 percent of $10,500 for half a year). Thus,

$$i = \frac{\$1.025}{\$10,000} = 10.25\%$$

This 10.25 percent return means that a bank offering a 10 percent interest rate compounded semi-annually would pay more interest to its customers than a competitor offering a simple (non-compounded) rate of, say, 10.2 percent.

Similarly, late-payment fees on credit card accounts can boost the actual interest rate paid on credit card balances to extremely high levels. Furthermore, low "teaser" rates designed to attract new customers often contain fine print that raises the interest rate to 16 percent, or even 28 percent, if there is a late payment on the account.

"Let the borrower (or depositor) beware" remains a fitting motto in the world of credit.

Question

Assume that you borrow $5000 and pay back the $5000 plus $250 in interest at the end of the year. Assuming no inflation, what is the real interest rate? What would the interest rate be if the $250 of interest had been discounted at the time the loan was made? What would the interest rate be if you were required to repay the loan in twelve equal monthly installments?

Chapter Summary

LO18.1 Explain the nature of economic rent and how it is determined.

- Economic rent is the price paid for the use of land and other natural resources whose total supplies are fixed.

- Differences in land rent result from differences in demand, often stemming from differences in the fertility and climactic features of the land or differences in location. Rent is a surplus payment that is socially unnecessary since land would be available to the economy even without rental payments.

- Although land rent is a surplus payment rather than a cost to the economy as a whole, to individual firms and industries rental payments are correctly regarded as costs. The payment of land rents by individuals and firms is socially useful because it puts an opportunity cost on the use of land so that people have the incentive to put each piece of land to its best possible use.

LO18.2 Define interest and explain how interest rates vary based on risk, maturity, loan size, and taxability.

- Interest is the price paid for the use of money. Because money is not itself an economic resource, people do not value money for its own sake; they value it for its purchasing power.

- The interest rate on money loans determines the interest income earned by households for providing capital to firms.

- Interest rates vary in size because loans differ as to risk, maturity, and amount.

- The pure rate of interest is the hypothetical interest rate that would serve purely and solely to compensate lenders for their willingness to patiently forgo alternative consumption and investment opportunities until their money is repaid. The pure rate of interest is the interest rate on virtually risk-free long-term Government of Canada bonds.

LO18.3 Explain the loanable funds theory of interest rates.

- In the loanable funds theory, the equilibrium interest rate is determined by the demand for and supply of loanable funds. Other things equal, an increase in the supply of loanable funds reduces the equilibrium interest rate, whereas a decrease in supply increases it; increases in the demand for loanable funds raise the equilibrium interest rate, whereas decreases in demand reduce it.

LO18.4   Demonstrate how interest rates relate to the time value of money.

- The time value of money is the idea that $1 today has more value than $1 sometime in the future because the $1 today can be placed in an interest-bearing account and earn compound interest over time. Future value is the amount to which a current amount of money will grow through interest compounding. Present value is the current value of some money payment to be received in the future.

LO18.5   Explain the role of interest rates in allocating capital, allocating R&D spending, and helping to determine the economy's total output of goods and services.

- The equilibrium interest rate influences the level of investment and helps ration financial and physical capital to specific firms and industries. Similarly, this rate influences the size and composition of R&D spending. The real interest rate, not the nominal rate, is critical to investment and R&D decisions.

LO18.6   Relate why economic profits occur, and how profits, along with losses, allocate resources among alternative uses.

- As residual claimants, entrepreneurs receive a firm's accounting profits (total revenue minus explicit costs) in exchange for assuming the uninsurable risks associated with running a business. An entrepreneur can earn an economic profit (total revenue minus both explicit and implicit costs, including a normal profit) if his firm's accounting profit exceeds the normal profit that his entrepreneurship could on average earn in other business ventures.

- The corporate form of business organization has allowed the millions who own corporate stock to share in the financial risks and economic profits engendered by entrepreneurship. Profits are the key energizer of business firms within the capitalist system. Profit expectations influence innovation and investment activities and, therefore, the economy's levels of employment and economic growth. The basic function of profits and losses, however, is to allocate resources in accordance with consumers' preferences.

Terms and Concepts

economic rent

incentive function

pure rate of interest

loanable funds theory of interest

time value of money

compound interest

future value

present value

nominal interest rate

real interest rate

explicit costs

implicit costs

economic (pure) profit

insurable risks

uninsurable risks

normal profit

Discussion Questions

1. How does the economist's use of the term *rent* differ from everyday usage? Explain the following statement: Though rent need not be paid by society to make land available, rental payments are very useful in guiding land into the most productive uses.   [**LO18.1**]

2. Explain why economic rent is a surplus payment when viewed by the economy as a whole, but is a cost of production from the standpoint of individual firms and industries. Explain: Land rent performs no incentive function in the economy.   [**LO18.1**]

3. If money is not an economic resource, why is interest paid and received for its use? What considerations account for the fact that interest rates differ greatly on various types of loans? Use those considerations to explain the relative sizes of the interest rates on the following: [**LO18.2**]

   a. A 10-year $1000 government bond

   b. A $20 pawnshop loan

   c. A 30-year mortgage loan on a $175,000 house

   d. A 24-month $12,000 bank loan to finance the purchase of an automobile

   e. A 60-day $100 loan from a personal finance company

4. Why is the supply of loanable funds upsloping? Why is the demand for loanable funds downsloping? Explain the equilibrium interest rate. List some factors that might cause it to change.   [**LO18.3**]

5. Here is the deal: You can pay your college or university tuition at the beginning of the academic year or the same amount at the end of the academic year. You either already have the money in an interest-bearing account or will have to borrow it. Which situation would you choose? Explain your financial reasoning. Relate your answer to the time value of money, present value, and future value.   [**LO18.4**]

6. What are the major economic functions of the interest rate? How might the fact that many businesses finance their investment activities internally affect the efficiency with which the interest rate performs its functions?   [**LO18.5**]

7. Distinguish between nominal and real interest rates. Which is more relevant in making investment and R&D decisions? If the nominal interest rate is 12 percent and the inflation rate is 8 percent, what is the real rate of interest?   [**LO18.5**]

8. How do accounting profit and economic profit differ? Why is economic profit smaller than accounting profit? What are the three basic sources of economic profit? Classify each of the following according to those sources: [**LO18.6**]

   a. A firm's profit from developing and patenting a new medication that greatly reduces cholesterol and thus diminishes the likelihood of heart disease and stroke

   b. A restaurant's profit that results from construction of a new highway past its door

   c. The profit received by a firm due to an unanticipated change in consumer tastes

9. Why is the distinction between insurable and uninsurable risks significant for the theory of profit? Carefully evaluate the following statement: "All economic profit can be traced to either uncertainty or the desire to avoid it." What are the major functions of economic profit?   [**LO18.6**]

Review Questions

1. When using a supply-and-demand model to illustrate how land rents are set, economists typically draw the supply curve as a vertical line because   [**LO18.1**]

   a. The supply of land is fixed

   b. The supply of land is perfectly inelastic

   c. The quantity supplied of land does not increase when rents go up

   d. All of the above

2. In the 1980s land prices in Japan surged upward in a speculative bubble. Land prices then fell for eleven straight years between 1990 and 2001. What can we safely assume happened to *land rent* in Japan over those eleven years? Use graphical analysis to illustrate your answer.   [**LO18.1**]

3. Angela puts $1000 in a savings account that pays 3 percent per year. What is the future value of her money one year from now?   [**LO16.4**]

   a. $970

   b. $1000

   c. $1003

   d. $1030

4. As shown in Table 18-2, $1000 invested at 10 percent compound interest will grow into $1331 after three years. What is the present value of $2662 in three years if it is discounted back to the present at a 10 percent compound interest rate? (*Hint:* $2662 is twice as much as $1331.)   [**LO18.4**]

5. Entrepreneurs are the residual claimants at their respective firms. This means that they   [**LO18.6**]

   a. Only get paid if there is any money left over after all the other factors of production have been paid

   b. Must bear the financial risks of running their firms

   c. Receive whatever accounting profits or losses their firms generate

   d. All of the above

Problems

1. Suppose that you own a 10-hectare plot of land that you would like to rent out to wheat farmers. For them, bringing in a harvest involves $30 per hectare for seed, $80 per hectare for fertilizer, and $70 per hectare for equipment rentals and labour. With these inputs, the land will yield 40 bushels of wheat per hectare. If the price at which wheat can be sold is $5 per bushel, and if farmers want to earn a normal profit of $10 per hectare, what is the most that any farmer would pay to rent your 10 hectares? What if the price of wheat rose to $6 per bushel?   [**LO18.1**]

2. Suppose that the demand for loanable funds for car loans in the Vancouver area is $10 million per month at an interest rate of 10 percent per year, $11 million at an interest rate of 9 percent per year, $12 million at an interest rate of 8 percent per year, and so on. If the supply of loanable funds is fixed at $15 million, what will be the equilibrium interest rate? If the government imposes a usury law and says that car loans cannot exceed 3 percent per year, how big will the monthly shortage (or excess demand) for car loans be? What if the usury limit is raised to 7 percent per year?   [**LO18.3**]

3. To fund its wars against Napoleon, the British government sold consol bonds. They were referred to as "perpetuities" because they would pay £3 every year in perpetuity (forever). If a citizen could purchase a consol for £25, what would its annual interest rate be? What if the price were £50? £100? Bonds are known as "fixed income" securities because the future payments that they will make to investors are fixed by the bond agreement in advance. Do the interest rates bonds and other investments that offer fixed future payments vary directly or inversely with their current prices?   [**LO18.4**]

4. Suppose that the interest rate is 4 percent. What is the future value of $100 four years from now? How much of the future value is total interest? By how much would total interest be greater at a 6 percent interest rate than at a 4 percent interest rate?   [**LO18.4**]

5. You are currently a worker earning $60,000 per year but are considering becoming an entrepreneur. You will not switch unless you can expect to earn an accounting profit that is, on average, at least as great as your current salary. You look into opening a small grocery store. Suppose that the store has annual costs of $150,000 for labour, $40,000 for rent, and $30,000 for equipment. There is a 50 percent probability that revenues will be $200,000 and a 50 percent probability that revenues will be $400,000.   [**LO18.6**]

   a. In the low-revenue situation, what will your accounting profit or loss be? In the high-revenue situation?

   b. On average, how much do you expect your revenue to be? Your accounting profit? Your economic profit? Will you quit your job and try your hand at being an entrepreneur?

   c. Suppose the government imposes a 25 percent tax on accounting profits. This tax is only levied if a firm is earning positive accounting profits. What will your after-tax accounting profit be in the low-revenue case? In the high-revenue case? What will your average after-tax accounting profit be? What about your average after-tax economic profit? Will you now want to quit your job and try your hand at being an entrepreneur?

   d. Other things equal, does the imposition of the 25 percent profit tax increase or decrease the supply of entrepreneurship in the economy?

CHAPTER 19

International Trade*

LEARNING OBJECTIVES

LO19.1 Define comparative advantage and demonstrate how specialization and trade add to a nation's output.

LO19.2 Describe how differences between world prices prompt exports and imports.

LO19.3 Analyze the economic effects of tariffs and quotas.

Backpackers in the wilderness like to think they are "leaving the world behind," but, like Atlas, they carry the world on their shoulders. Much of their equipment is imported—knives from Switzerland, rain gear from South Korea, cameras from Japan, aluminum pots from England, sleeping bags from China, hiking boots from Italy, and compasses from Finland. Moreover, they may have driven to the trailheads in Japanese-made Toyotas or German-made BMWs while they sipped coffee from Colombia and snacked on bananas from Honduras.

International trade and the global economy affect all of us daily, whether we are hiking in the wilderness, driving our cars, listening to music, or working at our jobs. We cannot leave the world behind. We are enmeshed in a global web of economic relationships such as trading of goods and services, multinational corporations, cooperative ventures among the world's firms, and ties among the world's financial markets.

The focus of this chapter is the trading of goods and services. We provide an analysis of the benefits of international trade and the costs of protectionism.

Note to instructors: If you prefer to cover international trade early in your course, you can assign this chapter at the end of either Part 1 or Part 2. This chapter builds on the introductory ideas of opportunity costs, supply and demand analysis, and economic efficiency, but it does not require an understanding of either market failures or government failures.

19.1 The Economic Basis for Trade

LO19.1   Define comparative advantage and demonstrate how specialization and trade add to a nation's output.

Sovereign nations, like individuals and the regions of a nation, can gain by specializing in those products they can produce with greatest relative efficiency and trading them for those goods they cannot produce as efficiently. The simple answer to the question "Why do nations trade?" is "Because it is beneficial." The benefits that emerge relate to three underlying facts:

- The distribution of natural, human, and capital resources among nations is uneven; nations differ in their endowments of economic resources.

- Efficient production of various goods requires different technologies or combinations of resources.

- Products are differentiated as to quality and other nonprice attributes. Some people may prefer certain imported goods to similar goods made domestically.

To recognize the character and interaction of these three facts, think of different countries in the world. China, for example, has a large labour force and therefore relatively inexpensive skilled labour. As a result, China can produce efficiently (at low cost) a variety of **labour-intensive goods** such as textiles, electronics, apparel, toys, and sporting goods.

In contrast, Australia has vast amounts of land and can inexpensively produce such **land-intensive goods** as wheat, wool, and meat. Brazil has the soil, tropical climate, rainfall, and ready supply of unskilled labour that are needed for the efficient, low-cost production of vegetables. Industrially advanced economies with relatively large amounts of capital can produce inexpensively those goods that require much capital to produce, including such **capital-intensive goods** as airplanes agricultural equipment, machinery, and chemicals.

Also, regardless of their resource intensities, nations can develop individual products that are in demand worldwide because of their special qualities: fashions from Italy, chocolates from Belgium, computer software from the United States, and watches from Switzerland.

The distribution of resources, technology, and product distinctiveness among nations is relatively stable in short time periods but certainly can change over time. When that distribution changes, the relative efficiency and success that nations have in producing and selling goods also changes. For example, in the past few decades South Korea has upgraded the quality of its labour force and has greatly expanded its stock of capital. Although South Korea was primarily an exporter of agricultural products and raw materials a half-century ago, it now exports large quantities of manufactured goods. Similarly, the new technologies that gave us synthetic fibres and synthetic rubber drastically altered the resource mix needed to produce these goods and changed the relative efficiency of nations in manufacturing them.

As national economies evolve, the size and quality of their labour forces may change, the volume and composition of their capital stocks may shift, new technologies may develop, and even the quality of land and the quantity of natural resources may be altered. As such changes take place, the relative efficiency with which a nation can produce specific goods will also change. As economists would say, comparative advantage can and does sometimes change.

Comparative Advantage

In an open economy (one with an international sector), a country produces more of certain goods (exports) and fewer of other goods (imports) than it would otherwise. Thus, the country shifts some labour and other resources toward export industries and away from import industries. For example, in the presence of international trade, Canada uses more resources to make telecommunication equipment and to grow wheat, and fewer resources to make television sets and sew clothes. So we ask, "Do such shifts of resources make economic sense? Do they enhance total output in Canada and thus the standard of living of Canadians?"

The answers are in the affirmative. Specialization and international trade increase the productivity of Canadian resources and allow it to obtain greater total output than otherwise would be possible. These benefits are the result of exploiting both *absolute advantages* and *comparative advantages*. A country is said to have an **absolute advantage** over other producers of a product if it is the most efficient producer of that product (by which we mean that it can produce more output of that product from any given amount of resource inputs than can any other producer). A country is said to have a **comparative advantage** over other producers if it can produce the product at a lower opportunity cost (by which we mean that it must forgo less output of alternative products when allocating resources to producing the product in question).

In 1776 Adam Smith used the concept of absolute advantage to argue for international specialization and trade. His point was that nations would be better off if they each specialized in the production of those goods and services in which they had an absolute advantage and were therefore the most efficient producers:

> It is the maxim of every prudent master of a family, never to attempt to make at home what it will cost him more to make than to buy. The taylor does not attempt to make his own shoes, but buys them of the shoemaker. The shoemaker does not attempt to make his own clothes, but employs a taylor. The farmer attempts to make neither the one nor the other, but employs those different artificers. . . .
>
> What is prudence in the conduct of every private family, can scarce be folly in that of a great kingdom. If a foreign country can supply us with a commodity cheaper than we can make it, better buy it of them with some part of the produce of our own industry, employed in a way in which we have some advantage.[1]

In the early 1800s, David Ricardo extended Smith's idea by demonstrating that it is advantageous for a country to specialize and trade with another country even if it is more productive in all economic activities than that other country. Stated more formally, a nation does not need Smith's absolute advantage—total superiority in the efficiency with which it produces products—to benefit from specialization and trade. It needs only a comparative advantage.

THE BASIC PRINCIPLE

The central concept underlying comparative advantage can be illustrated by posing a problem. Suppose that Madison, a chartered accountant (CA), is also a swifter house painter than Mason, the professional painter she is thinking of hiring. Also assume that Madison can earn $50 per hour doing accounting and must pay Mason $15 per hour. And suppose that Madison would need 30 hours to paint her house but Mason would need 40 hours. Finally, assume Madison receives no special pleasure from painting.

All nations, regardless of their labour, land, or capital intensity, can find special niches for products that are in demand worldwide.

© Zanskar/Dreamstime

Should Madison take time off from accounting to paint her own house or should she hire the painter? Madison's opportunity cost of painting her house is $1500 (= 30 hours × $50 per hour of sacrificed income). The cost of hiring Mason is only $600 (= 40 hours × $15 per hour paid to the painter). Although Madison is better at both accounting and painting, she will get her house painted at a lower cost by specializing in accounting and using some of the proceeds to hire the house painter.

Note that Madison has an absolute advantage in both accounting and painting; she can do accounting and paint more efficiently than our hypothetical house painter. Despite this, Madison should hire a house painter because of her *comparative advantage*.

Similarly, Mason can reduce his cost of obtaining accounting services by specializing in painting and using some of his income to hire Madison to prepare his income tax forms. Suppose Mason would need 10 hours to prepare his income tax return, but Mason could handle this task in 2 hours. Mason would sacrifice $150 of income (= 10 hours × $15 per hour of sacrificed time) to get a task done that he could hire out for $100 (= 2 hours × $50 per CA hour). By specializing in painting and hiring Madison to prepare his tax return, Mason *lowers his cost of getting the tax return prepared*.

We will see that what is true for our CA and house painter is also true for nations. Specializing on the basis of comparative advantage enables nations to reduce the cost of obtaining goods and services they desire.

With this simple example in mind, let's turn to an international trade model to understand the gains from specialization and trade.

---

[1] Adam Smith, *The Wealth of Nations* (originally published 1776; New York: Modern Library, 1937), p. 424.

QUICK REVIEW 19.1

- International trade enables nations to specialize, increase productivity, and increase the amount of output available for consumption.

- A country is said to have an *absolute advantage* over the other producers of a product if it can produce the product more efficiently, by which we mean that it can produce more of the product from any given amount of resource inputs than can any other producer.

- A country is said to have a *comparative advantage* over the other producers of a product if it can produce the product at a lower opportunity cost, by which we mean that it must forgo less of the output of alternative products when allocating resources to producing the product in question.

Two Isolated Nations

Our goal is to place the idea of comparative advantage into the context of trading nations. Our method is to build a simple model that relies on the familiar concepts of production possibilities curves. Suppose the world economy has just two nations, Canada and Brazil. For simplicity, we assume the labour forces in Canada and Brazil are of equal sizes. Each can produce both steel and soybeans, but at differing levels of economic efficiency. Suppose Canadian and Brazilian domestic production possibilities curves for soybeans and steel are as shown in Figures 19-1a and 19-1b. Note three realities relating to these production possibilities curves:

- **Constant Costs**   The "curves" are drawn as straight lines, in contrast to the concave-from-the-origin production possibilities frontiers introduced in Chapter 1. This means the law of increasing costs has been replaced with the assumption of constant costs. This substitution simplifies our discussion but does not change our analysis and conclusions. Later we will consider the effect of the more realistic increasing opportunity costs.

- **Different Costs**   The production possibilities curves of Canada and Brazil reflect different resource mixes and levels of technological progress. Specifically, the differing slopes of the two curves reflect the numbers in the figures and reveal that the opportunity costs of producing steel and soybeans differ between the two nations.

FIGURE 19-1   Production Possibilities Curve

The two production possibilities lines show the amounts of soybeans and steel (a) Canada and (b) Brazil can produce domestically. The curves for both countries are straight lines because we are assuming constant costs. (a) As reflected by the slope of *VB* in the left graph, the opportunity-cost ratio in Canada is 1 steel = 1 soybean. (b) The production possibilities curve *vb* in the right graph has a steeper slope, reflecting the different opportunity-cost ratio in Brazil of 2 soybeans = 1 steel. The difference in the opportunity-cost ratios between the two countries defines their comparative advantages and is the basis for specialization and international trade.

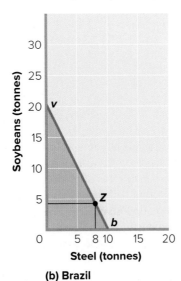

(a) Canada

(b) Brazil

• *Canada Has Absolute Advantage in Both*   A producer (an individual, firm, or country) has an *absolute advantage* over another producer if it can produce more of a product than the other producer using the same amount of resources. Because of our convenient assumption that the Canadian and Brazilian labour forces are of equal size, the two production possibilities curves show that Canada has an *absolute advantage* in producing both products. If Canada and Brazil use their entire (equal-size) labour forces to produce either steel or soybeans, Canada can produce more of either than Brazil. There are greater production possibilities in Canada using the same number of workers as in Brazil. So output per worker—labour productivity—in Canada exceeds that in Brazil in producing both products.

OPPORTUNITY-COST RATIO IN CANADA

In Figure 19-1a, with full employment, Canada will operate on its production possibilities curve. On that curve, it can increase its output of steel from 0 to 30 tonnes by forgoing an output of 30 tonnes of soybeans output. So the slope of the production possibilities curve is -1 ($= -30$ soybeans/$+30$ steel), meaning 1 tonne of steel must be sacrificed for each extra tonne of soybeans. In Canada the **opportunity-cost ratio** (domestic exchange rate) for the two products is 1 tonne of steel (S_t) for 1 tonne of soybeans (S_{oy}), or

$$1S_t = 1S_{oy}$$

Within its borders, Canada can "exchange" a tonne of steel from itself for a tonne of soybeans from itself. Our constant-cost assumption means this exchange or opportunity cost equation prevails for all possible moves from one point to another along Canada's production possibilities curve.

OPPORTUNITY-COST RATIO IN BRAZIL

Brazil's production possibilities curve in Figure 19-1b represents a different opportunity cost ratio. In Brazil, 2 tonnes of soybeans must be given up to obtain 1 tonne of steel. The slope of the production possibilities curve is -2 ($= -2$ soybeans/$+1$ steel). This means that in Brazil the domestic cost ratio for the two goods is 1 tonne of steel for 2 tonnes of soybeans, or

$$1S_t = 2S_{oy}$$

Self-Sufficiency Output Mix

If Canada and Brazil are isolated and are assumed to be self-sufficient, each must choose some output mix on its production possibilities curve. It will select the mix that provides the greatest total utility, or satisfaction. Assume point A in Figure 19-1a is the optimal output mix in Canada. The choice of this combination of 18 tonnes of steel and 12 tonnes of soybeans equates the marginal benefit and marginal cost of both goods. Suppose Brazil's optimal product mix is 8 tonnes of steel and 4 tonnes of soybeans, indicated by point B in Figure 19-1b. These choices by the two countries are reflected in column 1, Table 19-1.

Specialization Based on Comparative Advantage

As we have seen, a producer (an individual, firm, or nation) has a comparative advantage in producing a particular product if it can produce that product at a lower opportunity cost than other producers. Comparative advantage is the key determinant in whether nations can gain from specialization and trade. In fact, absolute advantage turns out to be irrelevant.

In our example, Canada has an absolute advantage over Brazil in producing both steel and soybeans. But it is still the case that Canada can gain from specialization and trade with Brazil. That is because what actually matters is whether the opportunity costs of producing the two products (steel and soybeans) differ in the two countries. If they do, then each nation will enjoy a comparative advantage in one of the products, meaning that it can produce that product at a lower opportunity cost than the other country. As a result, total output can increase if each country specializes in the production of the good in which it has the lower opportunity cost.

The idea is summarized in the **principle of comparative advantage**, which says that total output will be greatest when each good is produced by the nation that has the lowest domestic opportunity cost for that good. In our two-nation illustration, Canada has the lower domestic opportunity cost for steel; Canada need forgo only

TABLE 19-1	International Specialization According to Comparative Advantage and the Gains from Trade (in tonnes)				
Country	**(1)** **Outputs before specialization**	**(2)** **Outputs after specialization**	**(3)** **Amounts exported (−) and imported (+)**	**(4)** **Outputs available after trade**	**(5)** **Gains from specialization and trade (4) − (1)**
Canada	18 steel	30 steel	−10 steel	20 steel	2 steel
	12 soybeans	0 soybeans	+15 soybeans	15 soybeans	3 soybeans
Brazil	8 steel	0 steel	+10 steel	10 steel	2 steel
	4 soybeans	20 soybeans	−15 soybeans	5 soybeans	1 soybeans
Total output (steel and soybeans)	42	50		50	8

1 tonne of soybeans to produce 1 tonne of steel, whereas Brazil must forgo 2 tonnes of soybeans for 1 tonne of steel. Canada has a comparative (cost) advantage in steel and should specialize in steel production. The "world" (that is, Canada and Brazil) is not economizing in the use of its resources if a high-cost producer (Brazil) produces a specific product (steel) when a low-cost producer (Canada) could produce it. Having Brazil produce steel would mean that the world economy would have to give up more soybeans than is necessary to obtain a tonne of steel.

Brazil has the lower domestic opportunity cost for soybeans; it must sacrifice only ½ tonne of steel to produce 1 tonne of soybeans, while Canada must forgo 1 tonne of steel to produce 1 tonne of soybeans. Brazil has a comparative advantage in soybeans and should specialize in soybean production. Economizing requires that any particular good be produced by the nation with the lowest domestic opportunity cost, or the nation having a comparative advantage in that good. Canada should produce steel and Brazil should produce soybeans. Note that this conclusion holds even though Canada has an absolute advantage in both steel and soybeans.

A comparison of columns 1 and 2 of Table 19-1 verifies that specialization allows the world to get more output from its fixed amounts of resources. By specializing completely in steel, Canada can produce 30 tonnes of steel and no soybeans; Brazil, by specializing completely in soybeans, produces 20 tonnes of soybeans and no steel. These figures exceed the yields generated without specialization: 26 tonnes of steel (= 18 in Canada + 8 in Brazil) and 16 tonnes of soybeans (= 12 in Canada and 4 in Brazil). As a result, the world ends up with 4 more tonnes of steel (30 tonnes, compared with 26) *and* 4 more tonnes of soybeans (20 tonnes, compared with 16) than it would if there were self-sufficiency and unspecialized production.

Terms of Trade

We have just seen that specialization in production will allow for the largest possible amounts of both steel and soybeans to be produced. But with both countries specializing in the production of only one item, how will the soybeans produced by Brazil and the steel produced by Canada be divided between consumers in the two countries? The key turns out to be the **terms of trade**, the exchange ratio at which Canada and Brazil trade steel and soybeans. But consumers of each nation want *both* steel and soybeans. They can have both, if the two nations trade or exchange the two products. But what will be the terms of trade? At what exchange ratio will Canada and Brazil trade steel and soybeans?

Crucially, the terms of trade also establish whether each country will find it in its own better interest to bother specializing at all. This is because the terms of trade determine whether each country can "get a better deal" by specializing and trading than it could if it opted instead for self-sufficiency. To see how this works, note that because $1S_t = 1S_{oy}$ in Canada, Canada must get *more than* 1 tonne of soybeans for each tonne of steel exported; otherwise it will not benefit from exporting steel in exchange for Brazilian soybeans. Canada must get a better "price" (more soybeans) for its steel in the world market than it can get domestically or there is no gain from trade and it will not occur.

Similarly, because $1S_t = 2S_{oy}$ in Brazil, Brazil must obtain 1 tonne of steel by exporting some amount *less than* 2 tonnes of soybeans. Brazil must pay a lower "price" for steel in the world market than it must pay domestically or it will not want to trade. The international exchange ratio or terms of trade must lie somewhere between

$1S_t = 1S_{oy}$ (Canada's cost conditions)

and

$1S_t = 2S_{oy}$ (Brazil's cost conditions)

Where between these limits will the world exchange ratio fall? Canada will prefer a ratio close to $1S_t = 2S_{oy}$, say $1S_t = 1\frac{3}{4} S_{oy}$. Canada wants to get the most soybeans possible for each tonne of steel it exports. Similarly, Brazil wants a rate near $1S_t = 1S_{oy}$, say $1S_t = 1\frac{1}{4} S_{oy}$. Brazil wants to export the smallest quantity of soybeans possible for each tonne of steel it receives in exchange.

The actual exchange ratio depends on world supply and demand for the two products. If overall world demand for soybeans is weak relative to its supply and the demand for steel is strong relative to its supply, the exchange ratio will settle nearer the $1S_t = 2S_{oy}$ figure Canada prefers. If overall world demand for soybeans is great relative to its supply and if the demand for steel is weak relative to its supply, the ratio will settle nearer the $1S_t = 1S_{oy}$ level favourable to Brazil. (We will take up the topic of equilibrium world prices later in this chapter.)

Gains from Trade

Suppose the international exchange ratio or terms of trade is $1S_t = 1\frac{1}{2} S_{oy}$. The possibility of trading on these terms permits each nation to supplement its domestic production possibilities line with a **trading possibilities line**. This can be seen in Figure 19-2 (Key Graph). Just as a production possibilities line shows the amount of these products a full-employment economy can obtain by shifting resources from one to the other, a trading possibilities line shows the amounts of two products a nation can obtain by specializing in one product and trading for another. The trading possibilities lines in Figure 19-2 reflect the assumption that both nations specialize based on comparative advantage: Canada specializes completely in steel (point *B* in Figure 19-2a) and Brazil completely in soybeans (at point *v* in Figure 19-2b).

IMPROVED ALTERNATIVES

With specialization, Canada is no longer constrained by its domestic production possibilities line, which requires it to give up 1 tonne of steel for every tonne of soybeans it wants as it moves up its domestic production possibilities line, say from point *B*. Instead, Canada, through trade with Brazil, can get 1½ tonnes of soybeans for every tonne of steel it exports to Brazil, so long as Brazil has soybeans to export. Trading possibility line *BV′* thus represents the $1S_t = 1\frac{1}{2} S_{oy}$ trading ratio.

Specialization according to comparative advantage results in more efficient allocation of world resources.

© Darkop/Dreamstime.com

Similarly, Brazil, starting at, say, point *c*, no longer has to move down its domestic production possibilities curve, giving up 2 tonnes of soybeans for each tonne of steel it wants. It can now export just 1½ tonnes of soybeans for each tonne of steel it wants by moving down its trading possibilities line *vb′*.

Specialization and trade create a new exchange ratio between steel and soybeans, reflected in a nation's trading possibilities line. This exchange ratio is superior for both nations to the self-sufficiency exchange ratio embodied in the production possibilities line of each. By specializing in steel and trading for Brazil's soybeans, Canada can obtain more than 1 tonne of soybeans for 1 tonne of steel. By specializing in soybeans and trading for Canada's steel, Brazil can get 1 tonne of steel for less than 2 tonnes of soybeans. In both cases, self-sufficiency is undesirable.

KEY GRAPH

FIGURE 19-2   Trading Possibilities Lines and the Gains from Trade

As a result of international specialization and trade, Canada and Brazil both can have levels of output higher than those attainable on their domestic production possibilities curves. (a) Canada can move from point *A* on its domestic production possibilities curve to, say, *A'* on its trading possibilities line. (b) Brazil can move from *Z* to *Z'*.

(a) Canada

(b) Brazil

GREATER OUTPUT

By specializing according to comparative advantage and trading for those goods produced in nations with greater domestic efficiency, Canada and Brazil can achieve combinations of steel and soybeans beyond their individual production possibilities curves. Specialization according to comparative advantage results in a more efficient allocation of world resources, and larger outputs of both steel and soybeans are therefore available to both nations.

Suppose that at the $1S_t = 1\frac{1}{2} S_{oy}$ terms of trade, Canada exports 10 tonnes of steel to Brazil and in return Brazil exports 15 tonnes of soybeans to Canada. How do the new quantities of steel and soybeans available to the two nations compare with the optimal product mixes that existed before specialization and trade? Point A in Figure 19-2a reminds us that Canada chose 18 tonnes of steel and 12 tonnes of soybeans originally. But, by producing 30 tonnes of steel and no soybeans, and by trading 10 tonnes of steel for 15 tonnes of soybeans, Canada can obtain 20 tonnes of steel and 15 tonnes of soybeans. This new, superior combination of steel and soybeans is shown by point A' in Figure 19-2a. Compared with the non-trading figures of 18 tonnes of steel and 12 tonnes of soybeans, Canada's **gains from trade** are 2 tonnes of steel and 3 tonnes of soybeans.

Similarly, recall that Brazil's optimal product mix was 4 tonnes of soybeans and 8 tonnes of steel (point Z) before specialization and trade. Now, by specializing in soybeans and trading—producing 20 tonnes of soybeans and no steel and exporting 15 tonnes of its soybeans in exchange for 10 tonnes of Canadian steel—Brazil can have 5 tonnes of soybeans and 10 tonnes of steel. This new position is indicated by point Z' in Figure 19-2b. Brazil's gains from trade are 1 tonne of soybeans and 2 tonnes of steel.

Points A' and Z' in Figure 19-2 are superior economic positions to points A and Z. This fact is enormously important. We know that a nation can expand its production possibilities boundary by (1) expanding the quantity and improving the quality of its resources or (2) realizing technological progress. We have now established that international trade can enable a nation to get around the output constraint imposed by its production possibilities curve. The effects of international specialization and trade are the equivalent of having more and better resources or discovering improved production techniques.

WORKED PROBLEM 19.1   Gains from Trade

Table 19-1 summarizes the transactions and outcomes in our analysis. Please give it one final, careful review.

QUICK REVIEW 19.2

- The principle of comparative advantage says that total world output will be greatest when each good is produced by the nation that has the lowest domestic opportunity cost.

- The rate at which countries can trade units of one product for units of another product is referred to as the terms of trade.

- A trading possibilities line shows the amounts of two products that a nation can obtain by specializing in the production of one product and then trading for the other.

Trade with Increasing Costs

To explain the basic principles underlying international trade, we simplified our analysis in several ways. For example, we limited discussion to two products and two nations. But multiproduct/multinational analysis yields the same conclusions. We also assumed constant opportunity costs (linear production possibilities curves), which is a more substantive simplification. Let's consider the effect of allowing increasing opportunity costs (concave-from-the-origin production possibilities curves) to enter the picture.

Suppose Canada and Brazil are initially at positions on their concave production possibilities curves where their domestic cost ratios are $1S_t = 1S_{oy}$ and $1S_t = 2S_{oy}$, as they were in our constant-cost analysis. As before, comparative advantage indicates that Canada should specialize in steel and Brazil in soybeans. But now, as Canada begins to expand steel production, its $1S_t = 1S_{oy}$ cost ratio will *fall*; it will have to sacrifice *more than* 1 tonne of soybeans to

CONSIDER THIS

Misunderstanding the Gains from Trade

It is a common myth that the greatest benefit to be derived from international trade is greater domestic employment in the export sector. This suggests that exports are "good" because they increase domestic employment, whereas imports are "bad" because they deprive people of jobs at home. As we have demonstrated, the true benefit created by international trade is the overall increase in output available through specialization and exchange. A nation does not need international trade to

© Bloomberg via Getty Images

operate *on* its production possibilities curve. It can fully employ its resources, including labour, with or without international trade. International trade, however, enables a country to reach a point of consumption beyond its domestic production possibilities curve. The gain from trade to a nation is the extra output obtained from abroad—the imports obtained for less sacrifice of other goods than if they were produced at home.

get 1 additional tonne of steel. Resources are no longer perfectly shiftable between alternative uses, as the constant-cost assumption implied. Resources less and less suited to steel production must be allocated to the Canadian steel industry in expanding steel output, and this means increasing costs—the sacrifice of larger and larger amounts of soybeans for each additional tonne of steel.

Similarly, Brazil, starting from its $1S_t = 2S_{oy}$ cost ratio position, expands soybean production. But as it does, it will find that its $1S_t = 2S_{oy}$ cost ratio begins to *rise*. Sacrificing a tonne of steel will free resources that can be used to produce something less than 2 tonnes of soybeans, because these transferred resources are less suitable to soybean production.

As the Canadian cost ratio falls from $1S_t = 1S_{oy}$ and Brazil's rises from $1S_t = 2S_{oy}$, a point will be reached at which the cost ratios are equal in the two nations, perhaps at $1S_t = 1\frac{3}{4} S_{oy}$. At this point, the underlying basis for further specialization and trade—differing cost ratios—has disappeared. Most importantly, this point of equal cost ratios may be reached where Canada is still producing *some* soybeans along with its steel and Brazil is producing some steel along with its soybeans. *The primary effect of increasing costs is to make specialization less than complete.* For this reason we often find domestically produced products competing directly against identical or similar imported products within a particular economy.

The Case for Free Trade Restated

The case for free trade reduces to one compelling argument. Through free trade based on the principle of comparative advantage, the world economy can achieve a more efficient allocation of resources and a higher level of material well-being than without free trade.

Since the resource mixes and technological knowledge of each country are somewhat different, each nation can produce particular commodities at different real costs. Each nation should produce goods for which its domestic opportunity costs are lower than the domestic opportunity costs of other nations, and exchange these specialties for products for which its domestic opportunity costs are high relative to those of other nations. If each nation does this, the world can realize the advantages of specialization. The world and each free-trading nation can obtain a larger real income from the fixed supplies of resources available to it.

One side benefit of free trade is that it promotes competition and deters monopoly. The increased competition from foreign firms forces domestic firms to adopt the lowest-cost production techniques. It also compels them to be innovative with respect to both product quality and production methods, thereby contributing to economic growth. And free trade provides consumers with a wider range of product choices. The reasons to favour free trade are the same reasons to endorse competition.

A second side-benefit of free trade is that it links national interest and breaks down national animosities. Confronted with political disagreements, trading partners tend to negotiate rather than make war.

QUICK REVIEW 19.3

- International trade enables nations to specialize, improve the productivity of their resources, and obtain a larger output.

- Comparative advantage means total world output will be greatest when each good is produced by that nation having the lowest domestic opportunity cost.

- Specialization is less than complete among nations because opportunity costs normally rise as any specific nation produces more of a particular good.

19.2 Supply and Demand Analysis of Exports and Imports

LO19.2 Describe how differences between world prices prompt exports and imports.

Supply and demand analysis reveals how equilibrium prices and quantities of exports and imports are determined. The amount of a good or service that a nation will export or import depends on differences between equilibrium world and domestic prices. The interaction of *world* supply and demand determines **world price**, the price at which the quantities supplied and demanded are equal globally. *Domestic supply* and demand determine the equilibrium **domestic price**—the price that would prevail in a closed economy. It is a price at which domestic supply and demand are equal.

In the absence of trade, domestic prices in a closed economy may or may not equal world equilibrium prices. When economies are opened for international trade, differences between world and domestic prices motivate exports or imports. To see how, let's now look at the international effects of such price differences in a simple two-nation world consisting of Canada and the United States, which are both producing aluminum. We assume there are no trade barriers, such as tariffs and quotas, and no international transportation costs.

Supply and Demand in Canada

Figure 19-3a shows the domestic supply curve S_d and domestic demand curve D_d for aluminum in Canada. The intersection of S_d and D_d determines the equilibrium domestic price of $1.25 per kilogram and the equilibrium domestic quantity is 100 million kilograms. Domestic suppliers produce 100 million kilograms and sell them at $1.25. So there are no domestic surpluses or shortages of aluminum.

But what if the Canadian economy is opened to world trade and the *world price* of aluminum is above or below this $1.25 domestic price?

CANADIAN EXPORT SUPPLY

If the world aluminum price exceeds $1.25, Canadian firms will produce more than 100 million kilograms and export the excess domestic output to the rest of the world (United States). First, consider a world price of $1.50. We see from the supply curve S_d that Canadian aluminum firms will produce 125 million kilograms of aluminum at that price. The demand curve D_d tells us that Canadians will purchase only 75 million kilograms at $1.50. The outcome is a domestic surplus of 50 million kilograms of aluminum. Canadian producers will export these 50 million kilograms at the $1.50 world price.

What if the world price is $1.75? The supply curve shows that Canadian firms will produce 150 million kilograms of aluminum, while the demand curve tells us that Canadian consumers will buy only 50 million kilograms. So Canadian producers will export the domestic surplus of 100 million kilograms.

In Figure 19-3b we assign the quantity of surplus or shortage to the horizontal scale. The domestic surpluses—the Canadian exports—occurring at world prices above the $1.25 domestic equilibrium price are plotted in red. When the world and domestic prices are equal (= $1.25), the quantity of exports supplied is zero (point a). There is no surplus of domestic output to export. But when the world price is $1.50, Canadian firms export 50 million

FIGURE 19-3   Canadian Export Supply and Import Demand

(a) Domestic supply S_d and demand D_d at the domestic equilibrium price of aluminum at $1.25 per kilo. World prices above the $1.25 domestic price create domestic surpluses of aluminum. At prices below $1.25 there are domestic shortages. (b) Surpluses are exported (top curve), and shortages are met by importing aluminum (lower curve). The export supply curve shows the direct relationship between world prices and Canadian exports; the import demand curve portrays the inverse relationship between world prices and Canadian imports.

(a) Canadian domestic aluminum market

(b) Canadian export supply and import demand

kilograms of surplus aluminum (point *b*). At a $1.75 world price, the domestic surplus of 100 million kilograms is exported (point *c*).

The Canadian **export supply curve**, found by connecting points such as *a*, *b*, and *c*, shows the amount of aluminum that Canadian producers will export at each world price above $1.25. This curve *slopes upward*, revealing a direct or positive relationship between the world price and amount of Canadian exports. *As world prices increase relative to domestic prices, Canadian exports rise.*

CANADIAN IMPORT DEMAND

If the world price is below $1.25, Canada will end up importing aluminum. Consider a $1 world price. The supply curve in Figure 19-3a reveals that at that price Canadian firms will produce only 75 million kilograms of aluminum. But the demand curve shows that Canadians want to buy 125 million kilograms at that price. The result is a domestic shortage of 50 million kilograms. To satisfy that shortage, Canada will import 50 million kilograms of aluminum.

At an even lower $0.75 world price, Canadian producers will supply only 50 million kilograms. Because Canadian consumers want to buy 150 million kilograms, there is a domestic shortage of 100 million kilograms. Imports will flow to Canada to make up the difference. That is, at a $0.75 world price, Canadian firms supply 50 million kilograms and import 100 million kilograms.

In Figure 19-3b we plot the Canadian **import demand curve** from these data in blue. This *downsloping curve* shows the amounts of aluminum that will be imported at world prices below the $1.25 Canadian domestic price. The relationship between world prices and imports is inverse or negative. At a world price of $1.25, domestic output will satisfy Canadian demand; imports will be zero (point *a*). But at $1 Canadians will import 50 million kilograms of aluminum (point *x*); at $0.75, they will import 100 million kilograms (point *y*). Connecting points *a*, *x*, and *y* yields a *downsloping* Canadian import demand curve. *As world prices fall relative to domestic prices, Canadian imports increase.*

FIGURE 19-4 U.S. Export Supply and Import Demand

(a) At world prices above the $1 domestic price, production in the United States exceeds domestic consumption. At world prices below $1, domestic shortages occur. (b) Surpluses result in exports, and shortages result in imports. The U.S. export supply curve and import demand curve depict the relationships between world prices and exports or imports.

(a) United States domestic aluminum market

(b) United States export supply and import demand

Supply and Demand in the United States

We repeat our analysis in Figure 19-4, this time for the United States. (We have converted U.S. dollar prices to Canadian dollar prices via an assumed exchange rate.) Note that the domestic supply curve S_d and demand curve D_d for aluminum in the United States yield a domestic price of $1, which is $0.25 lower than the $1.25 Canadian domestic price.

The analysis proceeds exactly as for Canada. If the world price is $1, Americans will neither export nor import aluminum (which gives us point q in Figure 19-4b). At world prices above $1, U.S. firms will produce more aluminum than U.S. consumers will buy. The surplus will be exported. At a $1.25 world price, Figure 19-4a tells us that the United States will export a domestic surplus of 50 million kilograms (yielding point r). At $1.50 it will export a domestic surplus of 100 million kilograms (point s). Connecting these points yields the red, upsloping U.S. export supply curve that reflects the domestic surpluses (and thus exports) occurring when the world price exceeds the $1 U.S. domestic price.

At world prices below $1 domestic shortages occur in the United States. At a $0.75 world price, Figure 19-4a shows that U.S. consumers want to buy 125 million kilograms of aluminum but U.S. firms will produce only 75 million kilograms. The shortage will bring 50 million kilograms of imports to the United States (point t in Figure 19-4b). The blue U.S. import demand curve in that figure shows U.S. imports at world aluminum prices below the $1 U.S. domestic price.

Equilibrium World Price, Exports, and Imports

We now have the tools to determine the **equilibrium world price** of aluminum and the equilibrium world levels of exports and imports. Figure 19-5 combines the Canadian export supply curve and import demand curve in Figure 19-3b, and the U.S. export supply curve and import demand curve in Figure 19-4b. The two Canadian curves proceed rightward from the $1.25 domestic price; the two U.S. curves proceed rightward from the $1 U.S. domestic price.

FIGURE 19-5   Equilibrium World Price and Quantity of Exports and Imports

In a two-nation world, the equilibrium world price (= $1.125) is determined at the intersection of one nation's export supply curve and another nation's import demand curve. This intersection also decides the equilibrium volume of exports and imports. Here, the United States exports 25 million kilograms of aluminum to Canada.

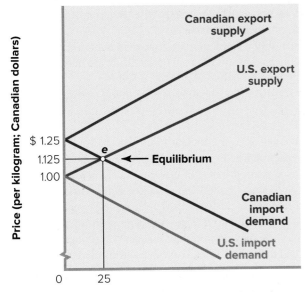

Quantity (millions of kilograms) of aluminum

International equilibrium occurs in this two-nation model where one nation's import demand curve intersects another nation's export supply curve. In this case Canada's import demand curve intersects America's export supply curve at *e*. There, the world price of aluminum is $1.125. The U.S. export supply curve indicates that the United States will export 25 million kilograms of aluminum at this price. Also at this price Canada will import 25 million kilograms from the United States, indicated by the Canadian import demand curve. The $1.125 world price equates the quantity of imports demanded and the quantity of exports supplied (= 25 million kilograms). Thus there will be world trade of 25 million kilograms of aluminum at $1.125 per kilogram.

Note that after trade, the single $1.125 world price will prevail in both Canada and the United States. Only one price for a standardized commodity can persist in a competitive market. With trade, all consumers can buy a kilogram of aluminum for $1.125 and all producers can sell it for that price.

WORKED PROBLEM 19.2   Equilibrium World Price, Exports, and Imports

Why would the United States willingly send 50 million kilograms of its aluminum output to Canada for consumption? After all, producing this output uses up scarce U.S. resources and drives up the price of aluminum for Americans. Americans are willing to export aluminum to Canada because they can gain the means—the earnings of Canadian dollars—to import other goods, say telecommunications equipment, from Canada.

QUICK REVIEW 19.4

- A nation will export a particular product if the world price exceeds the domestic price; it will import the product if the world price is less than the domestic price.

- In a two-country model, equilibrium world prices and equilibrium quantities of exports and imports occur when one nation's export supply curve intersects the other nation's import demand curve.

19.3 Trade Barriers and Export Subsidies

LO19.3 Analyze the economic effects of tariffs and quotas.

While a nation as a whole gains from trade, trade may harm particular domestic industries and their workers. Those industries might seek to preserve their economic positions by persuading their respective governments to protect them from imports—perhaps through tariffs, import quotas, or other trade barriers.

Indeed, the public may be won over by the apparent plausibility ("Cut imports and prevent domestic unemployment") and the patriotic ring ("Buy Canadian!") of the arguments. The alleged benefits of tariffs are immediate and clear-cut to the public, but the adverse effects cited by economists are obscure and dispersed over the entire economy. When political deal making is added in—"You back tariffs for the apparel industry in my province, and I'll back tariffs for the auto industry in your province"—the outcome can be a politically robust network of trade barriers. These impediments to free international trade can take several forms.

Tariffs are excise taxes or *duties* on the dollar values or physical quantities of imported goods. They may be imposed to obtain revenue or to protect domestic firms. A **revenue tariff** is usually applied to a product that is not being produced domestically, for example, tin, coffee, or bananas in the case of Canada. Rates on revenue tariffs tend to be modest and are designed to provide the federal government with revenue. A **protective tariff** is implemented to shield domestic producers from foreign competition. These tariffs impede free trade by increasing the prices of imported goods and therefore shifting sales toward domestic producers. Although protective tariffs are usually not high enough to stop the importation of foreign goods, they put foreign producers at a competitive disadvantage. A tariff on imported auto tires, for example, would make domestically produced tires more attractive to consumers.

An **import quota** is a limit on the quantities or total values of specific items that are imported in some period. Once a quota is filled, further imports of that product are choked off. Import quotas are more effective than tariffs in impeding international trade. With a tariff, a product can go on being imported in large quantities. But with an import quota, all imports are prohibited once the quota is filled.

A **nontariff barrier (NTB)** includes onerous licensing requirements, unreasonable standards pertaining to product quality, or simply bureaucratic hurdles and delays in customs procedures. Some nations require that importers of foreign goods obtain licences and then restrict the number of licences issued. Although many nations carefully inspect imported agricultural products to prevent the introduction of potentially harmful insects, some countries use lengthy inspections to impede imports. Japan and the European countries frequently require that their domestic importers of foreign goods obtain licences. By restricting the issuance of licences, governments can limit imports.

A **voluntary export restriction (VER)** is a trade barrier by which foreign firms "voluntarily" limit the amount of their exports to a particular country. VERs have the same effect as import quotas and are agreed to by exporters to avoid more stringent tariffs or quotas. In the late 1990s, for example, Canadian producers of softwood lumber (fir, spruce, cedar, pine) agreed to a VER on exports to the United States under the threat of a permanently higher U.S. tariff.

An **export subsidy** consists of a government payment to a domestic producer of export goods and is designed to aid that producer. By reducing production costs, the subsidies enable the domestic firm to charge a lower price and thus to sell more exports in world markets. Consider these two examples: (1) Some European governments have heavily subsidized Airbus Industries, a European firm that produces commercial aircraft. The subsidies help Airbus compete against the American firm Boeing. (2) Canada and other nations have subsidized domestic farmers to boost the domestic food supply. Such subsidies have artificially lowered export prices on agricultural produce.

Economic Impact of Tariffs

Once again we use supply and demand analysis to examine the economic effects of protective tariffs. Curves D_d and S_d in Figure 19-6 (Key Graph) show domestic demand and supply for a product in which a nation, say Canada, has a comparative *dis*advantage—for example, smartphones. (Disregard $S_d + Q$ for now.) Without world trade, the domestic price and output would be P_d and q respectively.

Assume now that the domestic economy is opened to world trade and that the Chinese, who have a comparative advantage in smartphones, begins to sell them in Canada. We assume that with free trade the domestic price cannot differ from the world price, which here is P_w. At P_w domestic consumption is d and domestic production is a. The horizontal distance between the domestic supply and demand curves at P_w represents imports of ad. Thus far, our analysis is similar to the analysis of world prices in Figure 19-3.

KEY GRAPH

FIGURE 19-6   The Economic Effects of a Protective Tariff or an Import Quota

A tariff that increases the price of a good from P_w to P_t will reduce domestic consumption from d to c. Domestic producers will be able to sell more output (b rather than a) at a higher price (P_t rather than P_w). Foreign exporters are injured because they sell less output (b–c rather than a–d). The shaded area indicates the amount of tariff paid by domestic consumers. An import quota of b–c units has the same effect as the tariff, with one exception: The amount represented by the shaded area will go to foreign producers rather than to the domestic government.

DIRECT EFFECTS

Suppose now that Canada imposes a tariff on each imported smartphone. This will raise the domestic price from P_w to P_t and has four effects.

1. *Decline in Consumption*   Consumption of smartphones in Canada declines from d to c as the higher price moves buyers up and to the left along their demand curve. The tariff prompts consumers to buy fewer smartphones and to reallocate a portion of their expenditures to less-desired substitute products. Canadian consumers are injured by the tariff, since they pay $P_t - P_w$ more for each of the c units they now buy at price P_t.

2. *Increased Domestic Production*   Canadian producers—who are *not* subject to the tariff—receive higher price P_t per unit. Because this new price is higher than the pre-tariff or world price of P_w, the domestic smartphone industry moves up and to the right along its supply curve S_d, increasing domestic output from a to b. Domestic producers thus enjoy both a higher price and expanded sales, which explains why domestic producers lobby for protective tariffs. But from a social point of view, the increased domestic production from b to a means that the tariff permits domestic producers of smartphones to bid resources away from other, more efficient, Canadian industries.

3. **Decline in Imports** Chinese producers are hurt. Although the sale price of each smartphone is higher by $P_t - P_w$, that amount accrues to the Canadian government, not to Chinese producers. The after-tariff world price, and thus the per-unit revenue to Chinese producers, remains at P_w, and the volume of Canadian imports (Chinese exports) falls from d–a to c–b.

4. **Tariff Revenue** The shaded rectangle indicates the amount of revenue that the tariff yields. Total revenue from the tariff is determined by multiplying the tariff, $P_t - P_w$ per unit, by the number of smartphones imported, c–b. This tariff revenue is a transfer of income from consumers to government and does *not* represent any net change in the nation's economic well-being. The result is that government gains a portion of what consumers lose by paying more for smartphones.

INDIRECT EFFECTS

Tariffs have a subtle effect beyond what our supply and demand diagram can show. Because China sells fewer smartphones in Canada, China will earn fewer dollars with which to buy Canadian exports. Canadian export industries must then cut production and release resources. These are highly efficient industries, as evidenced by their comparative advantage and ability to sell goods in world markets.

Tariffs directly promote the expansion of inefficient industries that do not have a comparative advantage; they also indirectly cause contraction of relatively efficient industries that do have a comparative advantage. We know that specialization and world trade lead to more efficient use of world resources and greater world output. But protective tariffs reduce world trade. Therefore, tariffs also reduce efficiency and the world's real output.

Economic Impact of Quotas

The economic impact of quotas is similar to that of a tariff with one salient difference: Although tariffs generate revenue for the Canadian government, a quota transfers that revenue to foreign producers.

Suppose in Figure 19-6 that, instead of imposing a tariff of $P_t - P_w$ per unit, Canada prohibits any Chinese imports of smartphones in excess of b–c units. In other words, an import quota of b–c smartphones is imposed on China. We have deliberately chosen the size of this quota to be the same amount as imports would be under a $P_t - P_w$ tariff so we are comparing equivalent situations. As a consequence of the quota, the supply of smartphones is $S_d + Q$ in Canada. This consists of the domestic supply plus the constant amount c–b ($= Q$) that importers will provide at each domestic price. The $S_d + Q$ supply curve does not exist below price P_w because Chinese producers would not export smartphones to Canada at any price *below* P_w; instead, they would sell them to other countries at the world market price of P_w.

Most of the economic results are the same as with a tariff. Prices of smartphones are higher (P_t instead of P_w) because imports have been reduced from d–a to c–b. Domestic consumption of smartphones is down from d–a to c–b. Canadian producers enjoy both a higher price (P_t rather than P_w) and increased sales (b rather than a).

The difference is that the price increase of $P_t - P_w$ paid by Canadian consumers on imports of c–b—the shaded area—no longer goes to the Canada Revenue Agency as tariff (tax) revenue, but flows to those Chinese firms that have acquired the quota rights to sell smartphones in Canada. The economic effects of a tariff are better for Canadian taxpayers than are those of a quota, other things equal. A tariff generates government revenue, which can be used to cut other taxes or to finance public goods and services that benefit Canadian citizens. In contrast, the higher price created by quotas results in additional revenue for foreign producers.

Net Costs of Tariffs and Quotas

Figure 19-6 shows that tariffs and quotas impose costs on domestic consumers but provide gains to domestic producers, and in the case of tariffs, revenue to the federal government. The consumer costs of trade restrictions are calculated by determining the effect they have on consumer prices. Protection raises the price of a product in three ways: (1) the price of the imported product goes up, (2) the higher price of imports causes some consumers to shift their purchases to higher-priced domestically produced goods, and (3) the prices of domestically produced goods rise because import competition has declined.

Study after study finds that the costs to consumers substantially exceed gains to producers, workers, other suppliers of resources in the protected industry, and to the government. A sizable net cost or efficiency loss to society arises from trade protection. Furthermore, industries employ large amounts of economic resources to influence politicians to pass and retain protectionist laws. Because these rent-seeking efforts divert resources away from more socially desirable purposes, trade restrictions impose these additional costs on society, as well.

Conclusion: The gains that Canadian trade barriers create for protected industries and their workers come at the expense of much greater losses for the entire economy. The result is economic inefficiency, reduced consumption, and lower standards of living.

QUICK REVIEW 19.5

- A tariff on a product increases its price, reduces its consumption, increases its domestic production, reduces its imports, and generates tariff revenue for government

- An import quota does the same, except a quota generates revenue for foreign producers rather than for the government imposing the quota.

The LAST WORD

Petition of the Candlemakers, 1845

© Robert W. Ginn/PhotoEdit

French economist Frédéric Bastiat (1801–1850) devastated the proponents of protectionism by satirically extending their reasoning to its logical and absurd conclusions.

Petition of the Manufacturers of Candles, Waxlights, Lamps, Candlesticks, Street Lamps, Snuffers, Extinguishers, and of the Producers of Oil Tallow, Rosin, Alcohol, and, Generally, of Everything Connected with Lighting.

TO MESSIEURS THE MEMBERS OF THE CHAMBER OF DEPUTIES.

Gentlemen—You are on the right road. You reject abstract theories, and have little consideration for cheapness and plenty. Your chief care is the interest of the producer. You desire to emancipate him from external competition, and reserve the national market for national industry.

We are about to offer you an admirable opportunity of applying your—what shall we call it? your theory? No; nothing is more deceptive than theory; your doctrine? your system? your principle? but you dislike doctrines, you abhor systems, and as for principles, you deny that there are any in social economy: we shall say, then, your practice, your practice without theory and without principle.

We are suffering from the intolerable competition of a foreign rival, placed, it would seem, in a condition so far superior to ours for the production of light, that he absolutely inundates our national market with it at a price fabulously reduced. The moment he shows himself, our trade leaves us—all consumers apply to him; and a branch of native industry, having countless ramifications, is all at once rendered completely stagnant. This rival ... is no other than the Sun.

What we pray for is, that it may please you to pass a law ordering the shutting up of all windows, skylights, dormer windows, outside and inside shutters, curtains, blinds, bull's-eyes; in a word, of all openings, holes, chinks, clefts, and fissures, by or through which the light of the sun has been in use to enter houses, to the prejudice of the meritorious manufacturers with which we flatter ourselves we have accommodated our country—a country which, in gratitude, ought not to abandon us now to a strife so unequal.

If you shut up as much as possible all access to natural light, and create a demand for artificial light, which of our French manufacturers will not be encouraged by it? If more tallow is consumed, then there must be more oxen and sheep; and, consequently, we shall behold the multiplication of artificial meadows, meat, wool, hides, and, above all, manure, which is the basis and foundation of all agricultural wealth.

The same remark applies to navigation. Thousands of vessels will proceed to the whale fishery; and, in a short time, we shall possess a navy capable of maintaining the honour of France, and gratifying the patriotic aspirations of your petitioners, the undersigned candlemakers and others.

Only have the goodness to reflect, Gentlemen, and you will be convinced that there is, perhaps, no Frenchman, from the wealthy coalmaster to the humblest vender of lucifer matches, whose lot will not be ameliorated by the success of this our petition.

Source: Frédéric Bastiat, *Economic Sophisms* (Irvington-on-Hudson, NY: The Foundation for Economic Education, Inc., 1996), abridged. Used with permission of Foundation for Economic Education, www.FEE.org.

Question

What was the central point that Bastiat was trying to make in his imaginary petition of the candlemakers?

Chapter Summary

LO19.1 Define comparative advantage and demonstrate how specialization and trade add to a nation's output.

- World trade is based on three considerations: the uneven distribution of economic resources among nations, the fact that efficient production of various goods requires particular techniques or combinations of resources, and the differentiated products produced among nations.

- Mutually advantageous specialization and trade are possible between any two nations if they have different opportunity cost ratios for any two products. By specializing based on comparative advantage, nations can obtain larger real incomes with fixed amounts of resources. The terms of trade determine how this increase in world output is shared by the trading nations. Increasing (rather than constant) costs limit specialization and trade.

LO19.2 Describe how differences between world prices prompt exports and imports.

- A nation's export supply curve shows the quantity of product it will export at world prices that exceed the domestic price—the

price in a closed, no-international-trade economy. Its import demand curve reveals the quantity of a product it will import at world prices below the domestic price. In a two-nation model, the equilibrium world price and the equilibrium quantities of exports and imports occur where one nation's import supply curve intersects the other nation's export demand curve.

LO19.3 Analyze the economic effects of tariffs and quotas.

- Trade barriers take the form of protective tariffs, quotas, nontariff barriers, and "voluntary" export restrictions. Export subsidies also distort international trade. Supply and demand analysis demonstrates that protective tariffs and quotas increase the prices and reduce the quantities demanded of affected goods. Sales by foreign exporters diminish; domestic producers, however, enjoy higher prices and enlarged sales. Consumer losses from trade restrictions greatly exceed producer and government gains, creating an efficiency loss to society.

Terms and Concepts

labour-intensive goods
land-intensive goods
capital-intensive goods
absolute advantage
comparative advantage
opportunity-cost ratio
principle of comparative advantage
terms of trade
trading possibilities line
gains from trade
world price

domestic price
export supply curve
import demand curve
equilibrium world price
tariffs
revenue tariff
protective tariff
import quota
nontariff barrier (NTB)
voluntary export restriction (VER)
export subsidy

Discussion Questions

1. Distinguish among land-, labour-, and capital-intensive goods, citing an example of each without resorting to book examples. How do these distinctions relate to international trade? How do distinctive products, unrelated to resource intensity, relate to international trade?   [**LO19.1**]

2. Explain the following: "Canada can make certain toys with greater productive efficiency than can China. Yet we import those toys from China." Relate your answer to the ideas of Adam Smith and David Ricardo.   [**LO19.1**]

3. Suppose Big Country can produce 80 units of X by using all its resources to produce X and 60 units of Y by devoting all its resources to Y. Comparative figures for Small Nation are 60 of X and 60 of Y. Assuming constant costs, in which product should each nation specialize? Explain why. What are the limits of the terms of trade between these two countries? How would rising costs (rather than constant costs) affect the extent of specialization and trade between these two countries?   [**LO19.1**]

4. What is an export demand curve? What is an import supply curve? How do such curves relate to the determination of the equilibrium world price of a tradable good?   [**LO19.2**]

5. Why is a quota more detrimental to an economy than a tariff that results in the same level of imports as the quota? What is the net outcome of either tariffs or quota for the world economy?   [**LO19.3**]

6. "The potentially valid arguments for tariff protection are also the most easily abused." (a) What are these particular arguments? (b) Why are they susceptible to abuse? (c) Evaluate the use of artificial trade barriers, such as tariffs and import quotas, as a means of achieving and maintaining full employment.   [**LO19.3**]

7. Evaluate the effectiveness of artificial trade barriers, such as tariffs and import quotas, as a way to achieve and maintain full employment throughout the Canadian economy. How might such policies reduce unemployment in one Canadian industry but increase it in another Canadian industry?   [**LO19.3**]

8. In 2014, manufacturing workers in Canada earned an average wage of $23.19 per hour. That same year, manufacturing workers in Mexico earned an average wage of $6.36 per hour. (a) How can Canadian manufacturers possibly compete? (b) Why isn't all manufacturing done in Mexico and other low-wage countries?   [**LO19.3**]

9. How might protective tariffs reduce both the imports and the exports of the nation that levies tariffs? In what way do foreign firms that "dump" their products onto the Canadian market in effect provide bargains to Canadian consumers? How might the import competition lead to quality improvements and cost reductions by Canadian firms?   [**LO19.3**]

Review Questions

1. In Country A, a worker can make 5 bicycles per hour. In Country B, a worker can make 7 bicycles per hour. Which country has an absolute advantage in making bicycles?   [**LO19.1**]

   a. Country A

   b. Country B

2. In Country A, the production of 1 bicycle requires using resources that could otherwise be used to produce 11 lamps. In Country B, the production of 1 bicycle requires using resources that could otherwise be used to produce 15 lamps. Which country has a comparative advantage in making bicycles?   [**LO19.1**]

   a. Country A

   b. Country B

3. True or False? If Country B has an absolute advantage over Country A in producing bicycles, it will also have a comparative advantage over Country A in producing bicycles.   [**LO19.1**]

4. Suppose that the opportunity-cost ratio for pears and apples is $4P : 1A$ in British Columbia but $1P : 2A$ in Ontario. Which province has the comparative advantage in producing apples?   [**LO19.1**]

   a. British Columbia

   b. Ontario

   c. Neither

5. Suppose that the opportunity-cost ratio for fish and lumber is $1F : 1L$ in Canada but $2F : 1L$ in Iceland. Then _____ should specialize in producing fish while _____ should specialize in producing lumber.   [**LO19.1**]

   a. Canada; Iceland

   b. Iceland; Canada

6. Suppose that the opportunity-cost ratio for watches and cheese is $1C : 1W$ in Switzerland but $1C : 4W$ in Japan. At which of the following international exchange ratios (terms of trade) will Switzerland and Japan be willing to specialize and engage in trade with each other? Select *one or more* answers from the choices shown.   [**LO19.1**]

   a. $1C \equiv 3W$

   b. $1C \equiv 1/2W$

   c. $1C \equiv 5W$

   d. $1/2C \equiv 1W$

   e. $2C \equiv 1W$

7. We see quite a bit of international trade in the real world. And trade is driven by specialization. So why don't we see full specialization—for instance, all cars in the world being made in South Korea, or all the mobile phones in the world being made in China? Choose the *best* answer from among the following choices.   [**LO19.1**]

   a. High tariffs

   b. Extensive import quotas

   c. Increasing opportunity costs

   d. Increasing returns

8. Which of the following are benefits of international trade? Select *one or more* answers from the choices shown.   [**LO19.1**]

   a. A more efficient allocation of resources

   b. A higher level of material well-being

   c. Gains from specialization

   d. Promoting competition

   e. Deterring monopoly

   f. Reducing the threat of war

9. True or False? If a country is open to international trade, the domestic price can differ from the international price. [**LO19.2**]

10. Suppose that the current international price of wheat is $6 per bushel and that Canada is currently exporting 30 million bushels per year. If Canada suddenly became a closed economy with respect to wheat, would the domestic price of wheat in Canada end up higher or lower than $6?   [**LO19.2**]

   a. Higher

   b. Lower

   c. The same

11. Suppose that if Iceland and Japan were both closed economies, the domestic price of fish would be $100 per tonne in Iceland and $90 per tonne in Japan. If the two countries decided to open up to international trade with each other, which of the following could be the equilibrium international price of fish once they begin trading?   [**LO19.2**]

   a. $75

   b. $85

   c. $95

   d. $105

12. Draw a domestic supply-and-demand diagram for a product in which Canada does not have a comparative advantage. What impact do foreign imports have on domestic price and quantity? On your diagram show a protective tariff that eliminates approximately one-half of the assumed imports. What are the price-quantity effects of this tariff on (a) domestic consumers, (b) domestic producers, and (c) foreign exporters? How would the effects of a quota that creates the same amount of imports differ?   [**LO19.3**]

13. Canadian apparel makers complain to Parliament about competition from China. Parliament decides to impose either a tariff or a quota on apparel imports from China. Which policy would Chinese apparel manufacturers prefer?   [**LO19.3**]

   a. Tariff

   b. Quota

Problems

1. Assume that the comparative-cost ratios of two products— baby formula and tuna fish—are as follows in the nations of Canswicki and Tunata: [**LO19.1**]

   Canswicki: 1 can baby formula = 2 cans tuna fish

   Tunata: 1 can baby formula = 4 cans tuna fish

   In what product should each nation specialize? Which of the following terms of trade would be acceptable to both nations: (a) 1 can baby formula = 2½ cans tuna fish; (b) 1 can baby formula = 1 can tuna fish; (c) 1 can baby formula = 5 cans tuna fish?

2. The following are hypothetical production possibilities tables for New Zealand and Spain.   [**LO19.1**]

New Zealand's Production Possibilities Table (millions of bushels)

PRODUCT	PRODUCTION ALTERNATIVES			
	A	**B**	**C**	**D**
Apples	0	20	40	60
Plums	15	10	5	0

Spain's Production Possibilities Table (millions of bushels)

PRODUCT	PRODUCTION ALTERNATIVES			
	R	**S**	**T**	**U**
Apples	0	20	40	60
Plums	60	40	20	0

Plot the production possibilities data for each of the two countries separately. Referring to your graphs,

   a. Determine each country's cost ratio of producing plums and apples.

   b. Determine which nation should specialize in which product.

   c. Determine the trading possibilities lines for each nation, if the actual terms of trade are 1 plum for 2 apples. (Plot these lines on your graph.)

   d. Suppose the optimum product mixes before specialization and trade were B in New Zealand and S in Spain. What are the gains from specialization and trade?

3. The following hypothetical production possibilities tables are for China and Canada. Assume that before specialization and trade the optimal product mix for China is alternative B and for Canada is alternative U.   [**LO19.1**]

PRODUCT	CHINA PRODUCTION POSSIBILITIES					
	A	**B**	**C**	**D**	**E**	**F**
Apparel (in thousands)	30	24	18	12	6	0
Chemicals (in tonnes)	0	6	12	18	24	30

PRODUCT	CANADIAN PRODUCTION POSSIBILITIES					
	R	**S**	**T**	**U**	**V**	**W**
Apparel (in thousands)	10	8	6	4	2	0
Chemicals (in tonnes)	0	4	8	12	16	20

a. Are comparative-cost conditions such that the two areas should specialize? If so, what product should each produce?

b. What is the total gain in apparel and chemical output that would result from such specialization?

c. What are the limits of the terms of trade? Suppose that the actual terms of trade are 1 unit of apparel for 1½ units of chemicals and that 4 units of apparel are exchanged for 6 units of chemicals. What are the gains from specialization and trade for each nation?

4. Refer to Figure 3-6. Assume that the graph depicts the Canadian domestic market for corn. How many bushels of corn, if any, will Canada export or import at a world price of $1, $2, $3, $4, and $5? Use this information to construct the Canadian export supply curve and import demand curve for corn. Suppose that the only other corn-producing nation is France, where the domestic price is $4. Which country will export corn. Which county will import it?   [**LO19.2**]

Glossary

A

absolute advantage What a region or nation is said to have as a result of its being able to produce more of good Z and good Y with fewer resources compared to other regions or nations.

absolute poverty A situation in which the basic material needs of an individual or a family (food, clothing, shelter) are not met.

accounting profit The total revenue of a firm less its explicit costs.

adverse selection problem A problem arising when information known to one party to a contract is not known to the other party, causing the latter to incur major costs.

aggregate A collection of specific economic units treated as one unit.

agribusinesses Large corporate firms in farming.

allocative efficiency The distribution of resources among firms and industries to produce the goods most wanted by society.

anchoring The tendency people have to unconsciously base, or "anchor," the valuation of an item they are currently thinking about on recently considered but logically irrelevant information.

asymmetric information A situation in which one party to a market transaction has much more information about a product or service than the other does.

average fixed cost (AFC) A firm's total fixed cost divided by output.

average product (AP) The total output divided by the quantity of that employed resource.

average revenue Total revenue from the sale of a product divided by the quantity of the product sold.

average total cost (ATC) A firm's total cost divided by output.

average variable cost (AVC) A firm's total variable cost divided by output.

B

backward induction A method for solving for the *subgame perfect Nash equilibrium* of a *sequential game* that is presented in *extensive form*.

barrier to entry Anything that artificially prevents the entry of firms into an industry.

barter The exchange of one good or service for another good or service.

behavioural economics The branch of economic theory that combines insights from economics, psychology, and biology to make more accurate predictions about human behaviour than conventional neoclassical economics, which is hampered by its core assumptions that people are fundamentally rational and almost entirely self-interested.

bilateral monopoly A market in which there is a single seller (monopoly) and a single buyer (monopsony).

break-even point An output at which a firm makes a normal profit but not an economic profit.

budget constraint The limit that a consumer's income (and the prices that must be paid for goods and services) imposes on the ability of that consumer to obtain goods and services.

budget deficit The amount by which the expenditures of the federal government exceed its revenues in any year.

budget line A schedule or curve that shows various combinations of two products a consumer can purchase with a specific money income.

businesses Economic entities (firms) that purchase factors of production and provide goods and services to the economy.

C

Canada Pension Plan (CPP) A national retirement plan funded by obligatory employer and employee contributions.

Canadian Wheat Marketing Board A board that maintained the price of wheat at board-determined levels through the control of product supply and that acted as the marketing agency for wheat producers up to 2012.

capital Human-made resources (buildings, machinery, and equipment) used to produce goods and services.

capital goods Goods that satisfy human wants indirectly by aiding the production of consumer goods.

capital-intensive goods Products that require a relatively large amount of capital to produce.

cartel A formal agreement among firms in an industry to set the price of a product and establish the outputs of the individual firms or to divide the market among them.

change in demand A change in the quantity demanded of a good or service at every price; a shift of the entire demand curve to the right (an increase in demand) or to the left (a decrease in demand).

change in quantity demanded A movement from one point to another on a fixed demand curve.

change in quantity supplied A movement from one point to another on a fixed supply curve.

change in supply A change in the quantity supplied of a good or service at every price; a shift of the supply curve to the left or right.

circular flow diagram Depiction of the flows of resources from households to firms and of products from firms to households. These flows are accompanied by reverse flows of money from firms to households and from households to firms.

Coase theorem The idea, first stated by economist Ronald Coase, that some externalities can be resolved through private negotiations among the affected parties.

cognitive biases Misperceptions or misunderstandings that cause *systematic errors*. Most result either (1) from *heuristics* that are prone to *systematic errors* or (2) because the brain is attempting to solve a type of problem (such as a calculus problem) for which it was not evolutionarily evolved and for which it has little innate capability.

collusion A situation in which firms act together and in agreement to fix prices, divide a market, or otherwise restrict competition.

command system An economic system in which most property resources are owned by the government and economic decisions are made by a central government body.

comparative advantage What a region or nation is said to have as a result of its being able to produce a product at a lower opportunity cost than other regions or nations.

compensating differences Differences in the wages received by workers in different jobs to compensate for nonmonetary differences in the jobs.

competition The presence in a market of a large number of independent buyers and sellers competing with one another and the freedom of buyers and sellers to enter and leave the market.

competition policy The laws and government actions designed to prevent monopoly and promote competition.

Competition Tribunal A government body adjudicating under a civil law framework that permits the issuing of remedial orders to restore and maintain competition in the market.

complementary good A product used together with another good.

compound interest The total interest that cumulates over time on money placed into an interest-bearing account.

conflict diamonds Diamonds mined and sold by combatants in war zones in Africa as a way to provide the currency needed to finance their military activities.

conglomerate merger The merger of a firm in one industry with a firm in another industry or region.

constant-cost industry An industry in which the entry of new firms has no effect on resource prices and thus no effect on production costs.

constant returns to scale The range of output between the points where economies of scale end and diseconomies of scale begin.

consumer equilibrium The combination of goods purchased that maximizes total utility by applying the utility-maximizing rule.

consumer goods Products and services that satisfy human wants directly.

consumer sovereignty Determination by consumers of the types and quantities of goods and services that will be produced with the scarce resources of the economy.

consumer surplus The difference between the maximum price consumers are willing to pay for a product and the actual price.

corporation A legal entity chartered by the federal or provincial government that operates as a distinct and separate body from the individuals who own it.

cost–benefit analysis Comparing the marginal costs with the marginal benefits to decide whether to employ more or less resources in that project.

creative destruction The hypothesis that the creation of new products and production methods simultaneously destroys the market power of firms that are wedded to existing products and older ways of doing business.

credible threat A statement of harmful intent by one party that the other party views as believable.

crop restriction In return for guaranteed prices for their crops, farmers agree to limit the number of hectares they plant in that crop.

cross elasticity of demand The ratio of the percentage change in quantity demanded of one good to the percentage change in price of some other good.

D

deadweight loss The loss of consumer surplus and producer surplus when output is either above or below its efficient level.

debt crisis An economic situation in which government debt has risen so high that the government is unable to borrow any more money.

decision node In a strategic game that is presented in extensive form, a point (node) at which a player must make a decision. The decision leads to either another decision node or a terminal node.

decreasing-cost industry An industry in which the entry of firms lowers resource prices and thus decreases production costs.

deficiency payments Subsidies that make up the difference between market prices and government-supported prices.

demand A schedule or curve that shows the various amounts of a product that consumers are willing and able to purchase at each of a series of possible prices during a specified period of time.

demand curve A curve illustrating the inverse (negative) relationship between the quantity demanded of a good or service and its price, other things equal.

demand-side market failure A market failure in which demand curves do not reflect consumers' full willingness to pay for goods or services.

demographers Scientists who study trends in human populations.

demographic transition When low birth rates and low death rates happen simultaneously.

dependent variable A variable that changes as a consequence of a change in some other (independent) variable; the effect or outcome.

deregulation The removal of most or even all of the government regulation and laws designed to supervise an industry. Sometimes undertaken to combat regulatory capture.

derived demand The demand for a factor that depends on the products it can be used to produce.

determinants of demand Factors other than price that determine the quantities demanded of a good or service.

determinants of supply Causes other than price that determine the quantities supplied of a good or service.

dictator game A mutually anonymous behavioural economics game in which one person (the dictator) unilaterally determines how to split an amount of money with a second player.

differentiated oligopoly An oligopoly in which the firms produce a differentiated product.

diffusion The spread of an *innovation* through its widespread imitation.

diminishing marginal utility As a consumer increases the consumption of a good or service, the marginal utility obtained from each additional unit of the good or service decreases.

direct relationship The (positive) relationship between two variables that change in the same direction, for example, product price and quantity supplied.

diseconomies of scale Increases in the average total cost of producing a product as the firm increases plant size (output) in the long run.

division of labour Dividing the work required to produce a product into a number of different tasks that are performed by different workers.

dollar votes Through their purchases in the product and resource markets, consumers and entrepreneurs determine the production of consumer and capital goods, respectively.

domestic price The price of a good or service within a country, determined by domestic demand and supply.

dominant strategy In game theory, an option that is better than any alternative option regardless of what the other firm does.

E

economic cost A value equal to the quantity of other products that cannot be produced when resources are instead used to make a particular product.

economic growth (1) An outward shift in the production possibilities curve that results from an increase in factor supplies or quality or an improvement in technology. (2) An increase either in real output (GDP) or in real output per capita.

economic perspective A viewpoint that envisions individuals and institutions making rational decisions by comparing the marginal benefits and marginal costs associated with their actions.

economic principle A statement about economic behaviour or the economy that enables prediction of the probable effects of certain actions.

economic problem The need to make choices because society's material wants for goods and services are unlimited, but the resources available to satisfy these wants are limited (scarce).

economic (pure) profit The total revenue of a firm less its economic costs (which includes both explicit costs and implicit costs); also called *above-normal profit*.

economic rent The price paid for the use of land and other natural resources, the supply of which is fixed (perfectly inelastic).

economic resources The land, labour, capital, and entrepreneurial ability that are used in the production of goods and services.

economics The social science concerned with how individuals, institutions, and society make optimal (best) choices under conditions of scarcity.

economic system A particular set of institutional arrangements and a coordinating mechanism for producing goods and services.

economies of scale Reductions in the average total cost of producing a product as the firm increases plant size (output) in the long run.

efficiency loss of a tax The loss of net benefits to society because a tax reduces the production and consumption of a taxed good below the level of allocative efficiency. Also called the *deadweight loss* of the tax.

efficiency losses (or deadweight losses) Reduction of combined consumer and producer surplus associated with underproduction or overproduction of a product.

elastic demand Product or resource demand with a price elasticity coefficient that is greater than 1.

elasticity of factor demand The percentage change in factor quantity divided by the percentage change in factor price.

employment insurance (EI) A program that insures workers against losing their incomes if they lose their jobs.

empty threat A statement of harmful intent that is easily dismissed by the second party because the threat is not viewed as believable.

endowment effect The tendency people have to put higher valuations on items they possess (are endowed with) than on identical items that they do not possess; perhaps caused by loss aversion.

entrepreneurial ability The human talents that combine the other resources to produce a product, make non-routine decisions, innovate, and bear risks.

entrepreneurs Individuals who provide entrepreneurial ability to firms by setting strategy, advancing innovations, and bearing the financial risk if their firms do poorly.

equality–efficiency trade-off The decrease in economic efficiency that may accompany a decrease in income inequality.

equilibrium position The combination of products that yields the greatest satisfaction or utility.

equilibrium price The price in a competitive market at which the quantity demanded and the quantity supplied are equal.

equilibrium quantity The quantity demanded and supplied at the equilibrium price in a competitive market.

equilibrium world price The price of an internationally traded product that equates the quantity of the product demanded by importers with the quantity of the product supplied by exporters.

excess capacity Plant or equipment that is underused because the firm is producing less than the minimum-ATC output.

excludability A situation in which sellers can keep people who do not pay for a product from obtaining its benefits.

exclusive unionism The practice of a labour union of restricting the supply of skilled union labour to increase the wages received by union members.

expected-rate-of-return curve As it relates to research and development (R&D), a curve showing the anticipated gain in profit, as a percentage of R&D expenditure, from an additional dollar spent on R&D.

explicit costs The monetary payments a firm must make to an outsider to obtain a resource.

export subsidy A government payment to a domestic producer of export goods, designed to aid that producer.

export supply curve An upsloping curve that shows the amount of a product domestic firms will export at each world price that is above the domestic price.

externality Benefit or cost from production or consumption accruing without compensation to nonbuyers and nonsellers of the product.

extraction costs All costs associated with extracting a natural resource and readying it for sale.

F

factor market A market in which households sell and firms buy factors of production.

factors of production Economic resources: land, labour, capital, and entrepreneurial ability.

fairness A person's opinion as to whether a price, wage, or allocation is considered morally or ethically acceptable.

fair-return price The price of a product that enables its producer to obtain a normal profit and that is equal to the average cost of producing it.

fast-second strategy An approach by a dominant firm in which it allows other firms in its industry to bear the risk of innovation and then quickly becomes the second firm to offer any successful new product or adopt any improved production process.

first-mover advantage In game theory, the benefit obtained by the party that moves first in a sequential game.

fiscal policy Changes in government spending and tax collections designed to achieve a full-employment and noninflationary domestic output.

fixed costs Costs that in total do not change when the firm changes its output.

four-firm concentration ratio The percentage of total industry sales accounted for by the top four firms in the industry.

framing effects In *prospect theory*, changes in people's decision making are caused by new information that alters the context or "frame of reference" that they use to judge whether options are viewed as gains or losses relative to the *status quo*.

freedom of choice The freedom of owners of property resources to employ or dispose of them as they see fit, and of consumers to spend their incomes in a manner that they think is appropriate.

freedom of enterprise The freedom of firms to obtain economic resources, to use these resources to produce products of the firm's own choosing, and to sell their products in markets of their choice.

free-rider problem The inability of potential providers of an economically desirable but indivisible good or service to obtain payment from those who benefit, because the exclusion principle is not applicable.

full employment Use of all available resources to produce want-satisfying goods and services.

future value The amount to which some current amount of money will grow if the interest earned on the amount is left to compound over time.

G

gains from trade The extra output that trading partners obtain through specialization of production and exchange of goods and services.

game theory The study of how people behave in strategic situations in which individuals must take into account not only their own possible actions but also the possible reactions of others.

Gini ratio A numerical measure of the overall dispersion of income.

government failure Inefficiencies in resource allocation caused by problems in the operation of the public sector (government).

Guaranteed Income Supplement (GIS) Money paid on application, subject to a means test, to those receiving an OAS pension who have an income below a certain level.

H

Herfindahl index The sum of the squared percentage market shares of all firms in the industry.

heuristics The brain's low-energy mental shortcuts for making decisions. They are "fast and frugal" and work well in most situations, but in other situations result in *systematic errors*.

homogeneous oligopoly An oligopoly in which the firms produce a standardized product.

horizontal axis The left–right or west–east axis on a graph or grid.

horizontal merger A merger between two competitors selling similar products in the same market.

households One or more persons occupying a housing unit, who buy businesses' goods and services in the product market using income derived from selling resources in the factor market.

human capital Any expenditure to improve the education, skills, health, or mobility of workers, with an expectation of greater productivity and thus a positive return on the investment.

I

imitation problem The potential for a firm's rivals to produce a close variation of (imitate) a firm's new product or process, greatly reducing the originator's profit from R&D and *innovation*.

immediate market period A period in which producers are unable to change the quantity of a product they produce in response to a change in its price.

imperfect competition The market models of monopoly, monopolistic competition, and oligopoly considered as a group.

implicit costs The monetary incomes a firm sacrifices when it uses a resource it owns rather than supplying the resource to the market.

import competition The competition domestic firms encounter from the products and services of foreign producers.

import demand curve A downsloping curve that shows the amount of a product an economy will import at each world price below the domestic price.

import quota A limit imposed by a nation on the quantity (or total value) of a good that may be imported during some period of time.

incentive function The inducement that an increase in the price of a commodity gives to sellers to make more of it available.

incentive pay plan A compensation structure, such as piece rates, commissions, royalties, bonuses, stock options, and profit sharing, that ties worker pay directly to performance.

inclusive unionism The practice of a labour union including as members all workers employed in an industry.

income effect A change in the price of a product changes a consumer's real income (purchasing power) and thus the quantity of the product purchased.

income elasticity of demand Measures the responsiveness of consumer purchases to income changes.

income inequality The unequal distribution of an economy's total income among households or families.

income mobility The movement of individuals and families from one income quintile to another over time.

increasing-cost industry An industry in which the entry of new firms raises resource prices and thus increases production costs.

independent variable The variable causing a change in some other (dependent) variable.

indifference curve A curve showing the different combinations of two products that yield the same satisfaction or utility to a consumer.

indifference map A series of indifference curves, each of which represents a different level of total utility, and that together show the preferences of the consumer.

individual transferable quota (ITQ) A limit on the total number or tonnage of fish that individual fishers can harvest during a particular time period.

inelastic demand Product or resource demand with a price elasticity coefficient that is less than 1.

inferior goods Goods or services whose consumption falls when income increases and rises when income decreases, price remaining constant.

innovation The first commercially successful introduction of a new product, use of a new method of production, or creation of a new form of business organization.

insurable risks Those risks for which it is possible to buy insurance.

interest-rate-cost-of-funds curve As it relates to research and development (R&D), a curve showing the interest rate a firm must pay to obtain any particular amount of funds to finance R&D.

interindustry competition The competition between the products of one industry and the products of another industry.

invention The conception of a new product or process combined with the first proof that it will work.

inverse relationship The (negative) relationship between two variables that change in opposite directions, for example, product price and quantity demanded.

inverted-U theory The idea that, other things equal, R&D expenditures as a percentage of sales rise with industry concentration, reach a peak at a *four-firm concentration ratio* of about 50 percent, and then fall as the ratio further increases.

investment Spending for the production and accumulation of capital.

invisible hand The tendency of firms and resource suppliers seeking to further their own self-interest in competitive markets to also promote the interest of society as a whole.

L

labour The physical and mental talents of individuals used in producing goods and services.

labour-intensive goods Products that require a relatively large amount of labour to produce.

labour market discrimination Equivalent labour resources being treated differently, even through their productive contributions are equal.

laissez-faire capitalism A hypothetical economic system in which the government's economic role is limited to protecting private property and establishing a legal environment appropriate to the operation of *markets* in which only mutually agreeable transactions take place between buyers and sellers.

land Natural resources used to produce goods and services.

land-intensive goods Products that require a relatively large amount of land to produce.

law of demand Other things equal, as price falls the quantity demanded rises, and vice versa.

law of diminishing marginal utility As a consumer increases consumption of a good or service, the marginal utility obtained from each additional unit of the good or service decreases.

law of diminishing returns The principle that as successive increments of a variable factor are added to a fixed factor, the marginal product of the variable factor will eventually decrease.

law of increasing opportunity costs As the production of a good increases, the opportunity cost of producing an additional unit rises.

law of supply The principle that, other things equal, an increase in the price of a product will increase the quantity of it supplied, and a decrease in the price of a product will decrease the quantity of it supplied.

least-cost combination of factors The quantity of each factor a firm must employ to produce a particular output at the lowest total cost.

legal cartel theory of regulation The hypothesis that some industries seek regulation or want to maintain regulation so that they may form a legal cartel.

loanable funds theory of interest The concept that the supply of and demand for loanable funds determines the equilibrium rate of interest.

loan guarantees A type of investment subsidy in which the government agrees to guarantee the money borrowed by a private company to fund investment projects if the private company itself fails to repay the loan.

logrolling The trading of votes by legislators to secure favourable outcomes on decisions concerning the provision of public goods and quasi-public goods.

long run A period of time long enough to enable producers to change the quantities of all the resources they employ.

long-run farm problem The tendency for agriculture to be a declining industry as technological progress increases supply relative to an inelastic and slowly increasing demand.

long-run supply curve A curve that shows the prices at which a purely competitive industry will make various quantities of the product available in the long run.

Lorenz curve A curve showing the distribution of income in an economy.

loss aversion In prospect theory, the property of most people's preferences that the pain generated by losses feels substantially more intense than the pleasure generated by gains.

M

macroeconomics The part of economics concerned with the economy as a whole.

marginal analysis The comparison of marginal (extra or additional) benefits and marginal costs, usually for decision making.

marginal cost = marginal benefit rule The rule that, for a government project, marginal benefit should equal marginal cost to produce maximum benefit to society.

marginal factor cost (MFC) The amount that each additional unit of a factor adds to the firm's total (factor) cost.

marginal product (MP) The extra output produced with one additional unit of a factor.

marginal productivity theory of income distribution The contention that the distribution of income is fair when each unit of each factor receives a money payment equal to its marginal contribution to the firm's revenue (its marginal revenue product).

marginal rate of substitution (MRS) The rate at which a consumer is prepared to substitute one good for another.

marginal revenue The change in total revenue that results from selling one more unit of a firm's product.

marginal revenue product (MRP) The change in total revenue from employing one additional unit of a factor.

marginal revenue productivity How much workers contribute to their employers' revenue.

marginal utility The extra utility a consumer obtains from the consumption of one additional unit of a product.

market Any institution or mechanism that brings together buyers and sellers of particular goods, services, or resources for the purpose of exchange.

market failures Situations in which markets do not function properly, whether by overproducing, underproducing, or failing to produce economically desirable goods.

market structure The characteristics of an industry that define the likely behaviour and performance of its firms.

market system An economic system in which property resources are privately owned and markets and prices are used to direct and coordinate economic activities.

median-voter model The theory that under majority rule the median (middle) voter will be in the dominant position to determine the outcome of an election.

medium of exchange Items sellers generally accept and buyers generally use to pay for a good or service.

mental accounting The tendency people have to create separate mental boxes (or accounts) in which they deal with particular financial transactions in isolation, rather than as part of an overall decision-making process that would consider how best to allocate their limited budgets across all possible options by using the utility-maximizing rule.

microeconomics The part of economics concerned with such individual units as industries, firms, and households.

midpoint formula A method for calculating price elasticity of demand or price elasticity of supply that averages the two prices and two quantities as the reference points for competing percentages.

minimum efficient scale (MES) The lowest level of output at which a firm can minimize long-run average costs.

minimum wage The lowest wage employers may legally pay for an hour of work.

monetary policy A central bank's changing of the money supply to influence interest rates and assist the economy in achieving price-level stability, full employment, and economic growth.

money Any item that is generally acceptable to sellers in exchange for goods and services.

monopolistic competition A market structure in which a relatively large number of sellers produce differentiated products.

monopoly A market structure in which one firm is the sole seller of a product or service.

monopsony A market structure in which there is only a single buyer.

moral hazard problem The possibility that individuals will change their behaviour as the result of a contract or agreement.

MR = MC rule A method of determining the total output at which economic profit is at a maximum (or losses are at a minimum).

MRP = MFC rule To maximize economic profit (or minimize losses) a firm should use the quantity of a factor at which its marginal revenue product is equal to its marginal factor cost.

mutual interdependence A situation in which a change in strategy (usually price) by one firm will affect the sales and profits of other firms.

myopia Refers to the difficulty human beings have with conceptualizing the more distant future. Leads to decisions that overly favour present and near-term options at the expense of more distant future possibilities.

N

Nash equilibrium In game theory, an outcome from which neither firm wants to deviate; the outcome that once achieved is stable and therefore lasting.

natural monopoly An industry in which economies of scale are so great that a single firm can produce the product at a lower average total cost than if more than one firm produced the product.

negative-sum game A game in which the gains and losses add up to some amount less than zero.

neoclassical economics The dominant and conventional branch of economic theory that attempts to predict human behaviour by building economic models based on simplifying assumptions about people's motives and capabilities. These include the assumption that people are fundamentally rational.

net benefits The total benefits of some activity or policy less the total costs of that activity or policy.

network effects Increases in the value of a product to each user, including existing users, as the total number of users rises.

nominal interest rate The interest rate expressed in terms of annual amounts currently charged for interest and not adjusted for inflation.

nominal wage The amount of money received by a worker per unit of time (hour, day, etc.).

non-renewable natural resources Resources that either are in actual fixed supply or that renew so slowly as to be in virtual fixed supply when viewed from a human time perspective.

noncash transfers Government transfer payments in the form of goods and services rather than money.

noncompeting groups Collections of workers in the economy who do not compete with each other for employment because the skills and training of the workers in any one group are substantially different from those of the workers in other groups.

nonexcludability The situation in which there is no effective way to prevent individuals from enjoying the benefit of a good once it has been created.

nonprice competition A selling strategy in which one firm tries to distinguish its product or service from all competing ones based on attributes other than price.

nonrivalry The situation in which the consumption of a good by one person does not preclude consumption of the good by others.

nontariff barrier (NTB) All restrictions other than tariffs that nations erect to impede international trade.

normal good A good or service whose consumption rises when income increases and falls when income decreases, price remaining constant.

normal profit The return flowing to those who provide the economy with the *economic resource* of *entrepreneurial ability*; the *total revenue* of a firm less its *economic costs* (which include both *explicit costs* and *implicit costs*); also called "pure profit" and "above-normal profit."

normative economics The part of economics involving value judgments about what the economy should be like.

O

occupational licensing Provincial or municipal governments' requiring a worker to satisfy certain specified requirements and obtain a licence from a licensing board before engaging in a particular occupation.

occupational segregation Crowding women or minorities into less desirable, lower-paying occupations.

Old Age Security (OAS) A pension paid on application at age 65 to everyone resident in Canada for at least ten years immediately before turning 65.

oligopoly A market structure in which a few large firms produce standardized or differentiated products.

one-time game In *game theory*, a game in which the parties select their optimal strategies in a single time period without regard to possible interaction in subsequent time periods.

opportunity cost The amounts of other products that must be forgone or sacrificed to produce a unit of a product.

opportunity-cost ratio An equality showing the number of units of two products that can be produced with the same resources.

optimal amount of R&D The level of R&D at which the marginal benefit and the marginal cost of R&D expenditures are equal.

optimal reduction of an externality The point at which society's marginal cost and marginal benefit of reducing that externality are equal.

other-things-equal assumption The assumption that factors other than those being considered are held constant.

output effect The phenomenon that an increase in the price of one input will increase a firm's production costs and reduce its level of output, thus reducing the demand for other inputs (and vice versa).

P

paradox of voting A situation in which paired-choice majority voting fails to provide a consistent ranking of society's preferences for public goods or services.

partnership An unincorporated firm owned and operated by two or more people.

patent An exclusive right given to inventors to produce and sell a new product or machine for twenty years from the time of patent application.

perfect competition A market structure in which a very large number of firms produce a standardized product.

perfectly competitive labour market A factor market in which a large number of firms demand a particular type of labour supplied by a large number of non-union workers.

perfectly elastic demand Quantity demanded can be any amount at a particular price.

perfectly inelastic demand Quantity demanded does not respond to a change in price.

Pigovian taxes A tax or charge levied on the production of a product that generates negative externalities. If set correctly, the tax will precisely offset the overallocation (overproduction) generated by the negative externality.

political corruption The abuse of power by government officials for personal gain.

positive economics The analysis of facts to establish cause-and-effect relationships.

positive-sum game A game in which the gains and losses add up to more than zero.

precommitments Actions taken ahead of time that make it difficult for the future self to avoid doing what the present self desires. See also *time inconsistency* and *self-control problems*.

present value Today's value of some amount of money that is to be received sometime in the future.

price ceiling A legally established maximum price for a good or service.

price discrimination Selling a product to different buyers at different prices when the price differences are not justified by differences in cost.

price elasticity of demand A measure of the responsiveness of buyers to a change in the price of a product or resource.

price elasticity of supply The ratio of the percentage change in quantity supplied of a product to the percentage change in its price.

price floor A legally established price above an equilibrium price.

price leadership An implicit understanding oligopolists use that has the dominant firm initiate price changes and all other firms follow.

price supports Government-supported minimum prices for agricultural products.

price-taker A firm in a purely competitive market that cannot change market price, but can only adjust to it.

price war Successive, competitive, and continued decreases in the prices charged by firms in an oligopolistic industry.

principal–agent problem A problem associated with possible differences in the interests of corporate shareholders (principals) and the executives (agents) they hire.

principle of comparative advantage The proposition that an individual, region, or nation will benefit if it specializes in producing goods for which its own *opportunity costs* are lower than the opportunity costs of a trading partner, and then exchanging some of the products in which it specializes for other desired products produced by others.

prisoner's dilemma A type of game between two players that shows the difficulty of cooperating when the two cannot communicate with each other, even when it is in their best interests to cooperate.

private goods Products or services that are individually consumed and that can be profitably provided by privately owned firms because they can exclude nonpayers from receiving the benefits.

private property The right of private persons and firms to obtain, own, control, employ, dispose of, and bequeath land, capital, and other property.

process innovation The development and use of new or improved production or distribution methods.

producer surplus The difference between the actual price producers receive for a product and the minimum acceptable price.

product differentiation A strategy in which one firm's product is distinguished from competing products by means of its design, related services, quality, location, or other attribute (except price).

product innovation The development and sale of a new or improved product (or service).

product market A market in which products are sold by firms and bought by households.

production possibilities curve A curve showing the different combinations of goods or services that can be produced in a full-employment, full-production economy where the available supplies of resources and technology are fixed.

productive efficiency The production of a good in the least costly way.

profit-maximizing combination of factors The quantity of each factor a firm must employ to maximize its profits or minimize its losses.

prospect theory A *behavioural economics* theory of preferences having three main features: (1) people evaluate options on the basis of whether they generate gains or losses relative to the status quo; (2) gains are subject to diminishing marginal utility, while losses are subject to diminishing marginal disutility; and (3) people are prone to loss aversion.

protective tariff A tariff designed to shield domestic producers of a good or service from the competition of foreign producers.

public choice theory The economic analysis of government decision making, politics, and elections.

public goods Goods or services that can be simultaneously consumed by everyone, and from which no one can be excluded, even if they don't pay for them.

public interest theory of regulation The theory that industrial regulation is necessary to keep a natural monopoly from charging monopoly prices and thus harming consumers and society.

pure rate of interest The hypothetical interest rate that would serve purely and solely to compensate lenders for their willingness to patiently forgo alternative consumption and investment opportunities until their money is repaid.

Q

quasi-public goods Goods provided by the government that fit the economist's definition of a public good but can be produced in such a way that exclusion would be possible.

R

rational behaviour Human behaviour based on comparison of marginal costs and marginal benefits; behaviour designed to maximize total utility.

rational decisions Decisions that maximize the chances of achieving a desired outcome.

real interest rate The interest rate expressed in dollars of constant value (adjusted for inflation); equal to the nominal interest rate less the expected rate of inflation.

real wage The amount of goods and services a worker can purchase with a nominal wage.

regulatory capture The situation that occurs when a governmental regulatory agency ends up being controlled by the industry that it is supposed to be regulating.

relative poverty An individual's or a family's low income relative to others in society.

renewable natural resources Resources that are capable of renewing themselves if they are harvested at moderate rates.

rent seeking The actions by persons, firms, or unions to gain special benefits from government at the taxpayers' or someone else's expense.

rent-seeking behaviour The actions by persons, firms, or unions to gain special benefits from government at taxpayers' or someone else's expense.

repeated game A game that is played again sometime after the previous game ends.

replacement rate The birth rate necessary to keep the size of a population constant without relying on immigration.

residual claimant The owners of a firm who in a market system are the rightful legal recipients (that is, are claimants) of whatever profit or loss remains (is residual) after all other input providers have been paid. The residual is compensation for providing the economic input of *entrepreneurial ability* and flows to the firm's owners.

revenue tariff A tariff designed to produce income for the federal government.

rivalry A situation in which when one person buys and consumes a product, it is not available for another person to buy and consume.

S

scarcity The limits placed on the amounts and types of goods and services available for consumption because there are limited economic resources from which to produce output.

scientific method The systematic pursuit of knowledge through formulating a problem, collecting data, and formulating and testing hypotheses to obtain theories, principles, and laws.

self-control problems Refers to the difficulty people have in sticking with earlier plans and avoiding suboptimal decisions when finally confronted with a particular decision-making situation. A manifestation of time inconsistency and potentially avoidable by using precommitments.

self-interest That which each firm, property owner, worker, and consumer believes is best for itself.

sequential game A game in which the parties make their moves in turn, with one party making the first move, followed by the other party making the next move, and so on.

short run A period of time in which producers are able to change the quantities of some but not all of the resources they employ.

short-run farm problem The sharp year-to-year changes in the prices of agricultural products and in the incomes of farmers.

short-run supply curve A curve that shows the quantities of the product a firm in a purely competitive industry will offer to sell at various prices in the short run.

shortage The amount by which the quantity demanded of a product exceeds the quantity supplied at a specific (below-equilibrium) price.

simultaneous consumption A product's ability to satisfy a large number of consumers at the same time.

simultaneous game A strategic interaction (game) between two or more parties (players) in which every player moves (makes a decision) at the same time.

slope of a straight line The ratio of the vertical change (the rise or fall) to the horizontal change (the run) between any two points on a line. The slope of an upsloping line is positive, reflecting a direct relationship between two variables; the slope of a downsloping line is negative, reflecting an inverse relationship between two variables.

social regulation Government regulation of the conditions under which goods are produced, the physical characteristics of goods, and the impact of the production on society.

socially optimal price The price of a product that results in the most efficient allocation of an economy's resources.

sole proprietorship An unincorporated firm owned and operated by one person.

special-interest effect Any result of government promotion of the interests (goals) of a small group at the expense of a much larger group.

specialization The use of the resources of an individual, a firm, a region, or a nation to produce one or a few goods and services.

start-ups Newly formed firms that are attempting to pioneer a new product or production method.

statistical discrimination Judging individuals on the average characteristic of the group to which they belong rather than on their own personal characteristics.

status quo The existing state of affairs; in prospect theory, the current situation from which gains and losses are calculated.

status quo bias The tendency most people have when making choices to select any option that is presented as the default (status quo) option. Explainable by prospect theory and loss aversion.

strategic behaviour Self-interested behaviour that takes into account the reactions of others.

subgame A subset of a larger game that begins with a single initial decision node. It includes all subsequent *decision nodes* and/or *terminal nodes*. Most easily seen in sequential games presented in strategic form.

subgame perfect Nash equilibrium In *sequential games*, a sequence of decisions made by the various players such that no player has an incentive to deviate.

substitute goods Products or services that can be used in place of each other.

substitution effect The phenomenon that a change in the price of a product changes the relative expensiveness of that good and hence changes the willingness to buy it rather than other goods.

supply A schedule or curve that shows the amounts of a product that producers are willing and able to make available for sale at each of a series of possible prices during a specific period.

supply curve A curve illustrating the positive (direct) relationship between the quantity supplied of a good or service and its price, other things equal.

supply-side market failure A market failure in which supply curves do not reflect the full cost of producing a good or service.

surplus The amount by which the quantity supplied of a product exceeds the quantity demanded at a specific (above-equilibrium) price.

systematic errors Suboptimal choices that (1) are not *rational decisions* because they do not maximize a person's chances of achieving his or her goals and (2) occur routinely, repeatedly, and predictably.

T

tariffs Taxes imposed by a nation on imported goods.

tax incidence The degree to which a tax falls on a particular person or group.

technological advance (1) Improvement in the quality of existing products, the invention of entirely new products, or the creation of new or better ways of producing or distributing products. (2) Any improvement in the methods by which resources are combined such that the same quantity of inputs can be made to yield a combination of outputs that is preferred to any combination of outputs that was previously possible.

terminal node In a *sequential game* presented in *extensive form*, a final outcome point (node) showing the payouts to each player if the game ends at that point.

terms of trade The rate at which units of one product can be exchanged for units of another product.

time inconsistency The human tendency to systematically misjudge at the present time what will actually end up being desired at a future time.

time value of money The idea that a specific amount of money is more valuable to a person the sooner it is received because the money can be placed in a financial account or investment and earn compound interest over time.

total allowable catch (TAC) A limit on the total number or tonnage of fish that fishers, collectively, can harvest during a particular time period.

total cost The sum of fixed cost and variable cost.

total fertility rate The average total number of children that a woman is expected to have during her lifetime.

total product (TP) The total output of a particular good or service produced by a firm.

total revenue (TR) The total number of dollars a seller receives from the sale of a product in a particular time period.

total-revenue test A test to determine elasticity of demand between any two prices, by noting what happens to total revenue when price changes.

total utility The total amount of satisfaction derived from the consumption of a single product or a combination of products.

trading possibilities line Shows the different combinations of two products that an economy is able to obtain when it specializes in the production of one product and exports it to obtain the other product.

tragedy of the commons The depletion of a shared (common) resource that occurs when, in the absence of strong property rights, it is in the best interests of each user to consume as much as possible rather than conserve it for future use.

tying contract A requirement imposed by a seller that a buyer purchase another (or other) of its products as a condition for buying a desired product.

U

ultimatum game A behavioural economics game in which a mutually anonymous pair of players interact to determine how an amount of money is going to be split. The first player suggests a division. The second player either accepts that proposal (in which case the split is made accordingly) or rejects it (in which case neither player gets anything).

unfunded liability A future government spending commitment (liability) for which the government has not legislated an offsetting revenue source.

uninsurable risks Those risks for which it is impossible to buy insurance.

unit elasticity Demand or supply with a price elasticity coefficient that is equal to 1.

user cost The cost to the user of extracting a resource; current extraction and use means lower future extraction and use.

utility The want-satisfying power of a good or service; the satisfaction or pleasure a consumer obtains from the consumption of a good or service (or from the consumption of a collection of goods and services).

utility-maximizing rule To obtain the greatest utility, the consumer should allocate money income so that the last dollar spent on each good or service yields the same marginal utility.

V

variable costs Costs that increase or decrease with a firm's output.

venture capital That part of household savings used to finance high-risk business enterprises in exchange for stock (and thus a share of any profit if the enterprises are successful).

vertical axis The up–down or north–south axis on a graph or grid.

vertical intercept The point at which a line meets the vertical axis of a graph.

vertical merger The merger of firms engaged in different stages of the production process of a final product.

very long run In microeconomics, a period of time long enough that technology can change and firms can introduce new products.

voluntary export restriction (VER) Voluntary limitations by countries or firms of their exports to a particular foreign nation.

W

wage differentials The difference between the wage received by one worker or group of workers and that received by another worker or group of workers.

wage rate A price paid per unit of labour services.

world price The international market price of a good or service, determined by world demand and supply.

X

X-inefficiency The production of output, whatever its level, at higher average (and total) cost than is necessary.

Z

zero-sum game A game in which the gains and losses add up to zero.

Index